Android Studio Quail Essentials

Kotlin Edition

Android Studio Quail Essentials – Kotlin Edition

ISBN: 978-1-965764-47-3

Rev: 1.0

Payload publishing

https://www.payloadbooks.com

Contents

Table of Contents

Chapter 1

1. Introduction

This book, fully updated for Android Studio Quail, teaches you how to develop Android-based applications using Kotlin.

Beginning with the basics, the book outlines how to set up an Android development and testing environment, followed by an introduction to programming in Kotlin, including data types, control flow, functions, lambdas, and object-oriented programming. Asynchronous programming using Kotlin coroutines and flow is also covered in detail.

Chapters also cover the Android Architecture Components, including view models, lifecycle management, Room database access, content providers, the Database Inspector, app navigation, live data, and data binding.

Topics such as intents, touchscreen handling, gesture recognition, and the integration of AI into Android apps are also included.

The concepts of material design are also covered in detail, including floating action buttons, Snackbars, tabbed interfaces, card views, and collapsing toolbars.

Other key features of Android Studio and Android are also covered in detail, including the Layout Editor, the ConstraintLayout and ConstraintSet classes, view binding, constraint chains, barriers, and direct reply notifications.

Chapters also cover advanced Android Studio features, such as Gradle build configuration, in-app billing, and submitting apps to the Google Play Developer Console.

Assuming you already have some programming experience, are ready to download Android Studio and the Android SDK, have access to a Windows, Mac, or Linux system, and have ideas for some apps to develop, you are ready to get started.

1.1 Downloading the Code Samples

The source code and Android Studio project files for the examples contained in this book are available for download at:

https://www.payloadbooks.com/product/quailkotlin

The steps to load a project from the code samples into Android Studio are as follows:

1. From the Welcome to Android Studio dialog, click on the Open button option.

2. In the project selection dialog, navigate to and select the folder containing the project to be imported and click on OK.

1.2 Feedback

We want you to be satisfied with your purchase of this book. If you find any errors in the book, or have any comments, questions or concerns please contact us at *info@payloadbooks.com*.

1.3 Errata

While we make every effort to ensure the accuracy of the content of this book, it is inevitable that a book covering a subject area of this size and complexity may include some errors and oversights. Any known issues with the book will be outlined, together with solutions, at the following URL:

https://www.payloadbooks.com/quail-kotlin-errata

If you find an error not listed in the errata, please let us know by emailing our technical support team at *info@payloadbooks.com*. They are there to help you and will work to resolve any problems you may encounter.

1.4 Download the Color eBook

Thank you for purchasing the print edition of this book. Your purchase includes a color copy of the book in PDF format.

If you would like to download the PDF version of this book, please email proof of purchase (for example, a receipt, delivery notice, or photo of the physical book) to *info@payloadbooks.com,* and we will provide you with a download link.

Chapter 2

2. Setting up an Android Studio Development Environment

Before any work can begin on developing an Android application, the first step is to configure a computer system to act as the development platform. This involves several steps consisting of installing the Android Studio Integrated Development Environment (IDE), including the Android Software Development Kit (SDK), the Kotlin plug-in and the OpenJDK Java development environment.

This chapter will cover the steps necessary to install the requisite components for Android application development on Windows, macOS, and Linux-based systems.

2.1 System requirements

Android application development may be performed on any of the following system types:

- Windows 10 or 11 64-bit
- macOS 12 or later running on Intel or Apple silicon
- Chrome OS device with Intel i5 or higher
- Linux systems with version 2.31 or later of the GNU C Library (glibc)
- Minimum of 16 GB of RAM
- Approximately 8 GB of available disk space
- 1280 x 800 minimum screen resolution

2.2 Downloading the Android Studio package

Most of the work involved in developing applications for Android will be performed using the Android Studio environment. The content and examples in this book were created based on Android Studio Quail 2026.1.2 using the Android API 37 SDK (CinnamonBun), which, at the time of writing, are the latest releases.

Android Studio is, however, subject to frequent updates, so a newer version may have been released since this book was published.

The latest release of Android Studio may be downloaded from the primary download page, which can be found at the following URL:

https://developer.android.com/studio/index.html

If this page provides instructions for downloading a newer version of Android Studio, there may be differences between this book and the software. A web search for "Android Studio Quail" should provide the option to download the older version if these differences become a problem. Alternatively, visit the following web page to find Android Studio Quail 2026.1.2 in the archives:

https://developer.android.com/studio/archive

2.3 Installing Android Studio

Once downloaded, the exact steps to install Android Studio differ depending on the operating system on which the installation is performed.

2.3.1 Installation on Windows

Locate the downloaded Android Studio installation executable file (named *android-studio-<version>-windows.exe*) in a Windows Explorer window and double-click on it to start the installation process, clicking the *Yes* button in the User Account Control dialog if it appears.

Once the Android Studio setup wizard appears, work through the various screens to configure the installation to meet your requirements in terms of the file system location into which Android Studio should be installed and whether or not it should be made available to other system users. When prompted to select the components to install, ensure that the *Android Studio* and *Android Virtual Device* options are all selected.

Although there are no strict rules on where Android Studio should be installed on the system, the remainder of this book will assume that the installation was performed into *C:\Program Files\Android\Android Studio* and that the Android SDK packages have been installed into the user's *AppData\Local\Android\sdk* sub-folder. Once the options have been configured, click the *Install* button to begin the installation process.

On versions of Windows with a Start menu, the newly installed Android Studio can be launched from the entry added to that menu during the installation. The executable may be pinned to the taskbar for easy access by navigating to the *Android Studio\bin* directory, right-clicking on the *studio64* executable, and selecting the *Pin to Taskbar* menu option (on Windows 11, this option can be found by selecting *Show more options* from the menu).

2.3.2 Installation on macOS

Android Studio for macOS is downloaded as a disk image (.dmg) file. Once the *android-studio-<version>-mac.dmg* file has been downloaded, locate it in a Finder window and double-click on it to open it, as shown in Figure 2-1:

Figure 2-1

To install the package, drag the Android Studio icon and drop it onto the Applications folder. The Android Studio package will then be installed into the Applications folder of the system, a process that will typically take a few seconds to complete.

To launch Android Studio, locate the executable in the Applications folder using a Finder window and double-click on it.

For future, easier access to the tool, drag the Android Studio icon from the Finder window and drop it onto the dock.

2.3.3 Installation on Linux

Having downloaded the Linux Android Studio package, open a terminal window, change directory to the location where Android Studio is to be installed, and execute the following command:

```
tar xvfz /<path to package>/android-studio-<version>-linux.tar.gz
```

Note that the Android Studio bundle will be installed into a subdirectory named *android-studio*. Therefore, assuming that the above command was executed in */home/demo*, the software packages will be unpacked into */home/demo/android-studio*.

To launch Android Studio, open a terminal window, change directory to the *android-studio/bin* sub-directory, and execute the following command:

```
./studio.sh
```

2.4 The Android Studio setup wizard

If you have previously installed an earlier version of Android Studio, the first time this new version is launched, a dialog may appear providing the option to import settings from a previous Android Studio version. If you have settings from a previous version and would like to import them into the latest installation, select the appropriate option and location. Alternatively, indicate that you do not need to import any previous settings and click the OK button to proceed.

If you are installing Android Studio for the first time, the initial dialog that appears once the setup process starts may resemble that shown in Figure 2-2 below:

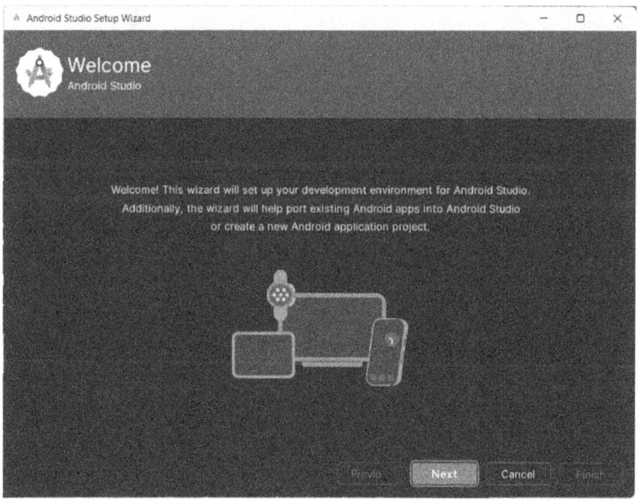

Figure 2-2

If this dialog appears, click the Next button to display the Install Type screen (Figure 2-3). On this screen, select the Standard installation option before clicking Next.

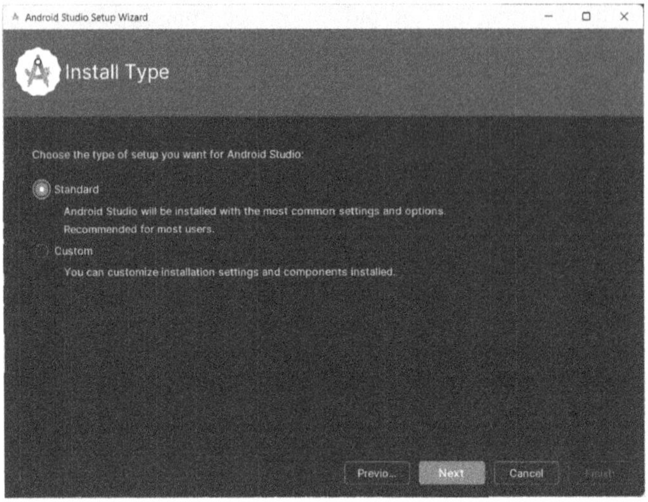

Figure 2-3

Click Next and review the options in the Verify Settings screen before proceeding to the License Agreement screen. Enable the Accept checkbox and click the Finish button to start the installation.

After these initial setup steps have been taken, click the Finish button to display the Welcome to Android Studio screen using your chosen UI theme:

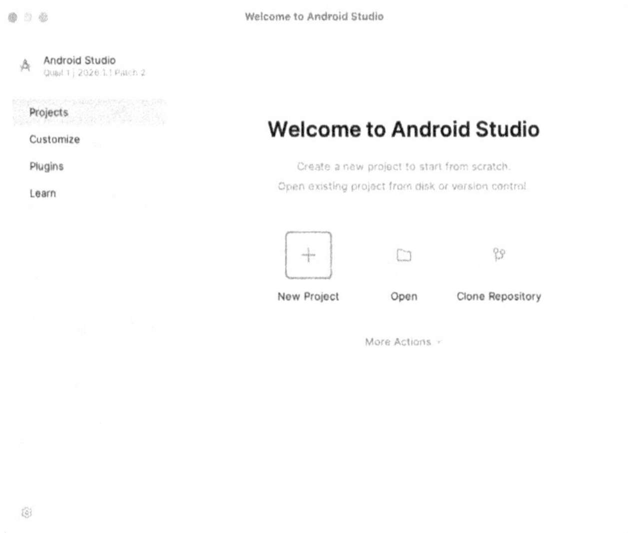

Figure 2-4

2.5 Installing additional Android SDK packages

The steps performed so far have installed the Android Studio IDE and the current set of default Android SDK packages. Before proceeding, it is worth taking some time to verify which packages are installed and to install any missing or updated packages.

This task can be performed by clicking on the *More Actions* link within the welcome dialog and selecting the *SDK Manager* option from the drop-down menu. Once invoked, the *Android SDK* screen of the Settings dialog will appear as shown in Figure 2-5:

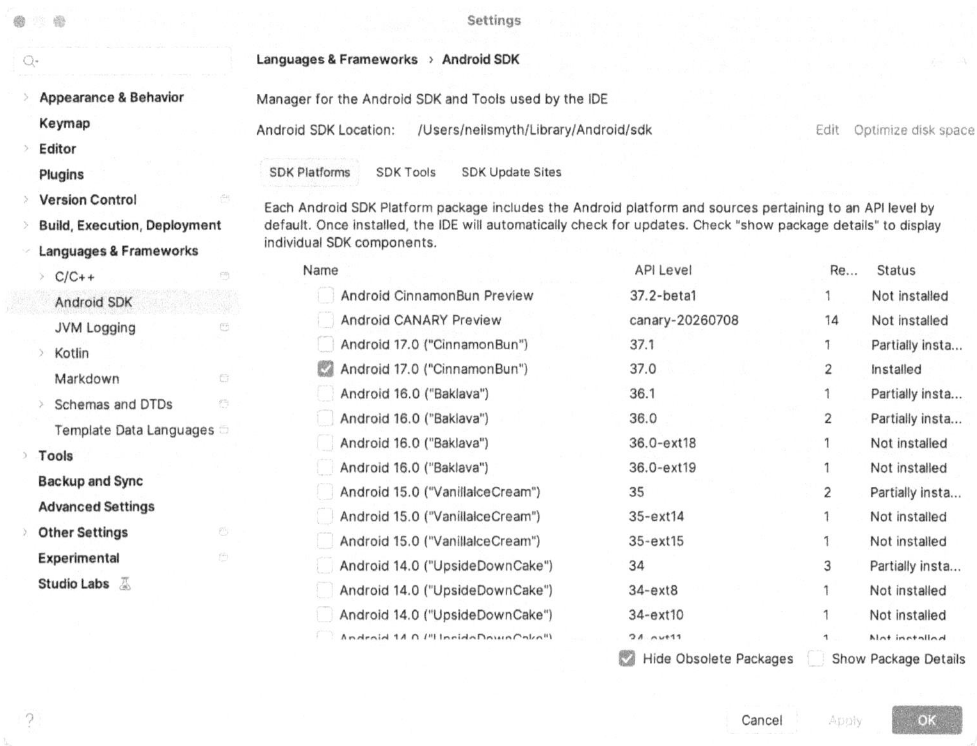

Figure 2-5

Google pairs each release of Android Studio with a maximum supported Application Programming Interface (API) level of the Android SDK. In the case of Android Studio Quail, this is Android API Level 37 (CinnamonBun). This information can be confirmed using the following link:

https://developer.android.com/studio/releases#api-level-support

Immediately after installing Android Studio for the first time, it is likely that only the latest supported version of the Android SDK has been installed. To install older versions of the Android SDK, select the checkboxes corresponding to the versions and click the *Apply* button. The rest of this book assumes that the Android API Level 37 (CinnamonBun) SDK is installed.

Most of the examples in this book will support older versions of Android as far back as Android 8.0 (Oreo). This ensures that the apps run on a wide range of Android devices. Within the list of SDK versions, enable the checkbox next to Android 8.0 (Oreo) and click the Apply button. Click the OK button to install the SDK in the resulting confirmation dialog. Subsequent dialogs will seek the acceptance of licenses and terms before performing the installation. Click Finish once the installation is complete.

It is also possible that updates will be listed as being available for the latest SDK. To access detailed information about the packages that are ready to be updated, enable the *Show Package Details* option located in the lower right-hand corner of the screen. This will display information similar to that shown in Figure 2-6:

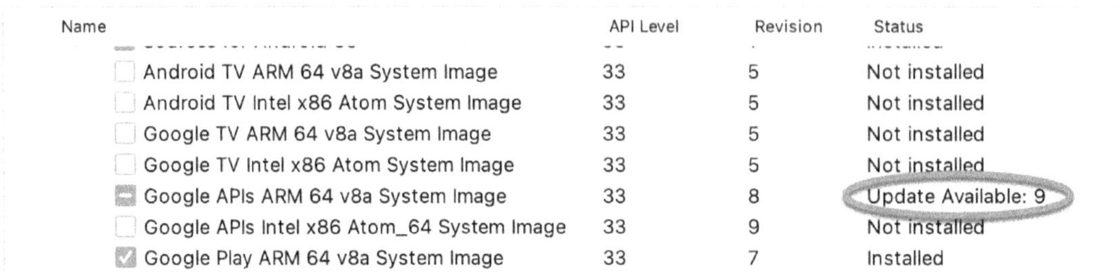

Figure 2-6

The above figure highlights the availability of an update. To install the updates, enable the checkbox to the left of the item name and click the *Apply* button.

In addition to the Android SDK packages, several tools are also installed for building Android applications. To view the currently installed packages and check for updates, remain within the SDK settings screen and select the SDK Tools tab as shown in Figure 2-7:

Figure 2-7

Within the Android SDK Tools screen, make sure that the following packages are listed as *Installed* in the Status column:

- Android SDK Build-tools
- Android SDK Command-line tools (latest)
- Android Emulator
- Android SDK Platform-tools
- Google Play Services
- Android Emulator hypervisor driver (installer)*
- Google USB Driver (Windows only)
- Layout Inspector image server for API 31-36

*Note that the Android Emulator hypervisor driver requires an Intel processor with VT-x support enabled or an AMD processor in SVM mode. It cannot be installed on Apple silicon-based Macs.

If any of the above packages are listed as *Not Installed* or requiring an update, select the checkboxes next to those packages and click the *Apply* button to initiate the installation process. If the hypervisor emulator settings dialog appears, select the recommended memory allocation:

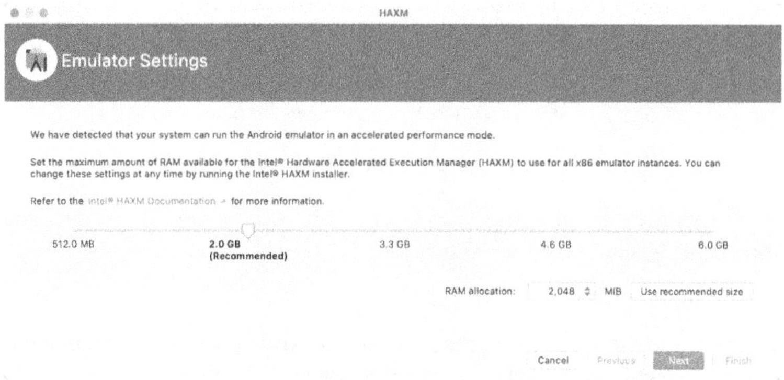

Figure 2-8

Once the installation is complete, review the package list and ensure that the selected packages are listed as *Installed* in the *Status* column. If any are listed as *Not installed,* make sure they are selected and click the *Apply* button again.

2.6 Setting up Command-line tools access

In the previous section, we installed the command-line tools for the Android SDK. As the name suggests, these tools are designed to be run from a command prompt or terminal window. To ensure that your operating system can locate these tools, you will need to add them to the system's PATH environment variable.

Regardless of your operating system, you will need to configure the PATH environment variable to include the following paths (where *<path_to_android_sdk_installation>* represents the file system location into which you installed the Android SDK):

```
<path_to_android_sdk_installation>/sdk/cmdline-tools/latest/bin
<path_to_android_sdk_installation>/sdk/platform-tools
```

You can identify the location of the SDK on your system by launching the SDK Manager and referring to the *Android SDK Location:* field located at the top of the settings panel, as highlighted in Figure 2-9:

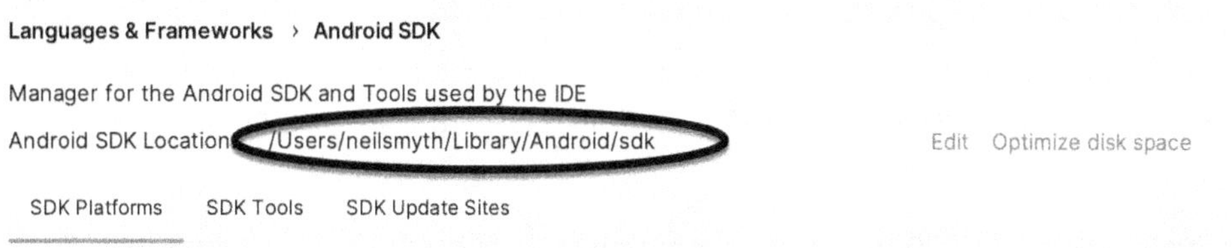

Figure 2-9

Once the location of the SDK has been identified, the steps to add this to the PATH variable are operating system dependent:

2.6.1 Windows 11

1. Right-click on the Start icon located in the taskbar and select Settings from the resulting menu. When the Settings dialog appears, scroll down the list of categories and select the "About" option. In the About screen, select *Advanced system settings* from the Related links section. When the System Properties window appears, click the *Environment Variables...* button.

2. In the Environment Variables dialog, locate the Path variable in the System variables list, select it, and click

the *Edit...* button. Using the *New* button in the edit dialog, add two new entries to the path. For example, assuming the Android SDK was installed into *C:\Users\demo\AppData\Local\Android\Sdk*, the following entries would need to be added:

```
C:\Users\demo\AppData\Local\Android\Sdk\cmdline-tools\latest\bin
C:\Users\demo\AppData\Local\Android\Sdk\platform-tools
```

3. Click OK in each dialog box and close the system properties control panel.

Open a command prompt window by pressing Windows + R on the keyboard and entering *cmd* into the Run dialog. Within the Command Prompt window, enter:

```
echo %Path%
```

The returned path variable value should include the paths to the Android SDK platform tools folders. Verify that the *platform-tools* value is correct by attempting to run the *adb* tool as follows:

```
adb
```

The tool should output a list of command-line options when executed.

Similarly, check the *tools* path setting by attempting to run the AVD Manager command-line tool (don't worry if the avdmanager tool reports a problem with Java - this will be addressed later):

```
avdmanager
```

If a message similar to the following message appears for one or both of the commands, it is most likely that an incorrect path was appended to the Path environment variable:

```
'adb' is not recognized as an internal or external command,
operable program or batch file.
```

2.6.2 Linux

This configuration can be achieved on Linux by adding a command to the *.bashrc* file in your home directory (specifics may differ depending on the particular Linux distribution in use). Assuming that the Android SDK bundle package was installed into */home/demo/Android/sdk*, the export line in the *.bashrc* file would read as follows:

```
export PATH=/home/demo/Android/sdk/platform-tools:/home/demo/Android/sdk/cmdline-tools/latest/bin:/home/demo/android-studio/bin:$PATH
```

Note also that the above command adds the *android-studio/bin* directory to the PATH variable. This will enable the *studio.sh* script to be executed regardless of the current directory within a terminal window.

2.6.3 macOS

Several techniques may be employed to modify the $PATH environment variable on macOS. Arguably the cleanest method is to add a new file in the */etc/paths.d* directory containing the paths to be added to $PATH. Assuming an Android SDK installation location of */Users/demo/Library/Android/sdk*, the path may be configured by creating a new file named *android-sdk* in the */etc/paths.d* directory containing the following lines:

```
/Users/demo/Library/Android/sdk/cmdline-tools/latest/bin
/Users/demo/Library/Android/sdk/platform-tools
```

Note that since this is a system directory, it will be necessary to use the *sudo* command when creating the file. For example:

```
sudo vim /etc/paths.d/android-sdk
```

The above command uses the Vim text editor to create and edit the *android-sdk* file. If you are not familiar with this editor, run the *vimtutor* command to quickly learn the basics.

2.7 Android Studio memory management

Android Studio is a large and complex software application with many background processes. Although Android Studio has been criticized in the past for providing less than optimal performance, Google has made significant performance improvements in recent releases and continues to do so with each new version. These improvements include allowing the user to configure the amount of memory used by both the Android Studio IDE and the background processes used to build and run apps. This allows the software to take advantage of systems with larger amounts of RAM.

If you are running Android Studio on a system with sufficient unused RAM to increase these values (this feature is only available on 64-bit systems with 5GB or more of RAM) and find that Android Studio performance appears to be degraded, it may be worth experimenting with these memory settings. Android Studio may also notify you that performance can be increased via a dialog similar to the one shown below:

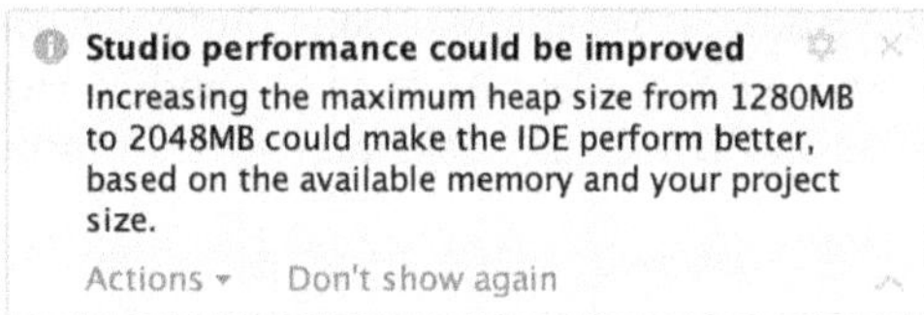

Figure 2-10

To view and modify the current memory configuration, select the *File -> Settings...* main menu option (*Android Studio -> Settings...* on macOS) and, in the resulting dialog, select *Appearance & Behavior* followed by the *Memory Settings* option listed under *System Settings* in the left-hand navigation panel, as illustrated in Figure 2-11 below:

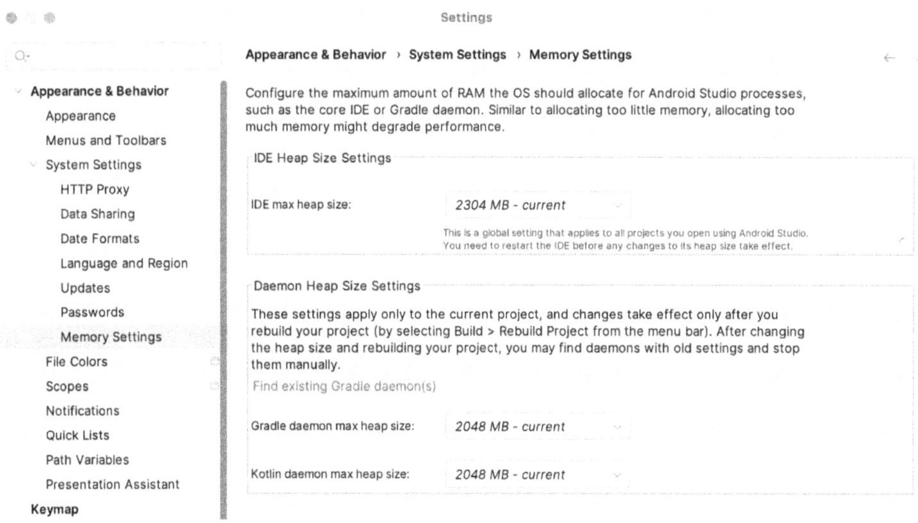

Figure 2-11

When changing the memory allocation, be sure not to allocate more memory than necessary or than your system can spare without slowing down other processes.

The IDE heap size setting adjusts the memory allocated to Android Studio and applies regardless of the currently loaded project. On the other hand, when a project is built and run from within Android Studio, several background processes (referred to as daemons) perform the task of compiling and running the app. When compiling and running large and complex projects, build time could be improved by adjusting the daemon heap settings. Unlike the IDE heap settings, these daemon settings apply only to the current project and can only be accessed when a project is open in Android Studio. To display the SDK Manager from within an open project, select the *Tools -> SDK Manager...* menu option from the main menu.

2.8 Updating Android Studio and the SDK

From time to time, new versions of Android Studio and the Android SDK are released. New versions of the SDK are installed using the Android SDK Manager. Android Studio will typically notify you when an update is ready to be installed.

To manually check for Android Studio updates, use the *Help -> Check for Updates...* menu option from the Android Studio main window (*Android Studio -> Check for Updates...* on macOS).

2.9 Summary

Before beginning the development of Android-based applications, the first step is to set up a suitable development environment. This consists of the Android SDKs and Android Studio IDE (which also includes the OpenJDK development environment). This chapter covers the steps necessary to install these packages on Windows, macOS, and Linux.

Chapter 3

3. Creating an Example Android App in Android Studio

The preceding chapters of this book have explained how to configure an environment suitable for developing Android applications using the Android Studio IDE. Before moving on to slightly more advanced topics, now is a good time to validate that all required development packages are installed and functioning correctly. The best way to achieve this goal is to create an Android application and compile and run it. This chapter will cover creating an Android application project using Android Studio. Once the project has been created, a later chapter will explore using the Android emulator environment to perform a test run of the application.

3.1 About the Project

The project created in this chapter takes the form of a rudimentary currency conversion calculator (so simple, in fact, that it only converts from dollars to euros and does so using an estimated conversion rate). The project will also use one of the most basic Android Studio project templates. This simplicity allows us to introduce some key aspects of Android app development without overwhelming the beginner by introducing too many concepts, such as the recommended app architecture and Android architecture components, at once. When following the tutorial in this chapter, rest assured that the techniques and code used in this initial example project will be covered in much greater detail later.

3.2 Creating a New Android Project

The first step in the application development process is to create a new project within the Android Studio environment. Begin, therefore, by launching Android Studio so that the "Welcome to Android Studio" screen appears as illustrated in Figure 3-1:

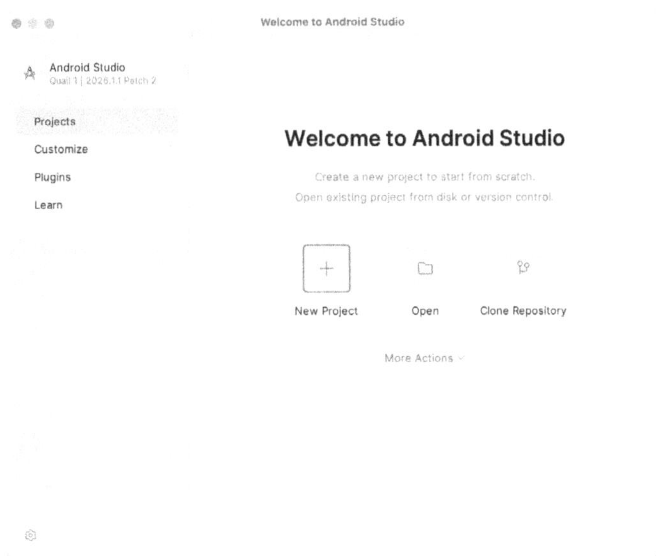

Figure 3-1

Once this window appears, Android Studio is ready for a new project to be created. To create the new project, click on the *New Project* option to display the first screen of the *New Project* wizard.

3.3 Creating an Activity

The next step is to define the type of initial activity to be created for the application. Options are available to create projects for Phone and Tablet, Wear OS, Television, Car, or XR headset devices. A range of different activity types is available when developing Android applications, many of which will be covered extensively in later chapters. For this example, however, select the *Phone and Tablet* option from the Templates panel, followed by the option to create an *Empty Views Activity.* The Empty Views Activity option creates a template user interface consisting of a single TextView object.

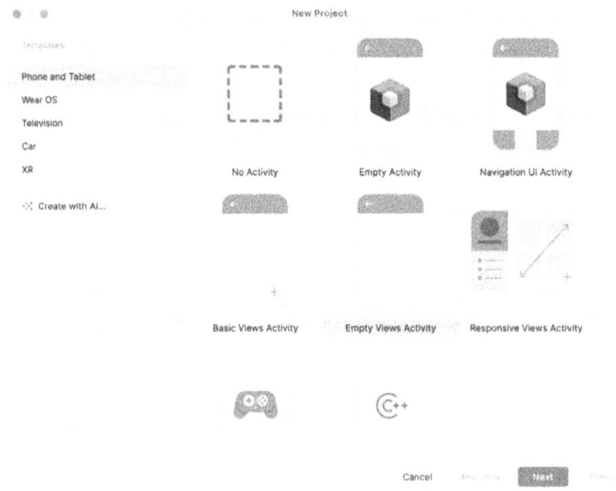

Figure 3-2

With the Empty Views Activity option selected, click *Next* to continue with the project configuration.

3.4 Defining the Project and SDK Settings

In the project configuration window (Figure 3-3), set the *Name* field to *AndroidSample*. The application name is the name by which the application will be referenced and identified within Android Studio and is also the name that would be used if the completed application were to go on sale in the Google Play store.

The *Package name* uniquely identifies the application within the Android application ecosystem. Although this can be set to any string that uniquely identifies your app, it is traditionally based on the reversed URL of your domain name followed by the application's name. For example, if your domain is *www.mycompany.com*, and the application has been named *AndroidSample*, then the package name might be specified as follows:

```
com.mycompany.androidsample
```

If you do not have a domain name, you can enter any other string into the Company Domain field, or you may use *example.com* for testing, though this will need to be changed before an application can be published:

```
com.example.androidsample
```

The *Save location* setting will default to a location in the folder named *AndroidStudioProjects* located in your home directory and may be changed by clicking on the folder icon to the right of the text field containing the current path setting.

Set the minimum SDK setting to API 26 (Oreo; Android 8.0). This minimum SDK will be used in most projects created in this book unless a necessary feature is only available in a more recent version. The objective here is to build an app using the latest Android SDK while retaining compatibility with devices running older versions of Android (in this case, as far back as Android 8.0). The text beneath the Minimum SDK setting will outline the percentage of Android devices currently in use on which the app will run. Click on the *Help me choose* button to see a full breakdown of the various Android versions still in use:

Figure 3-3

Finally, change the *Language* menu to *Kotlin* and select *Kotlin DSL (build.gradle.kts)* as the build configuration language before clicking *Finish* to create the project.

3.5 Modifying the Example Application

Once the project has been created, the main window will appear containing our AndroidSample project, as illustrated in Figure 3-4 below:

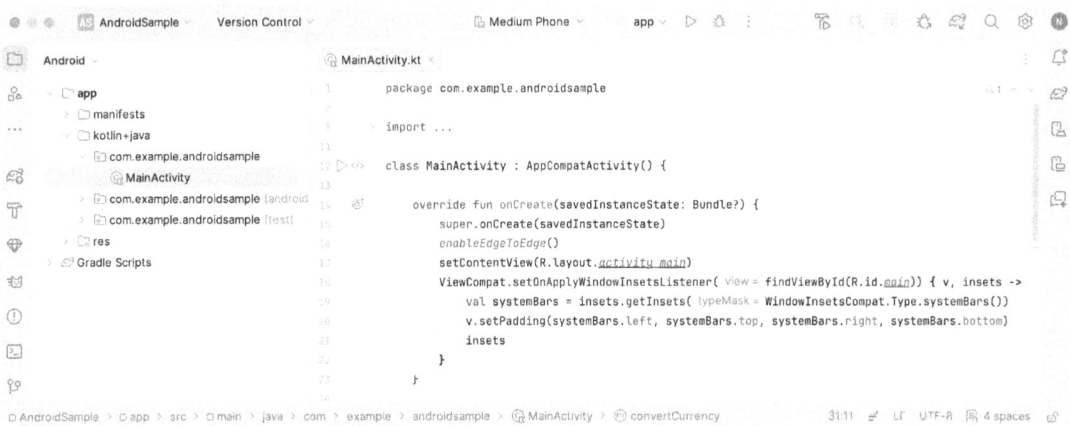

Figure 3-4

The newly created project and references to associated files are listed in the *Project* tool window on the left side of the main project window. The Project tool window has several modes in which information can be displayed. By default, this panel should be in *Android* mode. This setting is controlled by the menu at the top of the panel as highlighted in Figure 3-5. If the panel is not currently in Android mode, use the menu to switch mode:

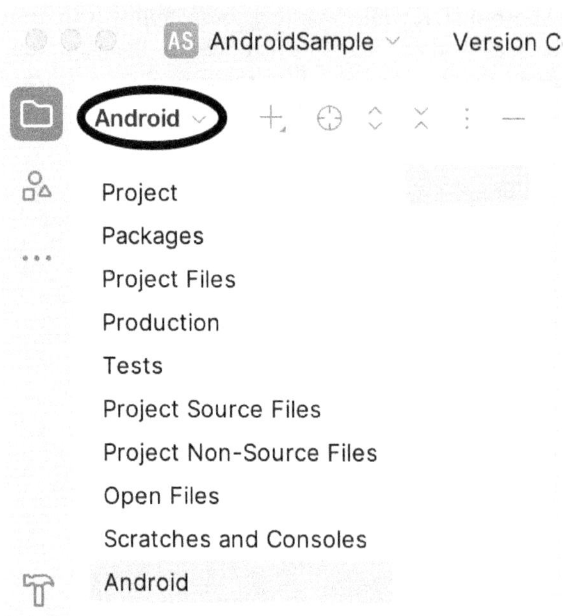

Figure 3-5

3.6 Modifying the User Interface

The user interface design for our activity is stored in a file named *activity_main.xml* which, in turn, is located under *app -> res -> layout* in the Project tool window file hierarchy. Once located in the Project tool window, double-click on the file to load it into the user interface Layout Editor tool, which will appear in the center panel of the Android Studio main window:

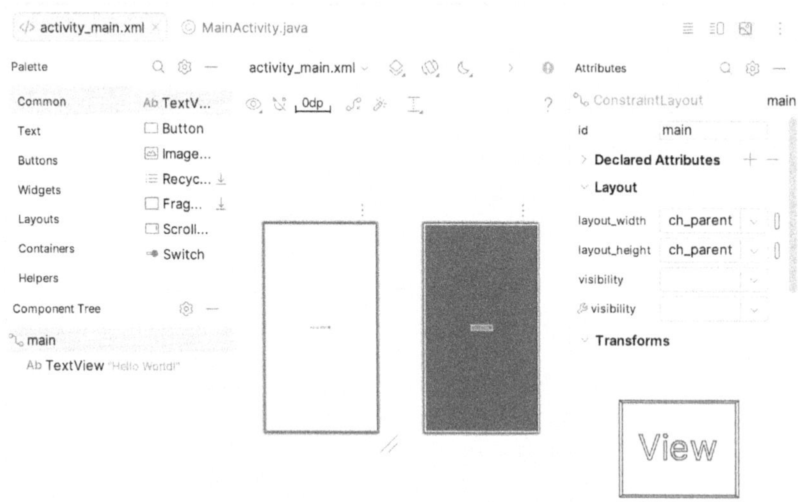

Figure 3-6

In the toolbar across the top of the Layout Editor window is a menu (currently set to *Pixel* in the above figure) which is reflected in the visual representation of the device within the Layout Editor panel. A range of other device options are available by clicking on this menu.

Use the System UI Mode button ( ) to turn Night mode on and off for the device screen layout. To change the orientation of the device representation between landscape and portrait, use the drop-down menu showing the icon.

As we can see in the device screen, the content layout already includes a label that displays a "Hello World!" message. Running down the left-hand side of the panel is a palette containing different categories of user interface components that may be used to construct a user interface, such as buttons, labels, and text fields. However, it should be noted that not all user interface components are visible to the user. One such category consists of *layouts*. Android supports a variety of layouts that provide different levels of control over how visual user interface components are positioned and managed on the screen. Though it is difficult to tell from looking at the visual representation of the user interface, the current design has been created using a ConstraintLayout. This can be confirmed by reviewing the information in the *Component Tree* panel, which, by default, is located in the lower left-hand corner of the Layout Editor panel and is shown in Figure 3-7:

Figure 3-7

As we can see from the component tree hierarchy, the user interface layout consists of a ConstraintLayout parent called *main* and a TextView child object.

Before proceeding, check that the Layout Editor's Autoconnect mode is enabled. This means that as components are added to the layout, the Layout Editor will automatically add constraints to ensure the components are correctly positioned for different screen sizes and device orientations (a topic that will be covered in much greater detail in future chapters). The Autoconnect button appears in the Layout Editor toolbar and is represented by a U-shaped icon. When disabled, the icon appears with a diagonal line through it (Figure 3-8). If necessary, re-enable Autoconnect mode by clicking on this button.

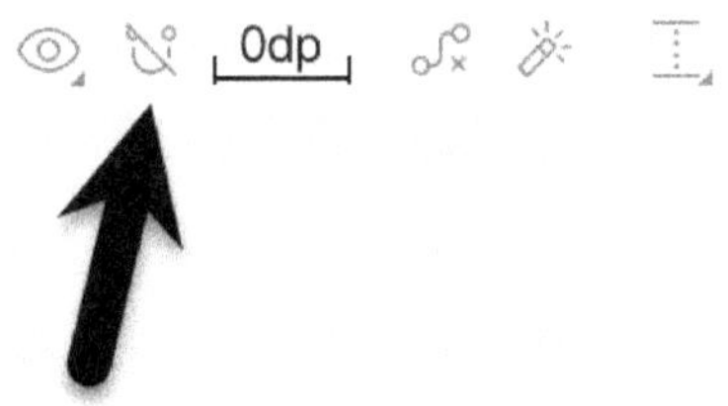

Figure 3-8

The next step in modifying the application is to add some additional components to the layout, the first of which will be a Button for the user to press to initiate the currency conversion.

The Palette panel consists of two columns, with the left-hand column containing a list of view component categories. The right-hand column lists the components contained within the currently selected category. In Figure 3-9, for example, the Button view is currently selected within the Buttons category:

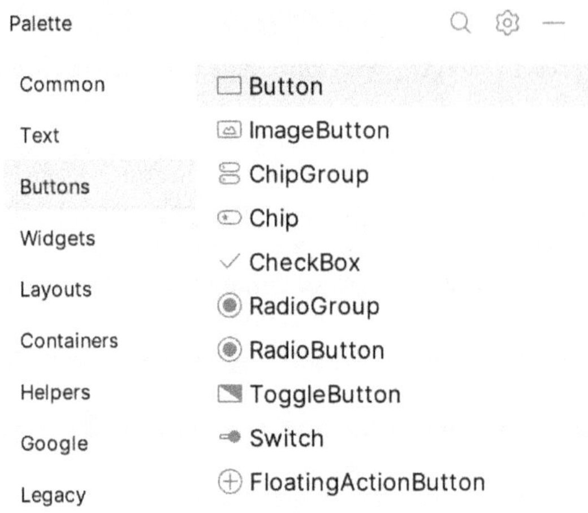

Figure 3-9

Click and drag the *Button* object from the Buttons list and drop it in the horizontal center of the user interface design so that it is positioned beneath the existing TextView widget:

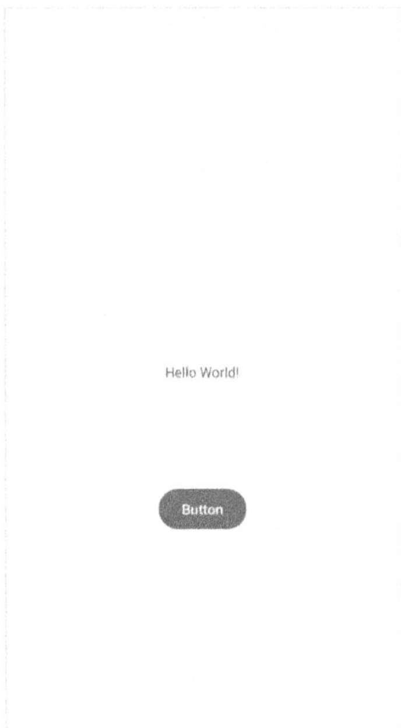

Figure 3-10

The next step is to change the text currently displayed by the Button component. The panel located to the right of the design area is the Attributes panel. This panel displays the attributes assigned to the currently selected component in the layout. Within this panel, locate the *text* property in the Common Attributes section and change the current value from "Button" to "Convert", as shown in Figure 3-11:

Figure 3-11

The second text property with a wrench next to it allows a text property to be set, which only appears within the Layout Editor tool but is not shown at runtime. This is useful for testing how a visual component and the layout will behave with different settings without running the app repeatedly.

Just in case the Autoconnect system failed to set all of the layout connections, click on the Infer Constraints button (Figure 3-12) to add any missing constraints to the layout:

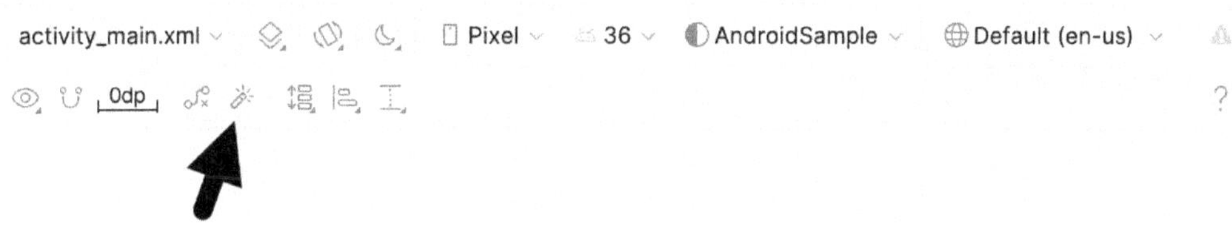

Figure 3-12

It is important to explain the warning button in the top right-hand corner of the Layout Editor tool, as indicated in Figure 3-13. This warning indicates potential problems with the layout. For details on any problems, click on the button:

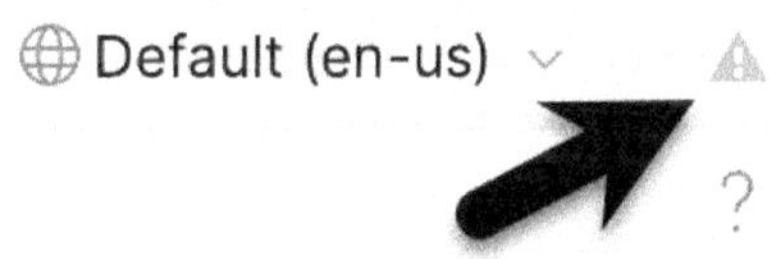

Figure 3-13

When clicked, the Problems tool window (Figure 3-14) will appear, describing the nature of the problems:

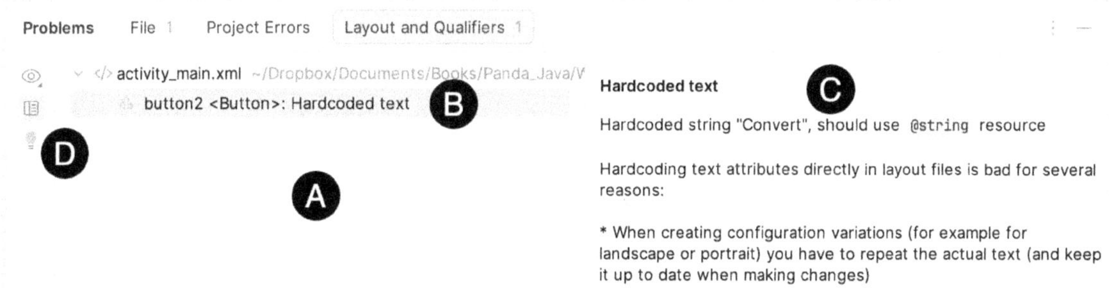

Figure 3-14

This tool window is divided into two panels. The left panel (marked A in the above figure) lists issues detected within the layout file. In our example, only the following problem is listed:

```
button <Button>: Hardcoded text
```

When an item is selected from the list (B), the right-hand panel will update to provide additional detail on the problem (C). In this case, the explanation reads as follows:

```
Hardcoded string "Convert", should use @string resource
```

This I18N message informs us that a potential issue exists concerning the future internationalization of the project ("I18N" comes from the fact that the word "internationalization" begins with an "I", ends with an "N" and has 18 letters in between). The warning reminds us that attributes and values such as text strings should be stored as *resources* wherever possible when developing Android applications. Doing so enables changes to the appearance of the application to be made by modifying resource files instead of changing the application source code. This can be especially valuable when translating a user interface to a different spoken language. If all of the text in a user interface is contained in a single resource file, for example, that file can be given to a translator, who will then perform the translation work and return the translated file for inclusion in the application. This enables multiple languages to be targeted without the necessity for any source code changes to be made. In this instance, we are going to create a new resource named *convert_string* and assign to it the string "Convert".

Begin by clicking on the Show Quick Fixes button (D) and selecting the *Extract string resource* option from the menu, as shown in Figure 3-15:

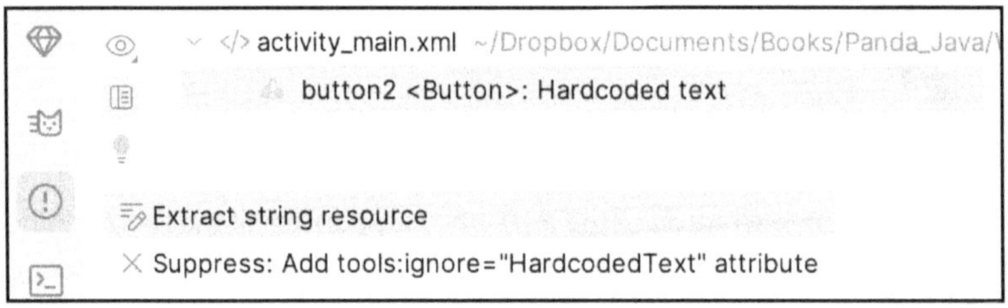

Figure 3-15

After selecting this option, the *Extract Resource* panel (Figure 3-16) will appear. Within this panel, change the resource name field to *convert_string* and leave the resource value set to *Convert* before clicking on the OK button:

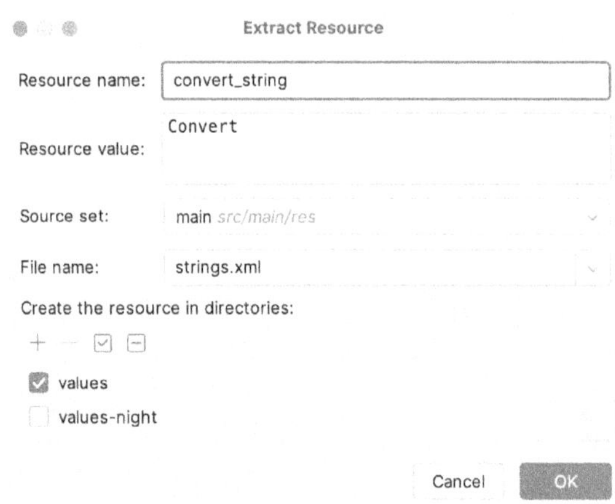

Figure 3-16

The next widget to be added is an EditText widget, into which the user will enter the dollar amount to be converted. From the Palette panel, select the Text category and click and drag a Number (Decimal) component onto the layout so that it is centered horizontally and positioned above the existing TextView widget. With the widget selected, use the Attributes tools window to set the *hint* property to "dollars". Click on the warning icon and extract the string to a resource named *dollars_hint*.

The code written later in this chapter will need to access the dollar value entered by the user into the EditText field. It will do this by referencing the id assigned to the widget in the user interface layout. The default id assigned to the widget by Android Studio can be viewed and changed from within the Attributes tool window when the widget is selected in the layout, as shown in Figure 3-17:

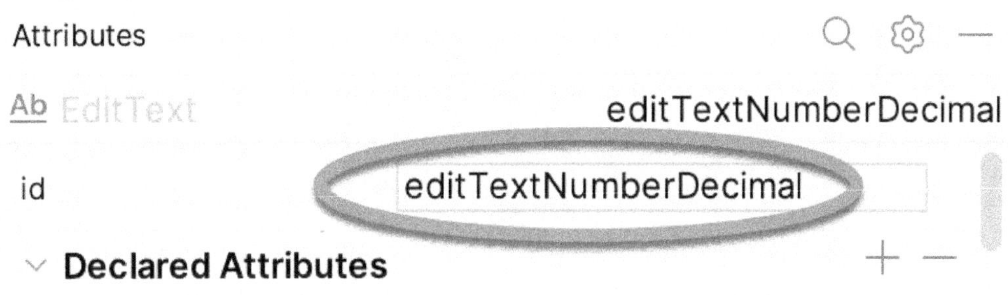

Figure 3-17

Change the id to *dollarText* and, in the Rename dialog, click on the *Refactor* button. This ensures that any references elsewhere within the project to the old id are automatically updated to use the new id:

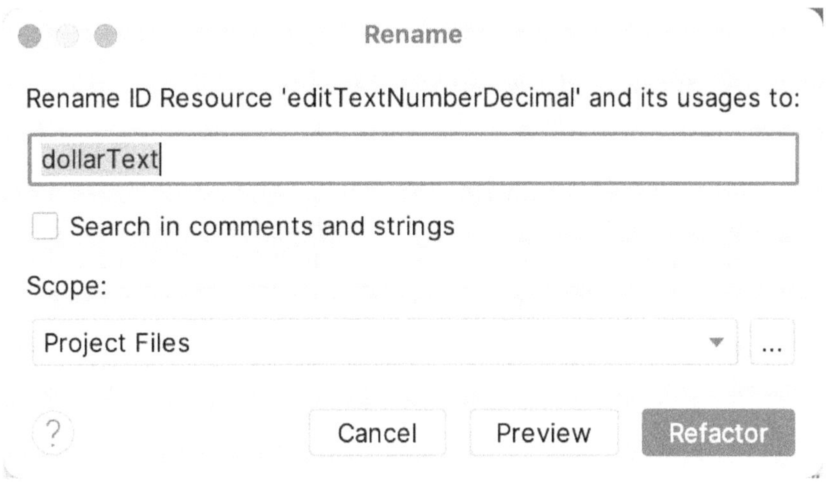

Figure 3-18

Repeat the steps to set the id of the TextView widget to *textView*, if necessary.

Add any missing layout constraints by clicking on the *Infer Constraints* button. At this point, the layout should resemble that shown in Figure 3-19:

Figure 3-19

3.7 Reviewing the Layout and Resource Files

Before moving on to the next step, we will look at some internal aspects of user interface design and resource handling. In the previous section, we changed the user interface by modifying the *activity_main.xml* file using the Layout Editor tool. In fact, all that the Layout Editor was doing was providing a user-friendly way to edit the underlying XML content of the file. In practice, there is no reason why you cannot modify the XML directly to make user interface changes, and, in some instances, this may actually be quicker than using the Layout Editor tool. In the top right-hand corner of the Layout Editor panel are the View Modes buttons marked A through C in Figure 3-20 below:

Figure 3-20

By default, the editor will be in *Design* mode (button C), whereby only the visual representation of the layout is displayed. In *Code* mode (A), the editor will display the XML for the layout, while in *Split* mode (B), both the layout and XML are displayed, as shown in Figure 3-21:

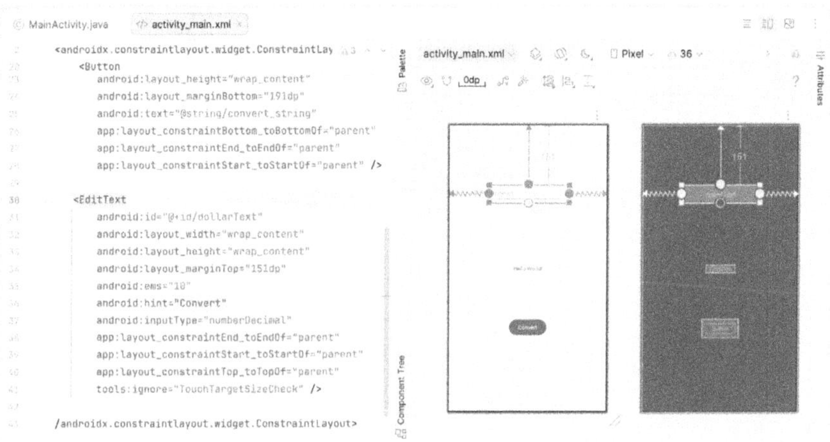

Figure 3-21

The button to the left of the View Modes button (marked B in Figure 3-20 above) is used to toggle between Code and Split modes quickly.

As can be seen from the structure of the XML file, the user interface consists of the ConstraintLayout component, which in turn, is the parent of the TextView, Button, and EditText objects. We can also see, for example, that the *text* property of the Button is set to our *convert_string* resource. Although complexity and content vary, all user interface layouts are structured in this hierarchical, XML-based way.

As changes are made to the XML layout, these will be reflected in the layout canvas. The layout may also be modified visually from within the layout canvas panel, with the changes appearing in the XML listing. To see this in action, switch to Split mode and modify the XML layout to change the background color of the ConstraintLayout to a shade of red as follows:

```
<?xml version="1.0" encoding="utf-8"?>
<androidx.constraintlayout.widget.ConstraintLayout xmlns:android="http://schemas.
android.com/apk/res/android"
    xmlns:app="http://schemas.android.com/apk/res-auto"
    xmlns:tools="http://schemas.android.com/tools"
    android:id="@+id/main"
    android:layout_width="match_parent"
    android:layout_height="match_parent"
    tools:context=".MainActivity"
    android:background="#ff2438" >
.
.
</androidx.constraintlayout.widget.ConstraintLayout>
```

Note that the layout color changes in real-time to match the new setting in the XML file. Note also that a small red square appears in the XML editor's left margin (also called the *gutter*) next to the line containing the color setting. This is a visual cue to the fact that the color red has been set on a property. Clicking on the red square will display a color chooser allowing a different color to be selected:

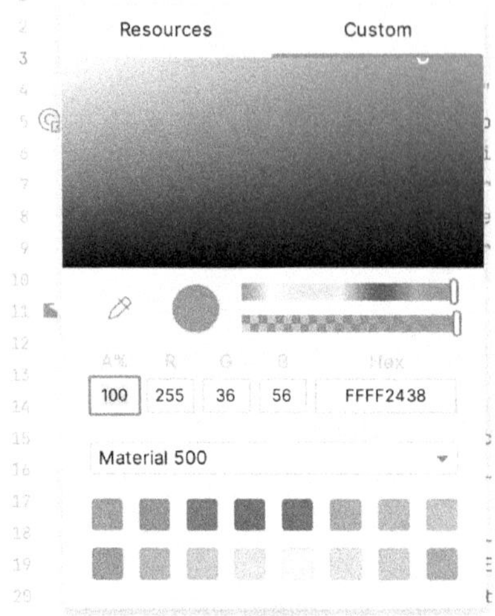

Figure 3-22

Before proceeding, delete the background property from the layout file so that the background returns to the default setting.

Finally, use the Project panel to locate the *app -> res -> values -> strings.xml* file and double-click on it to load it into the editor. Currently, the XML should read as follows:

```
<resources>
    <string name="app_name">AndroidSample</string>
    <string name="convert_string">Convert</string>
    <string name="dollars_hint">dollars</string>
</resources>
```

To demonstrate resources in action, change the string value currently assigned to the *convert_string* resource to "Convert to Euros" and then return to the Layout Editor tool by selecting the tab for the layout file in the editor panel. Note that the layout has picked up the new resource value for the string.

There is also a quick way to access the value of a resource referenced in an XML file. With the Layout Editor tool in Split or Code mode, click on the "@string/convert_string" property setting so that it highlights, and then press Ctrl-B on the keyboard (Cmd-B on macOS). Android Studio will subsequently open the *strings.xml* file and take you to the line in that file where this resource is declared. Use this opportunity to revert the string resource to the original "Convert" text and to add the following additional entry for a string resource that will be referenced later in the app code:

```
<resources>
    <string name="app_name">AndroidSample</string>
    <string name="convert_string">Convert</string>
    <string name="dollars_hint">dollars</string>
    <string name="no_value_string">No Value</string>
</resources>
```

Resource strings may also be edited using the Android Studio Translations Editor by clicking on the *Open editor* link in the top right-hand corner of the editor window. This will display the Translation Editor in the main panel of the Android Studio window:

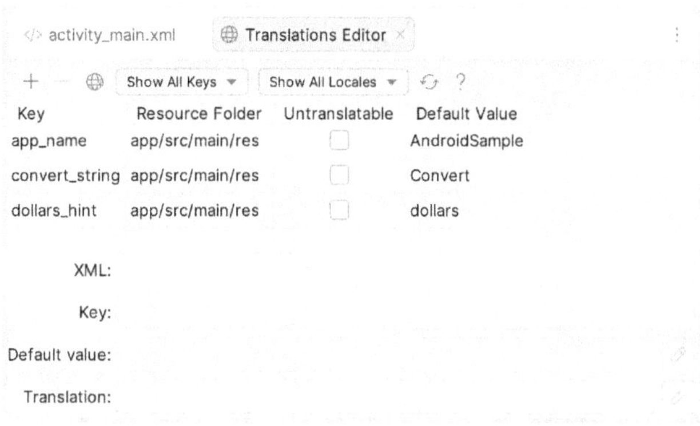

Figure 3-23

This editor allows the strings assigned to resource keys to be edited and for translations for multiple languages to be managed.

3.8 Adding Interaction

The final step in this example project is to make the app interactive so that when the user enters a dollar value into the EditText field and clicks the convert button, the converted euro value appears on the TextView. This involves the implementation of some event handling on the Button widget. Specifically, the Button needs to be configured so that a method in the app code is called when an *onClick* event is triggered. Event handling can be implemented in several ways and is covered in a later chapter entitled *"An Overview and Example of Android Event Handling"*. Return the layout editor to Design mode, select the Button widget in the layout editor, refer to the Attributes tool window, and specify a method named *convertCurrency* as shown below:

Figure 3-24

Next, double-click on the *MainActivity.kt* file in the Project tool window (*app -> kotlin+java -> <package name> -> MainActivity*) to load it into the code editor and add the code for the *convertCurrency* method to the class file so that it reads as follows, noting that it is also necessary to import some additional Android packages:

```
package com.example.androidsample

import android.os.Bundle
import androidx.activity.enableEdgeToEdge
import androidx.appcompat.app.AppCompatActivity
import androidx.core.view.ViewCompat
import androidx.core.view.WindowInsetsCompat
import android.view.View
import android.widget.EditText
import android.widget.TextView
```

```
class MainActivity : AppCompatActivity() {
    override fun onCreate(savedInstanceState: Bundle?) {
        super.onCreate(savedInstanceState)
.
.
        }
    }

    fun convertCurrency(view: View) {
        val dollarText: EditText = findViewById(R.id.dollarText)
        val textView: TextView = findViewById(R.id.textView)

        if (dollarText.text.isNotEmpty()) {
            val dollarValue = dollarText.text.toString().toFloat()
            val euroValue = dollarValue * 0.85f
            textView.text = euroValue.toString()
        } else {
            textView.text = getString(R.string.no_value_string)
        }
    }
}
```

The method begins by obtaining references to the EditText and TextView objects by making a call to a method named findViewById, passing through the id assigned within the layout file. A check is then made to ensure that the user has entered a dollar value, and if so, that value is extracted, converted from a String to a floating point value, and converted to euros. Finally, the result is displayed on the TextView widget.

If any of this is unclear, rest assured that these concepts will be covered in greater detail in later chapters. In particular, the topic of accessing widgets from within code using findByViewId and an introduction to an alternative technique referred to as *view binding* will be covered in the chapter entitled *"An Overview of Android View Binding"*.

3.9 Summary

While not excessively complex, several steps are involved in setting up an Android development environment. Having performed those steps, it is worth working through an example to ensure the environment is correctly installed and configured. In this chapter, we have created an example application and then used the Android Studio Layout Editor tool to modify the user interface layout. In doing so, we explored the importance of using resources wherever possible, particularly string values, and briefly touched on layouts. Next, we looked at the underlying XML used to store Android application user interface designs.

Finally, an onClick event was added to a Button connected to a method implemented to extract the user input from the EditText component, convert it from dollars to euros and then display the result on the TextView.

With the app ready for testing, the steps necessary to set up an emulator for testing purposes will be covered in detail in the next chapter.

Chapter 4

4. Creating an Android Virtual Device (AVD) in Android Studio

Although the Android Studio Preview panel allows us to see the layout we are designing, compiling and running an entire app will be necessary to thoroughly test that it works. An Android application may be tested by installing and running it on a physical device or in an Android Virtual Device (AVD) emulator environment. Before an AVD can be used, it must first be created and configured to match the specifications of a particular device model. In this chapter, we will work through creating such a virtual device using the Pixel 9 phone as a reference example.

4.1 About Android Virtual Devices

AVDs are emulators that allow Android applications to be tested without needing to install the application on a physical Android-based device. An AVD may be configured to emulate various hardware features, including screen size, memory capacity, and the presence or otherwise of features such as a camera, GPS navigation support, or an accelerometer. Several emulator templates are installed as part of the standard Android Studio installation, allowing AVDs to be configured for various devices. Custom configurations may be created to match any physical Android device by specifying properties such as processor type, memory capacity, and the size and pixel density of the screen.

An AVD session can appear as a separate window or embedded within the Android Studio window.

New AVDs are created and managed using the Android Virtual Device Manager, which may be used in command-line mode or with a more user-friendly graphical user interface. To create a new AVD, the first step is to launch the AVD Manager. This can be achieved from within the Android Studio environment by clicking the *Device Manager* button in the right-hand tool window bar, as indicated in Figure 4-1:

Figure 4-1

Once opened, the manager will appear as a tool window, as shown in Figure 4-2:

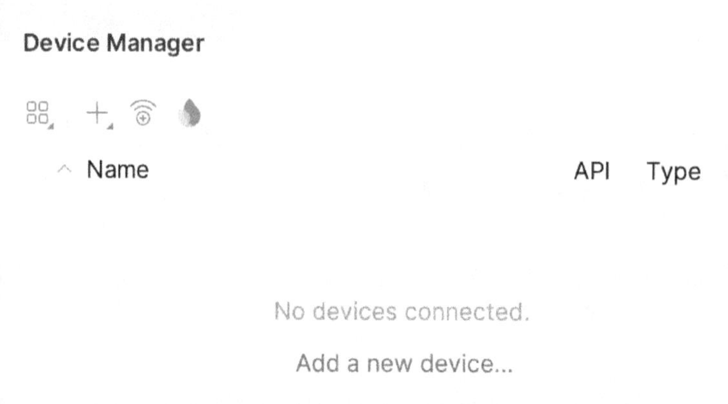

Figure 4-2

If you installed Android Studio for the first time on a computer (as opposed to upgrading an existing Android Studio installation), the installer might have created an initial AVD instance ready for use, as shown in Figure 4-3:

Figure 4-3

If this AVD is present on your system, you can use it to test apps. If no AVD was created, or you would like to create AVDs for different device types, follow the steps in the rest of this chapter.

To add a new AVD, click on the '+' button in the Device Manager toolbar and select the Create Virtual Device menu option:

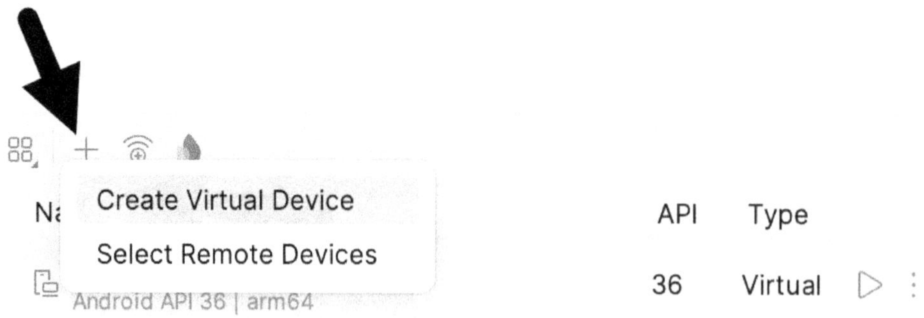

Figure 4-4

After selecting the option to create a virtual device, the Add Device dialog shown in Figure 4-5 dialog will appear:

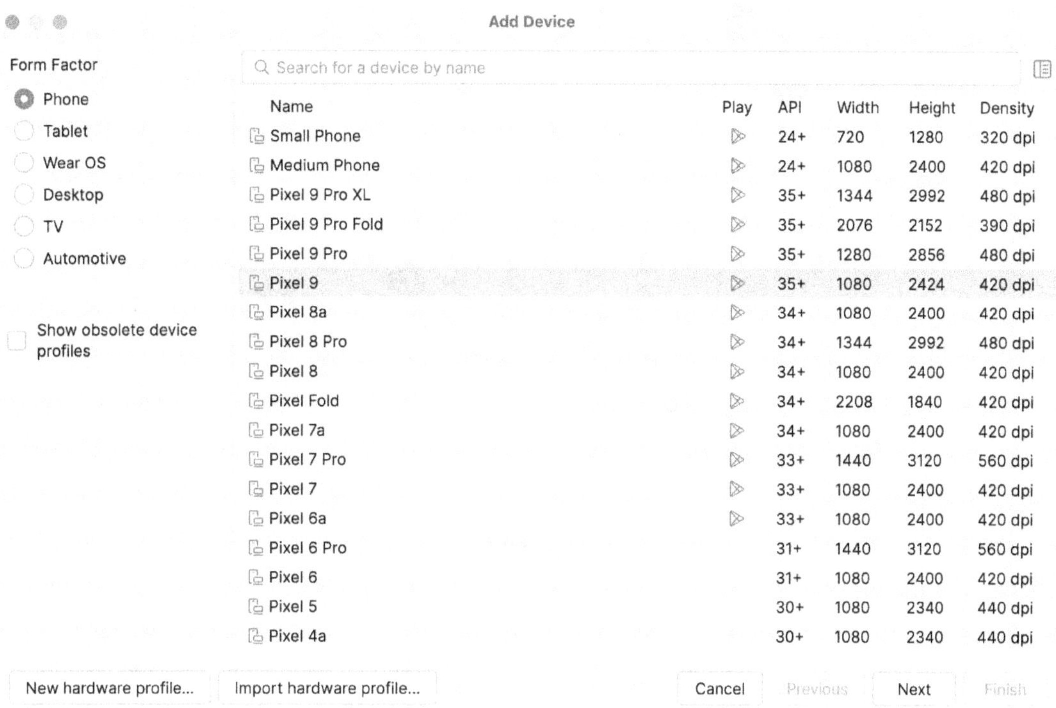

Figure 4-5

Within the dialog, perform the following steps to create a Pixel 9-compatible emulator:

1. Select the Phone option from the Form Factor panel to display the available Android phone AVD templates.
2. Select the *Pixel 9* device option and click *Next.*
3. On the configuration screen, select the latest Android version from the API menu (marked A in Figure 4-6).
4. Use the Services menu (B) to select which services to include in the emulator. Select the "Google Play Store" service option if you plan to complete the in-app billing chapters.
5. Select an image from the System Image list (C).
6. Enter a descriptive name (Pixel 9 API 36) into the name field (D) or accept the default name.
7. Review other configuration options by selecting the "Additional settings" tab (E). Available settings include device orientation, camera emulation options, simulated network speed and latency properties, and internal storage.
8. Click *Finish* to create the AVD.

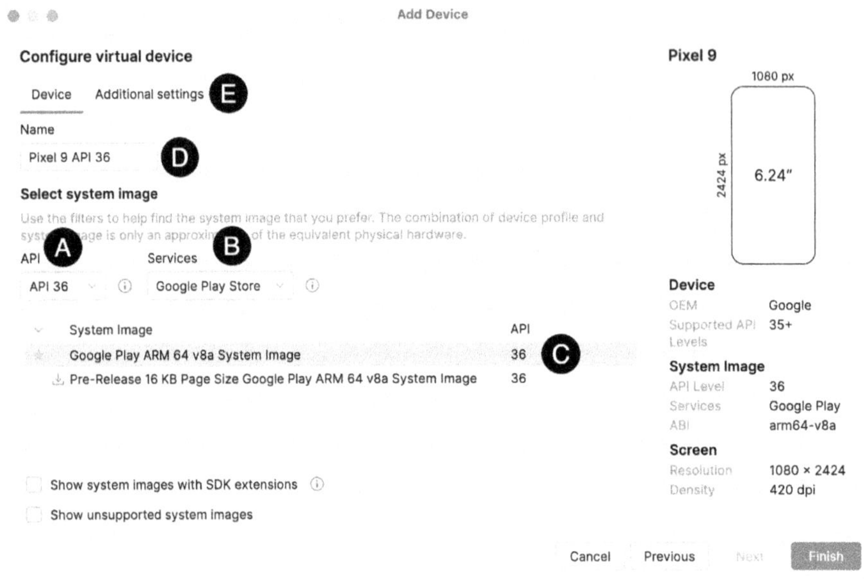

Figure 4-6

4.2 Remote Devices

An alternative to testing using an AVD emulator or your own Android device is to run the app on a remote device hosted by Google. To use this service, however, you will need to create a Firebase account and enable it within Android Studio. Firebase offers a free plan (called Spark) that provides 30 minutes of testing time a month per device model. Additional time will require an upgrade to the Blaze plan and the creation of a Google billing account.

Choosing the Select Remote Devices option from the menu shown in Figure 4-4 above will display the following dialog:

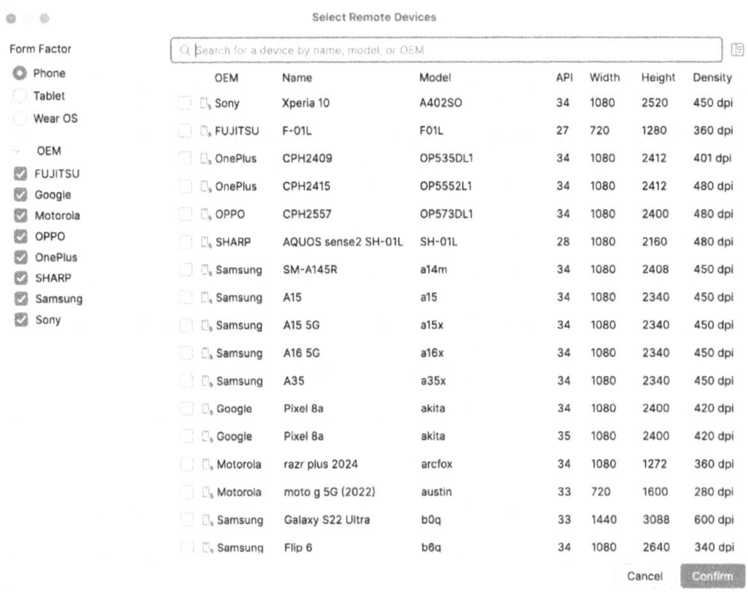

Figure 4-7

After selecting one or more remote devices and clicking the Confirm button, they will appear in the Device Manager tool window.

4.3 Starting the Emulator

To test the newly created AVD emulator, select the emulator from the Device Manager and click the Start button (the triangle located to the left of the menu button highlighted above). The emulator will appear embedded into the main Android Studio window and begin the startup process. The amount of time it takes for the emulator to start will depend on the configuration of both the AVD and the system on which it is running:

Figure 4-8

To hide and show the emulator tool window, click the Running Devices tool window button (marked A above). Click the "x" close button next to the tab (B) to exit the emulator. The emulator tool window can accommodate multiple emulator sessions, with each session represented by a tab. Figure 4-9, for example, shows a tool window with two emulator sessions:

Figure 4-9

To switch between sessions, click on the corresponding tab.

4.4 Running the Application in the AVD

With an AVD emulator configured, the example AndroidSample application created in the earlier chapter can now be compiled and run. With the AndroidSample project loaded into Android Studio, make sure that the newly created Pixel 9 AVD is displayed in the device menu (marked A in Figure 4-10 below), then either click the run button represented by a triangle (B), select the *Run -> Run 'app'* menu option or use the Ctrl-R keyboard shortcut:

Figure 4-10

The device menu (A) may be used to select a different AVD instance or physical device as the run target and also to run the app on multiple devices. The menu also provides access to the Device Manager as well as device connection configuration and troubleshooting options:

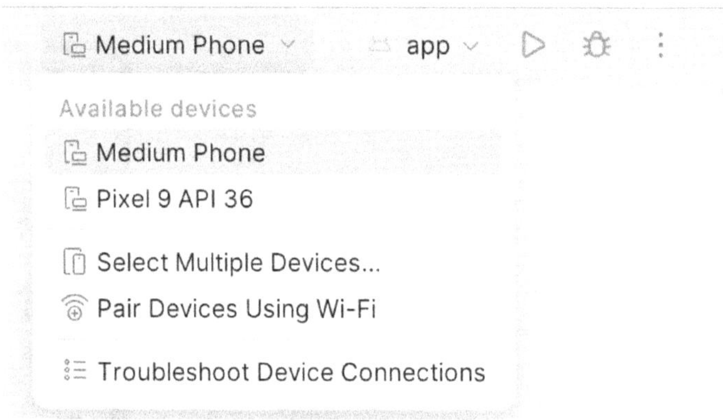

Figure 4-11

Once the application is installed and running, the user interface will appear within the emulator.

Once the run process begins, information will appear in the Run tool window. The Run tool window displays diagnostic information as the application package is installed and launched. If window does not open automatically, click the button shown in Figure 4-12:

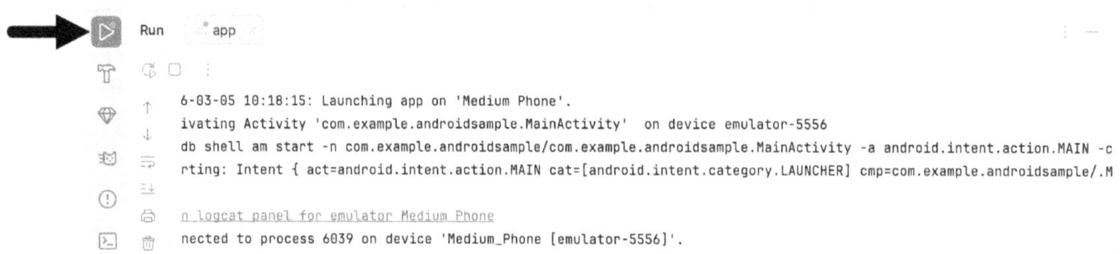

Figure 4-12

If problems are encountered during the launch process, the Run tool window will provide information to help isolate the problem's cause.

Assuming the application loads into the emulator and runs as expected, we have safely verified that the Android development environment is correctly installed and configured. With the app running, move the slider to verify that the app works as intended.

4.5 Running on Multiple Devices

The run target menu shown in Figure 4-11 above includes an option to run the app on multiple emulators and devices in parallel. When selected, this option displays the dialog in Figure 4-13, providing a list of the AVDs configured on the system and any attached physical devices. Enable the checkboxes next to the emulators or devices to be targeted before clicking on the Run button:

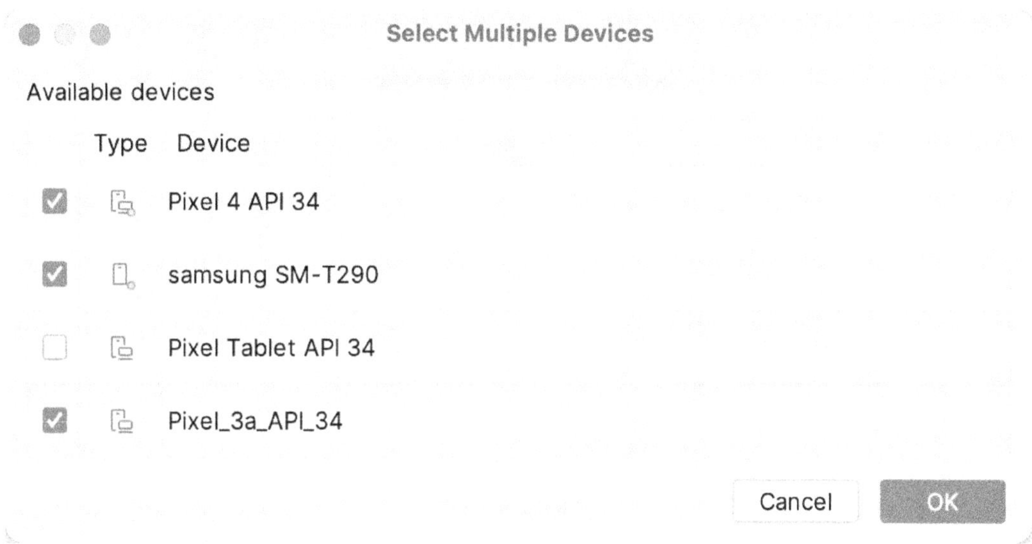

Figure 4-13

After clicking the Run button, Android Studio will launch the app on the selected emulators and devices.

4.6 Stopping a Running Application

To stop a running application, click the stop button located in the main toolbar, as shown in Figure 4-14:

Figure 4-14

An app may also be terminated using the Run tool window. Begin by displaying the *Run* tool window using the window bar button that becomes available when the app is running. Once the Run tool window appears, click the stop button highlighted in Figure 4-15 below:

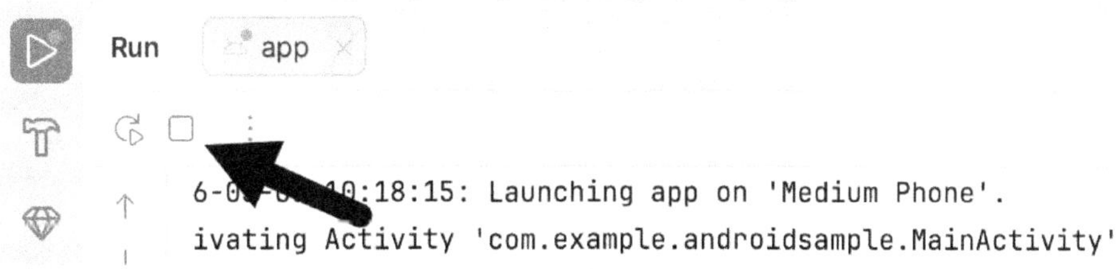

Figure 4-15

4.7 Supporting Dark Theme

To test how an app behaves when dark theme is enabled, click the Device UI Shortcuts button in the Running Devices tool window and enable the Dark Theme option in the resulting dialog:

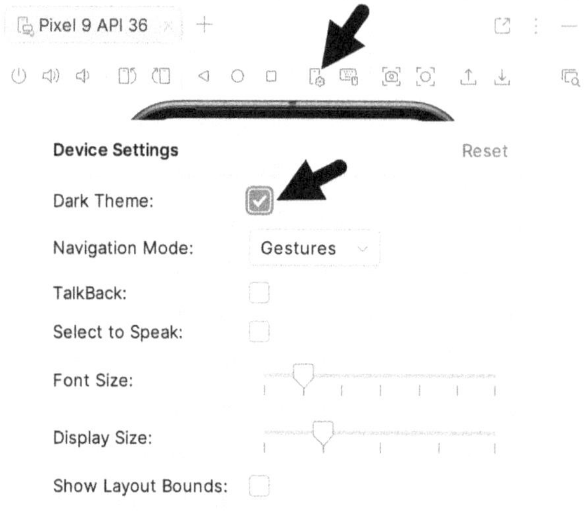

Figure 4-16

With dark theme enabled, the AndroidSample app will appear as shown in Figure 4-17:

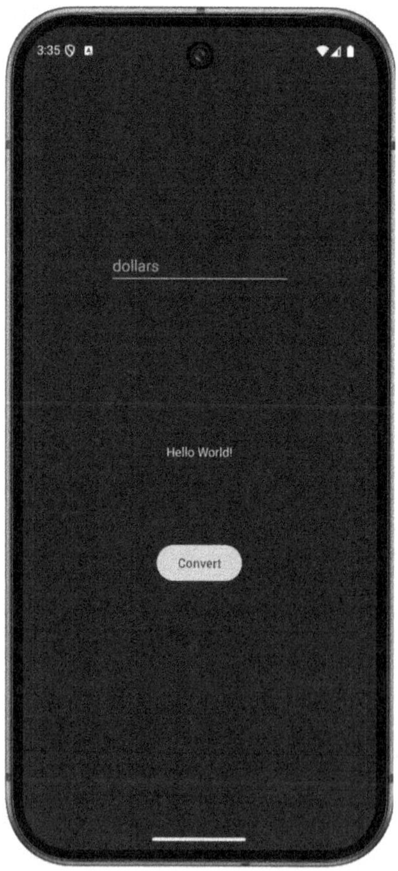

Figure 4-17

Use the Device UI Shortcuts dialog to turn off dark theme mode before continuing.

4.8 Running the Emulator in a Separate Window

So far in this chapter, we have only used the emulator as a tool window embedded within the main Android Studio window. The emulator can be configured to appear in a separate window within the Settings dialog, which can be displayed by clicking on the IDE and Project Settings button located in the Android Studio toolbar, as highlighted in Figure 4-18:

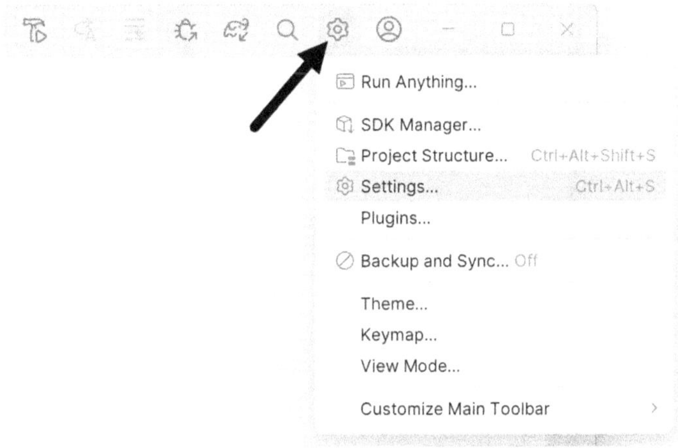

Figure 4-18

Within the Settings dialog, navigate to *Tools -> Emulator* in the side panel, and disable the *Launch in a tool window* option:

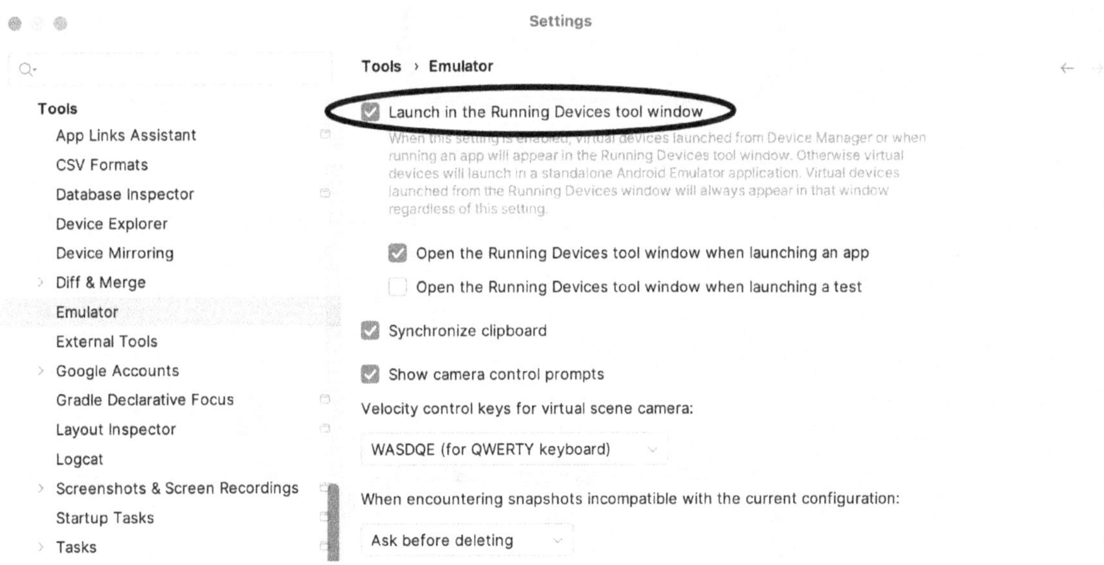

Figure 4-19

With the option disabled, click the Apply button followed by OK to commit the change, then exit the current emulator session by clicking on the close button on the tab marked B in Figure 4-8 above.

Run the sample app once again, at which point the emulator will appear as a separate window, as shown below:

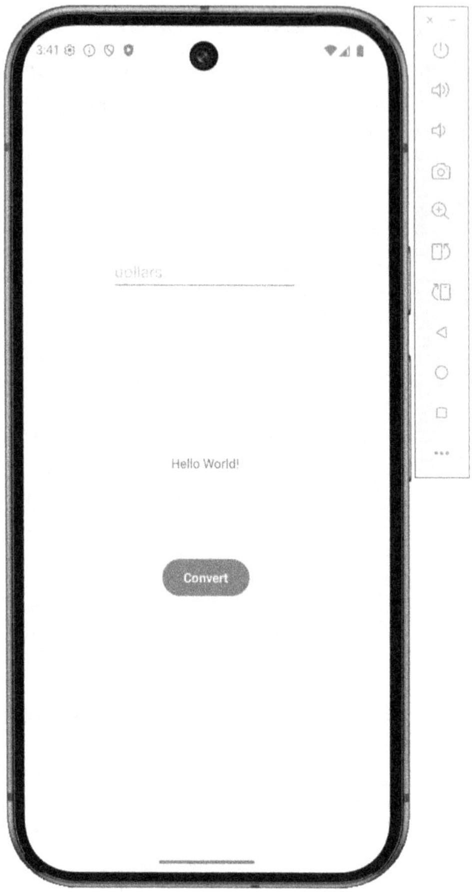

Figure 4-20

The choice of standalone or tool window mode is a matter of personal preference. If you prefer the emulator running in a tool window, return to the settings screen and re-enable the *Launch in a tool window* option. Before committing to standalone mode, however, keep in mind that the Running Devices tool window may also be detached from the main Android Studio window using the button indicated in Figure 4-21:

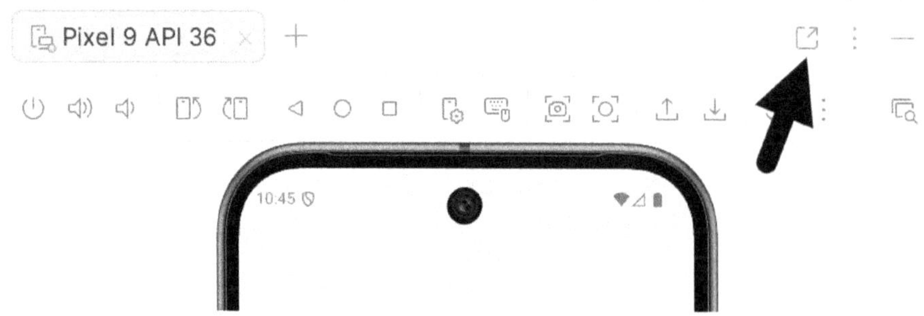

Figure 4-21

To re-dock the Running Devices tool window, click on the Dock button shown in Figure 4-22:

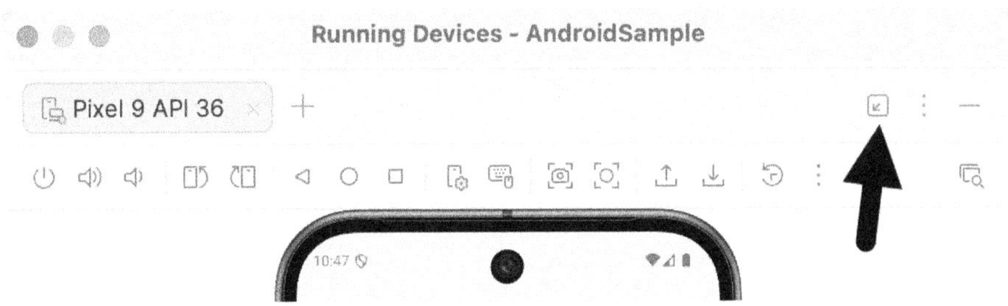

Figure 4-22

4.9 Removing the Device Frame

The emulator can be configured to appear with or without the device frame. To change the setting, exit the emulator, open the Device Manager, select the AVD from the list, and click on the menu button indicated by the arrow in Figure 4-23:

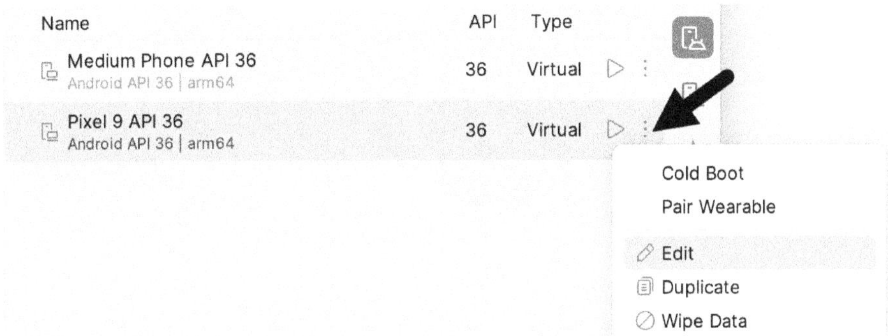

Figure 4-23

Select the Edit option and, in the configuration screen, select the "Additional settings" tab and change Device skin menu to [None] before clicking the Finish button:

Figure 4-24

Once the device frame has been disabled, the emulator will appear as shown in Figure 4-25 the next time it is launched:

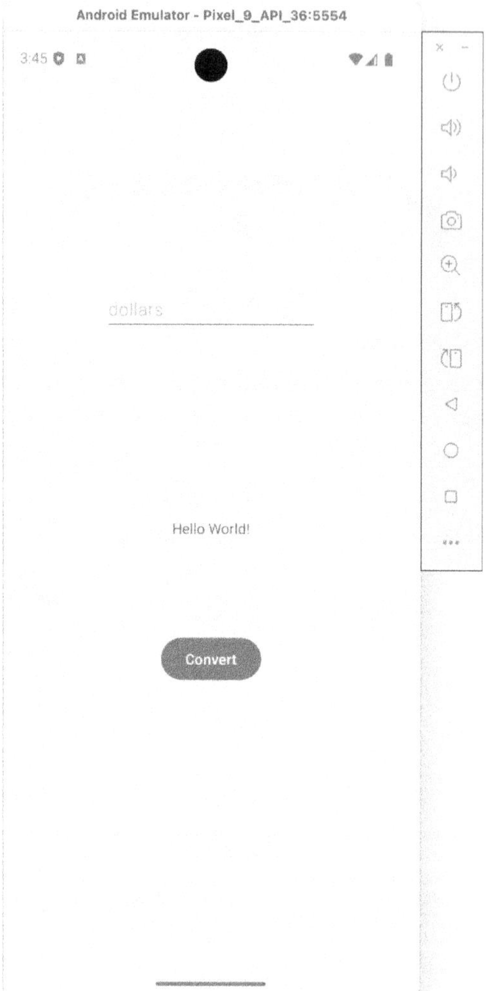

Figure 4-25

4.10 Summary

A typical application development process follows a cycle of coding, compiling, and running in a test environment. Android applications may be tested on a physical Android device or an Android Virtual Device (AVD) emulator. AVDs are created and managed using the Android Studio Device Manager tool, which may be used as a command-line tool or via a graphical user interface. When creating an AVD to simulate a specific Android device model, the virtual device should be configured with a hardware specification matching that of the physical device.

The AVD emulator session may be displayed as a standalone window or embedded into the main Android Studio user interface.

Chapter 5

5. Using and Configuring the Android Studio AVD Emulator

In this chapter, we will explore the features of the Android Studio AVD emulator, focusing on its configuration options to customize the environment in both standalone and tool window modes.

5.1 The Emulator Environment

When launched in a separate window, the emulator displays an initial splash screen during the loading process. Once loaded, the main emulator window appears, containing a representation of the chosen device type (in the case of Figure 5-1, this is a Pixel 4 device):

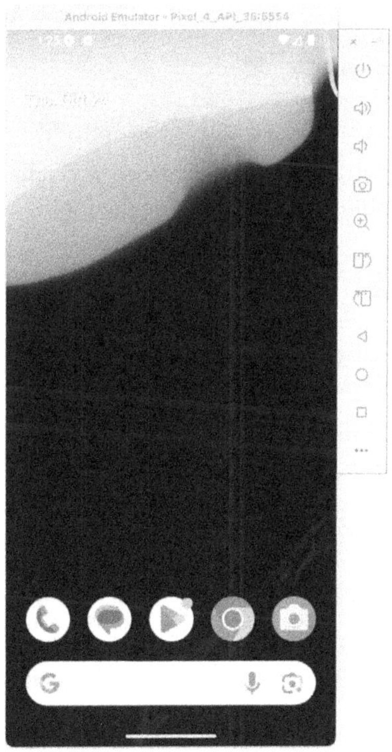

Figure 5-1

The toolbar positioned along the right-hand edge of the window provides quick access to the emulator controls and configuration options.

5.2 Emulator Toolbar Options

The emulator toolbar (Figure 5-2) provides access to a range of options relating to the appearance and behavior of the emulator environment.

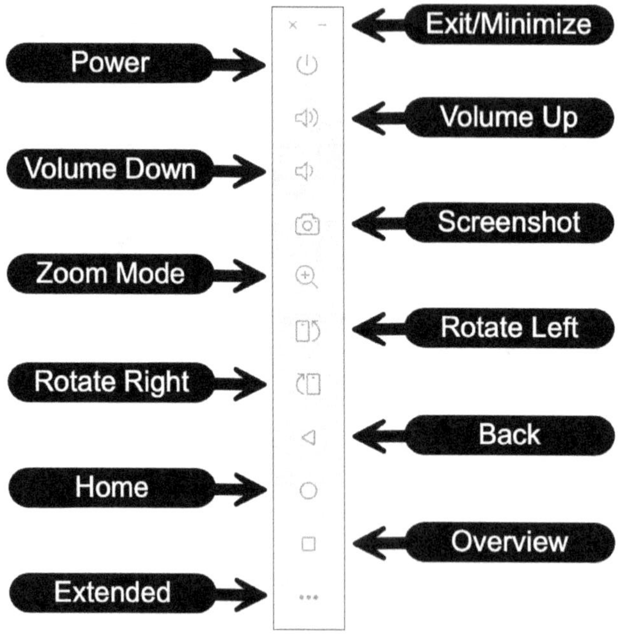

Figure 5-2

Each button in the toolbar has associated with it a keyboard accelerator which can be identified either by hovering the mouse pointer over the button and waiting for the tooltip to appear or via the help option of the extended controls panel.

Though many of the options contained within the toolbar are self-explanatory, each option will be covered for the sake of completeness:

- **Exit / Minimize** – The uppermost 'x' button in the toolbar exits the emulator session when selected, while the '-' option minimizes the entire window.
- **Power** – The Power button simulates the hardware power button on a physical Android device. Clicking and releasing this button will lock the device and turn off the screen. Clicking and holding this button will initiate the device "Power off" request sequence.
- **Volume Up / Down** – Two buttons that control the audio volume of playback within the simulator environment.
- **Take Screenshot** – Takes a screenshot of the content displayed on the device screen. The captured image is stored at the location specified in the Settings screen of the extended controls panel, as outlined later in this chapter.
- **Zoom Mode** – This button toggles in and out of zoom mode, details of which will be covered later in this chapter.
- **Rotate Left/Right** – Rotates the emulated device between portrait and landscape orientations.
- **Back** – Performs the standard Android "Back" navigation to return to a previous screen.
- **Home** – Displays the device's home screen.
- **Overview** – Simulates selection of the standard Android "Overview" navigation, which displays the currently running apps on the device.

- **Fold Device** – Simulates the folding and unfolding of a foldable device. This option is only available if the emulator is running a foldable device system image.
- **Extended Controls** – Displays the extended controls panel, allowing for the configuration of options such as simulated location and telephony activity, battery strength, cellular network type, and fingerprint identification.

5.3 Working in Zoom Mode

The zoom button located in the emulator toolbar switches in and out of zoom mode. When zoom mode is active, the toolbar button is depressed, and the mouse pointer appears as a magnifying glass when hovering over the device screen. Clicking the left mouse button will cause the display to zoom in relative to the selected point on the screen, with repeated clicking increasing the zoom level. Conversely, clicking the right mouse button decreases the zoom level. Toggling the zoom button off reverts the display to the default size.

Clicking and dragging while in zoom mode will define a rectangular area into which the view will zoom when the mouse button is released.

While in zoom mode, the screen's visible area may be panned using the horizontal and vertical scrollbars located within the emulator window.

5.4 Resizing the Emulator Window

The emulator window's size (and the device's corresponding representation) can be changed at any time by clicking and dragging on any of the corners or sides of the window.

5.5 Extended Control Options

The extended controls toolbar button displays the panel illustrated in Figure 5-3. By default, the display settings will be shown. Selecting a different category from the left-hand panel will display the corresponding group of controls:

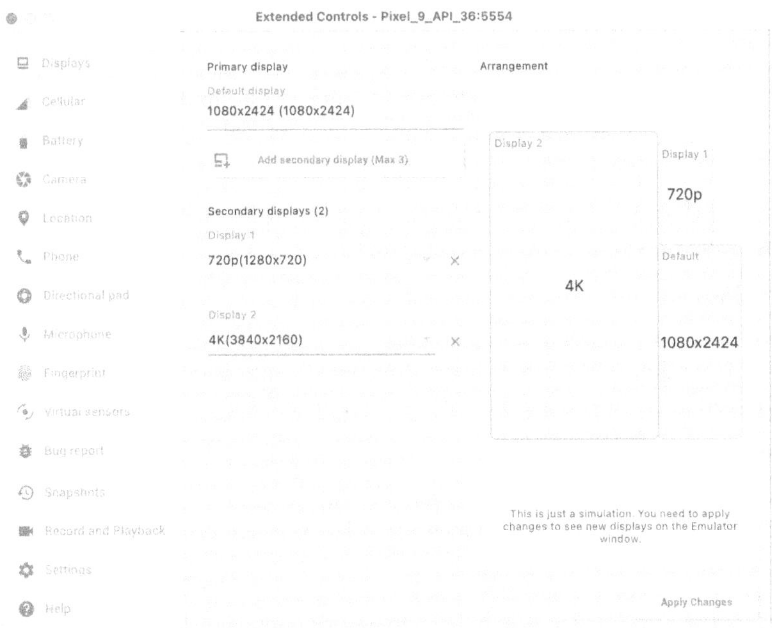

Figure 5-3

5.5.1 Displays

The display settings screen allows additional screen sizes to be added to the emulator so that apps can be tested in various device sizes. To add display sizes, click the "Add secondary display" button and change the screen dimensions using the drop-down menu. Click the Apply Changes button to create the displays, which will appear beside the default display in the emulator window. The emulator supports three secondary screens in addition to the default display.

5.5.2 Cellular

The type of cellular connection being simulated can be changed within the cellular settings screen. Options are available to simulate different network types (CSM, EDGE, HSDPA, etc.) in addition to a range of voice and data scenarios, such as roaming and denied access.

5.5.3 Battery

Various battery state and charging conditions can be simulated on this panel of the extended controls screen, including battery charge level, battery health, and whether the AC charger is currently connected.

5.5.4 Camera

The emulator simulates a 3D scene when the camera is active. This takes the form of the interior of a virtual building through which you can navigate by holding down the Option key (Alt on Windows) while using the mouse pointer and keyboard keys when recording video or before taking a photo within the emulator. This extended configuration option allows different images to be uploaded for display within the virtual environment.

5.5.5 Location

The location controls allow simulated location information to be sent to the emulator as decimal or sexagesimal coordinates. Location information can take the form of a single location or a sequence of points representing the device's movement, the latter being provided via a file in either GPS Exchange (GPX) or Keyhole Markup Language (KML) format. Alternatively, the integrated Google Maps panel may be used to select single points or travel routes visually.

5.5.6 Phone

The phone extended controls provide two straightforward but helpful simulations within the emulator. The first option simulates an incoming call from a designated phone number. This can be particularly useful when testing how an app handles high-level interrupts.

The second option allows the receipt of text messages to be simulated within the emulator session. As in the real world, these messages appear within the Message app and trigger the standard notifications within the emulator.

5.5.7 Directional Pad

A directional pad (D-Pad) is an additional set of controls either built into an Android device or connected externally (such as a game controller) that provides directional controls (left, right, up, down). The directional pad settings allow D-Pad interaction to be simulated within the emulator.

5.5.8 Microphone

The microphone settings allow the microphone to be enabled and virtual headset and microphone connections to be simulated. A button is also provided to launch the Voice Assistant on the emulator.

5.5.9 Fingerprint

Many Android devices are now supplied with built-in fingerprint detection hardware. The AVD emulator makes it possible to test fingerprint authentication without the need to test apps on a physical device containing a fingerprint sensor. Details on configuring fingerprint testing within the emulator will be covered later in this chapter.

5.5.10 Virtual Sensors

The virtual sensors option allows the accelerometer and magnetometer to be simulated to emulate the effects of the physical motion of a device, such as rotation, movement, and tilting through yaw, pitch, and roll settings.

5.5.11 Bug report

Use this screen if you encounter a problem while using the emulator and want to submit a bug report to Google.

5.5.12 Snapshots

Snapshots contain the state of the currently running AVD session to be saved and rapidly restored, making it easy to return the emulator to an exact state. Snapshots are covered later in this chapter.

5.5.13 Record and Playback

Allows the emulator screen and audio to be recorded and saved in WebM or animated GIF format.

5.5.14 Google Play

If the emulator is running a version of Android with Google Play Services installed, this option displays the current Google Play version. It also provides the option to update the emulator to the latest version.

5.5.15 Settings

The settings panel provides a small group of configuration options. Use this panel to choose a darker theme for the toolbar and extended controls panel, specify a file system location into which screenshots are to be saved, configure OpenGL support levels, and configure the emulator window to appear on top of other windows on the desktop.

5.5.16 Help

The Help screen contains three sub-panels containing a list of keyboard shortcuts, links to access the emulator online documentation, file bugs and send feedback, and emulator version information.

5.6 Working with Snapshots

When an emulator starts for the first time, it performs a *cold boot*, much like a physical Android device when powered on. This cold boot process can take some time to complete as the operating system loads and all the background processes are started. To avoid the necessity of going through this process every time the emulator is started, the system is configured to automatically save a snapshot (referred to as a *quick-boot snapshot*) of the emulator's current state each time it exits. The next time the emulator is launched, the quick-boot snapshot is loaded into memory, and execution resumes from where it left off previously, allowing the emulator to restart in a fraction of the time needed for a cold boot to complete.

The Snapshots screen of the extended controls panel can store additional snapshots at any point during the execution of the emulator. This saves the exact state of the entire emulator allowing the emulator to be restored to the exact point in time that the snapshot was taken. From within the screen, snapshots can be taken using the *Take Snapshot* button (marked A in Figure 5-4). To restore an existing snapshot, select it from the list (B) and click the run button (C) located at the bottom of the screen. Options are also provided to edit (D) the snapshot name and description and to delete (E) the currently selected snapshot:

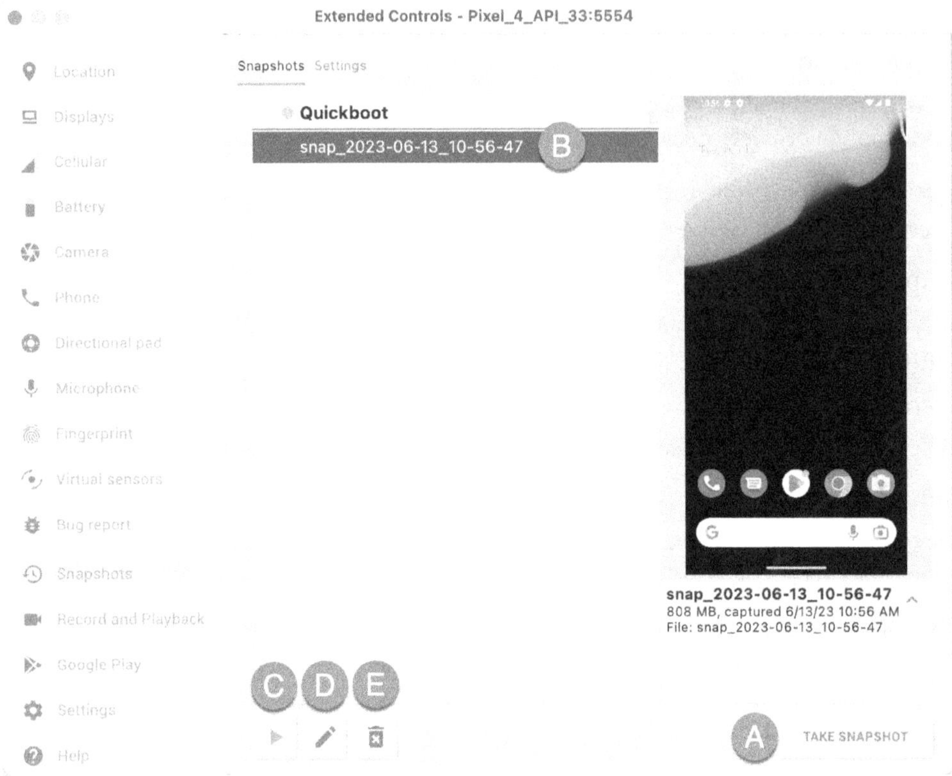

Figure 5-4

You can also choose whether to start an emulator using either a cold boot, the most recent quick-boot snapshot, or a previous snapshot by making a selection from the run target menu in the main toolbar, as illustrated in Figure 5-5:

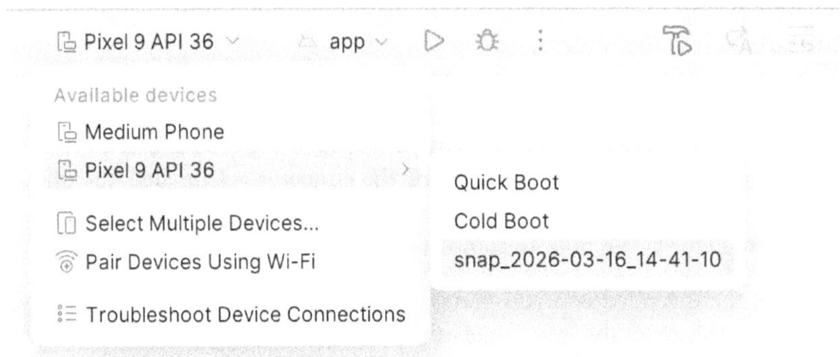

Figure 5-5

5.7 Configuring Fingerprint Emulation

The emulator allows up to 10 simulated fingerprints to be configured and used to test fingerprint authentication within Android apps (a topic covered in *"An Android Biometric Authentication Tutorial"*). Configuring simulated fingerprints begins by launching the emulator, opening the Settings app, and selecting the Security option.

Within the Security settings screen, select the fingerprint option. On the resulting information screen, click on the *Next* button to proceed to the Fingerprint setup screen. Before fingerprint security can be enabled, a backup screen unlocking method (such as a PIN) must be configured. Enter and confirm a suitable PIN and complete the PIN entry process by accepting the default notifications option.

Proceed through the remaining screens until the Settings app requests a fingerprint on the sensor. At this point, display the extended controls dialog, select the *Fingerprint* category in the left-hand panel, and make sure that *Finger 1* is selected in the main settings panel:

Figure 5-6

Click on the *Touch Sensor* button to simulate Finger 1 touching the fingerprint sensor. The emulator will report the successful addition of the fingerprint:

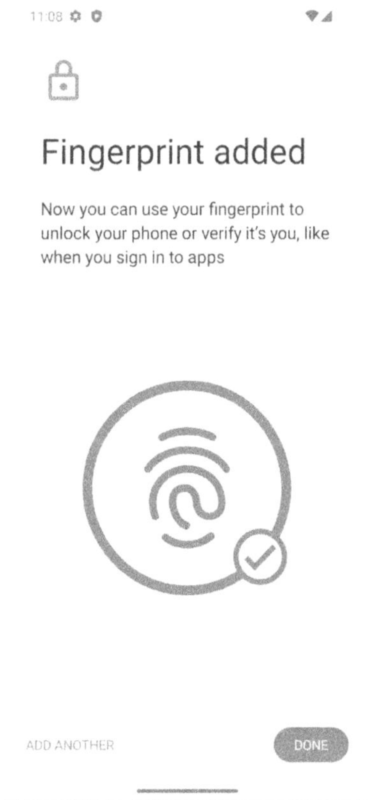

Figure 5-7

To add additional fingerprints, click on the *Add Another* button and select another finger from the extended controls panel menu before clicking on the *Touch Sensor* button again.

5.8 The Emulator in Tool Window Mode

As outlined in the previous chapter (*"Creating an Android Virtual Device (AVD) in Android Studio"*), Android Studio can be configured to launch the emulator in an embedded tool window so that it does not appear in a separate window. When running in this mode, the same controls available in standalone mode are provided in the toolbar, as shown in Figure 5-8:

Figure 5-8

From left to right, these buttons perform the following tasks (details of which match those for standalone mode):

- Power
- Volume Up
- Volume Down
- Rotate Left
- Rotate Right
- Back
- Home
- Overview
- Common Android Settings
- Hardware Input
- Screenshot
- Record Screen
- Backup App Data
- Restore App Data
- Snapshots
- Extended Controls
- Layout Inspector

5.9 Common Android Settings

The Common Android Settings button in the Running Devices toolbar provides quick access to several device configuration settings, including system font size, screen size, and dark mode. When clicked, the panel shown in Figure 5-9 will appear:

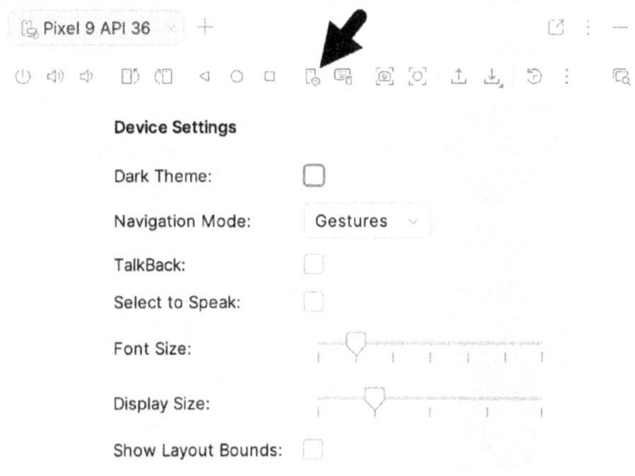

Figure 5-9

Changes made within this panel will be reflected instantly in the AVD session.

5.10 Creating a Resizable Emulator

In addition to emulators configured to match specific Android device models, Android Studio also provides a resizable AVD that allows you to switch between phone, tablet, and foldable device sizes. To create a resizable emulator, open the Device Manager tool window, click the '+' toolbar button, and select the Create Virtual Device menu option. In the Add Device dialog, type "Resizable" into the search bar and select the Resizable device profile:

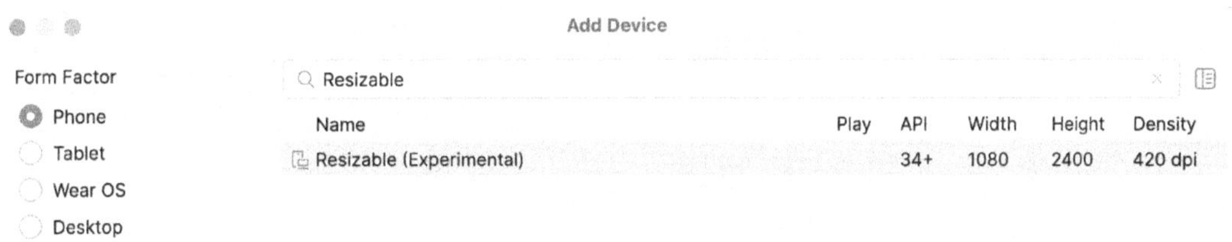

Figure 5-10

When you run an app on the new emulator within a tool window, the *Display mode* option will appear in the toolbar, allowing you to switch between emulator configurations as shown in Figure 5-11:

Figure 5-11

If the emulator is running in standalone mode, the Display mode option can be found in the side toolbar, as shown below:

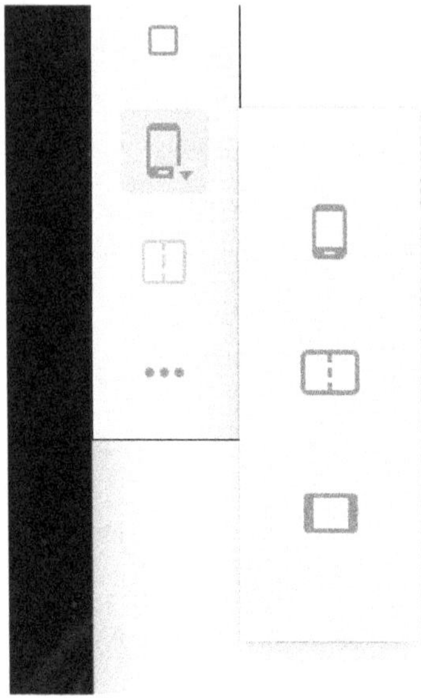

Figure 5-12

Once a foldable display mode has been selected, the Change posture menu may be used to test the app in open, closed, and half-open configurations:

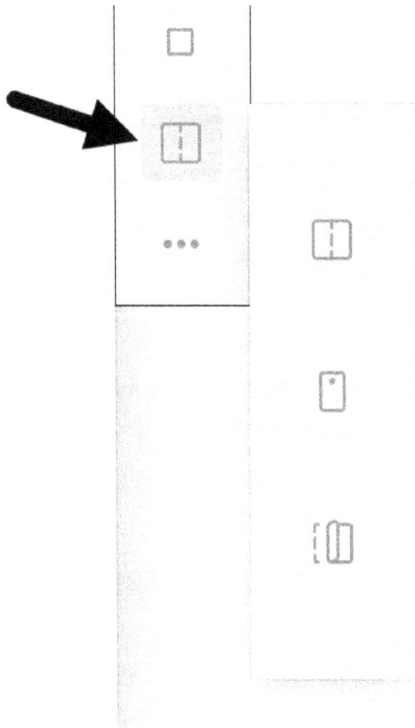

Figure 5-13

5.11 Summary

Android Studio contains an Android Virtual Device emulator environment designed to make it easier to test applications without running them on a physical Android device. This chapter has provided a brief tour of the emulator and highlighted key features available to configure and customize the environment to simulate different testing conditions.

Chapter 6

6. A Tour of the Android Studio User Interface

While it is tempting to plunge into running the example application created in the previous chapter, it involves using aspects of the Android Studio user interface, which are best described in advance.

Android Studio is a powerful and feature-rich development environment that is, to a large extent, intuitive to use. That being said, taking the time now to gain familiarity with the layout and organization of the Android Studio user interface will shorten the learning curve in later chapters of the book. With this in mind, this chapter will provide an overview of the various areas and components of the Android Studio environment.

6.1 The Welcome Screen

The welcome screen (Figure 6-1) is displayed any time that Android Studio is running with no projects currently open (open projects can be closed at any time by selecting the *File -> Close Project* menu option). If Android Studio was previously exited while a project was still open, the tool will bypass the welcome screen the next time it is launched, automatically opening the previously active project.

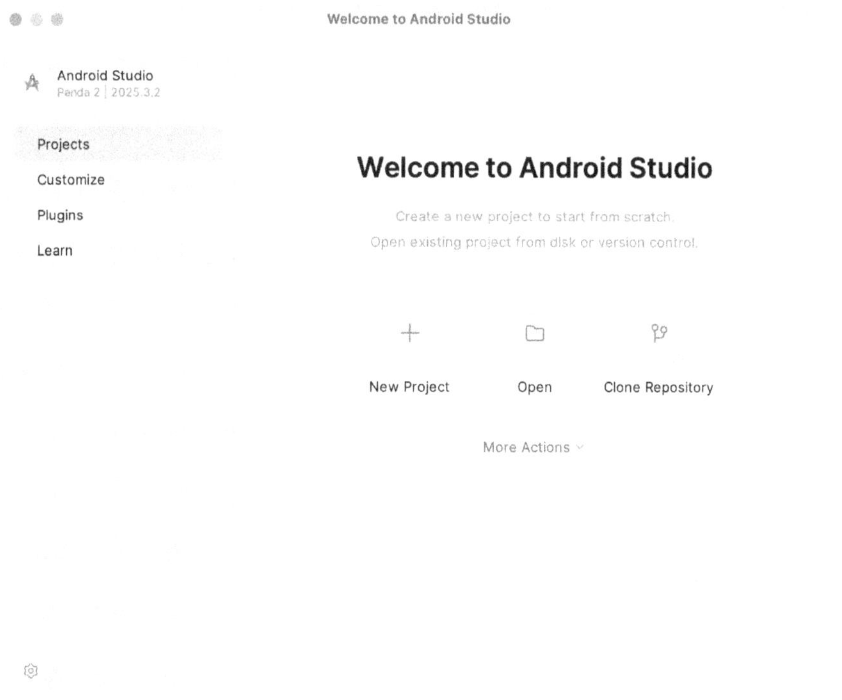

Figure 6-1

In addition to a list of recent projects, the welcome screen provides options for performing tasks such as opening and creating projects, along with access to projects currently under version control. In addition, the *Customize* screen provides options to change the theme and font settings used by both the IDE and the editor. Android

Studio plugins may be viewed, installed, and managed using the *Plugins* option.

Additional options are available by selecting the More Actions link or using the menu shown in Figure 6-2 when the list of recent projects replaces the More Actions link:

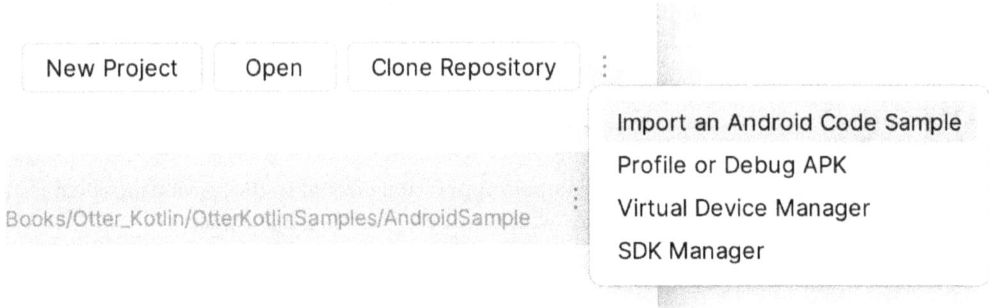

Figure 6-2

6.2 The Menu Bar

The Android Studio main window will appear when a new project is created, or an existing one is opened. When multiple projects are open simultaneously, each will be assigned its own main window. The precise configuration of the window will vary depending on the operating system Android Studio is running on and which tools and panels were displayed the last time the project was open. The appearance, for example, of the main menu bar will differ depending on the host operating system. On macOS, Android Studio follows the standard convention of placing the menu bar along the top edge of the desktop, as illustrated in Figure 6-3:

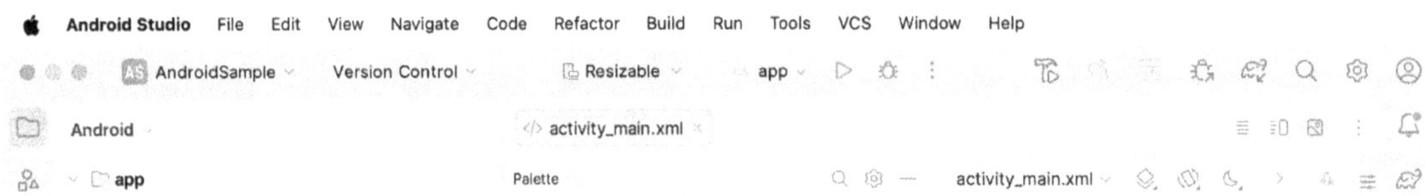

Figure 6-3

When Android Studio is running on Windows or Linux, however, the main menu is accessed via the button highlighted in Figure 6-4:

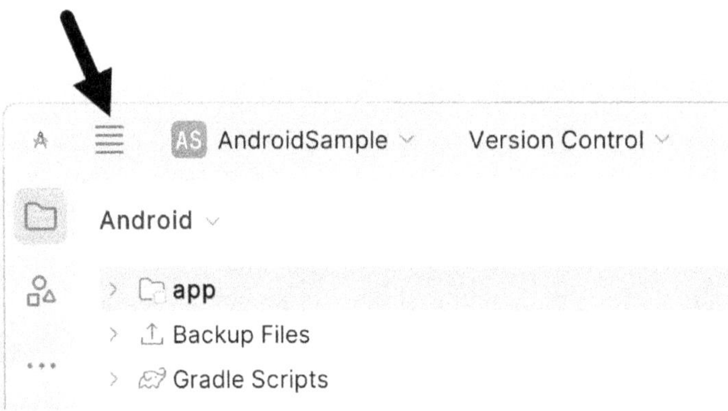

Figure 6-4

6.3 The Main Window

Once a project is open, the Android Studio main window will typically resemble that of Figure 6-5:

Figure 6-5

The various elements of the main window can be summarized as follows:

A – Toolbar – A selection of shortcuts to frequently performed actions. The toolbar buttons provide quick access to a select group of menu bar actions. The toolbar can be customized by right-clicking on the bar and selecting the *Customize Toolbar…* menu option. The toolbar menu shown in Figure 6-6 provides a convenient way to perform tasks such as creating and opening projects and switching between windows when multiple projects are open:

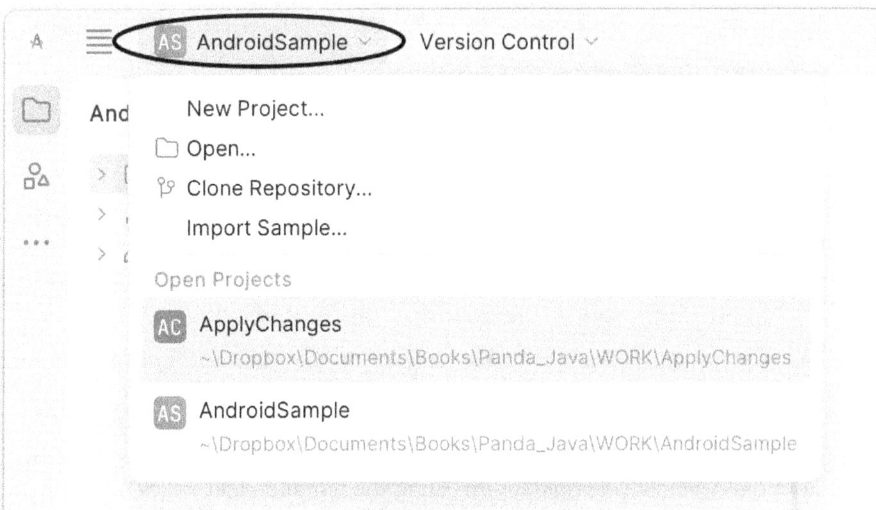

Figure 6-6

B – Navigation Bar – The navigation bar provides a convenient way to move around the files and folders that make up the project. Clicking on an element in the navigation bar will drop down a menu listing the sub-folders and files at that location, ready for selection. Similarly, clicking on a class name displays a menu listing methods contained within that class:

Figure 6-7

Select a method from the list to be taken to the corresponding location within the code editor. You can hide, display, and change the position of this bar using the *View -> Appearance -> Navigation Bar* menu option.

C – Editor Window – The editor window displays the content of the file on which the developer is currently working. When multiple files are open, each file is represented by a tab located along the top edge of the editor, as shown in Figure 6-8:

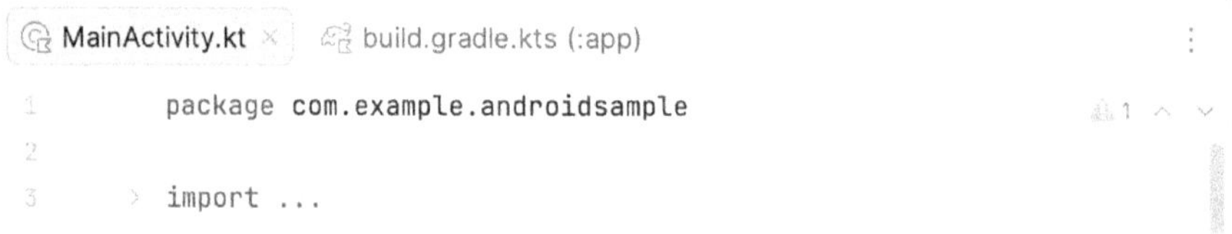

Figure 6-8

D – Status Bar – The status bar displays informational messages about the project and the activities of Android Studio. Hovering over items in the status bar will display a description of that field. Many fields are interactive, allowing users to click to perform tasks or obtain more detailed status information.

Figure 6-9

The widgets displayed in the status bar can be changed using the *View -> Appearance -> Status Bar Widgets* menu.

E – Project Tool Window – The project tool window provides a hierarchical overview of the project file structure allowing navigation to specific files and folders to be performed. The toolbar can be used to display the project in several different ways. The default setting is the *Android* view which is the mode primarily used in the remainder of this book.

The project tool window is just one of many available tools within the Android Studio environment.

6.4 The Tool Windows

In addition to the project view tool window, Android Studio also includes many other windows, which, when enabled, are displayed *tool window bars* that appear along the left and right edges of the main window and contain buttons for showing and hiding each of the tool windows. Figure 6-10 shows typical tool window bar configurations, though the buttons and their positioning may differ for your Android Studio installation.

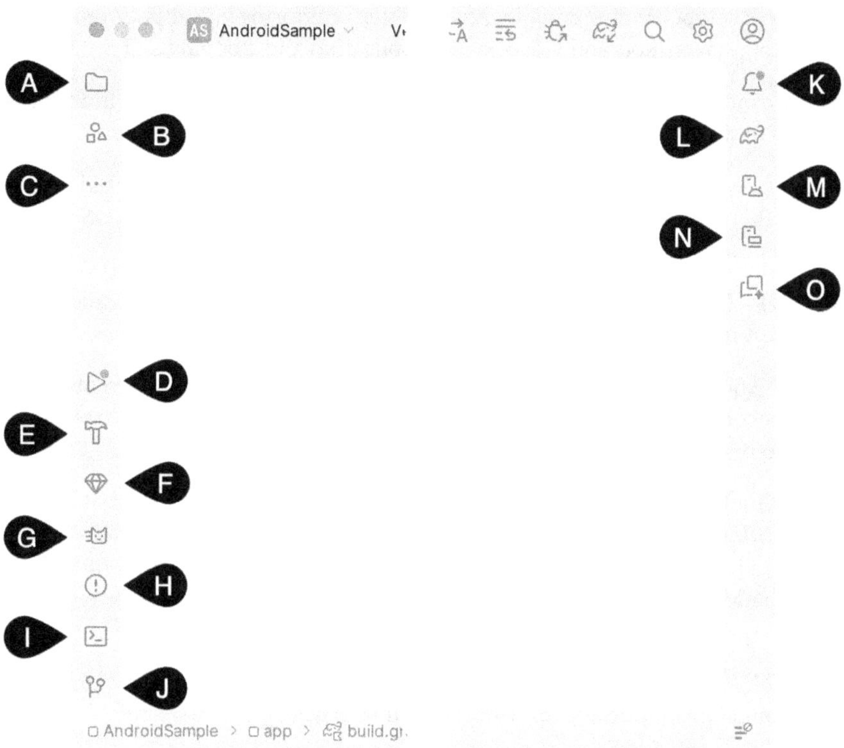

Figure 6-10

Clicking on a button will display the corresponding tool window, while a second click will hide the window. The location of a button in a tool window bar indicates the side of the window against which the window will appear when displayed. These positions can be changed by clicking and dragging the buttons to different locations in other window toolbars.

Android Studio offers a wide range of tool windows, the most commonly used of which are as follows:

- **Project (A)** – The project view provides an overview of the file structure that makes up the project allowing for quick navigation between files. Generally, double-clicking on a file in the project view will cause that file to be loaded into the appropriate editing tool.
- **Resource Manager (B)** - A tool for adding and managing resources and assets within the project, such as images, colors, and layout files.
- **More Tool Windows (C)** - Displays a menu containing additional tool windows not currently displayed in a tool window bar. When a tool window is selected from this menu, it will appear as a button in a tool window bar.
- **Run (D)** – The run tool window becomes available when an application is currently running and provides a view of the results of the run together with options to stop or restart a running process. If an application fails to install and run on a device or emulator, this window typically provides diagnostic information about the problem.
- **Build (E)** - Displays a real-time view of each process step while Android Studio builds the current project.
- **App Quality Insights (F)** - Provides access to the cloud-based Firebase app quality and crash analytics platform.

- **Logcat (G)** – The Logcat tool window provides access to the monitoring log output from a running application and options for taking screenshots and videos of the application and stopping and restarting a process.
- **Problems (H)** - A central location to view all of the current errors or warnings within the project. Double-clicking on an item in the problem list will take you to the problem file and location.
- **Terminal (I)** – Provides access to a terminal window on the system on which Android Studio is running. On Windows systems, this is the Command Prompt interface, while on Linux and macOS systems, this takes the form of a Terminal prompt.
- **Version Control (J)** - This tool window is used when the project files are under source code version control, allowing access to Git repositories and code change history.
- **Notifications (K)** - Android Studio occasionally displays notification popups for events such as project build completion or the successful launch of an app on a device or emulator. The Notifications tool window provides a central location to review the notification history.
- **Gradle (L)** – The Gradle tool window provides a view of the Gradle tasks that make up the project build configuration. The window lists the tasks involved in compiling the various elements of the project into an executable application. Right-click on a top-level Gradle task and select the *Open Gradle Config* menu option to load the Gradle build file for the current project into the editor. Gradle will be covered in greater detail later in this book.
- **Device Manager (M)** - Provides access to the Device Manager tool window where physical Android device connections and emulators may be added, removed, and managed.
- **Running Devices (N)** - Contains the AVD emulator if the option has been enabled to run the emulator in a tool window as outlined in the chapter entitled *"Creating an Android Virtual Device (AVD) in Android Studio"*.
- **AI Chat (O)** - Android Studio's AI powered coding assistant. This tool helps you develop your app by providing coding suggestions and solutions.
- **Assistant** - Display the Assistant panel, the content of which will differ depending on which Android Studio feature you are currently using.
- **App Inspection** - Provides access to the Database and Background Task inspectors. The Database Inspector allows you to inspect, query, and modify your app's databases while running. The Background Task Inspector allows background worker tasks created using WorkManager to be monitored and managed.
- **Bookmarks** – The Bookmarks tool window provides quick access to bookmarked files and code lines. For example, right-clicking on a file in the project view allows access to an Add to Bookmarks menu option. Similarly, you can bookmark a line of code in a source file by moving the cursor to that line and pressing the F11 key (F3 on macOS). All bookmarked items can be accessed through this tool window.
- **Build Variants** – The build variants tool window provides a quick way to configure different build targets for the current application project (for example, different builds for debugging and release versions of the application or multiple builds to target different device categories).
- **Device File Explorer** – Available via the *View -> Tool Windows -> Device File Explorer* menu, this tool window provides direct access to the filesystem of the currently connected Android device or emulator, allowing the filesystem to be browsed and files copied to the local filesystem.
- **Layout Inspector** - Provides a visual 3D rendering of the hierarchy of components that make up a user interface layout.

- **Structure** – The structure tool provides a high-level view of the structure of the source file currently displayed in the editor. This information includes a list of items such as classes, methods, and variables in the file. Selecting an item from the structure list will take you to that location in the source file in the editor window.
- **TODO** – As the name suggests, this tool provides a place to review items that have yet to be completed on the project. Android Studio compiles this list by scanning the source files that make up the project to look for comments that match specified TODO patterns. These patterns can be reviewed and changed by opening the Settings dialog and navigating to the *TODO* entry listed under *Editor*.

6.5 The Tool Window Menus

Each tool window has its own toolbar along the top edge. The menu buttons within these toolbars vary from one tool to the next, though all tool windows contain an Options menu (marked A in Figure 6-11):

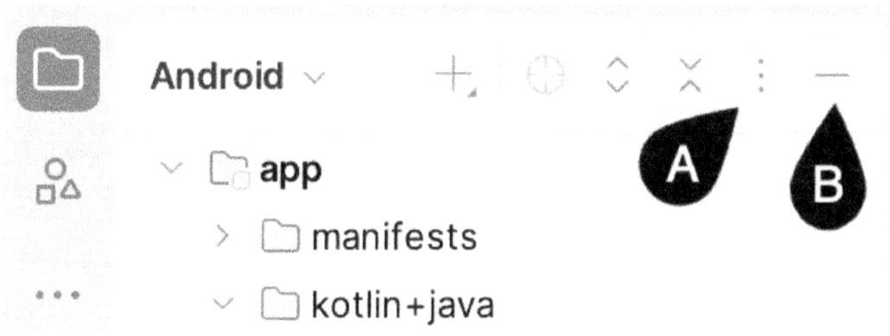

Figure 6-11

The Options menu allows various aspects of the window to be changed. Figure 6-12, for example, shows the Options menu for the Project tool window. Settings are available, for example, to undock a window and to allow it to float outside of the boundaries of the Android Studio main window, and to move and resize the tool panel:

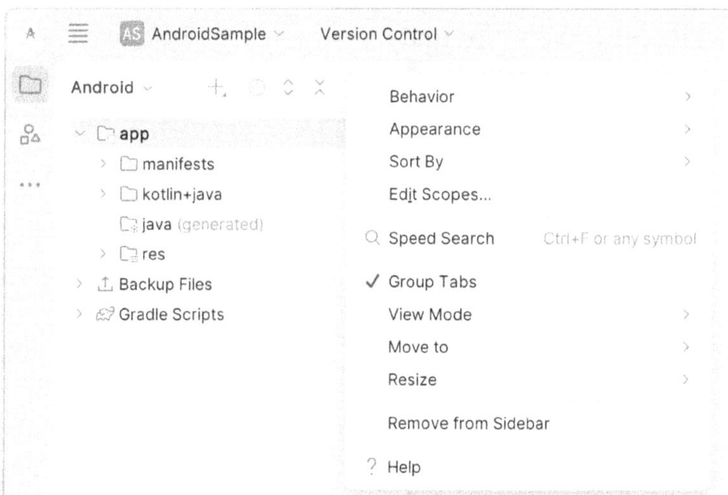

Figure 6-12

All tool windows also include a far-right button on the toolbar (marked B in Figure 6-11 above), providing an additional way to hide the tool window from view. A search of the items within a tool window can be performed by giving that window focus by clicking on it and then typing the search term (for example, the name of a file in the Project tool window). A search box will appear in the window's toolbar, and items matching the search highlighted.

6.6 Android Studio Keyboard Shortcuts

Android Studio includes many keyboard shortcuts to save time when performing common tasks. A complete keyboard shortcut keymap listing can be viewed and printed from within the Android Studio project window by selecting the *Help -> Keyboard Shortcuts PDF* menu option. You may also list and modify the keyboard shortcuts by opening the Settings dialog and clicking on the Keymap entry, as shown in Figure 6-13 below:

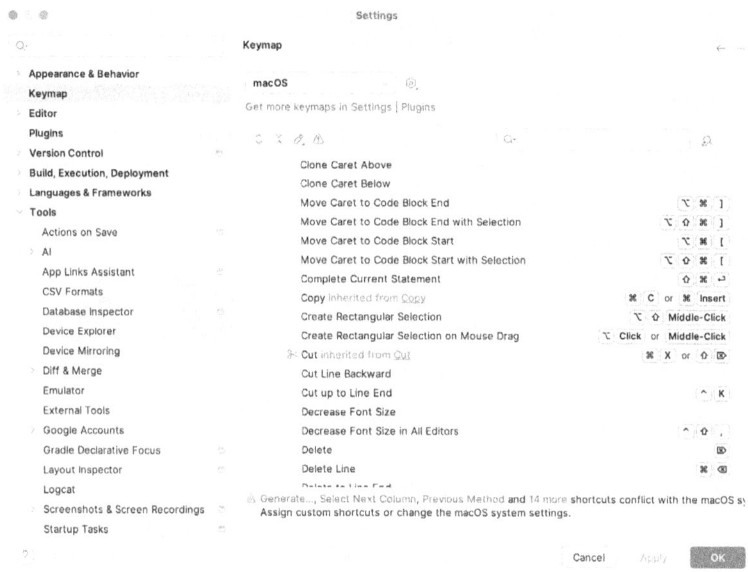

Figure 6-13

6.7 Switcher and Recent Files Navigation

Another useful mechanism for navigating within the Android Studio main window involves using the *Switcher*. Accessed via the Ctrl-Tab keyboard shortcut, the switcher appears as a panel listing both the tool windows and currently open files (Figure 6-14).

Figure 6-14

Once displayed, the switcher will remain visible as long as the Ctrl key remains depressed. Repeatedly tapping the Tab key while holding down the Ctrl key will cycle through the various selection options while releasing the

Ctrl key causes the currently highlighted item to be selected and displayed within the main window.

In addition to the Switcher, the Recent Files panel provides navigation to recently opened files (Figure 6-15). This can be accessed using the Ctrl-E keyboard shortcut (Cmd-E on macOS). Once displayed, either the mouse pointer can be used to select an option, or the keyboard arrow keys can be used to scroll through the file name and tool window options. Pressing the Enter key will select the currently highlighted item:

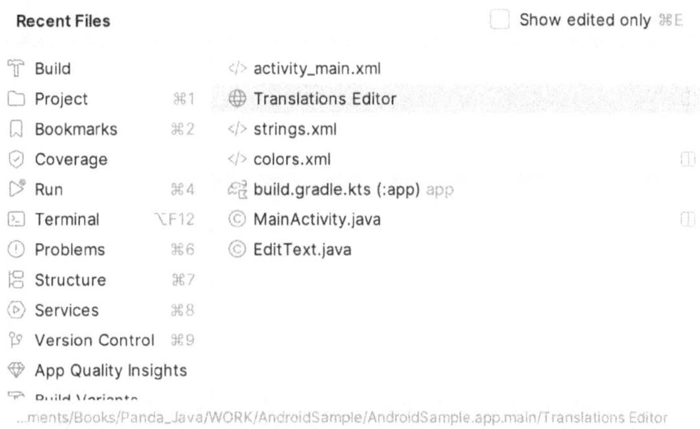

Figure 6-15

6.8 Changing the Android Studio Theme

The overall theme of the Android Studio environment may be changed using the Settings dialog. Once the settings dialog is displayed, select the *Appearance & Behavior* option in the left-hand panel, followed by *Appearance*. Then, change the setting of the *Theme* menu before clicking on the *OK* button. The themes available will depend on the platform but usually include options such as Islands Light, Islands Dark, Light, IntelliJ, Windows, High Contrast, and Darcula. Figure 6-16 shows an example of the main window with the Islands Dark theme selected:

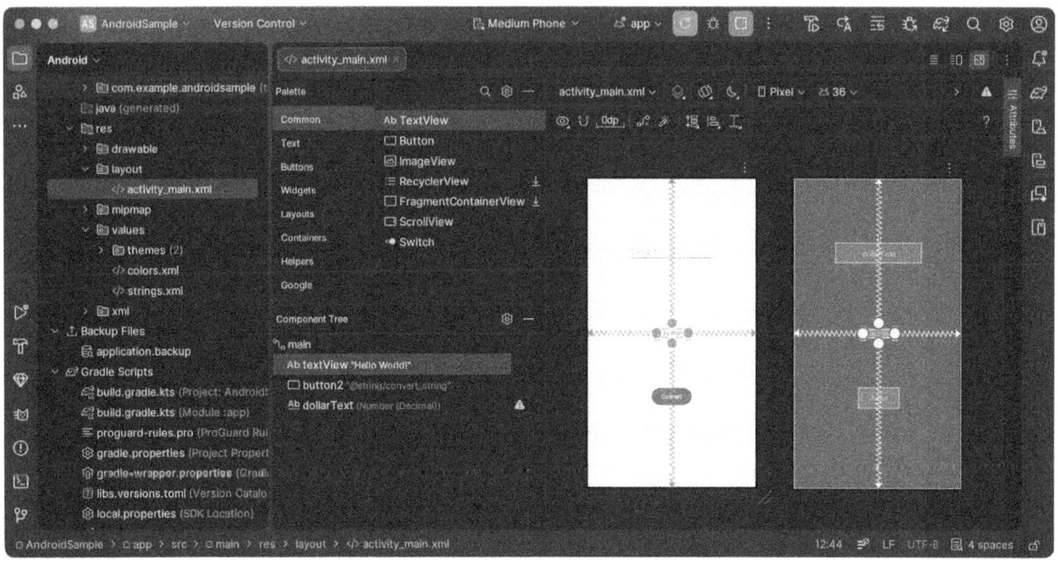

Figure 6-16

To synchronize the Android Studio theme with the operating system light and dark mode setting, enable the *Sync with OS* option and use the drop-down menu to control which theme to use for each mode:

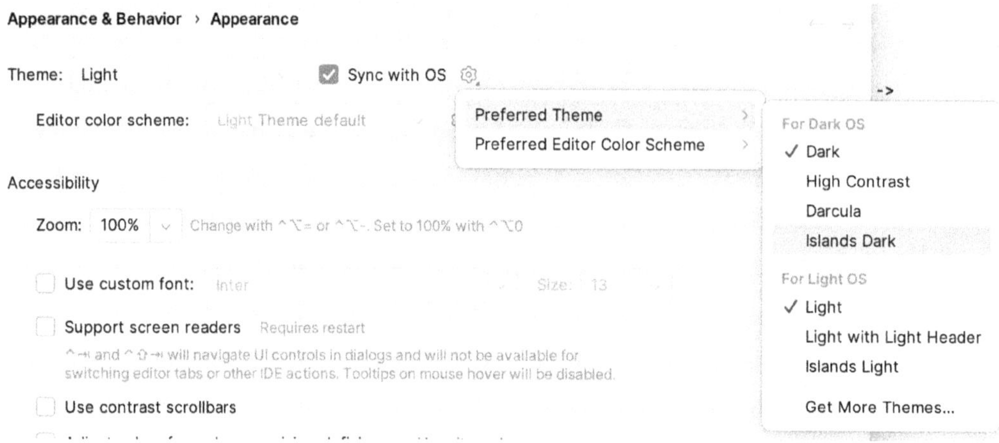

Figure 6-17

6.9 Summary

The primary elements of the Android Studio environment consist of the welcome screen and main window. Each open project is assigned its own main window, which, in turn, consists of a menu bar, toolbar, editing and design area, status bar, and a collection of tool windows. Tool windows appear on the sides of the main window.

There are very few actions within Android Studio that cannot be triggered via a keyboard shortcut. A keymap of default keyboard shortcuts can be accessed at any time from within the Android Studio main window.

Chapter 7

7. Testing Android Studio Apps on a Physical Android Device

While much can be achieved by testing applications using an Android Virtual Device (AVD), there is no substitute for performing real-world application testing on a physical Android device, and some Android features are only available on physical Android devices.

Communication with both AVD instances and connected Android devices is handled by the *Android Debug Bridge (ADB)*. This chapter explains how to configure the ADB environment to enable application testing on an Android device with macOS, Windows, and Linux-based systems.

7.1 An Overview of the Android Debug Bridge (ADB)

The primary purpose of the ADB is to facilitate interaction between a development system, in this case, Android Studio, and both AVD emulators and Android devices to run and debug applications. ADB allows you to connect to devices via WiFi or USB cable.

The ADB consists of a client, a server process running in the background on the development system, and a daemon background process running in either AVDs or real Android devices such as phones and tablets.

The ADB client can take a variety of forms. For example, a client is provided as a command-line tool named *adb* in the Android SDK *platform-tools* sub-directory. Similarly, Android Studio also has a built-in client.

A variety of tasks may be performed using the *adb* command-line tool. For example, active virtual or physical devices may be listed using the *devices* command-line argument. The following command output indicates the presence of an AVD on the system but no physical devices:

```
$ adb devices
List of devices attached
emulator-5554   device
```

7.2 Enabling USB Debugging ADB on Android Devices

Before ADB can connect to an Android device, that device must be configured to allow the connection. On phone and tablet devices running Android 6.0 or later, the steps to achieve this are as follows:

1. Open the Settings app on the device and select the *About tablet* or *About phone* option (on some versions of Android, this can be found on the *System* page of the Settings app).

2. On the *About* screen, scroll down to the *Build number* field (Figure 7-1) and tap it seven times until a message indicates that developer mode has been enabled. If the Build number is not listed on the About screen, it may be available via the *Software information* option. Alternatively, unfold the Advanced section of the list if available.

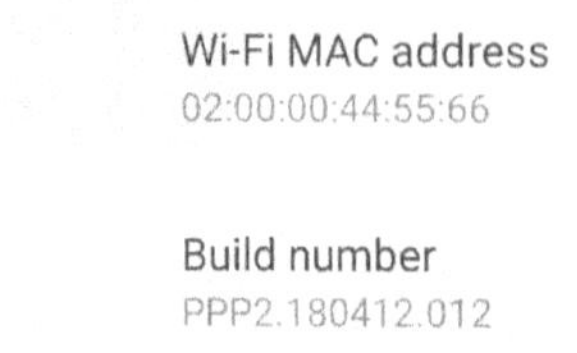

Figure 7-1

3. Return to the main Settings screen and note the appearance of a new option titled Developer options (on newer versions of Android, this option is listed on the System settings screen). Select this option, and on the resulting screen, locate the USB debugging option as illustrated in Figure 7-2:

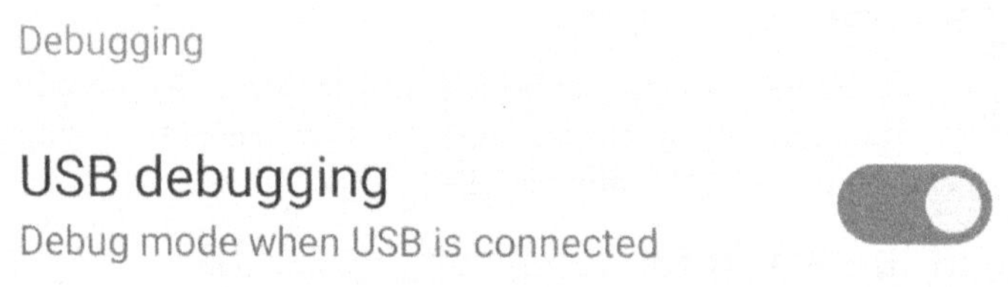

Figure 7-2

4. Enable the USB debugging option and tap the Allow button when confirmation is requested.

The device is now configured to accept debugging connections from ADB on the development system over a USB connection. All that remains is to configure the development system to detect the device when it is attached. While this is a relatively straightforward process, the steps differ depending on whether the development system runs Windows, macOS, or Linux. Note that the following steps assume that the Android SDK *platform-tools* directory is included in the operating system PATH environment variable as described in the chapter entitled *"Setting up an Android Studio Development Environment"*.

7.2.1 macOS ADB Configuration

To configure the ADB environment on a macOS system, connect the device to the computer system using a USB cable, open a terminal window, and execute the following command to restart the ADB server:

```
$ adb kill-server
$ adb start-server
* daemon not running. starting it now on port 5037 *
* daemon started successfully *
```

Once the server is successfully running, execute the following command to verify that the device has been detected:

```
$ adb devices
List of devices attached
74CE000600000001        offline
```

If the device is listed as *offline*, go to the Android device and check for the dialog shown in Figure 7-3 seeking permission to *Allow USB debugging*. Enable the checkbox next to the option that reads *Always allow from this computer* before clicking *OK*.

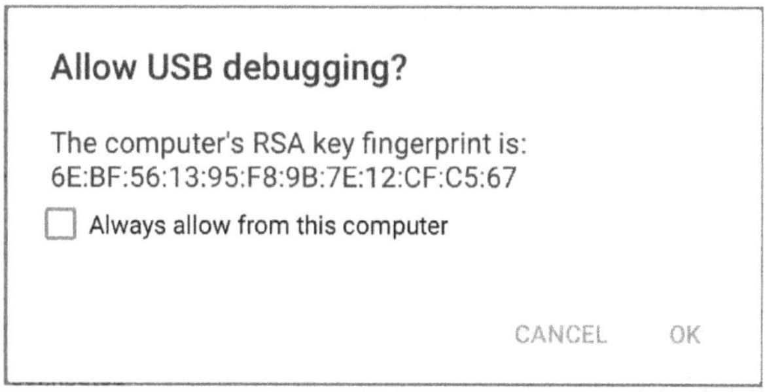

Figure 7-3

Repeating the *adb devices* command should now list the device as being available:

```
List of devices attached
015d41d4454bf80c        device
```

If the device is not listed, try logging out and back into the macOS desktop and rebooting the system if the problem persists.

7.2.2 Windows ADB Configuration

The first step in configuring a Windows-based development system to connect to an Android device using ADB is to install the appropriate USB drivers on the system. The USB drivers to install will depend on the model of the Android Device. If you have a Google device such as a Pixel phone, installing and configuring the Google USB Driver package on your Windows system will be necessary. Detailed steps to achieve this are outlined on the following web page:

https://developer.android.com/sdk/win-usb.html

For Android devices not supported by the Google USB driver, it will be necessary to download the drivers provided by the device manufacturer. A listing of drivers, together with download and installation information, can be obtained online at:

https://developer.android.com/tools/extras/oem-usb.html

With the drivers installed and the device now being recognized as the correct device type, open a Command Prompt window and execute the following command:

```
adb devices
```

This command should output information about the connected device similar to the following:

```
List of devices attached
HT4CTJT01906        offline
```

If the device is listed as *offline* or *unauthorized*, go to the device display and check for the dialog shown in Figure 7-3 seeking permission to *Allow USB debugging*. Enable the checkbox next to the option that reads *Always allow from this computer* before clicking *OK*. Repeating the *adb devices* command should now list the device as being ready:

```
List of devices attached
HT4CTJT01906    device
```

If the device is not listed, execute the following commands to restart the ADB server:

```
adb kill-server
adb start-server
```

If the device is still not listed, try executing the following command:

```
android update adb
```

Note that it may also be necessary to reboot the system.

7.2.3 Linux ADB Configuration

For this chapter, we will again use Ubuntu Linux as a reference example in configuring ADB on Linux to connect to a physical Android device for application testing.

Physical device testing on Ubuntu Linux requires the installation of a package named *android-tools-adb* which, in turn, requires the Android Studio user to be a member of the *plugdev* group. This is the default for user accounts on most Ubuntu versions and can be verified by running the *id* command. If the plugdev group is not listed, run the following command to add your account to the group:

```
sudo usermod -aG plugdev $LOGNAME
```

After the group membership requirement has been met, the *android-tools-adb* package can be installed by executing the following command:

```
sudo apt-get install android-tools-adb
```

Once the above changes have been made, reboot the Ubuntu system. Once the system has restarted, open a Terminal window, start the ADB server, and check the list of attached devices:

```
$ adb start-server
* daemon not running. starting it now on port 5037 *
* daemon started successfully *
$ adb devices
List of devices attached
015d41d4454bf80c        offline
```

If the device is listed as *offline* or *unauthorized*, go to the Android device and check for the dialog shown in Figure 7-3 seeking permission to *Allow USB debugging*. Enable the checkbox next to the option that reads *Always allow from this computer* before clicking *OK*.

7.3 Resolving USB Connection Issues

If you are unable to successfully connect to the device using the above steps, display the run target menu (Figure 7-4) and select the *Troubleshoot Device Connections* option:

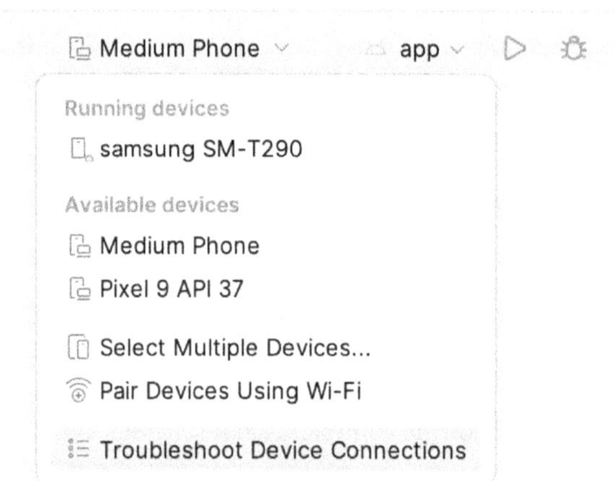

Figure 7-4

The connection assistant will scan for devices and report problems and possible solutions.

7.4 Enabling Wireless Debugging on Android Devices

Follow steps 1 through 3 from section 7.2 above, this time enabling the Wireless Debugging option as shown in Figure 7-5:

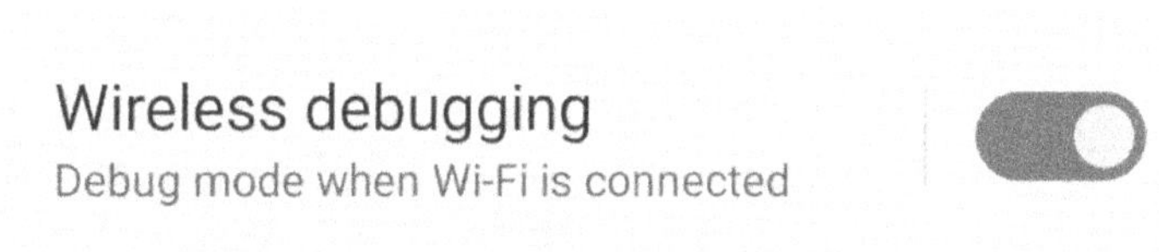

Figure 7-5

Next, tap the above Wireless debugging entry to display the screen shown in Figure 7-6:

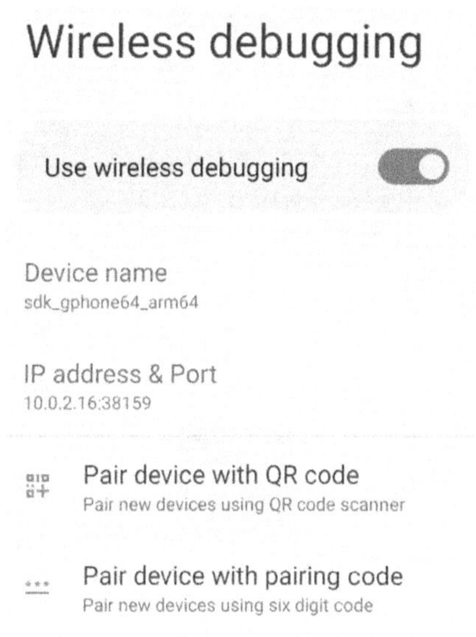

Figure 7-6

If your device has a camera, select *Pair device with QR code*, otherwise select the *Pair device with pairing code* option. Depending on your selection, the Settings app will either start a camera session or display a pairing code, as shown in Figure 7-7:

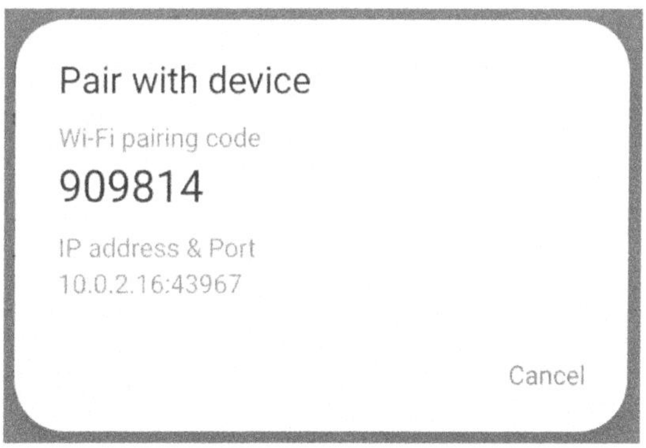

Figure 7-7

With an option selected, return to Android Studio and select the *Pair Devices Using WiFi* option from the run target menu as illustrated in Figure 7-8:

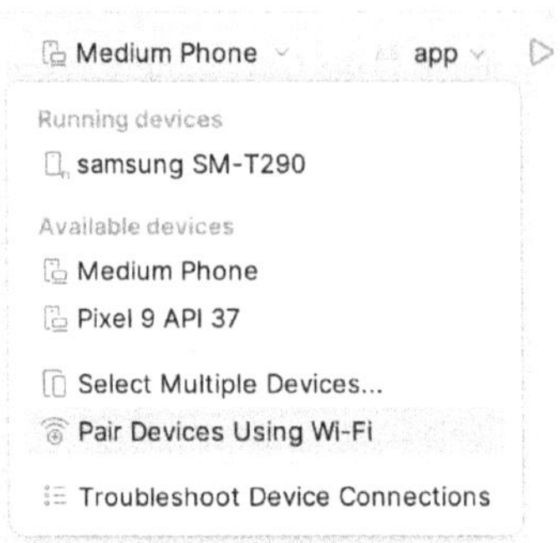

Figure 7-8

In the pairing dialog, select either *Pair using QR code* or *Pair using pairing code* depending on your previous selection in the Settings app on the device:

Figure 7-9

Either scan the QR code using the Android device or enter the pairing code displayed on the device screen into the Android Studio dialog (Figure 7-10) to complete the pairing process:

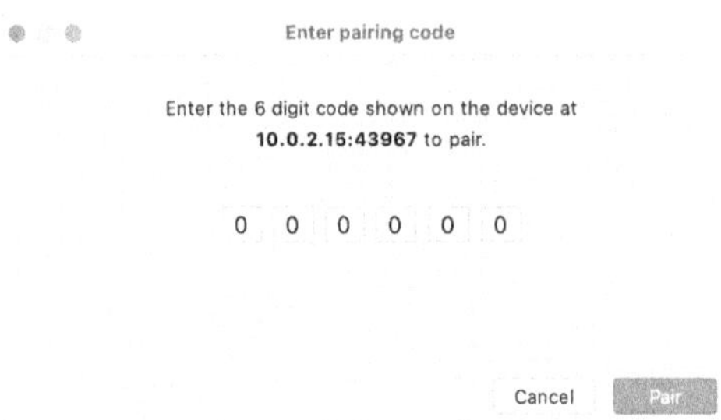

Figure 7-10

If the pairing process fails, try rebooting both the development system and the Android device and try again.

7.5 Testing the ADB Connection

Assuming that the ADB configuration has been successful on your chosen development platform, the next step is to try running the test application created in the chapter entitled *"Creating an Example Android App in Android Studio"* on the device. Launch Android Studio, open the AndroidSample project, and verify that the device appears in the device selection menu as highlighted in Figure 7-11:

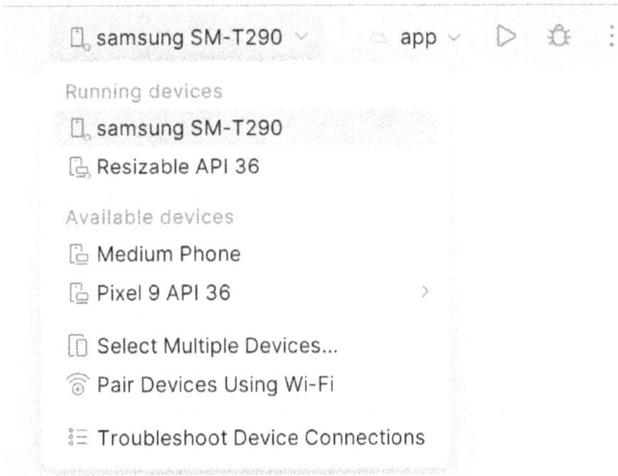

Figure 7-11

Select the device from the list and click the run button to install and run the app.

7.6 Device Mirroring

Device mirroring allows you to run an app on a physical device while viewing the display within Android Studio's Running Devices tool window. In other words, although your app is running on a physical device, it appears within Android Studio in the same way as an AVD instance.

With a device connected to Android Studio, display the *Running Devices* tool window and click the *Device Mirror settings* link to display the Settings dialog. Within the Settings dialog, enable the mirroring of physical Android devices and click on *OK*. On returning to the main window, Android Studio will mirror the display of the physical device in the Running Devices tool window.

7.7 Summary

While the Android Virtual Device emulator provides an excellent testing environment, it is essential to remember that there is no real substitute for ensuring an application functions correctly on a physical Android device.

By default, however, the Android Studio environment is not configured to detect Android devices as a target testing device. It is necessary, therefore, to perform some steps to load applications directly onto an Android device from within the Android Studio development environment via a USB cable or over a WiFi network. The exact steps to achieve this goal differ depending on the development platform. In this chapter, we have covered those steps for Linux, macOS, and Windows-based platforms.

Chapter 8

8. The Basics of the Android Studio Code Editor

Developing applications for Android involves a considerable amount of programming work which, by definition, involves typing, reviewing, and modifying lines of code. Unsurprisingly, most of a developer's time spent using Android Studio will typically involve editing code within the editor window.

The modern code editor must go far beyond the basics of typing, deleting, cutting, and pasting. Today the usefulness of a code editor is generally gauged by factors such as the amount by which it reduces the typing required by the programmer, ease of navigation through large source code files, and the editor's ability to detect and highlight programming errors in real-time as the code is being written. As will become evident in this chapter, these are just a few areas in which the Android Studio editor excels.

While not an exhaustive overview of the features of the Android Studio editor, this chapter aims to provide a guide to the tool's key features. Experienced programmers will find that some of these features are common to most code editors today, while a number are unique to this editing environment.

8.1 The Android Studio Editor

The Android Studio editor appears in the center of the main window when a Java, Kotlin, XML, or other text-based file is selected for editing. Figure 8-1, for example, shows a typical editor session with a Kotlin source code file loaded:

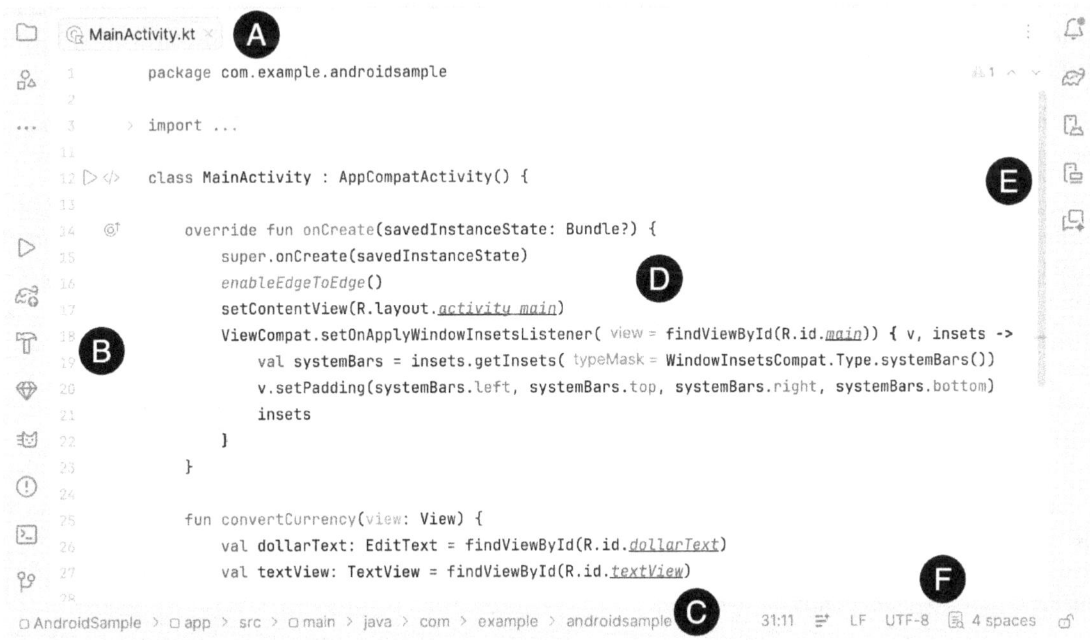

Figure 8-1

The elements that comprise the editor window can be summarized as follows:

A – Document Tabs – Android Studio can hold multiple files open for editing at anytime. As each file is opened, it is assigned a document tab displaying the file name in the tab bar along the editor window's top edge. A small drop-down menu will appear in the far right-hand corner of the tab bar when there is insufficient room to display all of the tabs. Clicking on this menu will drop down a list of additional open files. A wavy red line underneath a file name in a tab indicates that the code in the file contains one or more errors that need to be addressed before the project can be compiled and run.

Switching between files is a matter of clicking on the corresponding tab or using the Alt-Left and Alt-Right keyboard shortcuts. Navigation between files may also be performed using the Switcher mechanism (accessible via the Ctrl-Tab keyboard shortcut).

To detach an editor panel from the Android Studio main window so that it appears in a separate window, click on the tab and drag it to an area on the desktop outside the main window. To return the editor to the main window, click on the file tab in the separated editor window and drag and drop it onto the original editor tab bar in the main window.

B – The Editor Gutter Area - The editor uses the gutter area to display informational icons and controls. Some typical items in this gutter area are debugging breakpoint markers, controls to fold and unfold code blocks, bookmarks, XML file references, and line numbers. For example, Figure 8-2 shows the editor gutter area for the first few lines of the MainActivity class declaration in the *MainActivity.kt* file:

```
class MainActivity : AppCompatActivity() {

    override fun onCreate(savedInstanceState: Bundle?) {
```

Figure 8-2

Hovering the mouse pointer over a gutter icon will display a tooltip explanation. The above example includes a button to execute the main activity, an XML file reference, and an indication that the onCreate() method overrides a method in a parent class.

Line numbers are switched on by default but may be disabled by right-clicking in the gutter and selecting the *Appearance -> Show Line Numbers* menu option.

C – Code Structure Location - This bar at the bottom of the editor displays the cursor's current position as it relates to the overall structure of the code. In the following figure, for example, the bar indicates that the *convertCurrency* method is currently being edited and that this method is contained within the MainActivity class:

ComposeDemo > app > src > main > java > com > example > composedemo > MainActivity.kt > **DemoText**

Figure 8-3

Double-clicking an element within the bar will move the cursor to the corresponding location within the code file. For example, double-clicking on the *convertCurrency* entry will move the cursor to the top of the convertCurrency method within the source code. Similarly, clicking on the MainActivity entry displays a list of available code navigation points for selection:

Figure 8-4

D – The Editor Area – The main area where the user reviews, enters, and edits the code. Later sections of this chapter will cover the key features of the editing area in detail.

E – The Validation and Marker Sidebar – Android Studio incorporates a feature called "on-the-fly code analysis". This essentially means that as you are typing code, the editor analyzes the code to check for warnings and syntax errors. The indicators at the top of the validation sidebar will update in real-time to indicate the number of errors and warnings found as code is added. Clicking on this indicator will display a popup containing a summary of the issues found with the code in the editor, as illustrated in Figure 8-5:

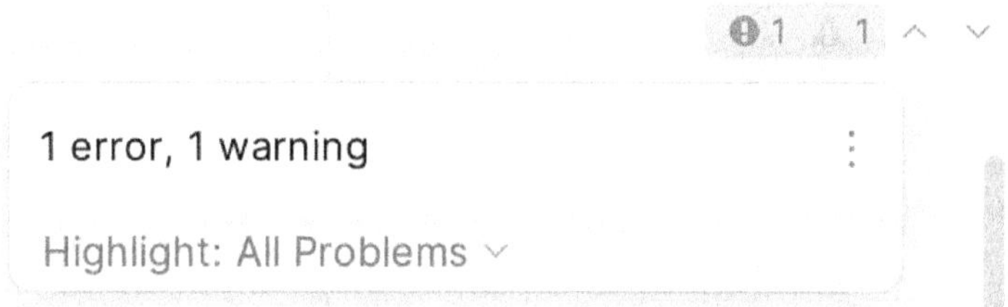

Figure 8-5

The up and down arrows move between the error locations within the code. A green check mark indicates that no warnings or errors have been detected.

The sidebar also displays markers at the locations where issues have been detected using the same color coding. Hovering the mouse pointer over a marker when the line of code is visible in the editor area will display a popup containing a description of the issue:

Figure 8-6

Hovering the mouse pointer over a marker for a line of code that is currently scrolled out of the viewing area of the editor will display a "lens" overlay containing the block of code where the problem is located (Figure 8-7) allowing it to be viewed without the necessity to scroll to that location in the editor:

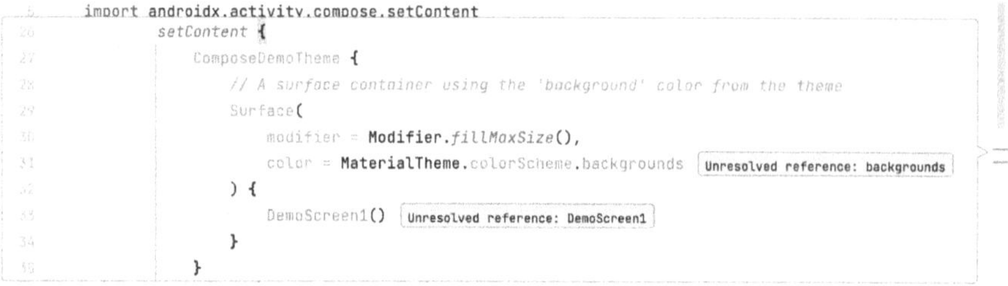

Figure 8-7

It is also worth noting that the lens overlay is not limited to warnings and errors in the sidebar. Hovering over any part of the sidebar will result in a lens appearing containing the code present at that location within the source file.

F – The Status Bar – Though the status bar is part of the main window, as opposed to the editor, it does contain some information about the currently active editing session. This information includes the current position of the cursor in terms of lines and characters and the encoding format of the file (UTF-8, ASCII, etc.). Clicking on these values in the status bar allows the corresponding setting to be changed. For example, clicking on the line number displays the Go to Line:Column dialog. Use the *View -> Appearance -> Status Bar Widgets* menu option to add and remove widgets. For example, the Memory Indicator is a helpful widget if you are experiencing performance problems with Android Studio.

Having provided an overview of the elements that comprise the Android Studio editor, the remainder of this chapter will explore the key features of the editing environment in more detail.

8.2 The Floating Code Toolbar

The floating code toolbar provides quick access to commonly performed tasks within the code editor. It automatically appears when code is selected within the editor, as illustrated in Figure 8-8 below:

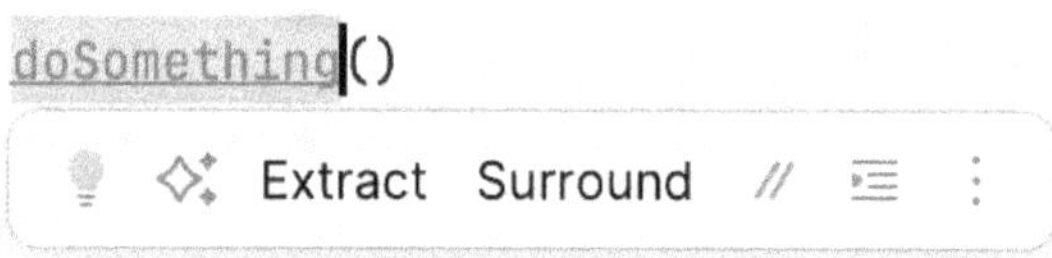

Figure 8-8

Hovering the mouse pointer over toolbar items displays the corresponding menu. The light bulb item, for example, is the context actions menu. It provides quick access to actions such as extracting the selected code to a separate file, launching an activity, or adding a new variable to a function. These menu options are context-sensitive and vary depending on the currently selected code:

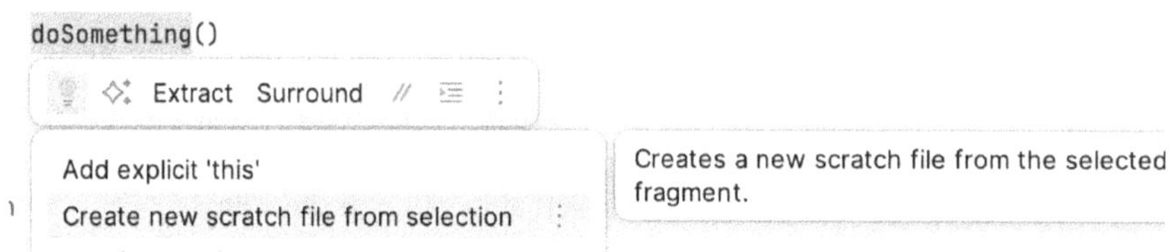

Figure 8-9

The preset toolbar items also include access to Gemini AI features, code reformatting, and code extraction, in addition to an option to add comment markers to the selected code. Use the More menu (highlighted in Figure 8-10) to customize or hide the toolbar:

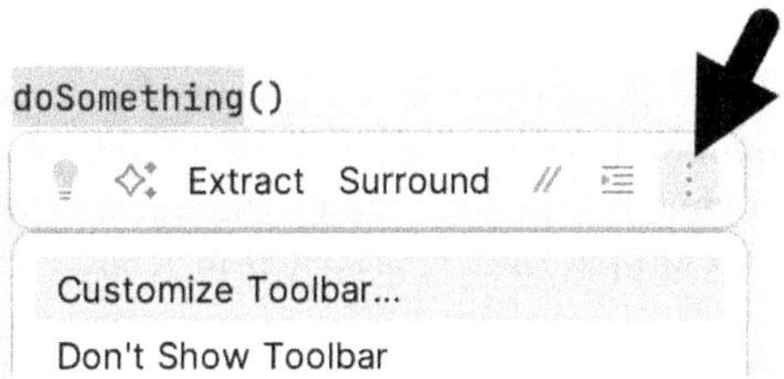

Figure 8-10

When the customize option is selected, the dialog shown in Figure 8-11 will appear, allowing items to be moved, edited, and deleted:

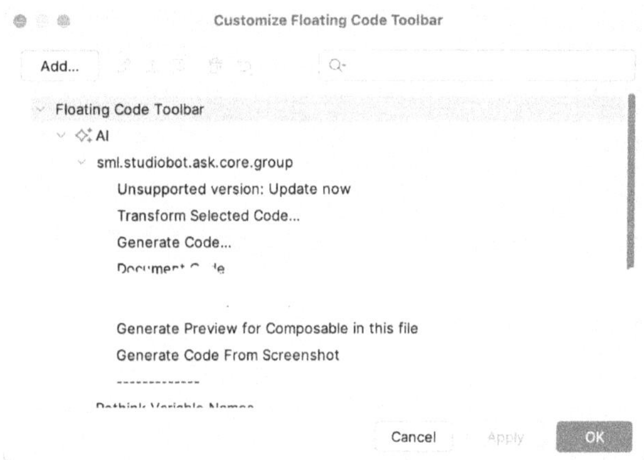

Figure 8-11

To add items, click the Add... button and make selections from the action list:

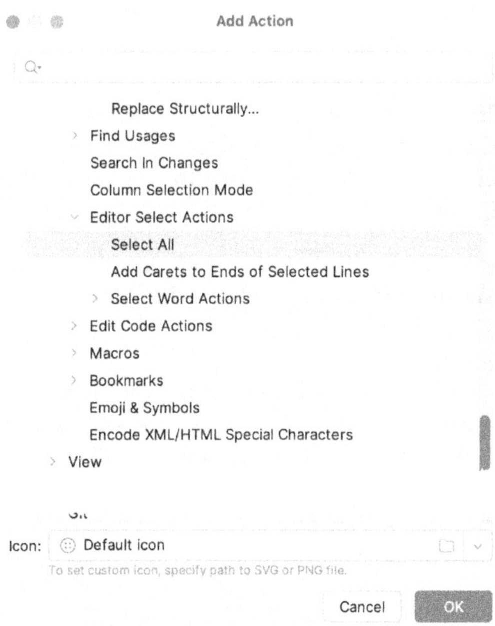

Figure 8-12

8.3 Splitting the Editor Window

By default, the editor will display a single panel showing the content of the currently selected file. A useful feature when working simultaneously with multiple source code files is the ability to split the editor into multiple panes. To split the editor, right-click on a file tab within the editor window and select either the Split Right or Split Down menu option. Figure 8-13, for example, shows the splitter in action with the editor split into three panels:

Figure 8-13

The orientation of a split panel may be changed at any time by right-clicking on the corresponding tab and selecting the Change Splitter Orientation menu option. Repeat these steps to unsplit a single panel, this time selecting the Unsplit option from the menu. All split panels may be removed by right-clicking on any tab and selecting the Unsplit All menu option.

Window splitting may be used to display different files or to provide multiple windows onto the same file, allowing different areas of the same file to be viewed and edited concurrently.

8.4 Code Completion

The Android Studio editor has a considerable amount of built-in knowledge of Kotlin programming syntax and the classes and methods that make up the Android SDK, as well as knowledge of your own code base. As code is typed, the editor scans what is being typed and, where appropriate, makes suggestions with regard to what might be needed to complete a statement or reference. When the editor detects a completion suggestion, a panel containing a list of suggestions will appear. In Figure 8-14, for example, the editor is suggesting possibilities for the beginning of a declaration:

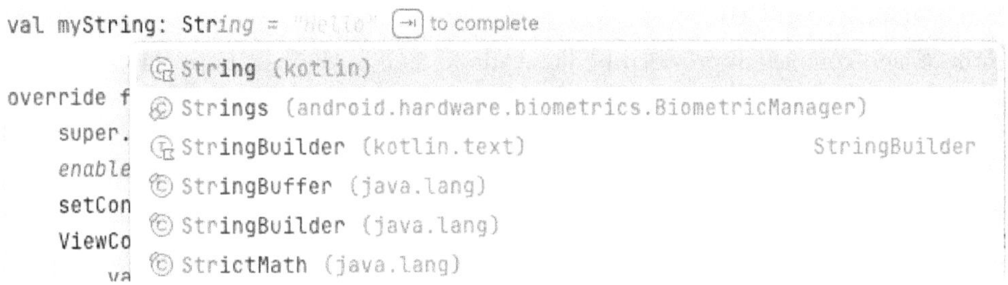

Figure 8-14

If none of the auto-completion suggestions are correct, keep typing, and the editor will continue to refine the suggestions where appropriate. To accept the topmost suggestion, press the Enter or Tab key on the keyboard. To select a different suggestion, use the arrow keys to move up and down the list, again using the Enter or Tab key to select the highlighted item.

Completion suggestions can be manually invoked using the Ctrl-Space keyboard sequence. This can be useful when changing a word or declaration in the editor. When the cursor is positioned over a word in the editor, that word will automatically highlight. Pressing Ctrl-Space will display a list of alternate suggestions. Press the Tab key to replace the current word with the highlighted item in the suggestion list.

In addition to the real-time auto-completion feature, the Android Studio editor also offers a Smart Completion system. Smart completion is invoked using the Shift-Ctrl-Space keyboard sequence and, when selected, will provide more detailed suggestions based on the current context of the code. Pressing the Shift-Ctrl-Space shortcut sequence a second time will provide more suggestions from a broader range of possibilities.

Code completion can be a matter of personal preference for many programmers. In recognition of this fact, Android Studio provides a high level of control over the auto-completion settings. These can be viewed and modified by opening the Settings dialog and choosing *Editor -> General -> Code Completion* from the settings panel, as shown in Figure 8-15:

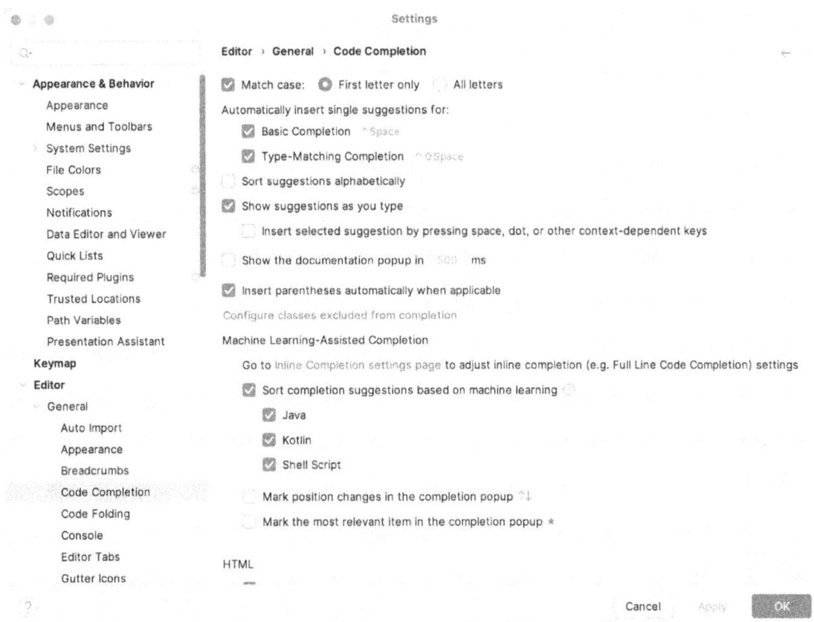

Figure 8-15

8.5 Statement Completion

Another form of auto-completion provided by the Android Studio editor is statement completion. This can be used to automatically fill out the parentheses and braces for items such as methods and loop statements. Statement completion is invoked using the Shift-Ctrl-Enter (Shift-Cmd-Enter on macOS) keyboard sequence. Consider, for example, the following code:

```
fun myMethod()
```

Having typed this code into the editor, triggering statement completion will cause the editor to add the braces to the method automatically:

```
fun myMethod() {


}
```

8.6 Parameter Information

It is also possible to ask the editor to provide information about the argument parameters a method accepts. With the cursor positioned between the brackets of a method call, the Ctrl-P (Cmd-P on macOS) keyboard sequence will display the parameters known to be accepted by that method, with the most likely suggestion highlighted in bold:

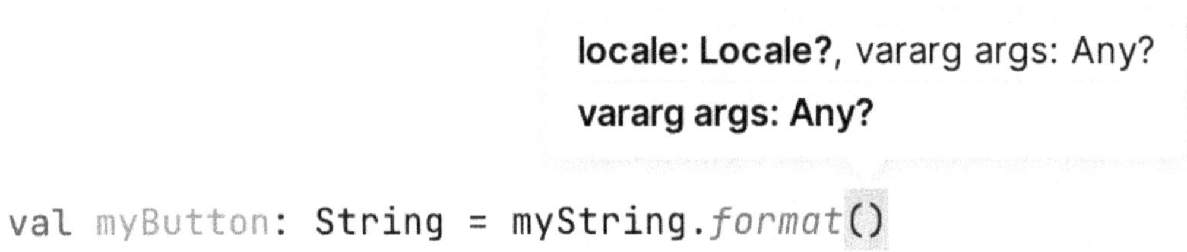

Figure 8-16

8.7 Parameter Name Hints

The code editor may be configured to display parameter name hints within method calls. Figure 8-17, for example, highlights the parameter name hints within the calls to the *make()* and *setAction()* methods of the Snackbar class:

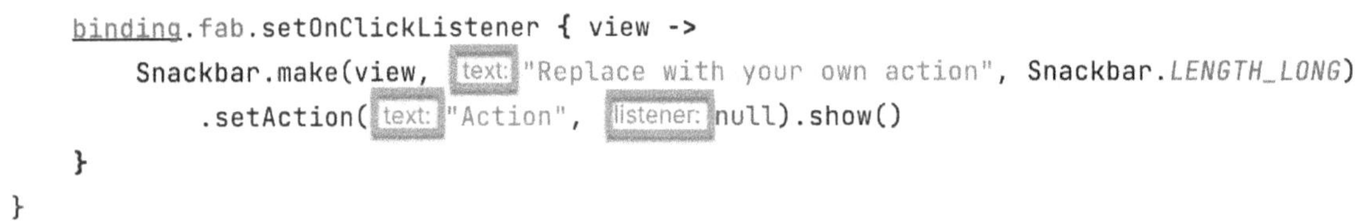

Figure 8-17

The settings for this mode may be configured by opening the Settings dialog and navigating to *Editor -> Inlay Hints -> Values -> Kotlin* in the side panel. Turn on or off the Parameter names option on the resulting screen for your chosen programming language. To adjust the hint settings, click on the *Exclude list...* link and make any necessary adjustments.

8.8 Code Generation

In addition to completing code as it is typed, the editor can, under certain conditions, also generate code for you. The list of available code generation options shown in Figure 8-18 can be accessed using the Alt-Insert (Cmd-N on macOS) keyboard shortcut when the cursor is at the location in the file where the code is to be generated.

Figure 8-18

For example, consider a situation where we want to be notified when an Activity in our project is about to be destroyed by the operating system. As outlined in a later chapter of this book, this can be achieved by overriding the *onStop()* lifecycle method of the Activity superclass. To have Android Studio generate a stub method for this, select the *Override Methods...* option from the code generation list and select the *onStop()* method from the resulting list of available methods:

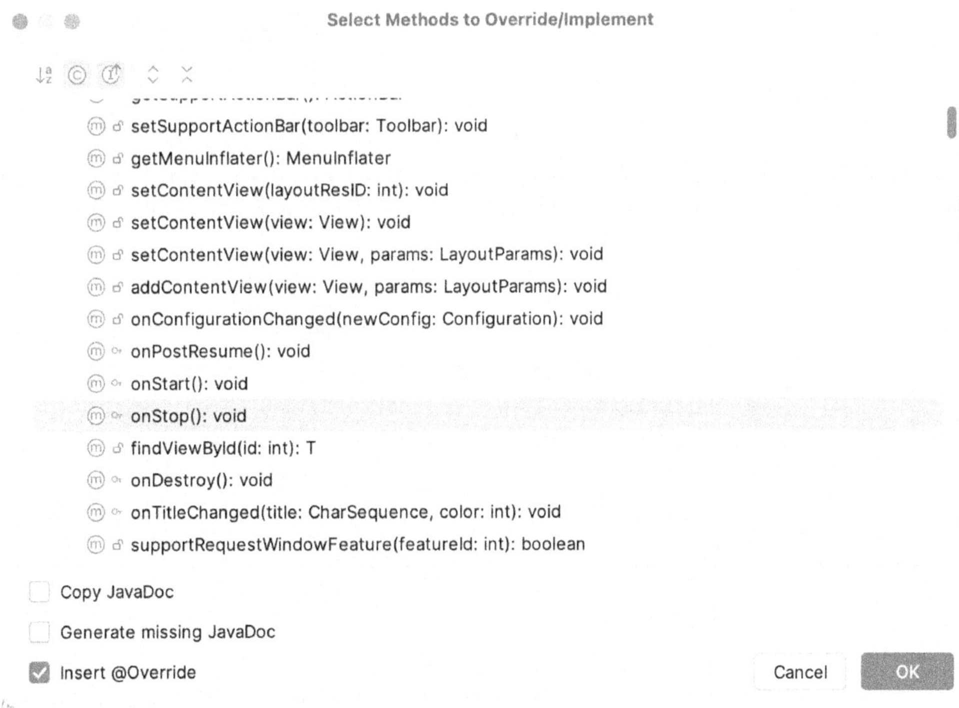

Figure 8-19

Having selected the method to override, clicking on OK will generate the stub method at the current cursor location in the Kotlin source file as follows:

```
override fun onStop() {
```

```
    super.onStop()
}
```

8.9 Code Folding

Once a source code file reaches a certain size, even the most carefully formatted and well-organized code can become overwhelming and challenging to navigate. Android Studio takes the view that it is not always necessary to have the content of every code block visible at all times. Code navigation can be made easier by using the *code folding* feature of the Android Studio editor. Code folding is controlled using disclosure arrows that appear at the beginning of each code block in a source file when the mouse pointer hovers in the gutter area. Figure 8-20, for example, highlights the disclosure arrow for a method declaration that is not currently folded:

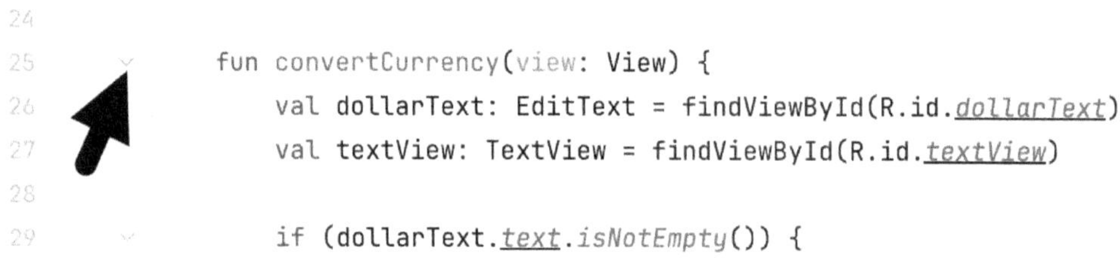

Figure 8-20

Clicking on this marker will fold the statement such that only the signature line is visible, as shown in Figure 8-21:

Figure 8-21

To unfold a collapsed section of code, click on the disclosure arrow in the editor gutter. To see the hidden code without unfolding it, hover the mouse pointer over the "{…}" indicator, as shown in Figure 8-22. The editor will then display the lens overlay containing the folded code block:

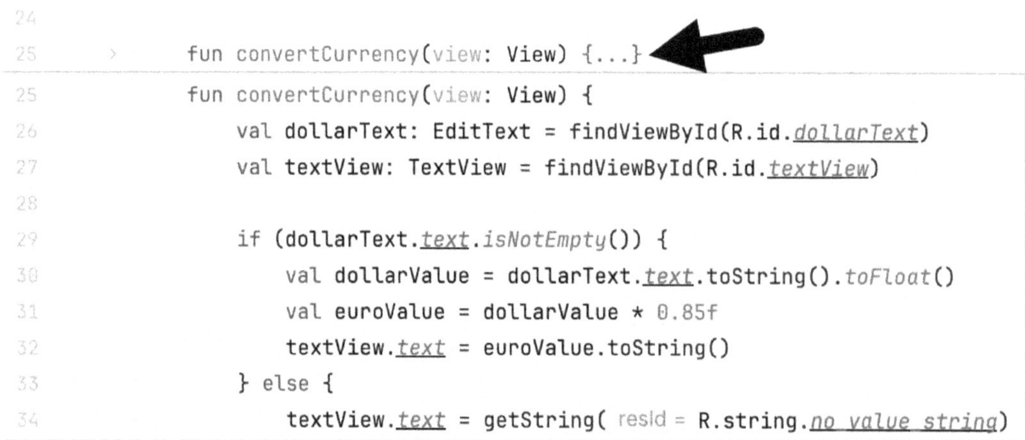

Figure 8-22

All of the code blocks in a file may be folded or unfolded using the Ctrl-Shift-Plus and Ctrl-Shift-Minus keyboard sequences (Cmd-Shift-Plus and Cmd-Shift-Minus on macOS).

By default, the Android Studio editor will automatically fold some code when a source file is opened. To configure the conditions under which this happens, navigate to the *Editor -> General -> Code Folding* entry in the Settings dialog (Figure 8-23):

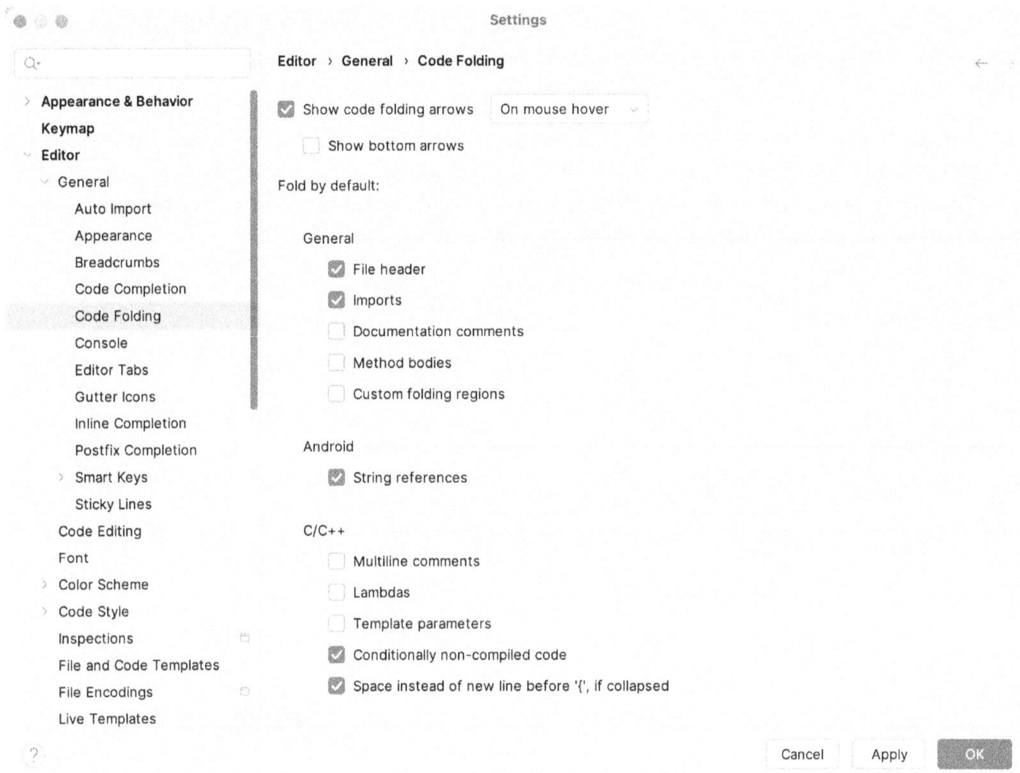

Figure 8-23

8.10 Quick Documentation Lookup

Context-sensitive Kotlin and Android documentation can be accessed by hovering the cursor over the declaration for which documentation is required or pressing the Ctrl-Q keyboard shortcut (Ctrl-J on macOS). This will display a panel containing the relevant reference documentation for the item. Figure 8-24, for example, shows the documentation for the Android Menu class.

Figure 8-24

8.11 Code Reformatting

In general, the Android Studio editor will automatically format code in terms of indenting, spacing, and nesting of statements and code blocks as they are added. In situations where lines of code need to be reformatted (a common occurrence, for example, when cutting and pasting sample code from a website), the editor provides a source code reformatting feature which, when selected, will automatically reformat code to match the prevailing code style.

Press the Ctrl-Alt-L (Cmd-Opt-L on macOS) keyboard shortcut sequence to reformat the source code. To display the Reformat Code dialog (Figure 8-25) use the Ctrl-Alt-Shift-L (Cmd-Opt-Shift-L on macOS). This dialog provides the option to reformat only the currently selected code, the entire source file currently active in the editor, or only code that has changed as a result of a source code control update:

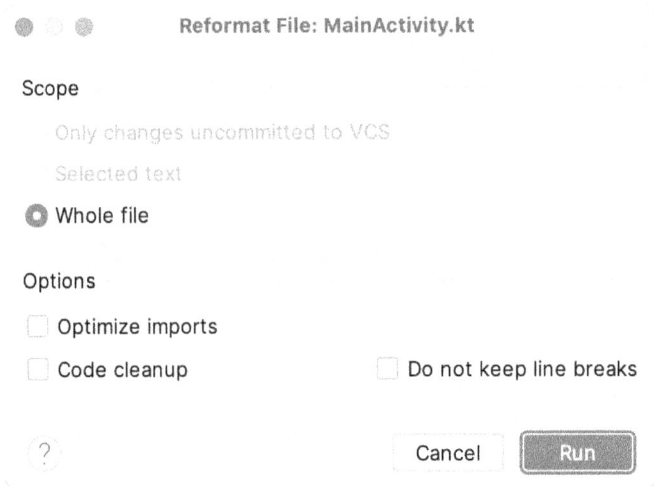

Figure 8-25

The full range of code style preferences can be changed by opening the Settings dialog and choosing Code Style in the side panel to access a list of supported programming and markup languages. Selecting a language will provide access to a vast array of formatting style options, all of which may be modified from the Android Studio default to match your preferred code style. To configure the settings for the Rearrange code option in the above dialog, for example, unfold the Code Style section, select Kotlin and, from the Kotlin settings, select the Arrangement tab.

8.12 Live Templates

As you write Android code, you will find that there are common constructs that are used frequently. For example, a common requirement is to display a popup message to the user using the Android Toast class. Live templates are a collection of common code constructs that can be entered into the editor by typing the initial characters followed by a special key (set to the Tab key by default) to insert template code. To experience this in action, type toast in the code editor followed by the Tab key, and Android Studio will insert the following code at the cursor position ready for editing:

```
Toast.makeText(, "", Toast.LENGTH_SHORT).show()
```

To list and edit existing templates, change the special key, or add your own templates, open the Settings dialog and select Live Templates from the Editor section of the left-hand navigation panel:

Figure 8-26

Add, remove, duplicate, or reset templates using the buttons marked A in Figure 8-26 above. To modify a template, select it from the list (B) and change the settings in the panel marked C.

8.13 Summary

The Android Studio editor goes to great lengths to reduce the typing needed to write code and make that code easier to read and navigate. This chapter covered key editor features, including code completion, code generation, editor window splitting, code folding, reformatting, documentation lookup, and live templates.

Chapter 9

9. An Overview of the Android Architecture

So far, in this book, steps have been taken to set up an environment suitable for developing Android applications using Android Studio. An initial step has also been taken into the application development process by creating an Android Studio application project.

However, before delving further into the practical matters of Android application development, it is essential to understand some of the more abstract concepts of both the Android SDK and Android development in general. Gaining a clear understanding of these concepts now will provide a sound foundation on which to build further knowledge.

Starting with an overview of the Android architecture in this chapter and continuing in the following few chapters of this book, the goal is to provide a detailed overview of the fundamentals of Android development.

9.1 The Android Software Stack

Android is structured as a software stack comprising applications, an operating system, a runtime environment, middleware, services, and libraries. This architecture can best be represented visually, as Figure 9-1 outlines. Each layer of the stack, and the corresponding elements within each layer, are tightly integrated and carefully tuned to provide the optimal application development and execution environment for mobile devices. The remainder of this chapter will work through the different layers of the Android stack, starting at the bottom with the Linux Kernel.

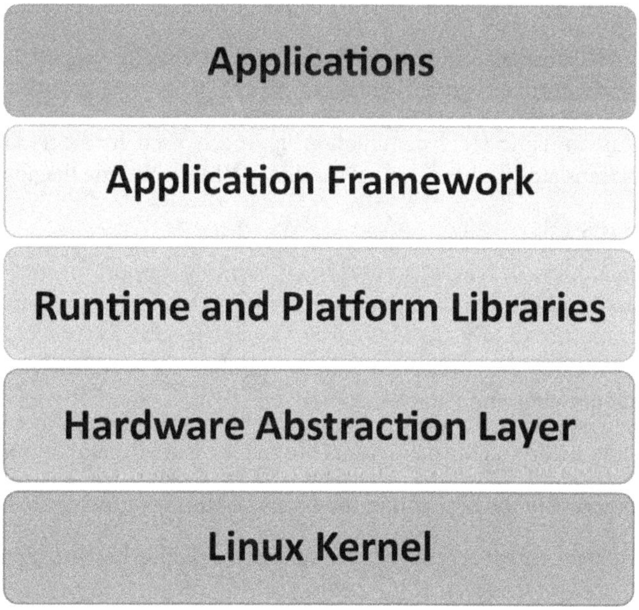

Figure 9-1

9.2 The Linux Kernel

Positioned at the bottom of the Android software stack, the Linux Kernel provides a level of abstraction between the device hardware and the upper layers of the Android software stack. The kernel provides preemptive multitasking, low-level core system services such as memory, process, and power management, and a network stack and device drivers for hardware such as the device display, WiFi, and audio.

The original Linux kernel was developed in 1991 by Linus Torvalds. It was combined with a set of tools, utilities, and compilers developed by Richard Stallman at the Free Software Foundation to create a complete operating system called GNU/Linux. Various Linux distributions have been derived from these basic underpinnings, such as Ubuntu and Red Hat Enterprise Linux.

However, it is important to note that Android uses only the Linux kernel. That said, it is worth noting that the Linux kernel was originally developed for use in traditional desktop and server computer systems. In fact, Linux is now most widely deployed in mission-critical enterprise server environments. It is a testament to both the power of today's mobile devices and the efficiency and performance of the Linux kernel that we find this software at the heart of the Android software stack.

9.3 Hardware Abstraction Layer

The Hardware Abstraction Layer (HAL) comprises a set of library modules that interface with device components such as the camera, microphone, and accelerometer. When the Android stack needs to access a hardware component, it uses the HAL library modules. Each Android device manufacturer has an abstraction layer for its specific hardware configuration, allowing the standard Android libraries and frameworks to run on any device without being altered for specific hardware.

9.4 Android Runtime – ART

When an Android app is built within Android Studio, it is compiled into an intermediate bytecode format (DEX format). When the application is subsequently loaded onto the device, the Android Runtime (ART) uses a process referred to as Ahead-of-Time (AOT) compilation to translate the bytecode down to the native instructions required by the device processor. This format is known as Executable and Linkable Format (ELF).

Each time the application is subsequently launched, the ELF executable version is run, resulting in faster application performance and improved battery life.

This contrasts with the Just-in-Time (JIT) compilation approach used in older Android implementations, whereby the bytecode was translated within a virtual machine (VM) each time the application was launched.

9.5 Android Libraries

In addition to a set of standard Java development libraries (providing support for such general-purpose tasks as string handling, networking, and file manipulation), the Android development environment also includes the Android Libraries. These are a set of Java-based libraries that are specific to Android development. Examples of libraries in this category include the application framework libraries in addition to those that facilitate user interface building, graphics drawing, and database access.

A summary of some key core Android libraries available to the Android developer is as follows:

- **android.app** – Provides access to the application model and is the cornerstone of all Android applications.
- **android.content** – Facilitates content access, publishing, and messaging between applications and application components.
- **android.database** – Used to access data published by content providers and includes SQLite database management classes.

- **android.graphics** – A low-level 2D graphics drawing API including colors, points, filters, rectangles, and canvases.
- **android.hardware** – Presents an API providing access to hardware such as the accelerometer and light sensor.
- **android.opengl** – A Java interface to the OpenGL ES 3D graphics rendering API.
- **android.os** – Provides applications with access to standard operating system services, including messages, system services, and inter-process communication.
- **android.media** – Provides classes to enable playback of audio and video.
- **android.net** – A set of APIs providing access to the network stack. Includes *android.net.wifi*, which provides access to the device's wireless stack.
- **android.print** – Includes a set of classes that enable content to be sent to configured printers from within Android applications.
- **android.provider** – A set of convenience classes that provide access to standard Android content provider databases such as those maintained by the calendar and contact applications.
- **android.text** – Used to render and manipulate text on a device display.
- **android.util** – A set of utility classes for performing tasks such as string and number conversion, XML handling and date and time manipulation.
- **android.view** – The fundamental building blocks of application user interfaces.
- **android.widget** - A rich collection of pre-built user interface components such as buttons, labels, list views, layout managers, radio buttons etc.
- **android.webkit** – A set of classes intended to allow web-browsing capabilities to be built into applications.

Having covered the Java-based libraries in the Android runtime, it is now time to turn our attention to the C/C++-based libraries in this layer of the Android software stack.

9.5.1 C/C++ Libraries

The Android runtime core libraries outlined in the preceding section are Java-based and provide the primary APIs for Android developers. It is important to note, however, that the core libraries do not perform much of the actual work and are, in fact, essentially Java "wrappers" around a set of C/C++-based libraries. When making calls, for example, to the *android.opengl* library to draw 3D graphics on the device display, the library ultimately makes calls to the *OpenGL ES* C++ library, which, in turn, works with the underlying Linux kernel to perform the drawing tasks.

C/C++ libraries are included to fulfill a broad and diverse range of functions, including 2D and 3D graphics drawing, Secure Sockets Layer (SSL) communication, SQLite database management, audio and video playback, bitmap and vector font rendering, display subsystem and graphic layer management and an implementation of the standard C system library (libc).

In practice, the typical Android application developer will access these libraries solely through the Java-based Android core library APIs. If direct access to these libraries is needed, this can be achieved using the Android Native Development Kit (NDK), the purpose of which is to call the native methods of non-Java or Kotlin programming languages (such as C and C++) from within Java code using the Java Native Interface (JNI).

9.6 Application Framework

The Application Framework is a set of services that collectively form the environment in which Android applications run and are managed. This framework implements the concept that Android applications are constructed from reusable, interchangeable, and replaceable components. This concept is taken a step further in that an application can also *publish* its capabilities along with any corresponding data so that other applications can find and reuse them.

The Android framework includes the following key services:

- **Activity Manager** – Controls all aspects of the application lifecycle and activity stack.
- **Content Providers** – Allows applications to publish and share data with other applications.
- **Resource Manager** – Provides access to non-code embedded resources such as strings, color settings, and user interface layouts.
- **Notifications Manager** – Allows applications to display alerts and notifications to the user.
- **View System** – An extensible set of views used to create application user interfaces.
- **Package Manager** – The system by which applications can find information about other applications currently installed on the device.
- **Telephony Manager** – Provides information to the application about the telephony services available on the device, such as status and subscriber information.
- **Location Manager** – Provides access to the location services allowing an application to receive updates about location changes.

9.7 Applications

Located at the top of the Android software stack are the applications. These comprise the native applications provided with the particular Android implementation (for example, web browser and email applications) and the third-party applications installed by the user after purchasing the device.

9.8 Summary

A good Android development knowledge foundation requires an understanding of the overall architecture of Android. Android is implemented as a software stack architecture consisting of a Linux kernel, a runtime environment, corresponding libraries, an application framework, and a set of applications. Applications are predominantly written in Java or Kotlin and compiled into bytecode format within the Android Studio build environment. When the application is subsequently installed on a device, this bytecode is compiled down by the Android Runtime (ART) to the native format used by the CPU. The key goals of the Android architecture are performance and efficiency, both in application execution and in the implementation of reuse in application design.

Chapter 10

10. The Anatomy of an Android App

Regardless of your prior programming experiences, be it Windows, macOS, Linux, or even iOS based, the chances are good that Android development is quite unlike anything you have encountered before.

Therefore, this chapter's objective is to provide an understanding of the high-level concepts behind the architecture of Android applications. In doing so, we will explore in detail the various components that can be used to construct an application and the mechanisms that allow these to work together to create a cohesive application.

10.1 Android Activities

Those familiar with object-oriented programming languages such as Java, Kotlin, C++, or C# will be familiar with the concept of encapsulating elements of application functionality into classes that are then instantiated as objects and manipulated to create an application. This is still true since Android applications are written in Java and Kotlin. Android, however, also takes the concept of reusable components to a higher level.

Android applications are created by combining one or more components known as *Activities*. An activity is a single, standalone module of application functionality that usually correlates directly to a single user interface screen and its corresponding functionality. An appointment application might, for example, have an activity screen that displays appointments set up for the current day. An appointment application might have an activity screen that displays appointments set up for the current day. The application might also utilize a second activity consisting of a screen where the user may enter new appointments.

Activities are intended as fully reusable and interchangeable building blocks that can be shared amongst different applications. An existing email application may contain an activity for composing and sending an email message. A developer might be writing an application that is also required to send an email message. Rather than develop an email composition activity specifically for the new application, the developer can use the activity from the existing email application.

Activities are created as subclasses of the Android *Activity* class and must be implemented so as to be entirely independent of other activities in the application. In other words, a shared activity cannot rely on being called at a known point in a program flow (since other applications may use the activity in unanticipated ways), and one activity cannot directly call methods or access instance data of another activity. This, instead, is achieved using *Intents* and *Content Providers*.

By default, an activity cannot return results to the activity from which it was invoked. If this functionality is required, the activity must be started explicitly as a *sub-activity* of the originating activity.

10.2 Android Fragments

As described above, an activity typically represents a single user interface screen within an app. One option is constructing the activity using a single user interface layout and one corresponding activity class file. A better alternative, however, is to break the activity into different sections. Each section is a *fragment* consisting of part of the user interface layout and a matching class file (declared as a subclass of the Android Fragment class). In this scenario, an activity becomes a container into which one or more fragments are embedded.

Fragments provide an efficient alternative to having each user interface screen represented by a separate activity. Instead, an app can have a single activity that switches between fragments, each representing a different app screen.

10.3 Android Intents

Intents are the mechanism by which one activity can launch another and implement the flow through the activities that make up an application. Intents consist of a description of the operation to be performed and, optionally, the data on which it is to be performed.

Intents can be *explicit*, in that they request the launch of a specific activity by referencing the activity by class name, or *implicit* by stating either the type of action to be performed or providing data of a specific type on which the action is to be performed. In the case of implicit intents, the Android runtime will select the activity to launch that most closely matches the criteria specified by the Intent using a process referred to as *Intent Resolution*.

10.4 Broadcast Intents

Another type of Intent, the *Broadcast Intent*, is a system-wide intent sent out to all applications that have registered an "interested" *Broadcast Receiver*. The Android system, for example, will typically send out Broadcast Intents to indicate changes in device status, such as the completion of system start-up, connection of an external power source to the device, or the screen being turned on or off.

A Broadcast Intent can be *normal* (asynchronous) in that it is sent to all interested Broadcast Receivers at more or less the same time or *ordered* in that it is sent to one receiver at a time where it can be processed and then either aborted or allowed to be passed to the next Broadcast Receiver.

10.5 Broadcast Receivers

Broadcast Receivers are the mechanism by which applications can respond to Broadcast Intents. A Broadcast Receiver must be registered by an application and configured with an *Intent Filter* to indicate the types of broadcast it is interested in. When a matching intent is broadcast, the receiver will be invoked by the Android runtime regardless of whether the application that registered the receiver is currently running. The receiver then has 5 seconds to complete required tasks (such as launching a Service, making data updates, or issuing a notification to the user) before returning. Broadcast Receivers operate in the background and do not have a user interface.

10.6 Android Services

Android Services are processes that run in the background and do not have a user interface. They can be started and managed from activities, Broadcast Receivers, or other Services. Android Services are ideal for situations where an application needs to continue performing tasks but does not necessarily need a user interface to be visible to the user. Although Services lack a user interface, they can still notify the user of events using notifications and *toasts* (small notification messages that appear on the screen without interrupting the currently visible activity) and are also able to issue Intents.

The Android runtime gives Services a higher priority than many other processes and will only be terminated as a last resort by the system to free up resources. If the runtime needs to kill a Service, however, it will be automatically restarted as soon as adequate resources become available. A Service can reduce the risk of termination by declaring itself as needing to run in the *foreground*. This is achieved by making a call to *startForeground()*. This is only recommended for situations where termination would be detrimental to the user experience (for example, if the user is listening to audio being streamed by the Service).

Example situations where a Service might be a practical solution include, as previously mentioned, the streaming of audio that should continue when the application is no longer active or a stock market tracking application that needs to notify the user when a share hits a specified price.

10.7 Content Providers

Content Providers implement a mechanism for the sharing of data between applications. Any application can provide other applications with access to its underlying data by implementing a Content Provider, including the ability to add, remove and query the data (subject to permissions). Access to the data is provided via a Universal Resource Identifier (URI) defined by the Content Provider. Data can be shared as a file or an entire SQLite database.

The native Android applications include several standard Content Providers allowing applications to access data such as contacts and media files. The Content Providers currently available on an Android system may be located using a *Content Resolver*.

10.8 The Application Manifest

The Application Manifest file is the glue that pulls together the various elements that comprise an application. Within this XML-based file, the application outlines the activities, services, broadcast receivers, data providers, and permissions that comprise the complete application.

10.9 Application Resources

In addition to the manifest file and the Dex files containing the byte code, an Android application package typically contains a collection of *resource files*. These files contain resources such as strings, images, fonts, and colors that appear in the user interface, together with the XML representation of the user interface layouts. These files are stored in the */res* sub-directory of the application project's hierarchy by default.

10.10 Application Context

When an application is compiled, a class named *R* is created containing references to the application resources. The application manifest file and these resources combine to create what is known as the *Application Context*. This context, represented by the Android *Context* class, may be used in the application code to gain access to the application resources at runtime. In addition, a wide range of methods may be called on an application's context to gather information and change the application's environment at runtime.

10.11 Summary

A number of different elements can be brought together to create an Android application. In this chapter, we have provided a high-level overview of Activities, Fragments, Services, Intents, and Broadcast Receivers and an overview of the manifest file and application resources.

Maximum reuse and interoperability are promoted by creating individual, standalone functionality modules in the form of activities and intents while implementing content providers to achieve data sharing between applications.

While activities are focused on areas where the user interacts with the application (an activity essentially equating to a single user interface screen and often made up of one or more fragments), background processing is typically handled by Services and Broadcast Receivers.

The components that make up the application are outlined for the Android runtime system in a manifest file which, combined with the application's resources, represents the application's context.

Much has been covered in this chapter that is likely new to the average developer. Rest assured, however, that extensive exploration and practical use of these concepts will be made in subsequent chapters to ensure a solid knowledge foundation on which to build your own applications.

Chapter 11

11. An Introduction to Kotlin

Android development is performed primarily using Android Studio which is, in turn, based on the IntelliJ IDEA development environment created by a company named JetBrains. Before the release of Android Studio 3.0, all Android apps were written using Android Studio and the Java programming language (with some occasional C++ code when needed).

Since the introduction of Android Studio 3.0, however, developers now have the option of creating Android apps using another programming language called Kotlin. Although detailed coverage of all features of this language is beyond the scope of this book (entire books can and have been written covering solely Kotlin), the objective of this and the following six chapters is to provide enough information to begin programming in Kotlin and quickly get up to speed developing Android apps using this programming language.

11.1 What is Kotlin?

Named after an island located in the Baltic Sea, Kotlin is a programming language created by JetBrains and follows Java in the tradition of naming programming languages after islands. Kotlin code is intended to be easier to understand and write and also safer than many other programming languages. The language, compiler, and related tools are all open source and available for free under the Apache 2 license.

The primary goals of the Kotlin language are to make code both concise and safe. Code is generally considered concise when it can be easily read and understood. Conciseness also plays a role when writing code, allowing code to be written more quickly and with greater efficiency. In terms of safety, Kotlin includes several features that improve the chances that potential problems will be identified when the code is being written instead of causing runtime crashes.

A third objective in the design and implementation of Kotlin involves interoperability with Java.

11.2 Kotlin and Java

Originally introduced by Sun Microsystems in 1995 Java is still by far the most popular programming language in use today. Until the introduction of Kotlin, it is quite likely that every Android app available on the market was written in Java. Since acquiring the Android operating system, Google has invested heavily in tuning and optimizing compilation and runtime environments for running Java-based code on Android devices.

Rather than try to re-invent the wheel, Kotlin is designed to both integrate with and work alongside Java. When Kotlin code is compiled it generates the same bytecode as that generated by the Java compiler enabling projects to be built using a combination of Java and Kotlin code. This compatibility also allows existing Java frameworks and libraries to be used seamlessly from within Kotlin code and also for Kotlin code to be called from within Java.

Kotlin's creators also acknowledged that while there were ways to improve on existing languages, there are many features of Java that did not need to be changed. Consequently, those familiar with programming in Java will find many of these skills to be transferable to Kotlin-based development. Programmers with Swift programming experience will also find much that is familiar when learning Kotlin.

11.3 Converting from Java to Kotlin

Given the high level of interoperability between Kotlin and Java, it is not essential to convert existing Java code to Kotlin since these two languages will comfortably co-exist within the same project. That being said, Java code can be converted to Kotlin from within Android Studio using a built-in Java to Kotlin converter. To convert an entire Java source file to Kotlin, load the file into the Android Studio code editor and select the *Code -> Convert Java File to Kotlin File* menu option. Alternatively, blocks of Java code may be converted to Kotlin by cutting the code and pasting it into an existing Kotlin file within the Android Studio code editor. Note when performing Java to Kotlin conversions that the Java code will not always convert to the best possible Kotlin code and that time should be taken to review and tidy up the code after conversion.

11.4 Kotlin and Android Studio

Support for Kotlin is provided within Android Studio via the Kotlin Plug-in which is integrated by default into Android Studio 3.0 or later.

11.5 Experimenting with Kotlin

When learning a new programming language, it is often useful to be able to enter and execute snippets of code. One of the best ways to do this with Kotlin is to use the Kotlin Playground (Figure 11-1) located at *https://play.kotlinlang.org:*

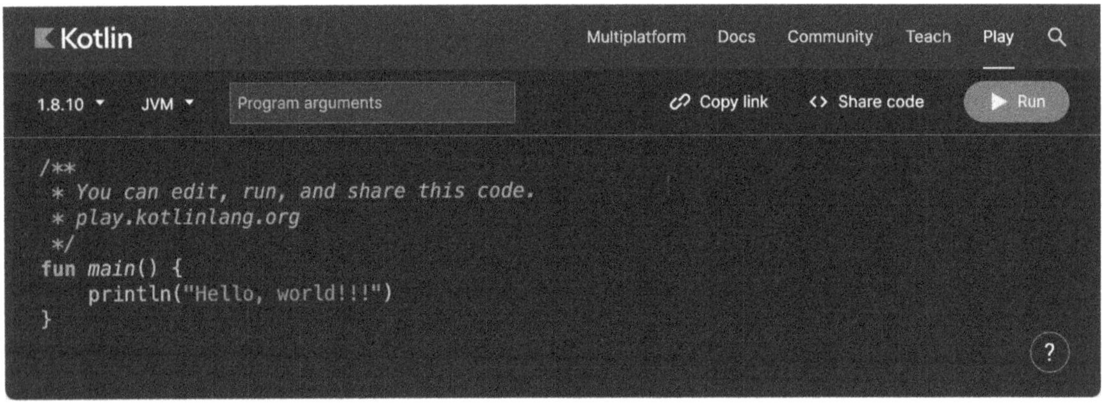

Figure 11-1

In addition to providing an environment in which Kotlin code may be quickly entered and executed, the playground also includes a set of examples and tutorials demonstrating key Kotlin features in action.

Try out some Kotlin code by opening a browser window, navigating to the playground, and entering the following into the main code panel:

```
fun main(args: Array<String>) {

    println("Welcome to Kotlin")

    for (i in 1..8) {
        println("i = $i")
    }
}
```

After entering the code, click on the Run button and note the output in the console panel:

Figure 11-2

11.6 Semi-colons in Kotlin

Unlike programming languages such as Java and C++, Kotlin does not require semi-colons at the end of each statement or expression line. The following, therefore, is valid Kotlin code:

```
val mynumber = 10
println(mynumber)
```

Semi-colons are only required when multiple statements appear on the same line:

```
val mynumber = 10; println(mynumber)
```

11.7 Summary

Kotlin is a programming language developed by JetBrains, the company that created the development environment on which Android Studio is based. Kotlin is intended to make code safer and easier to understand and write. Kotlin is also highly compatible with Java, allowing Java and Kotlin code to co-exist within the same projects. This interoperability ensures that most of the standard Java and Java-based Android libraries and frameworks are available for use when developing using Kotlin.

Kotlin support for Android Studio is provided via a plug-in bundled with Android Studio 3.0 or later. This plug-in also provides a converter to translate Java code to Kotlin.

When learning Kotlin, the online playground provides a useful environment for quickly trying out Kotlin code.

Chapter 12

12. Kotlin Data Types, Variables and Nullability

Both this and the following few chapters are intended to introduce the basics of the Kotlin programming language. This chapter will focus on the various data types available for use within Kotlin code. This will also include an explanation of constants, variables, type casting and Kotlin's handling of null values.

As outlined in the previous chapter, entitled *"An Introduction to Kotlin"* a useful way to experiment with the language is to use the Kotlin online playground environment. Before starting this chapter, therefore, open a browser window, navigate to *https://play.kotlinlang.org* and use the playground to try out the code in both this and the other Kotlin introductory chapters that follow.

12.1 Kotlin data types

When we look at the different types of software that run on computer systems and mobile devices, from financial applications to graphics-intensive games, it is easy to forget that computers are really just binary machines. Binary systems work in terms of 0 and 1, true or false, set and unset. All the data sitting in RAM, stored on disk drives and flowing through circuit boards and buses are nothing more than sequences of 1s and 0s. Each 1 or 0 is referred to as a bit and bits are grouped together in blocks of 8, each group being referred to as a byte. When people talk about 32-bit and 64-bit computer systems they are talking about the number of bits that can be handled simultaneously by the CPU bus. A 64-bit CPU, for example, is able to handle data in 64-bit blocks, resulting in faster performance than a 32-bit based system.

Humans, of course, don't think in binary. We work with decimal numbers, letters and words. For a human to easily ('easily' being a relative term in this context) program a computer, some middle ground between human and computer thinking is needed. This is where programming languages such as Kotlin come into play. Programming languages allow humans to express instructions to a computer in terms and structures we understand, and then compile that down to a format that can be executed by a CPU.

One of the fundamentals of any program involves data, and programming languages such as Kotlin define a set of *data types* that allow us to work with data in a format we understand when programming. For example, if we want to store a number in a Kotlin program we could do so with syntax similar to the following:

```
val mynumber = 10
```

In the above example, we have created a variable named *mynumber* and then assigned to it the value of 10. When we compile the source code down to the machine code used by the CPU, the number 10 is seen by the computer in binary as:

```
1010
```

Similarly, we can express a letter, the visual representation of a digit ('0' through to '9') or punctuation mark (referred to in computer terminology as *characters*) using the following syntax:

```
val myletter = 'c'
```

Once again, this is understandable by a human programmer, but gets compiled down to a binary sequence for the CPU to understand. In this case, the letter 'c' is represented by the decimal number 99 using the ASCII table (an internationally recognized standard that assigns numeric values to human readable characters). When converted to binary, it is stored as:

```
001100011
```

Now that we have a basic understanding of the concept of data types and why they are necessary we can take a closer look at some of the more commonly used data types supported by Kotlin.

12.1.1 Integer data types

Kotlin integer data types are used to store whole numbers (in other words, a number with no decimal places). Signed integers are capable of storing positive and negative whole numbers, while unsigned integers can only store positive numbers (including zero).

Kotlin provides support for 8-bit, 16-bit, 32-bit, and 64-bit integers, represented by the Byte, Short, Int, and Long types, respectively. The unsigned equivalent types are uByte, uShort, uInt, and uLong.

12.1.2 Floating point data types

The Kotlin floating-point data types are able to store values containing decimal places. For example, 4353.1223 would be stored in a floating-point data type. Kotlin provides two floating-point data types in the form of Float and Double. Which type to use depends on the size of value to be stored and the level of precision required. The Double type can be used to store up to 64-bit floating-point numbers. The Float data type, on the other hand, is limited to 32-bit floating-point numbers.

12.1.3 Boolean data type

Kotlin, like other languages, includes a data type for the purpose of handling true or false (1 or 0) conditions. Two Boolean constant values (*true* and *false*) are provided by Kotlin specifically for working with Boolean data types.

12.1.4 Character data type

The Kotlin Char data type is used to store a single character of rendered text such as a letter, numerical digit, punctuation mark or symbol. Internally characters in Kotlin are stored in the form of 16-bit Unicode grapheme clusters. A grapheme cluster is made of two or more Unicode code points that are combined to represent a single visible character.

The following lines assign a variety of different characters to Character type variables:

```
val myChar1 = 'f'
val myChar2 = ':'
val myChar3 = 'X'
```

Characters may also be referenced using Unicode code points. The following example assigns the 'X' character to a variable using Unicode:

```
val myChar4 = '\u0058'
```

Note the use of single quotes when assigning a character to a variable. This indicates to Kotlin that this is a Char data type as opposed to double quotes which indicate a String data type.

12.1.5 String data type

The String data type is a sequence of characters that typically make up a word or sentence. In addition to providing a storage mechanism, the String data type also includes a range of string manipulation features allowing strings to be searched, matched, concatenated and modified. Double quotes are used to surround single line strings during assignment, for example:

```
val message = "You have 10 new messages."
```

Alternatively, a multi-line string may be declared using triple quotes

```
val message = """You have 10 new messages,
                                    5 old messages
               and 6 spam messages."""
```

The leading spaces on each line of a multi-line string can be removed by making a call to the *trimMargin()* function of the String data type:

```
val message = """You have 10 new messages,
                                    5 old messages
               and 6 spam messages.""".trimMargin()
```

Strings can also be constructed using combinations of strings, variables, constants, expressions, and function calls using a concept referred to as string interpolation. For example, the following code creates a new string from a variety of different sources using string interpolation before outputting it to the console:

```
val username = "John"
val inboxCount = 25
val maxcount = 100
val message = "$username has $inboxCount messages. Message capacity remaining is
${maxcount - inboxCount} messages"

println(message)
```

When executed, the code will output the following message:

```
John has 25 messages. Message capacity remaining is 75 messages.
```

12.1.6 Escape sequences

In addition to the standard set of characters outlined above, there is also a range of special characters (also referred to as escape characters) available for specifying items such as a new line, tab or a specific Unicode value within a string. These special characters are identified by prefixing the character with a backslash (a concept referred to as escaping). For example, the following assigns a new line to the variable named newline:

```
var newline = '\n'
```

In essence, any character that is preceded by a backslash is considered to be a special character and is treated accordingly. This raises the question as to what to do if you actually want a backslash character. This is achieved by escaping the backslash itself:

```
var backslash = '\\'
```

The complete list of special characters supported by Kotlin is as follows:

- \n - New line
- \r - Carriage return
- \t - Horizontal tab
- \\ - Backslash
- \" - Double quote (used when placing a double quote into a string declaration)
- \' - Single quote (used when placing a single quote into a string declaration)
- \$ - Used when a character sequence containing a $ is misinterpreted as a variable in a string template.
- \unnnn – Double byte Unicode scalar where nnnn is replaced by four hexadecimal digits representing the

Unicode character.

12.2 Mutable variables

Variables are essentially locations in computer memory reserved for storing the data used by an application. Each variable is given a name by the programmer and assigned a value. The name assigned to the variable may then be used in the Kotlin code to access the value assigned to that variable. This access can involve either reading the value of the variable or, in the case of *mutable variables*, changing the value.

12.3 Immutable variables

Often referred to as a *constant,* an immutable variable is similar to a mutable variable in that it provides a named location in memory to store a data value. Immutable variables differ in one significant way in that once a value has been assigned, it cannot subsequently be changed.

Immutable variables are particularly useful if there is a value that is used repeatedly throughout the application code. Rather than use the value each time, it makes the code easier to read if the value is first assigned to a constant which is then referenced in the code. For example, it might not be clear to someone reading your Kotlin code why you used the value 5 in an expression. If, instead of the value 5, you use an immutable variable named *interestRate* the purpose of the value becomes much clearer. Immutable values also have the advantage that if the programmer needs to change a widely used value, it only needs to be changed once in the constant declaration and not each time it is referenced.

12.4 Declaring mutable and immutable variables

Mutable variables are declared using the *var* keyword and may be initialized with a value at creation time. For example:

```
var userCount = 10
```

If the variable is declared without an initial value, the type of the variable must also be declared (a topic that will be covered in more detail in the next section of this chapter). The following, for example, is a typical declaration where the variable is initialized after it has been declared:

```
var userCount: Int
userCount = 42
```

Immutable variables are declared using the *val* keyword.

```
val maxUserCount = 20
```

As with mutable variables, the type must also be specified when declaring the variable without initializing it:

```
val maxUserCount: Int
maxUserCount = 20
```

When writing Kotlin code, immutable variables should always be used in preference to mutable variables whenever possible.

12.5 Data types are objects

All of the above data types are objects, each of which provides a range of functions and properties that may be used to perform a variety of different type specific tasks. These functions and properties are accessed using so-called dot notation. Dot notation involves accessing a function or property of an object by specifying the variable name followed by a dot followed in turn by the name of the property to be accessed or function to be called.

A string variable, for example, can be converted to uppercase via a call to the *toUpperCase()* function of the String class:

```
val myString = "The quick brown fox"
val uppercase = myString.toUpperCase()
```

Similarly, the length of a string is available by accessing the length property:

```
val length = myString.length
```

Functions are also available within the String class to perform tasks such as comparisons and checking for the presence of a specific word. The following code, for example, will return a *true* Boolean value since the word "fox" appears within the string assigned to the *myString* variable:

```
val result = myString.contains("fox")
```

All of the number data types include functions for performing tasks such as converting from one data type to another such as converting an Int to a Float:

```
val myInt = 10
val myFloat = myInt.toFloat()
```

A detailed overview of all of the properties and functions provided by the Kotlin data type classes is beyond the scope of this book (there are hundreds). An exhaustive list for all data types can, however, be found within the Kotlin reference documentation available online at:

https://kotlinlang.org/api/latest/jvm/stdlib/kotlin/

12.6 Type annotations and type inference

Kotlin is categorized as a statically typed programming language. This essentially means that once the data type of a variable has been identified, that variable cannot subsequently be used to store data of any other type without inducing a compilation error. This contrasts to loosely typed programming languages where a variable, once declared, can subsequently be used to store other data types.

There are two ways in which the type of a variable will be identified. One approach is to use a type annotation at the point the variable is declared in the code. This is achieved by placing a colon after the variable name followed by the type declaration. The following line of code, for example, declares a variable named userCount as being of type Int:

```
val userCount: Int = 10
```

In the absence of a type annotation in a declaration, the Kotlin compiler uses a technique referred to as *type inference* to identify the type of the variable. When relying on type inference, the compiler looks to see what type of value is being assigned to the variable at the point that it is initialized and uses that as the type. Consider, for example, the following variable declarations:

```
var signalStrength = 2.231
val companyName = "My Company"
```

During compilation of the above lines of code, Kotlin will infer that the *signalStrength* variable is of type Double (type inference in Kotlin defaults to Double for all floating-point numbers) and that the companyName constant is of type String.

When a constant is declared without a type annotation it must be assigned a value at the point of declaration:

```
val bookTitle = "Android Studio Development Essentials"
```

If a type annotation is used when the constant is declared, however, the value can be assigned later in the code. For example:

```
val iosBookType = false
val bookTitle: String
```

```
if (iosBookType) {
        bookTitle = "iOS App Development Essentials"
} else {
        bookTitle = "Android Studio Development Essentials"
}
```

12.7 Nullable type

Kotlin nullable types are a concept that does not exist in most other programming languages (with the exception of the *optional* type in Swift). The purpose of nullable types is to provide a safe and consistent approach to handling situations where a variable may have a null value assigned to it. In other words, the objective is to avoid the common problem of code crashing with the null pointer exception errors that occur when code encounters a null value where one was not expected.

By default, a variable in Kotlin cannot have a null value assigned to it. Consider, for example, the following code:

```
val username: String = null
```

An attempt to compile the above code will result in a compilation error similar to the following:

```
Error: Null cannot be a value of a non-null string type String
```

If a variable is required to be able to store a null value, it must be specifically declared as a nullable type by placing a question mark (?) after the type declaration:

```
val username: String? = null
```

The *username* variable can now have a null value assigned to it without triggering a compiler error. Once a variable has been declared as nullable, a range of restrictions are then imposed on that variable by the compiler to prevent it being used in situations where it might cause a null pointer exception to occur. A nullable variable, cannot, for example, be assigned to a variable of non-null type as is the case in the following code:

```
val username: String? = null
val firstname: String = username
```

The above code will elicit the following error when encountered by the compiler:

```
Error: Type mismatch: inferred type is String? but String was expected
```

The only way that the assignment will be permitted is if some code is added to check that the value assigned to the nullable variable is non-null:

```
val username: String? = null

if (username != null) {
    val firstname: String = username
}
```

In the above case, the assignment will only take place if the username variable references a non-null value.

12.8 The safe call operator

A nullable variable also cannot be used to call a function or to access a property in the usual way. Earlier in this chapter, the *toUpperCase()* function was called on a String object. Given the possibility that this could cause a function to be called on a null reference, the following code will be disallowed by the compiler:

```
val username: String? = null
val uppercase = username.toUpperCase()
```

The exact error message generated by the compiler in this situation reads as follows:

```
Error: (Only safe (?.) or non-null asserted (!!.) calls are allowed on a nullable
receiver of type String?
```

In this instance, the compiler is essentially refusing to allow the function call to be made because no attempt has been made to verify that the variable is non-null. One way around this is to add some code to verify that something other than null value has been assigned to the variable before making the function call:

```
if (username != null) {
    val uppercase = username.toUpperCase()
}
```

A much more efficient way to achieve this same verification, however, is to call the function using the *safe call operator* (represented by ?.) as follows:

```
val uppercase = username?.toUpperCase()
```

In the above example, if the username variable is null, the *toUpperCase()* function will not be called and execution will proceed at the next line of code. If, on the other hand, a non-null value is assigned the *toUpperCase()* function will be called and the result assigned to the *uppercase* variable.

In addition to function calls, the safe call operator may also be used when accessing properties:

```
val uppercase = username?.length
```

12.9 Not-null assertion

The *not-null assertion* removes all of the compiler restrictions from a nullable type, allowing it to be used in the same ways as a non-null type, even if it has been assigned a null value. This assertion is implemented using double exclamation marks after the variable name, for example:

```
val username: String? = null
val length = username!!.length
```

The above code will now compile, but will crash with the following exception at runtime since an attempt is being made to call a function on a non existent object:

```
Exception in thread "main" kotlin.KotlinNullPointerException
```

Clearly, this causes the very issue that nullable types are designed to avoid. Use of the not-null assertion is generally discouraged and should only be used in situations where you are certain that the value will not be null.

12.10 Nullable types and the let function

Earlier in this chapter, we looked at how the safe call operator can be used when making a call to a function belonging to a nullable type. This technique makes it easier to check if a value is null without having to write an *if* statement every time the variable is accessed. A similar problem occurs when passing a nullable type as an argument to a function which is expecting a non-null parameter. As an example, consider the *times()* function of the Int data type. When called on an Int object and passed another integer value as an argument, the function multiplies the two values and returns the result. When the following code is executed, for example, the value of 200 will be displayed within the console:

```
val firstNumber = 10
val secondNumber = 20

val result = firstNumber.times(secondNumber)
print(result)
```

The above example works because the secondNumber variable is a non-null type. A problem, however, occurs if the secondNumber variable is declared as being of nullable type:

```
val firstNumber = 10
val secondNumber: Int? = 20

val result = firstNumber.times(secondNumber)
print(result)
```

Now the compilation will fail with the following error message because a nullable type is being passed to a function that is expecting a non-null parameter:

```
Error: Type mismatch: inferred type is Int? but Int was expected
```

A possible solution to this problem is to simply write an *if* statement to verify that the value assigned to the variable is non-null before making the call to the function:

```
val firstNumber = 10
val secondNumber: Int? = 20

if (secondNumber != null) {
    val result = firstNumber.times(secondNumber)
    print(result)
}
```

A more convenient approach to addressing the issue, however, involves use of the *let* function. When called on a nullable type object, the let function converts the nullable type to a non-null variable named *it* which may then be referenced within a lambda statement.

```
secondNumber?.let {
    val result = firstNumber.times(it)
    print(result)
}
```

Note the use of the safe call operator when calling the *let* function on secondVariable in the above example. This ensures that the function is only called when the variable is assigned a non-null value.

12.11 Late initialization (lateinit)

As previously outlined, non-null types need to be initialized when they are declared. This can be inconvenient if the value to be assigned to the non-null variable will not be known until later in the code execution. One way around this is to declare the variable using the *lateinit* modifier. This modifier designates that a value will be initialized with a value later. This has the advantage that a non-null type can be declared before it is initialized, with the disadvantage that the programmer is responsible for ensuring that the initialization has been performed before attempting to access the variable. Consider the following variable declaration:

```
var myName: String
```

Clearly, this is invalid since the variable is a non-null type but has not been assigned a value. Suppose, however, that the value to be assigned to the variable will not be known until later in the program execution. In this case, the lateinit modifier can be used as follows:

```
lateinit var myName: String
```

With the variable declared in this way, the value can be assigned later, for example:

```
myName = "John Smith"
print("My Name is " + myName)
```

Of course, if the variable is accessed before it is initialized, the code will fail with an exception:

```
lateinit var myName: String

print("My Name is " + myName)

Exception in thread "main" kotlin.UninitializedPropertyAccessException: lateinit
property myName has not been initialized
```

To verify whether a lateinit variable has been initialized, check the *isInitialized* property on the variable. To do this, we need to access the properties of the variable by prefixing the name with the '::' operator:

```
if (::myName.isInitialized) {
    print("My Name is " + myName)
}
```

12.12 The Elvis operator

The Kotlin Elvis operator can be used in conjunction with nullable types to define a default value that is to be returned if a value or expression result is null. The Elvis operator (?:) is used to separate two expressions. If the expression on the left does not resolve to a null value that value is returned, otherwise the result of the rightmost expression is returned. This can be thought of as a quick alternative to writing an if-else statement to check for a null value. Consider the following code:

```
if (myString != null) {
    return myString
} else {
    return "String is null"
}
```

The same result can be achieved with less coding using the Elvis operator as follows:

```
return myString ?: "String is null"
```

12.13 Type casting and type checking

When compiling Kotlin code, the compiler can typically infer the type of an object. Situations will occur, however, where the compiler is unable to identify the specific type. This is often the case when a value type is ambiguous or an unspecified object is returned from a function call. In this situation it may be necessary to let the compiler know the type of object that your code is expecting or to write code that checks whether the object is of a particular type.

Letting the compiler know the type of object that is expected is known as *type casting* and is achieved within Kotlin code using the *as* cast operator. The following code, for example, lets the compiler know that the result returned from the *getSystemService()* method needs to be treated as a KeyguardManager object:

```
val keyMgr = getSystemService(Context.KEYGUARD_SERVICE) as KeyguardManager
```

The Kotlin language includes both safe and unsafe cast operators. The above cast is an unsafe cast and will cause the app to throw an exception if the cast cannot be performed. A safe cast, on the other hand, uses the *as?* operator and returns null if the cast cannot be performed:

```
val keyMgr = getSystemService(Context.KEYGUARD_SERVICE) as? KeyguardManager
```

A type check can be performed to verify that an object conforms to a specific type using the *is* operator, for example:

```
if (keyMgr is KeyguardManager) {
```

```
    // It is a KeyguardManager object
}
```

12.14 Summary

This chapter has begun the introduction to Kotlin by exploring data types together with an overview of how to declare variables. The chapter has also introduced concepts such as nullable types, type casting and type checking and the Elvis operator, each of which is an integral part of Kotlin programming and designed specifically to make code writing less prone to error.

Chapter 13

13. Kotlin Operators and Expressions

So far, we have looked at using variables and constants in Kotlin and also described the different data types. Being able to create variables is only part of the story, however. The next step is to learn how to use these variables in Kotlin code. The primary method for working with data is in the form of *expressions*.

13.1 Expression syntax in Kotlin

The most basic expression consists of an *operator*, two *operands*, and an *assignment*. The following is an example of an expression:

```
val myresult = 1 + 2
```

In the above example, the (+) operator is used to add two operands (1 and 2) together. The *assignment operator* (=) subsequently assigns the result of the addition to a variable named *myresult*. The operands could have easily been variables (or a mixture of values and variables) instead of the actual numerical values used in the example.

In the remainder of this chapter, we will look at the basic types of operators available in Kotlin.

13.2 The Basic assignment operator

We have already looked at the most basic of assignment operators, the = operator. This assignment operator simply assigns the result of an expression to a variable. In essence, the = assignment operator takes two operands. The left-hand operand is the variable to which a value is to be assigned and the right-hand operand is the value to be assigned. The right-hand operand is, more often than not, an expression that performs some type of arithmetic or logical evaluation or a call to a function, the result of which will be assigned to the variable. The following examples are all valid uses of the assignment operator:

```
var x: Int // Declare a mutable Int variable
val y = 10 // Declare and initialize an immutable Int variable

x = 10 // Assign a value to x
x = x + y // Assign the result of x + y to x
x = y // Assign the value of y to x
```

13.3 Kotlin arithmetic operators

Kotlin provides a range of operators for creating mathematical expressions. These operators primarily fall into the category of *binary operators* in that they take two operands. The exception is the *unary negative operator* (-) which serves to indicate that a value is negative rather than positive. This contrasts with the *subtraction operator* (-) which takes two operands (i.e. one value to be subtracted from another). For example:

```
var x = -10 // Unary - operator used to assign -10 to variable x
x = x - 5 // Subtraction operator. Subtracts 5 from x
```

The following table lists the primary Kotlin arithmetic operators:

Operator	Description
-(unary)	Negates the value of a variable or expression
*	Multiplication

/	Division
+	Addition
-	Subtraction
%	Remainder/Modulo

Table 13-1

Note that multiple operators may be used in a single expression.

For example:

```
x = y * 10 + z - 5 / 4
```

13.4 Augmented assignment operators

In an earlier section, we looked at the basic assignment operator (=). Kotlin provides several operators designed to combine an assignment with a mathematical or logical operation. These are primarily of use when performing an evaluation where the result is to be stored in one of the operands. For example, one might write an expression as follows:

```
x = x + y
```

The above expression adds the value contained in variable x to the value contained in variable y and stores the result in variable x. This can be simplified using the addition augmented assignment operator:

```
x += y
```

The above expression performs the same task as $x = x + y$ but saves the programmer some typing.

Numerous augmented assignment operators are available in Kotlin. The most frequently used of which are outlined in the following table:

Operator	Description
x += y	Add x to y and place result in x
x -= y	Subtract y from x and place result in x
x *= y	Multiply x by y and place result in x
x /= y	Divide x by y and place result in x
x %= y	Perform Modulo on x and y and place result in x

Table 13-2

13.5 Increment and decrement operators

Another useful shortcut can be achieved using the Kotlin increment and decrement operators (also referred to as unary operators because they operate on a single operand). Consider the code fragment below:

```
x = x + 1 // Increase value of variable x by 1
x = x - 1 // Decrease value of variable x by 1
```

These expressions increment and decrement the value of x by 1. Instead of using this approach, however, it is quicker to use the ++ and -- operators. The following examples perform the same tasks as the examples above:

```
x++ // Increment x by 1
x-- // Decrement x by 1
```

These operators can be placed either before or after the variable name. If the operator is placed before the variable name, the increment or decrement operation is performed before any other operations are performed on the variable. For example, in the following code, x is incremented before it is assigned to y, leaving y with a value of 10:

```
var x = 9
val y = ++x
```

In the next example, however, the value of x (9) is assigned to variable y before the decrement is performed. After the expression is evaluated the value of y will be 9 and the value of x will be 8.

```
var x = 9
val y = x--
```

13.6 Equality operators

Kotlin also includes a set of logical operators useful for performing comparisons. These operators all return a Boolean result depending on the result of the comparison. These operators are *binary operators* in that they work with two operands.

Equality operators are most frequently used in constructing program control flow logic. For example, an *if* statement may be constructed based on whether one value matches another:

```
if (x == y) {
      // Perform task
}
```

The result of a comparison may also be stored in a Boolean variable. For example, the following code will result in a *true* value being stored in the variable result:

```
var result: Boolean
val x = 10
val y = 20

result = x < y
```

Clearly 10 is less than 20, resulting in a *true* evaluation of the *x* < *y* expression. The following table lists the full set of Kotlin comparison operators:

Operator	Description
x == y	Returns true if x is equal to y
x > y	Returns true if x is greater than y
x >= y	Returns true if x is greater than or equal to y
x < y	Returns true if x is less than y
x <= y	Returns true if x is less than or equal to y
x != y	Returns true if x is not equal to y

Table 13-3

13.7 Boolean logical operators

Kotlin also provides a set of so-called logical operators designed to return Boolean *true* or *false* values. These operators both return Boolean results and take Boolean values as operands. The key operators are NOT (!), AND (&&), and OR (||).

The NOT (!) operator simply inverts the current value of a Boolean variable or the result of an expression. For example, if a variable named *flag* is currently true, prefixing the variable with a '!' character will invert the value to false:

```
val flag = true // variable is true
```

```
val secondFlag = !flag // secondFlag set to false
```

The OR (||) operator returns true if one of its two operands evaluates to true, otherwise, it returns false. For example, the following code evaluates to true because at least one of the expressions on either side of the OR operator is true:

```
if ((10 < 20) || (20 < 10)) {
        print("Expression is true")
}
```

The AND (&&) operator returns true only if both operands are evaluated to be true. The following example will return false because only one of the two operand expressions evaluates to true:

```
if ((10 < 20) && (20 < 10)) {
      print("Expression is false")
}
```

13.8 Range operator

Kotlin includes a useful operator that allows a range of values to be declared. As will be seen in later chapters, this operator is invaluable when working with looping in program logic.

The syntax for the range operator is as follows:

```
x..y
```

This operator represents the range of numbers starting at x and ending at y where both x and y are included within the range (referred to as a closed range). The range operator 5..8, for example, specifies the numbers 5, 6, 7, and 8.

13.9 Bitwise operators

As previously discussed, computer processors work in binary. These are essentially streams of ones and zeros, each one referred to as a bit. Bits are formed into groups of 8 to form bytes. As such, it is not surprising that we, as programmers, will occasionally end up working at this level in our code. To facilitate this requirement, Kotlin provides a range of *bit operators*.

Those familiar with bitwise operators in other languages such as C, C++, C#, Objective-C, and Java will find nothing new in this area of the Kotlin language syntax. For those unfamiliar with binary numbers, now may be a good time to seek out reference materials on the subject to understand how ones and zeros are formed into bytes to form numbers. Other authors have done a much better job of describing the subject than we can do within the scope of this book.

For this exercise, we will be working with the binary representation of two numbers. First, the decimal number 171 is represented in binary as:

```
10101011
```

Second, the number 3 is represented by the following binary sequence:

```
00000011
```

Now that we have two binary numbers with which to work, we can begin to look at the Kotlin bitwise operators:

13.9.1 Bitwise inversion

The Bitwise inversion (also referred to as NOT) is performed using the *inv()* operation and has the effect of inverting all of the bits in a number. In other words, all the zeros become ones and all the ones become zeros. Taking our example 3 number, a Bitwise NOT operation has the following result:

```
00000011 NOT
```

```
========
11111100
```

The following Kotlin code, therefore, results in a value of -4:

```
val y = 3
val z = y.inv()

print("Result is $z")
```

13.9.2 Bitwise AND

The Bitwise AND is performed using the *and()* operation. It makes a bit-by-bit comparison of two numbers. Any corresponding position in the binary sequence of each number where both bits are 1 results in a 1 appearing in the same position of the resulting number. If either bit position contains a 0 then a zero appears in the result. Taking our two example numbers, this would appear as follows:

```
10101011 AND
00000011
========
00000011
```

As we can see, the only locations where both numbers have 1s are the last two positions. If we perform this in Kotlin code, therefore, we should find that the result is 3 (00000011):

```
val x = 171
val y = 3
val z = x.and(y)

print("Result is $z")
```

13.9.3 Bitwise OR

The bitwise OR also performs a bit-by-bit comparison of two binary sequences. Unlike the AND operation, the OR places a 1 in the result if there is a 1 in the first or second operand. Using our example numbers, the result will be as follows:

```
10101011 OR
00000011
========
10101011
```

If we perform this operation in Kotlin using the *or()* operation the result will be 171:

```
val x = 171
val y = 3
val z = x.or(y)

print("Result is $z")
```

13.9.4 Bitwise XOR

The bitwise XOR (commonly referred to as *exclusive OR* and performed using the *xor()* operation) performs a similar task to the OR operation except that a 1 is placed in the result if one or other corresponding bit positions in the two numbers is 1. If both positions are a 1 or a 0 then the corresponding bit in the result is set to a 0. For example:

```
10101011 XOR
```

```
00000011
========
10101000
```

The result, in this case, is 10101000 which converts to 168 in decimal. To verify this we can, once again, try some Kotlin code:

```
val x = 171
val y = 3
val z = x.xor(y)

print("Result is $z")
```

When executed, we get the following output from print:

```
Result is 168
```

13.9.5 Bitwise left shift

The bitwise left shift moves each bit in a binary number a specified number of positions to the left. Shifting an integer one position to the left has the effect of doubling the value.

As the bits are shifted to the left, zeros are placed in the vacated rightmost (low-order) positions. Note also that once the leftmost (high-order) bits are shifted beyond the size of the variable containing the value, those high -order bits are discarded:

```
10101011 Left Shift one bit
========
101010110
```

In Kotlin the bitwise left shift operator is performed using the *shl()* operation, passing through the number of bit positions to be shifted. For example, to shift left by 1 bit:

```
val x = 171
val z = x.shl(1)

print("Result is $z")
```

When compiled and executed, the above code will display a message stating that the result is 342 which, when converted to binary, equates to 101010110.

13.9.6 Bitwise right shift

A bitwise right shift is, as you might expect, the same as a left except that the shift takes place in the opposite direction. Shifting an integer one position to the right has the effect of halving the value.

Note that since we are shifting to the right, there is no opportunity to retain the lowermost bits regardless of the data type used to contain the result. As a result, the low-order bits are discarded. Whether or not the vacated high-order bit positions are replaced with zeros or ones depends on whether the *sign bit* used to indicate positive and negative numbers is set or not.

```
10101011 Right Shift one bit
========
01010101
```

The bitwise right shift is performed using the *shr()* operation passing through the shift count:

```
val x = 171
```

```
val z = x.shr(1)

print("Result is $z")
```

When executed, the above code will report the result of the shift as being 85, which equates to binary 01010101.

13.10 Summary

Operators and expressions provide the underlying mechanism by which variables and constants are manipulated and evaluated within Kotlin code. This can take the simplest of forms whereby two numbers are added using the addition operator in an expression and the result stored in a variable using the assignment operator. Operators fall into a range of categories, details of which have been covered in this chapter.

Chapter 14

14. Kotlin Control Flow

Regardless of the programming language used, application development is largely an exercise in applying logic, and much of the art of programming involves writing code that makes decisions based on one or more criteria. Such decisions define which code gets executed, how many times it is executed, and, conversely, which code gets bypassed when the program is running. This is often referred to as *control flow* since it controls the *flow* of program execution. Control flow typically falls into the categories of *looping control* (how often code is executed) and *conditional control flow* (whether or not code is executed). This chapter is intended to provide an introductory overview of both types of control flow in Kotlin.

14.1 Looping control flow

This chapter will begin by looking at control flow in the form of loops. Loops are essentially sequences of Kotlin statements that are to be executed repeatedly until a specified condition is met. The first looping statement we will explore is the *for* loop.

14.1.1 The Kotlin for-in Statement

The for-in loop is used to iterate over a sequence of items contained in a collection or number range.

The syntax of the for-in loop is as follows:

```
for ( <variable name> in <collection or range> ) {
    // code to be executed
}
```

In this syntax, *variable name* is the name to be used for a variable that will contain the current item from the collection or range through which the loop is iterating. The code in the body of the loop will typically use this name as a reference to the current item in the loop cycle. The *collection* or *range* references the item through which the loop is iterating. This could, for example, be an array of string values, a range operator, or even a string of characters.

Consider, for example, the following for-in loop construct:

```
for (index in 1..5) {
    println("Value of index is $index")
}
```

The loop begins by stating that the current item is to be assigned to a variable named *index*. The statement then declares a closed range operator to indicate that the for loop is to iterate through a range of numbers, starting at 1 and ending at 5. The body of the loop simply prints out a message to the console indicating the current value assigned to the *index* constant, resulting in the following output:

```
Value of index is 1
Value of index is 2
Value of index is 3
Value of index is 4
Value of index is 5
```

The for-in loop is of particular benefit when working with collections such as arrays. In fact, the for-in loop can be used to iterate through any object that contains more than one item. The following loop, for example, outputs each of the characters in the specified string:

```
for (index in "Hello") {
    println("Value of index is $index")
}
```

The operation of a for-in loop may be configured using the *downTo* and *until* functions. The downTo function causes the for loop to work backward through the specified collection until the specified number is reached. The following for loop counts backward from 100 until the number 90 is reached:

```
for (index in 100 downTo 90) {
    print("$index.. ")
}
```

When executed, the above loop will generate the following output:

```
100.. 99.. 98.. 97.. 96.. 95.. 94.. 93.. 92.. 91.. 90..
```

The until function operates in much the same way with the exception that counting starts from the bottom of the collection range and works up until (but not including) the specified endpoint (a concept referred to as a half-closed range):

```
for (index in 1 until 10) {
  print("$index.. ")
}
```

The output from the above code will range from the start value of 1 through to 9:

```
1.. 2.. 3.. 4.. 5.. 6.. 7.. 8.. 9..
```

The increment used on each iteration through the loop may also be defined using the step function as follows:

```
for (index in 0 until 100 step 10) {
    print("$index.. ")
}
```

The above code will result in the following console output:

```
0.. 10.. 20.. 30.. 40.. 50.. 60.. 70.. 80.. 90..
```

14.1.2 The while loop

The Kotlin *for* loop described previously works well when it is known in advance how many times a particular task needs to be repeated in a program. There will, however, be instances where code needs to be repeated until a certain condition is met, with no way of knowing in advance how many repetitions are going to be needed to meet that criterion. To address this need, Kotlin includes the *while* loop.

Essentially, the while loop repeats a set of tasks while a specified condition is met. The *while* loop syntax is defined as follows:

```
while ( <condition> ) {
      // Kotlin statements go here
}
```

In the above syntax, *condition* is an expression that will return either *true* or *false* and the *// Kotlin statements go here* comment represents the code to be executed while the condition expression is true. For example:

```
var myCount = 0

while  (myCount < 100) {
```

```
    myCount++
    println(myCount)
}
```

In the above example, the *while* expression will evaluate whether the *myCount* variable is less than 100. If it is already greater than 100, the code in the braces is skipped and the loop exits without performing any tasks.

If, on the other hand, *myCount* is not greater than 100 the code in the braces is executed and the loop returns to the while statement and repeats the evaluation of *myCount*. This process repeats until the value of *myCount* is greater than 100, at which point the loop exits.

14.1.3 The do ... while loop

It is often helpful to think of the *do ... while* loop as an inverted while loop. The *while* loop evaluates an expression before executing the code contained in the body of the loop. If the expression evaluates to *false* on the first check then the code is not executed. The *do ... while* loop, on the other hand, is provided for situations where you know that the code contained in the body of the loop will *always* need to be executed at least once. For example, you may want to keep stepping through the items in an array until a specific item is found. You know that you have to at least check the first item in the array to have any hope of finding the entry you need. The syntax for the *do ... while* loop is as follows:

```
do {
    // Kotlin statements here
} while ( <conditional expression> )
```

In the *do ... while* example below the loop will continue until the value of a variable named i equals 0:

```
var i = 10

do {
     i--
     println(i)
} while (i > 0)
```

14.1.4 Breaking from Loops

Having created a loop, it is possible that under certain conditions you might want to break out of the loop before the completion criteria have been met (particularly if you have created an infinite loop). One such example might involve continually checking for activity on a network socket. Once activity has been detected it will most likely be necessary to break out of the monitoring loop and perform some other task.

To break out of a loop, Kotlin provides the *break* statement which breaks out of the current loop and resumes execution at the code directly after the loop. For example:

```
var j = 10

for (i in 0..100)
{
    j += j

    if (j > 100) {
        break
    }
```

```
    println("j = $j")
}
```

In the above example, the loop will continue to execute until the value of j exceeds 100 at which point the loop will exit and execution will continue with the next line of code after the loop.

14.1.5 The continue statement

The *continue* statement causes all remaining code statements in a loop to be skipped, and execution to be returned to the top of the loop. In the following example, the *println* function is only called when the value of variable *i* is an even number:

```
var i = 1

while (i < 20)
{
    i += 1

    if (i % 2 != 0) {
        continue
    }

    println("i = $i")
}
```

The *continue* statement in the above example will cause the *println* call to be skipped unless the value of *i* can be divided by 2 with no remainder. If the *continue* statement is triggered, execution will skip to the top of the while loop and the statements in the body of the loop will be repeated (until the value of *i* exceeds 19).

14.1.6 Break and continue labels

Kotlin expressions may be assigned a label by preceding the expression with a label name followed by the @ sign. This label may then be referenced when using break and continue statements to designate where execution is to resume. This is particularly useful when breaking out of nested loops. The following code contains a for loop nested within another for loop. The inner loop contains a break statement which is executed when the value of j reaches 10:

```
for (i in 1..100) {

    println("Outer loop i = $i")

    for (j in 1..100) {
        println("Inner loop j = $j")
        if (j == 10) break
    }
}
```

As currently implemented, the break statement will exit the inner for loop but execution will resume at the top of the outer for loop. Suppose, however, that the break statement is required to also exit the outer loop. This can be achieved by assigning a label to the outer loop and referencing that label with the break statement as follows:

```
outerloop@ for (i in 1..100) {
```

```
    println("Outer loop i = $i")

    for (j in 1..100) {

        println("Inner loop j = $j")

        if (j == 10) break@outerloop
    }
}
```

Now when the value assigned to variable j reaches 10 the break statement will break out of both loops and resume execution at the line of code immediately following the outer loop.

14.2 Conditional control flow

In the previous chapter, we looked at how to use logical expressions in Kotlin to determine whether something is *true* or *false*. Since programming is largely an exercise in applying logic, much of the art of programming involves writing code that makes decisions based on one or more criteria. Such decisions define which code gets executed and, conversely, which code gets bypassed when the program is executing.

14.2.1 Using the if expressions

The *if* expression is perhaps the most basic of control flow options available to the Kotlin programmer. Programmers who are familiar with C, Swift, C++, or Java will immediately be comfortable using Kotlin if statements, although there are some subtle differences.

The basic syntax of the Kotlin *if* expression is as follows:

```
if ( <boolean expression> ) {
    // Kotlin code to be performed when expression evaluates to true
}
```

Unlike some other programming languages, it is important to note that the braces are optional in Kotlin if only one line of code is associated with the *if* expression. In fact, in this scenario, the statement is often placed on the same line as the if expression.

Essentially if the *Boolean expression* evaluates to *true* then the code in the body of the statement is executed. If, on the other hand, the expression evaluates to *false* the code in the body of the statement is skipped.

For example, if a decision needs to be made depending on whether one value is greater than another, we would write code similar to the following:

```
val x = 10

if (x > 9) println("x is greater than 9!")
```

Clearly, x is indeed greater than 9 causing the message to appear in the console panel.

At this point, it is important to notice that we have been referring to the if expression instead of the if statement. The reason for this is that unlike the if statement in other programming languages, the Kotlin if returns a result. This allows if constructs to be used within expressions. As an example, a typical if expression to identify the largest of two numbers and assign the result to a variable might read as follows:

```
if (x > y)
    largest = x
else
```

```
    largest = y
```

The same result can be achieved using the *if* statement within an expression using the following syntax:

```
<variable> = if ( <condition> ) <return_val_1> else <return_val_2>
```

The original example can, therefore be re-written as follows:

```
val largest = if (x > y) x else y
```

The technique is not limited to returning the values contained within the condition. The following example is also a valid use of if in an expression, in this case assigning a string value to the variable:

```
val largest = if (x > y) "x is greatest" else "y is greatest"
println(largest)
```

For those familiar with programming languages such as Java, this feature allows code constructs similar to ternary statements to be implemented in Kotlin.

14.2.2 Using if ... else … expressions

The next variation of the *if* expression allows us to also specify some code to perform if the expression in the if expression evaluates to *false*. The syntax for this construct is as follows:

```
if ( <boolean expression> ) {
    // Code to be executed if expression is true
} else {
    // Code to be executed if expression is false
}
```

The braces are, once again, optional if only one line of code is to be executed.

Using the above syntax, we can now extend our previous example to display a different message if the comparison expression evaluates to be *false*:

```
val x = 10

if (x > 9) println("x is greater than 9!")
    else println("x is less than 10!")
```

In this case, the second println statement will execute if the value of x is less than or equal to 9.

14.2.3 Using if ... else if ... Expressions

So far we have looked at *if* statements that make decisions based on the result of a single logical expression. Sometimes it becomes necessary to make decisions based on several different criteria. For this purpose, we can use the *if ... else if ...* construct, an example of which is as follows:

```
var x = 9

if (x == 10) println("x is 10")
    else if (x == 9) println("x is 9")
        else if (x == 8) println("x is 8")
            else println("x is less than 8")
}
```

14.2.4 Using the when statement

The Kotlin *when* statement provides a cleaner alternative to the *if ... else if ...* construct and uses the following syntax:

```
when (value) {
    match1 -> // code to be executed on match
    match2 -> // code to be executed on match
    .
    .
    else -> // default code to executed if no match
}
```

Using this syntax, the previous *if… else if…* construct can be rewritten to use the *when* statement:

```
when (x) {
    10 -> println ("x is 10")
    9 -> println("x is 9")
    8 -> println("x is 8")
    else ->  println("x is less than 8")
}
```

The *when* statement is similar to the *switch* statement found in many other programming languages.

14.3 Summary

The term *control flow* is used to describe the logic that dictates the execution path that is taken through the source code of an application as it runs. This chapter has looked at the two types of control flow provided by Kotlin (looping and conditional) and explored the various Kotlin constructs that are available to implement both forms of control flow logic.

Chapter 15

15. An Overview of Kotlin Functions and Lambdas

Kotlin functions and lambdas are a vital part of writing well-structured and efficient code and provide a way to organize programs while avoiding code repetition. In this chapter, we will look at how functions and lambdas are declared and used within Kotlin.

15.1 What is a function?

A function is a named block of code that can be called upon to perform a specific task. It can be provided data on which to perform the task and is capable of returning results to the code that called it. For example, if a particular arithmetic calculation needs to be performed in a Kotlin program, the code to perform the arithmetic can be placed in a function. The function can be programmed to accept the values on which the arithmetic is to be performed (referred to as parameters) and to return the result of the calculation. At any point in the program code where the calculation is required, the function is simply called, parameter values passed through as arguments and the result returned.

The terms parameter and argument are often used interchangeably when discussing functions. There is, however, a subtle difference. The values that a function can accept when it is called are referred to as parameters. At the point that the function is called and passed those values, however, they are referred to as arguments.

15.2 How to declare a Kotlin function

A Kotlin function is declared using the following syntax:

```
fun <function name> (<para name>: <para type>, <para name>: <para type>, ... ):
<return type> {
    // Function code
}
```

This combination of function name, parameters, and return type is referred to as the function *signature* or *type*. Explanations of the various fields of the function declaration are as follows:

- fun – The prefix keyword used to notify the Kotlin compiler that this is a function.
- <function name> - The name assigned to the function. This is the name by which the function will be referenced when it is called from within the application code.
- <para name> - The name by which the parameter is to be referenced in the function code.
- <para type> - The type of the corresponding parameter.
- <return type> - The data type of the result returned by the function. If the function does not return a result then no return type is specified.
- Function code - The code of the function that does the work.

As an example, the following function takes no parameters, returns no result, and simply displays a message:

```
fun sayHello() {
```

```
    println("Hello")
}
```

The following sample function, on the other hand, takes an integer and a string as parameters and returns a string result:

```
fun buildMessageFor(name: String, count: Int): String {
    return("$name, you are customer number $count")
}
```

15.3 Calling a Kotlin function

Once declared, functions are called using the following syntax:

```
<function name> (<arg1>, <arg2>, ... )
```

Each argument passed through to a function must match the parameters the function is configured to accept. For example, to call a function named sayHello that takes no parameters and returns no value, we would write the following code:

```
sayHello()
```

In the case of a message that accepts parameters, the function could be called as follows:

```
buildMessageFor("John", 10)
```

15.4 Single expression functions

When a function contains a single expression, it is not necessary to include the braces around the expression. All that is required is an equals sign (=) after the function declaration followed by the expression. The following function contains a single expression declared in the usual way:

```
fun multiply(x: Int, y: Int): Int {
    return x * y
}
```

Below is the same function expressed as a single line expression:

```
fun multiply(x: Int, y: Int): Int = x * y
```

When using single-line expressions, the return type may be omitted in situations where the compiler can infer the type returned by the expression making for even more compact code:

```
fun multiply(x: Int, y: Int) = x * y
```

15.5 Local functions

A local function is a function that is embedded within another function. In addition, a local function has access to all of the variables contained within the enclosing function:

```
fun main(args: Array<String>) {

    val name = "John"
    val count = 5

    fun displayString() {
        for (index in 0..count) {
            println(name)
        }
    }
```

```
    displayString()
}
```

15.6 Handling return values

To call a function named buildMessageFor that takes two parameters and returns a result, on the other hand, we might write the following code:

```
val message = buildMessageFor("John", 10)
```

To improve code readability, the parameter names may also be specified when making the function call:

```
val message = buildMessageFor(name = "John", count = 10)
```

In the above examples, we have created a new variable called message and then used the assignment operator (=) to store the result returned by the function.

15.7 Declaring default function parameters

Kotlin provides the ability to designate a default parameter value to be used if the value is not provided as an argument when the function is called. This simply involves assigning the default value to the parameter when the function is declared.

To see default parameters in action the buildMessageFor function will be modified so that the string "Customer" is used as a default if a customer name is not passed through as an argument. Similarly, the *count* parameter is declared with a default value of 0:

```
fun buildMessageFor(name: String = "Customer", count: Int = 0): String {
    return("$name, you are customer number $count")
}
```

When parameter names are used when making the function call, any parameters for which defaults have been specified may be omitted. The following function call, for example, omits the customer name argument but still compiles because the parameter name has been specified for the second argument:

```
val message = buildMessageFor(count = 10)
```

If parameter names are not used within the function call, however, only the trailing arguments may be omitted:

```
val message = buildMessageFor("John") // Valid
val message = buildMessageFor(10) // Invalid
```

15.8 Variable number of function parameters

It is not always possible to know in advance the number of parameters a function will need to accept when it is called within the application code. Kotlin handles this possibility through the use of the *vararg* keyword to indicate that the function accepts an arbitrary number of parameters of a specified data type. Within the body of the function, the parameters are made available in the form of an array object. The following function, for example, takes as parameters a variable number of String values and then outputs them to the console panel:

```
fun displayStrings(vararg strings: String)
{
    for (string in strings) {
        println(string)
    }
}

displayStrings("one", "two", "three", "four")
```

Kotlin does not permit multiple vararg parameters within a function and any single parameters supported by the function must be declared before the vararg declaration:

```
fun displayStrings(name: String, vararg strings: String)
{
    println(name)

    for (string in strings) {
        println(string)
    }
}
```

15.9 Lambda expressions

Having covered the basics of functions in Kotlin it is now time to look at the concept of lambda expressions. Essentially, lambdas are self-contained blocks of code. The following code, for example, declares a lambda, assigns it to a variable named sayHello, and then calls the function via the lambda reference:

```
val sayHello = { println("Hello") }
sayHello()
```

Lambda expressions may also be configured to accept parameters and return results. The syntax for this is as follows:

```
{<para name>: <para type>, <para name> <para type>, ... ->
    // Lambda expression here
}
```

The following lambda expression, for example, accepts two integer parameters and returns an integer result:

```
val multiply = { val1: Int, val2: Int -> val1 * val2 }
val result = multiply(10, 20)
```

Note that the above lambda examples have assigned the lambda code block to a variable. This is also possible when working with functions. Of course, the following syntax will execute the function and assign the result of that execution to a variable, instead of assigning the function itself to the variable:

```
val myvar = myfunction()
```

To assign a function reference to a variable, simply remove the parentheses and prefix the function name with double colons (::) as follows. The function may then be called simply by referencing the variable name:

```
val myvar = ::myfunction
myvar()
```

A lambda block may be executed directly by placing parentheses at the end of the expression including any arguments. The following lambda directly executes the multiplication lambda expression multiplying 10 by 20.

```
val result = { val1: Int, val2: Int -> val1 * val2 }(10, 20)
```

The last expression within a lambda serves as the expression's return value (hence the value of 200 being assigned to the result variable in the above multiplication examples). In fact, unlike functions, lambdas do not support the *return* statement. In the absence of an expression that returns a result (such as an arithmetic or comparison expression), simply declaring the value as the last item in the lambda will cause that value to be returned. The following lambda returns the Boolean true value after printing a message:

```
val result = { println("Hello"); true }()
```

Similarly, the following lambda simply returns a string literal:

```
val nextmessage = { println("Hello"); "Goodbye" }()
```

A particularly useful feature of lambdas and the ability to create function references is that they can be both passed to functions as arguments and returned as results. This concept, however, requires an understanding of function types and higher-order functions.

15.10 Higher-order functions

On the surface, lambdas and function references do not seem to be particularly compelling features. The possibilities that these features offer become more apparent, however, when we consider that lambdas and function references have the same capabilities as many other data types. In particular, these may be passed through as arguments to another function, or even returned as a result from a function.

A function that is capable of receiving a function or lambda as an argument, or returning one as a result is referred to as a *higher-order function.*

Before we look at what is, essentially, the ability to plug one function into another, it is first necessary to explore the concept of *function types*. The type of a function is dictated by a combination of the parameters it accepts and the type of result it returns. A function that accepts an Int and a Double as parameters and returns a String result for example is considered to have the following function type:

```
(Int, Double) -> String
```

To accept a function as a parameter, the receiving function simply declares the type of function it can accept.

As an example, we will begin by declaring two unit conversion functions:

```
fun inchesToFeet (inches: Double): Double {
    return inches * 0.0833333
}

fun inchesToYards (inches: Double): Double {
    return inches * 0.0277778
}
```

The example now needs an additional function, the purpose of which is to perform a unit conversion and print the result in the console panel. This function needs to be as general-purpose as possible, capable of performing a variety of different measurement unit conversions. To demonstrate functions as parameters, this new function will take as a parameter a function type that matches both the inchesToFeet and inchesToYards functions together with a value to be converted. Since the type of these functions is equivalent to (Double) -> Double, our general-purpose function can be written as follows:

```
fun outputConversion(value: Double, converterFunc: (Double) -> Double) {
    val result = converterFunc(value)
    println("Result of conversion is $result")
}
```

When the outputConversion function is called, it will need to be passed a function matching the declared type. That function will be called to perform the conversion and the result displayed in the console panel. This means that the same function can be called to convert inches to both feet and yards, simply by "plugging in" the appropriate converter function as a parameter, keeping in mind that it is the function reference that is being passed as an argument:

```
outputConversion(24, ::inchesToFeet)
outputConversion(24, ::inchesToYards)
```

Functions can also be returned as a data type simply by declaring the type of the function as the return type. The following function is configured to return either our inchesToFeet or inchesToYards function type (in other words, a function that accepts and returns a Double value) based on the value of a Boolean parameter:

```
fun decideFunction(feet: Boolean): (Double) -> Double
{
    if (feet) {
        return ::inchesToFeet
    } else {
        return ::inchesToYards
    }
}
```

When called, the function will return a function reference which can then be used to perform the conversion:

```
val converter = decideFunction(true)
val result = converter(22.4)
println(result)
```

15.11 Trailing lambdas

Trailing lambdas are expressions that are passed as the last argument when calling a function. They help make the code more concise and easier to read, and will be used extensively throughout the examples in this book. Unlike other arguments, the trailing lambda is placed outside the parentheses when calling a function. The syntax for calling a function with a trailing lambda is as follows:

```
myFunction(<arg1>, <arg2> ..) { <arg1_name>, <arg2_name>, ...
    // Lambda expression
}
```

The *outputConversion()* function declared in the previous section, for example, accepts a trailing lambda because *convertFunc* is the last argument.

The following statement passes a trailing lambda to *outputConversion()* to convert inches to meters:

```
outputConversion(22.5) { inches ->
    inches * 0.0254
}
```

15.12 Summary

Functions and lambda expressions are self-contained blocks of code that can be called upon to perform a specific task and provide a mechanism for structuring code and promoting reuse. This chapter has introduced the basic concepts of function and lambda declaration and implementation in addition to the use of higher-order functions that allow lambdas and functions to be passed as arguments and returned as results.

Chapter 16

16. The Basics of Object-Oriented Programming in Kotlin

Kotlin provides extensive support for developing object-oriented applications. The subject area of object-oriented programming is, however, large. As such, a detailed overview of object-oriented software development is beyond the scope of this book. Instead, we will introduce the basic concepts involved in object-oriented programming and then move on to explain the concept as it relates to Kotlin application development.

16.1 What is an object?

Objects (also referred to as instances) are self-contained modules of functionality that can be easily used and re-used as the building blocks for a software application.

Objects consist of data variables (called properties) and functions (called methods) that can be accessed and called on the object or instance to perform tasks and are collectively referred to as class members.

16.2 What is a class?

Much as a blueprint or architect's drawing defines what an item or a building will look like once it has been constructed, a class defines what an object will look like when it is created. It defines, for example, what the methods will do and what the properties will be.

16.3 Declaring a Kotlin class

Before an object can be instantiated, we first need to define the class 'blueprint' for the object. In this chapter, we will create a bank account class to demonstrate the basic concepts of Kotlin object-oriented programming.

In declaring a new Kotlin class we specify an optional parent class from which the new class is derived and also define the properties and methods that the class will contain. The basic syntax for a new class is as follows:

```
class NewClassName: ParentClass {
   // Properties
   // Methods
}
```

The Properties section of the declaration defines the variables and constants that are to be contained within the class. These are declared in the same way that any other variable would be declared in Kotlin.

The Methods sections define the methods that are available to be called on the class and instances of the class. These are essentially functions specific to the class that perform a particular operation when called upon and will be described in greater detail later in this chapter.

To create an example outline for our BankAccount class, we would use the following:

```
class BankAccount {


}
```

Now that we have the outline syntax for our class, the next step is to add some properties to it.

16.4 Adding properties to a class

A key goal of object-oriented programming is a concept referred to as data encapsulation. The idea behind data encapsulation is that data should be stored within classes and accessed only through methods defined in that class. Data encapsulated in a class are referred to as properties or instance variables.

Instances of our BankAccount class will be required to store some data, specifically a bank account number and the balance currently held within the account. Properties are declared in the same way any other variables are declared in Kotlin. We can, therefore, add these variables as follows:

```
class BankAccount {
    var accountBalance: Double = 0.0
    var accountNumber: Int = 0
}
```

Having defined our properties, we can now move on to defining the methods of the class that will allow us to work with our properties while staying true to the data encapsulation model.

16.5 Defining methods

The methods of a class are essentially code routines that can be called upon to perform specific tasks within the context of that class.

Methods are declared within the opening and closing braces of the class to which they belong and are declared using the standard Kotlin function declaration syntax.

For example, the declaration of a method to display the account balance in our example might read as follows:

```
class BankAccount {
    var accountBalance: Double = 0.0
    var accountNumber: Int = 0

    fun displayBalance()
    {
       println("Number $accountNumber")
       println("Current balance is $accountBalance")
    }
}
```

16.6 Declaring and initializing a class instance

So far, all we have done is define the blueprint for our class. To do anything with this class, we need to create instances of it. The first step in this process is to declare a variable to store a reference to the instance when it is created. We do this as follows:

```
val account1: BankAccount = BankAccount()
```

When executed, an instance of our BankAccount class will have been created and will be accessible via the account1 variable. Of course, the Kotlin compiler will be able to use inference here, making the type declaration optional:

```
val account1 = BankAccount()
```

16.7 Primary and secondary constructors

A class will often need to perform some initialization tasks at the point of creation. These tasks can be implemented using constructors within the class. In the case of the BankAccount class, it would be useful to be able to initialize the account number and balance properties with values when a new class instance is created. To achieve this, a *secondary constructor* can be declared within the class header as follows:

```
class BankAccount {

    var accountBalance: Double = 0.0
    var accountNumber: Int = 0

    constructor(number: Int, balance: Double) {
        accountNumber =  number
        accountBalance = balance
    }
.
.
}
```

When creating an instance of the class, it will now be necessary to provide initialization values for the account number and balance properties as follows:

```
val account1: BankAccount = BankAccount(456456234, 342.98)
```

A class can contain multiple secondary constructors allowing instances of the class to be initiated with different value sets. The following variation of the BankAccount class includes an additional secondary constructor for use when initializing an instance with the customer's last name in addition to the corresponding account number and balance:

```
class BankAccount {

    var accountBalance: Double = 0.0
    var accountNumber: Int = 0
    var lastName: String = ""

    constructor(number: Int,
                balance: Double) {
        accountNumber =  number
        accountBalance = balance
    }

    constructor(number: Int,
                balance: Double,
               name: String ) {
        accountNumber =  number
        accountBalance = balance
        lastName = name
    }
.
.
}
```

Instances of the BankAccount may now also be created as follows:

```
val account1: BankAccount = BankAccount(456456234, 342.98, "Smith")
```

It is also possible to use a *primary constructor* to perform basic initialization tasks. The primary constructor for a class is declared within the class header as follows:

```
class BankAccount (val accountNumber: Int, var accountBalance: Double) {
.
.
    fun displayBalance()
    {
        println("Number $accountNumber")
        println("Current balance is $accountBalance")
    }
}
```

Note that now both properties have been declared in the primary constructor, it is no longer necessary to also declare the variables within the body of the class. Since the account number will now not change after an instance of the class has been created, this property is declared as being immutable using the *val* keyword.

Although a class may only contain one primary constructor, Kotlin allows multiple secondary constructors to be declared in addition to the primary constructor. In the following class declaration the constructor that handles the account number and balance is declared as the primary constructor while the variation that also accepts the user's last name is declared as a secondary constructor:

```
class BankAccount (val accountNumber: Int, var accountBalance: Double) {

    var lastName: String = ""

    constructor(accountNumber: Int,
                accountBalance: Double,
                name: String ) : this(accountNumber, accountBalance) {

        lastName = name
    }
.
.
}
```

In the above example, two key points need to be noted. First, since the lastName property is referenced by a secondary constructor, the variable is not handled automatically by the primary constructor and must be declared within the body of the class and initialized within the constructor.

```
var lastName: String = ""
.
.
lastName = name
```

Second, although the accountNumber and accountBalance properties are accepted as parameters to the secondary constructor, the variable declarations are still handled by the primary constructor and do not need to be declared. To associate the references to these properties in the secondary constructor with the primary constructor, however, they must be linked back to the primary constructor using the *this* keyword:

```
... this(accountNumber, accountBalance)...
```

16.8 Initializer blocks

In addition to the primary and secondary constructors, a class may also contain *initializer blocks* which are called after the constructors. Since a primary constructor cannot contain any code, these methods are a particularly useful location for adding code to perform initialization tasks when an instance of the class is created. Initializer blocks are declared using the *init* keyword with the initialization code enclosed in braces:

```
class BankAccount (val accountNumber: Int, var accountBalance: Double) {

    init {
       // Initialization code goes here
    }
.
.
}
```

16.9 Calling methods and accessing properties

Now is probably a good time to recap what we have done so far in this chapter. We have now created a new Kotlin class named BankAccount. Within this new class, we declared primary and secondary constructors to accept and initialize account number, balance, and customer name properties. In the preceding sections, we also covered the steps necessary to create and initialize an instance of our new class. The next step is to learn how to call the instance methods and access the properties we built into our class. This is most easily achieved using dot notation.

Dot notation involves accessing a property, or calling a method by specifying a class instance followed by a dot followed in turn by the name of the property or method:

```
classInstance.propertyname
classInstance.methodname()
```

For example, to get the current value of our accountBalance instance variable:

```
val balance1 = account1.accountBalance
```

Dot notation can also be used to set values of instance properties:

```
account1.accountBalance = 6789.98
```

The same technique is used to call methods on a class instance. For example, to call the displayBalance method on an instance of the BankAccount class:

```
account1.displayBalance()
```

16.10 Custom accessors

When accessing the accountBalance property in the previous section, the code is making use of property accessors that are provided automatically by Kotlin. In addition to these default accessors, it is also possible to implement *custom accessors* that allow calculations or other logic to be performed before the property is returned or set.

Custom accessors are implemented by creating getter and optional corresponding setter methods containing the code to perform any tasks before returning the property. Consider, for example, that the BankAcccount class might need an additional property to contain the current balance less any recent banking fees. Rather than use a standard accessor, it makes more sense to use a custom accessor that calculates this value on request. The modified BankAccount class might now read as follows:

```
class BankAccount (val accountNumber: Int, var accountBalance: Double) {
```

```
    val fees: Double = 25.00

    val balanceLessFees: Double
        get() {
            return accountBalance - fees
        }

    fun displayBalance()
    {
       println("Number $accountNumber")
       println("Current balance is $accountBalance")
    }
}
```

The above code adds a getter that returns a computed property based on the current balance minus a fee amount. An optional setter could also be declared in much the same way to set the balance value less fees:

```
val fees: Double = 25.00

var balanceLessFees: Double
    get() {
        return accountBalance - fees
    }
    set(value) {
        accountBalance = value - fees
    }
.
.
}
```

The new setter takes as a parameter a Double value from which it deducts the fee value before assigning the result to the current balance property. Even though these are custom accessors, they are accessed in the same way as stored properties using dot-notation. The following code gets the current balance less the fees value before setting the property to a new value:

```
val balance1 = account1.balanceLessFees
account1.balanceLessFees = 12123.12
```

16.11 Nested and inner classes

Kotlin allows one class to be nested within another class. In the following code, for example, ClassB is nested inside ClassA:

```
class ClassA {
    class ClassB {
    }
}
```

In the above example, ClassB does not have access to any of the properties within the outer class. If access is required, the nested class must be declared using the *inner* directive. In the example below ClassB now has access to the myProperty variable belonging to ClassA:

```
class ClassA {
        var myProperty: Int = 10

    inner class ClassB {
            val result = 20 + myProperty
    }
}
```

16.12 Companion objects

A Kotlin class can also contain a companion object. A companion object contains methods and variables that are common to all instances of the class. In addition to being accessible within class instances, these properties are also accessible at the class level (in other words without the need to create an instance of the class).

The syntax for declaring a companion object within a class is as follows:

```
class ClassName: ParentClass {
   // Properties
   // Methods

   companion object {
        // properties
        // methods
    }
}
```

To experience a companion object example in action, enter the following into the Kotlin online playground at https://try.kotl.in:

```
class MyClass {

    fun showCount() {
        println("counter = " + counter)
    }

    companion object {
        var counter = 1

        fun counterUp() {
            counter += 1
        }
    }
}

fun main(args: Array<String>) {
    println(MyClass.counter)
}
```

The class contains a companion object consisting of a counter variable and a method to increment that variable. The class also contains a method to display the current counter value. The *main()* method simply displays the current value of the counter variable, but does so by calling the method on the class itself instead of a class instance:

```
println(MyClass.counter)
```

Modify the *main()* method to also increment the counter, displaying the current value both before and after:

```
fun main(args: Array<String>) {
    println(MyClass.counter)
    MyClass.counterUp()
    println(MyClass.counter)
}
```

Run the code and verify that the following output appears in the console:

```
1
2
```

Next, add some code to create an instance of MyClass before making a call to the *showCount()* method:

```
fun main(args: Array<String>) {
    println(MyClass.counter)
    MyClass.counterUp()
    println(MyClass.counter)

    val instanceA = MyClass()
    instanceA.showCount()
}
```

When executed, the following output will appear in the console:

```
1
2
counter = 2
```

Clearly, the class has access to the variables and methods contained within the companion object.

Another useful aspect of companion objects is that all instances of the containing class see the same companion object, including current variable values. To see this in action, create a second instance of MyClass and call the *showCount()* method on that instance:

```
fun main(args: Array<String>) {
    println(MyClass.counter)
    MyClass.counterUp()
    println(MyClass.counter)

    val instanceA = MyClass()
    instanceA.showCount()

    val instanceB = MyClass()
    instanceB.showCount()
}
```

When run, the code will produce the following console output:

```
1
2
```

```
counter = 2
counter = 2
```

Note that both instances return the incremented value of 2, showing that the two class instances are sharing the same companion object data.

16.13 Summary

Object-oriented programming languages such as Kotlin encourage the creation of classes to promote code reuse and the encapsulation of data within class instances. This chapter has covered the basic concepts of classes and instances within Kotlin together with an overview of primary and secondary constructors, initializer blocks, properties, methods, companion objects, and custom accessors.

Chapter 17

17. An Introduction to Kotlin Inheritance and Subclassing

In *"The Basics of Object-Oriented Programming in Kotlin"* we covered the basic concepts of object-oriented programming and worked through an example of creating and working with a new class using Kotlin. In that example, our new class was not specifically derived from a base class (though in practice, all Kotlin classes are ultimately derived from the *Any* class). In this chapter, we will provide an introduction to the concepts of subclassing, inheritance, and extensions in Kotlin.

17.1 Inheritance, classes, and subclasses

The concept of inheritance brings something of a real-world view to programming. It allows a class to be defined that has a certain set of characteristics (such as methods and properties) and then other classes to be created which are derived from that class. The derived class inherits all of the features of the parent class and typically then adds some features of its own. In fact, all classes in Kotlin are ultimately subclasses of the Any superclass which provides the basic foundation on which all classes are based.

By deriving classes, we create what is often referred to as a class hierarchy. The class at the top of the hierarchy is known as the base class or root class and the derived classes as subclasses or child classes. Any number of subclasses may be derived from a class. The class from which a subclass is derived is called the parent class or superclass.

Classes need not only be derived from a root class. For example, a subclass can also inherit from another subclass with the potential to create large and complex class hierarchies.

In Kotlin, a subclass can only be derived from a single direct parent class. This is a concept referred to as single inheritance.

17.2 Subclassing syntax

As a safety measure designed to make Kotlin code less prone to error, before a subclass can be derived from a parent class, the parent class must be declared as open. This is achieved by placing the *open* keyword within the class header:

```
open class MyParentClass {
   var myProperty: Int = 0
}
```

With a simple class of this type, the subclass can be created as follows:

```
class MySubClass : MyParentClass() {


}
```

For classes containing primary or secondary constructors, the rules for creating a subclass are slightly more complicated. Consider the following parent class which contains a primary constructor:

```
open class MyParentClass(var myProperty: Int) {
```

```
}
```

To create a subclass of this class, the subclass declaration references any base class parameters while also initializing the parent class using the following syntax:

```
class MySubClass(myProperty: Int) : MyParentClass(myProperty) {


}
```

If, on the other hand, the parent class contains one or more secondary constructors, the constructors must also be implemented within the subclass declaration and include a call to the secondary constructors of the parent class, passing through as arguments the values passed to the subclass secondary constructor. When working with subclasses, the parent class can be referenced using the *super* keyword. A parent class with a secondary constructor might read as follows:

```
open class MyParentClass {
    var myProperty: Int = 0

    constructor(number: Int) {
        myProperty = number
    }
}
```

The code for the corresponding subclass would need to be implemented as follows:

```
class MySubClass : MyParentClass {
    constructor(number: Int) : super(number)
}
```

If additional tasks need to be performed within the constructor of the subclass, this can be placed within curly braces after the constructor declaration:

```
class MySubClass : MyParentClass {

    constructor(number: Int) : super(number) {
        // Subclass constructor code here
    }
}
```

17.3 A Kotlin inheritance example

As with most programming concepts, the subject of inheritance in Kotlin is perhaps best illustrated with an example. In *"The Basics of Object-Oriented Programming in Kotlin"* we created a class named BankAccount designed to hold a bank account number and corresponding current balance. The BankAccount class contained both properties and methods. A simplified declaration for this class is reproduced below and will be used for the basis of the subclassing example in this chapter:

```
class BankAccount {

    var accountNumber = 0
    var accountBalance = 0.0

    constructor(number: Int, balance: Double) {
        accountNumber = number
```

```
        accountBalance = balance
    }

    fun displayBalance()
    {
       println("Number $accountNumber")
       println("Current balance is $accountBalance")
    }
}
```

Though this is a somewhat rudimentary class, it does everything necessary if all you need it to do is store an account number and account balance. Suppose, however, that in addition to the BankAccount class you also needed a class to be used for savings accounts. A savings account will still need to hold an account number and a current balance and methods will still be needed to access that data. One option would be to create an entirely new class, one that duplicates all of the functionality of the BankAccount class together with the new features required by a savings account. A more efficient approach, however, would be to create a new class that is a subclass of the BankAccount class. The new class will then inherit all the features of the BankAccount class but can then be extended to add the additional functionality required by a savings account. Before a subclass of the BankAccount class can be created, the declaration needs to be modified to declare the class as open:

```
open class BankAccount {
```

To create a subclass of BankAccount that we will call SavingsAccount, we simply declare the new class, this time specifying BankAccount as the parent class and add code to call the constructor on the parent class:

```
class SavingsAccount : BankAccount {
    constructor(accountNumber: Int, accountBalance: Double) :
         super(accountNumber, accountBalance)
}
```

Note that although we have yet to add any properties or methods, the class has inherited all the methods and properties of the parent BankAccount class. We could, therefore, create an instance of the SavingsAccount class and set variables and call methods in the same way we did with the BankAccount class in previous examples. That said, we haven't achieved anything unless we take steps to extend the class.

17.4 Extending the functionality of a subclass

So far, we have been able to create a subclass that contains all the functionality of the parent class. For this exercise to make sense, however, we now need to extend the subclass so that it has the features we need to make it useful for storing savings account information. To do this, we simply add the properties and methods that provide the new functionality, just as we would for any other class we might wish to create:

```
class SavingsAccount : BankAccount {
         var interestRate: Double = 0.0

    constructor(accountNumber: Int, accountBalance: Double) :
                            super(accountNumber, accountBalance)

    fun calculateInterest(): Double
    {
        return interestRate * accountBalance
    }
```

```
}
```

17.5 Overriding inherited methods

When using inheritance it is not unusual to find a method in the parent class that almost does what you need, but requires modification to provide the precise functionality you require. That being said, it is also possible you'll inherit a method with a name that describes exactly what you want to do, but it does not come close to doing what you need. One option in this scenario would be to ignore the inherited method and write a new method with an entirely new name. A better option is to override the inherited method and write a new version of it in the subclass.

Before proceeding with an example, three rules that must be obeyed when overriding a method. First, the overriding method in the subclass must accept the same number and type of parameters as the overridden method in the parent class. Second, the new method must have the same return type as the parent method. Finally, the original method in the parent class must be declared as open before the compiler will allow it to be overridden.

In our BankAccount class, we have a method named displayBalance that displays the bank account number and current balance held by an instance of the class. In our SavingsAccount subclass, we might also want to output the current interest rate assigned to the account. To achieve this, we simply declare a new version of the displayBalance method in our SavingsAccount subclass, prefixed with the *override* keyword:

```
class SavingsAccount : BankAccount {
    var interestRate: Double = 0.0

    constructor(accountNumber: Int, accountBalance: Double) :
               super(accountNumber, accountBalance)

    fun calculateInterest(): Double
    {
        return interestRate * accountBalance
    }

    override fun displayBalance()
    {
       println("Number $accountNumber")
       println("Current balance is $accountBalance")
       println("Prevailing interest rate is $interestRate")
     }
}
```

Before this code will compile, the displayBalance method in the BankAccount class must be declared as open:

```
open fun displayBalance()
{
   println("Number $accountNumber")
   println("Current balance is $accountBalance")
}
```

It is also possible to make a call to the overridden method in the superclass from within a subclass. The displayBalance method of the superclass could, for example, be called to display the account number and balance, before the interest rate is displayed, thereby eliminating further code duplication:

```
override fun displayBalance()
{
   super.displayBalance()
   println("Prevailing interest rate is $interestRate")
}
```

17.6 Adding a custom secondary constructor

As the SavingsAccount class currently stands, it makes a call to the secondary constructor from the parent BankAccount class which was implemented as follows:

```
constructor(accountNumber: Int, accountBalance: Double) :
             super(accountNumber, accountBalance)
```

Clearly this constructor takes the necessary steps to initialize both the account number and balance properties of the class. The SavingsAccount class, however, contains an additional property in the form of the interest rate variable. The SavingsAccount class, therefore, needs its own constructor to ensure that the interestRate property is initialized when instances of the class are created. Modify the SavingsAccount class one last time to add an additional secondary constructor allowing the interest rate to also be specified when class instances are initialized:

```
class SavingsAccount : BankAccount {

    var interestRate: Double = 0.0

    constructor(accountNumber: Int, accountBalance: Double) :
                 super(accountNumber, accountBalance)

    constructor(accountNumber: Int, accountBalance: Double, rate: Double) :
                        super(accountNumber, accountBalance) {
        interestRate = rate
    }
.
.
```

17.7 Using the SavingsAccount class

Now that we have completed work on our SavingsAccount class, the class can be used in some example code in much the same way as the parent BankAccount class:

```
val savings1 = SavingsAccount(12311, 600.00, 0.07)

println(savings1.calculateInterest())
savings1.displayBalance()
```

17.8 Summary

Inheritance extends the concept of object re-use in object-oriented programming by allowing new classes to be derived from existing classes, with those new classes subsequently extended to add new functionality. When an existing class provides some, but not all, of the functionality required by the programmer, inheritance allows that class to be used as the basis for a new subclass. The new subclass will inherit all the capabilities of the parent class, but may then be extended to add the missing functionality.

Chapter 18

18. An Overview of Android View Binding

An essential part of developing Android apps involves the interaction between the code and the views that make up the user interface layouts. This chapter will look at the options available for gaining access to layout views in code, emphasizing an option known as view binding. Once the basics of view bindings have been covered, the chapter will outline how to convert the AndroidSample project to use this approach.

18.1 Find View by Id

As outlined in the chapter entitled *"The Anatomy of an Android App"*, all of the resources that make up an application are compiled into a class named *R*. Amongst those resources are those that define layouts. Within the R class is a subclass named *layout*, which contains the layout resources, including the views that make up the user interface. Most apps will need to implement interaction between the code and these views, for example, when reading the value entered into the EditText view or changing the content displayed on a TextView.

Before the introduction of Android Studio 3.6, the most common option for gaining access to a view from within the app code involved writing code to manually find a view based on its id via the *findViewById()* method. For example:

```
val exampleView: TextView = findViewById(R.id.exampleView)
```

With the reference obtained, the view's properties can then be accessed. For example:

```
exampleView.text = "Hello"
```

While finding views by id is still a viable option, it has some limitations, the most significant disadvantage of *findViewById()* being that it is possible to obtain a reference to a view that has not yet been created within the layout, leading to a null pointer exception when an attempt is made to access the view's properties.

Since Android Studio 3.6, an alternative way of accessing views from the app code has been available in the form of *view binding*.

18.2 View Binding

When view binding is enabled in an app module, Android Studio automatically generates a binding class for each layout file. The layout views can be accessed from within the code using this binding class without using *findViewById()*.

The name of the binding class generated by Android Studio is based on the layout file name converted to so-called "camel case" with the word "Binding" appended to the end. For the *activity_main.xml* file, for example, the binding class will be called ActivityMainBinding.

Android Studio is inconsistent in using view bindings within project templates. For example, the Empty Views Activity template used when we created the AndroidSample project does not use view bindings. The Basic Views Activity template, on the other hand, is implemented using view binding. If you use a template that does not use view binding, it is important to know how to add it to your project.

18.3 Converting the AndroidSample project

In the remainder of this chapter, we will practice migrating to view bindings by converting the AndroidSample project to use view binding instead of *findViewById()*.

Begin, by copying the *AndroidSample* project folder project created in the chapter entitled *"Creating an Example Android App in Android Studio"* to a new folder named *AndroidSample_ViewBinding*. Next, start Android Studio and open the *AndroidSample_ViewBinding* project.

18.4 Enabling View Binding

To use view binding, some changes must first be made to the *build.gradle.kts* file for each module in which view binding is needed. In the case of the AndroidSample project, this will require a slight change to the *Gradle Scripts -> build.gradle.kts (Module: app)* file. Load this file into the editor, locate the *android* section and add an entry to enable the *viewBinding* property as follows:

```
plugins {
    alias(libs.plugins.android.application)
}

android {

    buildFeatures {
        viewBinding = true
    }
.
.
```

Once this change has been made, click on the Sync Now link at the top of the editor panel, then use the Build menu to clean and rebuild the project to ensure the binding class is generated. The next step is to use the binding class within the code.

18.5 Using View Binding

The first step in this process is to "inflate" the view binding class to access the root view within the layout. This root view will then be used as the content view for the layout.

The logical place to perform these tasks is within the *onCreate()* method of the activity associated with the layout. A typical *onCreate()* method will read as follows:

```
override fun onCreate(savedInstanceState: Bundle?) {
    super.onCreate(savedInstanceState)
    enableEdgeToEdge()
    setContentView(R.layout.activity_main)
    ViewCompat.setOnApplyWindowInsetsListener(findViewById(R.id.main)) {
                                                              v, insets ->
        val systemBars = insets.getInsets(WindowInsetsCompat.Type.systemBars())
        v.setPadding(systemBars.left, systemBars.top, systemBars.right,
                                   systemBars.bottom)
        insets
    }
}
```

To switch to using view binding, the view binding class will need to be imported and the class modified as follows. Note that since the layout file is named *activity_main.xml*, we can surmise that the binding class generated by Android Studio will be named ActivityMainBinding. Note that if you used a domain other than *com.example* when creating the project, the import statement below would need to be changed to reflect this:

```
.
.
import android.widget.EditText
import android.widget.TextView

import com.example.androidsample.databinding.ActivityMainBinding

class MainActivity : AppCompatActivity() {

    private lateinit var binding: ActivityMainBinding

    override fun onCreate(savedInstanceState: Bundle?) {
        super.onCreate(savedInstanceState)
        enableEdgeToEdge()
        setContentView(R.layout.activity_main)
        binding = ActivityMainBinding.inflate(layoutInflater)
        setContentView(binding.root)
        ViewCompat.setOnApplyWindowInsetsListener(binding.main) { v, insets ->
            val systemBars = insets.getInsets(WindowInsetsCompat.Type.
                                                  systemBars())
            v.setPadding(systemBars.left, systemBars.top, systemBars.right,
                                              systemBars.bottom)
            insets
        }
    }
.
.
```

Now that we have a reference to the binding, we can access the views by name as follows:

```
fun convertCurrency(view: View) {

    val dollarText: EditText = findViewById(R.id.dollarText)
    val textView: TextView = findViewById(R.id.textView)

    if (binding.dollarText.text.isNotEmpty()) {
        val dollarValue = binding.dollarText.text.toString().toFloat()
        val euroValue = dollarValue * 0.85f
        binding.textView.text = euroValue.toString()
    } else {
        binding.textView.text = getString(R.string.no_value_string)
    }
}
```

Compile and run the app and verify that the currency conversion process works as before.

18.6 Choosing an Option

Notwithstanding their failure to adopt view bindings in the Empty Views Activity project template, Google strongly recommends using view binding wherever possible. Therefore, view binding should be used when developing your own projects.

18.7 View Binding in the Book Examples

Any chapters in this book that rely on a project template that does not implement view binding will first be migrated. Instead of replicating the steps every time a migration needs to be performed, however, these chapters will refer you back here to refresh your memory (don't worry, after a few chapters, the necessary changes will become second nature). To help with the process, the following section summarizes the migration steps more concisely.

18.8 Migrating a Project to View Binding

The process for converting a project module to use view binding involves the following steps:

1. Edit the module-level Gradle build script file listed in the Project tool window as *Gradle Scripts -> build.gradle.kts (Module :app)*.

2. Locate the *android* section of the file and add an entry to enable the *viewBinding* property as follows:

```
android {

    buildFeatures {
        viewBinding = true
    }
.
.
```

3. Click on the *Sync Now* link at the top of the editor to resynchronize the project with these new build settings.

4. Edit the *MainActivity.kt* file and modify it to read as follows (where <*reverse domain*> represents the domain name used when the project was created and <*project name*> is replaced by the lowercase name of the project, for example, *androidsample*) and <*binding name*> is the name of the binding for the corresponding layout resource file (for example, the binding for *activity_main.xml* is ActivityMainBinding).

```
.
.
import <reverse domain>.<project name>.databinding.<binding name>

class MainActivity : AppCompatActivity() {

    private lateinit var binding: <binding name>

    override fun onCreate(savedInstanceState: Bundle?) {
        super.onCreate(savedInstanceState)
        setContentView(R.layout.activity_main)
        binding = <binding name>.inflate(layoutInflater)
        setContentView(binding.root)
       ViewCompat.setOnApplyWindowInsetsListener(binding.main) { v, insets ->
```

```
            val systemBars = insets.getInsets(WindowInsetsCompat.Type.
                                                systemBars())
            v.setPadding(systemBars.left, systemBars.top, systemBars.right,
                                                systemBars.bottom)
            insets
        }
    }
```

5. Access views by name as properties of the binding object.

18.9 Using AI to Perform the Conversion

An alternative to manually converting a project to use view binding is to ask Android Studio's Gemini AI agent to perform the task for us. This topic will be covered in the *"Introducing Gemini AI in Android Studio"* chapter.

18.10 Summary

Before the introduction of Android Studio 3.6, access to layout views from within the code of an app involved using the *findViewById()* method. An alternative is now available in the form of view bindings. View bindings consist of classes Android Studio automatically generates for each XML layout file. These classes contain bindings to each view in the corresponding layout, providing a safer option than the *findViewById()* method. However, as of Android Studio Quail, view bindings are not enabled by default in some project templates. Additional steps are required to enable and configure support within each project module manually.

19. Introducing Gemini AI in Android Studio

Much has changed since Alan Turing proposed a test to identify when a computer had become "intelligent." With recent breakthroughs in artificial intelligence from OpenAI and other companies, it is unsurprising that AI has found its way into Android app development with the integration of Google Gemini into Android Studio.

This chapter will explain the AI features available in Android Studio and explore how they can make your job as a developer easier.

19.1 Introducing Gemini AI

Originally called Bard, Gemini is an artificial intelligence technology developed by Google's DeepMind division. Gemini is categorized as a Large Language Model (LLM) generative artificial intelligence.

To 'train' Gemini, Google has fed it vast quantities of diverse content, including books, research papers, images, source code, and internet-scraped data. Gemini has then created a model from this data, which it uses to generate content in response to various inputs, such as questions, images, requests, or programming code.

Once Gemini has been enabled in Android Studio, it can generate sample code, explain how to achieve specific programming objectives, provide code completion suggestions, and improve or extend existing code.

19.2 Enabling Gemini AI in Android Studio

Before you can use Gemini in Android Studio, you must enable it. This process is straightforward but requires you to log in to your Google account within Android Studio. If you are not currently signed in, click the profile button in the Android Studio toolbar, followed by the sign-in button:

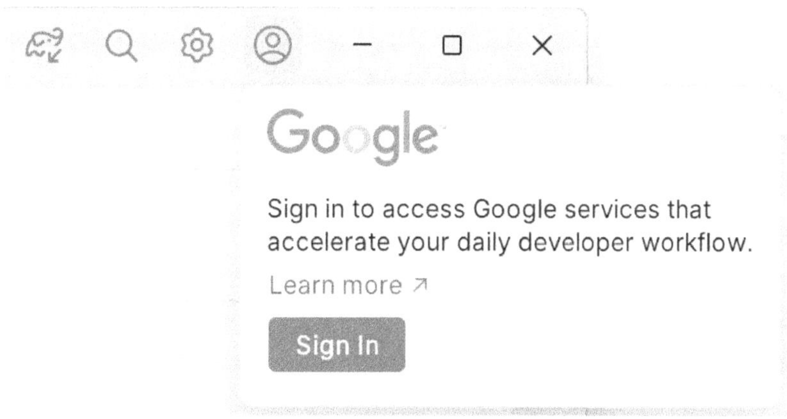

Figure 19-1

When the Sign-in wizard screen appears, ensure the Gemini in Android Studio option is enabled, as shown in Figure 19-2, before clicking the Finish button. Android Studio will open a browser window where you will complete the sign-in process and grant permission for Android Studio to access your account:

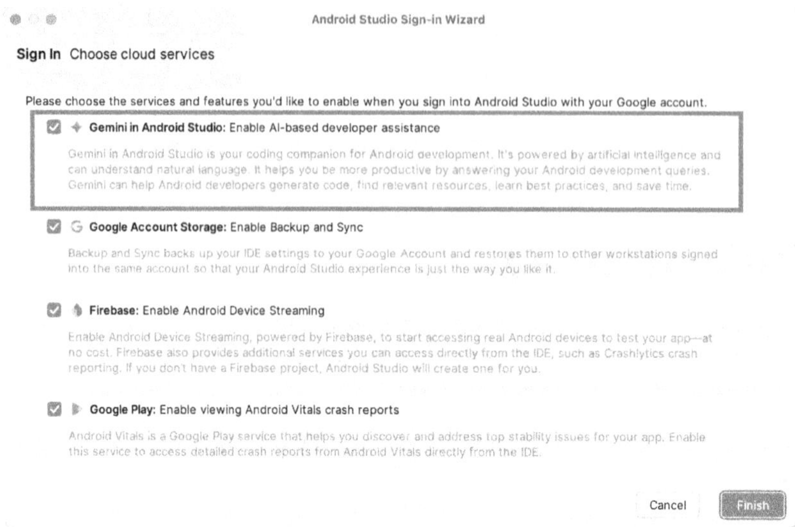

Figure 19-2

Once you have logged in and enabled Gemini, display the Gemini tool window by clicking the Chat button highlighted in Figure 19-3:

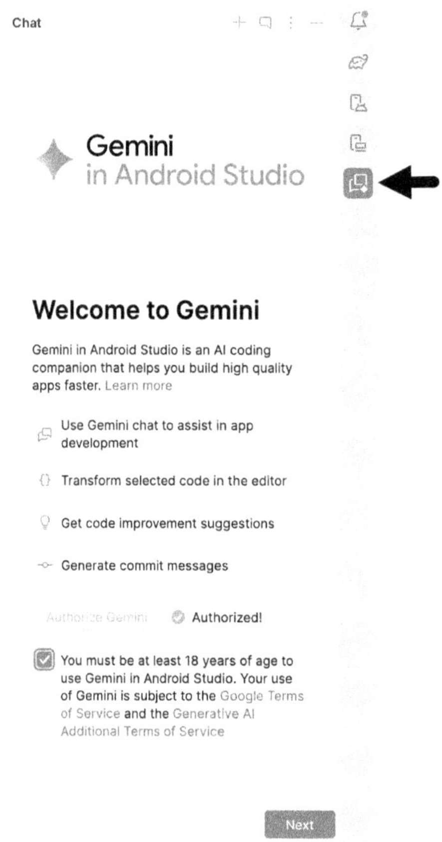

Figure 19-3

Select the checkbox to agree to the terms and conditions, then click the Next button to navigate through the remaining screens. You will need to decide whether to let Gemini access your project files. To get the most from Gemini, enable the Use all Gemini features and Apply to all projects options (Gemini's configuration settings can be reviewed and modified on the *Tools -> AI* page of the Android Studio Settings dialog):

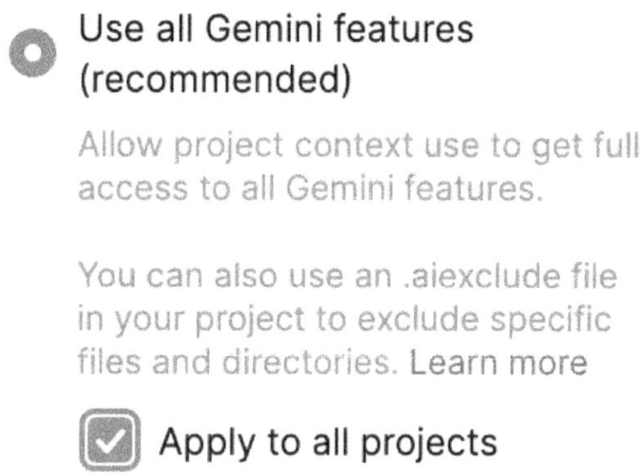

Figure 19-4

If you are concerned about Google accessing your code, you should choose the option to use the chat feature without project context:

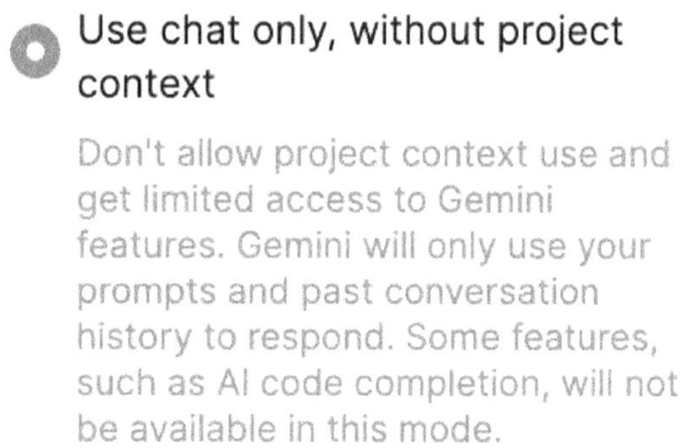

Figure 19-5

Note that without context, Gemini's features will be limited, and AI-assisted code completion within the code editor will be disabled. After making your selections, click Finish to begin using Gemini.

19.3 Google One Subscription

By default, you will be using the free Gemini base tier, which imposes limits on the number of AI responses Gemini will provide within a given period of time and restricts access to advanced models. For more advanced capabilities, you will either need a Google One subscription or set up a Google billing account and generate a Google AI Studio API key. Your current status is indicated in the bottom left corner of the Agent tool window. Hovering the mouse pointer over the indicator will explain the limitations and provide a link to a webpage where you can subscribe to Google One:

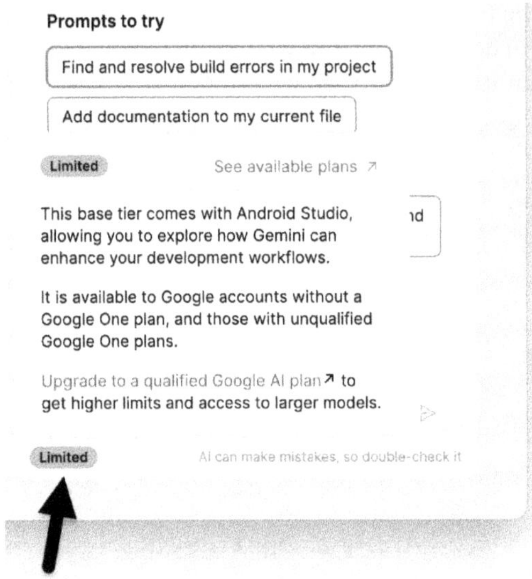

Figure 19-6

19.4 Using API Billing

Another option is to use "pay-as-you-go" billing by generating a Google AI Studio API key. To generate and apply the key, open the Android Studio settings dialog, navigate to the *Tools -> AI -> Model Providers* page, and click the *Get a Gemini API key* link:

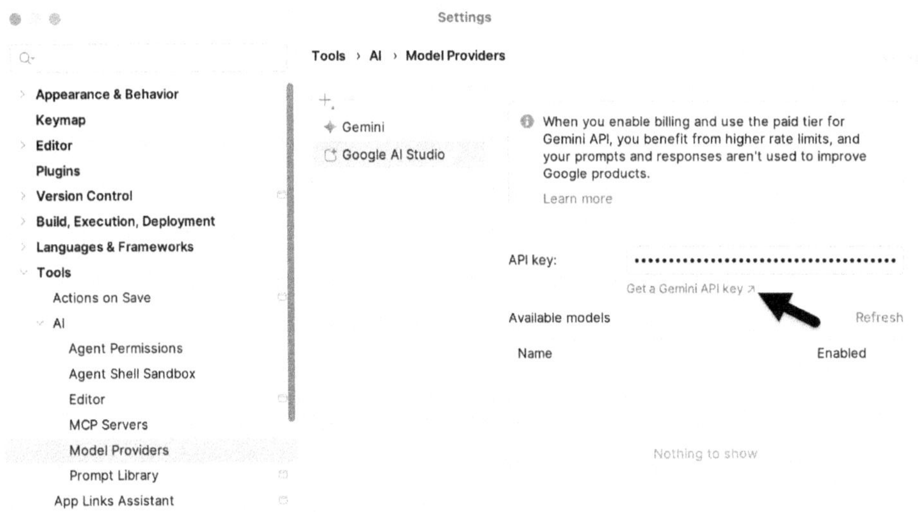

Figure 19-7

On the resulting Google AI Studio web page, click the button to create an API key and either import or create a Google Cloud project to associate with the key. Once the key has been generated, click the *Set up billing* link highlighted in Figure 19-8 and enter your payment information:

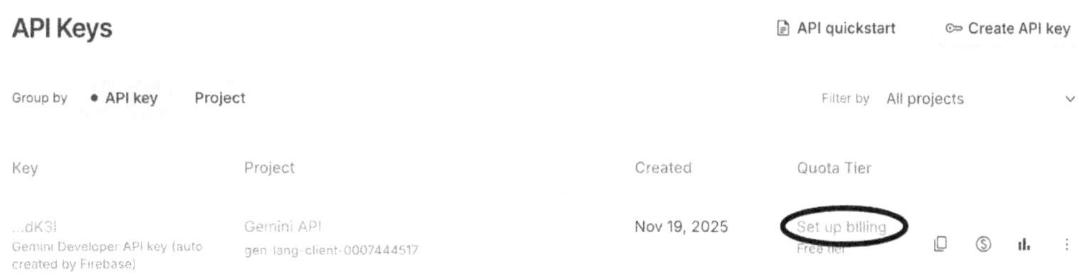

Figure 19-8

Once billing is configured, copy the API key, then return to Android Studio and enter it into the API key field. Once the key has been entered, click Apply, then Refresh to update the list of available models. Select the models you would like to use, then apply the changes and click on OK to close the Settings dialog:

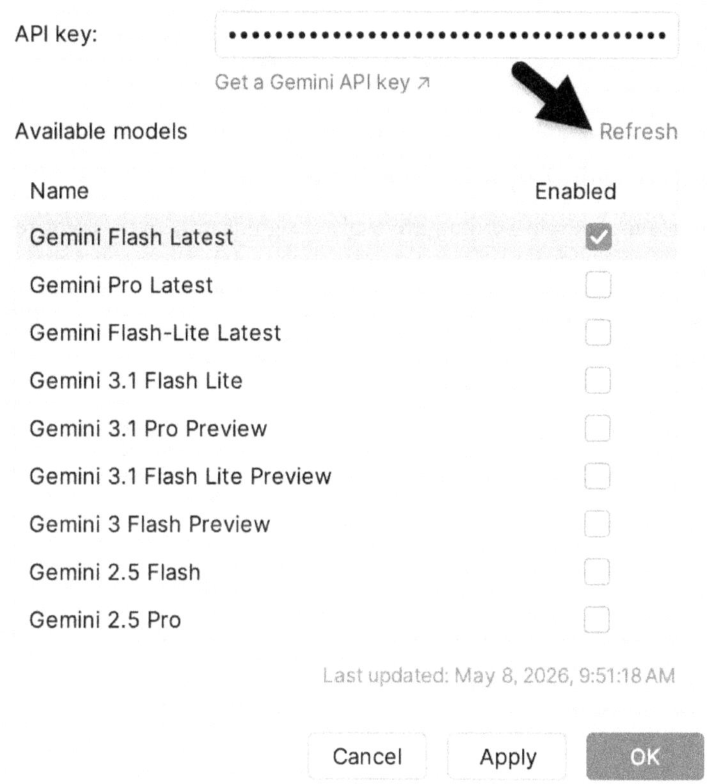

Figure 19-9

19.5 Selecting the Model

If you chose to upgrade the AI capabilities, use the Agent tool window menu highlighted in Figure 19-10 to select your preferred model before working with the agent:

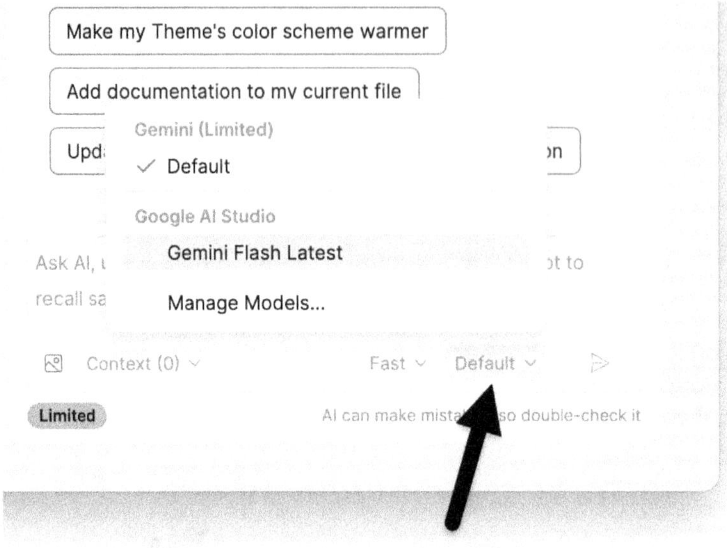

Figure 19-10

19.6 Understanding Agent Conversation Modes

The AI assistance features in Android Studio have evolved significantly over recent releases. Earlier versions separated interactions into distinct conversational modes such as Ask, Chat, and Agent. Each mode focused on a different style of interaction, ranging from simple informational questions to full project-aware automation. To change the current conversation mode settings, click the button indicated in Figure 19-11 and make a selection from the resulting menu:

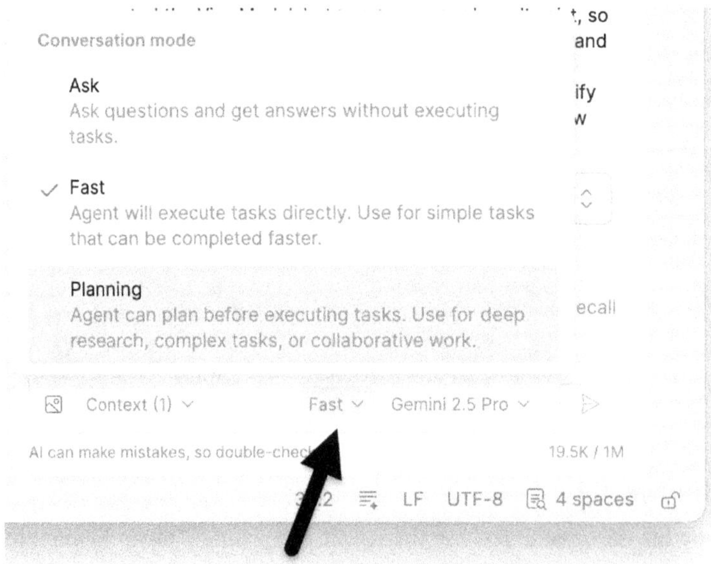

Figure 19-11

Recent Android Studio releases have simplified this interface and now typically present three primary interaction modes named Ask, Fast, and Planning. Although the names have changed, these newer modes are closely related to the concepts introduced in the earlier implementations.

Understanding the purpose of each mode is important because Gemini adjusts its behavior, reasoning depth, and project interaction level depending on the selected conversation style.

19.6.1 Ask Mode

Ask mode is the direct descendant of the original Ask-style interaction introduced in earlier Android Studio Gemini releases. This mode is designed primarily for questions, explanations, debugging assistance, and short conversational interactions.

In Ask mode, Gemini typically focuses on responding to the current request without performing extensive multi-step reasoning or large-scale project analysis, making us useful for tasks such as the following:

- Explaining error messages
- Clarifying APIs
- Understanding framework behavior
- Reviewing small code snippets
- Learning Android concepts

Typical prompts include:

```
What causes this Compose recomposition warning?
Explain how Room database migrations work.
Why is this coroutine leaking memory?
```

Unlike the more advanced modes, Ask mode generally emphasizes responsiveness and concise answers rather than deep architectural analysis or automated project modifications.

In practice, Ask mode behaves much like the original conversational assistant that appeared in the earliest Gemini-enabled versions of Android Studio.

19.6.2 Fast Mode

Fast mode represents the modern evolution of the earlier Chat and lightweight Agent experiences. This mode is optimized for speed while still maintaining greater contextual awareness of the project than Ask mode.

Fast mode is particularly useful when developers want Gemini to:

- Analyze larger portions of the codebase
- Suggest implementation approaches
- Generate or refactor code
- Navigate project structure
- Perform development tasks quickly

For example:

```
Convert this activity to use ViewModel state management.
Refactor this screen to use Material 3 components.
Find deprecated API usages in this module.
```

Compared to Ask mode, Fast mode typically performs broader project inspection and can reason across multiple files. However, its primary focus remains responsiveness and rapid task completion.

In earlier Android Studio versions, this behavior was often associated with Agent mode operating in a relatively lightweight conversational style.

19.6.3 Planning Mode

Planning mode is the most advanced conversational mode currently available in Android Studio. This mode is designed for complex reasoning tasks that require deeper analysis, multi-step planning, and a broader understanding of project architecture.

Rather than immediately generating code changes, Planning mode first attempts to reason about the problem, evaluate alternatives, and formulate a structured implementation strategy.

Planning mode is particularly valuable for:

- Large refactoring operations
- Architectural redesign
- Multi-module analysis
- Migration planning
- Dependency restructuring
- Complex debugging scenarios

An example prompt might read as follows:

```
Add a view model to the project, and implement the initialization code in
MainActivity to make it accessible to the DemoScreen composable.
```

Planning mode often produces more detailed reasoning before proposing modifications. In many cases, Gemini explains the implementation strategy first and then proceeds with individual development steps, seeking your permission at each step:

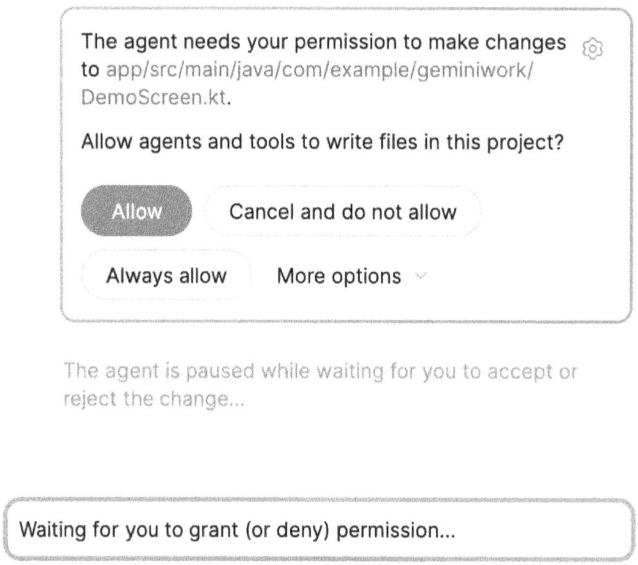

Figure 19-12

This mode reflects the most sophisticated aspects of the earlier Agent functionality, but with a stronger emphasis on deliberate reasoning and coordinated planning rather than immediate action.

19.7 Interacting with Gemini

You can chat with AI to get answers to questions about Android development or to ask it to perform tasks by typing a request into the Ask AI chat box (marked A in Figure 19-13), then clicking the send button (B):

Figure 19-13

Gemini can explain Android development concepts, show you how to accomplish a specific task, explain error messages, teach you how to use Android Studio features, and provide coding examples you can use in your projects. For example, you can ask Gemini how to draw a circle:

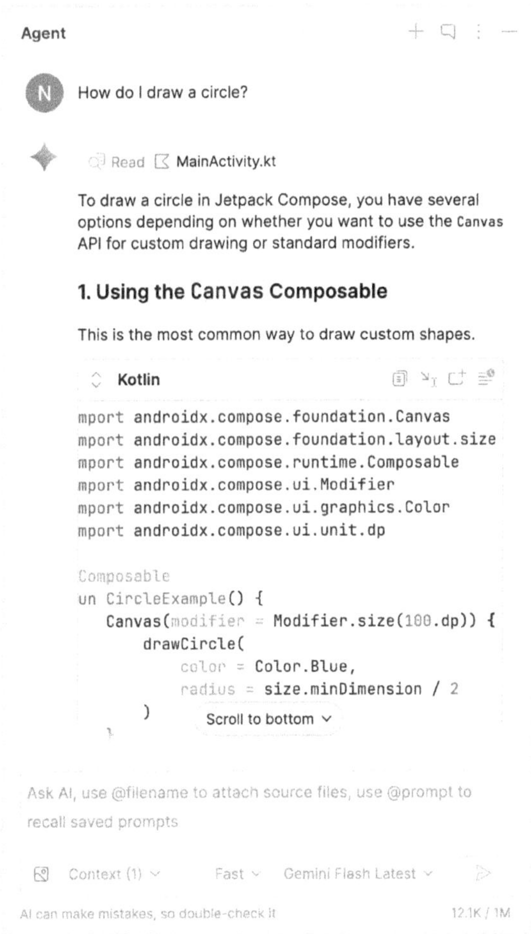

Figure 19-14

Gemini will explain how to draw a circle and provide example code. Above each code sample in Gemini's response is a collection of buttons, as shown in Figure 19-15:

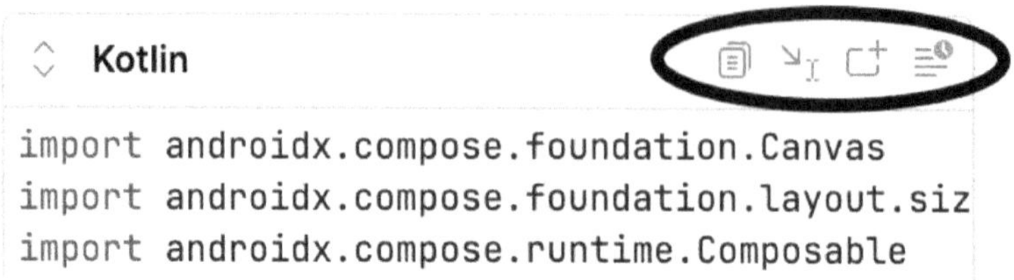

Figure 19-15

From left to right, the buttons perform the following tasks:

- **Copy** - Copies the sample code to the clipboard, ready to be pasted into your code.
- **Insert at Cursor** - Pastes the code at the code editor's current cursor location.
- **Insert into a New File** - Adds a new code file to the project containing the sample code.
- **Explore in Playground** - An experimental feature that places the code into a Kotlin Script file named *geminiplayground.kts,* where you can test small code examples. You can also interact with Gemini directly in the playground code file by prefixing questions with // @Gemini.

19.8 AI code prediction

Gemini can make code-completion suggestions as you type in the editor. It does this based on the code you are typing and an analysis of the rest of the project code. Gemini's ability to infer your intentions is so good that it can initially feel uncanny.

When code completion is enabled and active, the button highlighted in Figure 19-16 below will appear in the code editor's status bar:

Figure 19-16

Click this button to activate and deactivate code completion and to access the Gemini configuration settings.

A more advanced form of code completion, called Next Edit Prediction (NEP), is available if you are a Google One subscriber or have configured a billable Google AI Studio API key. Unlike inline code completion, which only makes suggestions at the current cursor position, NEP will make completion suggestions at multiple locations in the current file. To enable NEP, open the Android Studio Settings dialog, navigate to the *Tools -> AI -> Editor* screen, and enable the "AI next edit prediction" option marked A in Figure 19-17 below:

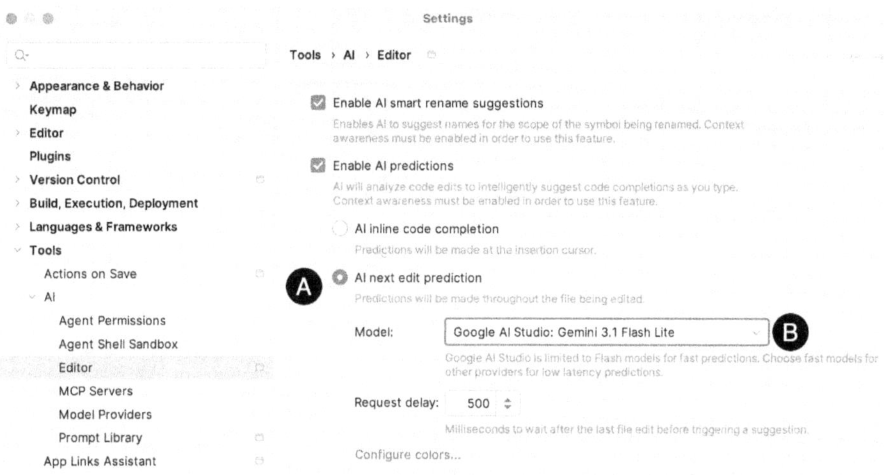

Figure 19-17

Note that an appropriate model must be selected using the menu mark B above to enable NEP.

Once NEP is enabled, the code editor will display markers indicating code prediction locations. When an edit prediction is available within a visible line of code, an arrow marker will appear in the editor margin, as shown in Figure 19-18:

Figure 19-18

If the predicted code location is above or below the currently visible code lines, an indicator similar to that shown in Figure 19-19 will appear:

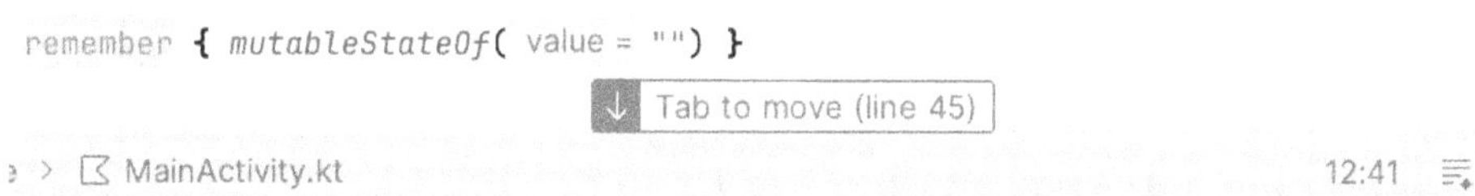

Figure 19-19

In a previous chapter, we demonstrated object-oriented programming by creating a bank account class. Suppose we are writing a similar class, but this time with Gemini code completion enabled. We might begin by creating the class as follows:

```
class BankAccount {
    var accountBalance = 0
}
```

After we declare the accountBalance variable and press enter, Gemini might suggest an additional variable named accountName. Assuming we want this variable, we can accept it by tapping the Tab key:

```
class BankAccount {
    var accountBalance = 0
    var accountName = ""
}
```

Next, Gemini suggests an account number variable:

```
class BankAccount {
    var accountBalance = 0
    var accountName = ""
    var accountNumber = 0
}
```

Once the variables have been declared, Gemini will suggest a method to deposit money into the account:

```
fun deposit(amount: Int) {
        accountBalance += amount
}
```

After we accept this method, Gemini will recommend the following withdrawal method:

```
fun withdraw(amount: Int) {
    if (accountBalance >= amount) {
        accountBalance -= amount
    }
}
```

Then, a transfer method:

```
fun transfer(otherAccount: BankAccount, amount: Int) {
    if (accountBalance >= amount) {
        accountBalance -= amount
        otherAccount.accountBalance += amount
    }
}
```

Gemini will continue to offer suggestions until you are satisfied that the class is complete. Consider that Gemini generated the above code entirely on the initial three lines of code with no additional input, and we can begin to appreciate the power of Gemini in Android Studio.

19.9 Transforming and documenting code

In addition to generating code, Gemini can modify, improve, and document existing code based on your instructions. To use transformation, highlight a section of code in the editor, right-click on it, and select the *AI -> Transform Selected Code...* menu option:

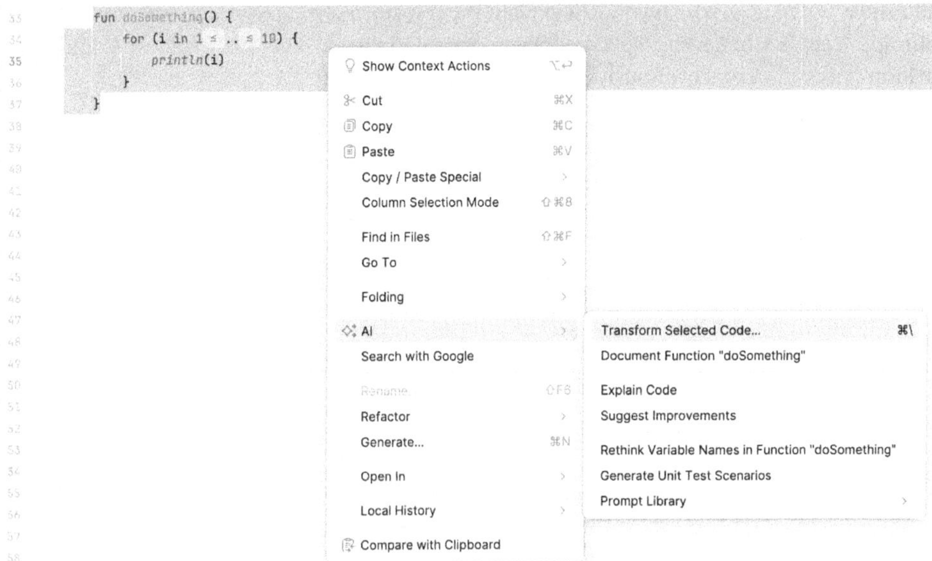

Figure 19-20

Alternatively, the toolbar shown below will appear whenever code is selected in the editor:

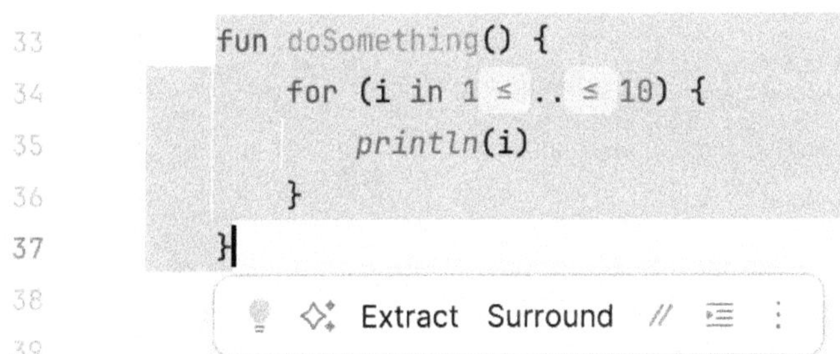

Figure 19-21

Hover the mouse pointer over the AI toolbar button and select the *Transform Selected Code...* menu option:

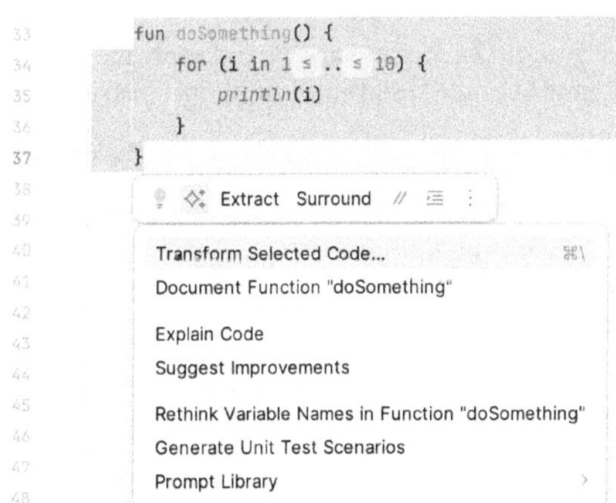

Figure 19-22

Gemini will display a dialog in which you will explain the transformation requirements. For example, we might find that our app freezes whenever a specific loop is executed. To resolve this issue, we could ask Gemini to execute the loop operation asynchronously:

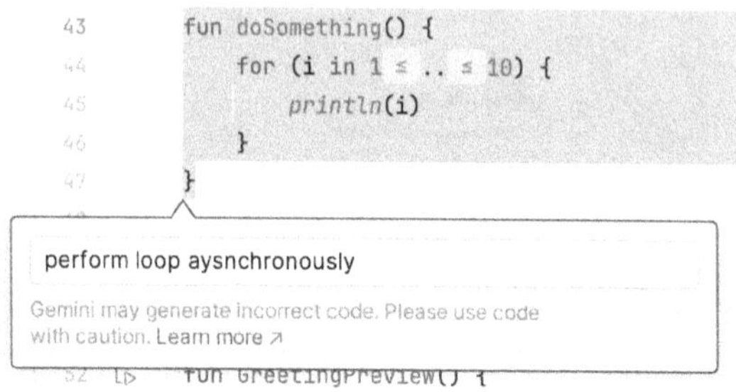

Figure 19-23

Pressing enter will start the transformation, and once it is complete, the proposed changes panel will appear. This panel displays the original code alongside the new code with the proposed changes highlighted:

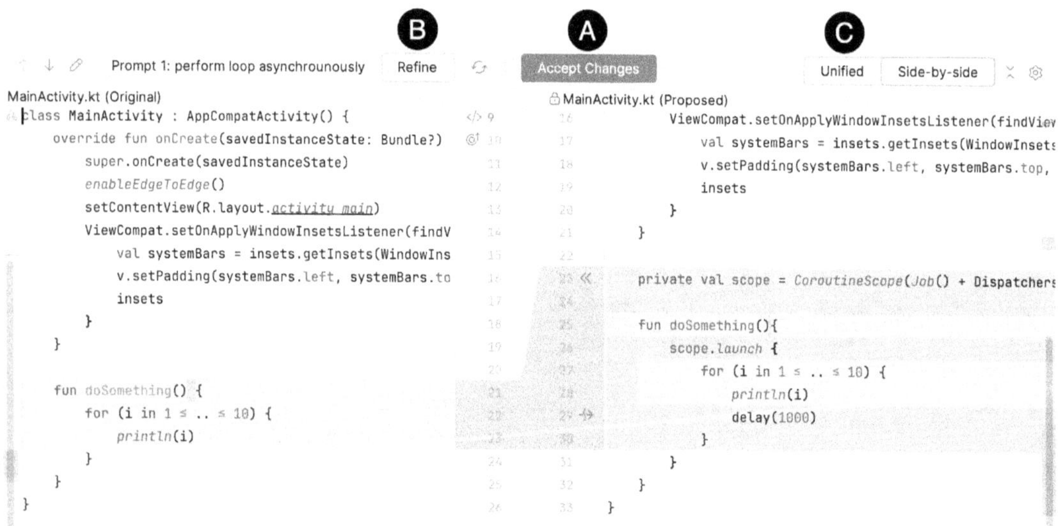

Figure 19-24

Click the button marked A in Figure 19-24 above to accept and apply the changes to the original code. If more changes are needed, click the Refine button (B) and enter additional instructions.

Use button C to switch between Unified (merged) mode and a side-by-side comparison, and to abandon the changes, close the window.

In the above example, our original code was as follows:

```
fun doSomething() {
    for (i in 1..10) {
        println(i)
    }
}
```

After the Gemini transformation, the code has been adapted to run the loop asynchronously:

```
import kotlinx.coroutines.Dispatchers
```

```
import kotlinx.coroutines.launch
import kotlinx.coroutines.withContext

fun doSomething() {
    CoroutineScope(Dispatchers.IO).launch {
        for (i in 1..10) {
            withContext(Dispatchers.Main){ println("i")}
        }
    }
}
```

Gemini can perform various transformation tasks, including improving code you have written and adding new functionality to existing code.

To ask Gemini to document code, highlight the code section and select the document option from the Gemini toolbar menu (the exact menu option will depend on the type of code selected). The following comment, for example, was generated by Gemini by highlighting the doSomething() function and selecting the *AI -> Document function "doSomething"* menu option:

```
/**
 * Launches a coroutine in the [GlobalScope] that iterates from 1 to 10,
 * printing each iteration index to the standard output.
 */
```

19.10 Smart Renaming

When writing code, it is common to need to change the names of classes, variables, and functions, particularly as a project grows in complexity. You might, for example, decide that a variable named "customer" referenced in multiple places in your code is too generic. One solution is to use Android Studio's refactoring feature to change all instances of the variable name to a new name of your choice. Gemini's smart renaming feature takes this concept further by scanning the code in the current context (for example, a class or function) and providing a list of alternative names that it believes will make your code more consistent and easier to understand.

To use smart renaming, right-click on a class or function name and select the *AI -> Rethink Names* menu option (the exact wording of the menu option will vary depending on the context of the code selection):

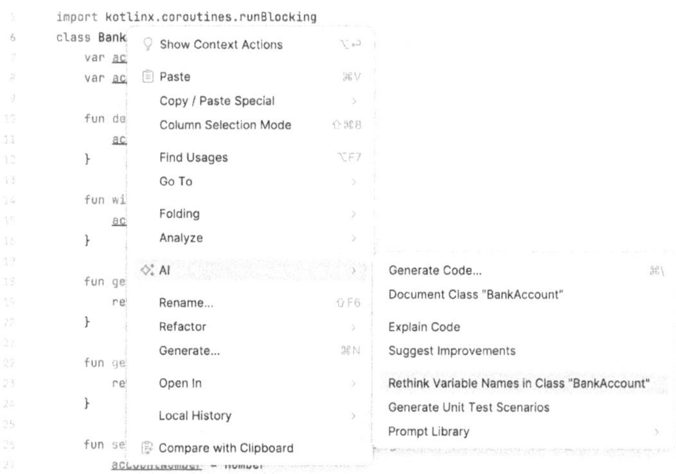

Figure 19-25

After Gemini has analyzed the code, the dialog shown in Figure 19-26 will appear, containing a list of renaming suggestions. Use the checkboxes to choose which suggestions to accept, then use the preview panel to review the code changes:

Figure 19-26

Click OK to accept the changes and apply them to your code.

19.11 Summary

With Gemini integrated into Android Studio, developers can now leverage AI assistance when developing Android apps. Once Gemini in Android Studio is activated, it can answer your questions, provide code examples, suggest code completions, and rewrite and extend existing code in ways that were unimaginable a few years ago.

Chapter 20

20. Understanding Android Application and Activity Lifecycles

In earlier chapters, we learned that Android applications run within processes and comprise multiple components in the form of activities, services, and broadcast receivers. This chapter aims to expand on this knowledge by looking at the lifecycle of applications and activities within the Android runtime system.

Regardless of the fanfare about how much memory and computing power resides in the mobile devices of today compared to the desktop systems of yesterday, it is important to keep in mind that these devices are still considered to be "resource constrained" by the standards of modern desktop and laptop-based systems, particularly in terms of memory. As such, a key responsibility of the Android system is to ensure that these limited resources are managed effectively and that the operating system and the applications running on it remain responsive to the user at all times. To achieve this, Android is given complete control over the lifecycle and state of the processes in which the applications run and the individual components that comprise those applications.

An important factor in developing Android applications, therefore, is to understand Android's application and activity lifecycle management models of Android, and how an application can react to the state changes likely to be imposed upon it during its execution lifetime.

20.1 Android Applications and Resource Management

The operating system views each running Android application as a separate process. If the system identifies that resources on the device are reaching capacity, it will take steps to terminate processes to free up memory.

When determining which process to terminate to free up memory, the system considers both the *priority* and *state* of all currently running processes, combining these factors to create what is referred to by Google as an *importance hierarchy*. Processes are then terminated, starting with the lowest priority and working up the hierarchy until sufficient resources have been liberated for the system to function.

20.2 Android Process States

Processes host applications, and applications are made up of components. Within an Android system, the current state of a process is defined by the highest-ranking active component within the application it hosts. As outlined in Figure 20-1, a process can be in one of the following five states at any given time:

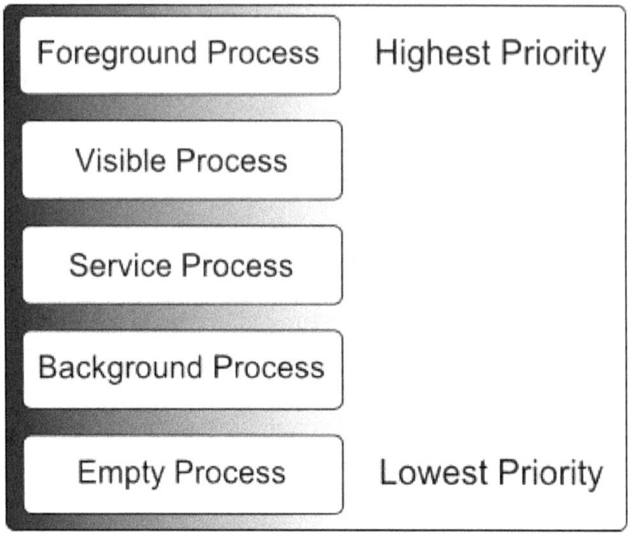

Figure 20-1

20.2.1 Foreground Process

These processes are assigned the highest level of priority. At any one time, there are unlikely to be more than one or two foreground processes active, which are usually the last to be terminated by the system. A process must meet one or more of the following criteria to qualify for foreground status:

- Hosts an activity with which the user is currently interacting.
- Hosts a Service connected to the activity with which the user is interacting.
- Hosts a Service that has indicated, via a call to *startForeground()*, that termination would disrupt the user experience.
- Hosts a Service executing either its *onCreate()*, *onResume()*, or *onStart()* callbacks.
- Hosts a Broadcast Receiver that is currently executing its *onReceive()* method.

20.2.2 Visible Process

A process containing an activity that is visible to the user but is not the activity with which the user is interacting is classified as a "visible process". This is typically the case when an activity in the process is visible to the user, but another activity, such as a partial screen or dialog, is in the foreground. A process is also eligible for visible status if it hosts a Service that is, itself, bound to a visible or foreground activity.

20.2.3 Service Process

Processes that contain a Service that has already been started and is currently executing.

20.2.4 Background Process

A process that contains one or more activities that are not currently visible to the user and does not host a Service that qualifies for *Service Process* status. Processes that fall into this category are at high risk of termination if additional memory needs to be freed for higher-priority processes. Android maintains a dynamic list of background processes, terminating processes in chronological order such that processes that were the least recently in the foreground are killed first.

20.2.5 Empty Process

Empty processes no longer contain active applications and are held in memory, ready to serve as hosts for newly launched applications. This is analogous to keeping the doors open and the engine running on a bus in anticipation of passengers arriving. Such processes are considered the lowest priority and are the first to be killed to free up resources.

20.3 Inter-Process Dependencies

Determining the highest priority process is more complex than outlined in the preceding section because processes can often be interdependent. As such, when determining the priority of a process, the Android system will also consider whether the process is in some way serving another process of higher priority (for example, a service process acting as the content provider for a foreground process). As a basic rule, the Android documentation states that a process can never be ranked lower than another process that it is currently serving.

20.4 The Activity Lifecycle

As we have previously determined, the state of an Android process is primarily determined by the status of the activities and components that make up the application it hosts. It is important to understand, therefore, that these activities also transition through different states during the execution lifetime of an application. The current state of an activity is determined, in part, by its position in something called the Activity Stack.

20.5 The Activity Stack

The runtime system maintains an *Activity Stack* for each application running on an Android device. When an application is launched, the first of the application's activities to be started is placed onto the stack. When a second activity is started, it is placed on the top of the stack, and the previous activity is *pushed* down. The activity at the top of the stack is called the *active* (or *running*) activity. When the active activity exits, it is *popped* off the stack by the runtime and the activity located immediately beneath it in the stack becomes the current active activity. For example, the activity at the top of the stack might exit because the task for which it is responsible has been completed. Alternatively, the user may have selected a "Back" button on the screen to return to the previous activity, causing the current activity to be popped off the stack by the runtime system and destroyed. A visual representation of the Android Activity Stack is illustrated in Figure 20-2.

As shown in the diagram, new activities are pushed onto the top of the stack when they are started. The current active activity is located at the top of the stack until it is either pushed down the stack by a new activity or popped off the stack when it exits or the user navigates to the previous activity. If resources become constrained, the runtime will kill activities, starting with those at the bottom of the stack.

The Activity Stack is what is referred to in programming terminology as a Last-In-First-Out (LIFO) stack in that the last item to be pushed onto the stack is the first to be popped off.

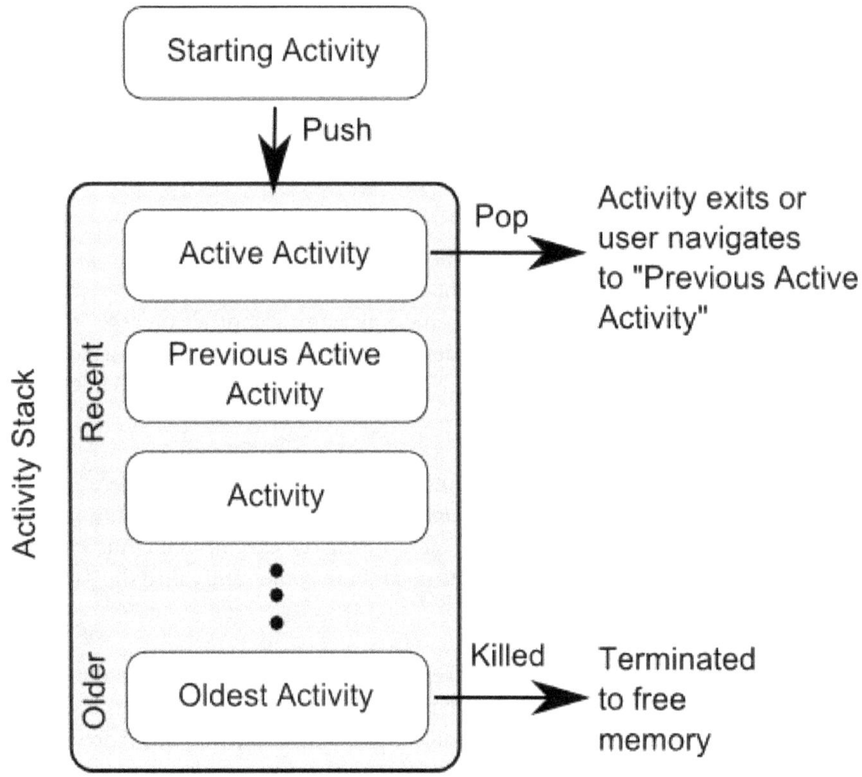

Figure 20-2

20.6 Activity States

An activity can be in one of several states during the course of its execution within an application:

- **Active / Running** – The activity is at the top of the Activity Stack, is the foreground task visible on the device screen, has focus, and is currently interacting with the user. This is the least likely activity to be terminated in the event of a resource shortage.
- **Paused** – The activity is visible to the user but does not currently have focus (typically because the current *active* activity partially obscures this activity). Paused activities are held in memory, remain attached to the window manager, retain all state information, and can quickly be restored to active status when moved to the top of the Activity Stack.
- **Stopped** – The activity is currently not visible to the user (in other words, it is obscured on the device display by other activities). As with paused activities, it retains all state and member information but is at higher risk of termination in low-memory situations.
- **Killed** – The runtime system has terminated the activity to free up memory and is no longer present on the Activity Stack. Such activities must be restarted if required by the application.

20.7 Configuration Changes

So far in this chapter, we have looked at two causes for the change in the state of an Android activity, namely the movement of an activity between the foreground and background and the termination of an activity by the runtime system to free up memory. In fact, there is a third scenario in which the state of an activity can dramatically change, which involves a change to the device configuration.

By default, any configuration change that impacts the appearance of an activity (such as rotating the orientation of the device between portrait and landscape or changing a system font setting) will cause the activity to be destroyed and recreated. The reasoning behind this is that such changes affect resources such as the layout of the user interface, and destroying and recreating impacted activities is the quickest way for an activity to respond to the configuration change. It is, however, possible to configure an activity so that the system does not restart it in response to specific configuration changes.

20.8 Handling State Change

It should be clear from this chapter that an application and, by definition, the components contained therein will transition through many states during its lifespan. Of particular importance is the fact that these state changes (up to and including complete termination) are imposed upon the application by the Android runtime subject to the user's actions and the availability of resources on the device.

In practice, however, these state changes are not imposed entirely without notice, and an application will, in most circumstances, be notified by the runtime system of the changes and given the opportunity to react accordingly. This will typically involve saving or restoring both internal data structures and user interface state, thereby allowing the user to switch seamlessly between applications and providing at least the appearance of multiple concurrently running applications.

Android provides two ways to handle the changes to the lifecycle states of the objects within an app. One approach involves responding to state change method calls from the operating system and is covered in detail in the next chapter entitled *"Handling Android Activity State Changes"*.

A new approach that Google recommends involves the lifecycle classes included with the Jetpack Android Architecture components, introduced in *"Modern Android App Architecture with Jetpack"* and explained in more detail in the chapter entitled *"Working with Android Lifecycle-Aware Components"*.

20.9 Summary

Mobile devices are typically considered to be resource constrained, particularly in terms of onboard memory capacity. Consequently, a prime responsibility of the Android operating system is to ensure that applications, and the operating system in general, remain responsive to the user.

Applications are hosted on Android within processes. Each application, in turn, comprises components in the form of activities and Services.

The Android runtime system has the power to terminate both processes and individual activities to free up memory. Process state is considered by the runtime system when deciding whether a process is a suitable candidate for termination. The state of a process largely depends upon the status of the activities hosted by that process.

The key message of this chapter is that an application moves through various states during its execution lifespan and has very little control over its destiny within the Android runtime environment. Those processes and activities not directly interacting with the user run a higher risk of termination by the runtime system. An essential element of Android application development, therefore, involves the ability of an application to respond to state change notifications from the operating system.

Chapter 21

21. Handling Android Activity State Changes

Based on the information outlined in the chapter entitled *"Understanding Android Application and Activity Lifecycles"* it is now evident that the activities and fragments that make up an application pass through various different states during the application's lifespan. The Android runtime system imposes the change from one state to the other and is, therefore, largely beyond the control of the activity itself. That does not, however, mean that the app cannot react to those changes and take appropriate actions.

The primary objective of this chapter is to provide a high-level overview of how an activity may be notified of a state change and outline the areas where it is advisable to save or restore state information. Having covered this information, the chapter will touch briefly on *activity lifetimes*.

21.1 New vs. Old Lifecycle Techniques

Until recently, there was a standard way to build lifecycle awareness into an app. This approach is covered in this chapter and involves implementing a set of methods (one for each lifecycle state) within an activity or fragment instance that the operating system calls when the lifecycle status of that object changes. This approach has remained unchanged since the early years of the Android operating system, and while still a viable option today, it does have some limitations, which will be explained later in this chapter.

With the introduction of the lifecycle classes with the Jetpack Android Architecture Components, a better approach to lifecycle handling is now available. This modern approach to lifecycle management (together with the Jetpack components and architecture guidelines) will be covered in detail in later chapters. It is still essential, however, to understand the traditional lifecycle methods for a couple of reasons. First, as an Android developer, you will not be completely insulated from the traditional lifecycle methods and will still use some of them. More importantly, understanding the older way of handling lifecycles will provide a sound foundation for learning the new approach later in the book.

21.2 The Activity and Fragment Classes

With few exceptions, an application's activities and fragments are created as subclasses of the Android AppCompatActivity class and Fragment classes, respectively.

Consider, for example, the *AndroidSample* project created in *"Creating an Example Android App in Android Studio"* and subsequently converted to use view binding. Load this project into the Android Studio environment and locate the *MainActivity.kt* file (located in *app -> kotlin+java -> <your domain> -> androidsample*). Having located the file, double-click on it to load it into the editor, where it should read as follows:

```
package com.example.androidsample
.
.
class MainActivity : AppCompatActivity() {

    private lateinit var binding: ActivityMainBinding
```

```
    override fun onCreate(savedInstanceState: Bundle?) {
        super.onCreate(savedInstanceState)
        enableEdgeToEdge()
        binding = ActivityMainBinding.inflate(layoutInflater)
        setContentView(binding.root)

        ViewCompat.setOnApplyWindowInsetsListener(binding.main) { v, insets ->
            val systemBars = insets.getInsets(
                        WindowInsetsCompat.Type.systemBars())
            v.setPadding(systemBars.left, systemBars.top, systemBars.right,
                        systemBars.bottom)
            insets
        }
    }

    fun convertCurrency(view: View) {
.
.
    }
}
```

When the project was created, we instructed Android Studio also to create an initial activity named *MainActivity.kt* As is evident from the above code, the MainActivity class is a subclass of the AppCompatActivity class.

A review of the reference documentation for the AppCompatActivity class would reveal that it is itself a subclass of the Activity class. This can be verified within the Android Studio editor using the *Hierarchy* tool window. With the *MainActivity.kt* file loaded into the editor, click on AppCompatActivity in the *class* declaration line and press the *Ctrl-H* keyboard shortcut. The hierarchy tool window will subsequently appear, displaying the class hierarchy for the selected class. As illustrated in Figure 21-1, AppCompatActivity is subclassed from the FragmentActivity class, which is itself ultimately a subclass of the Activity class:

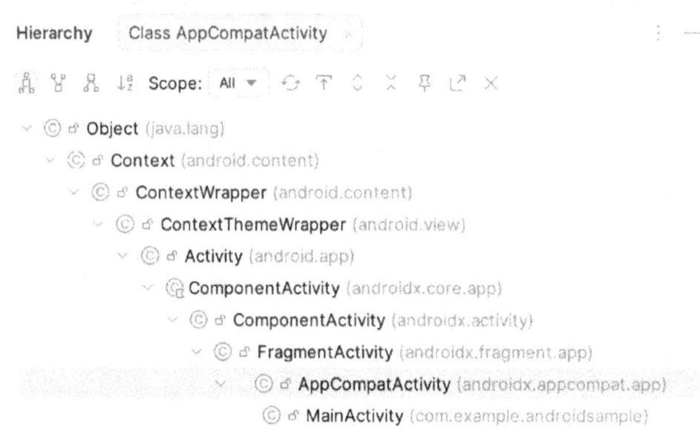

Figure 21-1

The Activity and Fragment classes contain a range of methods intended to be called by the Android runtime to notify the object when its state is changing. For this chapter, we will refer to these as the *lifecycle methods.* An activity or fragment class needs to *override* these methods and implement the necessary functionality to react accordingly to state changes.

One such method is named *onCreate()*, and, turning once again to the above code fragment, we can see that this method has already been overridden and implemented for us in the *MainActivity* class. In a later section, we will explore *onCreate()* and the other relevant lifecycle methods of the Activity and Fragment classes.

21.3 Dynamic State vs. Persistent State

A key objective of lifecycle management is ensuring that the state of the activity is saved and restored at appropriate times. When talking about *state* in this context, we mean the data currently being held within the activity and the appearance of the user interface. The activity might, for example, maintain a data model in memory that needs to be saved to a database, content provider, or file. Because it persists from one invocation of the application to another, such state information is referred to as the *persistent state.*

The appearance of the user interface (such as text entered into a text field but not yet committed to the application's internal data model) is referred to as the *dynamic state* since it is typically only retained during a single invocation of the application (and also referred to as *user interface state* or *instance state*).

Understanding the differences between these two states is important because the ways they are saved and the reasons for doing so differ.

The purpose of saving the persistent state is to avoid data loss that may result from an activity being killed by the runtime system while in the background. On the other hand, the dynamic state is saved and restored for slightly more complex reasons.

Consider, for example, that an application contains an activity (which we will refer to as *Activity A*) containing a text field and some radio buttons. During the course of using the application, the user enters some text into the text field and makes a selection from the radio buttons. However, before performing an action to save these changes, the user switches to another activity, causing *Activity A* to be pushed down the Activity Stack and placed into the background. After some time, the runtime system ascertains that memory is low and kills Activity A to free up resources. However, as far as the user is concerned, *Activity A* was placed in the background and is ready to be moved to the foreground at any time. On returning *Activity A* to the foreground, the user would reasonably expect the entered text and radio button selections to have been retained. In this scenario, however, a new instance of *Activity A* will have been created, and if the dynamic state is not saved and restored, the previous user input is lost.

Therefore, the primary purpose of saving dynamic state is to give the perception of seamless switching between foreground and background activities, regardless of the fact that activities may have been killed and restarted without the user's knowledge.

The mechanisms for saving persistent and dynamic states will become more apparent in the following sections of this chapter.

21.4 The Android Lifecycle Methods

As previously explained, the Activity and Fragment classes contain several lifecycle methods which act as event handlers when the state of an instance changes. The primary methods supported by the Android Activity and Fragment class are as follows:

- **onCreate(savedInstanceState: Bundle?)** – The method called when the activity is first created and the ideal location for most initialization tasks to be performed. The method is passed an argument in the form of a *Bundle* object that may contain dynamic state information (typically relating to the state of the user interface) from a prior invocation of the activity.
- **onRestart()** – Called when the activity is about to restart after having previously been stopped by the runtime system.

- **onStart()** – Always called immediately after the call to the *onCreate()* or *onRestart()* methods. This method indicates to the activity that it is about to become visible to the user. This call will be followed by a call to *onResume()* if the activity moves to the top of the activity stack, or *onStop()* if it is pushed down the stack by another activity.

- **onResume()** – Indicates that the activity is now at the top of the activity stack and is the activity with which the user is currently interacting.

- **onPause()** – Indicates that a previous activity is about to become the foreground activity. This call will be followed by a call to either the *onResume()* or *onStop()* method, depending on whether the activity moves back to the foreground or becomes invisible to the user. Steps may be taken within this method to store *persistent state* information not yet saved by the app. To avoid delays in switching between activities, time-consuming operations such as storing data to a database or performing network operations should be avoided within this method. This method should also ensure that any CPU-intensive tasks, such as animation, are stopped.

- **onStop()** – The activity is no longer visible to the user. The two possible scenarios following this call are a call to *onRestart()* if the activity moves to the foreground again or *onDestroy()* if the activity is terminated.

- **onDestroy()** – The activity is about to be destroyed, either voluntarily because the activity has completed its tasks and has called the *finish()* method or because the runtime is terminating it either to release memory or due to a configuration change (such as the orientation of the device changing). It is important to note that a call will not always be made to *onDestroy()* when an activity is terminated.

- **onConfigurationChanged()** – Called when a configuration change occurs for which the activity has indicated it is not to be restarted. The method is passed a Configuration object outlining the new device configuration, and it is then the responsibility of the activity to react to the change.

The following lifecycle methods only apply to the Fragment class:

- **onAttach()** - Called when the fragment is assigned to an activity.

- **onCreateView()** - Called to create and return the fragment's user interface layout view hierarchy.

- **onViewCreated()** - Called after *onCreateView()* returns.

- **onViewStatusRestored()** - The fragment's saved view hierarchy has been restored.

In addition to the lifecycle methods outlined above, there are two methods intended specifically for saving and restoring the *dynamic state* of an activity:

- **onRestoreInstanceState(savedInstanceState: Bundle?)** – This method is called immediately after a call to the *onStart()* method if the activity restarts from a previous invocation in which the state was saved. As with *onCreate()*, this method is passed a Bundle object containing the previous state data. This method is typically used when it makes more sense to restore a previous state after the initialization of the activity has been performed in *onCreate()* and *onStart()*.

- **onSaveInstanceState(outState: Bundle?)** – Called before an activity is destroyed so that the current *dynamic state* (usually relating to the user interface) can be saved. The method is passed the Bundle object into which the state should be saved and which is subsequently passed through to the *onCreate()* and *onRestoreInstanceState()* methods when the activity is restarted. Note that this method is only called when the runtime ascertains that dynamic state needs to be saved.

When overriding the above methods, it is important to remember that, except for *onRestoreInstanceState()* and *onSaveInstanceState()*, the method implementation must include a call to the corresponding method in the superclass. For example, the following method overrides the *onRestart()* method but also includes a call to the superclass instance of the method:

```
override fun onRestart() {
    super.onRestart()
    Log.i(TAG, "onRestart")
}
```

Failure to make this superclass call in method overrides will result in the runtime throwing an exception during execution. While calls to the superclass in the *onRestoreInstanceState()* and *onSaveInstanceState()* methods are optional (they can, for example, be omitted when implementing custom save and restoration behavior) there are considerable benefits to using them, a subject that will be covered in the chapter entitled *"Saving and Restoring the State of an Android Activity"*.

21.5 Lifetimes

The final topic to be covered involves an outline of the *entire*, *visible*, and *foreground* lifetimes through which an activity or fragment will transition during execution:

- **Entire Lifetime** –The term "entire lifetime" is used to describe everything that takes place between the initial call to the *onCreate()* method and the call to *onDestroy()* before the object terminates.
- **Visible Lifetime** – Covers the periods of execution between the call to *onStart()* and *onStop()*. During this period, the activity or fragment is visible to the user though it may not be the object with which the user is currently interacting.
- **Foreground Lifetime** – Refers to the periods of execution between calls to the *onResume()* and *onPause()* methods.

It is important to note that an activity or fragment may pass through the *foreground* and *visible* lifetimes multiple times during the course of the *entire* lifetime.

The concepts of lifetimes and lifecycle methods are illustrated in Figure 21-2:

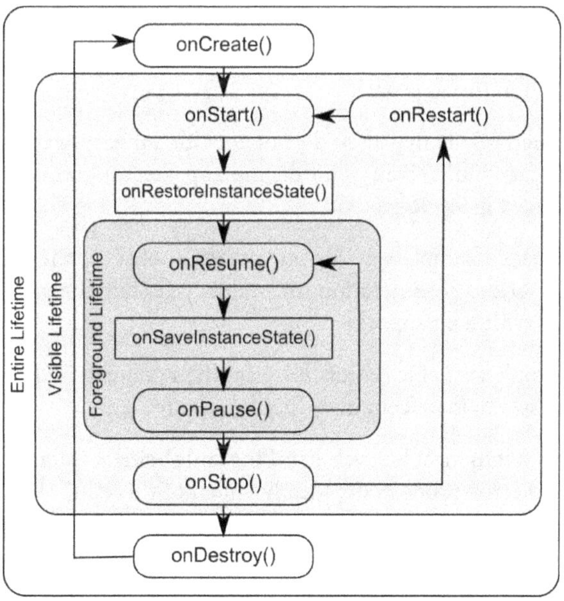

Figure 21-2

21.6 Foldable Devices and Multi-Resume

As discussed previously, an activity is considered to be in the resumed state when it has moved to the foreground and is the activity with which the user is currently interacting. On standard devices, an app can have one activity in the resumed state at any one time and all other activities are likely to be in the paused or stopped state.

For some time now, Android has included multi-window support, allowing multiple activities to appear simultaneously in either split-screen or freeform configurations. Although initially used primarily on large-screen tablet devices, this feature is likely to become more popular with the introduction of foldable devices.

On devices running Android 10 and on which multi-window support is enabled (as will be the case for most foldable devices), it will be possible for multiple app activities to be in the resumed state at the same time (a concept referred to as *multi-resume*) allowing those visible activities to continue functioning (for example streaming content or updating visual data) even when another activity currently has focus. Although multiple activities can be in the resumed state, only one of these activities will be considered the *topmost resumed activity* (in other words, the activity with which the user most recently interacted).

An activity can be notified that it has gained or lost the topmost resumed status by implementing the *onTopResumedActivityChanged()* callback method.

21.7 Disabling Configuration Change Restarts

As previously outlined, an activity may indicate that it is not to be restarted in the event of certain configuration changes. This is achieved by adding an *android:configChanges* directive to the activity element within the project manifest file. The following manifest file excerpt, for example, indicates that the activity should not be restarted in the event of configuration changes relating to orientation or device-wide font size:

```
<activity android:name=".MainActivity"
          android:configChanges="orientation|fontScale"
          android:label="@string/app_name">
```

21.8 Lifecycle Method Limitations

As discussed at the start of this chapter, lifecycle methods have been in use for many years and, until recently, were the only mechanism available for handling lifecycle state changes for activities and fragments. There are, however, areas for improvement in this approach.

One issue with the lifecycle methods is that they do not provide an easy way for an activity or fragment to discover its current lifecycle state at any given point during app execution. Instead, the object must track the state internally or wait for the next lifecycle method call.

Also, the methods do not provide a simple way for one object to observe the lifecycle state changes of other objects within an app. This is a serious consideration since a lifecycle state change in a given activity or fragment can impact many other objects within an app.

The lifecycle methods are also only available on subclasses of the Fragment and Activity classes. Therefore, it is impossible to build custom classes that are genuinely lifecycle aware.

Finally, the lifecycle methods result in most lifecycle handling code being written within the activity or fragment, which can lead to complex and error-prone code. Ideally, much of this code should reside in the other classes impacted by the state change. For example, an app that streams video might include a class designed specifically to manage the incoming stream. If the app needs to pause the stream when the main activity is stopped, the code to do so should reside in the streaming class, not the main activity.

All these problems and more are resolved using lifecycle-aware components, a topic that will be covered starting with the chapter entitled *"Modern Android App Architecture with Jetpack"*.

21.9 Summary

All activities are derived from the Android Activity class, which, in turn, contains several lifecycle methods that are designed to be called by the runtime system when the state of an activity changes. Similarly, the Fragment class contains several comparable methods. By overriding these methods, activities and fragments can respond to state changes and, where necessary, take steps to save and restore the current state of the activity and the application. Lifecycle state can be thought of as taking two forms. The persistent state refers to data that needs to be stored between application invocations (for example, to a file or database). Dynamic state, on the other hand, relates instead to the current appearance of the user interface.

Although lifecycle methods have some limitations that can be avoided using lifecycle-aware components, understanding these methods is essential to fully understand the new approaches to lifecycle management covered later in this book.

In this chapter, we have highlighted the lifecycle methods available to activities and covered the concept of activity lifetimes. In the next chapter, entitled *"Android Activity State Changes by Example"*, we will implement an example application that puts much of this theory into practice.

Chapter 22

22. Android Activity State Changes by Example

The previous chapters have discussed in detail the different states and lifecycles of the activities comprising an Android application. In this chapter, we will put the theory of handling activity state changes into practice by creating an example application. The purpose of this example application is to provide a real-world demonstration of an activity as it passes through various states within the Android runtime. In the next chapter, entitled *"Saving and Restoring the State of an Android Activity"*, the example project constructed in this chapter will be extended to demonstrate the saving and restoration of dynamic activity state.

22.1 Creating the State Change Example Project

The first step in this exercise is to create a new project. Launch Android Studio and, if necessary, close any currently open projects using the *File -> Close Project* menu option so that the Welcome screen appears.

Select the *New Project* option from the welcome screen and, within the resulting new project dialog, choose the Empty Views Activity template before clicking on the Next button.

Enter StateChange into the Name field and specify *com.ebookfrenzy.statechange* as the package name. Before clicking on the Finish button, change the Minimum API level setting to API 26: Android 8.0 (Oreo) and the Language menu to Kotlin. Upon completing the project creation process, the *StateChange* project should be listed in the Project tool window located along the left-hand edge of the Android Studio main window. Use the Gemini Agent or the steps outlined in section *18.8 Migrating a Project to View Binding* to convert the project to use view binding.

The next action to take involves the design of the user interface for the activity. This is stored in a file named *activity_main.xml* which should already be loaded into the Layout Editor tool. If it is not, navigate to it in the Project tool window where it can be found in the *app -> res -> layout* folder. Once located, double-clicking on the file will load it into the Android Studio Layout Editor tool.

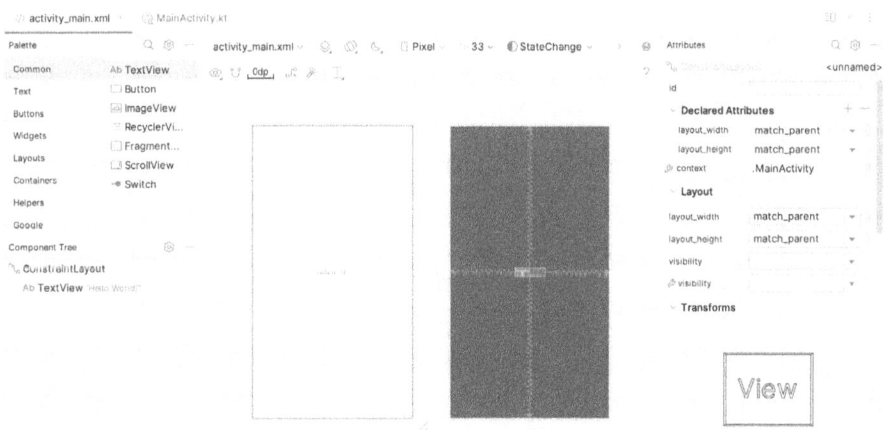

Figure 22-1

22.2 Designing the User Interface

With the user interface layout loaded into the Layout Editor tool, it is time to design the user interface for the example application. Instead of the "Hello World!" TextView currently in the user interface design, the activity requires an EditText view. Select the TextView object in the Component Tree panel and press the Delete key on the keyboard to remove it from the design.

From the Palette located on the left side of the Layout Editor, select the *Text* category and, from the list of text components, click and drag a *Plain Text* component over to the layout canvas. Move the component to the center of the display so that the center guidelines appear and drop it into place so that the layout resembles that of Figure 22-2.

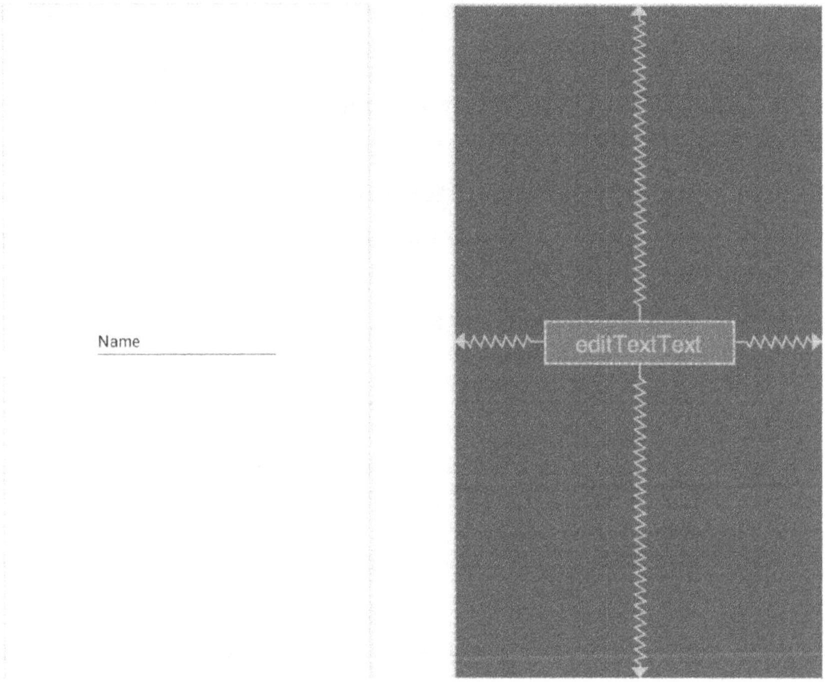

Figure 22-2

When using the EditText widget, it is necessary to specify an *input type* for the view. This defines the type of text or data the user will enter. For example, if the input type is set to *Phone*, the user will be restricted to entering numerical digits into the view. Alternatively, if the input type is set to *TextCapCharacters,* the input will default to upper-case characters. Input type settings may also be combined.

For this example, we will use the default input type to support general text input. To choose a different setting in the future, select the EditText widget in the layout and locate the inputType entry within the Attributes tool window. Next, click the flag icon to the left of the current setting to open the list of options, as shown in Figure 22-3 below. The Type menu provides options to restrict the input to text, numbers, dates and times, and phone numbers. The Variations menu provides additional options for the currently selected input type. For example, a variation is available for the text input type for email addresses as input.

Once a type and variation have been chosen, the input type may be customized further using the list of flag checkboxes:

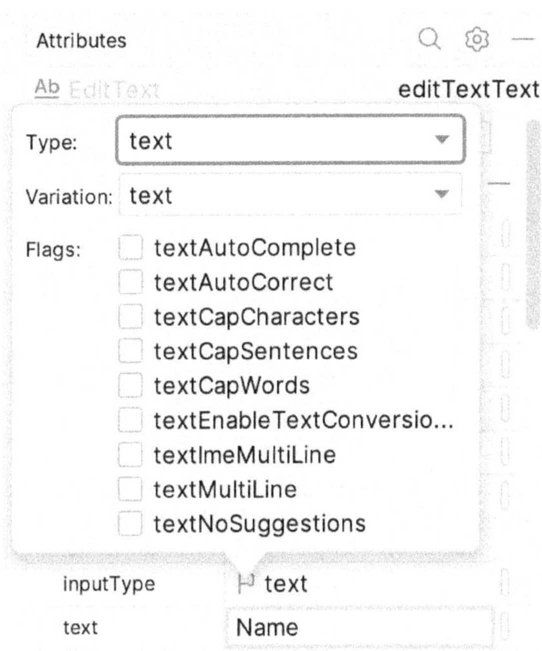

Figure 22-3

Remaining in the Attributes tool window, change the view's id to *editText* and click on the Refactor button in the resulting dialog.

By default, the EditText displays text which reads "Name". Remaining within the Attributes panel, delete this from the *text* property field so that the view is blank within the layout.

Before continuing, click the *Infer Constraints* button in the layout editor toolbar to add any missing constraints.

22.3 Overriding the Activity Lifecycle Methods

At this point, the project contains a single activity named *MainActivity*, derived from the Android *AppCompatActivity* class. The source code for this activity is contained within the *MainActivity.kt* file, which should already be open in an editor session and represented by a tab in the editor tab bar. If the file is no longer open, navigate to it in the Project tool window panel (*app -> kotlin+java -> com.ebookfrenzy.statechange -> MainActivity*) and double-click on it to load the file into the editor.

So far, the only lifecycle method overridden by the activity is the *onCreate()* method which has been implemented to call the superclass instance of the method before setting up the user interface for the activity. We will now modify this method to output a diagnostic message in the Android Studio Logcat panel each time it executes. For this, we will use the *Log* class, which requires that we import *android.util.Log* and declare a tag that will enable us to filter these messages in the log output:

```
package com.ebookfrenzy.statechange
.
.
import android.util.Log

import com.ebookfrenzy.statechange.databinding.ActivityMainBinding

class MainActivity : AppCompatActivity() {
```

```
    private lateinit var binding: ActivityMainBinding
    private val TAG = "StateChange"

    override fun onCreate(savedInstanceState: Bundle?) {
        super.onCreate(savedInstanceState)
.
.
        Log.i(TAG, "onCreate")
    }
}
.
.
```

The next task is to override more methods, each containing a corresponding log call. These override methods may be added manually or generated using the *Alt-Insert* keyboard shortcut as outlined in the chapter entitled *"The Basics of the Android Studio Code Editor"*. Note that the Log calls will still need to be added manually if the methods are being auto-generated:

```
override fun onStart() {
    super.onStart()
    Log.i(TAG, "onStart")
}

override fun onResume() {
    super.onResume()
    Log.i(TAG, "onResume")
}

override fun onPause() {
    super.onPause()
    Log.i(TAG, "onPause")
}

override fun onStop() {
    super.onStop()
    Log.i(TAG, "onStop")
}

override fun onRestart() {
    super.onRestart()
    Log.i(TAG, "onRestart")
}

override fun onDestroy() {
    super.onDestroy()
    Log.i(TAG, "onDestroy")
```

```
}

override fun onSaveInstanceState(outState: Bundle) {
    super.onSaveInstanceState(outState)
    Log.i(TAG, "onSaveInstanceState")
}

override fun onRestoreInstanceState(savedInstanceState: Bundle) {
    super.onRestoreInstanceState(savedInstanceState)
    Log.i(TAG, "onRestoreInstanceState")
}
```

22.4 Filtering the Logcat Panel

The purpose of the code added to the overridden methods in *MainActivity.kt* is to output logging information to the *Logcat* tool window, which is displayed using the button shown in Figure 22-4:

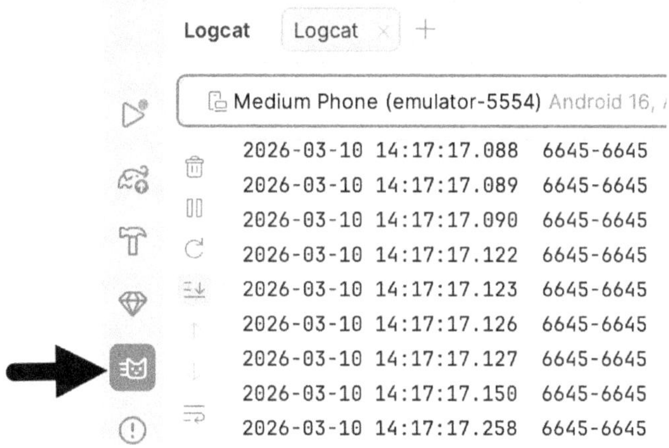

Figure 22-4

The Logcat tool window can be configured to display all events relating to the device or emulator session or restricted to those events that relate to the currently selected app. The output can also be restricted to only those log events that match a specified filter.

When displayed while the current app is running, the Logcat tool window will appear as shown in Figure 22-5 below:

Figure 22-5

The menu marked A in the above figure allows you to select the device or emulator for which log output will be displayed. This output appears in the output panel marked C. The log output can be filtered by entering options into the field marked B. The default key setting, *package:mine*, restricts the output to log messages generated by the current app package (in this case com.ebookfrenzy.statechange). Leaving this field blank will allow log output from the selected device or emulator to be displayed, including diagnostic messages generated by the operating system. Keys may also be combined to filter the output further. For example, we can configure the Logcat panel to display only messages associated with our StateChange tag as follows:

```
package:mine tag:StateChange
```

We can exclude output by prefixing the key with a minus (-) sign. In addition to the StateChange tag, we might have diagnostic messages using a different tag. To filter the log so that output from this second tag is excluded, we could enter the following key options:

```
package:mine tag:StateChange -tag:OtherTag
```

In addition to your own tag values, it is also possible to select from a range of predefined diagnostic tags built into Android. Logcat will display a list of matching tags as you type into the filter field, as shown in Figure 22-6:

Figure 22-6

Alternatively, use Ctrl-Space to access a complete list of filtering suggestions.

The *level* key may be used to control which messages are displayed based on severity. To filter out all messages except error messages, the following key would be used:

```
level:error
```

In addition to *error*, the Logcat panel supports *verbose, info*, *warn*, and *assert* level settings.

Logcat also supports multiple log panels, each with its own filter settings. To add another panel, click on the + button marked D in Figure 22-5 above. Switch between different panels using the corresponding tabs, or display them side-by-side by right-clicking on the currently displayed panel and selecting either the *Split-Right* or *Split-Down* menu option to arrange the panels horizontally or vertically. To rename a panel, right-click on the tab and select the *Rename Tab* option. Before proceeding, close all but one Logcat panel and configure the filter as follows:

```
package:mine tag:StateChange
```

22.5 Running the Application

For optimal results, the application should be run on a physical Android device or emulator. With the device configured and connected to the development computer, click on the run button in the Android Studio toolbar as shown in Figure 22-7 below:

Figure 22-7

Select the physical Android device or emulator from the *Choose Device* dialog if it appears (assuming you have not already configured it as the default target). After Android Studio has built the application and installed it on the device, it should start up and be running in the foreground.

A review of the Logcat panel should indicate which methods have so far been triggered:

Figure 22-8

22.6 Experimenting with the Activity

With the diagnostics working, it is time to exercise the application to understand the activity lifecycle state changes. To begin with, consider the initial sequence of log events in the Logcat panel:

```
onCreate
onStart
onResume
```

Clearly, the initial state changes are exactly as outlined in *"Understanding Android Application and Activity Lifecycles"*. Note, however, that a call was not made to *onRestoreInstanceState()* since the Android runtime detected that there was no state to restore in this situation.

Go to the device Home screen and note the sequence of method calls reported in the log as follows:

```
onPause
onStop
onSaveInstanceState
```

In this case, the runtime has noticed that the activity is no longer in the foreground, is not visible to the user, and has stopped the activity, but not without providing an opportunity for the activity to save the dynamic state. Depending on whether the runtime ultimately destroyed the activity or restarted it, the activity will either be notified it has been restarted via a call to *onRestart()* or will go through the creation sequence again when the user returns to the activity.

As outlined in *"Understanding Android Application and Activity Lifecycles"*, the destruction and recreation of an activity can be triggered by making a configuration change to the device, such as rotating from portrait to landscape. To see this in action, rotate the device while the *StateChange* application is in the foreground. When using the emulator, device rotation may be simulated using the rotation button located in the emulator toolbar. To complete the rotation, it may also be necessary to enable auto-rotation in the Settings app (*Settings -> Display & touch -> Auto-rotate screen*).

The resulting sequence of method calls in the log should read as follows:

```
onPause
onStop
onSaveInstanceState
onDestroy
onCreate
onStart
onRestoreInstanceState
onResume
```

Clearly, the runtime system has allowed the activity to save the state before being destroyed and restarted.

22.7 Summary

The adage that a picture is worth a thousand words holds just as true for examples when learning a new programming paradigm. In this chapter, we created an example Android application to demonstrate the different lifecycle states an activity will likely pass through. While developing the project in this chapter, we also looked at a mechanism for generating diagnostic logging information from within an activity.

In the next chapter, we will extend the *StateChange* example project to demonstrate how to save and restore an activity's dynamic state.

Chapter 23

23. Saving and Restoring the State of an Android Activity

If the previous few chapters have achieved their objective, it should now be clearer as to the importance of saving and restoring the state of a user interface at particular points in the lifetime of an activity.

In this chapter, we will extend the example application created in *"Android Activity State Changes by Example"* to demonstrate the steps involved in saving and restoring state when the runtime system destroys and recreates an activity.

A key component of saving and restoring dynamic state involves using the Android SDK *Bundle* class, a topic that will also be covered in this chapter.

23.1 Saving Dynamic State

As we have learned, an activity can save dynamic state information via a call from the runtime system to the activity's implementation of the *onSaveInstanceState()* method. Passed through as an argument to the method is a reference to a Bundle object into which the method must store any dynamic data that needs to be saved. The Bundle object is then stored by the runtime system on behalf of the activity and subsequently passed through as an argument to the activity's *onCreate()* and *onRestoreInstanceState()* methods if and when they are called. The data can then be retrieved from the Bundle object within these methods and used to restore the state of the activity.

23.2 Default Saving of User Interface State

In the previous chapter, the diagnostic output from the *StateChange* example application showed that an activity goes through several state changes when the device on which it is running is rotated sufficiently to trigger an orientation change.

Launch the *StateChange* application once again and enter some text into the EditText field before performing the device rotation (on devices or emulators running Android 9 or later, it may be necessary to tap the rotation button in the status bar to complete the rotation). Having rotated the device, the following state change sequence should appear in the Logcat window:

```
onPause
onStop
onSaveInstanceState
onDestroy
onCreate
onStart
onRestoreInstanceState
onResume
```

Clearly, this has resulted in the activity being destroyed and re-created. A review of the user interface of the running application, however, should show that the text entered into the EditText field has been preserved. Given that the activity was destroyed and recreated and we did not add any specific code to ensure the text was saved and restored, this behavior requires some explanation.

In fact, most view widgets included with the Android SDK already implement the behavior necessary to save and restore state when an activity is restarted automatically. The only requirement to enable this behavior is for the *onSaveInstanceState()* and *onRestoreInstanceState()* override methods in the activity to include calls to the equivalent methods of the superclass:

```
override fun onSaveInstanceState(outState: Bundle?) {
    super.onSaveInstanceState(outState)
    Log.i(TAG, "onSaveInstanceState")
}

override fun onRestoreInstanceState(savedInstanceState: Bundle?) {
    super.onRestoreInstanceState(savedInstanceState)
    Log.i(TAG, "onRestoreInstanceState")
}
```

The automatic saving of state for a user interface view can be disabled in the XML layout file by setting the *android:saveEnabled* property to *false*. The automatic state saving for a user interface view can be turned off in the XML layout file by setting the android:saveEnabled property to false. For this example, we will disable the automatic state-saving mechanism for the EditText view in the user interface layout and then add code to the application to manually save and restore the view's state.

To configure the EditText view such that state will not be saved and restored if the activity is restarted, edit the *activity_main.xml* file so that the entry for the view reads as follows (note that the XML can be edited by switching the Layout Editor to Code view mode as outlined in *"Creating an Example Android App in Android Studio"*):

```
<EditText
    android:id="@+id/editText"
    android:layout_width="wrap_content"
    android:layout_height="wrap_content"
    android:ems="10"
    android:inputType="text"
    android:saveEnabled="false"
    app:layout_constraintBottom_toBottomOf="parent"
    app:layout_constraintEnd_toEndOf="parent"
    app:layout_constraintStart_toStartOf="parent"
    app:layout_constraintTop_toTopOf="parent" />
```

After making the change, run the application, enter text, and rotate the device to verify that the text is no longer saved and restored.

23.3 The Bundle Class

For situations where state needs to be saved beyond the default functionality provided by the user interface view components, the Bundle class provides a container for storing data using a *key-value pair* mechanism. The *keys* take the form of string values, while the *values* associated with those *keys* can be a primitive value or any object that implements the Android *Parcelable* interface. A wide range of classes already implements the Parcelable interface. Custom classes may be made "parcelable" by implementing the set of methods defined in the Parcelable interface, details of which can be found in the Android documentation at:

https://developer.android.com/reference/android/os/Parcelable.html

The Bundle class also contains a set of methods that can be used to get and set key-value pairs for various data types, including both primitive types (including Boolean, char, double, and float values) and objects (such as Strings and CharSequences).

For this example, having disabled the automatic saving of text for the EditText view, we need to ensure that the text entered into the EditText field by the user is saved into the Bundle object and subsequently restored. This will demonstrate how to manually save and restore state within an Android application and will be achieved using the *putCharSequence()* and *getCharSequence()* methods of the Bundle class, respectively.

23.4 Saving the State

The first step in extending the *StateChange* application is to make sure that the text entered by the user is extracted from the EditText component within the *onSaveInstanceState()* method of the *MainActivity* activity and then saved as a key-value pair into the Bundle object.

To extract the text from the EditText object, we must first identify that object in the user interface. Clearly, this involves bridging the gap between the Kotlin code for the activity (contained in the *MainActivity.kt* source code file) and the XML representation of the user interface (contained within the *activity_main.xml* resource file). To extract the text entered into the EditText component, we need to gain access to that user interface object.

Each component within a user interface has associated with it a unique identifier. By default, the Layout Editor tool constructs the id for a newly added component from the object type. If more than one view of the same type is contained in the layout, the type name is followed by a sequential number (though this can, and should, be changed to something more meaningful by the developer). As can be seen by checking the *Component Tree* panel within the Android Studio main window when the *activity_main.xml* file is selected and the Layout Editor tool displayed, the EditText component has been assigned the id *editText*:

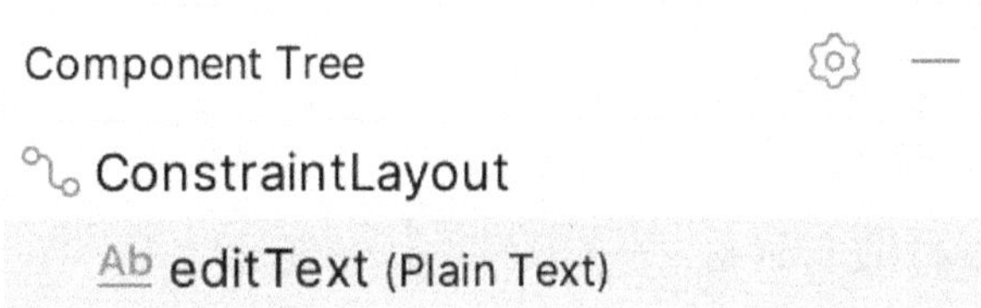

Figure 23-1

We can now obtain the text that the editText view contains via the object's text property, which, in turn, returns the current text:

```
val userText = binding.editText.text
```

Finally, we can save the text using the Bundle object's *putCharSequence()* method, passing through the key (this can be any string value, but in this instance, we will declare it as "savedText") and the *userText* object as arguments:

```
outState?.putCharSequence("savedText", userText)
```

Bringing this all together gives us a modified *onSaveInstanceState()* method in the *MainActivity.kt* file that reads as follows:

```
override fun onSaveInstanceState(outState: Bundle) {
    super.onSaveInstanceState(outState)
    Log.i(TAG, "onSaveInstanceState")

    val userText = binding.editText.text
    outState.putCharSequence("savedText", userText)
```

```
}
```

Now that steps have been taken to save the state, the next phase is to restore it when needed.

23.5 Restoring the State

The saved dynamic state can be restored in those lifecycle methods that are passed the Bundle object as an argument. This leaves the developer with the choice of using either *onCreate()* or *onRestoreInstanceState()*. The method to use will depend on the nature of the activity. In instances where state is best restored after the activity's initialization tasks have been performed, the *onRestoreInstanceState()* method is generally more suitable. For this example, we will add code to the *onRestoreInstanceState()* method to extract the saved state from the Bundle using the "savedText" key. We can then display the text on the editText component using the object's *setText()* method:

```
override fun onRestoreInstanceState(savedInstanceState: Bundle) {
    super.onRestoreInstanceState(savedInstanceState)
    Log.i(TAG, "onRestoreInstanceState")

    val userText = savedInstanceState.getCharSequence("savedText")
    binding.editText.setText(userText)
}
```

23.6 Testing the Application

All that remains is once again to build and run the *StateChange* application. Once running and in the foreground, touch the EditText component and enter some text before rotating the device to another orientation. Whereas the text changes were previously lost, the new text is retained within the editText component thanks to the code we have added to the activity in this chapter.

Having verified that the code performs as expected, comment out the *super.onSaveInstanceState()* and *super.onRestoreInstanceState()* calls from the two methods, re-launch the app and note that the text is still preserved after a device rotation. The default save and restoration system has essentially been replaced by a custom implementation, thereby providing a way to dynamically and selectively save and restore state within an activity.

23.7 Summary

The saving and restoration of dynamic state in an Android application is a matter of implementing the appropriate code in the appropriate lifecycle methods. For most user interface views, this is handled automatically by the Activity superclass. In other instances, this typically consists of extracting values and settings within the *onSaveInstanceState()* method and saving the data as key-value pairs within the Bundle object passed through to the activity by the runtime system.

State can be restored in either the *onCreate()* or the *onRestoreInstanceState()* methods of the activity by extracting values from the Bundle object and updating the activity based on the stored values.

In this chapter, we have used these techniques to update the *StateChange* project so that the Activity retains changes through the destruction and subsequent recreation of an activity.

Chapter 24

24. Understanding Android Views, View Groups and Layouts

With the possible exception of listening to streaming audio, a user's interaction with an Android device is primarily visual and tactile. All of this interaction occurs through the user interfaces of the applications installed on the device, including both the built-in applications and any third-party applications installed by the user. Therefore, it should come as no surprise that a critical element of developing Android applications involves designing and creating user interfaces.

This chapter covers the Android user interface structure, including an overview of the elements that can be combined to make up a user interface: Views, View Groups, and Layouts.

24.1 Designing for Different Android Devices

The term "Android device" covers many tablet and smartphone products with different screen sizes and resolutions. As a result, application user interfaces must now be carefully designed to ensure correct presentation on as wide a range of display sizes as possible. A key part of this is ensuring that the user interface layouts resize correctly when run on different devices. This can largely be achieved through careful planning and using the layout managers outlined in this chapter.

It is also essential to remember that most Android-based smartphones and tablets can be held by the user in both portrait and landscape orientations. A well-designed user interface should be able to adapt to such changes and make sensible layout adjustments to utilize the available screen space in each orientation.

24.2 Views and View Groups

Every item in a user interface is a subclass of the Android *View* class (to be precise *android.view.View*). The Android SDK provides a set of pre-built views that can be used to construct a user interface. Typical examples include standard items such as the Button, CheckBox, ProgressBar, and TextView classes. Such views are also referred to as *widgets* or *components*. For requirements not met by the widgets supplied with the SDK, new views may be created by subclassing and extending an existing class or creating an entirely new component by building directly on top of the View class.

A view can also comprise multiple other views (otherwise known as a *composite view*). Such views are subclassed from the Android *ViewGroup* class (*android.view.ViewGroup*), which is itself a subclass of *View*. An example of such a view is the RadioGroup, which is intended to contain multiple RadioButton objects such that only one can be in the "on" position at any one time. Regarding structure, composite views consist of a single parent view (derived from the ViewGroup class and otherwise known as a *container view* or *root element)* capable of containing other views (known as *child views*).

Another category of ViewGroup-based container view is that of the layout manager.

24.3 Android Layout Managers

In addition to the widget style views discussed in the previous section, the SDK also includes a set of views referred to as *layouts*. Layouts are container views (and, therefore, subclassed from ViewGroup) designed to control how child views are positioned on the screen.

The Android SDK includes the following layout views that may be used within an Android user interface design:

- **ConstraintLayout** – Introduced in Android 7, this layout manager is recommended for most layout requirements. ConstraintLayout allows the positioning and behavior of the views in a layout to be defined by simple constraint settings assigned to each child view. The flexibility of this layout allows complex layouts to be quickly and easily created without the necessity to nest other layout types inside each other, resulting in improved layout performance. ConstraintLayout is also tightly integrated into the Android Studio Layout Editor tool. Unless otherwise stated, this is the layout of choice for most of examples in this book.

- **LinearLayout** – Positions child views in a single row or column depending on the orientation selected. A *weight* value can be set on each child to specify how much of the layout space that child should occupy relative to other children.

- **TableLayout** – Arranges child views into a grid format of rows and columns. Each row within a table is represented by a *TableRow* object child, which, in turn, contains a view object for each cell.

- **FrameLayout** – The purpose of the FrameLayout is to allocate an area of the screen, typically to display a single view. If multiple child views are added, they will, by default, appear on top of each other and be positioned in the top left-hand corner of the layout area. Alternate positioning of individual child views can be achieved by setting gravity values on each child. For example, setting a *center_vertical* gravity value on a child will cause it to be positioned in the vertical center of the containing FrameLayout view.

- **RelativeLayout** – The RelativeLayout allows child views to be positioned relative to each other and the containing layout view through the specification of alignments and margins on child views. For example, child *View A* may be configured to be positioned in the vertical and horizontal center of the containing RelativeLayout view. *View B*, on the other hand, might also be configured to be centered horizontally within the layout view but positioned 30 pixels above the top edge of *View A*, thereby making the vertical position *relative* to that of *View A*. The RelativeLayout manager can be helpful when designing a user interface that must work on various screen sizes and orientations.

- **AbsoluteLayout** – Allows child views to be positioned at specific X and Y coordinates within the containing layout view. Using this layout is discouraged since it lacks the flexibility to respond to screen size and orientation changes.

- **GridLayout** – A GridLayout instance is divided by invisible lines that form a grid containing rows and columns of cells. Child views are then placed in cells and may be configured to cover multiple cells horizontally and vertically, allowing a wide range of layout options to be quickly and easily implemented. Gaps between components in a GridLayout may be implemented by placing a special type of view called a *Space* view into adjacent cells or setting margin parameters.

- **CoordinatorLayout** – Introduced as part of the Android Design Support Library with Android 5.0, the CoordinatorLayout is designed specifically for coordinating the appearance and behavior of the app bar across the top of an application screen with other view elements. When creating a new activity using the Basic Views Activity template, the parent view in the main layout will be implemented using a CoordinatorLayout instance. This layout manager will be covered in greater detail, starting with the chapter *"Working with the Floating Action Button and Snackbar"*.

When considering layouts in the user interface for an Android application, it is worth keeping in mind that, as outlined in the next section, these can be nested within each other to create a user interface design of just about any necessary level of complexity.

24.4 The View Hierarchy

Each view in a user interface represents a rectangular area of the display. A view is responsible for what is drawn in that rectangle and responding to events within that part of the screen (such as a touch event).

A user interface screen is comprised of a view hierarchy with a *root view* positioned at the top of the tree and child views positioned on branches below. The child of a container view appears on top of its parent view and is constrained to appear within the bounds of the parent view's display area. Consider, for example, the user interface illustrated in Figure 24-1:

Figure 24-1

In addition to the visible button and checkbox views, the user interface actually includes a number of layout views that control how the visible views are positioned. Figure 24-2 shows an alternative view of the user interface, this time highlighting the presence of the layout views in relation to the child views:

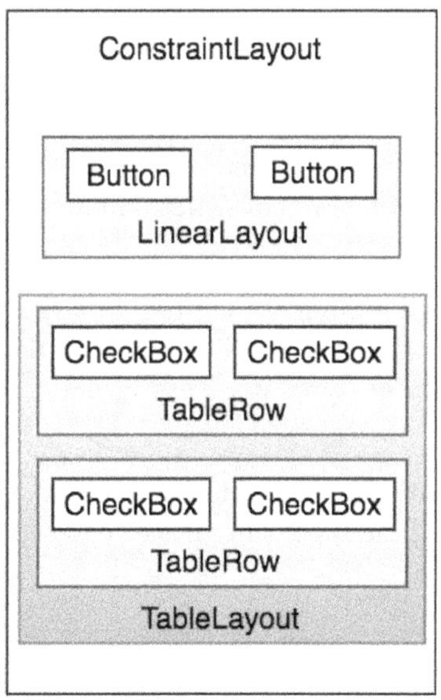

Figure 24-2

As was previously discussed, user interfaces are constructed in the form of a view hierarchy with a root view at the top. This being the case, we can also visualize the above user interface example in the form of the view tree illustrated in Figure 24-3:

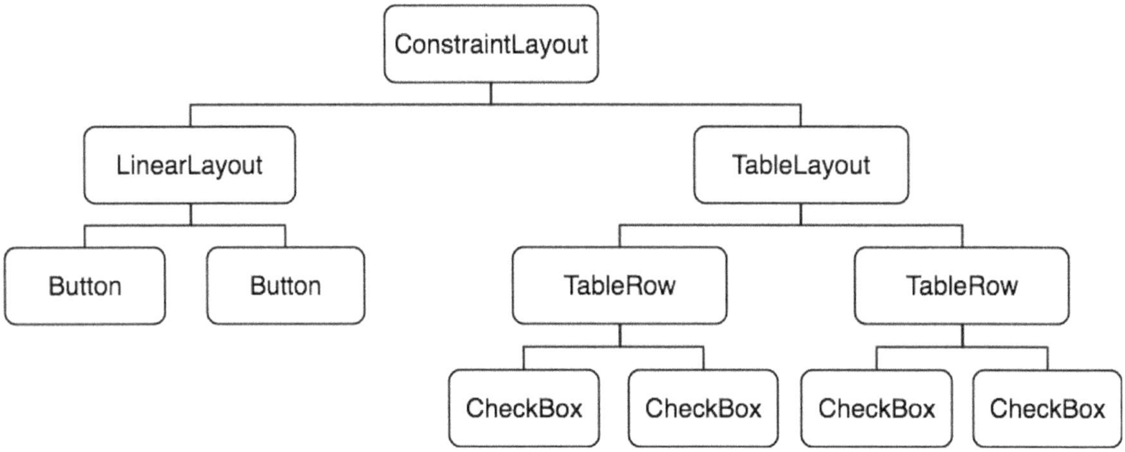

Figure 24-3

The view hierarchy diagram gives probably the clearest overview of the relationship between the various views that make up the user interface shown in Figure 24-1. When a user interface is displayed to the user, the Android runtime walks the view hierarchy, starting at the root view and working down the tree as it renders each view.

24.5 Creating User Interfaces

With a clearer understanding of the concepts of views, layouts and the view hierarchy, the following few chapters will focus on the steps involved in creating user interfaces for Android activities. In fact, there are three different approaches to user interface design: using the Android Studio Layout Editor tool, handwriting XML layout resource files or writing Kotlin code, each of which will be covered.

24.6 Summary

Each element within a user interface screen of an Android application is a view that is ultimately subclassed from the *android.view.View* class. Each view represents a rectangular area of the device display and is responsible both for what appears in that rectangle and for handling events that take place within the view's bounds. Multiple views may be combined to create a single *composite view*. The views within a composite view are children of a *container view* which is generally a subclass of *android.view.ViewGroup* (which is itself a subclass of *android.view.View*). A user interface is comprised of views constructed in the form of a view hierarchy.

The Android SDK includes a range of pre-built views that can be used to create a user interface. These include basic components such as text fields and buttons, in addition to a range of layout managers that can be used to control the positioning of child views. If the supplied views do not meet a specific requirement, custom views may be created, either by extending or combining existing views, or by subclassing *android.view.View* and creating an entirely new class of view.

User interfaces may be created using the Android Studio Layout Editor tool, handwriting XML layout resource files or by writing Kotlin code. Each of these approaches will be covered in the chapters that follow.

Chapter 25

25. A Guide to the Android Studio Layout Editor Tool

It is challenging to think of an Android application concept that does not require some form of user interface. Most Android devices come equipped with a touch screen and keyboard (either virtual or physical), and taps and swipes are the primary interaction between the user and the application. Invariably these interactions take place through the application's user interface.

A well-designed and implemented user interface, an essential factor in creating a successful and popular Android application, can vary from simple to highly complex, depending on the design requirements of the individual application. Regardless of the level of complexity, the Android Studio Layout Editor tool significantly simplifies the task of designing and implementing Android user interfaces.

25.1 Basic vs. Empty Views Activity Templates

As outlined in the chapter entitled *"The Anatomy of an Android App"*, Android applications comprise one or more activities. An activity is a standalone module of application functionality that usually correlates directly to a single user interface screen. As such, when working with the Android Studio Layout Editor, we are invariably work on the layout for an activity.

When creating a new Android Studio project, several templates are available to be used as the starting point for the user interface of the main activity. The most basic templates are the Basic Views Activity and Empty Views Activity templates. Although these seem similar at first glance, there are considerable differences between the two options. To see these differences within the layout editor, use the View Options menu to enable Show System UI, as shown in Figure 25-1 below:

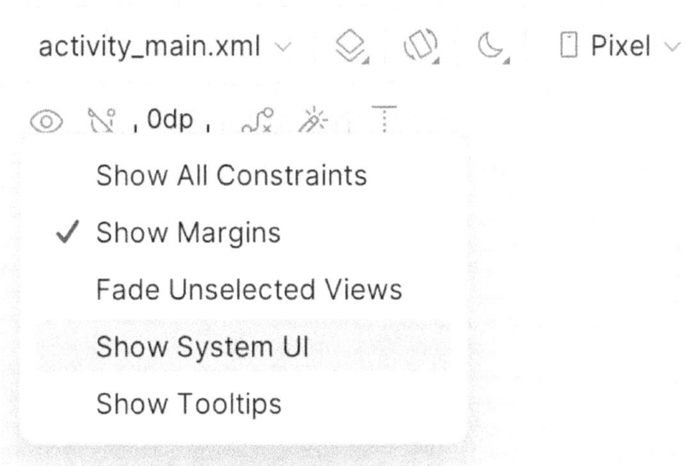

Figure 25-1

The Empty Views Activity template creates a single layout file consisting of a ConstraintLayout manager instance containing a TextView object, as shown in Figure 25-2:

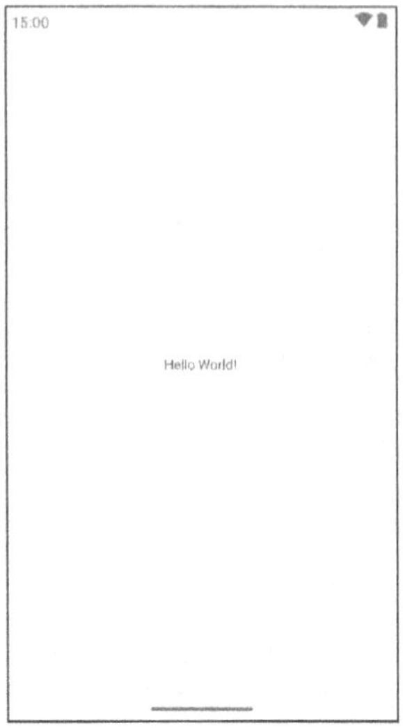

Figure 25-2

The Basic Views Activity, on the other hand, consists of multiple layout files. The top-level layout file has a CoordinatorLayout as the root view, a configurable app bar (which contains a toolbar) that appears across the top of the device screen (marked A in Figure 25-3), and a floating action button (the email button marked B). In addition to these items, the *activity_main.xml* layout file contains a reference to a second file named *content_main.xml* containing the content layout (marked C):

Figure 25-3

The Basic Views Activity contains layouts for two screens containing a button and a text view. This template aims to demonstrate how to implement navigation between multiple screens within an app. If an unmodified app using the Basic Views Activity template were to be run, the first of these two screens would appear (marked A in Figure 25-4). Pressing the Next button would navigate to the second screen (B), which, in turn, contains a button to return to the first screen:

Figure 25-4

This app behavior uses of two Android features referred to as *fragments* and *navigation*, which will be covered starting with the chapters entitled *"An Introduction to Android Fragments"* and *"An Overview of the Navigation Architecture Component"* respectively.

The *content_main.xml* file contains a special fragment, known as a Navigation Host Fragment which allows different content to be switched in and out of view depending on the settings configured in the *res -> layout -> nav_graph.xml* file. In the case of the Basic Views Activity template, the *nav_graph.xml* file is configured to switch between the user interface layouts defined in the *fragment_first.xml* and *fragment_second.xml* files based on the Next and Previous button selections made by the user.

The Empty Views Activity template is helpful if you need neither a floating action button nor a menu in your activity and do not need the special app bar behavior provided by the CoordinatorLayout, such as options to make the app bar and toolbar collapse from view during certain scrolling operations (a topic covered in the chapter entitled *"Working with the AppBar and Collapsing Toolbar Layouts"*). However, the Basic Views Activity is helpful because it provides these elements by default. In fact, it is often quicker to create a new activity using the Basic Views Activity template and delete the elements you do not require than to use the Empty Views Activity template and manually implement behavior such as collapsing toolbars, a menu, or a floating action button.

Since not all of the examples in this book require the features of the Basic Views Activity template, however, most of the examples in this chapter will use the Empty Views Activity template unless the example requires one or other of the features provided by the Basic Views Activity template.

For future reference, if you need a menu but not a floating action button, use the Basic Views Activity and follow these steps to delete the floating action button:

1. Double-click on the main *activity_main.xml* layout file in the Project tool window under *app -> res -> layout* to load it into the Layout Editor. With the layout loaded into the Layout Editor tool, select the floating action button and tap the keyboard *Delete* key to remove the object from the layout.

2. Locate and edit the Kotlin code for the activity (located under *app -> kotlin+java -> <package name> -> <activity class name>* and remove the floating action button code from the onCreate method as follows:

```
override fun onCreate(savedInstanceState: Bundle?) {
    super.onCreate(savedInstanceState)

    binding = ActivityMainBinding.inflate(layoutInflater)
    setContentView(binding.root)

    setSupportActionBar(binding.toolbar)

    val navController = findNavController(R.id.nav_host_fragment_content_main)
    appBarConfiguration = AppBarConfiguration(navController.graph)
    setupActionBarWithNavController(navController, appBarConfiguration)

    binding.fab.setOnClickListener { view ->
        Snackbar.make(view, "Replace with your own action", Snackbar.LENGTH_LONG)
            .setAnchorView(R.id.fab)
            .setAction("Action", null).show()
    }
}
```

If you need a floating action button but no menu, use the Basic Views Activity template and follow these steps:

1. Edit the main activity class file and delete the *onCreateOptionsMenu* and *onOptionsItemSelected* methods.
2. Select the *res -> menu* item in the Project tool window and tap the keyboard *Delete* key to remove the folder and corresponding menu resource files from the project.

If you need to use the Basic Views Activity template but need neither the navigation features nor the second content fragment, follow these steps:

1. Within the Project tool window, navigate to and double-click on the *app -> res -> navigation -> nav_graph.xml* file to load it into the navigation editor.
2. Within the editor, select the SecondFragment entry in the graph panel and tap the keyboard delete key to remove it from the graph.
3. Locate and delete the *SecondFragment.kt* (*app -> kotlin+java -> <package name> -> SecondFragment*) and *fragment_second.xml* (*app -> res -> layout -> fragment_second.xml*) files.
4. The final task is to remove some code from the FirstFragment class so that the Button view no longer navigates to the now non-existent second fragment when clicked. Locate the *FirstFragment.kt* file, double-click on it to load it into the editor, and remove the code from the *onViewCreated()* method so that it reads as follows:

```
override fun onViewCreated(view: View, savedInstanceState: Bundle?) {
    super.onViewCreated(view, savedInstanceState)

    binding.buttonFirst.setOnClickListener {
        findNavController().navigate(R.id.action_FirstFragment_to_SecondFragment)
    }
}
```

25.2 The Android Studio Layout Editor

As demonstrated in previous chapters, the Layout Editor tool provides a "what you see is what you get" (WYSIWYG) environment in which views can be selected from a palette and then placed onto a canvas representing the display of an Android device. Once a view has been placed on the canvas, it can be moved, deleted, and resized (subject to the constraints of the parent view). Moreover, various properties relating to the selected view may be modified using the Attributes tool window.

Under the surface, the Layout Editor tool constructs an XML resource file containing the definition of the user interface that is being designed. As such, the Layout Editor tool operates in three distinct modes: Design, Code, and Split.

25.3 Design Mode

In design mode, the user interface can be visually manipulated by directly working with the view palette and the graphical representation of the layout. Figure 25-5 highlights the key areas of the Android Studio Layout Editor tool in design mode:

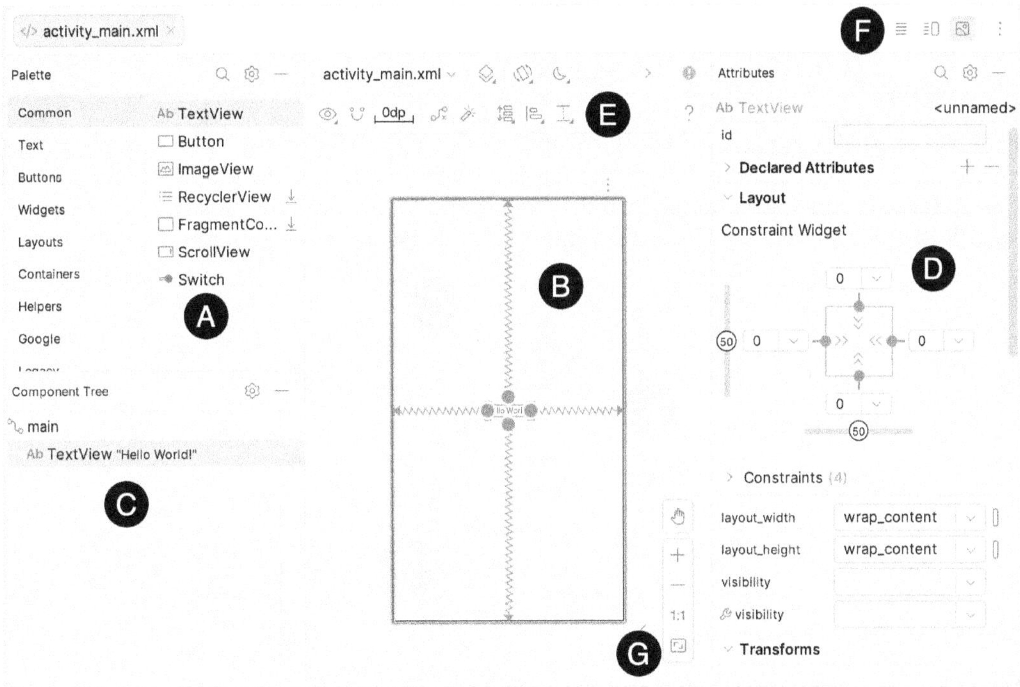

Figure 25-5

A - Palette – The palette provides access to the range of view components the Android SDK provides. These are grouped into categories for easy navigation. Items may be added to the layout by dragging a view component from the palette and dropping it at the desired position on the layout.

B - Device Screen – The device screen provides a visual "what you see is what you get" representation of the user interface layout as it is being designed. This layout allows direct design manipulation by allowing views to be selected, deleted, moved, and resized. The device model represented by the layout can be changed anytime using a menu in the toolbar.

C - Component Tree – As outlined in the previous chapter (*"Understanding Android Views, View Groups and Layouts"*), user interfaces are constructed using a hierarchical structure. The component tree provides a visual overview of the hierarchy of the user interface design. Selecting an element from the component tree will cause the corresponding view in the layout to be selected. Similarly, selecting a view from the device screen layout will select that view in the component tree hierarchy.

D – **Attributes** – All of the component views listed in the palette have associated with them a set of attributes that can be used to adjust the behavior and appearance of that view. The Layout Editor's attributes panel provides access to the attributes of the currently selected view in the layout allowing changes to be made.

E – **Toolbar** – The Layout Editor toolbar provides quick access to a wide range of options, including, amongst other options, the ability to zoom in and out of the device screen layout, change the device model currently displayed, rotate the layout between portrait and landscape and switch to a different Android SDK API level. The toolbar also has a set of context-sensitive buttons which will appear when relevant view types are selected in the device screen layout.

F – **Mode Switching Controls** – These three buttons provide a way to switch back and forth between the Layout Editor tool's Design, Code, and Split modes.

G - **Zoom and Pan Controls** - This control panel allows you to zoom in and out of the design canvas, grab the canvas, and pan around to find obscured areas when zoomed in.

25.4 The Palette

The Layout Editor palette is organized into two panels designed to make it easy to locate and preview view components for addition to a layout design. The category panel (marked A in Figure 25-6) lists the different categories of view components supported by the Android SDK. When a category is selected from the list, the second panel (B) updates to display a list of the components that fall into that category:

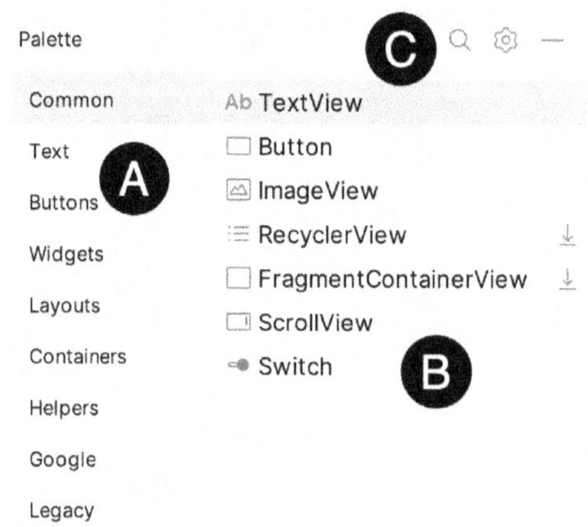

Figure 25-6

To add a component from the palette onto the layout canvas, select the item from the component list or the preview panel, drag it to the desired location on the canvas, and drop it into place.

A search for a specific component within the selected category may be initiated by clicking the search button (marked C in Figure 25-6 above) in the palette toolbar and typing in the component name. As characters are typed, matching results will appear in the component list panel. If you are unsure of the component's category, select the All Results category before or during the search operation.

25.5 Design Mode and Layout Views

The layout editor will appear in Design mode by default, as shown in Figure 25-5 above. This mode provides a visual representation of the user interface. Design mode can be selected by clicking on the button marked C in Figure 25-7:

Figure 25-7

When the Layout Editor tool is in Design mode, the layout can be viewed in two ways. The view shown in Figure 25-5 above is the Design view and shows the layout and widgets as they will appear in the running app. A second mode, the Blueprint view, can be shown instead of or concurrently with the Design view. The toolbar menu in Figure 25-8 provides options to display the Design, Blueprint, or both views. Settings are also available to adjust for color blindness. A fifth option, *Force Refresh Layout*, causes the layout to rebuild and redraw. This can be useful when the layout enters an unexpected state or is not accurately reflecting the current design settings:

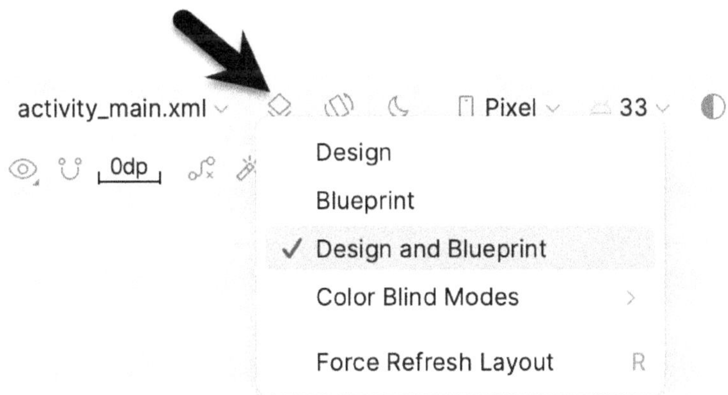

Figure 25-8

Whether to display the layout view, design view, or both is a matter of personal preference. A good approach is to begin with both displayed as shown in Figure 25-9:

Figure 25-9

25.6 Night Mode

To view the layout in night mode during the design work, select the menu shown in Figure 25-10 below and change the setting to *Night*:

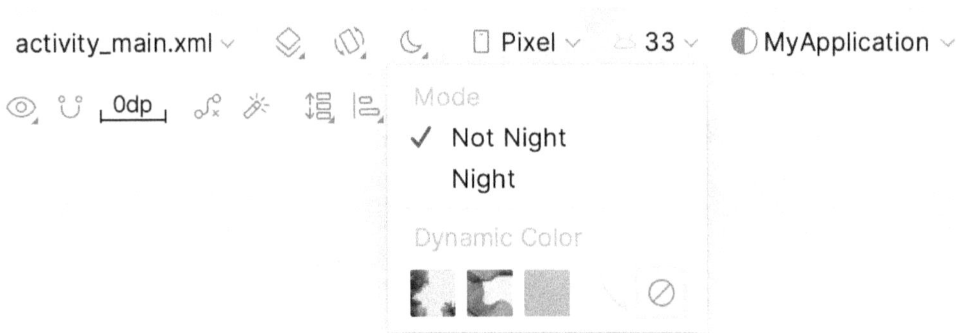

Figure 25-10

The mode menu also includes options for testing dynamic colors, a topic covered in the chapter *"A Material Design 3 Theming and Dynamic Color Tutorial"*.

25.7 Code Mode

It is important to remember when using the Android Studio Layout Editor tool that all it is doing is providing a user-friendly approach to creating XML layout resource files. The underlying XML can be viewed and directly edited during the design process by selecting the button marked A in Figure 25-7 above.

Figure 25-11 shows the Android Studio Layout Editor tool in Code mode, allowing changes to be made to the user interface declaration by modifying the XML:

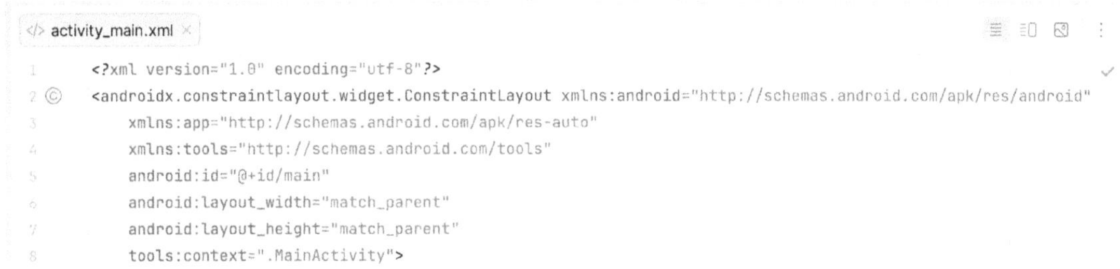

Figure 25-11

25.8 Split Mode

In Split mode, the editor shows the Design and Code views side-by-side, allowing the user interface to be modified visually using the design canvas and making changes directly to the XML declarations. Split mode is selected using the button marked B Figure 25-7 above.

Any changes to the XML are automatically reflected in the design canvas and vice versa. Figure 25-12 shows the editor in Split mode:

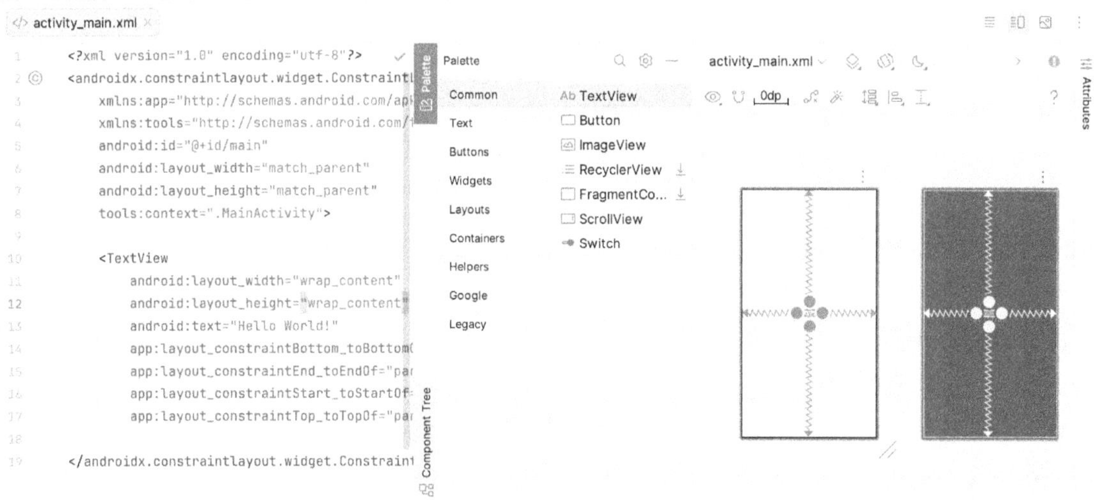

Figure 25-12

25.9 Setting Attributes

The Attributes panel provides access to all available settings for the currently selected component. Figure 25-13, for example, shows some of the attributes for the TextView widget:

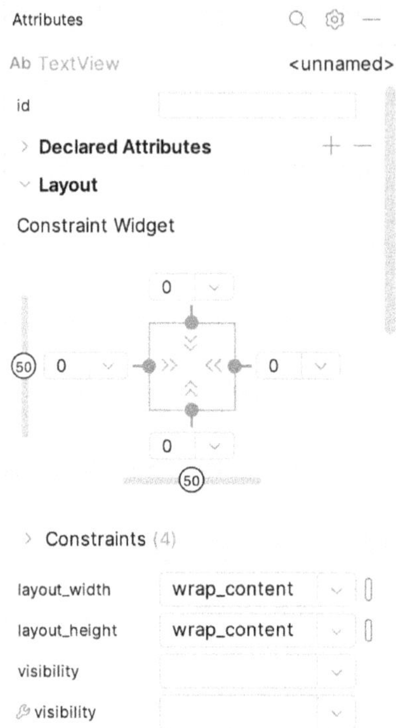

Figure 25-13

The Attributes tool window is divided into the following different sections.

- **id** - Contains the id property, which defines the name by which the currently selected object will be referenced in the app's source code.
- **Declared Attributes** - Contains all of the properties already assigned a value.
- **Layout** - The settings that define how the currently selected view object is positioned and sized relative to the screen and other objects in the layout.
- **Transforms** - Contains controls allowing the currently selected object to be rotated, scaled, and offset.
- **Common Attributes** - A list of attributes that commonly need to be changed for the class of view object currently selected.
- **All Attributes** - A complete list of all the attributes available for the currently selected object.

A search for a specific attribute may also be performed by selecting the search button in the toolbar of the attributes tool window and typing in the attribute name.

Some attributes contain a narrow button to the right of the value field. This indicates that the Resources dialog is available to assist in selecting a suitable property value. To display the dialog, click on the button. The appearance of this button changes to reflect whether or not the corresponding property value is stored in a resource file or hard-coded. If the value is stored in a resource file, the button to the right of the text property field will be filled in to indicate that the value is not hard-coded, as highlighted in Figure 25-14 below:

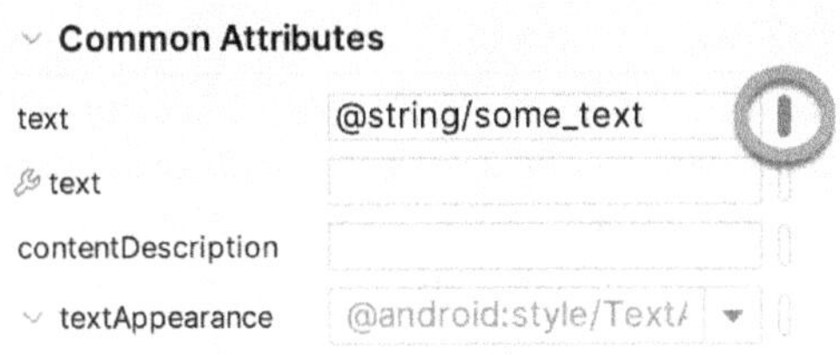

Figure 25-14

Attributes for which a finite number of valid options are available will present a drop-down menu (Figure 25-15) from which a selection may be made.

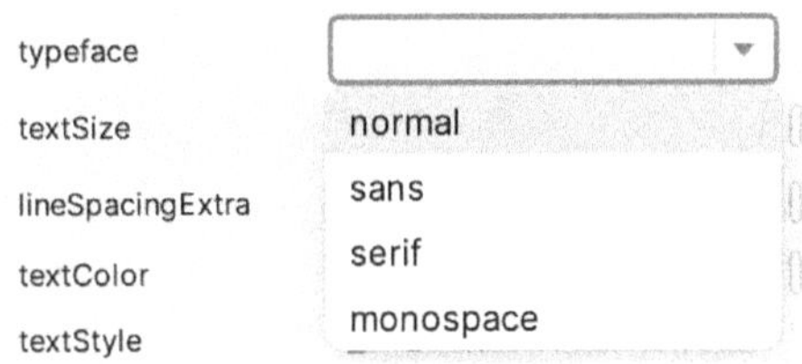

Figure 25-15

A dropper icon can be clicked to display the color selection palette. Similarly, when a flag icon appears, it can be clicked to display a list of options available for the attribute, while an image icon opens the resource manager panel allowing images and other resource types to be selected for the attribute.

25.10 Transforms

The transforms panel within the Attributes tool window (Figure 25-16) provides a set of controls and properties that control visual aspects of the currently selected object in terms of rotation, alpha (used to fade a view in and out), scale (size), and translation (offset from current position):

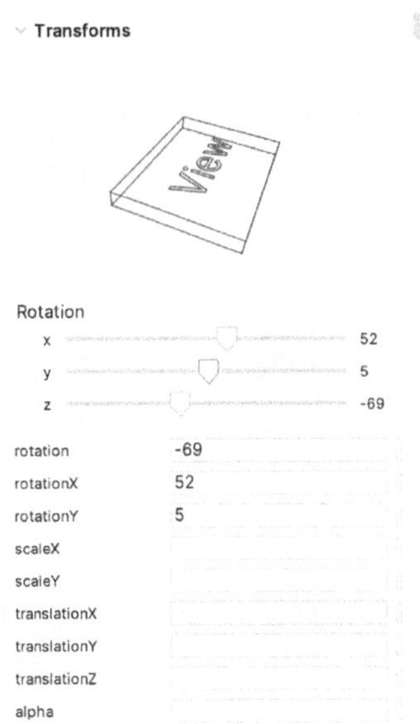

Figure 25-16

The panel contains a visual representation of the view, which updates as properties are changed. These changes are also reflected in the view within the layout canvas.

25.11 Tools Visibility Toggles

When reviewing the content of an Android Studio XML layout file in Code mode, you will notice that many attributes that define how a view appears and behaves begin with the *android:* prefix. This indicates that the attributes are set within the *android* namespace and will take effect when the app is run. The following excerpt from a layout file, for example, sets a variety of attributes on a Button view:

```
<Button
    android:id="@+id/button"
    android:layout_width="wrap_content"
    android:layout_height="wrap_content"
    android:text="Button"
.
.
```

In addition to the android namespace, Android Studio also provides a *tools* namespace. When attributes are set within this namespace, they only take effect within the layout editor preview. While designing a layout, you might find it helpful for an EditText view to display some text but require the view to be blank when the app runs. To achieve this, you would set the text property of the view using the tools namespace as follows:

```
<EditText
    android:id="@+id/editTextTextPersonName"
    android:layout_width="wrap_content"
    android:layout_height="wrap_content"
    android:ems="10"
    android:inputType="textPersonName"
    tools:text="Sample Text"
.
.
```

A tool attribute of this type is set in the Attributes tool window by entering the value into the property fields marked by the wrench icon, as shown in Figure 25-17:

Figure 25-17

Tools attributes are particularly useful for changing the visibility of a view during the design process. A layout may contain a view that is programmatically displayed and hidden when the app runs, depending on user actions. To simulate the hiding of the view, the following tools attribute could be added to the view XML declaration:

```
tools:visibility="invisible"
```

Although the view will no longer be visible when using the invisible setting, it is still present in the layout and occupies the same space it did when it was visible. To make the layout behave as though the view no longer exists, the visibility attribute should be set to *gone* as follows:

```
tools:visibility="gone"
```

In both examples above, the visibility settings only apply within the layout editor and will have no effect in the running app. To control visibility in both the layout editor and running app, the same attribute would be set using the *android* namespace:

```
android:visibility="gone"
```

While these visibility tools attributes are useful, having to manually edit the XML layout file is a cumbersome process. To make it easier to change these settings, Android Studio provides a set of toggles within the layout editor Component Tree panel. To access these controls, click in the margin to the right of the corresponding view in the panel. Figure 25-18, for example, shows the tools visibility toggle controls for a Button view named myButton:

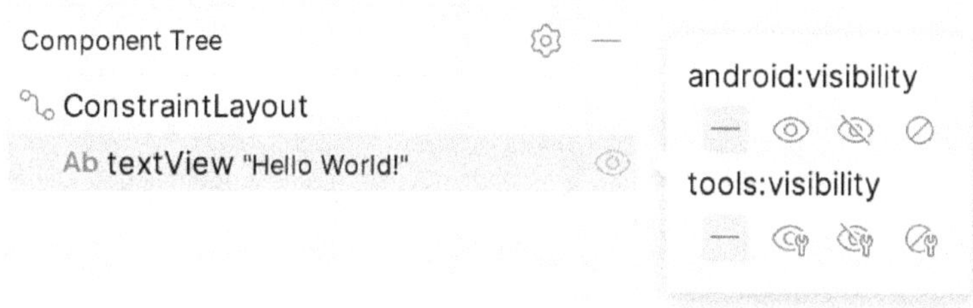

Figure 25-18

These toggles control the visibility of the corresponding view for both the android and tools namespaces and provide *not set*, *visible*, *invisible* and *gone* options. When conflicting attributes are set (for example, an android namespace toggle is set to visible while the tools value is set to invisible), the tools namespace takes precedence within the layout preview. When a toggle selection is made, Android Studio automatically adds the appropriate attribute to the XML view element in the layout file.

In addition to the visibility toggles in the Component Tree panel, the layout editor also includes the *tools visibility and position* menu shown highlighted in Figure 25-19 below:

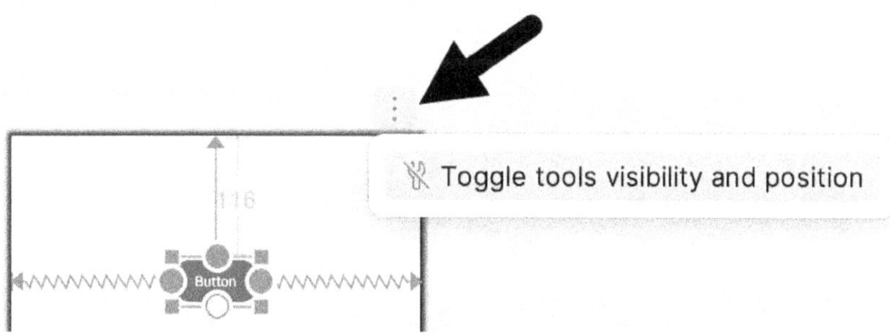

Figure 25-19

This button toggles the current tools visibility settings. If the Button view shown above currently has the tools visibility attribute set to *gone*, for example, toggling this button will make it visible. This makes it easy to quickly check the layout behavior as the view is added to and removed from the layout. This toggle is also useful for checking that the views in the layout are correctly constrained, a topic covered in the chapter entitled *"A Guide to Using ConstraintLayout in Android Studio"*.

25.12 Converting Views

Changing a view in a layout from one type to another (such as converting a TextView to an EditText) can be performed easily within the Android Studio layout editor by right-clicking on the view either within the screen layout or Component tree window and selecting the *Convert view...* menu option (Figure 25-20):

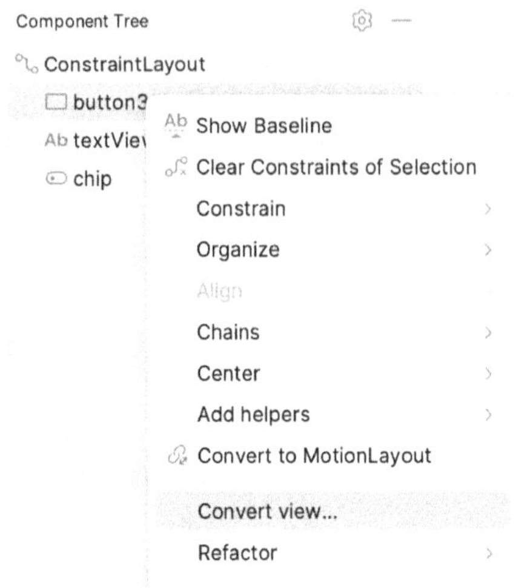

Figure 25-20

Once selected, a dialog containing a list of compatible view types to which the selected object is eligible for conversion will appear. Figure 25-21, for example, shows the types to which an existing TextView view may be converted:

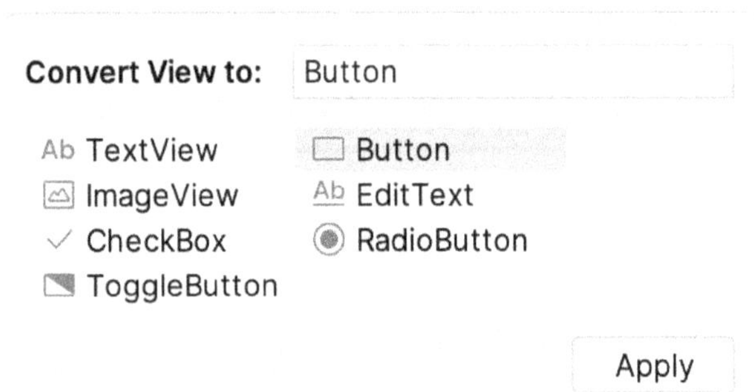

Figure 25-21

This technique is also helpful in converting layouts from one type to another (for example, converting a ConstraintLayout to a LinearLayout).

25.13 Displaying Sample Data

When designing layouts in Android Studio, situations will arise where the content to be displayed within the user interface will not be available until the app is completed and running. This can sometimes make it difficult to assess how the layout will appear at app runtime from within the layout editor. To address this issue, the layout editor allows sample data to be specified, which will populate views within the layout editor with sample images and data. This sample data only appears within the layout editor and is not displayed when the app runs. Sample data may be configured either by directly editing the XML for the layout or visually using the design-time helper by right-clicking on the widget in the design area and selecting the *Set Sample Data* menu option. The design-time helper panel will display a range of preconfigured options for sample data to be displayed on the selected view item, including combinations of text and images in various configurations. Figure 25-22, for example, shows the sample data options displayed when selecting sample data to appear in a RecyclerView list:

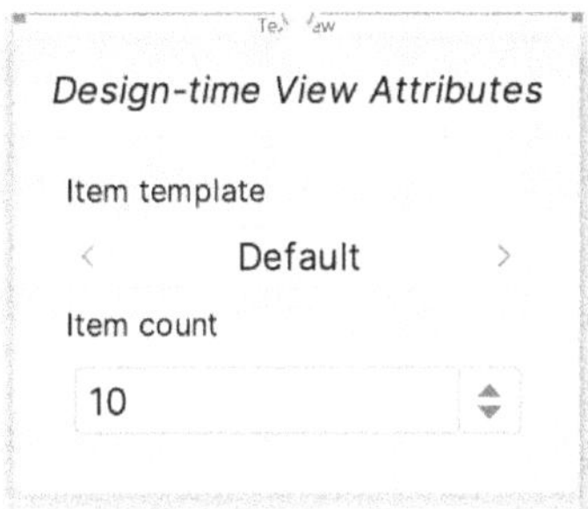

Figure 25-22

Alternatively, custom text and images may be provided for display during the layout design process. Since sample data is implemented as a *tools* attribute, the visibility of the data within the preview can be controlled using the toggle button highlighted in Figure 25-19 above.

25.14 Creating a Custom Device Definition

The device menu in the Layout Editor toolbar (Figure 25-23) provides a list of pre-configured device types, which, when selected, will appear as the device screen canvas. In addition to the pre-configured device types, any AVD instances previously configured within the Android Studio environment will also be listed within the menu. To add additional device configurations, display the device menu, select the *Add Device Definition* option and follow the steps outlined in the chapter entitled *"Creating an Android Virtual Device (AVD) in Android Studio"*.

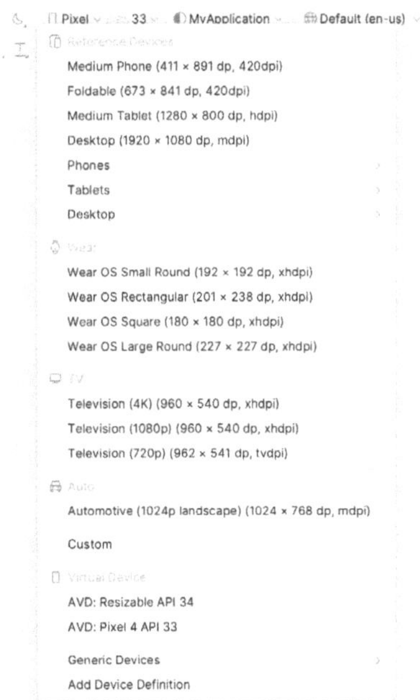

Figure 25-23

25.15 Changing the Current Device

As an alternative to the device selection menu, the current device format may be changed by selecting the *Custom* option from the device menu, clicking on the resize handle located next to the bottom right-hand corner of the device screen (Figure 25-24), and dragging to select an alternate device display format. As the screen resizes, markers will appear indicating the various size options and orientations available for selection:

Figure 25-24

25.16 Layout Validation

The layout validation option allows the user interface layout to be previewed simultaneously on a range of Pixel-sized screens. To access the layout validation tool window, select the *View -> Tool Windows -> Layout Validation* menu option. Once loaded, the panel will appear as shown in Figure 25-25, with the layout rendered on multiple device screen configurations:

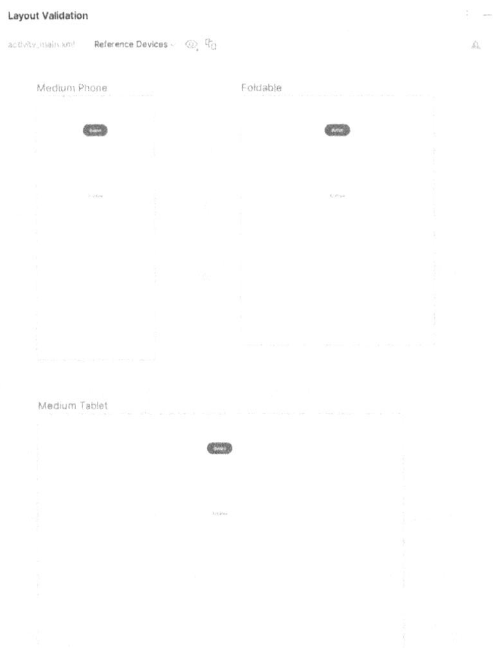

Figure 25-25

25.17 Summary

A key part of developing Android applications involves the creation of the user interface. This is performed within the Android Studio environment using the Layout Editor tool, which operates in three modes. In Design mode, view components are selected from a palette, positioned on a layout representing an Android device screen, and configured using a list of attributes. The underlying XML representing the user interface layout can be directly edited in Code mode. Split mode, on the other hand, allows the layout to be created and modified both visually and via direct XML editing. These modes combine to provide an extensive and intuitive user interface design environment.

The layout validation panel allows user interface layouts to be quickly previewed on various device screen sizes.

Chapter 26

26. A Guide to the Android ConstraintLayout

As discussed in the chapter entitled *"Understanding Android Views, View Groups and Layouts"*, Android provides several layout managers to design user interfaces. With Android 7, Google introduced a layout that addressed many of the shortcomings of the older layout managers. This layout, called ConstraintLayout, combines a simple, expressive, and flexible layout system with powerful features built into the Android Studio Layout Editor tool to ease the creation of responsive user interface layouts that adapt automatically to different screen sizes and changes in device orientation.

This chapter will outline the basic concepts of ConstraintLayout, while the next chapter will provide a detailed overview of how constraint-based layouts can be created using ConstraintLayout within the Android Studio Layout Editor tool.

26.1 How ConstraintLayout Works

In common with all other layouts, ConstraintLayout manages the positioning and sizing behavior of the visual components (also referred to as widgets) it contains. It does this based on the constraint connections set on each child widget.

To fully understand and use ConstraintLayout, it is essential to gain an appreciation of the following key concepts:

- Constraints
- Margins
- Opposing Constraints
- Constraint Bias
- Chains
- Chain Styles
- Guidelines
- Groups
- Barriers
- Flow

26.1.1 Constraints

Constraints are sets of rules that dictate how a widget is aligned and distanced relative to other widgets, the sides of the containing ConstraintLayout, and special elements called *guidelines*. Constraints also dictate how the user interface layout of an activity will respond to changes in device orientation or when displayed on devices of differing screen sizes. To be adequately configured, a widget must have sufficient constraint connections such that its position can be resolved by the ConstraintLayout layout engine in both the horizontal and vertical planes.

26.1.2 Margins

A margin is a form of constraint that specifies a fixed distance. Consider a Button object that needs to be positioned near the top right-hand corner of the device screen. This might be achieved by implementing margin constraints from the top and right-hand edges of the Button connected to the corresponding sides of the parent ConstraintLayout, as illustrated in Figure 26-1:

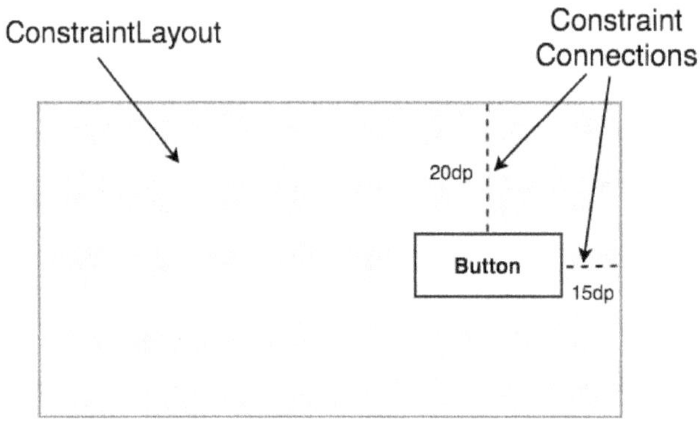

Figure 26-1

As indicated in the above diagram, each of these constraint connections has associated with it a margin value dictating the fixed distances of the widget from two sides of the parent layout. Under this configuration, regardless of screen size or the device orientation, the Button object will always be positioned 20 and 15 device-independent pixels (dp) from the top and right-hand edges of the parent ConstraintLayout, respectively, as specified by the two constraint connections.

While the above configuration will be acceptable for some situations, it does not provide any flexibility in terms of allowing the ConstraintLayout layout engine to adapt the position of the widget to respond to device rotation and to support screens of different sizes. To add this responsiveness to the layout, it is necessary to implement opposing constraints.

26.1.3 Opposing Constraints

Two constraints operating along the same axis on a single widget are considered *opposing constraints*. In other words, a widget with constraints on both its left and right-hand sides is considered to have horizontally opposing constraints. Figure 26-2, for example, illustrates the addition of both horizontally and vertically opposing constraints to the previous layout:

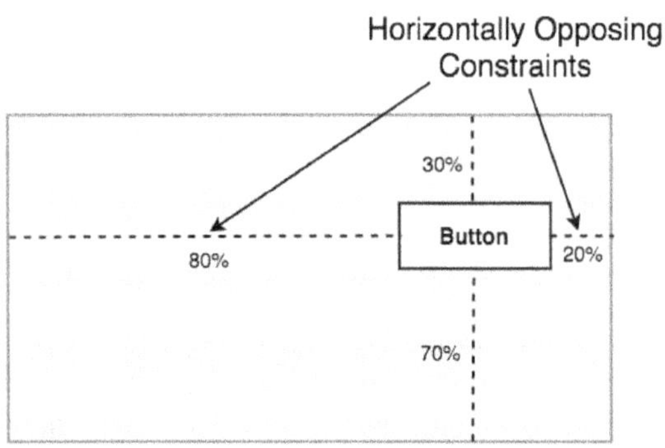

Figure 26-2

The key point to understand here is that once opposing constraints are implemented on a particular axis, the positioning of the widget becomes percentage rather than coordinate-based. Instead of being fixed at 20dp from the top of the layout, for example, the widget is now positioned at 30% from the top. In different orientations and when running on larger or smaller screens, the Button will always be in the same location relative to the dimensions of the parent layout.

It is now important to understand that the layout outlined in Figure 26-2 has been implemented using not only opposing constraints, but also by applying *constraint bias*.

26.1.4 Constraint Bias

It has now been established that a widget in a ConstraintLayout can potentially be subject to opposing constraint connections. By default, opposing constraints are equal, resulting in the corresponding widget being centered along the axis of opposition. Figure 26-3, for example, shows a widget centered within the containing ConstraintLayout using opposing horizontal and vertical constraints:

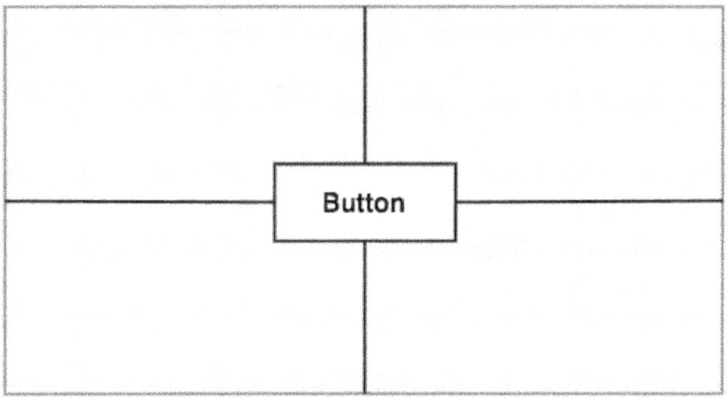

Widget Centered by Opposing Constraints

Figure 26-3

To allow for the adjustment of widget position in the case of opposing constraints, the ConstraintLayout implements a feature known as *constraint bias*. Constraint bias allows the positioning of a widget along the axis of opposition to be biased by a specified percentage in favor of one constraint. Figure 26-4, for example, shows the previous constraint layout with a 75% horizontal bias and 10% vertical bias:

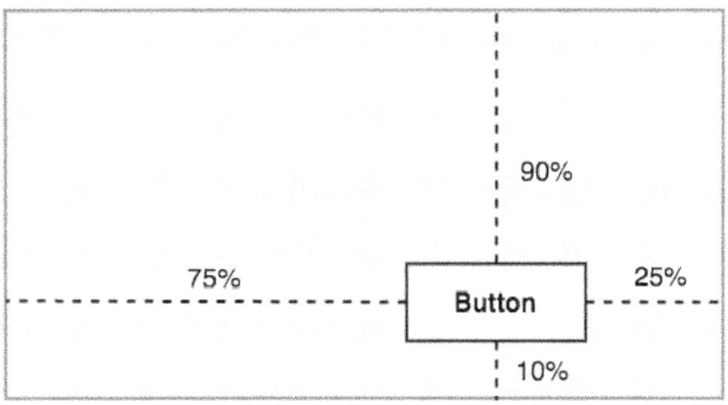

Widget Offset using Constraint Bias

Figure 26-4

The next chapter, entitled *"A Guide to Using ConstraintLayout in Android Studio"*, will cover these concepts in greater detail and explain how these features have been integrated into the Android Studio Layout Editor tool.

In the meantime, however, a few more areas of the ConstraintLayout class need to be covered.

26.1.5 Chains

ConstraintLayout chains provide a way for the layout behavior of two or more widgets to be defined as a group. Chains can be declared in either the vertical or horizontal axis and configured to define how the widgets in the chain are spaced and sized.

Widgets are chained when connected by bi-directional constraints. Figure 26-5, for example, illustrates three widgets chained in this way:

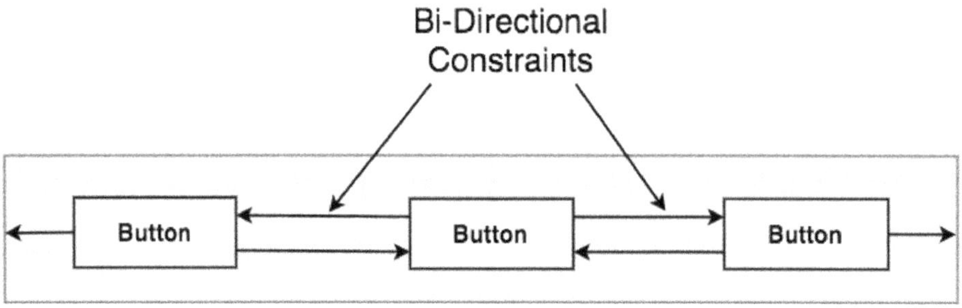

Figure 26-5

The first element in the chain is the *chain head* which translates to the top widget in a vertical chain or, in the case of a horizontal chain, the left-most widget. The layout behavior of the entire chain is primarily configured by setting attributes on the chain head widget.

26.1.6 Chain Styles

The layout behavior of a ConstraintLayout chain is dictated by the *chain style* setting applied to the chain head widget. The ConstraintLayout class currently supports the following chain layout styles:

- **Spread Chain** – The widgets within the chain are distributed evenly across the available space. This is the default behavior for chains.

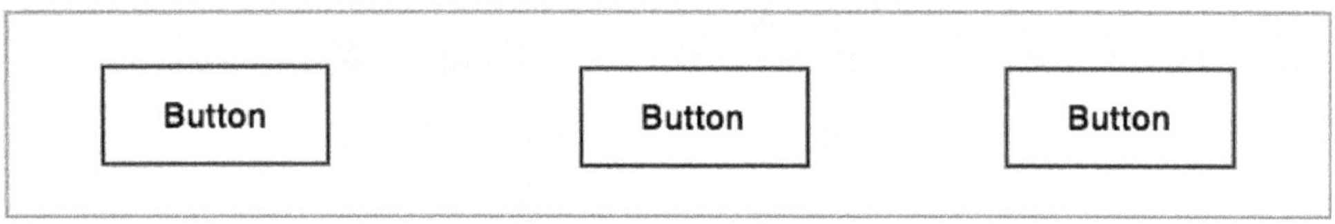

Figure 26-6

- **Spread Inside Chain** – The widgets within the chain are spread evenly between the chain head and the last widget. The head and last widgets are not included in the distribution of spacing.

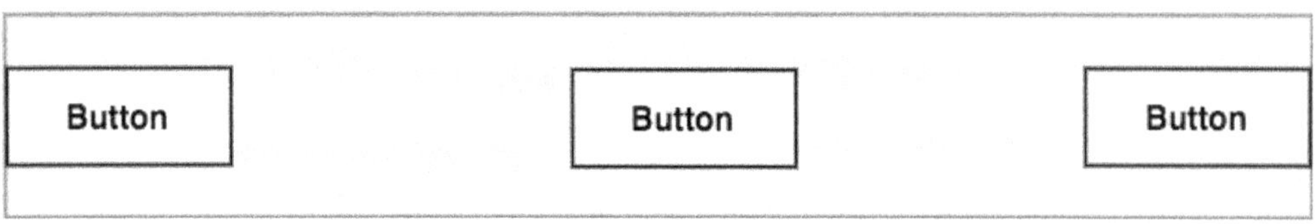

Figure 26-7

- **Weighted Chain** – Allows the space taken up by each widget in the chain to be defined via weighting properties.

Figure 26-8

- **Packed Chain** – The widgets that make up the chain are packed together without spacing. A bias may be applied to control the horizontal or vertical positioning of the chain relative to the parent container.

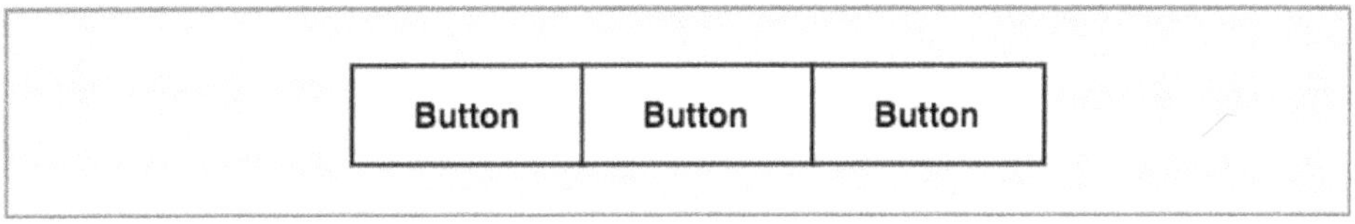

Figure 26-9

26.2 Baseline Alignment

So far, this chapter has only referred to constraints that dictate alignment relative to the sides of a widget (typically referred to as side constraints). A common requirement, however, is for a widget to be aligned relative to the content that it displays rather than the boundaries of the widget itself. To address this need, ConstraintLayout provides *baseline alignment* support.

For example, assume that the previous theoretical layout from Figure 26-1 requires a TextView widget to be positioned 40dp to the left of the Button. In this case, the TextView needs to be *baseline aligned* with the Button view. This means that the text within the Button needs to be vertically aligned with the text within the TextView. The additional constraints for this layout would need to be connected as illustrated in Figure 26-10:

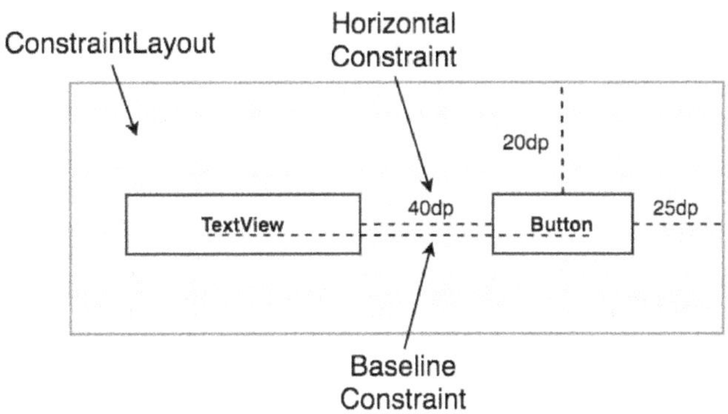

Figure 26-10

The TextView is now aligned vertically along the baseline of the Button and positioned 40dp horizontally from the Button object's left-hand edge.

26.3 Configuring Widget Dimensions

Controlling the dimensions of a widget is a key element of the user interface design process. The ConstraintLayout provides three options that can be set on individual widgets to manage sizing behavior. These settings are configured individually for height and width dimensions:

- **Fixed** – The widget is fixed to specified dimensions.

- **Match Constraint** –Allows the widget to be resized by the layout engine to satisfy the prevailing constraints.

Also referred to as the *AnySize* or MATCH_CONSTRAINT option.

- **Wrap Content** – The widget's size is dictated by its content (i.e., text or graphics).

26.4 Guideline Helper

Guidelines are special elements available within the ConstraintLayout that provide an additional target to which constraints may be connected. Multiple guidelines may be added to a ConstraintLayout instance which may, in turn, be configured in horizontal or vertical orientations. Once added, constraint connections may be established from widgets in the layout to the guidelines. This is particularly useful when multiple widgets must be aligned along an axis. In Figure 26-11, for example, three Button objects contained within a ConstraintLayout are constrained along a vertical guideline:

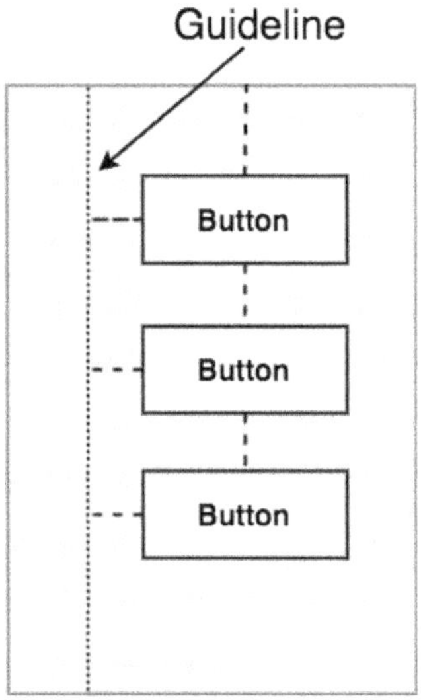

Figure 26-11

26.5 Group Helper

This feature of ConstraintLayout allows widgets to be placed into logical groups, and the visibility of those widgets controlled as a single entity. A Group is a list of references to other widgets in a layout. Once defined, changing the visibility attribute (visible, invisible, or gone) of the group instance will apply the change to all group members. This makes hiding and showing multiple widgets with a single attribute change easy. A single layout may contain multiple groups, and a widget can belong to more than one group. If a conflict occurs between groups, the last group to be declared in the XML file takes priority.

26.6 Barrier Helper

Rather like guidelines, barriers are virtual views that can be used to constrain views within a layout. As with guidelines, a barrier can be vertical or horizontal, and one or more views may be constrained to it (to avoid confusion, these will be referred to as *constrained views*). Unlike guidelines, where the guideline remains at a fixed position within the layout, however, the position of a barrier is defined by a set of so-called *reference views*. Barriers were introduced to address an issue that occurs with some frequency involving overlapping views. Consider, for example, the layout illustrated in Figure 26-12 below:

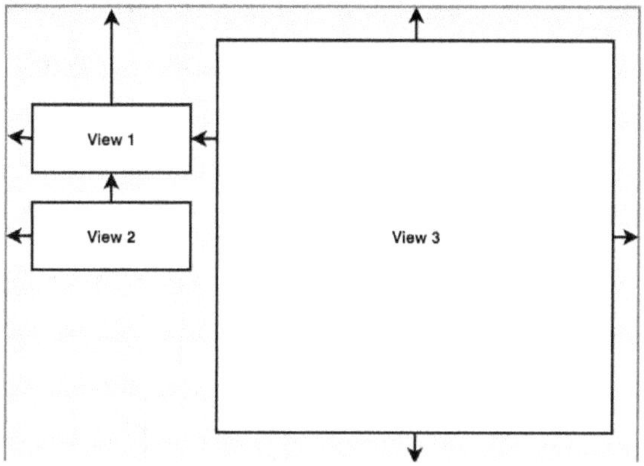

Figure 26-12

The key points to note about the above layout are that the width of View 3 is set to match constraint mode, and the left-hand edge of the view is connected to the right-hand edge of View 1. As currently implemented, an increase in width of View 1 will have the desired effect of reducing the width of View 3:

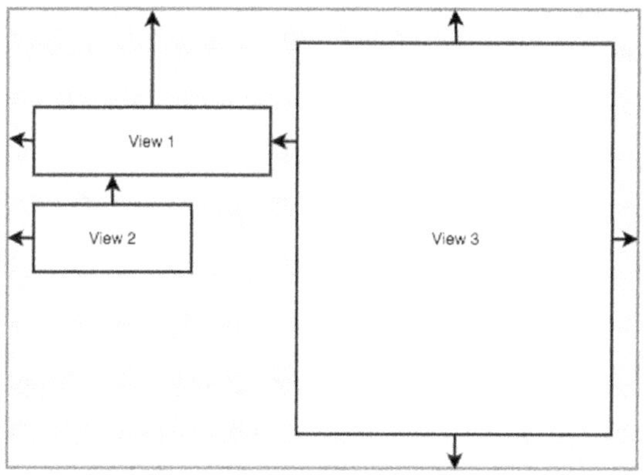

Figure 26-13

A problem arises, however, if View 2 increases in width instead of View 1:

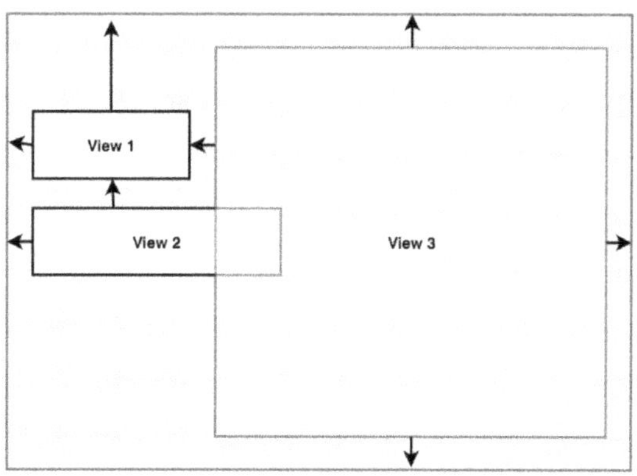

Figure 26-14

Because View 3 is only constrained by View 1, it does not resize to accommodate the increase in width of View

2, causing the views to overlap.

A solution to this problem is to add a vertical barrier and assign Views 1 and 2 as the barrier's *reference views* so that they control the barrier position. The left-hand edge of View 3 will then be constrained relative to the barrier, making it a *constrained view.*

Now when either View 1 or View 2 increases in width, the barrier will move to accommodate the widest of the two views, causing the width of View 3 to change relative to the new barrier position:

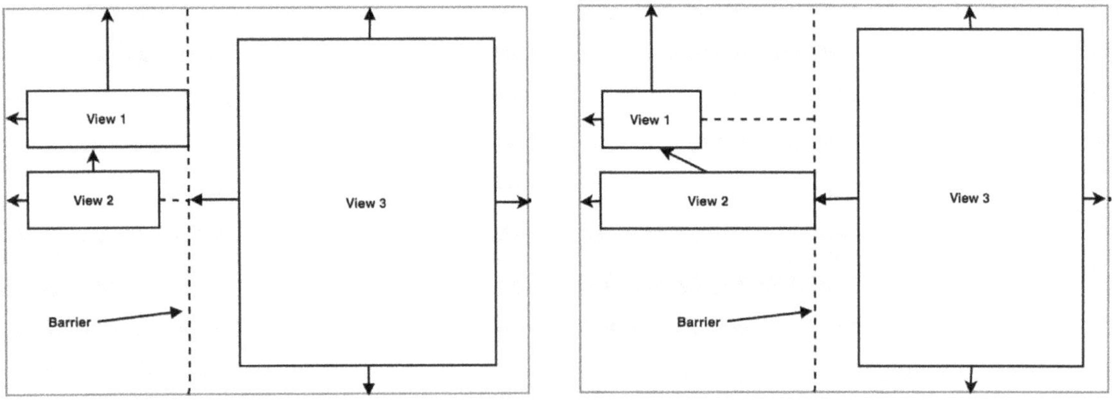

Figure 26-15

When working with barriers, there is no limit to the number of reference and constrained views that can be associated with a single barrier.

26.7 Flow Helper

The ConstraintLayout Flow helper allows groups of views to be displayed in a flowing grid-style layout. As with the Group helper, Flow contains references to the views it is responsible for positioning and provides various configuration options, including vertical and horizontal orientations, wrapping behavior (including the maximum number of widgets before wrapping), spacing, and alignment properties. Chain behavior may also be applied to a Flow layout, including spread, spread inside, and packed options.

Figure 26-16 represents the layout of five uniformly sized buttons positioned using a Flow helper instance in horizontal mode with no wrap settings:

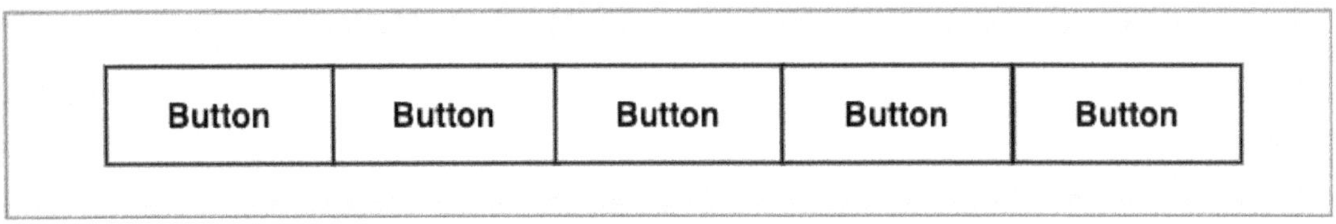

Figure 26-16

Figure 26-17 shows the same buttons in a horizontal flow configuration with wrapping set to occur after every third widget:

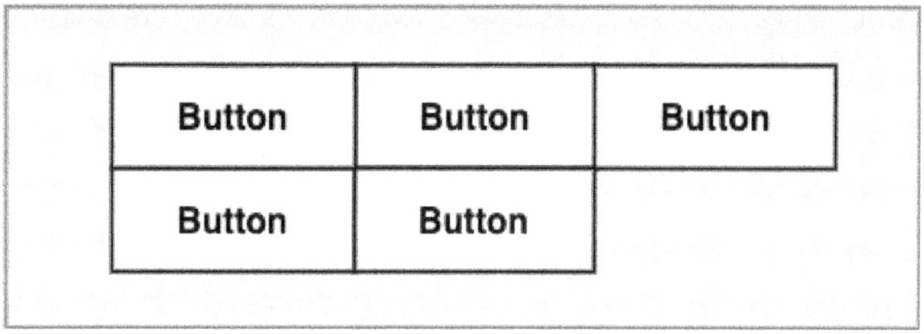

Figure 26-17

Figure 26-18, on the other hand, shows the buttons with wrapping set to chain mode using spread inside (the effects of which are only visible on the second row since the first row is full). The configuration also has the gap attribute set to add spacing between buttons:

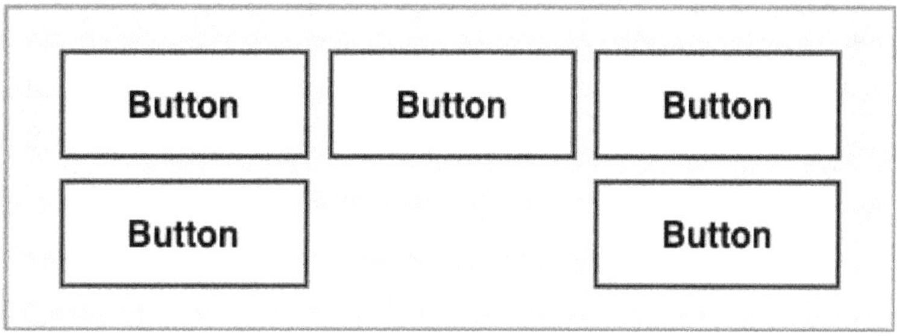

Figure 26-18

As a final demonstration of the flexibility of the Flow helper, Figure 26-19 shows five buttons of varying sizes configured in horizontal, packed chain mode with wrapping after each third widget. In addition, the grid content has been right-aligned by setting a horizontal-bias value of 1.0 (a value of 0.0 would cause left-alignment while 0.5 would center-align the grid content):

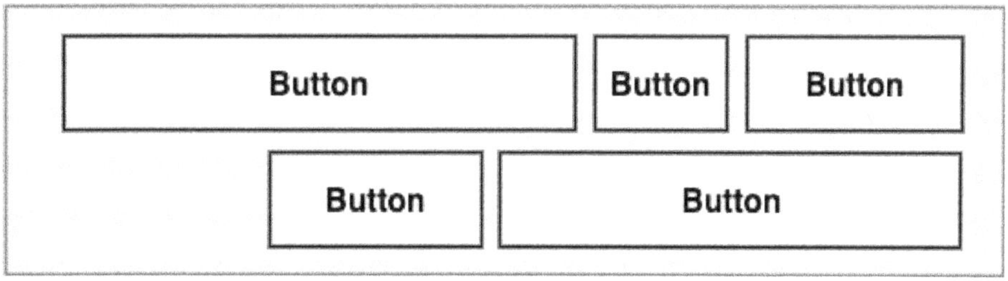

Figure 26-19

26.8 Ratios

The dimensions of a widget may be defined using ratio settings. A widget could, for example, be constrained using a ratio setting such that, regardless of any resizing behavior, the width is always twice the height dimension.

26.9 ConstraintLayout Advantages

ConstraintLayout provides a level of flexibility that allows many of the features of older layouts to be achieved with a single layout instance where it would previously have been necessary to nest multiple layouts. This can avoid the problems inherent in layout nesting by allowing so-called "flat" or "shallow" layout hierarchies to be designed, leading both to less complex layouts and improved user interface rendering performance at runtime.

ConstraintLayout was also implemented to address the wide range of Android device screen sizes available today. The flexibility of ConstraintLayout makes it easier for user interfaces to be designed that respond and adapt to the device on which the app is running.

Finally, as will be demonstrated in the chapter entitled *"A Guide to Using ConstraintLayout in Android Studio"*, the Android Studio Layout Editor tool has been enhanced specifically for ConstraintLayout-based user interface design.

26.10 ConstraintLayout Availability

Although introduced with Android 7, ConstraintLayout is provided as a separate support library from the main Android SDK and is compatible with older Android versions as far back as API Level 9 (Gingerbread). This allows apps that use this layout to run on devices running much older versions of Android.

26.11 Summary

ConstraintLayout is a layout manager introduced with Android 7. It is designed to ease the creation of flexible layouts that adapt to the size and orientation of the many Android devices on the market. ConstraintLayout uses constraints to control the alignment and positioning of widgets relative to the parent ConstraintLayout instance, guidelines, barriers, and the other widgets in the layout. ConstraintLayout is the default layout for newly created Android Studio projects and is recommended when designing user interface layouts. This simple yet flexible approach to layout management allows complex and responsive user interfaces to be easily implemented.

Chapter 27

27. A Guide to Using ConstraintLayout in Android Studio

As mentioned more than once in previous chapters, Google has made significant changes to the Android Studio Layout Editor tool, many of which were made solely to support user interface layout design using ConstraintLayout. Now that the basic concepts of ConstraintLayout have been outlined in the previous chapter, this chapter will explore these concepts in more detail while also outlining how the Layout Editor tool allows ConstraintLayout-based user interfaces to be designed and implemented.

27.1 Design and Layout Views

The chapter entitled *"A Guide to the Android Studio Layout Editor Tool"* explained that the Android Studio Layout Editor tool provides two ways to view the user interface layout of an activity in the form of Design and Layout (also known as blueprint) views. These views of the layout may be displayed individually or, as in Figure 27-1, side-by-side:

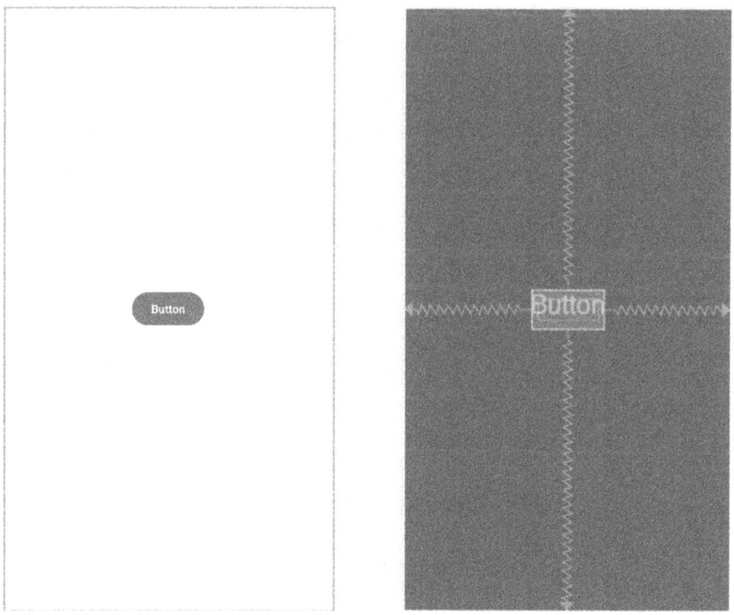

Figure 27-1

The Design view (positioned on the left in the above figure) presents a "what you see is what you get" representation of the layout, wherein the layout appears as it will within the running app. On the other hand, the Layout view displays a blueprint style of view where shaded outlines represent the widgets. As shown in Figure 27-1 above, the Layout view also displays the constraint connections (in this case, opposing constraints used to center a button within the layout). These constraints are also overlaid onto the Design view when a specific widget in the layout is selected or when the mouse pointer hovers over the design area, as illustrated in Figure 27-2:

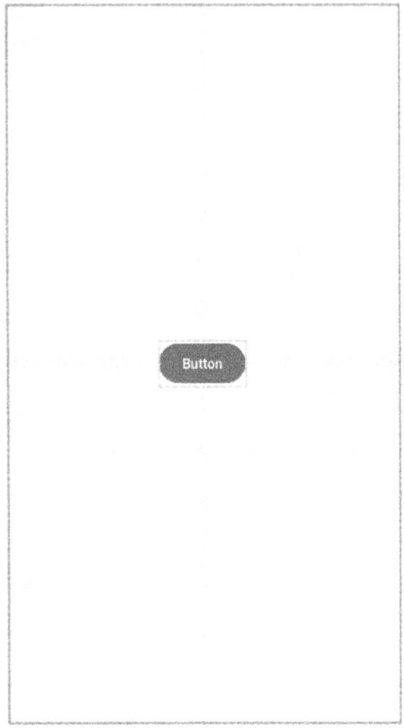

Figure 27-2

The appearance of constraint connections in both views can be changed using the View Options menu shown in Figure 27-3:

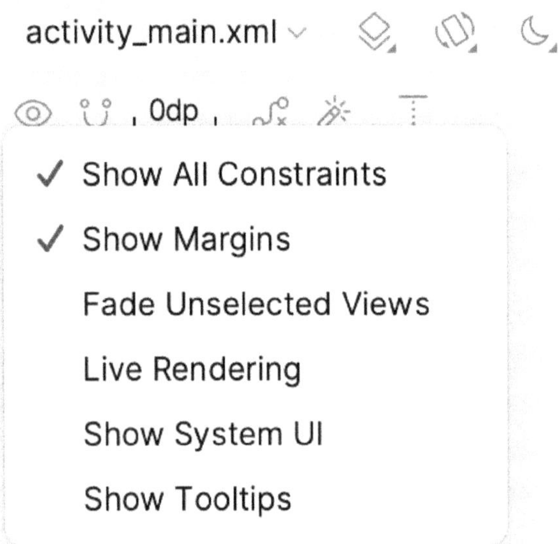

Figure 27-3

In addition to the two modes of displaying the user interface layout, the Layout Editor tool provides three ways of establishing the constraints required for a specific layout design.

27.2 Autoconnect Mode

Autoconnect, as the name suggests, automatically establishes constraint connections as items are added to the layout. Autoconnect mode may be turned on and off using the toolbar button indicated in Figure 27-4:

Figure 27-4

Autoconnect mode uses algorithms to decide the best constraints to establish based on the widget's position and the widget's proximity to both the sides of the parent layout and other elements. If any of the automatic constraint connections fail to provide the desired behavior, these may be changed manually, as outlined later in this chapter.

27.3 Inference Mode

Inference mode uses a heuristic approach involving algorithms and probabilities to automatically implement constraint connections after widgets have already been added to the layout. This mode is usually used when the Autoconnect feature has been turned off, and objects have been added to the layout without any constraint connections. This allows the layout to be designed by dragging and dropping objects from the palette onto the layout canvas and making size and positioning changes until the layout appears as required. Essentially, this involves "painting" the layout without worrying about constraints. Inference mode may also be used during the design process to fill in missing constraints within a layout.

Constraints are automatically added to a layout when the *Infer constraints* button (Figure 27-5) is clicked:

Figure 27-5

As with Autoconnect mode, there is always the possibility that the Layout Editor tool will infer incorrect constraints, though these may be modified and corrected manually.

27.4 Manipulating Constraints Manually

The third option for implementing constraint connections is to do so manually. When doing so, it will be helpful to understand the various handles that appear around a widget within the Layout Editor tool. Consider, for example, the widget shown in Figure 27-6:

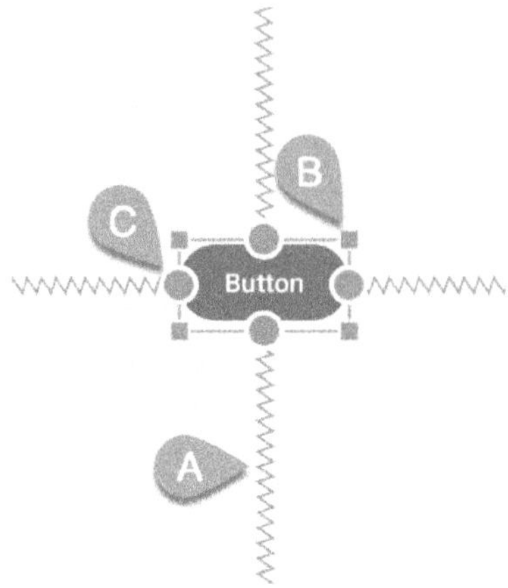

Figure 27-6

The spring-like lines (A) represent established constraint connections leading from the sides of the widget to the targets. The small square markers (B) in each corner of the object are resizing handles which, when clicked and dragged, serve to resize the widget. The small circle handles (C) located on each side of the widget are the side constraint anchors. To create a constraint connection, click on the handle and drag the resulting line to the element to which the constraint is to be connected (such as a guideline or the side of either the parent layout or another widget), as outlined in Figure 27-7. When connecting to the side of another widget, drag the line to the side constraint handle of that widget and release the line when the widget and handle are highlighted:

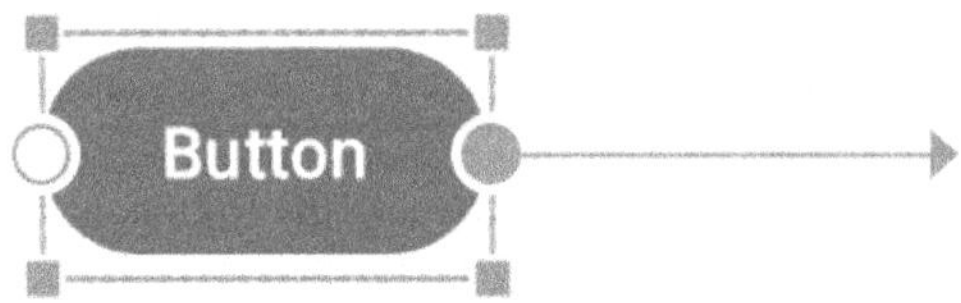

Figure 27-7

If the constraint line is dragged to a widget and released but not attached to a constraint handle, the layout editor will display a menu containing a list of the sides to which the constraint may be attached. In Figure 27-8, for example, the constraint can be attached to the top or bottom edge of the destination button widget:

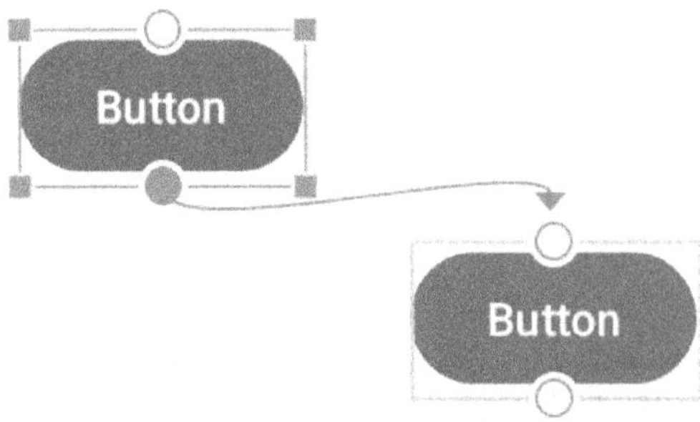

Figure 27-8

An additional marker indicates the anchor point for baseline constraints whereby the content within the widget (as opposed to outside edges) is used as the alignment point. To display this marker, right-click on the widget and select the *Show Baseline* menu option. To establish a constraint connection from a baseline constraint handle, hover the mouse pointer over the handle until it highlights before clicking and dragging to the target (such as the baseline anchor of another widget, as shown in Figure 27-9).

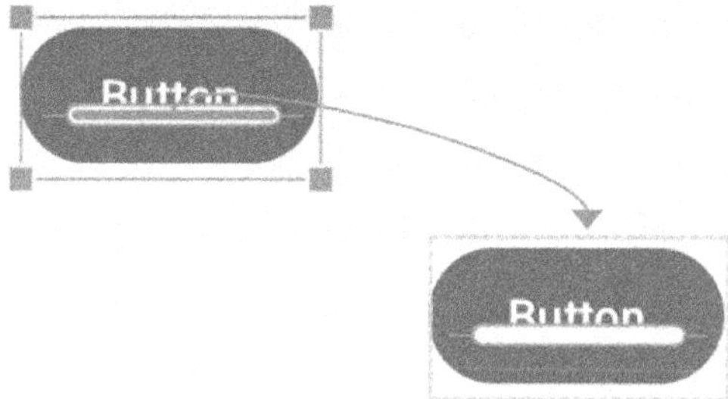

Figure 27-9

To hide the baseline anchors, right-click on the widget again and select the *Hide Baseline* menu option.

27.5 Adding Constraints in the Inspector

Constraints may also be added to a view within the Android Studio Layout Editor tool using the *Inspector* panel in the Attributes tool window, as shown in Figure 27-10. The square in the center represents the currently selected view, and the areas around the square the constraints, if any, applied to the corresponding sides of the view:

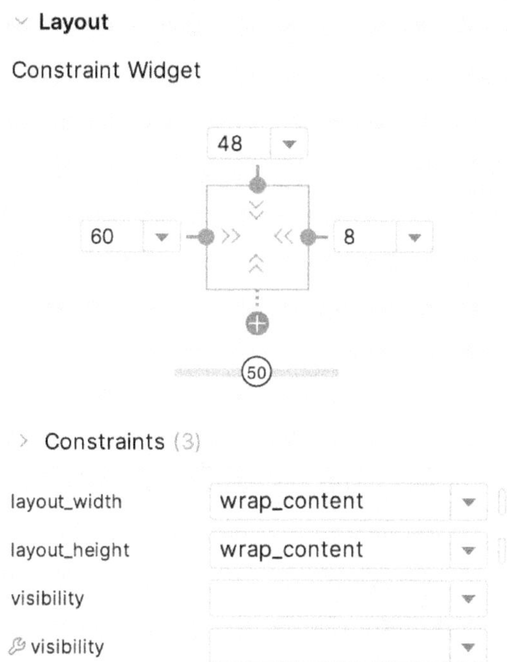

Figure 27-10

The absence of a constraint on the side of the view is represented by a dotted line leading to a blue circle containing a plus sign (as is the case with the view's bottom edge in the above figure). To add a constraint, click on this blue circle, and the layout editor will add a constraint connected to what it considers the most appropriate target within the layout.

27.6 Viewing Constraints in the Attributes Window

A list of constraints configured on the currently selected widget can be viewed by displaying the Constraints section of the Attributes tool window, as shown in Figure 27-11 below:

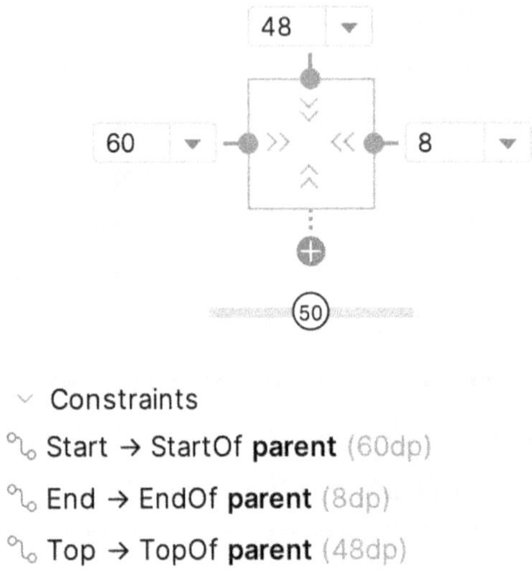

Figure 27-11

Clicking on a constraint in the list will select that constraint within the design layout.

27.7 Deleting Constraints

To delete an individual constraint, select the constraint either within the design layout or the Attributes tool window so that it highlights (in Figure 27-12, for example, the right-most constraint has been selected) and tap the keyboard delete key. The constraint will then be removed from the layout.

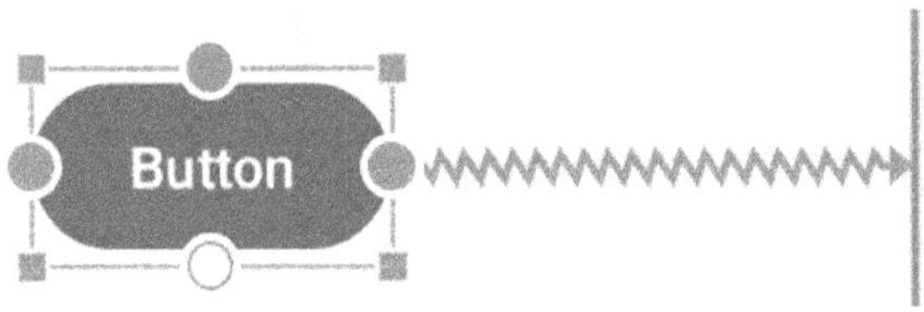

Figure 27-12

Another option is to hover the mouse pointer over the constraint anchor while holding down the Ctrl (Cmd on macOS) key and clicking on the anchor after it turns red:

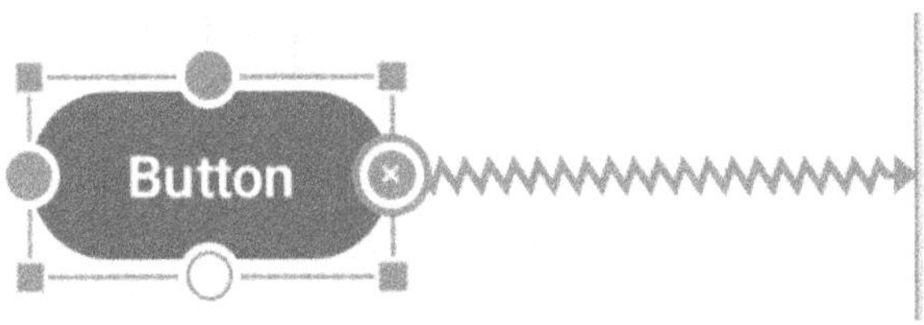

Figure 27-13

Alternatively, remove all of the constraints on a widget by right-clicking on it and selecting the *Clear Constraints of Selection* menu option.

To remove all of the constraints from every widget in a layout, use the toolbar button highlighted in Figure 27-14:

Figure 27-14

27.8 Adjusting Constraint Bias

The previous chapter outlined the concept of using bias settings to favor one opposing constraint over another. Bias within the Android Studio Layout Editor tool is adjusted using the *Inspector* located in the Attributes tool window and shown in Figure 27-15. The two sliders indicated by the arrows in the figure are used to control the bias of the currently selected widget's vertical and horizontal opposing constraints.

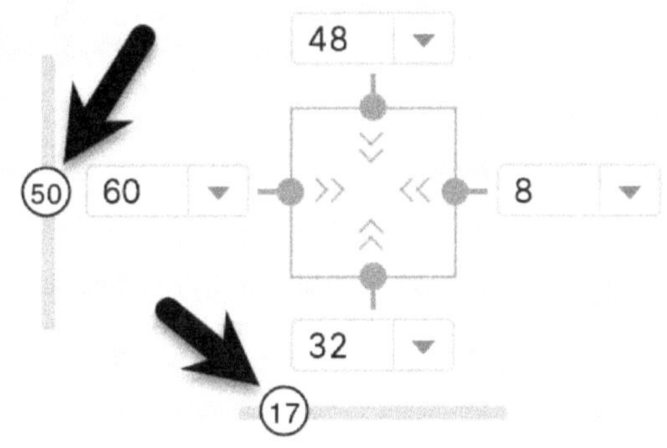

Figure 27-15

27.9 Understanding ConstraintLayout Margins

Constraints can be used with margins to implement fixed gaps between a widget and another element (such as another widget, a guideline, or the side of the parent layout). Consider, for example, the horizontal constraints applied to the Button object in Figure 27-16:

Figure 27-16

As currently configured, horizontal constraints run to the left and right edges of the parent ConstraintLayout. As such, the widget has opposing horizontal constraints indicating that the ConstraintLayout layout engine has some discretion in terms of the actual positioning of the widget at runtime. This allows the layout some flexibility to accommodate different screen sizes and device orientations. The horizontal bias setting can also control the widget's position right up to the right-hand side of the layout. Figure 27-17, for example, shows the same button with 100% horizontal bias applied:

Figure 27-17

ConstraintLayout margins can appear at the end of constraint connections and represent a fixed gap into which the widget cannot be moved, even when adjusting bias or responding to layout changes elsewhere in the activity. In Figure 27-18, the right-hand constraint now includes a 50dp margin into which the widget cannot be moved even though the bias is still set at 100%.

Figure 27-18

Existing margin values on a widget can be modified from within the Inspector. As shown in Figure 27-19, a drop-down menu is being used to change the right-hand margin on the currently selected widget to 16dp. Alternatively, clicking on the current value also allows a number to be typed into the field.

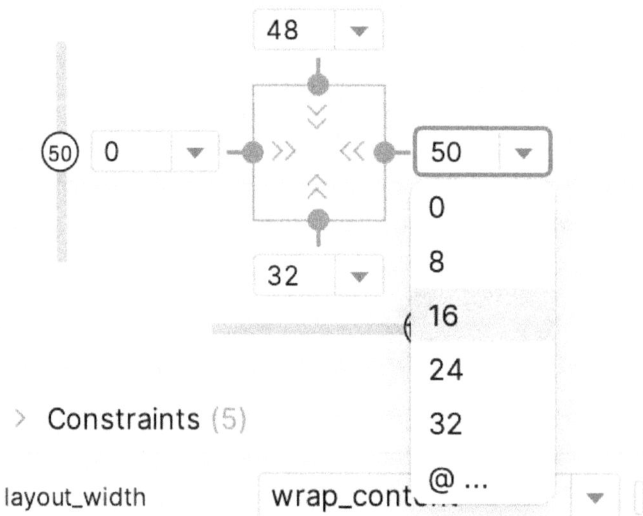

Figure 27-19

The default margin for new constraints can be changed at any time using the option in the toolbar highlighted in Figure 27-20:

Figure 27-20

27.10 The Importance of Opposing Constraints and Bias

As discussed in the previous chapter, opposing constraints, margins, and bias form the cornerstone of responsive layout design in Android when using the ConstraintLayout. When a widget is constrained without opposing constraint connections, those constraints are essentially margin constraints. This is indicated visually within the Layout Editor tool by solid straight lines accompanied by margin measurements, as shown in Figure 27-21.

Figure 27-21

The above constraints fix the widget at that position. The result is that if the device is rotated to landscape orientation, the widget will no longer be visible since the vertical constraint pushes it beyond the top edge of the device screen (as is the case in Figure 27-22). A similar problem will arise if the app is run on a device with a smaller screen than that used during the design process.

Figure 27-22

When opposing constraints are implemented, the constraint connection is represented by the jagged spring-like line (the spring metaphor is intended to indicate that the position of the widget is not fixed to absolute X and Y coordinates):

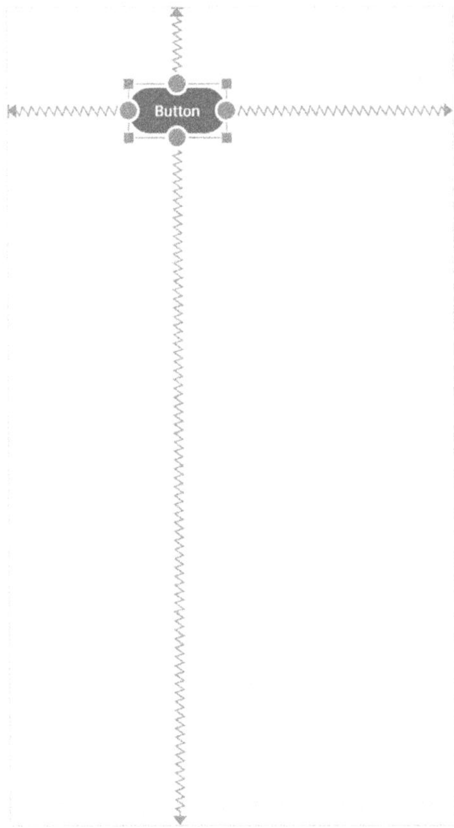

Figure 27-23

In the above layout, vertical and horizontal bias settings have been configured such that the widget will always be positioned 90% of the distance from the bottom and 35% from the left-hand edge of the parent layout. When rotated, therefore, the widget is still visible and positioned in the same location relative to the dimensions of the screen:

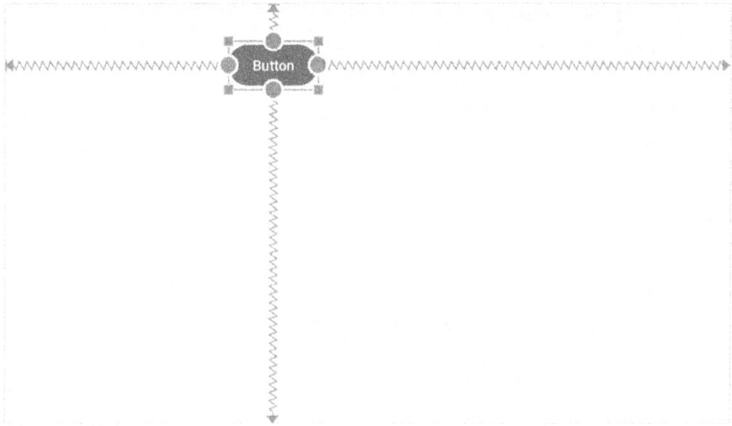

Figure 27-24

When designing a responsive and adaptable user interface layout, it is important to consider bias and opposing constraints when manually designing a user interface layout and correcting automatically created constraints.

27.11 Configuring Widget Dimensions

The inner dimensions of a widget within a ConstraintLayout can also be configured using the Inspector. As outlined in the previous chapter, widget dimensions can be set to wrap content, fixed, or match constraint modes. The prevailing settings for each dimension on the currently selected widget are shown within the square representing the widget in the Inspector, as illustrated in Figure 27-25:

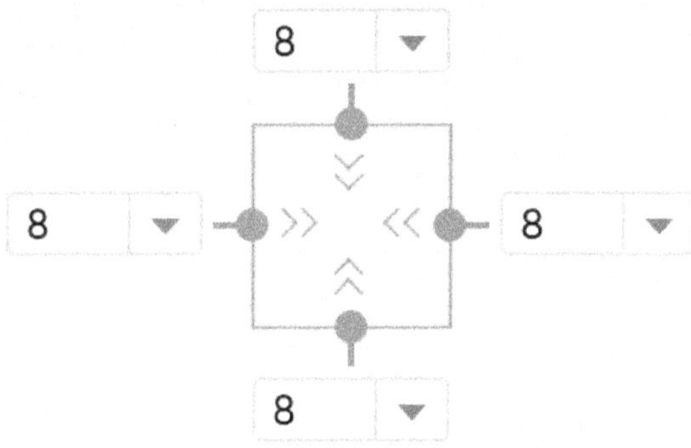

Figure 27-25

The above figure sets the horizontal and vertical dimensions to wrap content mode (indicated by the inward-pointing chevrons). The inspector uses the following visual indicators to represent the three dimension modes:

Fixed Size	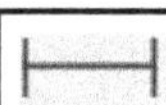
Match Constraint	
Wrap Content	

Table 27-1

To change the current setting, click on the indicator to cycle through the three settings.

In addition, a widget's size can be expanded horizontally or vertically to the maximum amount allowed by the constraints and other widgets in the layout using the Expand Horizontally and Expand Vertically options. These are accessible by right-clicking on a widget within the layout and selecting the Organize option from the resulting menu (Figure 27-26). When used, the currently selected widget will increase in size horizontally or vertically to fill the available space around it.

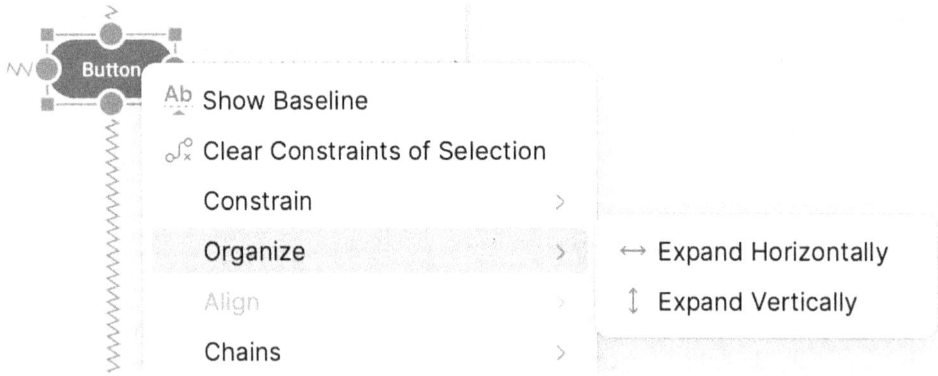

Figure 27-26

27.12 Design Time Tools Positioning

The chapter entitled *"A Guide to the Android Studio Layout Editor Tool"* introduced the concept of the *tools* namespace and explained how it can be used to set visibility attributes that only take effect within the layout editor. Behind the scenes, Android Studio also uses tools attributes to hold widgets in position when placed on the layout without constraints. Imagine, for example, a Button placed onto the layout while autoconnect mode is disabled. While the widget will appear to be in the correct position within the preview canvas, when the app is run, it will appear in the top left-hand corner of the screen. This is because the widget has no constraints to tell the ConstraintLayout parent where to position it.

The widget appears to be in the correct location in the layout editor because Android Studio has set absolute X and Y positioning tools attributes to keep it in the correct location until constraints can be added. Within the XML layout file, this might read as follows:

```
<Button
    android:id="@+id/button4"
    android:layout_width="wrap_content"
    android:layout_height="wrap_content"
    android:text="Button"
    tools:layout_editor_absoluteX="111dp"
    tools:layout_editor_absoluteY="88dp" />
```

Once adequate constraints have been added to the widget, the layout editor will remove these tools attributes. A useful technique for quickly identifying which widgets lack constraints without waiting for the app to run is to use the menu shown in Figure 27-27 to toggle tools position visibility. Any widgets that jump to the top left-hand corner are not fully constrained and are being held in place by temporary tools absolute X and Y positioning attributes.

Figure 27-27

27.13 Adding Guidelines

Guidelines provide additional elements to which constraints may be anchored. Guidelines are added by right-clicking on the layout and selecting either the *Vertical Guideline* or *Horizontal Guideline* menu option or using the toolbar menu options as shown in Figure 27-28:

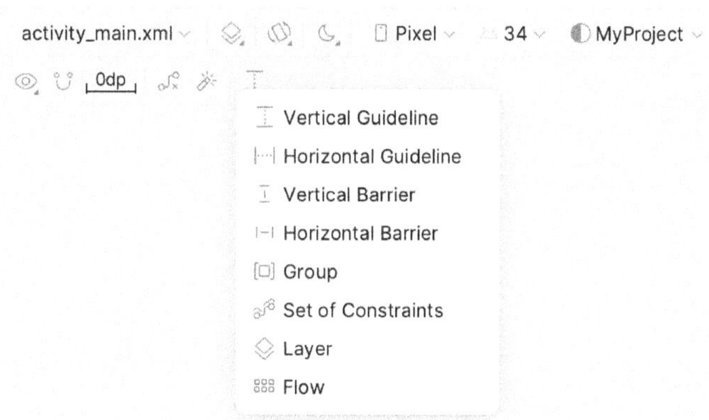

Figure 27-28

Alternatively, horizontal and vertical Guidelines may be dragged from the Helpers section of the Palette and dropped either onto the layout canvas or Component Tree panel as indicated by the arrows in Figure 27-29:

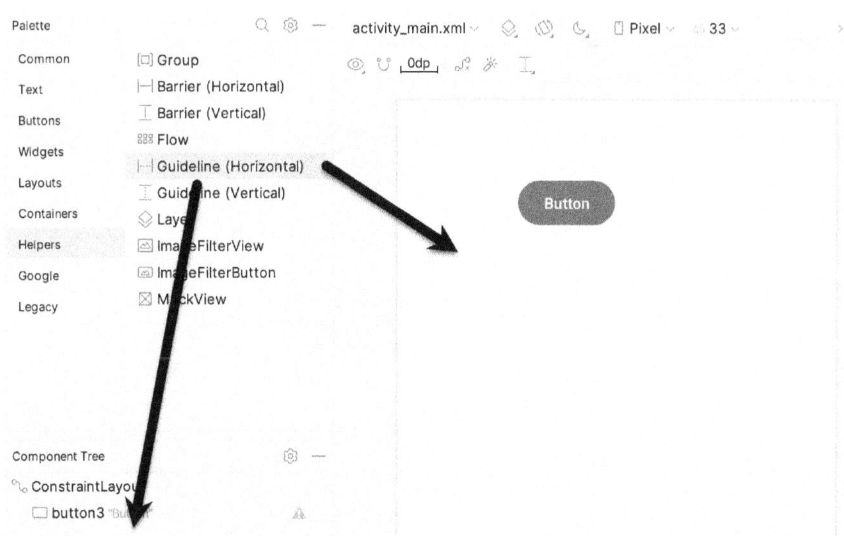

Figure 27-29

Once added, a guideline will appear as a dashed line in the layout and may be moved by clicking and dragging the line. To establish a constraint connection to a guideline, click on the constraint handler of a widget and drag it to the guideline before releasing. In Figure 27-30, the left sides of two Buttons are connected by constraints to a vertical guideline.

The position of a vertical guideline can be specified as an absolute distance from either the left or the right of the parent layout (or the top or bottom for a horizontal guideline). For example, the vertical guideline in the figure below is positioned at 97dp from the left-hand edge of the parent:

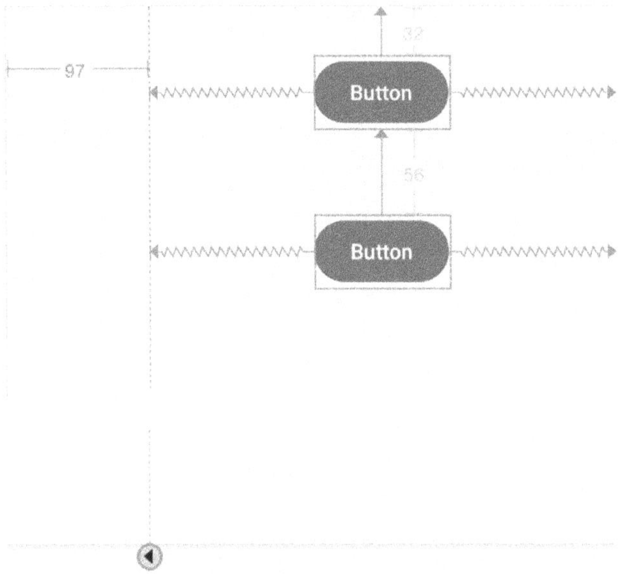

Figure 27-30

Alternatively, the guideline may be positioned as a percentage of the overall width or height of the parent layout. To switch between these three modes, select the guideline and click on the circle at the bottom or end of the guideline (depending on whether the guideline is vertical or horizontal). Figure 27-31, for example, shows a guideline positioned based on percentage:

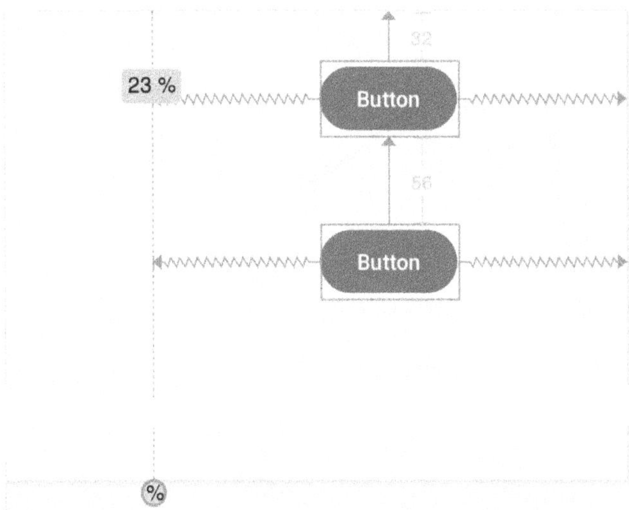

Figure 27-31

27.14 Adding Barriers

Barriers are added by right-clicking on the layout and selecting either the *Vertical* or *Horizontal Barrier* option from the *Add helpers* menu or using the toolbar menu options, as shown in Figure 27-28. Alternatively, locate the Barrier types in the Helpers section of the Palette and drag and drop them either onto the layout canvas or the Component Tree panel.

Once a barrier has been added to the layout, it will appear as an entry in the Component Tree panel:

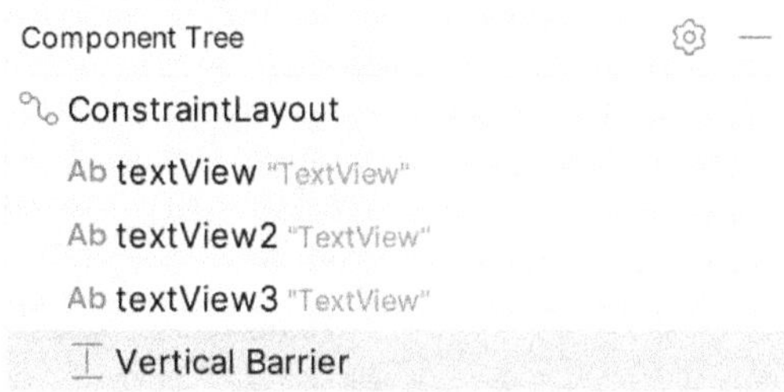

Figure 27-32

To add views as reference views (in other words, the views that control the position of the barrier), drag the widgets from within the Component Tree onto the barrier entry. In Figure 27-33, for example, widgets named textView2 and textView3 have been assigned as the reference widgets for the barrier:

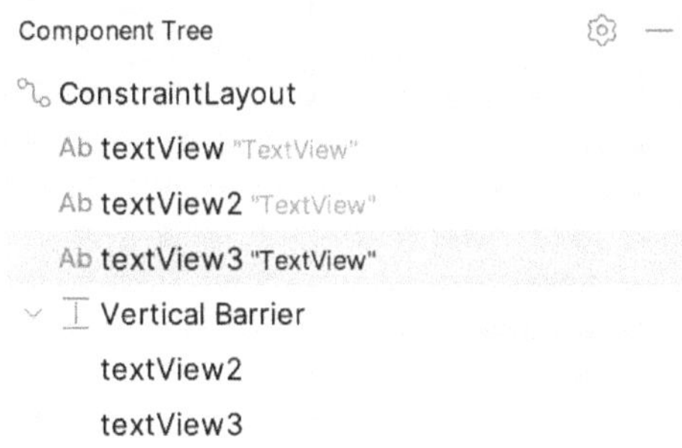

Figure 27-33

After the reference views have been added, the barrier needs to be configured to specify the direction of the barrier relative to those views. This is the *barrier direction* setting and is defined within the Attributes tool window when the barrier is selected in the Component Tree panel:

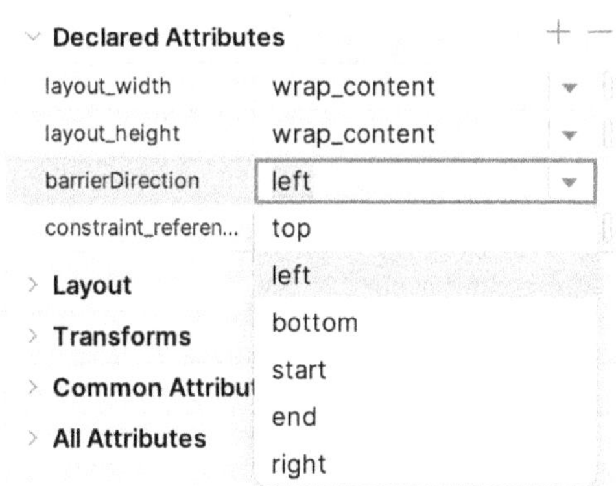

Figure 27-34

The following figure shows a layout containing a barrier declared with textView1 and textView2 acting as the reference views and textview3 as the constrained view. Since the barrier is pushing from the end of the reference views towards the constrained view, the barrier direction has been set to *end*:

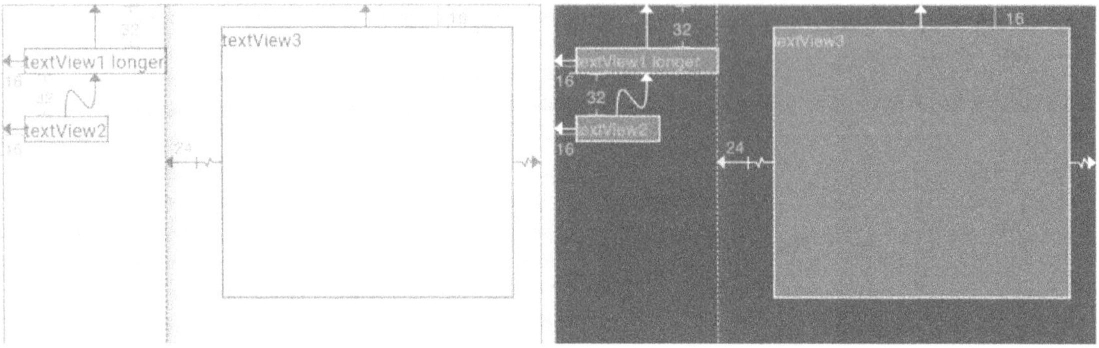

Figure 27-35

27.15 Adding a Group

To add a Group to a layout, right-click on the layout and select the *Group* option from the Add *helpers* menu or use the toolbar menu options shown in Figure 27-28. Alternatively, locate the Group item in the Helpers section of the Palette and drag and drop it either onto the layout canvas or Component Tree panel.

To add widgets to the group, select them in the Component Tree and drag and drop them onto the Group entry. Figure 27-36, for example, shows three selected widgets being added to a group:

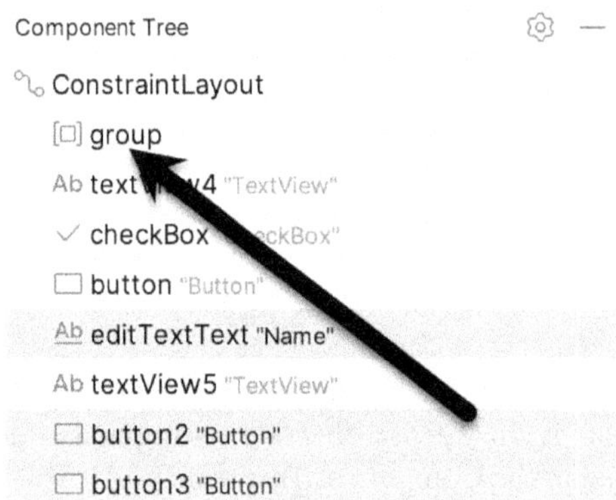

Figure 27-36

Any widgets referenced by the group will appear italicized beneath the group entry in the Component Tree, as shown in Figure 27-37. To remove a widget from the group, select it and tap the keyboard delete key:

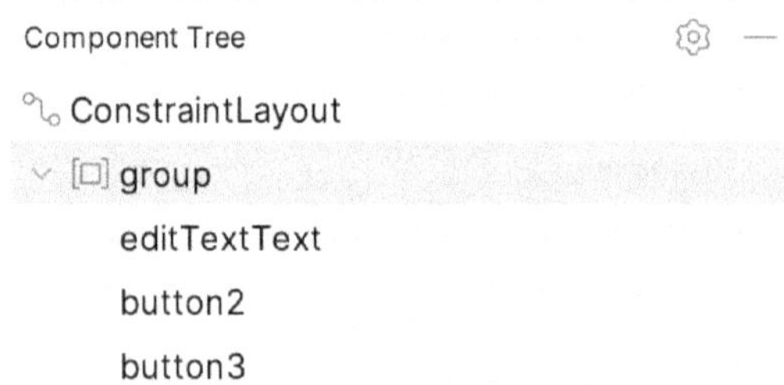

Figure 27-37

Once widgets have been assigned to the group, use the Constraints section of the Attributes tool window to modify the visibility setting:

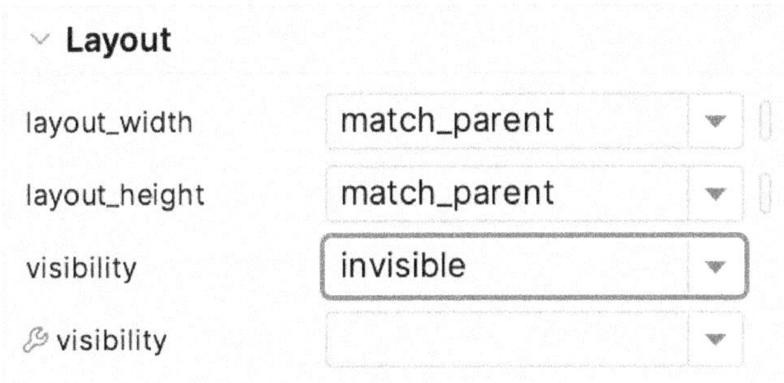

Figure 27-38

27.16 Working with the Flow Helper

Flow helpers may be added using either the menu or Palette, as outlined previously for the other helpers. As with the Group helper (Figure 27-36), widgets are added to a Flow instance by dragging them within the Component Tree onto the Flow entry. Having added a Flow helper and assigned widgets to it, select it in the Component Tree and use the Common Attributes section of the Attribute tool window to configure the flow layout behavior:

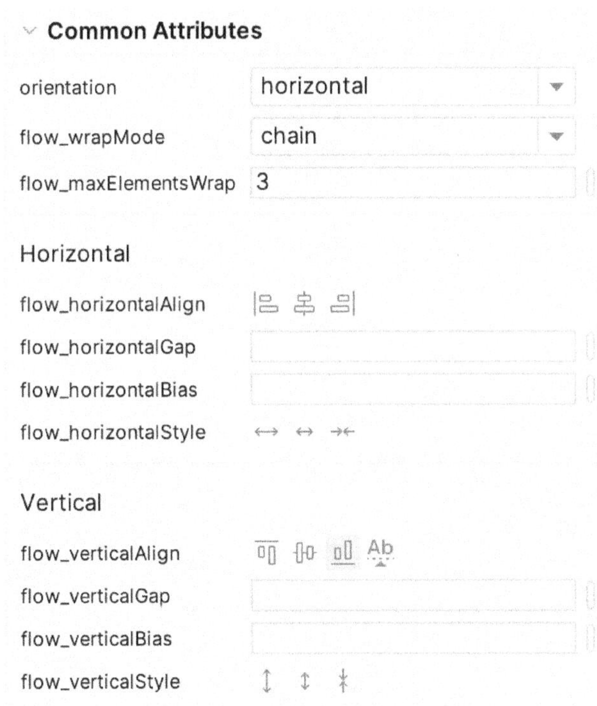

Figure 27-39

27.17 Widget Group Alignment and Distribution

The Android Studio Layout Editor tool provides a range of alignment and distribution actions that can be performed when two or more widgets are selected in the layout. Shift-click on each of the widgets to be included in the action, right-click on the layout and make a selection from the many options displayed in the Align menu:

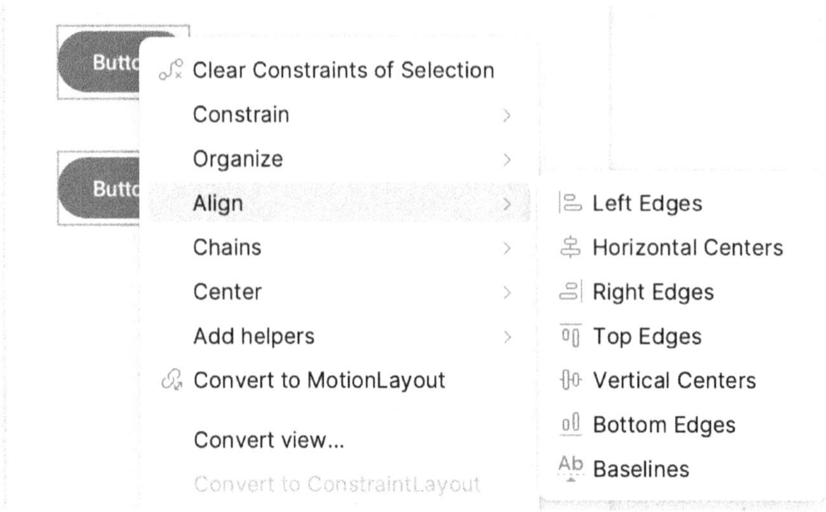

Figure 27-40

As shown in Figure 27-41 below, these options are also accessible via the Align button located in the Layout Editor toolbar:

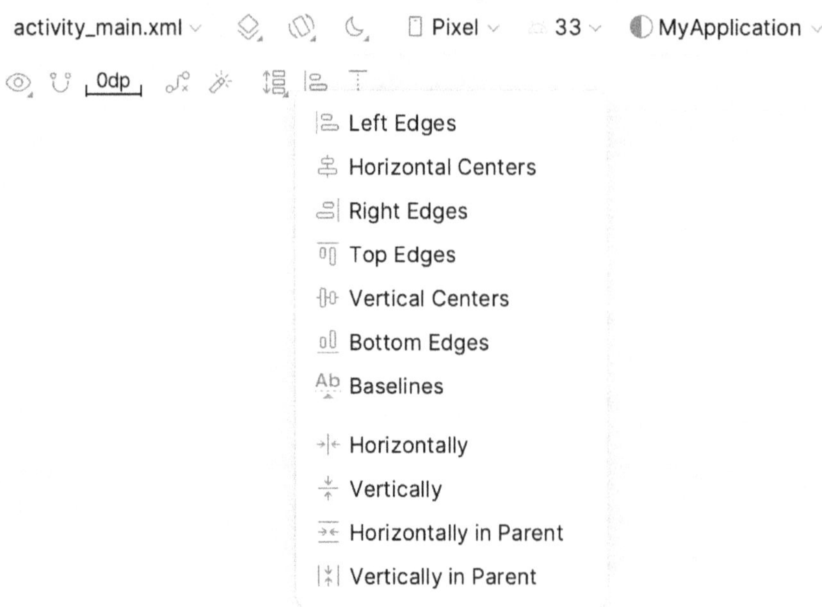

Figure 27-41

Similarly, the Pack menu (Figure 27-42) can be used to collectively reposition the selected widgets so that they are packed tightly together, either vertically or horizontally. It achieves this by changing the widgets' absolute x and y coordinates but does not apply any constraints. The two distribution options in the Pack menu, on the other hand, move the selected widgets so that they are spaced evenly apart in either vertical or horizontal axis and apply constraints between the views to maintain this spacing:

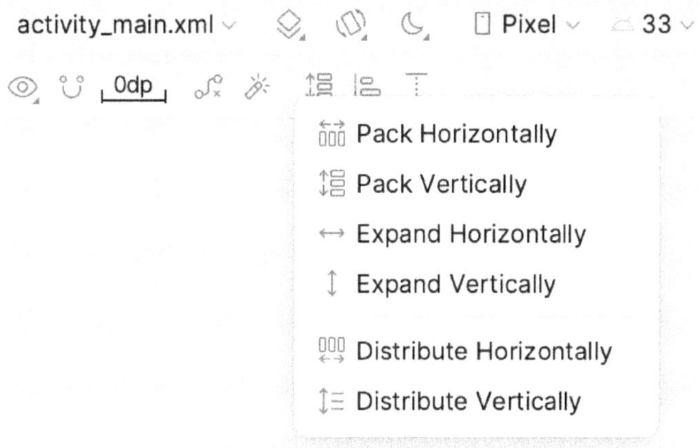

Figure 27-42

27.18 Converting other Layouts to ConstraintLayout

For existing user interface layouts that use one or more of the other Android layout classes (such as RelativeLayout or LinearLayout), the Layout Editor tool provides an option to convert the user interface to use the ConstraintLayout.

The Component Tree panel is displayed beneath the Palette when the Layout Editor tool is open and in Design mode. To convert a layout to ConstraintLayout, locate it within the Component Tree, right-click on it, and select the *Convert <current layout> to Constraint Layout* menu option:

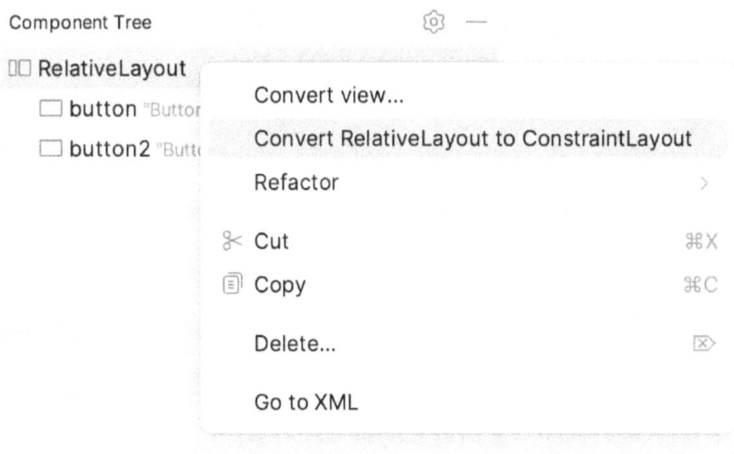

Figure 27-43

When this menu option is selected, Android Studio will convert the selected layout to a ConstraintLayout and use inference to establish constraints designed to match the layout behavior of the original layout type.

27.19 Summary

A redesigned Layout Editor tool combined with ConstraintLayout makes designing complex user interface layouts with Android Studio a relatively fast and intuitive process. This chapter has covered the concepts of constraints, margins, and bias in more detail while also exploring how ConstraintLayout-based design has been integrated into the Layout Editor tool.

Chapter 28

28. Working with ConstraintLayout Chains and Ratios in Android Studio

The previous chapters have introduced the key features of the ConstraintLayout class and outlined the best practices for ConstraintLayout-based user interface design within the Android Studio Layout Editor. Although the concepts of ConstraintLayout chains and ratios were outlined in the chapter entitled *"A Guide to the Android ConstraintLayout"*, we have not yet addressed how to use these features within the Layout Editor. Therefore, this chapter's focus is to provide practical steps on how to create and manage chains and ratios when using the ConstraintLayout class.

28.1 Creating a Chain

Chains may be implemented by adding a few lines to an activity's XML layout resource file or by using some chain-specific features of the Layout Editor.

Consider a layout consisting of three Button widgets constrained to be positioned in the top-left, top-center, and top-right of the ConstraintLayout parent, as illustrated in Figure 28-1:

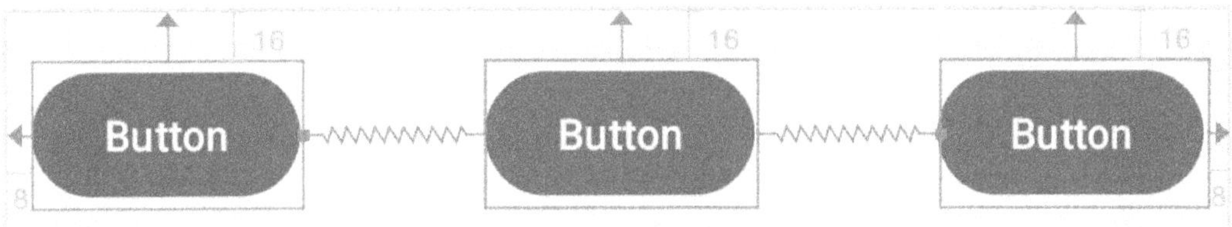

Figure 28-1

To represent such a layout, the XML resource layout file might contain the following entries for the button widgets:

```
<Button
    android:id="@+id/button1"
    android:layout_width="wrap_content"
    android:layout_height="wrap_content"
    android:layout_marginStart="8dp"
    android:layout_marginTop="16dp"
    android:text="Button"
    app:layout_constraintHorizontal_bias="0.5"
    app:layout_constraintStart_toStartOf="parent"
    app:layout_constraintTop_toTopOf="parent" />

<Button
    android:id="@+id/button2"
    android:layout_width="wrap_content"
    android:layout_height="wrap_content"
```

```
    android:layout_marginEnd="8dp"
    android:layout_marginStart="8dp"
    android:layout_marginTop="16dp"
    android:text="Button"
    app:layout_constraintHorizontal_bias="0.5"
    app:layout_constraintEnd_toStartOf="@+id/button3"
    app:layout_constraintStart_toEndOf="@+id/button1"
    app:layout_constraintTop_toTopOf="parent" />

<Button
    android:id="@+id/button3"
    android:layout_width="wrap_content"
    android:layout_height="wrap_content"
    android:layout_marginEnd="8dp"
    android:layout_marginTop="16dp"
    android:text="Button"
    app:layout_constraintHorizontal_bias="0.5"
    app:layout_constraintEnd_toEndOf="parent"
    app:layout_constraintTop_toTopOf="parent" />
```

As currently configured, there are no bi-directional constraints to group these widgets into a chain. To address this, additional constraints need to be added from the right-hand side of button1 to the left side of button2 and from the left side of button3 to the right side of button2 as follows:

```
<Button
    android:id="@+id/button1"
    android:layout_width="wrap_content"
    android:layout_height="wrap_content"
    android:layout_marginStart="8dp"
    android:layout_marginTop="16dp"
    android:text="Button"
    app:layout_constraintHorizontal_bias="0.5"
    app:layout_constraintStart_toStartOf="parent"
    app:layout_constraintTop_toTopOf="parent"
    app:layout_constraintEnd_toStartOf="@+id/button2" />

<Button
    android:id="@+id/button2"
    android:layout_width="wrap_content"
    android:layout_height="wrap_content"
    android:layout_marginEnd="8dp"
    android:layout_marginStart="8dp"
    android:layout_marginTop="16dp"
    android:text="Button"
    app:layout_constraintHorizontal_bias="0.5"
    app:layout_constraintEnd_toStartOf="@+id/button3"
    app:layout_constraintStart_toEndOf="@+id/button1"
```

```
    app:layout_constraintTop_toTopOf="parent" />

<Button
    android:id="@+id/button3"
    android:layout_width="wrap_content"
    android:layout_height="wrap_content"
    android:layout_marginEnd="8dp"
    android:layout_marginTop="16dp"
    android:text="Button"
    app:layout_constraintHorizontal_bias="0.5"
    app:layout_constraintEnd_toEndOf="parent"
    app:layout_constraintTop_toTopOf="parent"
    app:layout_constraintStart_toEndOf="@+id/button2" />
```

With these changes, the widgets now have bi-directional horizontal constraints configured. This constitutes a ConstraintLayout chain represented visually within the Layout Editor by chain connections, as shown in Figure 28-2 below. Note that the chain has defaulted to the *spread* chain style in this configuration.

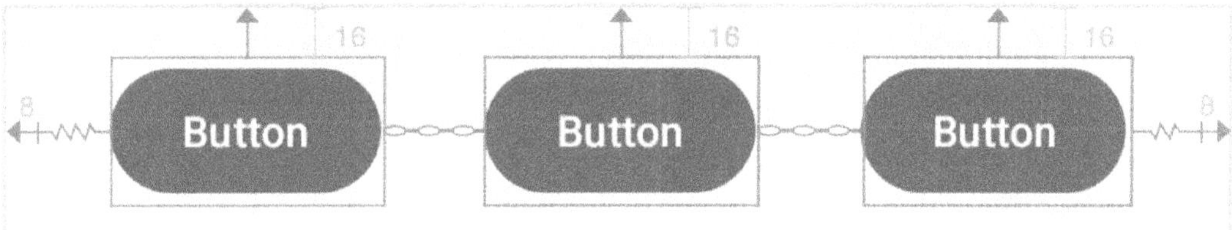

Figure 28-2

A chain may also be created by right-clicking on one of the views and selecting the *Chains -> Create Horizontal Chain* or *Chains -> Create Vertical Chain* menu options.

28.2 Changing the Chain Style

If no chain style is configured, the ConstraintLayout will default to the spread chain style. The chain style can be altered by right-clicking any of the widgets in the chain and selecting the *Cycle Chain Mode* menu option. Each time the menu option is clicked, the style will switch to another setting in the order of spread, spread inside, and packed.

Alternatively, the style may be specified in the Attributes tool window unfolding the *layout_constraints* property and changing either the *horizontal_chainStyle* or *vertical_chainStyle* property depending on the orientation of the chain:

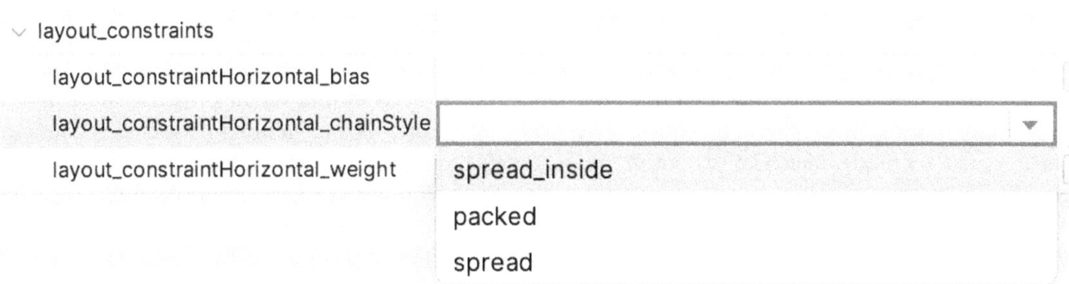

Figure 28-3

28.3 Spread Inside Chain Style

Figure 28-4 illustrates the effect of changing the chain style to the *spread inside* chain style using the above techniques:

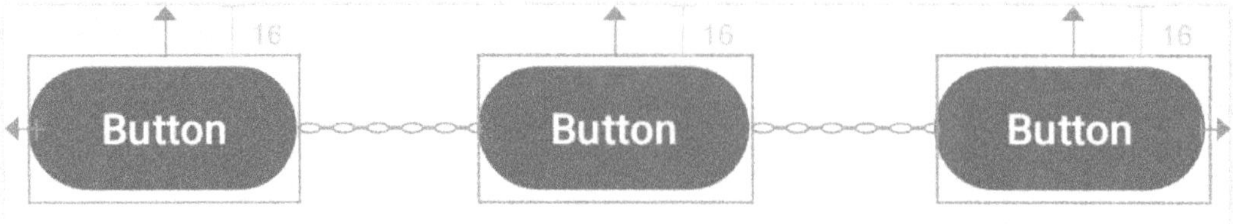

Figure 28-4

28.4 Packed Chain Style

Using the same technique, changing the chain style property to *packed* causes the layout to change, as shown in Figure 28-5:

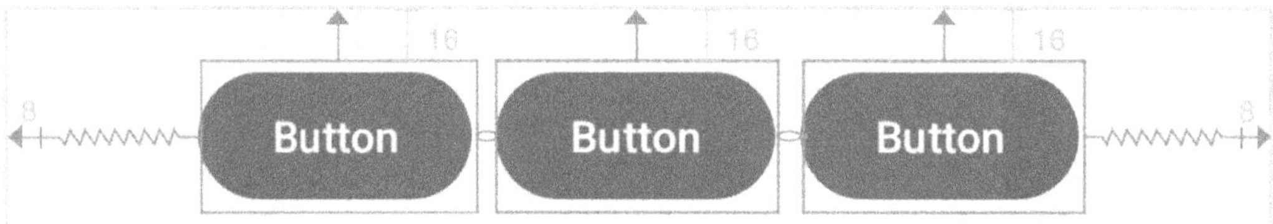

Figure 28-5

28.5 Packed Chain Style with Bias

The positioning of the packed chain may be influenced by applying a bias value. The bias can be between 0.0 and 1.0, with 0.5 representing the parent's center. Bias is controlled by selecting the chain head widget and assigning a value to the *layout_constraintHorizontal_bias* or *layout_constraintVertical_bias* attribute in the Attributes panel. Figure 28-6 shows a packed chain with a horizontal bias setting of 0.2:

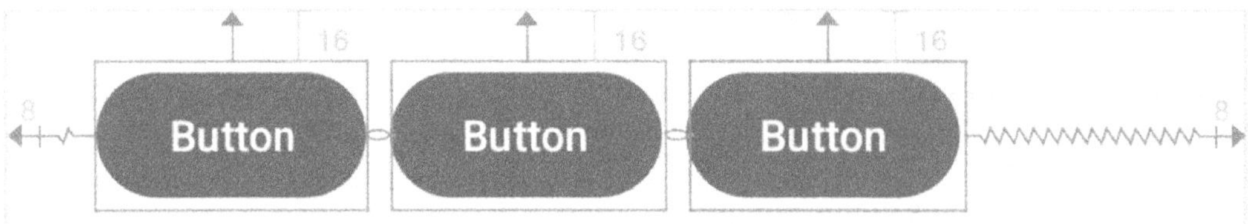

Figure 28-6

28.6 Weighted Chain

The final area of chains to explore involves weighting the individual widgets to control how much space each widget in the chain occupies within the available space. A weighted chain may only be implemented using the spread chain style, and any widget within the chain that responds to the weight property must have the corresponding dimension property (height for a vertical chain and width for a horizontal chain) configured for *match constraint* mode. Match constraint mode for a widget dimension may be configured by selecting the widget, displaying the Attributes panel, and changing the dimension to *match_constraint* (equivalent to 0dp). In Figure 28-7, for example, the *layout_width* constraint for a button has been set to *match_constraint (0dp)* to indicate that the width of the widget is to be determined based on the prevailing constraint settings:

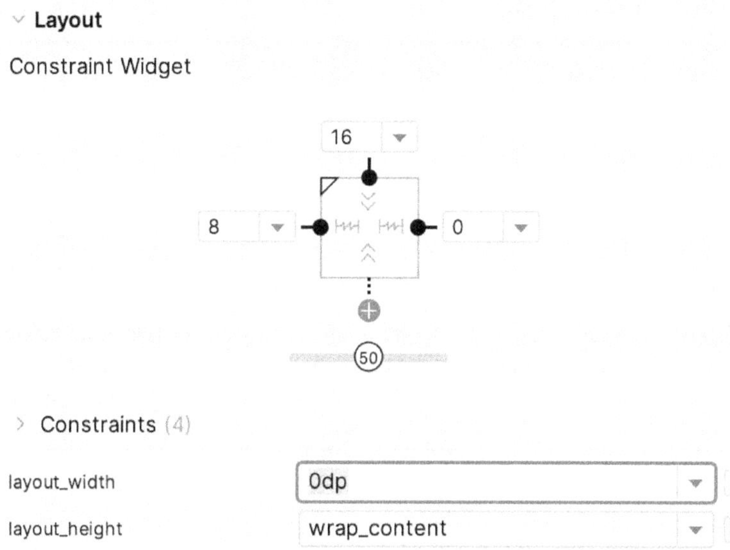

Figure 28-7

Assuming that the spread chain style has been selected and all three buttons have been configured such that the width dimension is set to match the constraints, the widgets in the chain will expand equally to fill the available space:

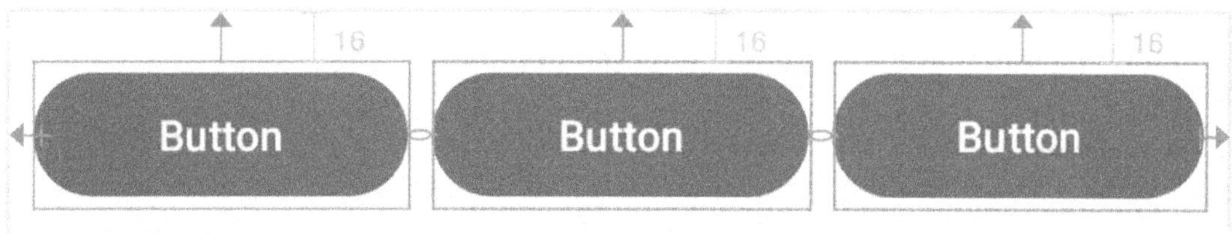

Figure 28-8

The amount of space occupied by each widget relative to the other widgets in the chain can be controlled by adding weight properties to the widgets. Figure 28-9 shows the effect of setting the *layout_constraintHorizontal_weight* property to 4 on button1, and to 2 on both button2 and button3:

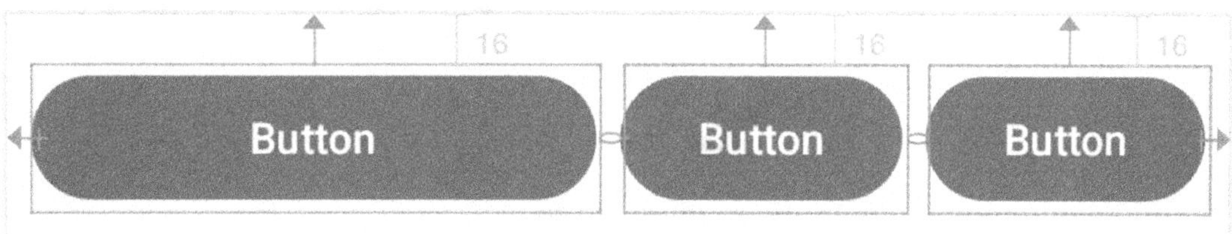

Figure 28-9

As a result of these weighting values, button1 occupies half of the space (4/8), while button2 and button3 each occupy one-quarter (2/8) of the space.

28.7 Working with Ratios

ConstraintLayout ratios allow one widget dimension to be sized relative to the widget's other dimension (also referred to as aspect ratio). For example, an aspect ratio setting could be applied to an ImageView to ensure that its width is always twice its height.

A dimension ratio constraint is configured by setting the constrained dimension to match constraint mode and configuring the *layout_constraintDimensionRatio* attribute on that widget to the required ratio. This ratio value may be specified as a float value or a *width:height* ratio setting. The following XML excerpt, for example, configures a ratio of 2:1 on an ImageView widget:

```
<ImageView
        android:layout_width="0dp"
        android:layout_height="100dp"
        android:id="@+id/imageView"
        app:layout_constraintDimensionRatio="2:1" />
```

The above example demonstrates how to configure a ratio when only one dimension is set to *match constraint*. A ratio may also be applied when both dimensions are set to match constraint mode. This involves specifying the ratio preceded with either an H or a W to indicate which of the dimensions is constrained relative to the other.

Consider, for example, the following XML excerpt for an ImageView object:

```
<ImageView
    android:layout_width="0dp"
    android:layout_height="0dp"
    android:id="@+id/imageView"
    app:layout_constraintBottom_toBottomOf="parent"
    app:layout_constraintRight_toRightOf="parent"
    app:layout_constraintLeft_toLeftOf="parent"
    app:layout_constraintTop_toTopOf="parent"
    app:layout_constraintDimensionRatio="W,1:3" />
```

In the above example, the height will be defined subject to the constraints applied to it. In this case, constraints have been configured such that it is attached to the top and bottom of the parent view, essentially stretching the widget to fill the entire height of the parent. On the other hand, the width dimension has been constrained to be one-third of the ImageView's height dimension. Consequently, whatever size screen or orientation the layout appears on, the ImageView will always be the same height as the parent and the width one-third of that height.

The same results may also be achieved without manually editing the XML resource file. Whenever a widget dimension is set to match constraint mode, a ratio control toggle appears in the Inspector area of the property panel. Figure 28-10, for example, shows the layout width and height attributes of a button widget set to match constraint mode and 100dp respectively, and highlights the ratio control toggle in the widget sizing preview:

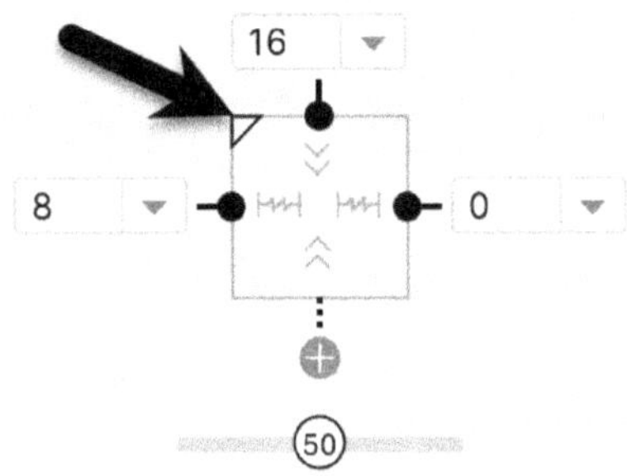

Figure 28-10

By default, the ratio sizing control is toggled off. Clicking on the control enables the ratio constraint and displays an additional field where the ratio may be changed:

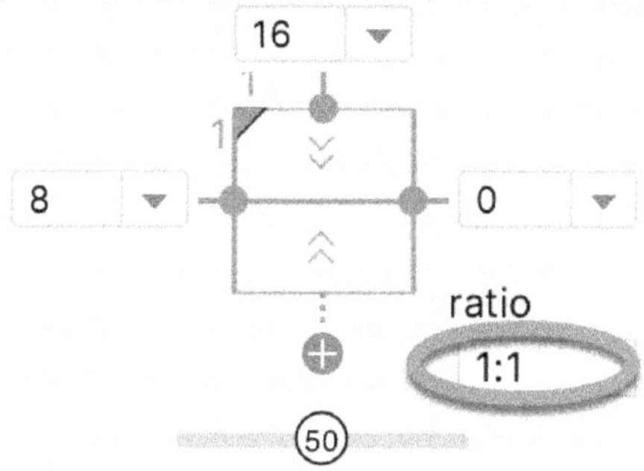

Figure 28-11

28.8 Summary

Both chains and ratios are powerful features of the ConstraintLayout class intended to provide additional options for designing flexible and responsive user interface layouts within Android applications. As outlined in this chapter, the Android Studio Layout Editor has been enhanced to make it easier to use these features during the user interface design process.

29. An Android Studio Layout Editor ConstraintLayout Tutorial

The easiest and most productive way to design a user interface for an Android application is to use the Android Studio Layout Editor tool. This chapter will provide an overview of how to create a ConstraintLayout-based user interface using this approach. The exercise included in this chapter will also be used as an opportunity to outline the creation of an activity starting with a "bare-bones" Android Studio project.

Having covered the use of the Android Studio Layout Editor, the chapter will also introduce the Layout Inspector tool.

29.1 An Android Studio Layout Editor Tool Example

The first step in this phase of the example is to create a new Android Studio project. Launch Android Studio and close any previously opened projects by selecting the *File -> Close Project* menu option.

Select the *New Project* option from the welcome screen, select the Empty Views Activity template, and click Next. Enter *LayoutSample* into the Name field and specify *com.ebookfrenzy.layoutsample* as the package name. Before clicking the Finish button, change the Minimum API level setting to API 26: Android 8.0 (Oreo) and the Language menu to Kotlin.

29.2 Preparing the Layout Editor Environment

Locate and double-click on the *activity_main.xml* layout file in the *app -> res -> layout* folder to load it into the Layout Editor tool. Since this tutorial aims to gain experience with the use of constraints, turn off the Autoconnect feature using the button located in the Layout Editor toolbar. Once disabled, the button will appear with a line through it, as is the case in Figure 29-1:

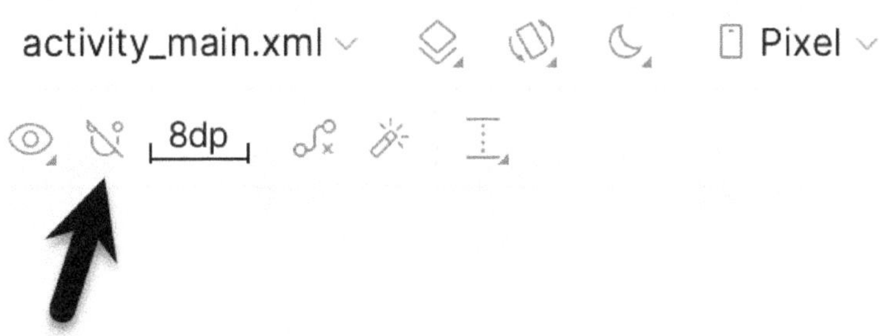

Figure 29-1

If the default margin value to the right of the Autoconnect button is not set to 8dp, click on it and select 8dp from the resulting panel.

The user interface design will also use the ImageView object to display an image. Before proceeding, this image should be added to the project, ready for use later in the chapter. This file is named *GalaxyS23.webp* and can be found in the *project_icons* folder of the sample code download available from the following URL:

https://www.payloadbooks.com/product/quailkotlin

Within Android Studio, display the Resource Manager tool window (*View -> Tool Windows -> Resource Manager*). Locate the *GalaxyS23.webp* image in the file system navigator for your operating system and drag and drop the image onto the Resource Manager tool window. In the resulting dialog, click *Next*, followed by the *Import* button, to add the image to the project. The image should now appear in the Resource Manager, as shown in Figure 29-2 below:

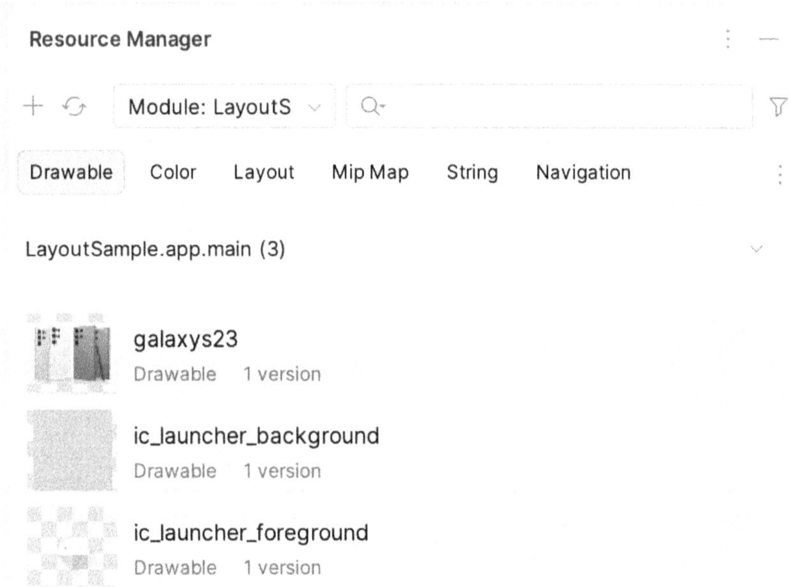

Figure 29-2

The image will also appear in the *res -> drawable* section of the Project tool window:

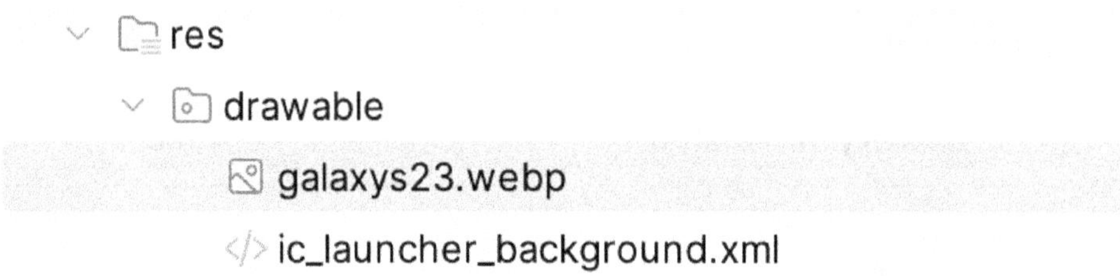

Figure 29-3

29.3 Adding the Widgets to the User Interface

Select and delete the "Hello World" TextView, then, from within the *Common* palette category, drag an ImageView object into the center of the display view. Note that horizontal and vertical dashed lines appear, indicating the center axes of the display. When centered, release the mouse button to drop the view into position. Once placed within the layout, the Resources dialog will appear, seeking the image to be displayed within the view. In the search bar at the top of the dialog, enter "galaxy" to locate the *galaxys23.png* resource, as illustrated in Figure 29-4.

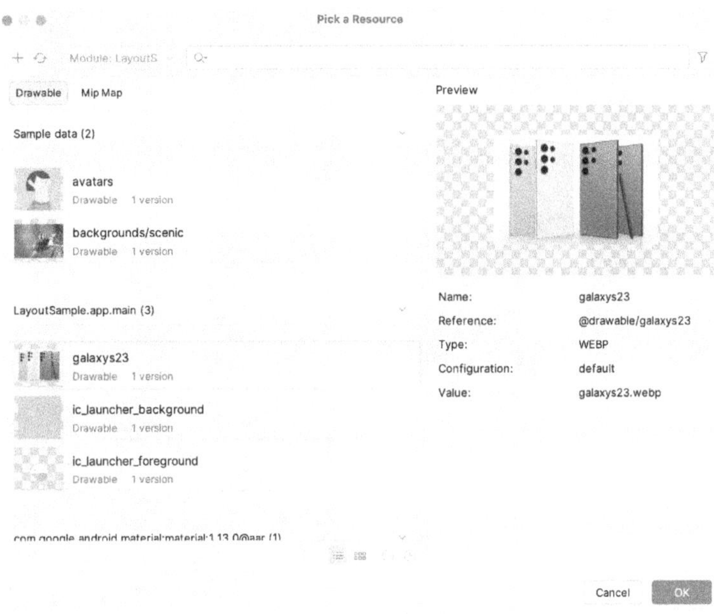

Figure 29-4

Select the image and click OK to assign it to the ImageView object. If necessary, adjust the size of the ImageView using the resize handles and reposition it in the center of the layout. At this point, the layout should match Figure 29-5:

Figure 29-5

Click and drag a TextView object from the *Common* section of the palette and position it to appear above the ImageView, as illustrated in Figure 29-6.

Using the Attributes panel, unfold the *textAppearance* attribute entry in the Common Attributes section, change the *textSize* property to 24sp, the *textAlignment* setting to center, and the text to "Samsung Galaxy S23".

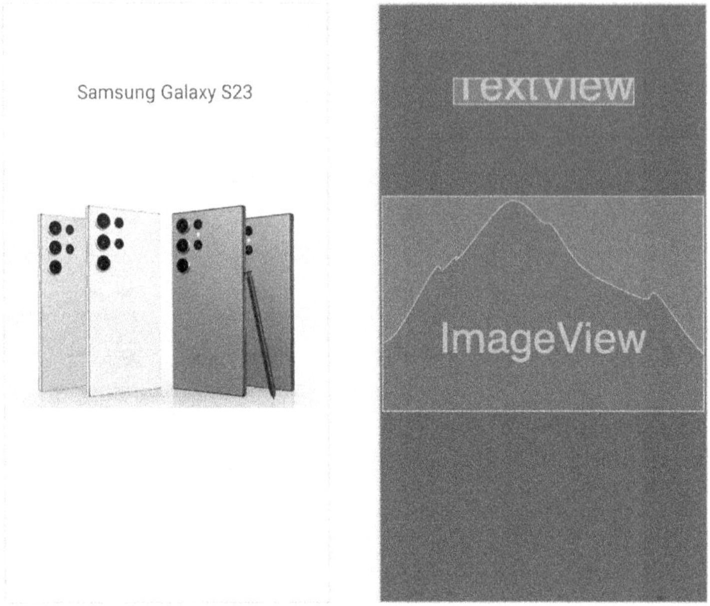

Figure 29-6

Next, add three Button widgets along the bottom of the layout and set the text attributes of these views to "Buy Now", "Pricing", and "Details". The completed layout should now match Figure 29-7:

Figure 29-7

At this point, the widgets are not sufficiently constrained for the layout engine to be able to position and size the widgets at runtime. Were the app to run now, all of the widgets would be positioned in the top left-hand corner of the display.

With the widgets added to the layout, use the device rotation menu located in the Layout Editor toolbar (indicated by the arrow in Figure 29-8) to view the user interface in landscape orientation:

Figure 29-8

The absence of constraints results in a layout that fails to adapt to the change in device orientation, leaving the content off-center and with part of the image and all three buttons positioned beyond the screen's viewable area. Some work still needs to be done to make this a responsive user interface.

29.4 Adding the Constraints

Constraints are the key to creating layouts that adapt to device orientation changes and different screen sizes. Begin by rotating the layout back to portrait orientation and selecting the TextView widget above the ImageView. With the widget selected, establish constraints from the left, right and top sides of the TextView to the corresponding sides of the parent ConstraintLayout, as shown in Figure 29-9. Set the spacing on the top constraint to 16:

Figure 29-9

With the TextView widget constrained, select the ImageView instance and establish opposing constraints on the left and right sides, each connected to the corresponding sides of the parent layout. Next, establish a constraint connection from the top of the ImageView to the bottom of the TextView and from the bottom of the ImageView to the top of the center Button widget. If necessary, click and drag the ImageView to remain positioned in the vertical center of the layout.

With the ImageView still selected, use the Inspector in the attributes panel to change the top and bottom margins on the ImageView to 24 and 8, respectively, and to change both the widget height and width dimension properties to *match_constraint* so that the widget will resize to match the constraints. These settings will allow the layout engine to enlarge and reduce the size of the ImageView when necessary to accommodate layout changes:

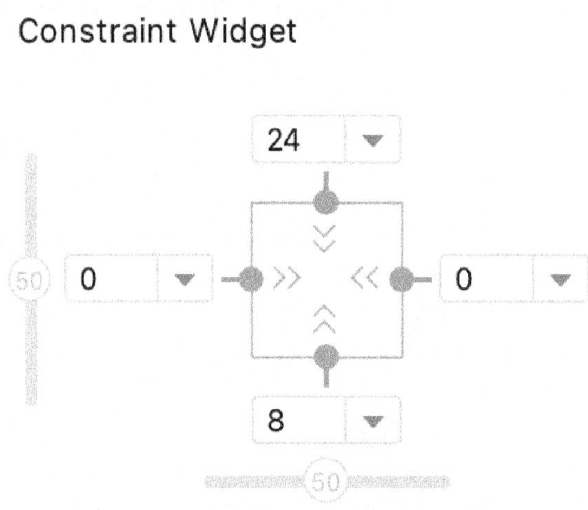

Figure 29-10

Figure 29-11 shows the currently implemented constraints for the ImageView relative to the other elements in the layout:

Figure 29-11

The final task is to add constraints to the three Button widgets. For this example, the buttons will be placed in a chain. Begin by turning on Autoconnect within the Layout Editor by clicking the toolbar button highlighted in Figure 29-1.

Next, click on the Buy Now button and then shift-click on the other two buttons to select all three. Right-click on the Buy Now button and select the *Chains -> Create Horizontal Chain* menu option from the resulting menu. By default, the chain will be displayed using the spread style, which is the correct behavior for this example.

Finally, establish a constraint between the bottom of the Buy Now button and the bottom of the layout with a margin of 8. Repeat this step for the remaining buttons.

On completion of these steps, the buttons should be constrained as outlined in Figure 29-12:

Figure 29-12

29.5 Testing the Layout

With the constraints added to the layout, rotate the screen into landscape orientation and verify that the layout adapts to accommodate the new screen dimensions.

While the Layout Editor tool provides a good visual environment in which to design user interface layouts, when it comes to testing, there is no substitute for testing the running app. Launch the app on a physical Android device or emulator session and verify that the user interface reflects the layout created in the Layout Editor. Figure 29-13, for example, shows the running app in landscape orientation:

Figure 29-13

The user interface design is now complete. Designing a more complex user interface layout is a continuation of the steps outlined above. Drag and drop views onto the display, position, constrain and set properties as needed.

29.6 Using the Layout Inspector

The hierarchy of components comprising a user interface layout may be viewed using the Layout Inspector tool. The app must be running on a device or emulator running Android API 29 or later to access this information. Once the app is running, display the Running Devices tool window using the button marked A in Figure 29-14, then click the button marked B to display the Layout Inspector:

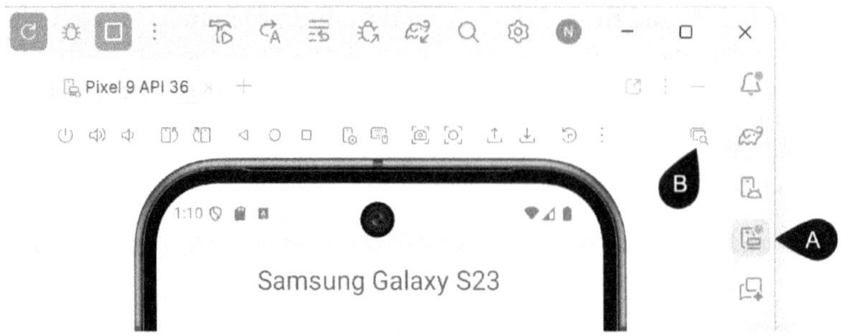

Figure 29-14

Once the inspector loads, the leftmost panel (marked A in Figure 29-15) shows the hierarchy of components that make up the user interface layout. The top panel (B) visually represents the layout design. Clicking on a widget in the hierarchy list will cause that item to highlight in visual layout, making it easy to find where a visual component is situated relative to the overall layout hierarchy.

The right-most panel (C) contains all the property settings for the currently selected component, allowing for an in-depth analysis of the component's internal configuration. Where appropriate, the value cell will contain a link to the location of the property setting within the project source code.

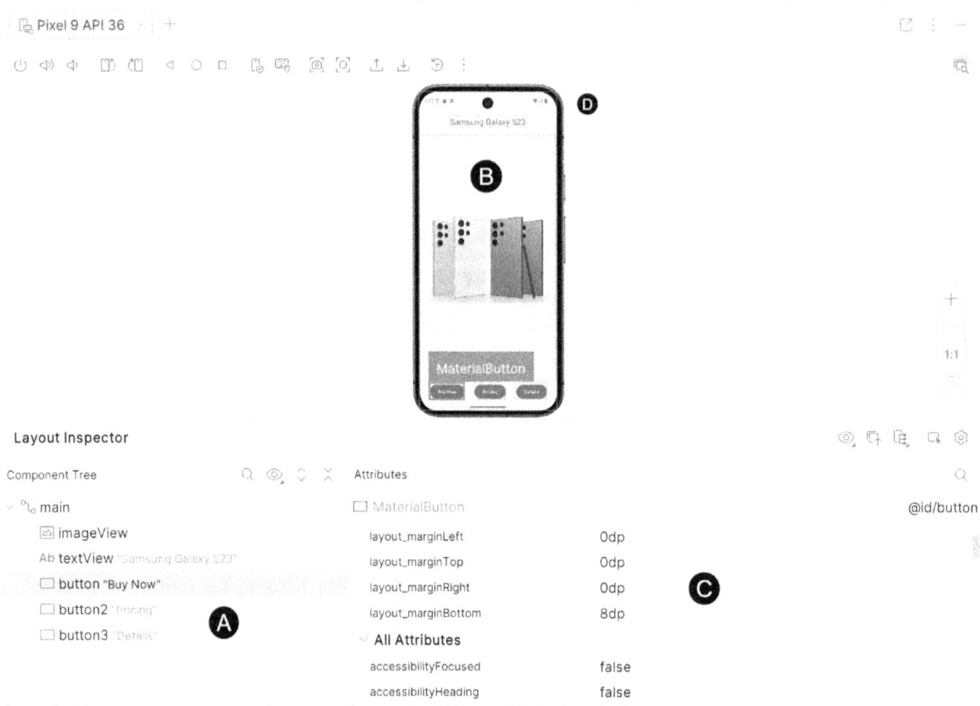

Figure 29-15

29.7 Summary

The Layout Editor tool in Android Studio has been tightly integrated with the ConstraintLayout class. This chapter has worked through creating an example user interface intended to outline how a ConstraintLayout-based user interface can be implemented using the Layout Editor tool to add widgets and set constraints. This chapter also introduced the Live Layout Inspector tool, which is useful for analyzing the structural composition of a user interface layout.

Chapter 30

30. Manual XML Layout Design in Android Studio

While the design of layouts using the Android Studio Layout Editor tool greatly improves productivity, it is still possible to create XML layouts by manually editing the underlying XML. This chapter will introduce the basics of the Android XML layout file format.

30.1 Manually Creating an XML Layout

The structure of an XML layout file is quite straightforward and follows the hierarchical approach of the view tree. The first line of an XML resource file should ideally include the following standard declaration:

```
<?xml version="1.0" encoding="utf-8"?>
```

This declaration should be followed by the root element of the layout, typically a container view such as a layout manager. This is represented by opening and closing tags and any properties that need to be set on the view. The following XML, for example, declares a ConstraintLayout view as the root element and sets *match_parent* attributes such that it fills all the available space of the device display:

```
<?xml version="1.0" encoding="utf-8"?>
<androidx.constraintlayout.widget.ConstraintLayout
    xmlns:android="http://schemas.android.com/apk/res/android"
    xmlns:app="http://schemas.android.com/apk/res-auto"
    xmlns:tools="http://schemas.android.com/tools"
    android:layout_width="match_parent"
    android:layout_height="match_parent"
    android:paddingLeft="16dp"
    android:paddingRight="16dp"
    android:paddingTop="16dp"
    android:paddingBottom="16dp"
    tools:context=".MainActivity">
</androidx.constraintlayout.widget.ConstraintLayout>
```

In the above example, the layout element is also configured with padding on each side of 16dp (density-independent pixels). Any specification of spacing in an Android layout must be specified using one of the following units of measurement:

- **in** – Inches.
- **mm** – Millimeters.
- **pt** – Points (1/72 of an inch).
- **dp** – Density-independent pixels. An abstract unit of measurement based on the physical density of the device display relative to a 160dpi display baseline.
- **sp** – Scale-independent pixels. Similar to dp but scaled based on the user's font preference.

- **px** – Actual screen pixels. Use is not recommended since different displays will have different pixels per inch. Use *dp* in preference to this unit.

Any children that need to be added to the ConstraintLayout parent must be *nested* within the opening and closing tags. In the following example, a Button widget has been added as a child of the ConstraintLayout:

```
<?xml version="1.0" encoding="utf-8"?>
<androidx.constraintlayout.widget.ConstraintLayout
    xmlns:android="http://schemas.android.com/apk/res/android"
    xmlns:app="http://schemas.android.com/apk/res-auto"
    xmlns:tools="http://schemas.android.com/tools"
    android:layout_width="match_parent"
    android:layout_height="match_parent"
    tools:context=".MainActivity">

    <Button
        android:text="My Button"
        android:layout_width="wrap_content"
        android:layout_height="wrap_content"
        android:id="@+id/button" />

</androidx.constraintlayout.widget.ConstraintLayout>
```

As currently implemented, the button has no constraint connections. At runtime, therefore, the button will appear in the top left-hand corner of the screen (though indented 16dp by the padding assigned to the parent layout). If opposing constraints are added to the sides of the button, however, it will appear centered within the layout:

```
<Button
    android:text="My Button"
    android:layout_width="wrap_content"
    android:layout_height="wrap_content"
    android:id="@+id/button"
    app:layout_constraintBottom_toBottomOf="parent"
    app:layout_constraintEnd_toEndOf="parent"
    app:layout_constraintStart_toStartOf="parent"
    app:layout_constraintTop_toTopOf="parent" />
```

To add a second widget to the layout, embed it within the body of the ConstraintLayout element. The following modification, for example, adds a TextView widget to the layout:

```
<?xml version="1.0" encoding="utf-8"?>
<androidx.constraintlayout.widget.ConstraintLayout
    xmlns:android="http://schemas.android.com/apk/res/android"
    xmlns:app="http://schemas.android.com/apk/res-auto"
    xmlns:tools="http://schemas.android.com/tools"
    android:layout_width="match_parent"
    android:layout_height="match_parent"
    android:paddingLeft="16dp"
    android:paddingTop="16dp"
```

```
    android:paddingRight="16dp"
    android:paddingBottom="16dp"
    tools:context=".MainActivity">

    <Button
        android:text="@string/button_string"
        android:layout_width="wrap_content"
        android:layout_height="wrap_content"
        android:id="@+id/button"
        app:layout_constraintBottom_toBottomOf="parent"
        app:layout_constraintEnd_toEndOf="parent"
        app:layout_constraintStart_toStartOf="parent"
        app:layout_constraintTop_toTopOf="parent" />

    <TextView
        android:text="My Text"
        android:layout_width="wrap_content"
        android:layout_height="wrap_content"
        android:id="@+id/textView" />

</androidx.constraintlayout.widget.ConstraintLayout>
```

Once again, the absence of constraints on the newly added TextView will cause it to appear in the top left-hand corner of the layout at runtime. The following modifications add opposing constraints connected to the parent layout to center the widget horizontally, together with a constraint connecting the bottom of the TextView to the top of the button:

```
<TextView
    android:text="My Text"
    android:layout_width="wrap_content"
    android:layout_height="wrap_content"
    android:id="@+id/textView"
    android:layout_marginTop="8dp"
    android:layout_marginBottom="8dp"
    app:layout_constraintBottom_toTopOf="@+id/button"
    app:layout_constraintEnd_toEndOf="parent"
    app:layout_constraintStart_toStartOf="parent"
    app:layout_constraintTop_toTopOf="parent" />
```

Also, note that the Button and TextView views have several attributes declared. Both views have been assigned IDs and configured to display text strings represented by string resources named *button_string* and *text_string*, respectively. Additionally, the *wrap_content* height and width properties have been declared on both objects so that they are sized to accommodate the content (in this case, the text referenced by the string resource value).

Viewed from within the Preview panel of the Layout Editor in Design mode, the above layout will be rendered as shown in Figure 30-1:

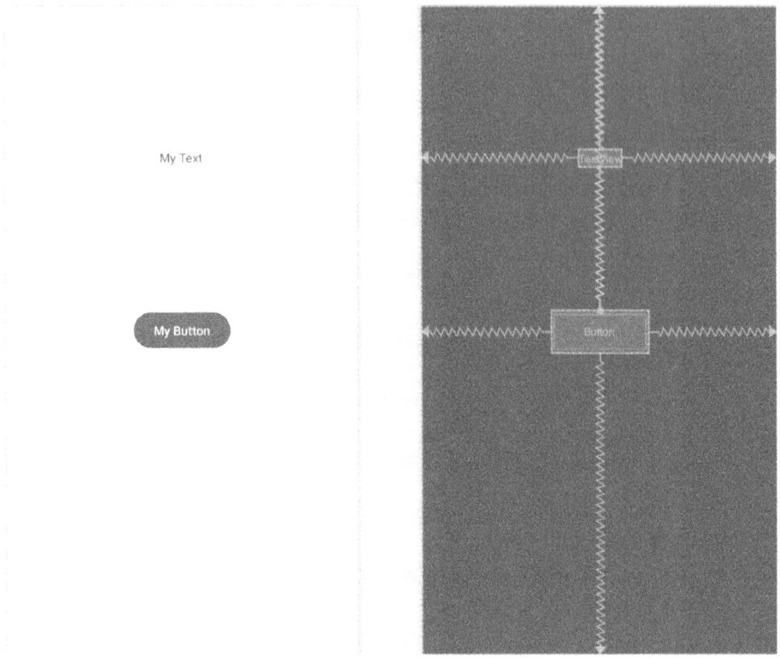

Figure 30-1

30.2 Manual XML vs. Visual Layout Design

When to write XML manually as opposed to using the Layout Editor tool in design mode is a matter of personal preference. There are, however, advantages to using design mode.

First, design mode will generally be quicker because it avoids the need to type XML lines. Additionally, design mode avoids the need to learn the intricacies of the various property values of the Android SDK view classes. Rather than continually referring to the Android documentation to find the correct keywords and values, most properties can be located by referring to the Attributes panel.

All the advantages of design mode aside, it is important to remember that the two approaches to user interface design are in no way mutually exclusive. As an application developer, you will likely create user interfaces within design mode while performing fine-tuning and layout tweaks of the design by directly editing the generated XML resources. Both views of the interface design are displayed side-by-side within the Android Studio environment, making it easy to work seamlessly on both the XML and the visual layout.

30.3 Summary

The Android Studio Layout Editor tool provides a visually intuitive method for designing user interfaces. Using a drag-and-drop paradigm combined with a set of property editors, the tool provides considerable productivity benefits to the application developer.

User interface designs may also be implemented by manually writing the XML layout resource files, the format of which is well-structured and easily understood.

The fact that the Layout Editor tool generates XML resource files means that these two approaches to interface design can be combined to provide a "best of both worlds" approach to user interface development.

31. Managing Constraints using Constraint Sets

Until this point in the book, all user interface design tasks have been performed using the Android Studio Layout Editor tool, either in text or design mode. An alternative to writing XML resource files or using the Android Studio Layout Editor is to write Kotlin code to directly create, configure and manipulate the view objects comprising an Android activity's user interface. This chapter will explore some advantages and disadvantages of writing Kotlin code to create a user interface before describing key concepts such as view properties and the creation and management of layout constraints.

In the next chapter, an example project will be created and used to demonstrate some of the typical steps involved in this approach to Android user interface creation.

31.1 Kotlin Code vs. XML Layout Files

There are several advantages to using XML resource files to design a user interface instead of writing Kotlin code. In fact, Google goes to considerable lengths in the Android documentation to extol the virtues of XML resources over Kotlin code. As discussed in the previous chapter, one key advantage of the XML approach is using the Android Studio Layout Editor tool, which generates XML resources. A second advantage is that once an application has been created, changes to user interface screens can be made by modifying the XML file, thereby avoiding recompiling the application. Also, even when-hand writing XML layouts, it is possible to get instant feedback on the appearance of the user interface using the preview feature of the Android Studio Layout Editor tool. To test the appearance of a Kotlin-created user interface, the developer will inevitably cycle through a loop of writing code, compiling, and testing to complete the design work.

Regarding the strengths of the Kotlin coding approach to layout creation, the most significant advantage that Kotlin has over XML resource files comes into play when dealing with dynamic user interfaces. XML resource files are inherently most useful when defining static layouts, which are unlikely to change significantly from one invocation of an activity to the next. Kotlin code, on the other hand, is ideal for creating user interfaces dynamically at run-time. This is particularly useful when the user interface may appear differently each time the activity executes, subject to external factors.

Knowledge of working with user interface components in Kotlin code can also be useful when dynamic changes to a static XML resource-based layout must be performed in real-time as the activity is running.

Finally, some developers prefer to write Kotlin code than to use layout tools and XML, regardless of the advantages offered by the latter approaches.

31.2 Creating Views

As previously established, the Android SDK includes a toolbox of view classes to meet most basic user interface design needs. The creation of a view in Kotlin is a matter of creating instances of these classes, passing through as an argument a reference to the activity with which that view is to be associated.

The first view (typically a container view to which additional child views can be added) is displayed to the user via a call to the *setContentView()* activity method. Additional views may be added to the root view via calls to the object's *addView()* method.

When working with Kotlin code to manipulate views contained in XML layout resource files, it is necessary to obtain the ID of the view. The same rule holds true for views created in Kotlin. As such, it is necessary to assign an ID to any view for which certain types of access will be required in subsequent Kotlin code. This is achieved via a call to the *setId()* method of the view object in question. In later code, the ID for a view may be obtained via the object's *id property*.

31.3 View Attributes

Each view class has associated with it a range of *attributes*. These property settings are set directly on the view instances and generally define how the view object will appear or behave. Examples of attributes are the text that appears on a Button object or the background color of a ConstraintLayout view. Each view class within the Android SDK has a pre-defined set of methods that allow the user to *set* and *get* these property values. The Button class, for example, has a *setText()* method, which can be called from within Kotlin code to set the text displayed on the button to a specific string value. On the other hand, the background color of a ConstraintLayout object can be set with a call to the object's *setBackgroundColor()* method.

31.4 Constraint Sets

While property settings are internal to view objects and dictate how a view appears and behaves, *constraint sets* control how a view appears relative to its parent view and other sibling views. Every ConstraintLayout instance has associated with it a set of constraints that define how its child views are positioned and constrained.

The key to working with constraint sets in Kotlin code is the *ConstraintSet* class. This class contains a range of methods that allow tasks such as creating, configuring, and applying constraints to a ConstraintLayout instance. In addition, the current constraints for a ConstraintLayout instance may be copied into a ConstraintSet object and applied to other layouts (with or without modifications).

A ConstraintSet instance is created just like any other Kotlin object:

```
val set = ConstraintSet()
```

Once a constraint set has been created, methods can be called on the instance to perform a wide range of tasks.

31.4.1 Establishing Connections

The *connect()* method of the ConstraintSet class is used to establish constraint connections between views. The following code configures a constraint set in which the left-hand side of a Button view is connected to the right-hand side of an EditText view with a margin of 70dp:

```
set.connect(button1.id, ConstraintSet.LEFT,
        editText1.id, ConstraintSet.RIGHT, 70)
```

31.4.2 Applying Constraints to a Layout

Once the constraint set is configured, it must be applied to a ConstraintLayout instance before it will take effect. A constraint set is applied via a call to the *applyTo()* method, passing through a reference to the layout object to which the settings are to be applied:

```
set.applyTo(myLayout)
```

31.4.3 Parent Constraint Connections

Connections between a child view and its parent ConstraintLayout may also be established by referencing the ConstraintSet.PARENT_ID constant. In the following example, the constraint set is configured to connect the top edge of a Button view to the top of the parent layout with a margin of 100dp:

```
set.connect(button1.id, ConstraintSet.TOP,
        ConstraintSet.PARENT_ID, ConstraintSet.TOP, 100)
```

31.4.4 Sizing Constraints

Several methods are available for controlling the sizing behavior of views. The following code, for example, sets the horizontal size of a Button view to *wrap_content* and the vertical size of an ImageView instance to a maximum of 250dp:

```
set.constrainWidth(button1.id, ConstraintSet.WRAP_CONTENT)
set.constrainMaxHeight(imageView1.id, 250)
```

31.4.5 Constraint Bias

As outlined in the chapter entitled *"A Guide to Using ConstraintLayout in Android Studio"*, when a view has opposing constraints, it is centered along the axis of the constraints (i.e., horizontally or vertically). This centering can be adjusted by applying a bias along the particular constraint axis. When using the Android Studio Layout Editor, this is achieved using the controls in the Attributes tool window. When working with a constraint set, however, bias can be added using the *setHorizontalBias()* and *setVerticalBias()* methods, referencing the view ID and the bias as a floating point value between 0 and 1.

The following code, for example, constrains the left and right-hand sides of a Button to the corresponding sides of the parent layout before applying a 25% horizontal bias:

```
set.connect(button1.id, ConstraintSet.LEFT,
        ConstraintSet.PARENT_ID, ConstraintSet.LEFT, 0)
set.connect(button1.id, ConstraintSet.RIGHT,
                ConstraintSet.PARENT_ID, ConstraintSet.RIGHT, 0)
set.setHorizontalBias(button1.id, 0.25f)
```

31.4.6 Alignment Constraints

Alignments may also be applied using a constraint set. The full set of alignment options available with the Android Studio Layout Editor may also be configured using a constraint set via the *centerVertically()* and *centerHorizontally()* methods, both of which take various arguments depending on the alignment being configured. In addition, the *center()* method may be used to center a view between two other views.

In the code below, button2 is positioned so that it is aligned horizontally with button1:

```
set.centerHorizontally(button2.id, button1.id)
```

31.4.7 Copying and Applying Constraint Sets

The current constraint set for a ConstraintLayout instance may be copied into a constraint set object using the *clone()* method. The following line of code, for example, copies the constraint settings from a ConstraintLayout instance named *myLayout* into a constraint set object:

```
set.clone(myLayout)
```

Once copied, the constraint set may be applied directly to another layout or, as in the following example, modified before being applied to the second layout:

```
val set = ConstraintSet()
set.clone(myLayout)
set.constrainWidth(button1.id, ConstraintSet.WRAP_CONTENT)
set.applyTo(mySecondLayout)
```

31.4.8 ConstraintLayout Chains

Vertical and horizontal chains may also be created within a constraint set using the *createHorizontalChain()* and *createVerticalChain()* methods. The syntax for using these methods is as follows:

```
createVerticalChain(int topId, int topSide, int bottomId,
```

```
    int bottomSide, int[] chainIds, float[] weights, int style)
```

Based on the above syntax, the following example creates a horizontal spread chain that starts with button1 and ends with button4. In between these views are button2 and button3 with weighting set to zero for both:

```
val set = ConstraintSet()
val chainViews = intArrayOf( button2.id, button3.id )
val chainWeights = floatArrayOf(0f, 0f)

set.createHorizontalChain(button1.id, ConstraintSet.LEFT,
                          button4.id, ConstraintSet.RIGHT,
                          chainViews, chainWeights,
                          ConstraintSet.CHAIN_SPREAD)
```

A view can be removed from a chain by passing the ID of the view to be removed through to either the *removeFromHorizontalChain()* or *removeFromVerticalChain()* methods. A view may be added to an existing chain using either the *addToHorizontalChain()* or *addToVerticalChain()* methods. In both cases, the methods take as arguments the IDs of the views between which the new view is to be inserted as follows:

```
set.addToHorizontalChain(newViewId, leftViewId, rightViewId)
```

31.4.9 Guidelines

Guidelines are added to a constraint set using the *create()* method and then positioned using the *setGuidelineBegin()*, *setGuidelineEnd()*, or *setGuidelinePercent()* methods. In the following code, a vertical guideline is created and positioned 50% across the width of the parent layout. The left side of a button view is then connected to the guideline with no margin:

```
val set = ConstraintSet()

set.create(R.id.myGuideline, ConstraintSet.VERTICAL_GUIDELINE)
set.setGuidelinePercent(R.id.myGuideline, 0.5f)

set.connect(button.id, ConstraintSet.LEFT,
   R.id.myGuideline, ConstraintSet.RIGHT, 0)

set.applyTo(layout)
```

31.4.10 Removing Constraints

A constraint may be removed from a view in a constraint set using the *clear()* method, passing through as arguments the view ID and the anchor point for which the constraint is to be removed:

```
set.clear(button.id, ConstraintSet.LEFT)
```

Similarly, all of the constraints on a view may be removed in a single step by referencing only the view in the *clear()* method call:

```
set.clear(button.id)
```

31.4.11 Scaling

The scale of a view within a layout may be adjusted using the ConstraintSet *setScaleX()* and *setScaleY()* methods which take as arguments the view on which the operation is to be performed together with a float value indicating the scale. In the following code, a button object is scaled to twice its original width and half the height:

```
set.setScaleX(mybutton.id, 2f)
set.setScaleY(myButton.id, 0.5f)
```

31.4.12 Rotation

A view may be rotated on either the X or Y axis using the *setRotationX()* and *setRotationY()* methods, respectively, both of which must be passed the ID of the view to be rotated and a float value representing the degree of rotation to be performed. The pivot point on which the rotation is to take place may be defined via a call to the *setTransformPivot()*, *setTransformPivotX()*, and *setTransformPivotY()* methods. The following code rotates a button view 30 degrees on the Y axis using a pivot point located at point 500, 500:

```
set.setTransformPivot(button.id, 500, 500)
set.setRotationY(button.id, 30)
set.applyTo(layout)
```

Having covered the theory of constraint sets and user interface creation from within Kotlin code, the next chapter will work through creating an example application to put this theory into practice. For more details on the ConstraintSet class, refer to the reference guide at the following URL:

https://developer.android.com/reference/androidx/constraintlayout/widget/ConstraintSet

31.5 Summary

As an alternative to writing XML layout resource files or using the Android Studio Layout Editor tool, Android user interfaces may also be dynamically created in Kotlin code.

Creating layouts in Kotlin code consists of creating instances of view classes and setting attributes on those objects to define required appearance and behavior.

How a view is positioned and sized relative to its ConstraintLayout parent view and any sibling views are defined using constraint sets. A constraint set is represented by an instance of the ConstraintSet class, which, once created, can be configured using a wide range of method calls to perform tasks such as establishing constraint connections, controlling view sizing behavior, and creating chains.

With the basics of the ConstraintSet class covered in this chapter, the next chapter will work through a tutorial that puts these features to practical use.

Chapter 32

32. An Android ConstraintSet Tutorial

The previous chapter introduced the basic concepts of creating and modifying user interface layouts in Kotlin code using the ConstraintLayout and ConstraintSet classes. This chapter will put these concepts into practice by creating an example layout created entirely in Kotlin code and without using the Android Studio Layout Editor tool.

32.1 Creating the Example Project in Android Studio

Launch Android Studio and select the *New Project* option from the welcome screen and, within the resulting new project dialog, choose the Empty Views Activity template before clicking on the Next button.

Enter *KotlinLayout* into the Name field and specify *com.ebookfrenzy.kotlinlayout* as the package name. Before clicking on the Finish button, change the Minimum API level setting to API 26: Android 8.0 (Oreo) and the Language menu to Kotlin.

Once the project has been created, the *MainActivity.kt* file should automatically load into the editing panel. As we have come to expect, Android Studio has created a template activity and overridden the *onCreate()* method, providing an ideal location for Kotlin code to be added to create a user interface.

32.2 Adding Views to an Activity

The *onCreate()* method is currently designed to use a resource layout file for the user interface. Begin, therefore, by deleting the following lines from the method:

```
override fun onCreate(savedInstanceState: Bundle?) {
    super.onCreate(savedInstanceState)
    enableEdgeToEdge()
    setContentView(R.layout.activity_main)
    ViewCompat.setOnApplyWindowInsetsListener(findViewById(R.id.main)) {
            v, insets ->
        val systemBars = insets.getInsets(WindowInsetsCompat.Type.systemBars())
        v.setPadding(systemBars.left, systemBars.top,
                systemBars.right, systemBars.bottom)
        insets
    }
}
```

The next modification is to add a ConstraintLayout object with a single Button view child to the activity. This involves the creation of new instances of the ConstraintLayout and Button classes. The Button view then needs to be added as a child to the ConstraintLayout view, which, in turn, is displayed via a call to the *setContentView()* method of the activity instance:

```
package com.ebookfrenzy.kotlinlayout
.
```

```
.
import androidx.constraintlayout.widget.ConstraintLayout
import android.widget.Button
import android.widget.EditText

class MainActivity : AppCompatActivity() {

    override fun onCreate(savedInstanceState: Bundle?) {
        super.onCreate(savedInstanceState)
        configureLayout()
    }

    private fun configureLayout() {
        val myButton = Button(this)
        val myLayout = ConstraintLayout(this)
        myLayout.addView(myButton)
        setContentView(myLayout)
    }
}
```

When new instances of user interface objects are created in this way, the constructor methods must be passed the context within which the object is being created, which, in this case, is the current activity. Since the above code resides within the activity class, the context is referenced by the standard *this* keyword:

```
val myButton = Button(this)
```

Once the above additions have been made, compile and run the application (either on a physical device or an emulator). Once launched, the visible result will be a button containing no text appearing in the top left-hand corner of the ConstraintLayout view, as shown in Figure 32-1:

Figure 32-1

32.3 Setting View Attributes

For this exercise, we need the background of the ConstraintLayout view to be blue and the Button view to display text that reads “Press Me” on a yellow background. These tasks can be achieved by setting attributes on the views in the Kotlin code as outlined in the following code fragment. To allow the text on the button to be easily translated to other languages, it will be added as a String resource. Within the Project tool window, locate the *app -> res -> values -> strings.xml* file and modify it to add a resource value for the “Press Me” string:

```
<resources>
    <string name="app_name">KotlinLayout</string>
    <string name="press_me">Press Me</string>
</resources>
```

Although this is the recommended way to handle strings directly referenced in code, many subsequent code samples will directly enter strings into the code to avoid repetition of this step throughout the remainder of the book.

Once the string is stored as a resource, it can be accessed from within the code as follows:

```
getString(R.string.press_me)
```

With the string resource created, add code to the *configureLayout()* method to set the button text and color attributes:

```
.
.
import android.graphics.Color
.
.
    private fun configureLayout() {
        val myButton = Button(this)
        myButton.text = getString(R.string.press_me)
        myButton.setBackgroundColor(Color.YELLOW)

        val myLayout = ConstraintLayout(this)
        myLayout.setBackgroundColor(Color.BLUE)

        myLayout.addView(myButton)
        setContentView(myLayout)

    }
}
.
.
```

When the application is compiled and run, the layout will reflect the property settings such that the layout will appear with a blue background, and the button will display the assigned text on a yellow background.

32.4 Creating View IDs

When the layout is complete, it will consist of a Button and an EditText view. Before these views can be referenced within the methods of the ConstraintSet class, they must be assigned unique view IDs. The first step in this process is to create a new resource file containing these ID values.

Right-click on the *app -> res -> values* folder, select the *New -> Values Resource File* menu option, and name the new resource file *id.xml*. With the resource file created, edit it so that it reads as follows:

```
<?xml version="1.0" encoding="utf-8"?>
<resources>
    <item name="myButton" type="id" />
    <item name="myEditText" type="id" />
</resources>
```

At this point in the tutorial, only the Button has been created, so edit the *configureLayout()* method to assign the corresponding ID to the object:

```
fun configureLayout() {
```

```
    val myButton = Button(this)
    myButton.text = getString(R.string.press_me)
    myButton.setBackgroundColor(Color.YELLOW)
    myButton.id = R.id.myButton
.
.
```

32.5 Configuring the Constraint Set

Without constraints, the ConstraintLayout view has placed the Button view in the display's top left corner. To instruct the layout view to place the button in a different location, in this case, centered both horizontally and vertically, it will be necessary to create a ConstraintSet instance, initialize it with the appropriate settings and apply it to the parent layout.

For this example, the button needs to be configured so that the width and height are constrained to the size of the text it displays and the view centered within the parent layout. Edit the *configureLayout()* method once more to make these changes:

```
.
.
import androidx.constraintlayout.widget.ConstraintSet
.
.
private fun configureLayout() {
    val myButton = Button(this)
    myButton.text = getString(R.string.press_me)
    myButton.setBackgroundColor(Color.YELLOW)
    myButton.id = R.id.myButton

    val myLayout = ConstraintLayout(this)
    myLayout.setBackgroundColor(Color.BLUE)

    myLayout.addView(myButton)
    setContentView(myLayout)

    val set = ConstraintSet()

    set.constrainHeight(myButton.id,
        ConstraintSet.WRAP_CONTENT)
    set.constrainWidth(myButton.id,
        ConstraintSet.WRAP_CONTENT)

    set.connect(myButton.id, ConstraintSet.START,
            ConstraintSet.PARENT_ID, ConstraintSet.START, 0)
    set.connect(myButton.id, ConstraintSet.END,
            ConstraintSet.PARENT_ID, ConstraintSet.END, 0)
    set.connect(myButton.id, ConstraintSet.TOP,
            ConstraintSet.PARENT_ID, ConstraintSet.TOP, 0)
```

```
    set.connect(myButton.id, ConstraintSet.BOTTOM,
            ConstraintSet.PARENT_ID, ConstraintSet.BOTTOM, 0)

    set.applyTo(myLayout)
}
```

With the initial constraints configured, compile and run the application and verify that the Button view now appears in the center of the layout:

Figure 32-2

32.6 Adding the EditText View

The next item to be added to the layout is the EditText view. The first step is to create the EditText object, assign the ID as declared in the *id.xml* resource file and add it to the layout. The code changes to achieve these steps now need to be made to the *configureLayout()* method as follows:

```
private fun configureLayout() {
    val myButton = Button(this)
    myButton.text = getString(R.string.press_me)
    myButton.setBackgroundColor(Color.YELLOW)
    myButton.id = R.id.myButton

    val myEditText = EditText(this)
    myEditText.id = R.id.myEditText

    val myLayout = ConstraintLayout(this)
    myLayout.setBackgroundColor(Color.BLUE)

    myLayout.addView(myButton)
    myLayout.addView(myEditText)

    setContentView(myLayout)
```

```
.
.
}
```

The EditText widget is intended to be sized subject to the content it displays, centered horizontally within the layout, and positioned 70dp above the existing Button view. Add code to the *configureLayout()* method so that it reads as follows:

```
.
.
set.constrainHeight(myEditText.id,
                ConstraintSet.WRAP_CONTENT)
set.constrainWidth(myEditText.id,
                ConstraintSet.WRAP_CONTENT)

set.connect(myEditText.id, ConstraintSet.LEFT,
      ConstraintSet.PARENT_ID, ConstraintSet.LEFT, 0)
set.connect(myEditText.id, ConstraintSet.RIGHT,
      ConstraintSet.PARENT_ID, ConstraintSet.RIGHT, 0)
set.connect(myEditText.id, ConstraintSet.BOTTOM,
      myButton.id, ConstraintSet.TOP, 70)

set.applyTo(myLayout)
```

A test run of the application should show the EditText field centered above the button with a margin of 70dp.

32.7 Converting Density Independent Pixels (dp) to Pixels (px)

The next task in this exercise is to set the width of the EditText view to 200dp. As outlined in the chapter entitled *"An Android Studio Layout Editor ConstraintLayout Tutorial"*, when setting sizes and positions in user interface layouts, it is better to use density independent-pixels (dp) rather than pixels (px). To set a position using dp, it is necessary to convert a dp value to a px value at runtime, considering the density of the device display. In order, therefore, to set the width of the EditText view to 200dp, the following code needs to be added to the class:

```
package com.ebookfrenzy.kotlinlayout
.
.
import android.content.res.Resources
import android.util.TypedValue

class MainActivity : AppCompatActivity() {

    override fun onCreate(savedInstanceState: Bundle?) {
        super.onCreate(savedInstanceState)
        configureLayout()
    }

    private fun convertToPx(value: Int): Int {
        val r = resources
        return TypedValue.applyDimension(
```

```
            TypedValue.COMPLEX_UNIT_DIP, value.toFloat(),
            r.displayMetrics
        ).toInt()
    }

    private fun configureLayout() {
        val myButton = Button(this)
        myButton.text = getString(R.string.press_me)
        myButton.setBackgroundColor(Color.YELLOW)
        myButton.id = R.id.myButton

        val myEditText = EditText(this)
        myEditText.id = R.id.myEditText

        myEditText.width = convertToPx(200)
.
.
```

Compile and run the application one more time and note that the width of the EditText view has changed, as illustrated in Figure 32-3:

Figure 32-3

32.8 Summary

The example activity created in this chapter has created a similar user interface (the change in background color and view type notwithstanding) as that created in the earlier *"Manual XML Layout Design in Android Studio"* chapter. If nothing else, this chapter should have provided an appreciation of the level to which the Android Studio Layout Editor tool and XML resources shield the developer from many of the complexities of creating Android user interface layouts.

There are, however, instances where it makes sense to create a user interface in Kotlin. For example, this approach is most useful when creating dynamic user interface layouts.

Chapter 33

33. A Guide to Using Apply Changes in Android Studio

Now that some of the basic concepts of Android development using Android Studio have been covered, this is a good time to introduce the Android Studio Apply Changes feature. As all experienced developers know, every second spent waiting for an app to compile and run is better spent writing and refining code.

33.1 Introducing Apply Changes

In early versions of Android Studio, each time a change to a project needed to be tested, Android Studio would recompile the code, convert it to Dex format, generate the APK package file, and install it on the device or emulator. Having performed these steps, the app would finally be launched and ready for testing. Even on a fast development system, this process takes considerable time to complete. It is not uncommon for it to take a minute or more for this process to complete for a large application.

Apply Changes, in contrast, allows many code and resource changes within a project to be reflected nearly instantaneously within the app while it is already running on a device or emulator session.

Consider, for example, an app being developed in Android Studio which has already been launched on a device or emulator. If changes are made to resource settings or the code within a method, Apply Changes will push the updated code and resources to the running app and dynamically "swap" the changes. The changes are then reflected in the running app without the need to build, deploy and relaunch the entire app. This often allows changes to be tested in a fraction of the time without Apply Changes.

33.2 Understanding Apply Changes Options

Android Studio provides three options for applying changes to a running app in the form of *Run App*, *Apply Changes and Restart Activity* and *Apply Code Changes*. These options can be summarized as follows:

- **Run App** - Stops the currently running app and restarts it. If no changes have been made to the project since it was last launched, this option will restart the app. If, on the other hand, changes have been made to the project, Android Studio will rebuild and re-install the app onto the device or emulator before launching it.

- **Apply Code Changes** - This option can be used when the only changes made to a project involve modifications to the body of existing methods or when a new class or method has been added. When selected, the changes will be applied to the running app without needing to restart the app or the currently running activity. This mode cannot, however, be used when changes have been made to any project resources, such as a layout file. Other restrictions include removing methods, changing a method signature, renaming classes, and other structural code changes. It is also impossible to use this option when changes have been made to the project manifest.

- **Apply Changes and Restart Activity** - When selected, this mode will dynamically apply any code or resource changes made within the project and restart the activity without re-installing or restarting the app. Unlike the Apply Code changes option, this can be used when changes have been made to the code and resources of the project. However, the same restrictions involving some structural code changes and manifest modifications apply.

33.3 Using Apply Changes

When a project has been loaded into Android Studio but is not yet running on a device or emulator, it can be launched as usual using either the run (marked A in Figure 33-1) or debug (B) button located in the toolbar:

Figure 33-1

After the app has launched and is running, a stop button (marked A in Figure 33-2) will appear, and the *Apply Changes and Restart Activity* (B) and *Apply Code Changes* (C) buttons will be enabled:

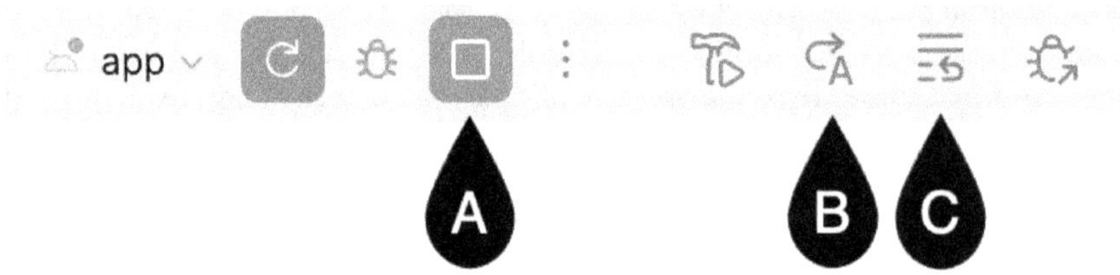

Figure 33-2

If the changes cannot be applied when one of the Apply Changes buttons is selected, Android Studio will display a message indicating the failure and an explanation. Figure 33-3, for example, shows the message displayed by Android Studio when the *Apply Code Changes* option is selected after a change has been made to a resource file:

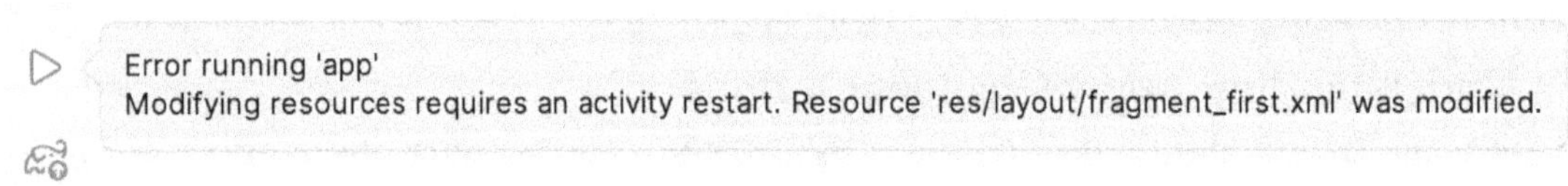

Figure 33-3

In this situation, the solution is to use the *Apply Changes and Restart Activity* option (for which a link is provided). Similarly, the following message will appear when an attempt to apply changes that involve the removal of a method is made:

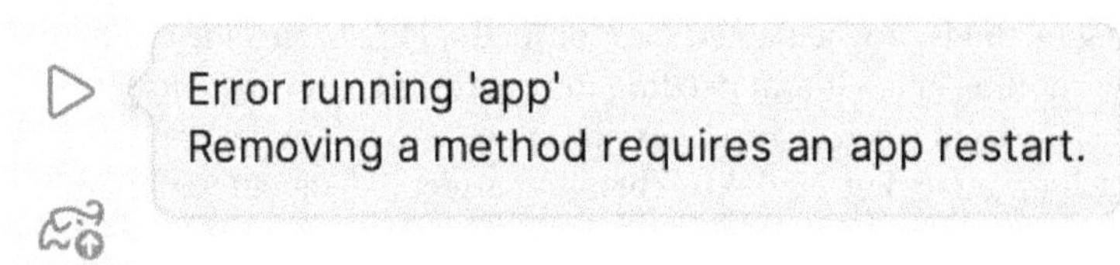

Figure 33-4

In this case, the only option is to click on the *Run App* button to re-install and restart the app. As an alternative to manually selecting the correct option, Android Studio may be configured to automatically fall back to performing a Run App operation.

33.4 Configuring Apply Changes Fallback Settings

The Apply Changes fallback settings are located in the Android Studio Settings dialog. Within the Settings dialog, select the *Build, Execution, Deployment* entry in the left-hand panel, followed by *Deployment*, as shown in Figure 33-5:

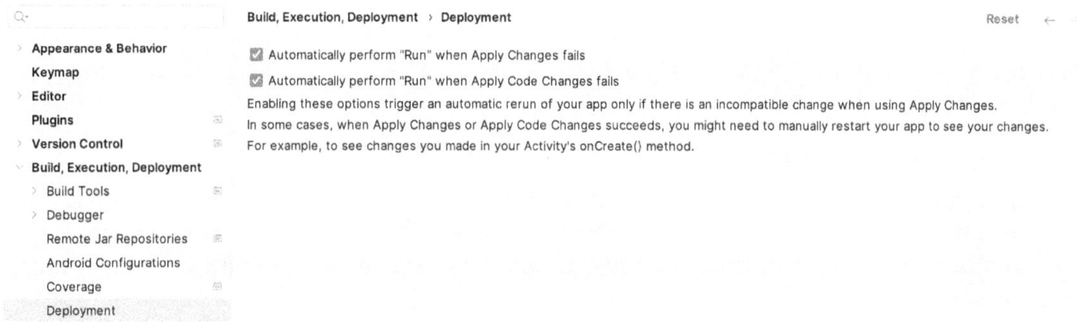

Figure 33-5

Once the required options have been enabled, click on Apply, followed by the OK button to commit the changes and dismiss the dialog. After these defaults have been enabled, Android Studio will automatically re-install and restart the app when necessary.

33.5 An Apply Changes Tutorial

Launch Android Studio, select the New Project option from the welcome screen, and choose the Basic Views Activity template within the resulting new project dialog before clicking the Next button.

Enter *ApplyChanges* into the Name field and specify *com.ebookfrenzy.applychanges* as the package name. Before clicking the Finish button, change the Minimum API level setting to API 26: Android 8.0 (Oreo) and the Language menu to Kotlin.

33.6 Using Apply Code Changes

Begin by clicking the run button and selecting an emulator or physical device as the run target. After clicking the run button, track the time before the example app appears on the device or emulator.

Once running, click on the action button (the button displaying an envelope icon in the screen's lower right-hand corner). Note that a Snackbar instance appears, displaying text which reads "Replace with your own action", as shown in Figure 33-6:

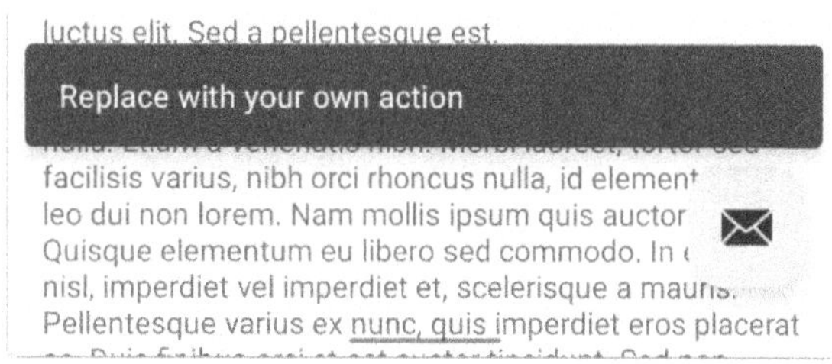

Figure 33-6

Once the app is running, the Apply Changes buttons should have been enabled, indicating that certain project changes can be applied without reinstalling and restarting the app. To see this in action, edit the *MainActivity.kt* file, locate the *onCreate* method, and modify the action code so that a different message is displayed when the action button is selected:

```
binding.fab.setOnClickListener { view ->
    Snackbar.make(view, "Apply Changes is Amazing!", Snackbar.LENGTH_LONG)
        .setAnchorView(R.id.fab)
        .setAction("Action", null).show()
}
```

With the code change implemented, click the *Apply Code Changes* button and note that a message appears within a few seconds indicating the app has been updated. Tap the action button and note that the new message is now displayed in the Snackbar.

33.7 Using Apply Changes and Restart Activity

Any resource change will require the use of the *Apply Changes and Restart Activity* option. Within Android Studio, select the *app -> res -> layout -> fragment_first.xml* layout file. With the Layout Editor tool in Design mode, select the default TextView component and change the text property in the attributes tool window to "Hello Android".

Ensure that the fallback options outlined in *"Configuring Apply Changes Fallback Settings"* above are turned off before clicking on the *Apply Code Changes* button. Note that the request fails because this change involves project resources. Click on the *Apply Changes and Restart Activity* button and verify that the activity restarts and displays the new text on the TextView widget.

33.8 Using Run App

As previously described, removing a method requires the complete re-installation and restart of the running app. To experience this, edit the *MainActivity.kt* file and add a new method after the *onCreate* method as follows:

```
fun demoMethod() {
}
```

Use the *Apply Code Changes* button and confirm that the changes are applied without re-installing the app.

Next, delete the new method and verify that clicking on either of the two Apply Changes buttons will result in the request failing. The only way to run the app after such a change is to click the Run App button.

33.9 Summary

Apply Changes is a feature of Android Studio designed to significantly accelerate the code, build and run cycle performed when developing an app. The Apply Changes feature can push updates to the running application, in many cases, without reinstalling or restarting the app. Apply Changes provides several different levels of support depending on the nature of the modification being applied to the project.

Chapter 34

34. A Guide to Gradle Version Catalogs

A newly created Android Studio project will consist of approximately 80 files automatically generated by Android Studio. When you click on the Run button, Android Studio uses a build system called Gradle to generate additional files, compile the source code, resolve library dependencies, and create the installable application package. After the build is completed, the project folder will contain approximately 700 files.

This chapter explains how the Gradle build system determines which libraries to include in the build process and how you can use this system to add library dependencies to your projects.

34.1 Library and Plugin Dependencies

In the earlier chapter titled *"An Overview of the Android Architecture"* we talked briefly about the Java API Framework and the libraries that it contains. When Gradle is building a project, it needs to know which libraries are required to complete the build and their respective version numbers. For example, a project might depend on version 2.6.0 of the Room Database runtime library (*androidx.room:room-runtime*). Unfortunately, when we write Room Database code in our project, Gradle does not automatically add the corresponding library dependency to the build configuration. Instead, we must add this ourselves via Gradle *build files* and the *version catalog*.

34.2 Project Gradle Build File

Every Android Studio has a project-level Gradle file that you can find by navigating to *Gradle Scripts -> build.gradle.kts (<Project name>)* in the Project tool window. The primary purpose of this file is to define the plugins that do the work of building the entire project and will typically read as follows:

```
plugins {
    alias(libs.plugins.android.application) apply false
}
```

In practice, changes to this file are only necessary on rare occasions.

34.3 Module Gradle Build Files

An Android Studio project will consist of one or more *modules*, each with its own build configuration and library dependencies. A new project will contain a single module, the gradle build file for which will be listed in the *Gradle Scripts* folder as *build.gradle.kts (Module: app)* and will, in part, read as follows:

```
plugins {
    alias(libs.plugins.android.application) apply false
}

android {
.
.
}
```

```
dependencies {
    implementation(libs.androidx.core.ktx)
    implementation(libs.androidx.appcompat)
    implementation(libs.material)
    implementation(libs.androidx.activity)
    implementation(libs.androidx.constraintlayout)
    testImplementation(libs.junit)
    androidTestImplementation(libs.androidx.junit)
    androidTestImplementation(libs.androidx.espresso.core)
}
```

The *plugins* section once again contains the plugins needed to build the project and, in most cases, will mirror those declared in the project-level build file. When a module needs plugins that are not required by other modules, they are declared here.

The *dependencies* section contains a list of the libraries on which the module depends and which must be resolved for a successful build.

34.4 Version Catalog File

Earlier, we mentioned besides the library names, dependencies must also include library version numbers. You will have noticed, however, that none of the configuration files reviewed so far include version information. This is where the *version catalog* file comes in. The version catalog can be found in a file named *libs.versions.toml* located in the Project tool window's *Gradle Scripts* folder. An example version catalog file is listed below:

```
[versions]
agp = "9.1.0"
coreKtx = "1.18.0"
junit = "4.13.2"
junitVersion = "1.2.1"
espressoCore = "3.7.0"
appcompat = "1.7.1"
material = "1.13.0"
activity = "1.10.1"
constraintlayout = "2.2.1"

[libraries]
.
.
androidx-core-ktx = { group = "androidx.core", name = "core-ktx", version.ref = 
"coreKtx" }
appcompat = { group = "androidx.appcompat", name = "appcompat", version.ref = 
"appcompat" }
material = { group = "com.google.android.material", name = "material", version.
ref = "material" }
.
.
[plugins]
android-application = { id = "com.android.application", version.ref = "agp" }
```

The catalog is divided into sections labeled [versions], [libraries], and [plugins]. To help understand how the catalog works, we will use the *material* library as an example. In the [libraries] section, the *material* library is declared as follows:

```
material = { group = "com.google.android.material", name = "material",  version.
ref = "material" }
```

The *group* entry above tells us the actual name of the Material library group in the Java API framework is *com.google.android.material*, while the *versions.ref* assignment declares how the library will be referenced in the [versions] catalog section. The declaration is assigned to a value named "material" which is the name by which the library will be referenced in the module-level build files.

Referring to the [versions] section, we find that the library has been assigned version 1.11.0:

```
material = "1.13.0"
```

Finally, the library is declared in the *dependencies* section of the module-level build file as follows:

```
dependencies {
.
.
    implementation(libs.material)
}
```

Note that the syntax for referencing the library in the build file is to prefix the name used in the [libraries] catalog entry with "*libs.*".

Although we have focused on a library for this example, the syntax is the same for plugins.

34.5 Adding Dependencies

You will need to add dependencies to several projects in this book, and in each case, we will step you through the process. As an example, we will demonstrate adding the Room Database runtime library dependency to our earlier hypothetical project. First, we must add the following entry to the [libraries] section of the *libs.versions.toml* version catalog file:

```
[libraries]
.
.
androidx-roomruntime = {  group = "androidx.room", name = "room-runtime",
version.ref = "roomRuntime" }
```

Next, the version number is added to the [versions] catalog section:

```
[versions]
.
.
roomRuntime = "2.6.1"
```

Finally, the library is added to the dependencies section of the module-level gradle build file:

```
dependencies {
.
.
    implementation(libs.androidx.room.runtime)
}
```

Another example is the *androidx.navigation:navigation-fragment-ktx* library. In this case, the library group is *androidx.navigation* and the name is *navigation-fragment-ktx*. The library would be declared in the version catalog as follows:

```
[versions]
.
.
navigationFragmentKtx = "2.8.9"

[libraries]
.
.
navigation-fragment-ktx = { group = "androidx.navigation", name = "navigation-
fragment-ktx", version.ref = "navigationFragmentKtx" }
```

Once the library has been added to the catalog, the gradle build file dependency would read as follows:

```
dependencies {
.
.
    implementation(libs.navigation.fragment.ktx)
.
.
```

34.6 Library Updates

While declaring library and plugin dependencies is primarily a manual task, one thing that Android Studio will do for you is let you know when a more recent library version is available. It does this by highlighting the version number while you are editing the catalog file. Hovering the mouse pointer over the highlighted number will display the panel shown in Figure 34-1, providing the option to change to the latest version:

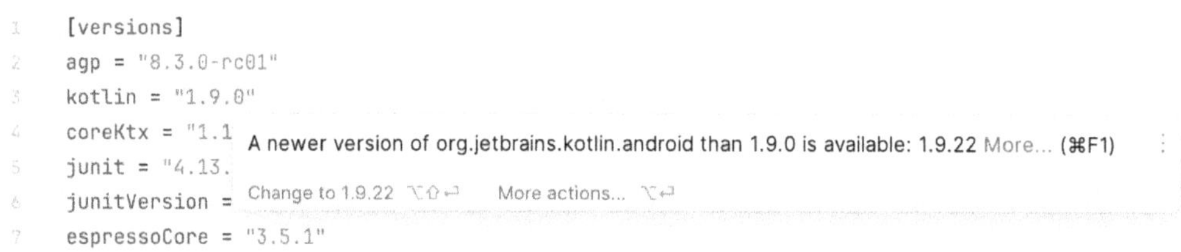

Figure 34-1

34.7 Summary

Android Studio projects are built using the Gradle build system in a process involving several steps. One of these steps is to resolve and include any required libraries for the project to compile successfully. While a newly created project will include the basic libraries and plugins necessary for a simple app, more complex projects will have additional dependencies. These dependencies are declared in the module-level Gradle build files. To provide version consistency across project modules and a single location to add new libraries or update version numbers, Gradle uses a version catalog file. As your code uses more libraries and plugins, you must edit the build and catalog files to add these dependencies.

Chapter 35

35. An Overview and Example of Android Event Handling

Much has been covered in the previous chapters relating to the design of user interfaces for Android applications. However, an area that has yet to be covered involves how a user's interaction with the user interface triggers the underlying activity to perform a task. In other words, from the previous chapters, we know how to create a user interface containing a button view but not how to make something happen within the application when the user touches it.

Therefore, this chapter's primary objective is to provide an overview of event handling in Android applications together with an Android Studio-based example project.

35.1 Understanding Android Events

Android events can take various forms but are usually generated in response to an external action. The most common form of events, particularly for devices such as tablets and smartphones, involve some form of interaction with the touch screen. Such events fall into the category of *input events*.

The Android framework maintains an *event queue* into which events are placed as they occur. Events are then removed from the queue on a first-in, first-out (FIFO) basis. In the case of an input event, such as a touch on the screen, the event is passed to the view positioned at the location on the screen where the touch took place. In addition to the event notification, the view is also passed a range of information (depending on the event type) about the nature of the event, such as the coordinates of the point of contact between the user's fingertip and the screen.

To handle an event that has been passed, the view must have an *event listener* in place. The Android View class, from which all user interface components are derived, contains a range of event listener interfaces, each containing an abstract declaration for a callback method. To be able to respond to an event of a particular type, a view must register the appropriate event listener and implement the corresponding callback. For example, if a button is to respond to a *click* event (the equivalent of the user touching and releasing the button view as though clicking on a physical button), it must both register the *View.onClickListener* event listener (via a call to the target view's *setOnClickListener()* method) and implement the corresponding *onClick()* callback method. If a "click" event is detected on the screen at the location of the button view, the Android framework will call the *onClick()* method of that view when that event is removed from the event queue. It is, of course, within the implementation of the onClick() callback method that any tasks or other methods called in response to the button click should be performed.

35.2 Using the android:onClick Resource

Before exploring event listeners in more detail, it is worth noting that a shortcut is available when all that is required is for a callback method to be called when a user "clicks" on a button view in the user interface. Consider a user interface layout containing a button view named *button1* with the requirement that when the user touches the button, a method called *buttonClick()* declared in the activity class is called. All that is required to implement this behavior is to write the *buttonClick()* method (which takes as an argument a reference to the view that triggered the click event) and add a single line to the declaration of the button view in the XML file. For example:

```
<Button
        android:id="@+id/button1"
        android:layout_width="wrap_content"
        android:layout_height="wrap_content"
        android:onClick="buttonClick"
        android:text="Click me" />
```

This provides a simple way to capture click events. It does not, however, provide the range of options offered by event handlers, which is the topic of the rest of this chapter. As outlined in later chapters, the onClick property also has limitations in layouts involving fragments. When working within Android Studio Layout Editor, the onClick property can be found and configured in the Attributes panel when a suitable view type is selected in the device screen layout.

35.3 Event Listeners and Callback Methods

In the example activity outlined later in this chapter, the steps involved in registering an event listener and implementing the callback method will be covered in detail. Before doing so, however, it is worth taking some time to outline the event listeners available in the Android framework and the callback methods associated with each one.

- **onClickListener** – Used to detect click style events whereby the user touches and then releases an area of the device display occupied by a view. Corresponds to the *onClick()* callback method, which is passed a reference to the view that received the event as an argument.

- **onLongClickListener** – Used to detect when the user maintains the touch over a view for an extended period. Corresponds to the *onLongClick()* callback method, which is passed as an argument the view that received the event.

- **onTouchListener** – Used to detect any contact with the touch screen, including individual or multiple touches and gesture motions. Corresponding with the *onTouch()* callback, this topic will be covered in greater detail in the chapter entitled *"Android Touch and Multi-touch Event Handling"*. The callback method is passed as arguments the view that received the event and a MotionEvent object.

- **onCreateContextMenuListener** – Listens for the creation of a context menu as the result of a long click. Corresponds to the *onCreateContextMenu()* callback method. The callback is passed the menu, the view that received the event and a menu context object.

- **onFocusChangeListener** – Detects when focus moves away from the current view due to interaction with a trackball or navigation key. Corresponds to the *onFocusChange()* callback method, which is passed the view that received the event and a Boolean value to indicate whether focus was gained or lost.

- **onKeyListener** – Used to detect when a key on a device is pressed while a view has focus. Corresponds to the *onKey()* callback method. It is passed as arguments the view that received the event, the KeyCode of the physical key that was pressed, and a KeyEvent object.

35.4 An Event Handling Example

In the remainder of this chapter, we will create an Android Studio project designed to demonstrate the implementation of an event listener and corresponding callback method to detect when the user has clicked on a button. The code within the callback method will update a text view to indicate that the event has been processed.

Select the *New Project* option from the welcome screen and, within the resulting new project dialog, choose the Empty Views Activity template before clicking the Next button.

Enter *EventExample* into the Name field and specify *com.ebookfrenzy.eventexample* as the package name. Before clicking on the Finish button, change the Minimum API level setting to API 26: Android 8.0 (Oreo) and the Language menu to Kotlin. Using the Gemini Agent or the steps outlined in section *18.8 Migrating a Project to View Binding*, convert the project to use view binding.

35.5 Designing the User Interface

The user interface layout for the *MainActivity* class in this example will consist of a ConstraintLayout, a Button, and a TextView, as illustrated in Figure 35-1.

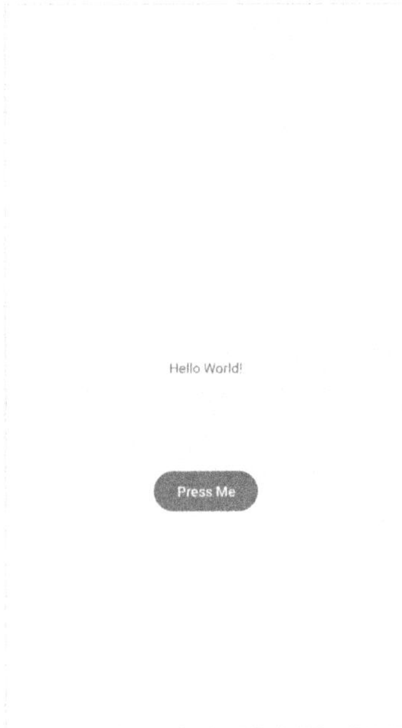

Figure 35-1

Locate and select the *activity_main.xml* file created by Android Studio (located in the Project tool window under *app -> res -> layouts*) and double-click on it to load it into the Layout Editor tool.

Ensure that Autoconnect is enabled, then drag a Button widget from the palette and move it so that it is positioned in the horizontal center of the layout and beneath the existing TextView widget. When correctly positioned, drop the widget into place so that the autoconnect system adds appropriate constraints.

Select the "Hello World!" TextView widget and use the Attributes panel to set the ID to *statusText*. Repeat this step to change the ID of the Button widget to *myButton*.

Add any missing constraints by clicking on the *Infer Constraints* button in the layout editor toolbar.

With the Button widget selected, use the Attributes panel to set the text property to Press Me. Extract the text string on the button to a resource named *press_me*.

With the user interface layout completed, the next step is registering the event listener and callback method.

35.6 The Event Listener and Callback Method

For this example, an *onClickListener* needs to be registered for the *myButton* view. This is achieved by calling the *setOnClickListener()* method of the button view, passing through a new *onClickListener* object as an argument, and implementing the *onClick()* callback method. Since this task only needs to be performed when the activity is created, a good location is the *onCreate()* method of the MainActivity class.

If the *MainActivity.kt* file is already open within an editor session, select it by clicking on the tab in the editor panel. Alternatively, locate it within the Project tool window by navigating to (*app -> kotlin+java -> com.ebookfrenzy.eventexample -> MainActivity*) and double-click on it to load it into the code editor. Once loaded, locate the template *onCreate()* method and modify it to obtain a reference to the button view, register the event listener, and implement the *onClick()* callback method:

```
package com.ebookfrenzy.eventexample
.
.
import android.view.View

import com.ebookfrenzy.eventexample.databinding.ActivityMainBinding

class MainActivity : AppCompatActivity() {

    private lateinit var binding: ActivityMainBinding

    override fun onCreate(savedInstanceState: Bundle?) {
.
.
        binding.myButton.setOnClickListener(object : View.OnClickListener {
            override fun onClick(v: View?) {

            }
        })
    }
}
```

The above code has registered the event listener on the button and implemented the *onClick()* method. In fact, the code to configure the listener can be made more efficient by using a lambda as follows:

```
override fun onCreate(savedInstanceState: Bundle?) {
    super.onCreate(savedInstanceState)
.
.
    binding.myButton.setOnClickListener(object : View.OnClickListener {
        override fun onClick(v: View?) {

        }
    })

    binding.myButton.setOnClickListener {
    }
}
```

If the application were to be run at this point, however, there would be no indication that the event listener installed on the button was working since there is, as yet, no code implemented within the body of the lambda. The goal for the example is to have a message appear on the TextView when the button is clicked, so some further code changes need to be made:

```
override fun onCreate(savedInstanceState: Bundle?) {
    super.onCreate(savedInstanceState)
.
.
    binding.myButton.setOnClickListener {
        binding.statusText.text = "Button clicked"
    }
}
```

Complete this tutorial phase by compiling and running the application on either an AVD emulator or a physical Android device. On touching and releasing the button view (otherwise known as "clicking"), the text view should change to display the "Button clicked" text.

35.7 Consuming Events

The detection of standard clicks (as opposed to long clicks) on views is a straightforward case of event handling. The example will now be extended to include the detection of long click events, which occur when the user clicks and holds a view on the screen and, in doing so, cover the topic of event consumption.

Consider the code for the *onClick* listener code in the above section of this chapter. The lambda code assigned to the listener does not return any value and is not required to do so.

On the other hand, the code assigned to the *onLongClickListener* is required to return a Boolean value to the Android framework. The purpose of this return value is to indicate to the Android runtime whether or not the callback has consumed the event. If the callback returns a true value, the framework discards the event. If, on the other hand, the callback returns a false value, the Android framework will consider the event still to be active and pass it along to the next matching event listener registered on the same view.

As with many programming concepts, this is best demonstrated with an example. The first step is to add an event listener for long clicks to the button view in the example activity:

```
override fun onCreate(savedInstanceState: Bundle?) {
.
.
    binding.myButton.setOnClickListener {
        binding.statusText.text = "Button clicked"
    }

    binding.myButton.setOnLongClickListener {
        binding.statusText.text = "Long button click"
        true
    }
}
```

When a long click is detected, the lambda code will display "Long button click" on the text view. Note, however, that the callback method returns a *true* value to indicate that it has consumed the event. Run the application and press and hold the Button view until the "Long button click" text appears in the text view. On releasing the button, the text view displays the "Long button click" text indicating that the onClick listener code was not called.

Next, modify the code so that the onLongClick listener now returns a *false* value:

```
binding.myButton.setOnLongClickListener {
```

```
    statusText.text = "Long button click"
    false
}
```

Once again, compile and run the application and perform a long click on the button until the long click message appears. However, after releasing the button this time, note that the onClick listener is also triggered, and the text changes to "Button clicked". This is because the *false* value returned by the *onLongClick* listener code indicated to the Android framework that the event was not consumed by the method and was eligible to be passed on to the next registered listener on the view. In this case, the runtime ascertained that the onClickListener on the button was also interested in events of this type and subsequently called the *onClick* listener code.

35.8 Summary

A user interface is of little practical use if the views it contains do not do anything in response to user interaction. Android bridges the gap between the user interface and the back-end code of the application through the concepts of event listeners and callback methods. The Android View class defines a set of event listeners which can be registered on view objects. Each event listener also has associated with it a callback method.

When an event takes place on a view in a user interface, that event is placed into an event queue and handled on a first-in, first-out basis by the Android runtime. If the view on which the event took place has registered a listener that matches the type of event, the corresponding callback method or lambda expression is called. This code then performs any tasks required by the activity before returning. Some callback methods are required to return a Boolean value to indicate whether the event needs to be passed on to other event listeners registered on the view or discarded by the system.

Now that the basics of event handling have been covered, the next chapter will explore touch events with a particular emphasis on handling multiple touches.

Chapter 36

36. Android Touch and Multi-touch Event Handling

Most Android-based devices use a touch screen as the primary interface between the user and the device. The previous chapter introduced how a touch on the screen translates into an action within a running Android application. There is, however, much more to touch event handling than responding to a single finger tap on a view object. Most Android devices can, for example, detect more than one touch at a time. Nor are touches limited to a single point on the device display. Touches can be dynamic as the user slides one or more contact points across the screen's surface.

An application can also interpret touches as a gesture. Consider, for example, that a horizontal swipe is typically used to turn the page of an eBook or how a pinching motion can zoom in and out of an image displayed on the screen.

An application can also interpret touches as a *gesture*. Consider, for example, that a horizontal swipe is typically used to turn the page of an eBook or how a pinching motion can zoom in and out of an image displayed on the screen.

This chapter will explain the handling of touches that involve motion and explore the concept of intercepting multiple concurrent touches. The topic of identifying distinct gestures will be covered in the next chapter.

36.1 Intercepting Touch Events

A view object can intercept touch events by registering an onTouchListener event listener and implementing the corresponding onTouch() callback method or lambda. The following code, for example, ensures that any touches on a ConstraintLayout view instance named *myLayout* result in a call to a lambda expression:

```
binding.myLayout.setOnTouchListener {v: View, m: MotionEvent ->
    // Perform tasks here
    true
}
```

Of course, the above code could also be implemented by using a function instead of a lambda as follows, though the lambda approach results in more compact and readable code:

```
binding.myLayout.setOnTouchListener(object : View.OnTouchListener {
    override fun onTouch(v: View, m: MotionEvent): Boolean {
        // Perform tasks here
        return true
    }
})
```

As indicated in the code example, the lambda expression is required to return a Boolean value indicating to the Android runtime system whether or not the event should be passed on to other event listeners registered on the same view or discarded. The method is passed both a reference to the view on which the event was triggered and an object of type *MotionEvent*.

36.2 The MotionEvent Object

The MotionEvent object passed through to the *onTouch()* callback method is the key to obtaining information about the event. Information within the object includes the location of the touch within the view and the type of action performed. The MotionEvent object is also the key to handling multiple touches.

36.3 Understanding Touch Actions

An important aspect of touch event handling involves identifying the type of action the user performed. The type of action associated with an event can be obtained by making a call to the *getActionMasked()* method of the MotionEvent object, which was passed through to the *onTouch()* callback method. When the first touch on a view occurs, the MotionEvent object will contain an action type of ACTION_DOWN together with the coordinates of the touch. When that touch is lifted from the screen, an ACTION_UP event is generated. Any motion of the touch between the ACTION_DOWN and ACTION_UP events will be represented by ACTION_MOVE events.

When more than one touch is performed simultaneously on a view, the touches are referred to as *pointers*. In a multi-touch scenario, pointers begin and end with event actions of type ACTION_POINTER_DOWN and ACTION_POINTER_UP, respectively. To identify the index of the pointer that triggered the event, the *getActionIndex()* callback method of the MotionEvent object must be called.

36.4 Handling Multiple Touches

The chapter entitled *"An Overview and Example of Android Event Handling"* began exploring event handling within the narrow context of a single-touch event. In practice, most Android devices can respond to multiple consecutive touches (though it is important to note that the number of simultaneous touches that can be detected varies depending on the device).

As previously discussed, each touch in a multi-touch situation is considered by the Android framework to be a *pointer*. Each pointer, in turn, is referenced by an *index* value and assigned an *ID*. The current number of pointers can be obtained via a call to the *getPointerCount()* method of the current MotionEvent object. The ID for a pointer at a particular index in the list of current pointers may be obtained via a call to the MotionEvent *getPointerId()* method. For example, the following code excerpt obtains a count of pointers and the ID of the pointer at index 0:

```
binding.myLayout.setOnTouchListener {v: View, m: MotionEvent ->
    val pointerCount = m.pointerCount
    val pointerId = m.getPointerId(0)
    true
}
```

Note that the pointer count will always be greater than or equal to 1 when the *onTouch* listener is triggered (since at least one touch must have occurred for the callback to be triggered).

A touch on a view, particularly one involving motion across the screen, will generate a stream of events before the point of contact with the screen is lifted. An application will likely need to track individual touches over multiple touch events. While the ID of a specific touch gesture will not change from one event to the next, it is important to remember that the index value will change as other touch events come and go. When working with a touch gesture over multiple events, the ID value must be used as the touch reference to ensure the same touch is being tracked. When calling methods that require an index value, this should be obtained by converting the ID for a touch to the corresponding index value via a call to the *findPointerIndex()* method of the *MotionEvent* object.

36.5 An Example Multi-Touch Application

The example application created in the remainder of this chapter will track up to two touch gestures as they move across a layout view. As the events for each touch are triggered, the coordinates, index, and ID for each touch will be displayed on the screen.

Select the *New Project* option from the welcome screen and, within the resulting new project dialog, choose the Empty Views Activity template before clicking on the Next button.

Enter *MotionEvent* into the Name field and specify *com.ebookfrenzy.motionevent* as the package name. Before clicking the Finish button, change the Minimum API level setting to API 26: Android 8.0 (Oreo) and the Language menu to Kotlin.

Adapt the project to use view binding using the Gemini Agent or the steps in section *18.8 Migrating a Project to View Binding*.

36.6 Designing the Activity User Interface

The user interface for the application's sole activity is to consist of a ConstraintLayout view containing two TextView objects. Within the Project tool window, navigate to *app -> res -> layout* and double-click on the *activity_main.xml* layout resource file to load it into the Android Studio Layout Editor tool.

Select and delete the default "Hello World!" TextView widget and then, with autoconnect enabled, drag and drop a new TextView widget so that it is centered horizontally and positioned at the 16dp margin line on the top edge of the layout:

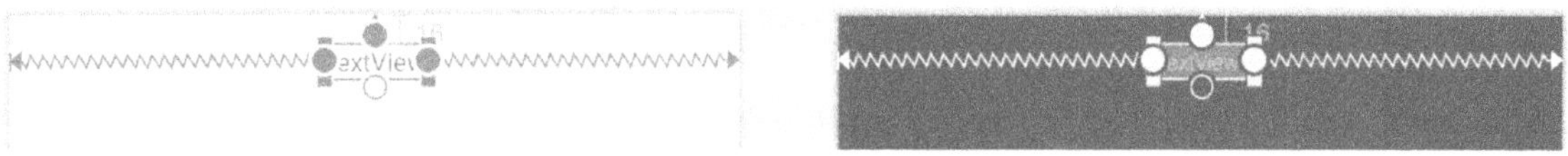

Figure 36-1

Drag a second TextView widget and position and constrain it so that a 32dp margin distances it from the bottom of the first widget:

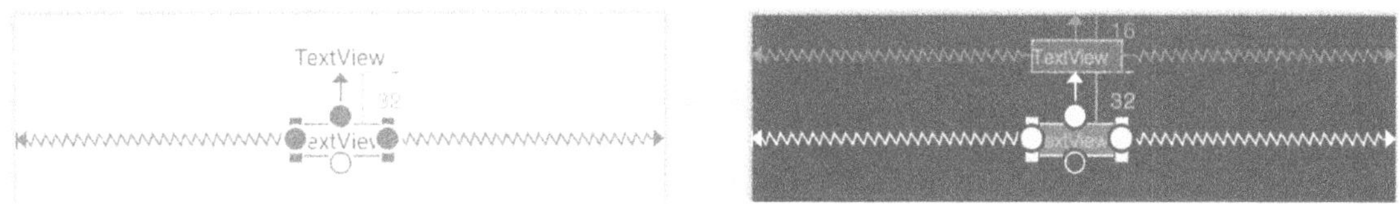

Figure 36-2

Using the Attributes tool window, change the IDs for the TextView widgets to *textView1* and *textView2*, respectively. Change the text displayed on the widgets to read "Touch One Status" and "Touch Two Status" and extract the strings to resources using the warning button in the top right-hand corner of the Layout Editor.

36.7 Implementing the Touch Event Listener

To receive touch event notification, it will be necessary to register a touch listener on the layout view within the *onCreate()* method of the *MainActivity* activity class. Select the *MainActivity.kt* tab from the Android Studio editor panel to display the source code. Within the *onCreate()* method, add code to register the touch listener and implement code which, in this case, is going to call a second method named *handleTouch()* to which is passed the MotionEvent object:

```
package com.ebookfrenzy.motionevent
```

```
import androidx.appcompat.app.AppCompatActivity
import android.os.Bundle
import android.view.MotionEvent

import com.ebookfrenzy.motionevent.databinding.ActivityMainBinding

class MainActivity : AppCompatActivity() {

    private lateinit var binding: ActivityMainBinding

    override fun onCreate(savedInstanceState: Bundle?) {
.
.
        binding.root.setOnTouchListener {_, m: MotionEvent ->
            handleTouch(m)
            true
        }
    }
}
```

When we designed the user interface, the parent ConstraintLayout was not assigned an ID that would allow us to access it via the view binding mechanism. Since this layout component is the topmost component in the UI layout hierarchy, we have been able to reference it using the *root* binding property in the code above.

Before testing the application, the final task is to implement the *handleTouch()* method called by the listener. The code for this method reads as follows:

```
private fun handleTouch(m: MotionEvent)
{
    val pointerCount = m.pointerCount

    for (i in 0 until pointerCount)
    {
        val x = m.getX(i)
        val y = m.getY(i)
        val id = m.getPointerId(i)
        val action = m.actionMasked
        val actionIndex = m.actionIndex

        val actionString = when (action) {
                MotionEvent.ACTION_DOWN -> "DOWN"
                MotionEvent.ACTION_UP -> "UP"
                MotionEvent.ACTION_POINTER_DOWN -> "PNTR DOWN"
                MotionEvent.ACTION_POINTER_UP -> "PNTR UP"
                MotionEvent.ACTION_MOVE -> "MOVE"
                else -> ""
            }
```

```
        val touchStatus =
                "Action: $actionString Index: $actionIndex ID: $id X: $x Y: $y"

        if (id == 0)
            binding.textView1.text = touchStatus
        else
            binding.textView2.text = touchStatus
    }
}
```

Before compiling and running the application, it is worth taking the time to walk through this code systematically to highlight the tasks performed.

The code begins by identifying how many pointers are currently active on the view:

```
val pointerCount = m.pointerCount
```

Next, the *pointerCount* variable initiates a for loop, which performs tasks for each active pointer. The first few lines of the loop obtain the X and Y coordinates of the touch together with the corresponding event ID, action type, and action index. Lastly, a string variable is declared:

```
for (i in 0 until pointerCount)
{
    val x = m.getX(i)
    val y = m.getY(i)
    val id = m.getPointerId(i)
    val action = m.actionMasked
    val actionIndex = m.actionIndex
    var actionString: String
```

Since action types equate to integer values, a *when* statement is used to convert the action type to a more meaningful string value, which is stored in the previously declared *actionString* variable:

```
val actionString = when (action) {
    MotionEvent.ACTION_DOWN -> "DOWN"
    MotionEvent.ACTION_UP -> "UP"
    MotionEvent.ACTION_POINTER_DOWN -> "PNTR DOWN"
    MotionEvent.ACTION_POINTER_UP -> "PNTR UP"
    MotionEvent.ACTION_MOVE -> "MOVE"
    else -> ""
}
```

Finally, the string message is constructed using the *actionString* value, the action index, touch ID, and X and Y coordinates. The ID value is then used to decide whether the string should be displayed on the first or second TextView object:

```
val touchStatus =
   "Action: $actionString Index: $actionIndex ID: $id X: $x Y: $y"

if (id == 0)
    binding.textView1.text = touchStatus
else
```

```
    binding.textView2.text = touchStatus
```

36.8 Running the Example Application

Compile and run the application and, once launched, experiment with single and multiple touches on the screen and note that the text views update to reflect the events as illustrated in Figure 36-3. When running on an emulator, multiple touches may be simulated by holding down the Ctrl (Cmd on macOS) key while clicking the mouse button (note that simulating multiple touches may not work if the emulator is running in a tool window):

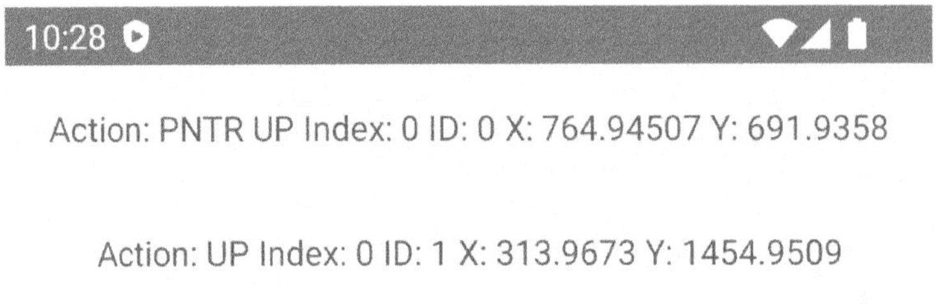

Figure 36-3

36.9 Summary

Activities receive notifications of touch events by registering an onTouchListener event listener and implementing the onTouch() callback method, which, in turn, is passed a MotionEvent object when called by the Android runtime. This object contains information about the touch, such as the type of touch event, the coordinates of the touch, and a count of the number of touches currently in contact with the view.

When multiple touches are involved, each point of contact is referred to as a pointer, with each assigned an index and an ID. While the index of a touch can change from one event to another, the ID will remain unchanged until the touch ends.

This chapter has worked through creating an example Android application designed to display the coordinates and action type of up to two simultaneous touches on a device display.

Having covered touches in general, the next chapter (entitled *"Detecting Common Gestures Using the Android Gesture Detector Class"*) will look further at touchscreen event handling through gesture recognition.

Chapter 37

37. Detecting Common Gestures Using the Android Gesture Detector Class

The term "gesture" defines a contiguous sequence of interactions between the touch screen and the user. A typical gesture begins at the point that the screen is first touched and ends when the last finger or pointing device leaves the display surface. When correctly harnessed, gestures can be implemented to communicate between the user and the application. Swiping motions to turn the pages of an eBook or a pinching movement involving two touches to zoom in or out of an image are prime examples of how gestures can interact with an application.

The Android SDK provides mechanisms for the detection of both common and custom gestures within an application. Common gestures involve interactions such as a tap, double tap, long press, or a swiping motion in either a horizontal or a vertical direction (referred to in Android nomenclature as a *fling*).

This chapter explores using the Android GestureDetector class to detect common gestures performed on the display of an Android device. The next chapter, *"Implementing Custom Gesture and Pinch Recognition on Android"*, will cover detecting more complex, custom gestures such as circular motions and pinches.

37.1 Implementing Common Gesture Detection

When a user interacts with the display of an Android device, the *onTouchEvent()* method of the currently active application is called by the system and passed MotionEvent objects containing data about the user's contact with the screen. This data can be interpreted to identify if the motion on the screen matches a common gesture such as a tap or a swipe. This can be achieved with minimal programming effort by using the Android GestureDetector class. This class is designed to receive motion event information from the application and trigger method calls based on the type of common gesture, if any, detected.

The basic steps in detecting common gestures are as follows:

1. Declaration of a class which implements the GestureDetector.OnGestureListener interface including the required *onFling()*, *onDown()*, *onScroll()*, *onShowPress()*, *onSingleTapUp()* and *onLongPress()* callback methods. Note that this can be either an entirely new or an enclosing activity class. If double-tap gesture detection is required, the class must also implement the GestureDetector.OnDoubleTapListener interface and include the corresponding *onDoubleTap()* method.

2. Creation of an instance of the Android GestureDetector class, passing through an instance of the class created in step 1 as an argument.

3. An optional call to the *setOnDoubleTapListener()* method of the GestureDetector instance to enable double tap detection if required.

4. Implementation of the *onTouchEvent()* callback method on the enclosing activity, which, in turn, must call the *onTouchEvent()* method of the GestureDetector instance, passing through the current motion event object as an argument to the method.

Once implemented, the result is a set of methods within the application code that will be called when a gesture of a particular type is detected. The code within these methods can then be implemented to perform any tasks that need to be performed in response to the corresponding gesture.

In the remainder of this chapter, we will work through creating an example project intended to put the above steps into practice.

37.2 Creating an Example Gesture Detection Project

This project aims to detect the full range of common gestures currently supported by the GestureDetector class and to display status information to the user indicating the type of gesture that has been detected.

Select the *New Project* option from the welcome screen and, within the resulting new project dialog, choose the Empty Views Activity template before clicking on the Next button.

Enter *CommonGestures* into the Name field and specify *com.ebookfrenzy.commongestures* as the package name. Before clicking the Finish button, change the Minimum API level setting to API 26: Android 8.0 (Oreo) and the Language menu to Kotlin.

Adapt the project to use view binding using the Gemini Agent or the steps outlined in section *18.8 Migrating a Project to View Binding.*

Once the new project has been created, navigate to the *app -> res -> layout -> activity_main.xml* file in the Project tool window and double-click on it to load it into the Layout Editor tool.

Within the Layout Editor tool, select the "Hello, World!" TextView component and, in the Attributes tool window, enter *gestureStatusText* as the ID. Finally, set the textSize to 20sp and enable the bold textStyle:

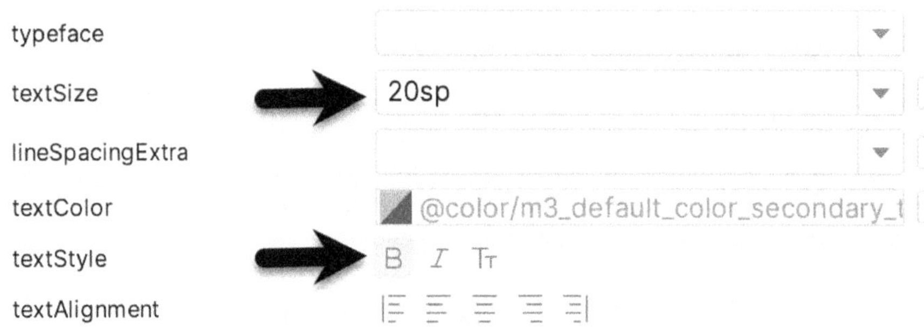

Figure 37-1

37.3 Implementing the Listener Class

As previously outlined, it is necessary to create a class that implements the GestureDetector.OnGestureListener interface and, if double tap detection is required, the GestureDetector.OnDoubleTapListener interface. While this can be an entirely new class, it is also perfectly valid to implement this within the current activity class. Therefore, we will modify the MainActivity class to implement these listener interfaces for this example. Edit the *MainActivity.kt* file so that it reads as follows:

```
package com.ebookfrenzy.commongestures

import androidx.appcompat.app.AppCompatActivity
import android.os.Bundle
import android.view.GestureDetector
import android.view.MotionEvent
```

```
.
.
class MainActivity : AppCompatActivity(),
   GestureDetector.OnGestureListener, GestureDetector.OnDoubleTapListener
{
.
.
```

Declaring that the class implements the listener interfaces mandates that the corresponding methods also be implemented in the class:

```
class MainActivity : AppCompatActivity(),
   GestureDetector.OnGestureListener, GestureDetector.OnDoubleTapListener
{
.
.
    override fun onDown(event: MotionEvent): Boolean {
        binding.gestureStatusText.text = "onDown"
        return true
    }

    override fun onFling(event1: MotionEvent?, event2: MotionEvent,
                         velocityX: Float, velocityY: Float): Boolean {
        binding.gestureStatusText.text = "onFling"
        return true
    }

    override fun onLongPress(event: MotionEvent) {
        binding.gestureStatusText.text = "onLongPress"
    }

    override fun onScroll(e1: MotionEvent?, e2: MotionEvent,
                          distanceX: Float, distanceY: Float): Boolean {
        binding.gestureStatusText.text = "onScroll"
        return true
    }

    override fun onShowPress(event: MotionEvent) {
        binding.gestureStatusText.text = "onShowPress"
    }

    override fun onSingleTapUp(event: MotionEvent): Boolean {
        binding.gestureStatusText.text = "onSingleTapUp"
        return true
    }

    override fun onDoubleTap(event: MotionEvent): Boolean {
```

```
        binding.gestureStatusText.text = "onDoubleTap"
        return true
    }

    override fun onDoubleTapEvent(event: MotionEvent): Boolean {
        binding.gestureStatusText.text = "onDoubleTapEvent"
        return true
    }

    override fun onSingleTapConfirmed(event: MotionEvent): Boolean {
        binding.gestureStatusText.text = "onSingleTapConfirmed"
        return true
    }
}
```

Note that many of these methods return *true*. This indicates to the Android Framework that the method has consumed the event and does not need to be passed to the next event handler in the stack.

37.4 Creating the GestureDetector Instance

With the activity class now updated to implement the listener interfaces, the next step is to create an instance of the GestureDetector class. Since this only needs to be performed once at the point that the activity is created, the best place for this code is in the *onCreate()* method. Since we also want to detect double taps, the code also needs to call the *setOnDoubleTapListener()* method of the GestureDetector instance:

```
.
.
class MainActivity : AppCompatActivity(), GestureDetector.OnGestureListener,
GestureDetector.OnDoubleTapListener
{
    private lateinit var binding: ActivityMainBinding
    var gDetector: GestureDetector? = null

    override fun onCreate(savedInstanceState: Bundle?) {
.
.
        this.gDetector = GestureDetector(this, this)
        gDetector?.setOnDoubleTapListener(this)
    }
.
.
```

37.5 Implementing the onTouchEvent() Method

If the application were to be compiled and run at this point, nothing would happen if gestures were performed on the device display. This is because no code has been added to intercept touch events and to pass them through to the GestureDetector instance. To achieve this, it is necessary to override the *onTouchEvent()* method within the activity class and implement it such that it calls the *onTouchEvent()* method of the GestureDetector instance. Remaining in the *MainActivity.kt* file, therefore, implement this method so that it reads as follows:

```
override fun onTouchEvent(event: MotionEvent): Boolean {
```

```
    this.gDetector?.onTouchEvent(event)
    // Be sure to call the superclass implementation
    return super.onTouchEvent(event)
}
```

37.6 Testing the Application

Compile and run the application on either a physical Android device or an AVD emulator. Once launched, experiment with swipes, presses, scrolling motions, and double and single taps. Note that the text view updates to reflect the events as illustrated in Figure 37-2:

Figure 37-2

37.7 Summary

Any physical contact between the user and the touchscreen display of a device can be considered a "gesture". Lacking the physical keyboard and mouse pointer of a traditional computer system, gestures are widely used as a method of interaction between the user and the application. While a gesture can comprise just about any sequence of motions, there is a widely used set of gestures with which users of touchscreen devices have become familiar. Some of these so-called "common gestures" can be easily detected within an application by using the Android Gesture Detector classes. In this chapter, the use of this technique has been outlined both in theory and through the implementation of an example project.

Having covered common gestures in this chapter, the next chapter will look at detecting a wider range of gesture types, including the ability to design and detect your own gestures.

Chapter 38

38. Implementing Custom Gesture and Pinch Recognition on Android

The previous chapter covered the detection of what is referred to as "common gestures" from within an Android application. In practice, however, a gesture can conceivably involve just about any sequence of touch motions on the display of an Android device. In recognition of this, the Android SDK allows custom gestures of just about any nature to be defined by the application developer and used to trigger events when performed by the user. This is a multi-stage process, the details of which are the topic of this chapter.

38.1 The Android Gesture Builder Application

The Android SDK allows developers to design custom gestures stored in a gesture file bundled with an Android application package. These custom gesture files are most easily created using the Gesture Builder application. Creating a gestures file involves launching the Gesture Builder application on a physical device or emulator and "drawing" the gestures that will need to be detected by the application. Once the gestures have been designed, the file containing the gesture data can be downloaded and added to the application project. Within the application code, the file is loaded into an instance of the *GestureLibrary* class, which can be used to search for matches to any gestures the user performs on the device display.

38.2 The GestureOverlayView Class

To facilitate the detection of gestures within an application, the Android SDK provides the GestureOverlayView class. This transparent view can be placed over other views in the user interface to detect gestures.

38.3 Detecting Gestures

Gestures are detected by loading the gestures file created using the Gesture Builder app and then registering a *GesturePerformedListener* event listener on an instance of the GestureOverlayView class. The enclosing class is then declared to implement both the *OnGesturePerformedListener* interface and the corresponding *onGesturePerformed* callback method required by that interface. If the listener detects a gesture, the Android runtime system triggers a call to the onGesturePerformed callback method.

38.4 Identifying Specific Gestures

When a gesture is detected, the *onGesturePerformed* callback method is called and passed as arguments a reference to the GestureOverlayView object on which the gesture was detected, together with a Gesture object containing information about the gesture.

With access to the Gesture object, the GestureLibrary can compare the detected gesture to those contained in the gestures file previously loaded into the application. The GestureLibrary reports the probability that the gesture performed by the user matches an entry in the gestures file by calculating a *prediction score* for each gesture. A prediction score of 1.0 or greater is generally accepted as a good match between a gesture stored in the file and that performed by the user on the device display.

38.5 Installing and Running the Gesture Builder Application

The easiest way to create a gestures file is to use an app allowing gesture motions to be captured and saved. Although Google originally provided an app for this purpose, it has not been maintained adequately for use on more recent versions of Android. Fortunately, an alternative is available in the form of the Gesture Builder Tool app, which is available from the Google Play Store at the following URL:

https://play.google.com/store/apps/details?id=migueldp.runeforge

38.6 Creating a Gestures File

Once the Gesture Builder Tool has loaded, click on the *Create New Gesture* button at the bottom of the device screen and "draw" a gesture using a circular motion on the gray canvas, as illustrated in Figure 38-1. Assuming that the gesture appears as required (represented by the yellow line on the device screen), click on the save button to add the gesture to the gestures file, entering "Circle Gesture" when prompted for a name:

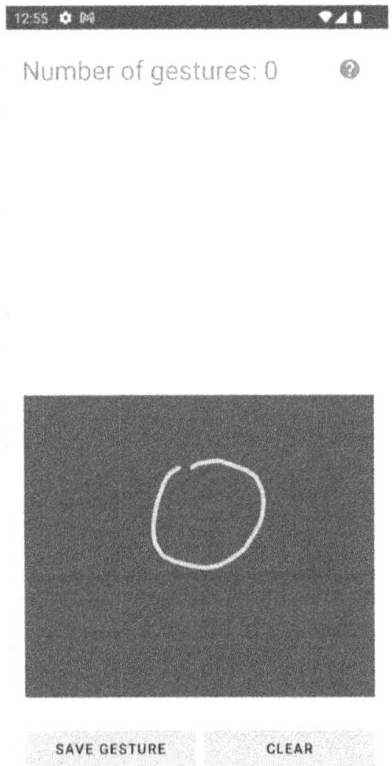

Figure 38-1

After the gesture has been saved, the Gesture Builder Tool will display a list of currently defined gestures that will consist solely of the new *Circle Gesture*.

38.7 Creating the Example Project

Select the *New Project* option from the welcome screen and, within the resulting new project dialog, choose the Empty Views Activity template before clicking on the Next button.

Enter *CustomGestures* into the Name field and specify *com.ebookfrenzy.customgestures* as the package name. Before clicking the Finish button, change the Minimum API level setting to API 26: Android 8.0 (Oreo) and the Language menu to Kotlin. Adapt the project to use view binding using the Gemini Agent or the steps outlined in section *18.8 Migrating a Project to View Binding.*

38.8 Extracting the Gestures File from the SD Card

As each gesture was created within the Gesture Builder application, it was added to a file named *gesture.txt*, located in the storage of the emulator or device on which the app was running. However, before this file can be added to an Android Studio project, it must be copied off the device storage and saved to the local file system. This is most easily achieved using the Android Studio Device File Explorer tool window. Display this tool using the *View -> Tool Windows -> Device File Explorer* menu option. Once displayed, select the device or emulator on which the gesture file was created from the drop-down menu, then navigate through the filesystem to the following folder:

```
/storage/emulated/0/Android/data/migueldp.runeforge/files/gestures.txt
```

Locate the *gesture.txt* file in this folder, right-click on it, select the *Save As...* menu option, and save the file to a temporary location as a file named *gestures*.

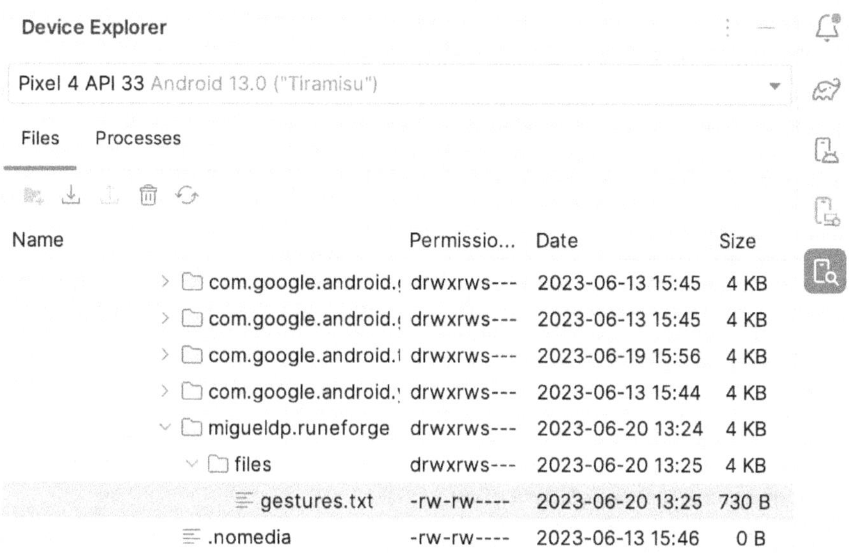

Figure 38-2

Once the gestures file has been created and pulled from the device storage, it can be added to an Android Studio project as a resource file.

38.9 Adding the Gestures File to the Project

Within the Android Studio Project tool window, locate and right-click on the *res* folder (located under *app*) and select *New -> Directory* from the resulting menu. In the New Directory dialog, enter *raw* as the folder name and tap the keyboard enter key. Using the appropriate file explorer utility for your operating system type, locate the *gestures* file previously pulled from the device storage and copy and paste it into the new *raw* folder in the Project tool window.

38.10 Designing the User Interface

This example application calls for a user interface consisting of a ConstraintLayout view with a GestureOverlayView layered on it to intercept any gestures the user performs. Locate the *app -> res -> layout -> activity_main.xml* file, double-click on it to load it into the Layout Editor tool, and select and delete the default TextView widget.

Switch the layout editor Code mode and modify the XML so that it reads as follows:

```
<?xml version="1.0" encoding="utf-8"?>
<androidx.constraintlayout.widget.ConstraintLayout
    xmlns:android="http://schemas.android.com/apk/res/android"
    xmlns:app="http://schemas.android.com/apk/res-auto"
    xmlns:tools="http://schemas.android.com/tools"
    android:layout_width="match_parent"
    android:layout_height="match_parent"
```

```
    tools:context=".MainActivity" >

    <android.gesture.GestureOverlayView
        android:id="@+id/gOverlay"
        android:layout_width="0dp"
        android:layout_height="0dp"
        app:layout_constraintBottom_toBottomOf="parent"
        app:layout_constraintEnd_toEndOf="parent"
        app:layout_constraintStart_toStartOf="parent"
        app:layout_constraintTop_toTopOf="parent" />

</androidx.constraintlayout.widget.ConstraintLayout>
```

38.11 Loading the Gestures File

Now that the gestures file has been added to the project, the next step is to write some code to load the file when the activity starts. For this project, the code to achieve this will be added to the MainActivity class as follows:

```
package com.ebookfrenzy.customgestures

import androidx.appcompat.app.AppCompatActivity
import android.os.Bundle
import android.gesture.GestureLibraries
import android.gesture.GestureLibrary
import android.gesture.GestureOverlayView
import android.gesture.GestureOverlayView.OnGesturePerformedListener

import com.ebookfrenzy.customgestures.databinding.ActivityMainBinding

class MainActivity : AppCompatActivity(), OnGesturePerformedListener {

    private lateinit var binding: ActivityMainBinding
    private var gLibrary: GestureLibrary? = null

    override fun onCreate(savedInstanceState: Bundle?) {
.
.
        gestureSetup()
    }

    private fun gestureSetup()  {
        gLibrary = GestureLibraries.fromRawResource(this,
                R.raw.gestures)
        if (gLibrary?.load() == false) {
            finish()
        }
    }
.
```

```
.
}
```

In addition to some necessary import directives, the above code also creates a *GestureLibrary* instance named *gLibrary* and then loads into it the contents of the *gesture* file located in the *raw* resources folder. The activity class has also been modified to implement the *OnGesturePerformedListener* interface, which requires adding the onGesturePerformed callback method (which will be created later in this chapter).

38.12 Registering the Event Listener

For the activity to receive a notification that the user has performed a gesture on the screen, it is necessary to register the *OnGesturePerformedListener* event listener on the *gLayout* view as outlined in the following code fragment:

```
private fun gestureSetup() {
    gLibrary = GestureLibraries.fromRawResource(this,
            R.raw.gesture)
    if (gLibrary?.load() == false) {
        finish()
    }

    binding.gOverlay.addOnGesturePerformedListener(this)
}
```

38.13 Implementing the onGesturePerformed Method

All that remains before an initial test run of the application can be performed is to implement the *OnGesturePerformed* callback method. This is the method that will be called when a gesture is performed on the GestureOverlayView instance:

```
package com.ebookfrenzy.customgestures
.
.
import android.widget.Toast
import android.gesture.Gesture

class MainActivity : AppCompatActivity(), OnGesturePerformedListener {
.
.
    override fun onGesturePerformed(overlay: GestureOverlayView,
                           gesture: Gesture) {

        val predictions = gLibrary?.recognize(gesture)

        predictions?.let {
            if (it.size > 0 && it[0].score > 1.0) {
                val action = it[0].name
                Toast.makeText(this, action, Toast.LENGTH_SHORT).show()
            }
        }
    }
```

```
}
```

When the Android runtime detects a gesture on the gesture overlay view object, the *onGesturePerformed* method is called. Passed through as arguments are a reference to the GestureOverlayView object on which the gesture was detected together with an object of type *Gesture*. The Gesture class is designed to hold the information that defines a specific gesture (essentially a sequence of timed points on the screen depicting the path of the strokes that comprise a gesture).

The Gesture object is passed through to the *recognize()* method of our *gLibrary* instance to compare the current gesture with each gesture loaded from the *gesture* file. Once this task is complete, the *recognize()* method returns an ArrayList object containing a Prediction object for each comparison performed. The list is ranked in order from the best match (at position 0 in the array) to the worst. Contained within each prediction object is the name of the corresponding gesture from the *gesture* file and a prediction score indicating how closely it matches the current gesture.

The code in the above method, therefore, takes the prediction at position 0 (the closest match), makes sure it has a score of greater than 1.0, and then displays a Toast message (an Android class designed to display notification pop-ups to the user) displaying the name of the matching gesture.

38.14 Testing the Application

Build and run the application on an emulator or a physical Android device and perform the circle gesture on the display. When performed, the toast notification should appear containing the name of the detected gesture. Note that when a gesture is recognized, it is outlined on the display with a bright yellow line, while gestures about which the overlay is uncertain appear as a faint yellow line. While useful during development, this is probably not ideal for a real-world application. Therefore, there is still some more configuration work to do.

38.15 Configuring the GestureOverlayView

By default, the GestureOverlayView is configured to display yellow lines during gestures. The color that draws recognized and unrecognized gestures can be defined via the *android:gestureColor* and *android:uncertainGestureColor* attributes. For example, to hide the gesture lines, modify the *activity_main.xml* file in the example project as follows:

```
<android.gesture.GestureOverlayView
    android:id="@+id/gOverlay"
    android:layout_width="0dp"
    android:layout_height="0dp"
    app:layout_constraintBottom_toBottomOf="parent"
    app:layout_constraintEnd_toEndOf="parent"
    app:layout_constraintStart_toStartOf="parent"
    app:layout_constraintTop_toTopOf="parent"
    android:gestureColor="#00000000"
    android:uncertainGestureColor="#00000000" />
```

On re-running the application, gestures should now be invisible (since they are drawn in white on the white background of the ConstraintLayout view).

38.16 Intercepting Gestures

The GestureOverlayView is, as previously described, a transparent overlay that may be positioned over the top of other views. This leads to the question of whether events intercepted by the gesture overlay should be passed on to the underlying views when a gesture has been recognized. This is controlled via the *android:eventsInterceptionEnabled* property of the GestureOverlayView instance. When set to true, the gesture events are not passed to the underlying views when a gesture is recognized. This can be a particularly useful setting when gestures are being performed over a view that might be configured to scroll in response to certain gestures. Setting this property to *true* will avoid gestures also being interpreted as instructions to the underlying view to scroll in a particular direction.

38.17 Detecting Pinch Gestures

Before moving on from touch handling in general and gesture recognition in particular, the last topic of this chapter is handling pinch gestures. While it is possible to create and detect a wide range of gestures using the steps outlined in the previous sections of this chapter, it is, in fact, not possible to detect a pinching gesture (where two fingers are used in a stretching and pinching motion, typically to zoom in and out of a view or image) using the techniques discussed so far.

The simplest method for detecting pinch gestures is to use the Android *ScaleGestureDetector* class. In general terms, detecting pinch gestures involves the following three steps:

1. Declaration of a new class which implements the SimpleOnScaleGestureListener interface, including the required *onScale()*, *onScaleBegin()*, and *onScaleEnd()* callback methods.

2. Creation of an instance of the ScaleGestureDetector class, passing through an instance of the class created in step 1 as an argument.

3. Implementing the *onTouchEvent()* callback method on the enclosing activity, which, in turn, calls the *onTouchEvent()* method of the ScaleGestureDetector class.

In the remainder of this chapter, we will create an example designed to demonstrate the implementation of pinch gesture recognition.

38.18 A Pinch Gesture Example Project

Select the *New Project* option from the welcome screen and, within the resulting new project dialog, choose the Empty Views Activity template before clicking on the Next button.

Enter *PinchExample* into the Name field and specify *com.ebookfrenzy.pinchexample* as the package name. Before clicking on the Finish button, change the Minimum API level setting to API 26: Android 8.0 (Oreo) and the Language menu to Kotlin. Convert the project to use view binding using the Gemini Agent or by following the steps in *18.8 Migrating a Project to View Binding*.

Within the *activity_main.xml* file, select the default TextView object and use the Attributes tool window to set the ID to *myTextView*.

Locate and load the *MainActivity.kt* file into the Android Studio editor and modify the file as follows:

```
package com.ebookfrenzy.pinchexample

import androidx.appcompat.app.AppCompatActivity
import android.os.Bundle
import android.view.MotionEvent
import android.view.ScaleGestureDetector
import android.view.ScaleGestureDetector.SimpleOnScaleGestureListener

import com.ebookfrenzy.pinchexample.databinding.ActivityMainBinding

class MainActivity : AppCompatActivity() {
```

```
    private lateinit var binding: ActivityMainBinding
    private var scaleGestureDetector: ScaleGestureDetector? = null

    override fun onCreate(savedInstanceState: Bundle?) {
        super.onCreate(savedInstanceState)
.
.
        scaleGestureDetector = ScaleGestureDetector(this,
                    MyOnScaleGestureListener())
    }

    override fun onTouchEvent(event: MotionEvent): Boolean {
        scaleGestureDetector?.onTouchEvent(event)
        return true
    }

    inner class MyOnScaleGestureListener : SimpleOnScaleGestureListener() {
        override fun onScale(detector: ScaleGestureDetector): Boolean {
            val scaleFactor = detector.scaleFactor
            if (scaleFactor > 1) {
                binding.myTextView.text = "Zooming In"
            } else {
                binding.myTextView.text = "Zooming Out"
            }
            return true
        }

        override fun onScaleBegin(detector: ScaleGestureDetector): Boolean {
            return true
        }

        override fun onScaleEnd(detector: ScaleGestureDetector) {
        }
    }
}
```

The code declares a new class named MyOnScaleGestureListener, extending the Android SimpleOnScaleGestureListener class. This interface requires that three methods (*onScale()*, *onScaleBegin()*, and *onScaleEnd()*) be implemented. In this instance, the *onScale()* method identifies the scale factor and displays a message on the text view indicating the type of pinch gesture detected.

Within the *onCreate()* method, a new *ScaleGestureDetector* instance is created, passing through a reference to the enclosing activity and an instance of our new *MyOnScaleGestureListener* class as arguments. Finally, an *onTouchEvent()* callback method is implemented for the activity, which calls the corresponding *onTouchEvent()* method of the *ScaleGestureDetector* object, passing through the MotionEvent object as an argument.

Compile and run the application on an emulator or physical Android device and perform pinching gestures on the screen, noting that the text view displays either the zoom-in or zoom-out message depending on the pinching motion. Pinching gestures may be simulated within the emulator in stand-alone mode by holding down the Ctrl (or macOS Cmd) key and clicking and dragging the mouse pointer, as shown in Figure 38-3:

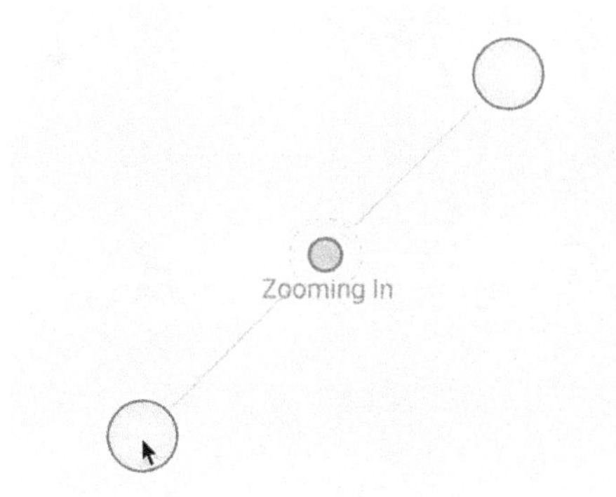

Figure 38-3

38.19 Summary

A gesture is the motion of points of contact on a touch screen involving one or more strokes and can be used as a method of communication between the user and the application. Android allows gestures to be designed using the Gesture Builder application. Once created, gestures can be saved to a gestures file and loaded into an activity at application runtime using the GestureLibrary.

Gestures can be detected on areas of the display by overlaying existing views with instances of the transparent *GestureOverlayView* class and implementing an *OnGesturePerformedListener* event listener. Using the GestureLibrary, a ranked list of matches between a gesture performed by the user and the gestures stored in a gestures file may be generated, using a prediction score to decide whether a gesture is a close enough match.

Pinch gestures may be detected by implementing the ScaleGestureDetector class, an example of which was also provided in this chapter.

Chapter 39

39. An Introduction to Android Fragments

As you progress through the chapters of this book, it will become increasingly evident that many of the design concepts behind the Android system were conceived to promote the reuse of and interaction between the different elements that make up an application. One such area that will be explored in this chapter involves using Fragments.

This chapter will provide an overview of the basics of fragments in terms of what they are and how they can be created and used within applications. The next chapter will work through a tutorial designed to show fragments in action when developing applications in Android Studio, including the implementation of communication between fragments.

39.1 What is a Fragment?

A fragment is a self-contained, modular section of an application's user interface and corresponding behavior that can be embedded within an activity. Fragments can be assembled to create an activity during the application design phase and added to or removed from an activity during application runtime to create a dynamically changing user interface.

Fragments may only be used as part of an activity and cannot be instantiated as standalone application elements. However, a fragment can be considered a functional "sub-activity" with its own lifecycle similar to that of a full activity.

Fragments are stored in the form of XML layout files. They may be added to an activity by placing appropriate <fragment> elements in the activity's layout file or through code within the activity's class implementation.

39.2 Creating a Fragment

The two components that make up a fragment are an XML layout file and a corresponding Kotlin class. The XML layout file for a fragment takes the same format as a layout for any other activity layout and can contain any combination and complexity of layout managers and views. The following XML layout, for example, is for a fragment consisting of a ConstraintLayout with a red background containing a single TextView with a white foreground:

```
<?xml version="1.0" encoding="utf-8"?>
<androidx.constraintlayout.widget.ConstraintLayout
    xmlns:android="http://schemas.android.com/apk/res/android"
    xmlns:app="http://schemas.android.com/apk/res-auto"
    xmlns:tools="http://schemas.android.com/tools"
    android:id="@+id/constraintLayout"
    android:layout_width="match_parent"
    android:layout_height="match_parent"
    android:background="@android:color/holo_red_dark"
    tools:context=".FragmentOne">
```

```
    <TextView
        android:id="@+id/textView1"
        android:layout_width="wrap_content"
        android:layout_height="wrap_content"
        android:text="My First Fragment"
        android:textAppearance="@style/TextAppearance.AppCompat.Large"
        android:textColor="@color/white"
        app:layout_constraintBottom_toBottomOf="parent"
        app:layout_constraintEnd_toEndOf="parent"
        app:layout_constraintStart_toStartOf="parent"
        app:layout_constraintTop_toTopOf="parent" />
</androidx.constraintlayout.widget.ConstraintLayout>
```

The corresponding class to go with the layout must be a subclass of the Android *Fragment* class. This class should, at a minimum, override the *onCreateView()* method, which is responsible for loading the fragment layout. For example:

```
package com.example.myfragmentdemo

import android.os.Bundle
import android.view.LayoutInflater
import android.view.View
import android.view.ViewGroup
import androidx.fragment.app.Fragment

class FragmentOne : Fragment() {

    private var _binding: FragmentTextBinding? = null
    private val binding get() = _binding!!

    override fun onCreateView(
        inflater: LayoutInflater, container: ViewGroup?,
        savedInstanceState: Bundle?
    ): View? {
        _binding = FragmentTextBinding.inflate(inflater, container, false)
        return binding.root
    }
}
```

In addition to the *onCreateView()* method, the class may also override the standard lifecycle methods.

Once the fragment layout and class have been created, the fragment is ready to be used within application activities.

39.3 Adding a Fragment to an Activity using the Layout XML File

Fragments may be incorporated into an activity by writing Kotlin code or embedding the fragment into the activity's XML layout file. Regardless of the approach used, a key point to be aware of is that when the support library is being used for compatibility with older Android releases, any activities using fragments must be implemented as a subclass of *FragmentActivity* instead of the *AppCompatActivity* class:

```
package com.example.myFragmentDemo

import androidx.fragment.app.FragmentActivity
import android.os.Bundle

class MainActivity : FragmentActivity() {
.
.
```

Fragments are embedded into activity layout files using the FragmentContainerView class. The following example layout embeds the fragment created in the previous section of this chapter into an activity layout:

```
<?xml version="1.0" encoding="utf-8"?>
<androidx.constraintlayout.widget.ConstraintLayout
    xmlns:android="http://schemas.android.com/apk/res/android"
    xmlns:app="http://schemas.android.com/apk/res-auto"
    xmlns:tools="http://schemas.android.com/tools"
    android:layout_width="match_parent"
    android:layout_height="match_parent"
    tools:context=".MainActivity">

    <androidx.fragment.app.FragmentContainerView
        android:id="@+id/fragment2"
        android:name="com.ebookfrenzy.myfragmentdemo.FragmentOne"
        android:layout_width="0dp"
        android:layout_height="wrap_content"
        android:layout_marginStart="32dp"
        android:layout_marginEnd="32dp"
        app:layout_constraintBottom_toBottomOf="parent"
        app:layout_constraintEnd_toEndOf="parent"
        app:layout_constraintStart_toStartOf="parent"
        app:layout_constraintTop_toTopOf="parent"
        tools:layout="@layout/fragment_one" />
</androidx.constraintlayout.widget.ConstraintLayout>
```

The key properties within the <fragment> element are *android:name*, which must reference the class associated with the fragment, and *tools:layout*, which must reference the XML resource file containing the fragment's layout.

Once added to the layout of an activity, fragments may be viewed and manipulated within the Android Studio Layout Editor tool. Figure 39-1, for example, shows the above layout with the embedded fragment within the Android Studio Layout Editor:

Figure 39-1

39.4 Adding and Managing Fragments in Code

The ease of adding a fragment to an activity via the activity's XML layout file comes at the cost of the activity not being able to remove the fragment at runtime. To achieve full dynamic control of fragments during runtime, those activities must be added via code. This has the advantage that the fragments can be added, removed, and even made to replace one another dynamically while the application is running.

When using code to manage fragments, the fragment will still consist of an XML layout file and a corresponding class. The difference comes when working with the fragment within the hosting activity. There is a standard sequence of steps when adding a fragment to an activity using code:

1. Create an instance of the fragment's class.
2. Pass any additional intent arguments through to the class instance.
3. Obtain a reference to the fragment manager instance.
4. Call the *beginTransaction()* method on the fragment manager instance. This returns a fragment transaction instance.
5. Call the *add()* method of the fragment transaction instance, passing through as arguments the resource ID of the view that is to contain the fragment and the fragment class instance.
6. Call the *commit()* method of the fragment transaction.

The following code, for example, adds a fragment defined by the FragmentOne class so that it appears in the container view with an ID of LinearLayout1:

```
val firstFragment = FragmentOne()
```

```
firstFragment.arguments = intent.extras
val transaction = fragmentManager.beginTransaction()
transaction.add(R.id.LinearLayout1, firstFragment)
transaction.commit()
```

The above code breaks down each step into a separate statement for clarity. The last four lines can, however, be abbreviated into a single line of code as follows:

```
supportFragmentManager.beginTransaction().add(
      R.id.LinearLayout1, firstFragment).commit()
```

Once added to a container, a fragment may subsequently be removed via a call to the *remove()* method of the fragment transaction instance, passing through a reference to the fragment instance that is to be removed:

```
transaction.remove(firstFragment)
```

Similarly, one fragment may be replaced with another by a call to the *replace()* method of the fragment transaction instance. This takes as arguments the ID of the view containing the fragment and an instance of the new fragment. The replaced fragment may also be placed on what is referred to as the *back* stack so that it can be quickly restored if the user navigates back to it. This is achieved by making a call to the *addToBackStack()* method of the fragment transaction object before making the *commit()* method call:

```
val secondFragment = FragmentTwo()
transaction.replace(R.id.LinearLayout1, secondFragment)
transaction.addToBackStack(null)
transaction.commit()
```

39.5 Handling Fragment Events

As previously discussed, a fragment is like a sub-activity with its layout, class, and lifecycle. The view components (such as buttons and text views) within a fragment can generate events like regular activity. This raises the question of which class receives an event from a view in a fragment, the fragment itself, or the activity in which the fragment is embedded. The answer to this question depends on how the event handler is declared.

In the chapter entitled *"An Overview and Example of Android Event Handling"*, two approaches to event handling were discussed. The first method involved configuring an event listener and callback method within the activity's code. For example:

```
binding.button.setOnClickListener { // Code to be performed on button click }
```

In the case of intercepting click events, the second approach involved setting the *android:onClick* property within the XML layout file:

```
<Button
    android:id="@+id/button1"
    android:layout_width="wrap_content"
    android:layout_height="wrap_content"
    android:onClick="onClick"
    android:text="Click me" />
```

The general rule for events generated by a view in a fragment is that if the event listener were declared in the fragment class using the event listener and callback method approach, the event would be handled first by the fragment. However, if the *android:onClick* resource is used, the event will be passed directly to the activity containing the fragment.

39.6 Implementing Fragment Communication

Once one or more fragments are embedded within an activity, the chances are good that some form of communication will need to take place between the fragments and the activity and between one fragment and another. Good practice dictates that fragments do not communicate directly with one another. All communication should take place via the encapsulating activity.

To communicate with a fragment, the activity must identify the fragment object via the ID assigned to it. Once this reference has been obtained, the activity can call the public methods of the fragment object.

Communicating in the other direction (from fragment to activity) is a little more complicated. In the first instance, the fragment must define a listener interface, which is then implemented within the activity class. For example, the following code declares a ToolbarListener interface on a fragment named ToolbarFragment. The code also declares a variable in which a reference to the activity will later be stored:

```
class ToolbarFragment : Fragment() {

    var activityCallback: ToolbarFragment.ToolbarListener? = null

    interface ToolbarListener {
        fun onButtonClick(fontsize: Int, text: String)
    }
.
.
}
```

The above code dictates that any class that implements the ToolbarListener interface must also implement a callback method named *onButtonClick* which, in turn, accepts an integer and a String as arguments.

Next, the *onAttach()* method of the fragment class needs to be overridden and implemented. This method is called automatically by the Android system when the fragment has been initialized and associated with an activity. The method is passed a reference to the activity in which the fragment is contained. The method must store a local reference to this activity and verify that it implements the ToolbarListener interface:

```
override fun onAttach(context: Context?) {
    super.onAttach(context)
    try {
        activityCallback = context as ToolbarListener
    } catch (e: ClassCastException) {
        throw ClassCastException(context?.toString()
           + " must implement ToolbarListener")
    }
}
```

Upon execution of this example, a reference to the activity will be stored in the local *activityCallback* variable, and an exception will be thrown if that activity does not implement the ToolbarListener interface.

The next step is to call the callback method of the activity from within the fragment. When and how this happens depends entirely on the circumstances under which the activity needs to be contacted by the fragment. The following code, for example, calls the callback method on the activity when a button is clicked:

```
override fun onButtonClick(arg1: Int, arg2: String) {
   activityCallback.onButtonClick(arg1, arg2)
```

```
}
```

All that remains is to modify the activity class to implement the ToolbarListener interface. For example:

```
class MainActivity : FragmentActivity(),
      ToolbarFragment.ToolbarListener {

    override fun onButtonClick(arg1: Int, arg2: String) {
         // Implement code for callback method
    }
.
.
}
```

As we can see from the above code, the activity declares that it implements the ToolbarListener interface of the ToolbarFragment class and then proceeds to implement the *onButtonClick()* method as required by the interface.

39.7 Summary

Fragments provide a powerful mechanism for creating reusable modules of user interface layout and application behavior, which, once created, can be embedded in activities. A fragment consists of a user interface layout file and a class. Fragments may be utilized in an activity by adding the fragment to the activity's layout file or writing code to manage the fragments at runtime. Fragments added to an activity in code can be removed and replaced dynamically at runtime. All communication between fragments should be performed via the activity within which the fragments are embedded.

Having covered the basics of fragments in this chapter, the next chapter will work through a tutorial designed to reinforce the techniques outlined in this chapter.

Chapter 40

40. Using Fragments in Android Studio - An Example

As outlined in the previous chapter, fragments provide a convenient mechanism for creating reusable modules of application functionality consisting of both sections of a user interface and the corresponding behavior. Once created, fragments can be embedded within activities.

Having explored the general theory of fragments in the previous chapter, this chapter aims to create an example Android application using Android Studio designed to demonstrate the actual steps involved in creating and using fragments and implementing communication between one fragment and another within an activity.

40.1 About the Example Fragment Application

The application created in this chapter will consist of a single activity and two fragments. The user interface for the first fragment will contain a toolbar consisting of an EditText view, a SeekBar, and a Button, all contained within a ConstraintLayout view. The second fragment will consist solely of a TextView object within a ConstraintLayout view.

The two fragments will be embedded within the main activity of the application and communication implemented such that when the button in the first fragment is pressed, the text entered into the EditText view will appear on the TextView of the second fragment using a font size dictated by the position of the SeekBar in the first fragment.

Since this application is intended to work on earlier versions of Android, we will need to use the appropriate Android support library.

40.2 Creating the Example Project

Select the *New Project* option from the welcome screen and, within the resulting new project dialog, choose the Empty Views Activity template before clicking on the Next button.

Enter *FragmentExample* into the Name field and specify *com.ebookfrenzy.fragmentexample* as the package name. Before clicking the Finish button, change the Minimum API level setting to API 26: Android 8.0 (Oreo) and the Language menu to Kotlin. Modify the project to use view binding using the Gemini Agent or the steps outlined in *18.8 Migrating a Project to View Binding.*

40.3 Creating the First Fragment Layout

The next step is to create the user interface for the first fragment used within our activity.

This user interface will consist of an XML layout file and a fragment class. While these could be added manually, it is quicker to ask Android Studio to create them for us. Within the project tool window, locate the *app -> kotlin + kotlin+java -> com.ebookfrenzy.fragmentexample* entry and right-click on it. From the resulting menu, select the *New -> Fragment -> Gallery...* option to display the dialog shown in Figure 40-1 below:

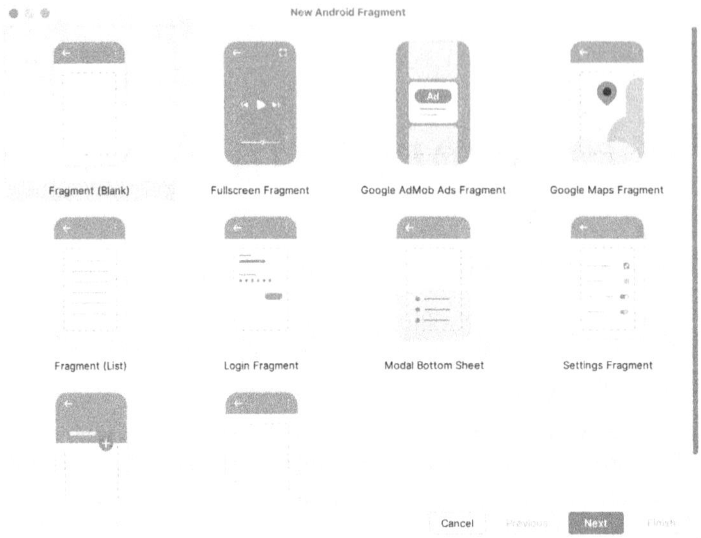

Figure 40-1

Select the *Fragment (Blank)* template before clicking the Next button. On the subsequent screen, name the fragment *ToolbarFragment* with a layout file named *fragment_toolbar*:

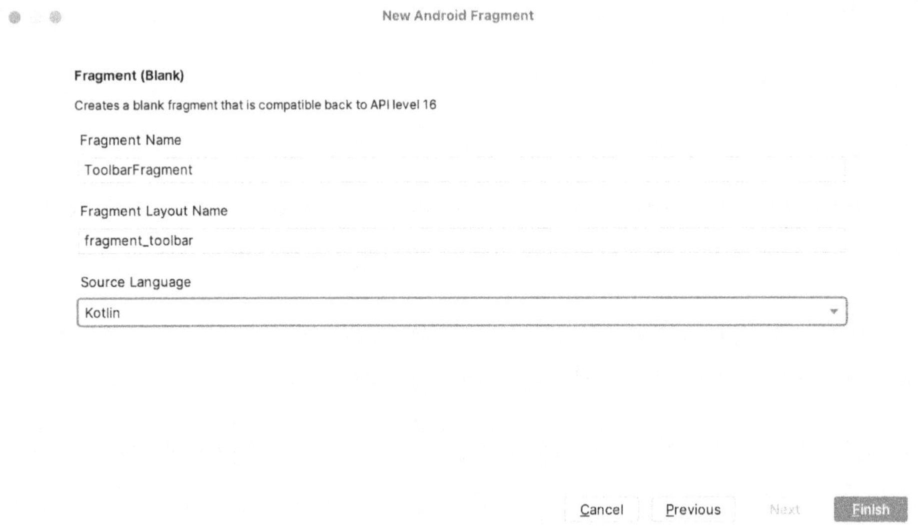

Figure 40-2

Load the *fragment_toolbar.xml* file into the layout editor using Design mode. Next, right-click on the FrameLayout entry in the Component Tree panel and select the *Convert FrameLayout to ConstraintLayout* menu option, accepting the default settings in the confirmation dialog. Change the id from to *constraintLayout*. Ensure that Autoconnect mode is enabled, then select and delete the default TextView and add Plain Text, Seekbar, and Button widgets to the layout so that their positions match those shown in Figure 40-3. Finally, change the view ids to *editText1*, *seekBar1*, and *button1*, respectively.

Change the text on the button to read "Change Text", extract the text to a string resource named *change_text,* and remove the Name text from the EditText view. Finally, set the *layout_width* property of the Seekbar to *match_constraint* with margins set to 16dp on the left and right edges.

Use the *Infer constraints* toolbar button to add any missing constraints, at which point the layout should match that shown in Figure 40-3 below:

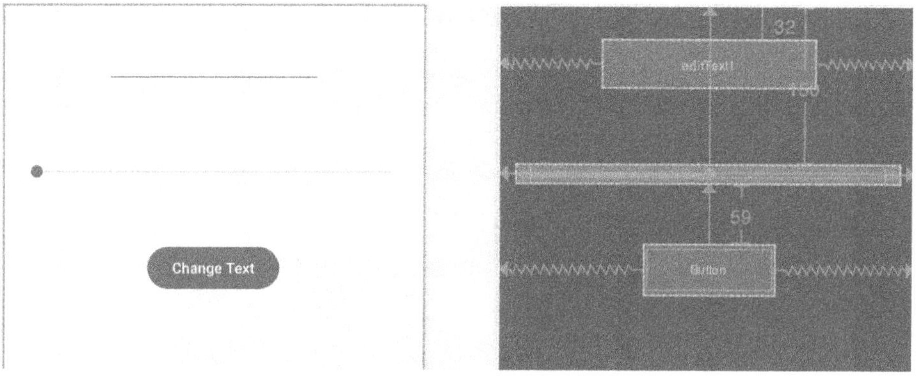

Figure 40-3

40.4 Migrating a Fragment to View Binding

As with the Empty Views Activity template, Android Studio does not enable view binding support when new fragments are added to a project. Therefore, we will need to perform this migration before moving to the next step of this tutorial. Begin by editing the *ToolbarFragment.kt* file and importing the binding for the fragment as follows:

```
import com.ebookfrenzy.fragmentexample.databinding.FragmentToolbarBinding
```

Next, locate the *onCreateView()* method and make the following declarations and changes (which also include adding the *onDestroyView()* method to ensure that the binding reference is removed when the fragment is destroyed):

```
.
.
private var _binding: FragmentToolbarBinding? = null
private val binding get() = _binding!!
.
.
override fun onCreateView(
    inflater: LayoutInflater, container: ViewGroup?,
    savedInstanceState: Bundle?
): View? {
    return inflater.inflate(R.layout.fragment_toolbar, container, false)
    _binding = FragmentToolbarBinding.inflate(inflater, container, false)
    return binding.root
}

override fun onDestroyView() {
    super.onDestroyView()
    _binding = null
}
```

Once these changes are complete, the fragment is ready to use view binding.

40.5 Adding the Second Fragment

Repeating the steps to create the toolbar fragment, add another blank fragment named TextFragment with a layout file named *fragment_text*. Once again, convert the FrameLayout container to a ConstraintLayout (changing the id to *constraintLayout2*) and remove the default TextView.

Drag a drop a TextView widget from the palette and position it in the center of the layout, using the *Infer constraints* button to add any missing constraints. Change the id of the TextView to *textView2*, the text to read "Fragment Two" and modify the *textSize* attribute to 24sp.

On completion, the layout should match that shown in Figure 40-4:

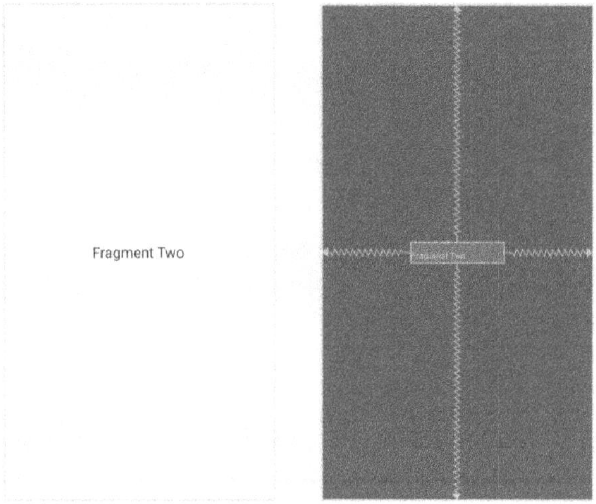

Figure 40-4

Repeat the steps performed in the previous section to migrate the TextFragment class to use view binding as follows:

```
.
.
import com.ebookfrenzy.fragmentexample.databinding.FragmentTextBinding
.
.
private var _binding: FragmentTextBinding? = null
private val binding get() = _binding!!
.
.
override fun onCreateView(
    inflater: LayoutInflater, container: ViewGroup?,
    savedInstanceState: Bundle?
): View? {
    return inflater.inflate(R.layout.fragment_text, container, false)
    _binding = FragmentTextBinding.inflate(inflater, container, false)
    return binding.root
}
```

40.6 Adding the Fragments to the Activity

The main activity for the application has associated with it an XML layout file named *activity_main.xml*. For this example, the fragments will be added to the activity using the <fragment> element within this file. Using the Project tool window, navigate to the *app -> res -> layout* section of the *FragmentExample* project and double-click on the *activity_main.xml* file to load it into the Android Studio Layout Editor tool.

With the Layout Editor tool in Design mode, select and delete the default TextView object from the layout and select the *Common* category in the palette. Drag the *FragmentContainerView* component from the list of views and drop it onto the layout so that it is centered horizontally and positioned such that the dashed line appears, indicating the top layout margin:

Figure 40-5

On dropping the fragment onto the layout, a dialog will appear displaying a list of Fragments available within the current project, as illustrated in Figure 40-6:

Figure 40-6

Select the ToolbarFragment entry from the list and click OK to dismiss the Fragments dialog. Once added, click the red warning button in the top right-hand corner of the layout editor to display the Problems tool window. An *unknown fragments* message will indicate that the Layout Editor tool needs to know which fragment to display during the preview session. Select the Unknown fragment item, then click on the *Pick Layout...* link in the right-hand panel as shown in Figure 40-7:

Figure 40-7

In the resulting dialog (Figure 40-8), select the *fragment_toolbar* entry and then click OK:

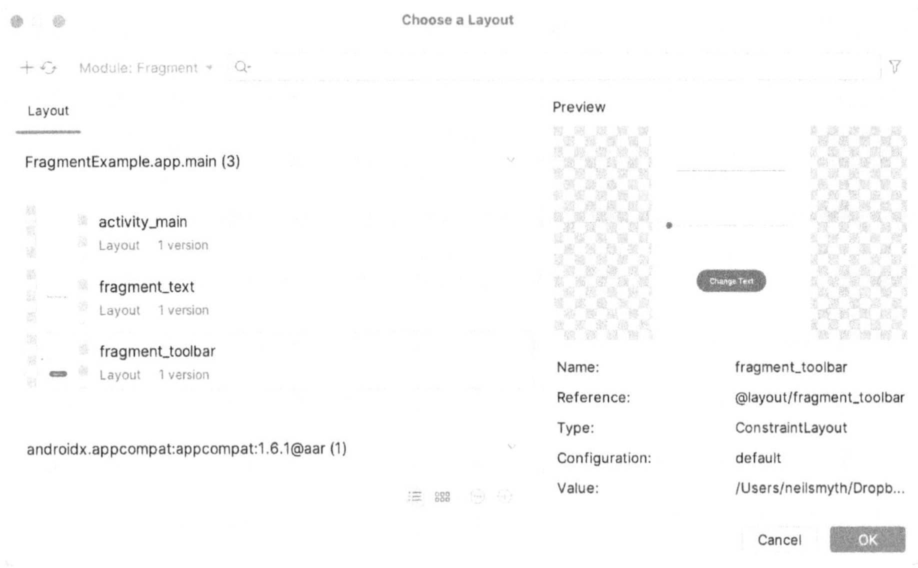

Figure 40-8

With the fragment selected, change the *layout_width* property to *match_constraint* so that it occupies the full width of the screen. Click and drag another *FragmentContainerView* entry from the palette and position it so that it is centered horizontally and located beneath the bottom edge of the first fragment. When prompted, select the *TextFragment* entry from the fragment dialog before clicking OK. Display the Problems tool window and repeat the previous steps, this time selecting the *fragment_text* layout. Use the *Infer constraints* button to establish any missing layout constraints.

Note that the fragments are now visible in the layout, as demonstrated in Figure 40-9:

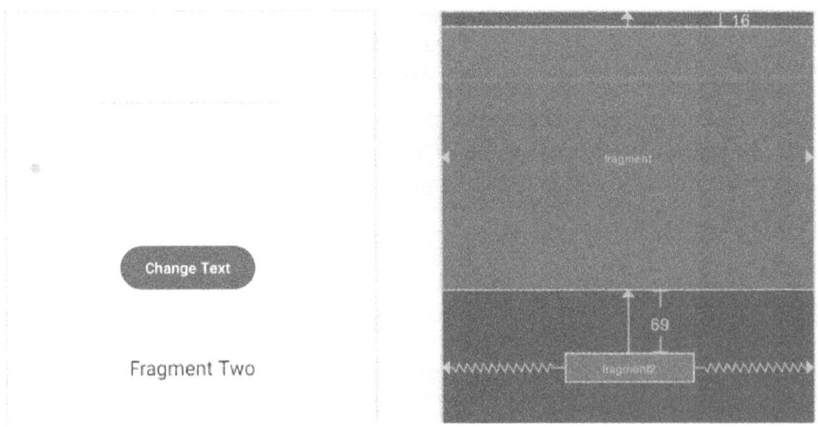

Figure 40-9

Before proceeding to the next step, select the TextFragment instance in the layout and, within the Attributes tool window, change the ID of the fragment to *text_fragment*.

40.7 Making the Toolbar Fragment Talk to the Activity

When the user touches the button in the toolbar fragment, the fragment class will need to extract the text from the EditText view and the current value of the SeekBar and send them to the text fragment. As outlined in *"An Introduction to Android Fragments"*, fragments should not communicate with each other directly, instead using the activity in which they are embedded as an intermediary.

The first step in this process is ensuring that the toolbar fragment responds to the clicked button. We also need to implement some code to keep track of the value of the SeekBar view. For this example, we will implement these listeners within the ToolbarFragment class. Select the *ToolbarFragment.kt* file and modify it so that it reads as shown in the following listing:

```
package com.ebookfrenzy.fragmentexample
.
.
import android.widget.SeekBar
import android.content.Context
.
.
class ToolbarFragment : Fragment(), SeekBar.OnSeekBarChangeListener {
.
.
    var seekvalue = 10
.
.
    override fun onViewCreated(view: View, savedInstanceState: Bundle?) {
        super.onViewCreated(view, savedInstanceState)

        binding.seekBar1.setOnSeekBarChangeListener(this)
        binding.button1.setOnClickListener { v: View -> buttonClicked(v) }
    }

    private fun buttonClicked(view: View) {

    }

    override fun onProgressChanged(seekBar: SeekBar, progress: Int,
                                   fromUser: Boolean) {
        seekvalue = progress
    }

    override fun onStartTrackingTouch(arg0: SeekBar) {
    }

    override fun onStopTrackingTouch(arg0: SeekBar) {
    }
.
.
}
```

Before moving on, we need to take some time to explain the above code changes. First, the class is declared as implementing the OnSeekBarChangeListener interface. This is because the user interface contains a SeekBar instance, and the fragment needs to receive notifications when the user slides the bar to change the font size. Implementation of the OnSeekBarChangeListener interface requires that the *onProgressChanged()*, *onStartTrackingTouch()*, and *onStopTrackingTouch()* methods be implemented. These methods have been implemented, but only the *onProgressChanged()* method is required to perform a task, in this case, storing the new value in a variable named seekvalue, which was declared at the start of the class. Also declared is a variable to store a reference to the EditText object.

The *onViewCreated()* method has been added to set up an onClickListener on the button, which is configured to call a method named *buttonClicked()* when a click event is detected. This method is also then implemented, though it does not do anything at this point.

The next phase of this process is to set up the listener that will allow the fragment to call the activity when the button is clicked. This follows the mechanism outlined in the previous chapter:

```
class ToolbarFragment : Fragment(), SeekBar.OnSeekBarChangeListener {
.
.
    var seekvalue = 10

    var activityCallback: ToolbarFragment.ToolbarListener? = null

    interface ToolbarListener {
        fun onButtonClick(fontSize: Int, text: String)
    }

    override fun onAttach(context: Context) {
        super.onAttach(context)
        try {
            activityCallback = context as ToolbarListener
        } catch (e: ClassCastException) {
            throw ClassCastException(context.toString()
                                        + " must implement ToolbarListener")
        }
    }
.
.
    private fun buttonClicked(view: View) {
        activityCallback?.onButtonClick(seekvalue,
                binding.editText1.text.toString())
    }
.
.
}
```

The above implementation will result in a method named *onButtonClick()* belonging to the activity class being called when the user clicks the button. All that remains, therefore, is to declare that the activity class implements the newly created ToolbarListener interface and to implement the *onButtonClick()* method.

Since the Android Support Library is being used for fragment support in earlier Android versions, the activity also needs to be changed to subclass from *FragmentActivity* instead of *AppCompatActivity*. Bringing these requirements together results in the following modified *MainActivity.kt* file:

```
package com.ebookfrenzy.fragmentexample
.
.
import androidx.appcompat.app.AppCompatActivity
import androidx.fragment.app.FragmentActivity
.
.
class MainActivity : FragmentActivity(),
                                ToolbarFragment.ToolbarListener {
.
.
    override fun onButtonClick(fontSize: Int, text: String) {

    }
}
```

With the code changes as they currently stand, the toolbar fragment will detect when the user clicks the button and call a method on the activity passing through the content of the EditText field and the current setting of the SeekBar view. It is now the job of the activity to communicate with the Text Fragment and to pass along these values so that the fragment can update the TextView object accordingly.

40.8 Making the Activity Talk to the Text Fragment

As *"An Introduction to Android Fragments"* outlined, an activity can communicate with a fragment by obtaining a reference to the fragment class instance and then calling public methods on the object. As such, within the TextFragment class, we will now implement a public method named *changeTextProperties()* which takes as arguments an integer for the font size and a string for the new text to be displayed. The method will then use these values to modify the TextView object. Within the Android Studio editing panel, locate and modify the *TextFragment.kt* file to add this new method:

```
package com.ebookfrenzy.fragmentexample
.
.
class TextFragment : Fragment() {
.
.
    fun changeTextProperties(fontSize: Int, text: String)
    {
        binding.textView2.textSize = fontSize.toFloat()
        binding.textView2.text = text
    }
.
.
}
```

When the TextFragment fragment was placed in the activity's layout, it was given an ID of *text_fragment*. Using this ID, it is now possible for the activity to obtain a reference to the fragment instance and call the *changeTextProperties()* method on the object. Edit the *MainActivity.kt* file and modify the *onButtonClick()*

method as follows:

```
override fun onButtonClick(fontSize: Int, text: String) {

    val textFragment = supportFragmentManager.findFragmentById(
                            R.id.text_fragment) as TextFragment

    textFragment.changeTextProperties(fontSize, text)
}
```

40.9 Testing the Application

With the coding for this project now complete, the last remaining task is to run the application. When the application is launched, the main activity will start and will, in turn, create and display the two fragments. When the user touches the button in the toolbar fragment, the *onButtonClick()* method of the activity will be called by the toolbar fragment and passed the text from the EditText view and the current value of the SeekBar. The activity will then call the *changeTextProperties()* method of the second fragment, which will modify the TextView to reflect the new text and font size:

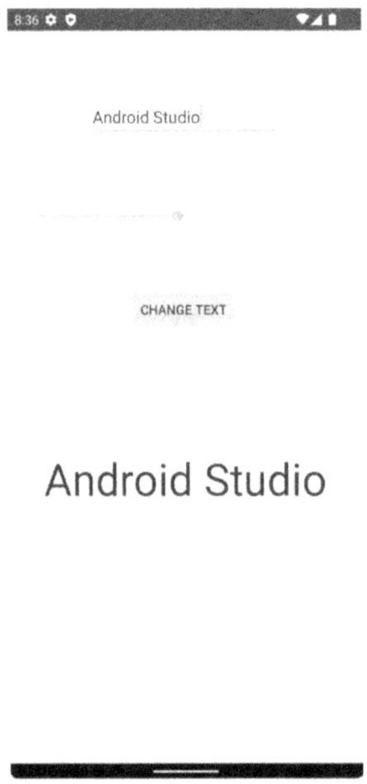

Figure 40-10

40.10 Summary

The goal of this chapter was to work through creating an example project to demonstrate the steps involved in using fragments within an Android application. Topics covered included using the Android Support Library for compatibility with Android versions predating the introduction of fragments, including fragments within an activity layout, and implementing inter-fragment communication.

Chapter 41

41. Modern Android App Architecture with Jetpack

For many years, Google did not recommend a specific approach to building Android apps other than to provide tools and development kits while letting developers decide what worked best for a particular project or individual programming style. That changed in 2017 with the introduction of the Android Architecture Components, which, in turn, became part of Android Jetpack when it was released in 2018.

This chapter provides an overview of the concepts of Jetpack, Android app architecture recommendations, and some key architecture components. Once the basics have been covered, these topics will be covered in more detail and demonstrated through practical examples in later chapters.

41.1 What is Android Jetpack?

Android Jetpack consists of Android Studio, the Android Architecture Components, the Android Support Library, and a set of guidelines recommending how an Android App should be structured. The Android Architecture Components are designed to make it quicker and easier to perform common tasks when developing Android apps while also conforming to the key principle of the architectural guidelines.

While all Android Architecture Components will be covered in this book, this chapter will focus on the key architectural guidelines and the ViewModel, LiveData, and Lifecycle components while introducing Data Binding and Repositories.

Before moving on, it is important to understand that the Jetpack approach to app development is optional. While highlighting some of the shortcomings of other techniques that have gained popularity over the years, Google stopped short of completely condemning those approaches to app development. Google is taking the position that while there is no right or wrong way to develop an app, there is a recommended way.

41.2 The "Old" Architecture

In the chapter entitled *"Creating an Example Android App in Android Studio"*, an Android project was created consisting of a single activity that contained all of the code for presenting and managing the user interface together with the back-end logic of the app. Until the introduction of Jetpack, the most common architecture followed this paradigm with apps consisting of multiple activities (one for each screen within the app), with each activity class to some degree mixing user interface and back-end code.

This approach led to a range of problems related to the lifecycle of an app (for example, an activity is destroyed and recreated each time the user rotates the device leading to the loss of any app data that had not been saved to some form of persistent storage) as well as issues such as inefficient navigation involving launching a new activity for each app screen accessed by the user.

41.3 Modern Android Architecture

At the most basic level, Google now advocates single-activity apps where different screens are loaded as content within the same activity.

Modern architecture guidelines also recommend separating different areas of responsibility within an app into entirely separate modules (a concept referred to as "separation of concerns"). One of the keys to this approach is the ViewModel component.

41.4 The ViewModel Component

The purpose of ViewModel is to separate the user interface-related data model and logic of an app from the code responsible for displaying and managing the user interface and interacting with the operating system. When designed this way, an app will consist of one or more UI Controllers, such as an activity, together with ViewModel instances responsible for handling the data those controllers need.

The ViewModel only knows about the data model and corresponding logic. It knows nothing about the user interface and does not attempt to directly access or respond to events relating to views within the user interface. When a UI controller needs data to display, it asks the ViewModel to provide it. Similarly, when the user enters data into a view within the user interface, the UI controller passes it to the ViewModel for handling.

This separation of responsibility addresses the issues relating to the lifecycle of UI controllers. Regardless of how often the UI controller is recreated during the lifecycle of an app, the ViewModel instances remain in memory, thereby maintaining data consistency. For example, a ViewModel used by an activity will remain in memory until the activity finishes, which, in the single activity app, is not until the app exits.

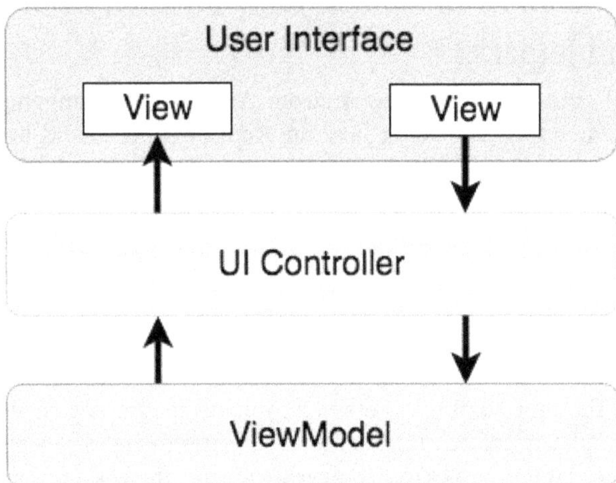

Figure 41-1

41.5 The LiveData Component

Consider an app that displays real-time data, such as the current price of a financial stock. The app could use a stock price web service to continuously update the data model within the ViewModel with the latest information. This real-time data is of use only if it is displayed to the user promptly. There are only two ways that the UI controller can ensure that the latest data is displayed in the user interface. One option is for the controller to continuously check with the ViewModel to determine if the data has changed since it was last displayed. However, the problem with this approach is that it could be more efficient. To maintain the real-time nature of the data feed, the UI controller would have to run on a loop, continuously checking for the data to change.

A better solution would be for the UI controller to receive a notification when a specific data item within a ViewModel changes. This is made possible by using the LiveData component. LiveData is a data holder that allows a value to become *observable*. In basic terms, an observable object can notify other objects when changes to its data occur, thereby solving the problem of ensuring that the user interface always matches the data within the ViewModel.

This means, for example, that a UI controller interested in a ViewModel value can set up an observer, which will, in turn, be notified when that value changes. In our hypothetical application, for example, the stock price would be wrapped in a LiveData object within the ViewModel, and the UI controller would assign an observer to the value, declaring a method to be called when the value changes. When triggered by data change, this method will read the updated value from the ViewModel and use it to update the user interface.

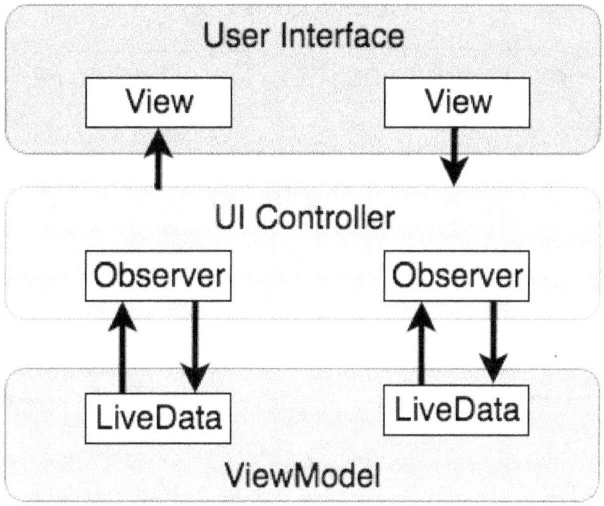

Figure 41-2

A LiveData instance may also be declared as mutable, allowing the observing entity to update the underlying value held within the LiveData object. The user might, for example, enter a value in the user interface that needs to overwrite the value stored in the ViewModel.

Another of the key advantages of using LiveData is that it is aware of the *lifecycle state* of its observers. If, for example, an activity contains a LiveData observer, the corresponding LiveData object will know when the activity's lifecycle state changes and respond accordingly. If the activity is paused (perhaps the app is put into the background), the LiveData object will stop sending events to the observer. Suppose the activity has just started or resumes after being paused. In that case, the LiveData object will send a LiveData event to the observer so that the activity has the most up-to-date value. Similarly, the LiveData instance will know when the activity is destroyed and remove the observer to free up resources.

So far, we've only talked about UI controllers using observers. In practice, however, an observer can be used within any object that conforms to the Jetpack approach to lifecycle management.

41.6 ViewModel Saved State

Android allows the user to place an active app in the background and return to it after performing other tasks on the device (including running other apps). When a device runs low on resources, the operating system will rectify this by terminating background app processes, starting with the least recently used app. However, when the user returns to the terminated background app, it should appear in the same state as when it was placed in the background, regardless of whether it was terminated. In terms of the data associated with a ViewModel, this can be implemented using the ViewModel Saved State module. This module allows values to be stored in the app's *saved state* and restored in case of system-initiated process termination. This topic will be covered later in the *"An Android ViewModel Saved State Tutorial"* chapter.

41.7 LiveData and Data Binding

Android Jetpack includes the Data Binding Library, which allows data in a ViewModel to be mapped directly to specific views within the XML user interface layout file. In the AndroidSample project created earlier, code had to be written to obtain references to the EditText and TextView views and to set and get the text properties to reflect data changes. Data binding allows the LiveData value stored in the ViewModel to be referenced directly within the XML layout file avoiding the need to write code to keep the layout views updated.

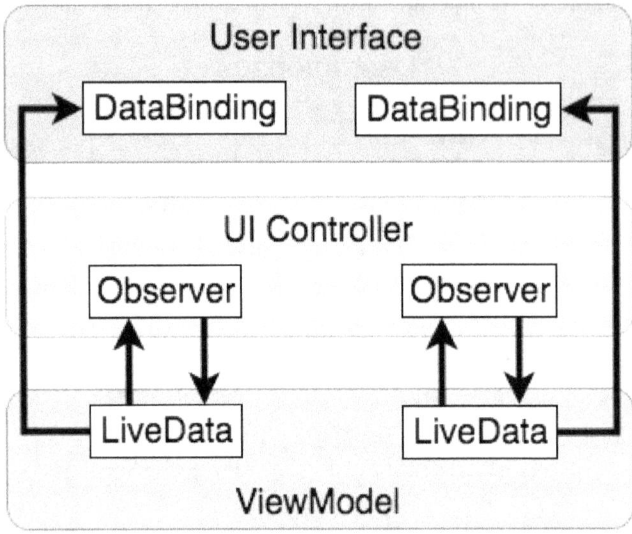

Figure 41-3

Data binding will be covered in greater detail, starting with the chapter *"An Overview of Android Jetpack Data Binding"*.

41.8 Android Lifecycles

The duration from when an Android component is created to the point that it is destroyed is called the *lifecycle*. During this lifecycle, the component will change between different lifecycle states, usually under the operating system's control and in response to user actions. An activity, for example, will begin in the *initialized* state before transitioning to the *created* state. Once the activity runs, it will switch to the *started* state, from which it will cycle through various states, including *created*, *started*, *resumed*, and *destroyed*.

Many Android Framework classes and components allow other objects to access their current state. *Lifecycle observers* may also be used so that an object receives a notification when the lifecycle state of another object changes. The ViewModel component uses this technique behind the scenes to identify when an observer has restarted or been destroyed. This functionality is not limited to Android framework and architecture components. It may also be built into any other classes using a set of lifecycle components included with the architecture components.

Objects that can detect and react to lifecycle state changes in other objects are said to be *lifecycle-aware*. In contrast, objects that provide access to their lifecycle state are called *lifecycle owners*. The chapter entitled "*Working with Android Lifecycle-Aware Components*" will cover Lifecycles in greater detail.

41.9 Repository Modules

If a ViewModel obtains data from one or more external sources (such as databases or web services, it is important to separate the code involved in handling those data sources from the ViewModel class. Failure to do this would, after all, violate the separation of concerns guidelines. To avoid mixing this functionality with the ViewModel, Google's architecture guidelines recommend placing this code in a separate *Repository* module.

A repository is not an Android architecture component but a Kotlin class created by the app developer that is responsible for interfacing with the various data sources. The class then provides an interface to the ViewModel, allowing that data to be stored in the model.

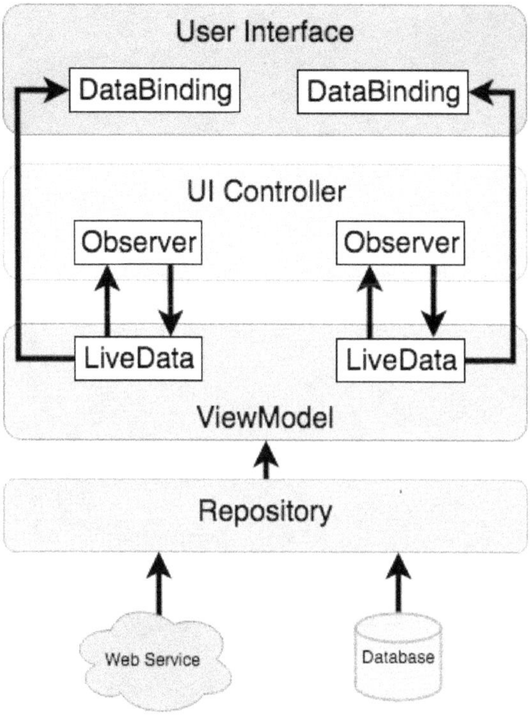

Figure 41-4

41.10 Summary

Until recently, Google has tended not to recommend any particular approach to structuring an Android app. That has now changed with the introduction of Android Jetpack, consisting of tools, components, libraries, and architecture guidelines. Google now recommends that an app project be divided into separate modules, each responsible for a particular area of functionality, otherwise known as "separation of concerns".

In particular, the guidelines recommend separating the view data model of an app from the code responsible for handling the user interface. In addition, the code responsible for gathering data from data sources such as web services or databases should be built into a separate repository module instead of being bundled with the view model.

Android Jetpack includes the Android Architecture Components, designed to make developing apps that conform to the recommended guidelines easier. This chapter has introduced the ViewModel, LiveData, and Lifecycle components. These will be covered in more detail, starting with the next chapter. Other architecture components not mentioned in this chapter will be covered later in the book.

Chapter 42

42. An Android ViewModel Tutorial

The previous chapter introduced the fundamental concepts of Android Jetpack and outlined the basics of modern Android app architecture. Jetpack defines a set of recommendations describing how an Android app project should be structured while providing a set of libraries and components that make it easier to conform to these guidelines to develop reliable apps with less coding and fewer errors.

To help reinforce and clarify the information provided in the previous chapter, this chapter will step through creating an example app project that uses the ViewModel component. The next chapter will further enhance this example by including LiveData and data binding support.

42.1 About the Project

In the chapter entitled *"Creating an Example Android App in Android Studio"*, a project named AndroidSample was created in which all of the code for the app was bundled into the main Activity class file. In the following chapter, an AVD emulator was created and used to run the app. While the app was running, we experienced first-hand the problems that occur when developing apps in this way when the data displayed on a TextView widget was lost during a device rotation.

This chapter will implement the same currency converter app, using the ViewModel component and following the Google app architecture guidelines to avoid Activity lifecycle complications.

42.2 Creating the ViewModel Example Project

When the AndroidSample project was created, the Empty Views Activity template was chosen as the basis for the project. However, the Basic Views Template template will be used for this project.

Select the *New Project* option from the welcome screen and, within the resulting new project dialog, choose the *Basic Views Activity* template before clicking on the Next button.

Enter *ViewModelDemo* into the Name field and specify *com.ebookfrenzy.viewmodeldemo* as the package name. Before clicking on the Finish button, change the Minimum API level setting to API 26: Android 8.0 (Oreo) and the Language menu to Kotlin.

42.3 Removing Unwanted Project Elements

As outlined in the *"A Guide to the Android Studio Layout Editor Tool"*, the Basic Views Activity template includes features not required by all projects. Before adding the ViewModel to the project, we first need to remove the navigation features, the second content fragment, and the floating action button as follows:

1. Double-click on the *activity_main.xml* layout file in the Project tool window, select the floating action button, and tap the keyboard delete key to remove the object from the layout.

2. Edit the *MainActivity.kt* file and remove the floating action button code from the onCreate method as follows:

```
override fun onCreate(savedInstanceState: Bundle?) {
.
.
    binding.fab.setOnClickListener { view ->
```

```
            Snackbar.make(view, "Replace with your own action", Snackbar.LENGTH_LONG)
                .setAnchorView(R.id.fab)
                .setAction("Action", null).show()
        }
}
```

3. Within the Project tool window, navigate to and double-click on the *app -> res -> navigation -> nav_graph.xml* file to load it into the navigation editor.

4. Within the editor, select the SecondFragment entry in the graph panel and tap the keyboard delete key to remove it from the graph.

5. Locate and delete the *SecondFragment.kt* and *fragment_second.xml* files.

6. The final task is to remove some code from the FirstFragment class so that the Button view no longer navigates to the now non-existent second fragment when clicked. Edit the *FirstFragment.kt* file and remove the code from the *onViewCreated()* method so that it reads as follows:

```
override fun onViewCreated(view: View, savedInstanceState: Bundle?) {
    super.onViewCreated(view, savedInstanceState)

    binding.buttonFirst.setOnClickListener {
        findNavController().navigate(R.id.action_FirstFragment_to_SecondFragment)
    }
}
```

42.4 Designing the Fragment Layout

The next step is to design the layout of the fragment. First, locate the *fragment_first.xml* file in the Project tool window and double-click on it to load it into the layout editor. Once the layout has loaded, select and delete the existing Button, TextView, and ConstraintLayout components. Next, right-click on the NestedScrollView instance in the Component Tree panel and select the *Convert NestedScrollView to ConstraintLayout* menu option as shown in Figure 42-1, and accept the default settings in the resulting dialog:

Figure 42-1

Select the converted ConstraintLayout component and use the Attributes tool window to change the id to *constraintLayout*.

Add a new TextView, position it in the center of the layout, and change the id to *resultText*. Next, drag a Number (Decimal) view from the palette and position it above the existing TextView. With the view selected in the layout, refer to the Attributes tool window and change the id to *dollarText*.

Drag a Button widget onto the layout to position it below the TextView, and change the text attribute to read "Convert". With the button still selected, change the id property to *convertButton*. At this point, the layout should resemble that illustrated in Figure 42-2 (note that the three views have been constrained using a vertical chain):

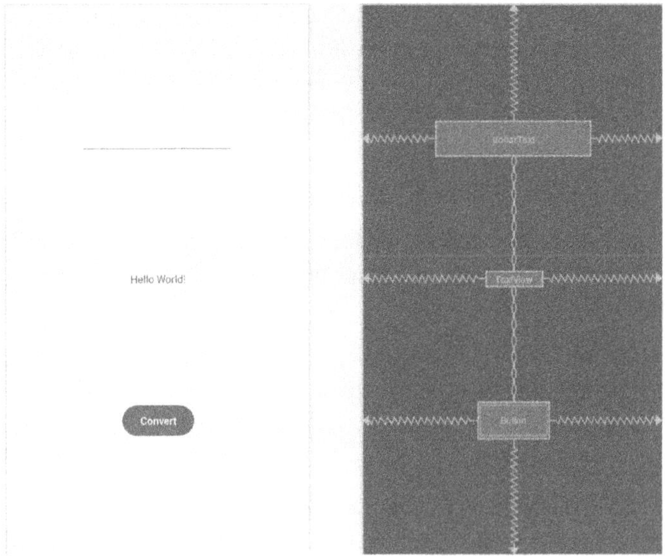

Figure 42-2

Finally, click on the warning icon in the top right-hand corner of the layout editor and convert the hard-coded strings to resources.

42.5 Implementing the View Model

With the user interface layout completed, the data model for the app needs to be created within the view model. Begin by locating the *com.ebookfrenzy.viewmodeldemo* entry in the Project tool window, right-clicking on it, and selecting the *New -> Kotlin Class/File* menu option. Name the new class MainViewModel and press the keyboard enter key. Edit the new class file so that it reads as follows:

```
package com.ebookfrenzy.viewmodeldemo

import androidx.lifecycle.ViewModel

class MainViewModel : ViewModel() {

    private val rate = 0.74f
    private var dollarText = ""
    private var result: Float = 0f

    fun setAmount(value: String) {
        this.dollarText = value
        result = value.toFloat() * rate
    }

    fun getResult(): Float {
        return result
    }
}
```

The class declares variables to store the current dollar string value and the converted amount together with getter and setter methods to provide access to those data values. When called, the *setAmount()* method takes the current dollar amount as an argument and stores it in the local *dollarText* variable. The dollar string value is converted to a floating point number, multiplied by a fictitious exchange rate, and the resulting euro value is stored in the *result* variable. The *getResult()* method, on the other hand, returns the current value assigned to the *result* variable.

42.6 Associating the Fragment with the View Model

There needs to be some way for the fragment to obtain a reference to the ViewModel to access the model and observe data changes. A Fragment or Activity maintains references to the ViewModels on which it relies for data using an instance of the ViewModelProvider class.

A ViewModelProvider instance is created using the ViewModelProvider class from within the Fragment. When called, the class initializer is passed a reference to the current Fragment or Activity and returns a ViewModelProvider instance as follows:

```
val viewModelProvider = ViewModelProvider(this)
```

Once the ViewModelProvider instance has been created, an index value can be used to request a specific ViewModel class. The provider will then either create a new instance of that ViewModel class or return an existing instance, for example:

```
val viewModel = ViewModelProvider(this)[MyViewModel::class.java]
```

Edit the *FirstFragment.kt* file and override the *onCreate()* method to set up the ViewModelProvider:

```
.
.
import androidx.lifecycle.ViewModelProvider
.
.
class FirstFragment : Fragment() {
.
.
    private lateinit var viewModel: MainViewModel

    override fun onCreate(savedInstanceState: Bundle?) {
        super.onCreate(savedInstanceState)
        viewModel = ViewModelProvider(this)[MainViewModel::class.java]
    }
.
.
```

With access to the model view, code can now be added to the Fragment to begin working with the data model.

42.7 Modifying the Fragment

The fragment class needs to be updated to react to button clicks and interact with the data values stored in the ViewModel. The class will also need references to the three views in the user interface layout to react to button clicks, extract the current dollar value, and display the converted currency amount.

In the chapter entitled *"Creating an Example Android App in Android Studio"*, the onClick property of the Button widget was used to designate the method to be called when the user clicks the button. Unfortunately, this property can only call methods on an Activity and cannot be used to call a method in a Fragment. To overcome this limitation, we must add some code to the Fragment class to set up an onClick listener on the button. This can be achieved in the *onViewCreated()* lifecycle method in the *FirstFragment.kt* file as outlined below:

```
override fun onViewCreated(view: View, savedInstanceState: Bundle?) {
    super.onViewCreated(view, savedInstanceState)

    binding.convertButton.setOnClickListener {

    }
}
```

With the listener added, any code placed within the *onClick()* method will be called whenever the user clicks the button.

42.8 Accessing the ViewModel Data

When the button is clicked, the *onClick()* method needs to read the current value from the EditText view, confirm that the field is not empty, and then call the *setAmount()* method of the ViewModel instance. The method will then need to call the ViewModel's *getResult()* method and display the converted value on the TextView widget.

Since LiveData has yet to be used in the project, it will also be necessary to get the latest result value from the ViewModel each time the Fragment is created.

Remaining in the *FirstFragment.kt* file, implement these requirements as follows in the *onViewCreated()* method:

```
.
.
override fun onViewCreated(view: View, savedInstanceState: Bundle?) {
    super.onViewCreated(view, savedInstanceState)

    binding.resultText.text = viewModel.getResult().toString()

    binding.convertButton.setOnClickListener {
        if (binding.dollarText.text.isNotEmpty()) {
            viewModel.setAmount(binding.dollarText.text.toString())
            binding.resultText.text = viewModel.getResult().toString()
        } else {
            binding.resultText.text = "No Value"
        }
    }
}
```

42.9 Testing the Project

With this project development phase completed, build and run the app on the simulator or a physical device, enter a dollar value, and click the Convert button. The converted amount should appear on the TextView, indicating that the UI controller and ViewModel re-structuring is working as expected.

When the original AndroidSample app was run, rotating the device caused the value displayed on the *resultText* TextView widget to be lost. Repeat this test now with the ViewModelDemo app and note that the current euro value is retained after the rotation. This is because the ViewModel remained in memory as the Fragment was destroyed and recreated, and code was added to the *onViewCreated()* method to update the TextView with the result data value from the ViewModel each time the Fragment re-started.

While this is an improvement on the original AndroidSample app, much more can be done to simplify the project by using LiveData and data binding, both of which are the topics of the next chapters.

42.10 Summary

In this chapter, we revisited the AndroidSample project created earlier in the book and created a new version of the project structured to comply with the Android Jetpack architectural guidelines. The example project also demonstrated the use of ViewModels to separate data handling from user interface-related code. Finally, the chapter showed how the ViewModel approach avoids problems handling Fragment and Activity lifecycles.

Chapter 43

43. An Android Jetpack LiveData Tutorial

The previous chapter began building an app to conform to the recommended Jetpack architecture guidelines. These initial steps involved implementing the data model for the app user interface within a ViewModel instance.

This chapter will further enhance the app design using the LiveData architecture component. Once LiveData support has been added to the project in this chapter, the next chapters (starting with *"An Overview of Android Jetpack Data Binding"*) will use the Jetpack Data Binding library to eliminate even more code from the project.

43.1 LiveData - A Recap

LiveData was previously introduced in the *"Modern Android App Architecture with Jetpack"* chapter. As described earlier, the LiveData component can be used as a wrapper around data values within a view model. Once contained in a LiveData instance, those variables become observable to other objects within the app, typically UI controllers such as Activities and Fragments. This allows the UI controller to receive a notification whenever the underlying LiveData value changes. An observer is set up by creating an instance of the Observer class and defining an *onChange()* method to be called when the LiveData value changes. Once the Observer instance has been created, it is attached to the LiveData object via a call to the LiveData object's *observe()* method.

LiveData instances can be declared mutable using the MutableLiveData class, allowing both the ViewModel and UI controller to change the underlying data value.

43.2 Adding LiveData to the ViewModel

Launch Android Studio, open the ViewModelDemo project created in the previous chapter, and open the *MainViewModel.kt* file, which should currently read as follows:

```
package com.ebookfrenzy.viewmodeldemo

import androidx.lifecycle.ViewModel

class MainViewModel : ViewModel() {

    private val rate = 0.74f
    private var dollarText = ""
    private var result: Float = 0f

    fun setAmount(value: String) {
        this.dollarText = value
        result = value.toFloat() * rate
    }

    fun getResult(): Float {
        return result
```

```
    }
}
```

This stage in the chapter aims to wrap the *result* variable in a MutableLiveData instance (the object will need to be mutable so that the value can be changed each time the user requests a currency conversion). Begin by modifying the class so that it now reads as follows, noting that an additional package needs to be imported when making use of LiveData:

```
package com.ebookfrenzy.viewmodeldemo

import androidx.lifecycle.ViewModel
import androidx.lifecycle.MutableLiveData

class MainViewModel : ViewModel() {

    private val rate = 0.74f
    private var dollarText = ""
    private var result: Float = 0f
    private var result: MutableLiveData<Float> = MutableLiveData()

    fun setAmount(value: String) {
        this.dollarText = value
        result = value.toFloat() * rate
    }

    fun getResult(): Float {
        return result
    }
}
```

Now that the result variable is contained in a mutable LiveData instance, both the *setAmount()* and *getResult()* methods must be modified. In the case of the *setAmount()* method, a value can no longer be assigned to the result variable using the assignment (=) operator. Instead, the LiveData *setValue()* method must be called, passing through the new value as an argument. As currently implemented, the *getResult()* method is declared to return a Float value and must be changed to return a MutableLiveData object. Making these remaining changes results in the following class file:

```
package com.ebookfrenzy.viewmodeldemo

import androidx.lifecycle.ViewModel
import androidx.lifecycle.MutableLiveData

class MainViewModel : ViewModel() {

    private val rate = 0.74f
    private var dollarText = ""
    private var result: MutableLiveData<Float> = MutableLiveData()

    fun setAmount(value: String) {
```

```
        this.dollarText = value
        result = value.toFloat() * rate
        result.value = value.toFloat() * rate
    }
    fun getResult(): Float {
    fun getResult(): MutableLiveData<Float> {
        return result
    }
}
```

43.3 Implementing the Observer

Now that the conversion result is contained within a LiveData instance, the next step is configuring an observer within the UI controller, which, in this example, is the FirstFragment class. Locate the *FirstFragment.kt* class (*app -> kotlin+java -> <package name> -> FirstFragment*), double-click on it to load it into the editor, and modify the *onViewCreated()* method to create a new Observer instance named *resultObserver*:

```
.
.
import androidx.lifecycle.Observer
.
.
override fun onViewCreated(view: View, savedInstanceState: Bundle?) {
    super.onViewCreated(view, savedInstanceState)

    binding.resultText.text = viewModel.getResult().toString()

    val resultObserver = Observer<Float> {
        result -> binding.resultText.text = result.toString()
    }
.
.
}
```

The *resultObserver* instance declares lambda code which, when called, is passed the current result value, which it then converts to a string and displays on the resultText TextView object. The next step is to add the observer to the result LiveData object, a reference that can be obtained via a call to the *getResult()* method of the ViewModel object. Since updating the result TextView is now the responsibility of the *onChanged()* callback method, the existing lines of code to perform this task can now be deleted:

```
override fun onViewCreated(view: View, savedInstanceState: Bundle?) {
    super.onViewCreated(view, savedInstanceState)

    binding.resultText.text = viewModel.getResult().toString()

    val resultObserver = Observer<Float> {
            result -> binding.resultText.text = result.toString()
    }

    viewModel.getResult().observe(viewLifecycleOwner, resultObserver)
```

```
    binding.convertButton.setOnClickListener {
        if (binding.dollarText.text.isNotEmpty()) {
            viewModel.setAmount(binding.dollarText.text.toString())
            binding.resultText.text = viewModel.getResult().toString()
        } else {
            binding.resultText.text = "No Value"
        }
    }
}
```

Compile and run the app, enter a value into the dollar field, click on the Convert button, and verify that the converted euro amount appears on the TextView. This confirms that the observer received notification that the result value had changed and called the *onChanged()* method to display the latest data.

Note in the above implementation of the *onViewCreated()* method that the line of code responsible for displaying the current result value each time the method was called was removed. This was originally put in place to ensure that the displayed value was recovered if the Fragment was recreated for any reason. Because LiveData monitors the lifecycle status of its observers, this step is no longer necessary. When LiveData detects that the UI controller was recreated, it automatically triggers any associated observers and provides the latest data. Verify this by rotating the device while a euro value is displayed on the TextView object and confirming that the value is not lost.

Before moving on to the next chapter, close the project, copy the ViewModelDemo project folder, and save it as ViewModelDemo_LiveData to be used later when saving the ViewModel state.

43.4 Summary

This chapter demonstrated the use of the Android LiveData component to ensure that the data displayed to the user always matches that stored in the ViewModel. This relatively simple process consisted of wrapping a ViewModel data value within a LiveData object and setting up an observer within the UI controller subscribed to the LiveData value. Each time the LiveData value changes, the observer is notified, and the *onChanged()* method is called and passed the updated value.

Adding LiveData support to the project has gone some way towards simplifying the design of the project. Additional and significant improvements are also possible using the Data Binding Library, details of which will be covered in the next chapter.

Chapter 44

44. An Overview of Android Jetpack Data Binding

In the chapter entitled *"Modern Android App Architecture with Jetpack"*, we introduced the concept of Android Data Binding. We explained how it is used to directly connect the views in a user interface layout to the methods and data located in other objects within an app without the need to write code. This chapter will provide more details on data binding, emphasizing how data binding is implemented within an Android Studio project. The tutorial in the next chapter (*"An Android Jetpack Data Binding Tutorial"*) will provide a practical example of data binding in action.

44.1 An Overview of Data Binding

The Android Jetpack Data Binding Library provides data binding support, primarily providing a simple way to connect the views in a user interface layout to the data stored within the app's code (typically within ViewModel instances). Data binding also provides a convenient way to map user interface controls, such as Button widgets, to event and listener methods within other objects, such as UI controllers and ViewModel instances.

Data binding becomes particularly powerful when used in conjunction with the LiveData component. Consider, for example, an EditText view bound to a LiveData variable within a ViewModel using data binding. When connected in this way, any changes to the data value in the ViewModel will automatically appear within the EditText view, and when using two-way binding, any data typed into the EditText will automatically be used to update the LiveData value. Perhaps most impressive is that this can be achieved with no code beyond that necessary to initially set up the binding.

Connecting an interactive view, such as a Button widget, to a method within a UI controller traditionally required that the developer write code to implement a listener method to be called when the button is clicked. Data binding makes this as simple as referencing the method to be called within the Button element in the layout XML file.

44.2 The Key Components of Data Binding

An Android Studio project is not configured for data binding support by default. Several elements must be combined before an app can begin using data binding. These involve the project build configuration, the layout XML file, data binding classes, and the use of the data binding expression language. While this may appear overwhelming at first, when taken separately, these are quite simple steps that, once completed, are more than worthwhile in terms of saved coding effort. Each element will be covered in detail in the remainder of this chapter. Once these basics have been covered, the next chapter will work through a detailed tutorial demonstrating these steps.

44.2.1 The Project Build Configuration

Before a project can use data binding, it must be configured to use the Android Data Binding Library and to enable support for data binding classes and the binding syntax. Fortunately, this can be achieved with just a few lines added to the module level *build.gradle.kts* file (the one listed as *build.gradle.kts (Module: app)* under *Gradle Scripts* in the Project tool window). The following lists a partial build file with data binding enabled:

.

```
.
android {

    buildFeatures {
        dataBinding = true
    }
.
.
```

44.2.2 The Data Binding Layout File

As we have seen in previous chapters, the user interfaces for an app are typically contained within an XML layout file. Before the views contained within one of these layout files can take advantage of data binding, the layout file must be converted to a *data binding layout file*.

As outlined earlier in the book, XML layout files define the hierarchy of components in the layout, starting with a top-level or *root view*. Invariably, this root view takes the form of a layout container such as a ConstraintLayout, FrameLayout, or LinearLayout instance, as is the case in the *fragment_main.xml* file for the ViewModelDemo project:

```
<?xml version="1.0" encoding="utf-8"?>
<androidx.constraintlayout.widget.ConstraintLayout
    xmlns:android="http://schemas.android.com/apk/res/android"
    xmlns:app="http://schemas.android.com/apk/res-auto"
    xmlns:tools="http://schemas.android.com/tools"
    android:id="@+id/main"
    android:layout_width="match_parent"
    android:layout_height="match_parent"
    tools:context=".ui.main.MainFragment">
.
.
</androidx.constraintlayout.widget.ConstraintLayout>
```

To use data binding, the layout hierarchy must have a *layout* component as the root view, which, in turn, becomes the parent of the current root view.

In the case of the above example, this would require that the following changes be made to the existing layout file:

```
<?xml version="1.0" encoding="utf-8"?>

<layout xmlns:app="http://schemas.android.com/apk/res-auto"
    xmlns:tools="http://schemas.android.com/tools"
    xmlns:android="http://schemas.android.com/apk/res/android">

        <androidx.constraintlayout.widget.ConstraintLayout
            xmlns:android="http://schemas.android.com/apk/res/android"
            xmlns:app="http://schemas.android.com/apk/res-auto"
            xmlns:tools="http://schemas.android.com/tools"
            android:id="@+id/main"
            android:layout_width="match_parent"
```

```
        android:layout_height="match_parent"
        tools:context=".ui.main.MainFragment">
.
.
    </androidx.constraintlayout.widget.ConstraintLayout>
</layout>
```

44.2.3 The Layout File Data Element

The data binding layout file needs some way to declare the classes within the project to which the views in the layout are to be bound (for example, a ViewModel or UI controller). Having declared these classes, the layout file will need a variable name to reference those instances within binding expressions.

This is achieved using the *data* element, an example of which is shown below:

```
<?xml version="1.0" encoding="utf-8"?>

<layout xmlns:app="http://schemas.android.com/apk/res-auto"
    xmlns:tools="http://schemas.android.com/tools"
    xmlns:android="http://schemas.android.com/apk/res/android">

    <data>
        <variable
            name="myViewModel"
            type="com.ebookfrenzy.myapp.ui.main.MainViewModel" />
    </data>

    <androidx.constraintlayout.widget.ConstraintLayout
        android:id="@+id/main"
        android:layout_width="match_parent"
        android:layout_height="match_parent"
        tools:context=".ui.main.MainFragment">
.
.
</layout>
```

The above data element declares a new variable named *myViewModel* of type MainViewModel (note that it is necessary to declare the full package name of the MyViewModel class when declaring the variable).

The data element can import other classes that may then be referenced within binding expressions elsewhere in the layout file. For example, if you have a class containing a method that needs to be called on a value before it is displayed to the user, the class could be imported as follows:

```
<data>
        <import type="com.ebookfrenzy.MyFormattingTools" />
        <variable
            name="viewModel"
            type="com.ebookfrenzy.myapp.ui.main.MainViewModel" />
    </data>
```

44.2.4 The Binding Classes

For each class referenced in the *data* element within the binding layout file, Android Studio will automatically generate a corresponding *binding class*. This subclass of the Android ViewDataBinding class will be named based on the layout filename using word capitalization and the *Binding* suffix. Therefore, the binding class for a layout file named *fragment_main.xml* file will be named *FragmentMainBinding*. The binding class contains the bindings specified within the layout file and maps them to the variables and methods within the bound objects.

Although the binding class is generated automatically, code must be written to create an instance of the class based on the corresponding data binding layout file. Fortunately, this can be achieved by making use of the DataBindingUtil class.

The initialization code for an Activity or Fragment will typically set the content view or "inflate" the user interface layout file. This means that the code opens the layout file, parses the XML, and creates and configures all of the view objects in memory. In the case of an existing Activity class, the code to achieve this can be found in the *onCreate()* method and will read as follows:

```
setContentView(R.layout.activity_main)
```

In the case of a Fragment, this takes place in the *onCreateView()* method:

```
return inflater.inflate(R.layout.fragment_main, container, false)
```

All that is needed to create the binding class instances within an Activity class is to modify this initialization code as follows:

```
lateinit var binding: ActivityMainBinding

binding = DataBindingUtil.inflate(
                inflater, R.layout.activity_main, container, false)
```

In the case of a Fragment, the code would read as follows:

```
lateinit var binding: FragmentMainBinding

binding = DataBindingUtil.inflate(
                inflater, R.layout.fragment_main, container, false)

binding.setLifecycleOwner(this)

return binding.root
```

44.2.5 Data Binding Variable Configuration

As outlined above, the data binding layout file contains the *data* element, which contains *variable* elements consisting of variable names and the class types to which the bindings are to be established. For example:

```
<data>
    <variable
        name="viewModel"
        type="com.ebookfrenzy.viewmodeldemo.ui.main.MainViewModel" />
    <variable
        name="uiController"
        type="com.ebookfrenzy.viewmodeldemo_databinding.ui.main.MainFragment" />
</data>
```

In the above example, the first variable knows that it will be binding to an instance of a ViewModel class of type MainViewModel but has yet to be connected to an actual MainViewModel object instance. This requires the additional step of assigning the MainViewModel instance used within the app to the variable declared in the layout file. This is performed via a call to the *setVariable()* method of the data binding instance, a reference to which was obtained in the previous chapter:

```
var MainViewModel mViewModel =
          ViewModelProvider(this).get(MainViewModel::class.java)
binding.setVariable(mViewModel, viewModel)
```

The second variable in the above data element references a UI controller class in the form of a Fragment named MainFragment. In this situation, the code within a UI controller (be it an Activity or Fragment) would need to assign itself to the variable as follows:

```
binding.setVariable(uiController, this)
```

44.2.6 Binding Expressions (One-Way)

Binding expressions define how a particular view interacts with bound objects. For example, a binding expression on a Button might declare which method on an object is called in response to a click. Alternatively, a binding expression might define which data value stored in a ViewModel is to appear within a TextView and how it is to be presented and formatted.

Binding expressions use a declarative language that allows logic and access to other classes and methods to decide how bound data is used. Expressions can, for example, include mathematical expressions, method calls, string concatenations, access to array elements, and comparison operations. In addition, all standard Java language libraries are imported by default, so many things that can be achieved in Java or Kotlin can also be performed in a binding expression. As already discussed, the data element may also be used to import custom classes to add more capability to expressions.

A binding expression begins with an @ symbol followed by the expression enclosed in curly braces ({}).

Consider, for example, a ViewModel instance containing a variable named *result*. Assume that this class has been assigned to a variable named *viewModel* within the data binding layout file and needs to be bound to a TextView object so that the view always displays the latest result value. If this value were stored as a String object, this would be declared within the layout file as follows:

```
<TextView
    android:id="@+id/resultText"
    android:layout_width="wrap_content"
    android:layout_height="wrap_content"
    android:text="@{viewModel.result}"
    app:layout_constraintBottom_toBottomOf="parent"
    app:layout_constraintEnd_toEndOf="parent"
    app:layout_constraintStart_toStartOf="parent"
    app:layout_constraintTop_toTopOf="parent" />
```

In the above XML, the *text* property is set to the value stored in the *result* LiveData property of the viewModel object.

Consider, however, that the result is stored within the model as a Float value instead of a String. That being the case, the above expression would cause a compilation error. Clearly, the Float value must be converted to a string before the TextView can display it. To resolve issues such as this, the binding expression can include the necessary steps to complete the conversion using the standard Java language classes:

```
android:text="@{String.valueOf(viewModel.result)}"
```

When running the app after making this change, it is important to be aware that the following warning may appear in the Android Studio console:

```
warning: myViewModel.result.getValue() is a boxed field but needs to be un-boxed
to execute String.valueOf(viewModel.result.getValue()).
```

Values in Java can take the form of primitive values such as the *boolean* type (referred to as being *unboxed*) or wrapped in a Java object such as the *Boolean* type and accessed via reference to that object (i.e., *boxed*). The unboxing process involves unwrapping the primitive value from the object.

To avoid this message, wrap the offending operation in a *safeUnbox()* call as follows:

```
android:text="@{String.valueOf(safeUnbox(myViewModel.result))}"
```

String concatenation may also be used. For example, to include the word "dollars" after the result string value, the following expression would be used:

```
android:text='@{String.valueOf(safeUnbox(myViewModel.result)) + " dollars"}'
```

Note that since the appended result string is wrapped in double quotes, the expression is now encapsulated with single quotes to avoid syntax errors.

The expression syntax also allows ternary statements to be declared. In the following expression, the view will display different text depending on whether or not the result value is greater than 10.

```
@{myViewModel.result > 10 ? "Out of range" : "In range"}
```

Expressions may also be constructed to access specific elements in a data array:

```
@{myViewModel.resultsArray[3]}
```

44.2.7 Binding Expressions (Two-Way)

The type of expression covered so far is called *one-way binding*. In other words, the layout is constantly updated as the corresponding value changes, but changes to the value from within the layout do not update the stored value.

A *two-way binding*, on the other hand, allows the data model to be updated in response to changes in the layout. An EditText view, for example, could be configured with a two-way binding so that when the user enters a different value, that value is used to update the corresponding data model value. When declaring a two-way expression, the syntax is similar to a one-way expression except that it begins with @=. For example:

```
android:text="@={myViewModel.result}"
```

44.2.8 Event and Listener Bindings

Binding expressions may also trigger method calls in response to events on a view. A Button view, for example, can be configured to call a method when clicked. In the chapter entitled *"Creating an Example Android App in Android Studio"*, for example, the onClick property of a button was configured to call a method within the app's main activity named *convertCurrency()*. Within the XML file, this was represented as follows:

```
android:onClick="convertCurrency"
```

The *convertCurrency()* method was declared along the following lines:

```
fun convertCurrency(view: View) {
.
.
}
```

Note that this type of method call is always passed a reference to the view on which the event occurred. The same effect can be achieved in data binding using the following expression (assuming the layout has been bound to a class with a variable name of *uiController*):

```
android:onClick="@{uiController::convertCurrency}"
```

Another option, and one which provides the ability to pass parameters to the method, is referred to as a *listener binding*. The following expression uses this approach to call a method on the same viewModel instance with no parameters:

```
android:onClick='@{() -> myViewModel.methodOne()}'
```

The following expression calls a method that expects three parameters:

```
android:onClick='@{() -> myViewModel.methodTwo(viewModel.result, 10, "A
String")}'
```

Binding expressions provide a rich and flexible language to bind user interface views to data and methods in other objects. This chapter has only covered the most common use cases. To learn more about binding expressions, review the Android documentation online at:

```
https://developer.android.com/topic/libraries/data-binding/expressions
```

44.3 Summary

Android data bindings provide a system for creating connections between the views in a user interface layout and the data and methods of other objects within the app architecture without writing code. Once some initial configuration steps have been performed, data binding involves using binding expressions within the view elements of the layout file. These binding expressions can be either one-way or two-way and may also be used to bind methods to be called in response to events such as button clicks within the user interface.

Chapter 45

45. An Android Jetpack Data Binding Tutorial

So far in this book, we have covered the basic concepts of modern Android app architecture and looked in more detail at the ViewModel and LiveData components. The concept of data binding was also covered in the previous chapter and will now be used in this chapter to modify the ViewModelDemo app further.

45.1 Removing the Redundant Code

If you still need to, copy the ViewModelDemo project folder and save it as ViewModelDemo_LiveData for the next chapter. Once copied, open the original ViewModelDemo project, ready to implement data binding.

Before implementing data binding within the ViewModelDemo app, the power of data binding will be demonstrated by deleting all of the code within the project that will no longer be needed by the end of this chapter.

Launch Android Studio, open the ViewModelDemo project, edit the *FirstFragment.kt* file, and modify the code as follows:

```
package com.ebookfrenzy.viewmodeldemo
.
.
import androidx.lifecycle.Observer

class FirstFragment : Fragment() {
.
.
    override fun onViewCreated(view: View, savedInstanceState: Bundle?) {
        super.onViewCreated(view, savedInstanceState)

        val resultObserver = Observer<Float> {
                result -> binding.resultText.text = result.toString()
        }

        viewModel.getResult().observe(viewLifecycleOwner, resultObserver)

        binding.convertButton.setOnClickListener {
            if (binding.dollarText.text.isNotEmpty()) {
                viewModel.setAmount(binding.dollarText.text.toString())
            } else {
                binding.resultText.text = "No Value"
            }
        }
```

```
    }
}
```

Next, edit the *MainViewModel.kt* file and continue deleting code as follows (note also the conversion of the *dollarText* variable to LiveData):

```
package com.ebookfrenzy.viewmodeldemo

import androidx.lifecycle.ViewModel
import androidx.lifecycle.MutableLiveData

class MainViewModel : ViewModel() {

    private val rate = 0.74f
    private var dollarText = ""
    var dollarValue: MutableLiveData<String> = MutableLiveData()
    private var result: MutableLiveData<Float> = MutableLiveData()

    fun setAmount(value: String) {
        this.dollarText = value
        result.value = value.toFloat() * rate
    }

    fun getResult(): MutableLiveData<Float> {
        return result
    }
}
```

Though we'll add a few additional lines of code in implementing data binding, data binding has significantly reduced the amount of code that needs to be written.

45.2 Enabling Data Binding

The first step in using data binding is to enable it within the Android Studio project. This involves adding a new property to the *Gradle Scripts -> build.gradle.kts (Module :app)* file. First, however, we need to add an entry to the plugins section of the *libs.version.toml* file as follows:

```
.
.
[plugins]
legacy-kapt = { id = "com.android.legacy-kapt", version.ref = "agp" }
.
.
```

Within the *build.gradle.kts* file, add the element below to enable data binding within the project, and apply the Kotlin *kapt* plugin. This plugin is required to process the data binding annotations that will be added to the fragment XML layout file later in the chapter:

```
plugins {
    alias(libs.plugins.android.application)
    alias(libs.plugins.legacy.kapt)
}
```

```
android {
.
.
    buildFeatures {
        viewBinding = true
        dataBinding = true
    }
.
.
}
```

Once the entry has been added, a bar will appear across the top of the editor screen containing a *Sync Now* link. Click this to resynchronize the project with the new build configuration settings.

45.3 Adding the Layout Element

As described in *"An Overview of Android Jetpack Data Binding"*, the layout hierarchy must have a layout component as the root view to use data binding. This requires that the following changes be made to the *fragment_first.xml* layout file (*app -> res -> layout -> fragment_first.xml*). Open this file in the layout editor tool, switch to Code mode, and make these changes:

```
<?xml version="1.0" encoding="utf-8"?>

<layout xmlns:app="http://schemas.android.com/apk/res-auto"
    xmlns:tools="http://schemas.android.com/tools"
    xmlns:android="http://schemas.android.com/apk/res/android">

        <androidx.constraintlayout.widget.ConstraintLayout
            xmlns:android="http://schemas.android.com/apk/res/android"
            xmlns:app="http://schemas.android.com/apk/res-auto"
            xmlns:tools="http://schemas.android.com/tools"
            android:id="@+id/main"
            android:layout_width="match_parent"
            android:layout_height="match_parent"
            tools:context=".FirstFragment">
.
.
        </androidx.constraintlayout.widget.ConstraintLayout>
</layout>
```

Once these changes have been made, switch back to Design mode and note that the new root view, though invisible in the layout canvas, is now listed in the component tree, as shown in Figure 45-1:

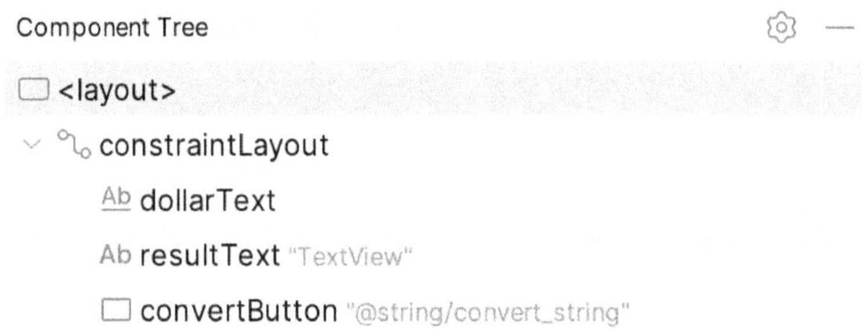

Figure 45-1

Build and run the app to verify that adding the layout element has not changed the user interface appearance.

45.4 Adding the Data Element to Layout File

The next step in converting the layout file to a data binding layout file is to add the *data* element. For this example, the layout will be bound to MainViewModel, so edit the *fragment_first.xml* file to add the data element as follows:

```
<?xml version="1.0" encoding="utf-8"?>

<layout xmlns:app="http://schemas.android.com/apk/res-auto"
    xmlns:tools="http://schemas.android.com/tools"
    xmlns:android="http://schemas.android.com/apk/res/android">

    <data>
        <variable
            name="myViewModel"
            type="com.ebookfrenzy.viewmodeldemo.MainViewModel" />
    </data>

    <androidx.constraintlayout.widget.ConstraintLayout
        android:id="@+id/main"
        android:layout_width="match_parent"
        android:layout_height="match_parent"
        tools:context=".FirstFragment">
.
.
</layout>
```

Build and rerun the app to ensure these changes take effect.

45.5 Working with the Binding Class

The next step is to modify the *FirstFragment.kt* file code to inflate the data binding. This is best achieved by rewriting the *onCreateView()* method:

```
.
.
import androidx.databinding.DataBindingUtil
.
```

```
.
class FirstFragment : Fragment() {

    private var _binding: FragmentMainBinding? = null
    private val binding get() = _binding!!

    private lateinit var viewModel: MainViewModel
    lateinit var binding: FragmentFirstBinding

    override fun onCreateView(inflater: LayoutInflater, container: ViewGroup?,
                              savedInstanceState: Bundle?): View {

        _binding = FragmentMainBinding.inflate(inflater, container, false)
        binding = DataBindingUtil.inflate(
                inflater, R.layout.fragment_first, container, false)

        binding.lifecycleOwner = this
        return binding.root
    }

    override fun onDestroyView() {
        super.onDestroyView()
        _binding = null
    }
.
.
```

The old code inflated the *fragment_first.xml* layout file (in other words, created the layout containing all of the view objects) and returned a reference to the root view (the top-level layout container). The Data Binding Library contains a utility class that provides a special inflation method which, in addition to constructing the UI, also initializes and returns an instance of the layout's data binding class. The new code calls this method and stores a reference to the binding class instance in a variable:

```
binding = DataBindingUtil.inflate(
                inflater, R.layout.fragment_first, container, false)
```

The binding object must only remain in memory for as long as the fragment is present. To ensure that the instance is destroyed when the fragment goes away, the current fragment is declared as the lifecycle owner for the binding object.

```
binding.lifecycleOwner = this
return binding.getRoot
```

45.6 Assigning the ViewModel Instance to the Data Binding Variable

At this point, the data binding knows it will be binding to an instance of a class of type MainViewModel but has yet to be connected to an actual MainViewModel object. This requires the additional step of assigning the MainViewModel instance used within the app to the viewModel variable declared in the layout file. Add this code to the *onViewCreated()* method in the FirstFragment.kt file as follows:

```
.
```

```
.
import com.ebookfrenzy.viewmodeldemo.BR.myViewModel
.
.
override fun onViewCreated(view: View, savedInstanceState: Bundle?) {
    super.onViewCreated(view, savedInstanceState)
    binding.setVariable(myViewModel, viewModel)
}
.
.
```

If Android Studio reports myViewModel as undefined, rebuild the project using the *Build -> Make Project* menu option to force the class to be generated. With these changes made, the next step is to insert some binding expressions into the view elements of the data binding layout file.

45.7 Adding Binding Expressions

The first binding expression will bind the resultText TextView to the result value within the model view. Edit the *fragment_first.xml* file, locate the resultText element, and modify the text property so that the element reads as follows:

```
<TextView
    android:id="@+id/resultText"
    android:layout_width="wrap_content"
    android:layout_height="wrap_content"
    android:text="TextView"
    android:text='@{safeUnbox(myViewModel.result) == 0.0 ? "Enter value" :
String.valueOf(safeUnbox(myViewModel.result)) + " euros"}'
    app:layout_constraintBottom_toBottomOf="parent"
    app:layout_constraintEnd_toEndOf="parent"
    app:layout_constraintStart_toStartOf="parent"
    app:layout_constraintTop_toTopOf="parent" />
```

The expression begins by checking if the result value is currently zero and, if it is, displays a message instructing the user to enter a value. However, if the result is not zero, the value is converted to a string and concatenated with the word "euros" before being displayed to the user.

The result value only requires a one-way binding in that the layout does not ever need to update the value stored in the ViewModel. The *dollarValue* EditText view, on the other hand, needs to use two-way binding so that the data model can be updated with the latest value entered by the user and to allow the current value to be redisplayed in the view in the event of a lifecycle event such as that triggered by a device rotation. The *dollarText* element should now be declared as follows:

```
<EditText
    android:id="@+id/dollarText"
    android:layout_width="wrap_content"
    android:layout_height="wrap_content"
    android:layout_marginTop="96dp"
    android:ems="10"
    android:importantForAutofill="no"
    android:inputType="numberDecimal"
```

```
    android:text="@={myViewModel.dollarValue}"
    app:layout_constraintEnd_toEndOf="parent"
    app:layout_constraintHorizontal_bias="0.502"
    app:layout_constraintStart_toStartOf="parent"
    app:layout_constraintTop_toTopOf="parent" />
```

Now that these initial binding expressions have been added, a method must be written to perform the conversion when the user clicks on the Button widget.

45.8 Adding the Conversion Method

When the Convert button is clicked, it will call a method on the ViewModel to perform the conversion calculation and place the euro value in the *result* LiveData variable. Add this method now within the *MainViewModel.kt* file:

```
.
.
class MainViewModel : ViewModel() {

    private val rate = 0.74f
    var dollarValue: MutableLiveData<String> = MutableLiveData()
    var result: MutableLiveData<Float> = MutableLiveData()

    fun convertValue() {
        dollarValue.let {
            if (!it.value.equals("")) {
                result.value = it.value?.toFloat()?.times(rate)
            } else {
                result.value = 0f
            }
        }
    }
}
```

Note that a zero value is assigned to the *result* LiveData variable in the absence of a valid dollar value. This ensures that the binding expression assigned to the *resultText* TextView displays the "Enter value" message if no value has been entered by the user.

45.9 Adding a Listener Binding

The final step before testing the project is to add a listener binding expression to the Button element within the layout file to call the *convertValue()* method when the button is clicked. Edit the *fragment_first.xml* file in Code mode once again, locate the *convertButton* element, and add an onClick entry as follows:

```
<Button
    android:id="@+id/convertButton"
    android:layout_width="wrap_content"
    android:layout_height="wrap_content"
    android:onClick="@{() -> myViewModel.convertValue()}"
    android:text="@string/convert_text"
    app:layout_constraintBottom_toBottomOf="parent"
    app:layout_constraintEnd_toEndOf="parent"
```

```
    app:layout_constraintHorizontal_bias="0.5"
    app:layout_constraintStart_toStartOf="parent"
    app:layout_constraintTop_toBottomOf="@+id/resultText" />
```

45.10 Testing the App

Compile and run the app and test that entering a value into the dollar field and clicking on the Convert button displays the correct result on the TextView (together with the "euros" suffix) and that the "Enter value" prompt appears if a conversion is attempted while the dollar field is empty. Also, verify that information displayed in the user interface is retained through a device rotation.

45.11 Summary

The primary goal of this chapter has been to work through the steps involved in setting up a project to use data binding and to demonstrate the use of one-way, two-way, and listener binding expressions. The chapter also provided a practical example of how much code writing is saved by using data binding in conjunction with LiveData to connect the user interface views with the back-end data and logic of the app.

Chapter 46

46. An Android ViewModel Saved State Tutorial

The preservation and restoration of app state is about presenting the user with continuity in appearance and behavior after an app is placed in the background. Users expect to be able to switch from one app to another and, on returning to the original app, find it in the exact state it was in before the switch took place.

As outlined in the chapter entitled *"Understanding Android Application and Activity Lifecycles"*, when the user places an app in the background, that app becomes eligible for termination by the operating system if resources become constrained. When the user attempts to return the terminated app to the foreground, Android relaunches the app in a new process. Since this is all invisible to the user, it is the app's responsibility to restore itself to the same state it was in when it was originally placed in the background instead of presenting itself in its "initial launch" state. In the case of ViewModel-based apps, much of this behavior can be achieved using the ViewModel *Saved State module.*

46.1 Understanding ViewModel State Saving

As outlined in the previous chapters, the ViewModel brings many benefits to app development, including UI state restoration in the event of configuration changes such as a device rotation. To see this in action, run the ViewModelDemo app (or, if you still need to create the project, load into Android Studio the *ViewModelDemo_LiveData* project from the sample code download accompanying the book).

Once running, enter a dollar value and convert it to euros. With both the dollar and euro values displayed, rotate the device or emulator and note that both values are still visible once the app has responded to the orientation change.

Unfortunately, this behavior does not extend to the termination of a background app process. With the app still running, tap the device home button to place the ViewModelDemo app in the background, then terminate it by opening the Terminal tool window and running the following command (where *<package name>* is the name you used when the project was created, for example, *com.ebookfrenzy.viewmodeldemo*):

```
adb shell am kill <package name>
```

If the *adb* command is not found, refer to the chapter *"Setting up an Android Studio Development Environment"* for steps to set up your Android Studio environment.

Once the app has been terminated, return to the device or emulator and select the app from the launcher (do not re-run the app from within Android Studio). Once the app appears, it will do so as if it was just launched, with the last dollar and euro values lost. From the user's perspective, however, the app was restored from the background and should still have contained the original data. In this case, the app has failed to provide the continuity that users have come to expect from Android apps.

46.2 Implementing ViewModel State Saving

Basic ViewModel state saving is made possible through the introduction of the ViewModel Saved State library. This library extends the ViewModel class to include support for maintaining state through the termination and subsequent relaunch of a background process.

The key to saving state is the SavedStateHandle class which is used to save and restore the state of a view model instance. A SavedStateHandle object contains a key-value map that allows data values to be saved and restored by referencing corresponding keys.

To support state saving, a different kind of ViewModel subclass needs to be declared, in this case containing a constructor which can receive a SavedStateHandle instance. Once declared, ViewModel instances of this type can be created by including a SavedStateViewModelFactory object at creation time. Consider the following code excerpt from a standard ViewModel declaration:

```
package com.ebookfrenzy.viewmodeldemo

import androidx.lifecycle.ViewModel
import androidx.lifecycle.MutableLiveData

class MainViewModel : ViewModel() {
.
.
}
```

The code to create an instance of this class would likely resemble the following:

```
private lateinit var viewModel: MainViewModel

viewModel = ViewModelProvider(this).get(MainViewModel::class.java)
```

A ViewModel subclass designed to support saved state, on the other hand, would need to be declared as follows:

```
package com.ebookfrenzy.viewmodeldemo

import androidx.lifecycle.ViewModel
import androidx.lifecycle.MutableLiveData
import androidx.lifecycle.SavedStateHandle

class MainViewModel(private val savedStateHandle: SavedStateHandle) : ViewModel()
{
.
.
}
```

When instances of the above ViewModel are created, the *ViewModelProvider* class initializer must be passed a SavedStateViewModelFactory instance as follows:

```
private lateinit var viewModel: MainViewModel

val factory = SavedStateViewModelFactory(activity.application, this)
viewModel = ViewModelProvider(this, factory).get(MainViewModel::class.java)
```

46.3 Saving and Restoring State

An object or value can be saved from within the ViewModel by passing it through to the *set()* method of the SavedStateHandle instance, providing the key string by which it is to be referenced when performing a retrieval:

```
val NAME_KEY = "Customer Name"
```

```
savedStateHandle.set(NAME_KEY, customerName)
```

When used with LiveData objects, a previously saved value may be restored using the *getLiveData()* method of the SavedStateHandle instance, once again referencing the corresponding key as follows:

```
var restoredName: LiveData<String> = savedStateHandle.getLiveData(NAME_KEY)
```

To restore a normal (non-LiveData) object, use the SavedStateHandle *get()* method:

```
var restoredName: String? = savedStateHandle.get(NAME_KEY)
```

Other useful SavedStateHandle methods include the following:

- **contains(String key)** - Returns a boolean value indicating whether the saved state contains a value for the specified key.
- **remove(String key)** - Removes the value and key from the saved state. Returns the value that was removed.
- **keys()** - Returns a String set of all keys contained within the saved state.

46.4 Adding Saved State Support to the ViewModelDemo Project

With the basics of ViewModel Saved State covered, the ViewModelDemo app can be extended to include this support. Begin by loading the ViewModelDemo_LiveData project created in *"An Android Jetpack LiveData Tutorial"* into Android Studio (a copy of the project is also available in the sample code download).

Next, modify the *MainViewModel.kt* file so the constructor accepts a SavedStateHandle instance. Also, import androidx.lifecycle.SavedStateHandle, declare a key string constant, and modify the *result* LiveData variable so that the value is now obtained from the saved state:

```
package com.ebookfrenzy.viewmodeldemo

import androidx.lifecycle.ViewModel
import androidx.lifecycle.MutableLiveData
import androidx.lifecycle.SavedStateHandle

const val RESULT_KEY = "Euro Value"

class MainViewModel(private val savedStateHandle: SavedStateHandle) : ViewModel()
{

    private val rate = 0.74f
    private var dollarText = ""
    private var result: MutableLiveData<Float> =
                savedStateHandle.getLiveData(RESULT_KEY)
.
.
```

Remaining within the *MainViewModel.kt* file, modify the *setAmount()* method to include code to save the result value each time a new euro amount is calculated:

```
fun setAmount(value: String) {
    this.dollarText = value
    val convertedValue = value.toFloat() * rate
    result.value = convertedValue
```

```
    savedStateHandle[RESULT_KEY]
}
```

With the changes to the ViewModel complete, open the *FirstFragment.kt* file and make the following alterations to include a Saved State factory instance during the ViewModel creation process:

```
.
.
import androidx.lifecycle.SavedStateViewModelFactory
.
.
override fun onCreate(savedInstanceState: Bundle?) {
.
.
        activity?.application?.let {
            val factory = SavedStateViewModelFactory(it, this)
            viewModel =
                ViewModelProvider(this, factory)[MainViewModel::class.java]
        }
    }
.
.
}
```

With the screen UI populated with dollar and euro values, place the app into the background, terminate it using the *adb* tool, and then relaunch it from the device or emulator screen. After restarting, the previous currency amounts should still be visible in the TextView and EditText components, confirming that the state was successfully saved and restored.

46.5 Summary

A well-designed app should always present the user with the same state when brought forward from the background, regardless of whether the operating system terminated the process containing the app in the interim. When working with ViewModels, this can be achieved by taking advantage of the ViewModel Saved State module. This involves modifying the ViewModel constructor to accept a SavedStateHandle instance which, in turn, can be used to save and restore data values via a range of method calls. When the ViewModel instance is created, it must be passed a SavedStateViewModelFactory instance. Once these steps have been implemented, the app will automatically save and restore state during a background termination.

47. Working with Android Lifecycle-Aware Components

The earlier chapter, *"Understanding Android Application and Activity Lifecycles"* described the use of lifecycle methods to track lifecycle state changes within a UI controller such as an activity or fragment. One of the main problems with these methods is that they place the burden of handling lifecycle changes onto the UI controller. On the surface, this might seem like the logical approach since the UI controller is, after all, the object going through the state change. However, the fact is that the code typically impacted by the state change invariably resides in other classes within the app. This led to complex code appearing in the UI controller that needed to manage and manipulate other objects in response to changes in the lifecycle state. This scenario is best avoided when following the Android architectural guidelines.

A much cleaner and more logical approach would be for the objects within an app to be able to observe the lifecycle state of other objects and to be responsible for taking any necessary actions in response to the changes. For example, the class responsible for tracking a user's location could observe the lifecycle state of a UI controller and suspend location updates when the controller enters a paused state. Tracking would then be restarted when the controller enters the resumed state. This is made possible by the classes and interfaces provided by the Lifecycle package bundled with the Android architecture components.

This chapter will introduce the terminology and key components that enable lifecycle awareness to be built into Android apps.

47.1 Lifecycle Awareness

An object is said to be *lifecycle-aware* if it can detect and respond to changes in the lifecycle state of other objects within an app. Some Android components, LiveData being a prime example, are already lifecycle-aware. Configuring any class to be lifecycle-aware is also possible by implementing the LifecycleObserver interface within the class.

47.2 Lifecycle Owners

Lifecycle-aware components can only observe the status of objects that are *lifecycle owners*. Lifecycle owners implement the LifecycleOwner interface and are assigned a companion *Lifecycle object* responsible for storing the current state of the component and providing state information to *lifecycle observers*. Most standard Android Framework components (such as activity and fragment classes) are lifecycle owners. Custom classes may also be configured as lifecycle owners using the LifecycleRegistry class and implementing the LifecycleObserver interface. For example:

```
class SampleOwner(override val lifecycle: Lifecycle): LifecycleOwner {

    private val lifecycleRegistry: LifecycleRegistry

    init {
        lifecycleRegistry = LifecycleRegistry(this)
        lifecycle.addObserver(DemoObserver())
    }
```

```
}
```

Unless the lifecycle owner is a subclass of another lifecycle-aware component, the class will need to trigger lifecycle state changes via calls to methods of the LifecycleRegistry class. The *markState()* method can be used to trigger a lifecycle state change passing through the new state value:

```
fun resuming() {
    lifecycleRegistry.markState(Lifecycle.State.RESUMED)
}
```

The above call will also result in a call to the corresponding event handler. Alternatively, the LifecycleRegistry *handleLifecycleEvent()* method may be called and passed the lifecycle event to be triggered (which will also result in the lifecycle state changing). For example:

```
lifecycleRegistry.handleLifecycleEvent(Lifecycle.Event.ON_START)
```

47.3 Lifecycle Observers

To observe the state of a lifecycle owner, a lifecycle-aware component must implement the DefaultLifecycleObserver interface and override methods for any lifecycle change events it needs to observe.

```
class DemoObserver: DefaultLifecycleObserver {
    // Lifecycle event methods go here
}
```

An instance of this observer class is then created and added to the list of observers maintained by the Lifecycle object.

```
lifecycle.addObserver(DemoObserver())
```

An observer may be removed from the Lifecycle object anytime if it no longer needs to track the lifecycle state.

Figure 47-1 illustrates the relationship between the key elements that provide lifecycle awareness:

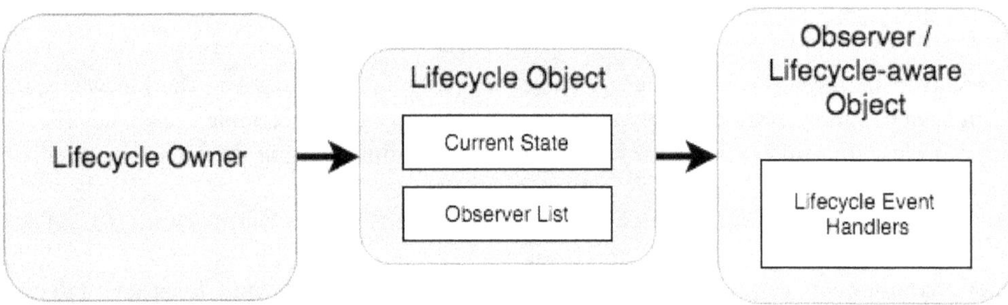

Figure 47-1

47.4 Lifecycle States and Events

When the status of a lifecycle owner changes, the assigned Lifecycle object will be updated with the new state. At any given time, a lifecycle owner will be in one of the following five states:

- Lifecycle.State.INITIALIZED
- Lifecycle.State.CREATED
- Lifecycle.State.STARTED
- Lifecycle.State.RESUMED
- Lifecycle.State.DESTROYED

The Lifecycle object will trigger events on any observers added to the list as the component transitions through the different states. The following event methods are available to be overridden within the lifecycle observer:

- onCreate()
- onResume()
- onPause()
- onStop()
- onStart()
- onDestroy()

The following code, for example, overrides the DefaultLifecycleObserver *onResume()* method:

```
override fun onResume(owner: LifecycleOwner) {
    // Perform tasks in response to Resume status event
}
```

The flowchart in Figure 47-2 illustrates the sequence of state changes for a lifecycle owner and the lifecycle events that will be triggered on observers between each state transition:

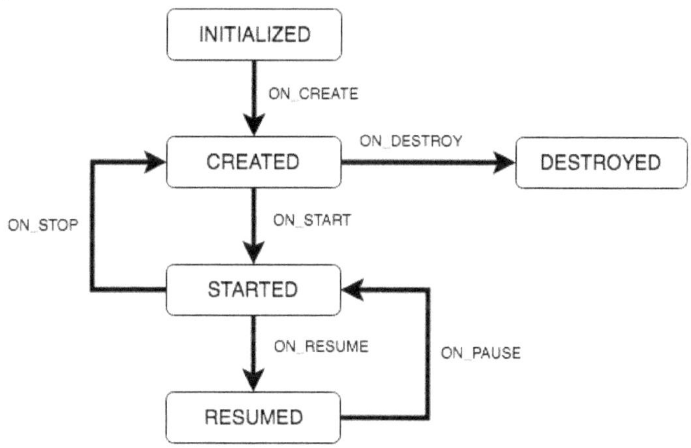

Figure 47-2

47.5 Summary

This chapter has introduced the basics of lifecycle awareness and the classes and interfaces of the Android Lifecycle package included with Android Jetpack. The package contains several classes and interfaces for creating lifecycle owners, observers, and lifecycle-aware components. A lifecycle owner has assigned to it a Lifecycle object that maintains a record of the owner's state and a list of subscribed observers. When the owner's state changes, the observer is notified via lifecycle event methods to respond to the change.

The next chapter will create an Android Studio project that demonstrates how to work with and create lifecycle-aware components, including the creation of both lifecycle observers and owners and the handling of lifecycle state changes and events.

Chapter 48

48. An Android Jetpack Lifecycle Awareness Tutorial

The previous chapter provided an overview of lifecycle awareness and outlined the key classes and interfaces that make this possible within an Android app project. This chapter will build on this knowledge base by building an Android Studio project to highlight lifecycle awareness in action.

48.1 Creating the Example Lifecycle Project

Select the *New Project* quick start option from the welcome screen and, within the resulting new project dialog, choose the Empty Views Activity template before clicking on the Next button.

Enter *LifecycleDemo* into the Name field and specify *com.ebookfrenzy.lifecycledemo* as the package name. Before clicking on the Finish button, change the Minimum API level setting to API 26: Android 8.0 (Oreo) and the Language menu to Kotlin.

48.2 Creating a Lifecycle Observer

As previously discussed, activities and fragments already implement the LifecycleOwner interface and are ready to be observed by other objects. To see this in practice, the next step in this tutorial is to add a new class to the project that will be able to observe the MainActivity instance.

To add the new class, right-click on a*pp -> kotlin+java -> com.ebookfrenzy.lifecycledemo* in the Project tool window and select *New -> Kotlin Class/File...* from the resulting menu. In the New Class dialog, name the class DemoObserver, select Class from the list, and press the keyboard Return key to create the *DemoObserver.kt* file. The new file should automatically open in the editor, where it will read as follows:

```
package com.ebookfrenzy.lifecycledemo

class DemoObserver {
}
```

Remaining in the editor, modify the class file to declare that it will be implementing the DefaultLifecycleObserver interface:

```
package com.ebookfrenzy.lifecycledemo

import androidx.lifecycle.DefaultLifecycleObserver

class DemoObserver: DefaultLifecycleObserver {
}
```

The next step is to override the lifecycle methods of the DefaultLifecycleObserver class. For this example, all events will be handled, each outputting a message to the Logcat panel displaying the event type. Update the observer class as outlined in the following listing:

```
package com.ebookfrenzy.lifecycledemo
```

```
import android.util.Log
import androidx.lifecycle.DefaultLifecycleObserver
import androidx.lifecycle.LifecycleOwner

class DemoObserver: DefaultLifecycleObserver {

    private val TAG = "DemoObserver"

    override fun onCreate(owner: LifecycleOwner) {
        Log.i(TAG, "onCreate")
    }

    override fun onResume(owner: LifecycleOwner) {
        Log.i(TAG, "onResume")
    }

    override fun onPause(owner: LifecycleOwner) {
        Log.i(TAG, "onPause")
    }

    override fun onStart(owner: LifecycleOwner) {
        Log.i(TAG, "onStart")
    }

    override fun onStop(owner: LifecycleOwner) {
        Log.i(TAG, "onStop")
    }

    override fun onDestroy(owner: LifecycleOwner) {
        Log.i(TAG, "onDestroy")
    }
}
```

With the DemoObserver class completed, the next step is to add it as an observer on the MainActivity class.

48.3 Adding the Observer

Observers are added to lifecycle owners via calls to the *addObserver()* method of the owner's Lifecycle object, a reference to which is obtained via a call to the *getLifecycle()* method. Edit the *MainActivity.kt* class file and edit the *onCreate()* method to add an observer:

```
.
.
import com.ebookfrenzy.lifecycledemo.DemoObserver
.
.
override fun onCreate(savedInstanceState: Bundle?) {
    super.onCreate(savedInstanceState)
```

```
.
.
    lifecycle.addObserver(DemoObserver())
}
```

With the observer class created and added to the lifecycle owner's Lifecycle object, the app is ready to be tested.

48.4 Testing the Observer

Since the DemoObserver class outputs diagnostic information to the Logcat console, it will be easier to see the output if a filter is configured to display only the DemoObserver messages. Using the steps outlined previously in *"Android Activity State Changes by Example"*, display the Logcat panel and enter the following keys into the filter field:

```
package:mine tag:DemoObserver
```

On successful launch of the app, the Logcat output should indicate the following lifecycle state changes and events:

```
onCreate
onStart
onResume
```

With the app still running, perform a device rotation to trigger the destruction and recreation of the activity, generating the following additional output:

```
onPause
onStop
onDestroy
onCreate
onStart
onResume
```

Before moving to the next section in this chapter, take some time to compare the output from the app with the flow chart in Figure 47-2 of the previous chapter.

48.5 Creating a Lifecycle Owner

The final task in this chapter is to create a custom lifecycle owner class and demonstrate how to trigger events and modify the lifecycle state from within that class.

Add a new class by right-clicking on the *app -> kotlin+java -> com.ebookfrenzy.lifecycledemo* entry in the Project tool window and selecting the *New -> Kotlin Class/File...* menu option. Name the class DemoOwner in the Create Class dialog and select the Class option before tapping the keyboard Return key. With the new *DemoOwner.kt* file loaded into the code editor, modify it as follows:

```
package com.ebookfrenzy.lifecycledemo

import androidx.lifecycle.Lifecycle
import androidx.lifecycle.LifecycleOwner
import androidx.lifecycle.LifecycleRegistry

class DemoOwner(override val lifecycle: Lifecycle): LifecycleOwner {
}
```

The class will need a LifecycleRegistry instance initialized with a reference to itself and a *getLifecycle()* method configured to return the LifecycleRegistry instance. Declare a variable to store the LifecycleRegistry reference and a constructor to initialize the LifecycleRegistry instance:

```
package com.ebookfrenzy.lifecycledemo

import androidx.lifecycle.Lifecycle
import androidx.lifecycle.LifecycleOwner
import androidx.lifecycle.LifecycleRegistry

class DemoOwner(override val lifecycle: Lifecycle): LifecycleOwner {

    private val lifecycleRegistry: LifecycleRegistry = LifecycleRegistry(this)

    init {

    }
}
```

Next, the class must notify the registry of lifecycle state changes. This can be achieved by marking the state with the *markState()* method of the LifecycleRegistry object or by triggering lifecycle events using the *handleLifecycleEvent()* method. What constitutes a state change within a custom class will depend on the purpose of the class. For this example, we will add some methods that trigger lifecycle events when called:

```
.
.
fun startOwner() {
    lifecycleRegistry.handleLifecycleEvent(Lifecycle.Event.ON_START)
}

fun stopOwner() {
    lifecycleRegistry.handleLifecycleEvent(Lifecycle.Event.ON_STOP)
}
.
.
```

The last change within the DemoOwner class is to add the DemoObserver class as the observer. This call will be made by adding the following to the class constructor:

```
init {
    lifecycle.addObserver(DemoObserver())
}
```

Load the *MainActivity.kt* file into the code editor, locate the *onCreate()* method, and add code to create an instance of the DemoOwner class and to call the *startOwner()* and *stopOwner()* methods. Note also that the call to add the DemoObserver as an observer has been removed. Although a single observer can be used with multiple owners, it is removed in this case to avoid duplicated and confusing output within the Logcat tool window:

```
.
.
import com.ebookfrenzy.lifecycledemo.DemoOwner
```

```
.
.
private lateinit var demoOwner: DemoOwner

override fun onCreate(savedInstanceState: Bundle?) {
.
.
    demoOwner = DemoOwner(this.lifecycle)
    demoOwner.startOwner()
    demoOwner.stopOwner()
}
```

48.6 Testing the Custom Lifecycle Owner

Build and run the app one final time, refer to the Logcat tool window, and confirm that the observer detected the create, start, and stop lifecycle events in the following order:

```
onCreate
onStart
onStop
```

Note that the "created" state changes were triggered even though code was not added to the DemoOwner class to do this manually. These were triggered automatically when the owner instance was first created and when the ON_STOP event was handled.

48.7 Summary

This chapter has provided a practical demonstration of implementing lifecycle awareness within an Android app, including creating a lifecycle observer and designing and implementing a basic lifecycle owner class.

49. An Overview of the Navigation Architecture Component

Very few Android apps today consist of just a single screen. In reality, most apps comprise multiple screens through which the user navigates using screen gestures, button clicks, and menu selections. Before the introduction of Android Jetpack, implementing navigation within an app was largely a manual coding process with no easy way to view and organize potentially complex navigation paths. However, this situation has improved considerably with the introduction of the Android Navigation Architecture Component combined with support for navigation graphs in Android Studio.

49.1 Understanding Navigation

Every app has a home screen that appears after the app has launched and after any splash screen has appeared (a splash screen being the app branding screen that appears temporarily while the app loads). The user will typically perform tasks from this home screen, resulting in other screens appearing. These screens will usually take the form of other activities and fragments within the app. For example, a messaging app may have a home screen listing current messages from which users can navigate to another screen to access a contact list or a settings screen. The contacts list screen, in turn, might allow the user to navigate to other screens where new users can be added or existing contacts updated. Graphically, the app's *navigation graph* might be represented as shown in Figure 49-1:

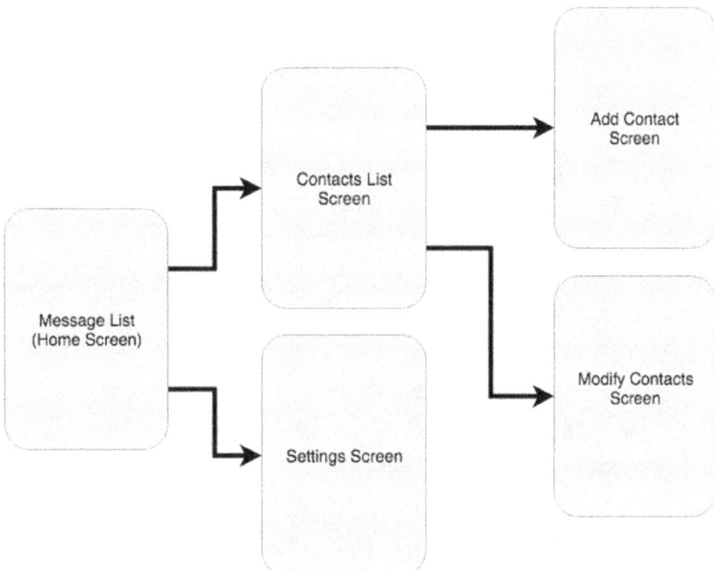

Figure 49-1

Each screen that makes up an app, including the home screen, is referred to as a *destination* and is usually a fragment or activity. The Android navigation architecture uses a *navigation stack* to track the user's path through the destinations within the app. When the app first launches, the home screen is the first destination placed onto the stack and becomes the *current destination*. When the user navigates to another destination, that screen becomes the current destination and is *pushed* onto the stack above the home destination. As the user navigates to other screens, they are also pushed onto the stack. Figure 49-2, for example, shows the current state of the navigation stack for the hypothetical messaging app after the user has launched the app and is navigating to the "Add Contact" screen:

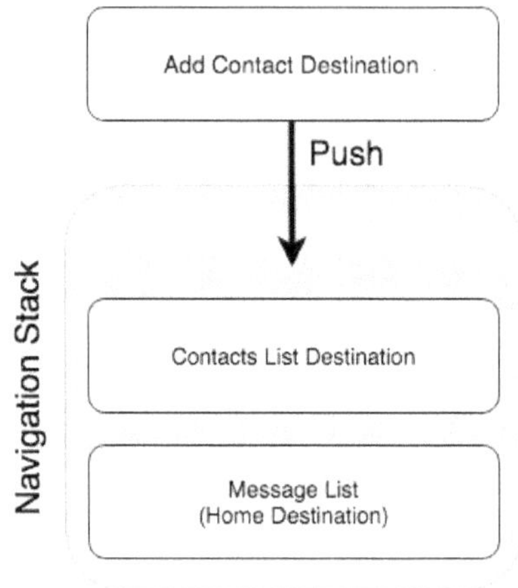

Figure 49-2

As the user navigates back through the screens using the system back button, each destination is *popped* off the stack until the home screen is once again the only destination on the stack. In Figure 49-3, the user has navigated back from the Add Contact screen, popping it off the stack and making the Contacts List screen the current destination:

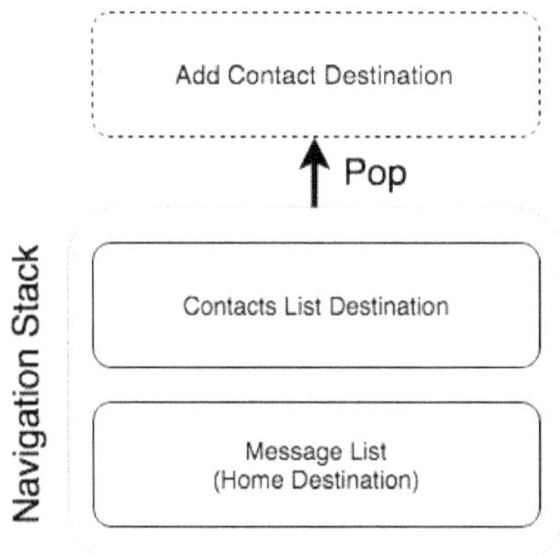

Figure 49-3

All of the work involved in navigating between destinations and managing the navigation stack is handled by a *navigation controller*, represented by the NavController class.

Adding navigation to an Android project using the Navigation Architecture Component is a straightforward process involving a navigation host, navigation graph, navigation actions, and minimal code writing to obtain a reference to, and interact with, the navigation controller instance.

49.2 Declaring a Navigation Host

A navigation host is a special fragment (NavHostFragment) embedded into the user interface layout of an activity and serves as a placeholder for the destinations through which the user will navigate. Figure 49-4, for example, shows a typical activity screen and highlights the area represented by the navigation host fragment:

Figure 49-4

A NavHostFragment can be placed into an activity layout within the Android Studio layout editor either by dragging and dropping an instance from the Containers section of the palette or by manually editing the XML as follows:

```
<?xml version="1.0" encoding="utf-8"?>
<FrameLayout xmlns:android="http://schemas.android.com/apk/res/android"
    xmlns:app="http://schemas.android.com/apk/res-auto"
    xmlns:tools="http://schemas.android.com/tools"
    android:id="@+id/container"
    android:layout_width="match_parent"
    android:layout_height="match_parent"
    tools:context=".MainActivity" >

    <androidx.fragment.app.FragmentContainerView
        android:id="@+id/demo_nav_host_fragment"
        android:name="androidx.navigation.fragment.NavHostFragment"
        android:layout_width="match_parent"
        android:layout_height="match_parent"
        app:defaultNavHost="true"
        app:navGraph="@navigation/navigation_graph" />
</FrameLayout>
```

The points of note in the above navigation host fragment element are the reference to the NavHostFragment in the *name* property, the setting of *defaultNavHost* to true, and the assignment of the file containing the navigation graph to the *navGraph* property.

When the activity launches, this navigation host fragment is replaced by the home destination designated in the navigation graph. As the user navigates through the app screens, the host fragment will be replaced by the appropriate fragment for the destination.

49.3 The Navigation Graph

A navigation graph is an XML file that contains the destinations that will be included in the app navigation. In addition to these destinations, the file contains navigation actions that define navigation between destinations and optional arguments for passing data from one destination to another. Android Studio includes a navigation graph editor that can be used to design graphs and implement actions either visually or by manually editing the XML.

Figure 49-5 shows the Android Studio navigation graph editor in Design mode:

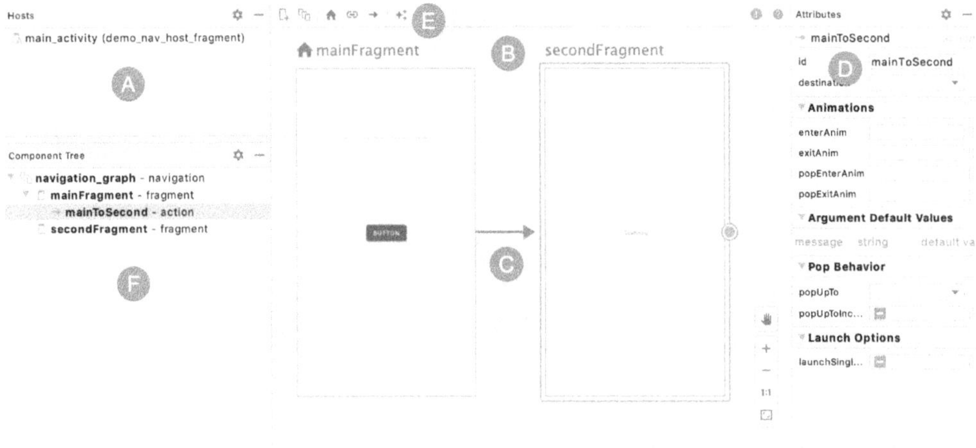

Figure 49-5

The destinations list (A) lists all destinations within the graph. Selecting a destination from the list will locate and select the corresponding destination in the graph (particularly useful for locating specific destinations in a large graph). The navigation graph panel (B) contains a dialog for each destination representing the user interface layout. In this example, this graph contains two destinations named mainFragment and secondFragment. Arrows between destinations (C) represent navigation action connections. Actions are added by hovering the mouse pointer over the edge of the origin until a circle appears, then clicking and dragging from the circle to the destination. The Attributes panel (D) allows the properties of the currently selected destination or action connection to be viewed and modified. In the above figure, the attributes for the action are displayed. New destinations are added by clicking on the button marked E and selecting options from a menu. Options are available to add existing fragments or activities as destinations or to create new blank fragment destinations. The Component Tree panel (F) provides a hierarchical overview of the navigation graph.

The underlying XML for the navigation graph can be viewed and modified by switching the editor into Code mode. The following XML listing represents the navigation graph for the destinations and action connection shown in Figure 49-5 above:

```
<?xml version="1.0" encoding="utf-8"?>
<navigation xmlns:android="http://schemas.android.com/apk/res/android"
    xmlns:app="http://schemas.android.com/apk/res-auto"
    xmlns:tools="http://schemas.android.com/tools"
    android:id="@+id/navigation_graph"
    app:startDestination="@id/mainFragment">

    <fragment
        android:id="@+id/mainFragment"
```

```
        android:name="com.ebookfrenzy.navigationdemo.ui.main.MainFragment"
        android:label="fragment_main"
        tools:layout="@layout/fragment_main" >
        <action
            android:id="@+id/mainToSecond"
            app:destination="@id/secondFragment" />
    </fragment>
    <fragment
        android:id="@+id/secondFragment"
        android:name="com.ebookfrenzy.navigationdemo.SecondFragment"
        android:label="fragment_second"
        tools:layout="@layout/fragment_second" >
    </fragment>
</navigation>
```

Navigation graphs can also be split over multiple files to improve organization and promote reuse. When structured in this way, *nested graphs* are embedded into *root graphs*. To create a nested graph, shift-click on the destinations to be nested, right-click over the first destination and select the *Move to Nested Graph -> New Graph* menu option. The nested graph will then appear as a new node in the graph. Double-click on the nested graph node to load the graph file into the editor to access the nested graph.

49.4 Accessing the Navigation Controller

Navigating from one destination to another usually occurs in response to an event within an app, such as a button click or menu selection. Before a navigation action can be triggered, the code must first obtain a reference to the navigation controller instance. This requires a call to the *findNavController()* method of the Navigation or NavHostFragment classes. The following code, for example, can be used to access the navigation controller of an activity. Note that for the code to work, the activity must contain a navigation host fragment:

```
val controller: NavController =
         Navigation.findNavController(activity, R.id.demo_nav_host_fragment)
```

In this case, the method call is passed a reference to the activity and the id of the NavHostFragment embedded in the activity's layout.

Alternatively, the navigation controller associated with any view may be identified by passing that view to the method:

```
val controller: NavController = Navigation.findNavController(button)
```

The final option finds the navigation controller for a fragment by calling the *findNavController()* method of the NavHostFragment class, passing through a reference to the fragment:

```
val controller: NavController = NavHostFragment.findNavController(fragment)
```

49.5 Triggering a Navigation Action

Once the navigation controller has been found, a navigation action is triggered by calling the controller's *navigate()* method and passing through the resource id of the action to be performed. For example:

```
controller.navigate(R.id.goToContactsList)
```

The id of the action is defined within the Attributes panel of the navigation graph editor when an action connection is selected.

49.6 Passing Arguments

Data may be passed from one destination to another during a navigation action by using arguments declared within the navigation graph file. An argument consists of a name, type, and an optional default value and may be added manually within the XML or using the Attributes panel when an action arrow or destination is selected within the graph. In Figure 49-6, for example, an integer argument named *contactsCount* has been declared with a default value of 0:

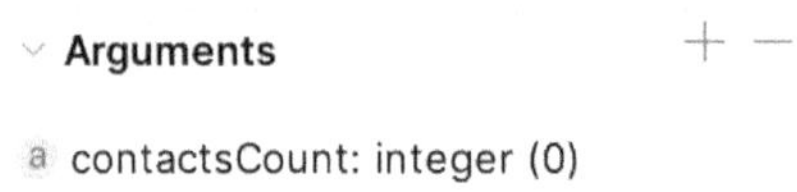

Figure 49-6

Once added, arguments are placed within the XML element of the receiving destination, for example:

```
<fragment
    android:id="@+id/secondFragment"
    android:name="com.ebookfrenzy.navigationdemo.SecondFragment"
    android:label="fragment_second"
    tools:layout="@layout/fragment_second" >
    <argument
        android:name="contactsCount"
        android:defaultValue=0
        app:type="integer" />
</fragment>
```

The Navigation Architecture Component provides two techniques for passing data between destinations. One approach involves placing the data into a Bundle object that is passed to the destination during an action, where it is then unbundled and the arguments extracted.

The main drawback to this particular approach is that it is not "type safe". In other words, if the receiving destination treats an argument as a different type than it was declared (for example, treating a string as an integer) this error will not be caught by the compiler and will likely cause problems at runtime.

A better option, which is used in this book, is *safeargs*. Safeargs is a plugin for the Android Studio Gradle build system which automatically generates special classes that allow arguments to be passed in a type-safe way. The safeargs approach to argument passing will be described and demonstrated in the next chapter (*"An Android Jetpack Navigation Component Tutorial"*).

49.7 Summary

Navigation within the context of an Android app user interface refers to the ability of a user to move back and forth between different screens. Once time-consuming to implement and difficult to organize, Android Studio and the Navigation Architecture Component now make it easier to implement and manage navigation within Android app projects.

The different screens within an app are referred to as destinations and are usually represented by fragments or activities. All apps have a home destination, including the screen displayed when the app first loads. The content area of this layout is replaced by a navigation host fragment which is swapped out for other destination fragments as the user navigates the app. The navigation path is defined by the navigation graph file consisting of destinations and the actions that connect them together with any arguments to be passed between destinations. Navigation is handled by navigation controllers, which, in addition to managing the navigation stack, provide methods to initiate navigation actions from within app code.

Chapter 50

50. An Android Jetpack Navigation Component Tutorial

The previous chapter described the Android Jetpack Navigation Component and how it integrates with the navigation graphing features of Android Studio to provide an easy way to implement navigation between the screens of an Android app. In this chapter, a new Android Studio project will be created that uses these navigation features to implement an example app containing multiple screens. In addition to demonstrating the use of the Android Studio navigation graph editor, the example project will also implement the passing of data between origin and destination screens using type-safe arguments.

50.1 Creating the NavigationDemo Project

Select the *New Project* option from the welcome screen and, within the resulting new project dialog, choose the Empty Views Activity template before clicking on the Next button.

Enter *NavigationDemo* into the Name field and specify *com.ebookfrenzy.navigationdemo* as the package name. Before clicking on the Finish button, change the Minimum API level setting to API 26: Android 8.0 (Oreo) and the Language menu to Kotlin.

50.2 Adding Navigation to the Build Configuration

A new Empty Views Activity project does not include the Navigation component libraries in the build configuration files by default. The next step is to add the navigation library to the build configuration. Start by editing the *Gradle Scripts -> libs.version.toml* file and modify it as follows (keeping in mind that a more recent version of the libraries may now be available):

```
[versions]
.
.
navigationFragmentKtx = "2.9.7"

[libraries]
.
.
androidx-navigation-fragment-ktx = { group = "androidx.navigation", name =
"navigation-fragment-ktx", version.ref = "navigationFragmentKtx" }
```

Next, open the *Gradle Scripts -> build.gradle.kts (Module: app)* file and add the following directive to the *dependencies* section. Also, take this opportunity to enable view binding for this module:

```
.
.
android {

    buildFeatures {
        viewBinding = true
```

```
    }
.
.
dependencies {
    implementation(libs.androidx.navigation.fragment.ktx)
.
.
```

After adding the navigation dependencies to the file, click on the *Sync Now* link to resynchronize the build configuration for the project.

50.3 Creating the Navigation Graph Resource File

With the navigation libraries added to the build configuration, the navigation graph resource file can now be added to the project. As outlined in *"An Overview of the Navigation Architecture Component"*, this is an XML file containing the fragments and activities through which the user will be able to navigate, together with the actions to perform the transitions and any data to be passed between destinations.

Within the Project tool window, locate the *res* folder (*app -> res*), right-click on it, and select the *New ->Android Resource File* menu option:

Figure 50-1

After selecting the menu item, the New Resource File dialog will appear. In this dialog, name the file *navigation_graph* and change the Resource type menu to Navigation as outlined in Figure 50-2 before clicking on the OK button to create the file.

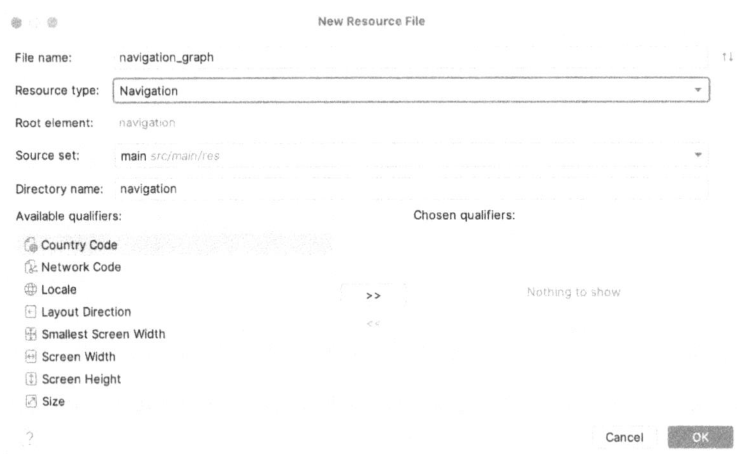

Figure 50-2

After the navigation graph resource file has been added to the project, it will appear in the main panel, ready for adding new destinations. Switch the editor to Code mode and review the XML for the graph before any destinations are added:

```
<?xml version="1.0" encoding="utf-8"?>
```

```
<navigation xmlns:android="http://schemas.android.com/apk/res/android"
    xmlns:app="http://schemas.android.com/apk/res-auto"
    android:id="@+id/navigation_graph">
</navigation>
```

Switch back to Design mode within the editor and note that the Host section of the Destinations panel indicates that no navigation host fragments have been detected within the project:

Figure 50-3

Before adding any destinations to the navigation graph, the next step is to add a navigation host fragment to the project.

50.4 Declaring a Navigation Host

For this project, the navigation host fragment will be contained within the user interface layout of the main activity. First, locate the main activity layout file in the Project tool window (*app -> res -> layout -> activity_main.xml*), load it into the layout editor tool, and delete the default TextView component.

With the layout editor in Design mode, drag a NavHostFragment element from the Containers section of the Palette and drop it onto the container area of the activity layout, as indicated by the arrow in Figure 50-4:

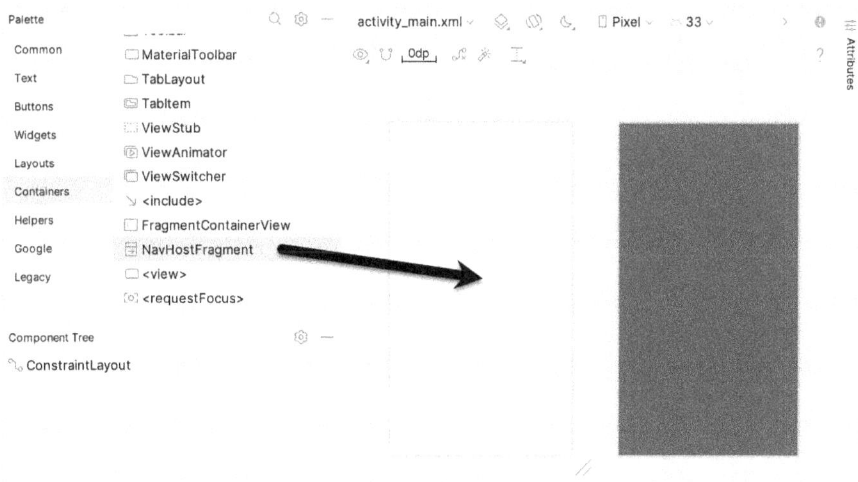

Figure 50-4

Select the *navigation_graph.xml* file created in the previous section from the resulting Navigation Graphs dialog and click on the OK button.

With the newly added NavHostFragment instance selected in the layout, use the Attributes tool window to change the element's ID to *demo_nav_host_fragment* before clicking on the *Infer constraints* button.

Switch the layout editor to Code mode and review the XML file. Note that the editor has correctly configured the navigation graph property to reference the *navigation_graph.xml* file and that the *defaultNavHost* property has been set to *true*:

```
<?xml version="1.0" encoding="utf-8"?>
<androidx.constraintlayout.widget.ConstraintLayout
xmlns:android="http://schemas.android.com/apk/res/android"
    xmlns:app="http://schemas.android.com/apk/res-auto"
    xmlns:tools="http://schemas.android.com/tools"
    android:layout_width="match_parent"
    android:layout_height="match_parent"
    tools:context=".MainActivity">

    <androidx.fragment.app.FragmentContainerView
        android:id="@+id/demo_nav_host_fragment"
        android:name="androidx.navigation.fragment.NavHostFragment"
        android:layout_width="409dp"
        android:layout_height="729dp"
        app:defaultNavHost="true"
        app:layout_constraintBottom_toBottomOf="parent"
        app:layout_constraintEnd_toEndOf="parent"
        app:layout_constraintStart_toStartOf="parent"
        app:layout_constraintTop_toTopOf="parent"
        app:navGraph="@navigation/navigation_graph" />
</androidx.constraintlayout.widget.ConstraintLayout>
```

Return to the *navigation_graph.xml* file and confirm that the NavHostFragment instance has been detected (it may be necessary to close and reopen the file before the change appears):

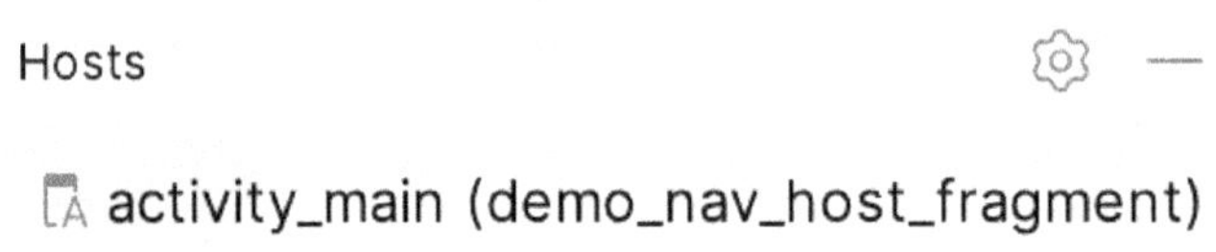

Figure 50-5

50.5 Adding Navigation Destinations

Remaining in the navigation graph, it is time to add the first destination. Click on the new destination button as shown in Figure 50-6 to select or create a destination:

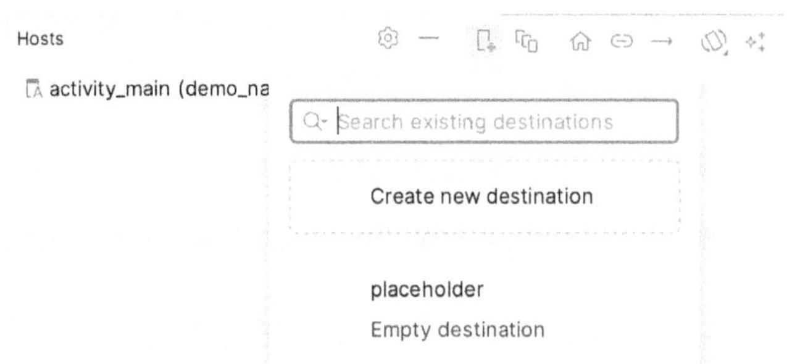

Figure 50-6

Next, select the *Create new destination* option from the menu. In the resulting dialog, select the Fragment (Blank) template, name the new fragment *FirstFragment* and the layout *fragment_first* before clicking on the Finish button. After a short delay while the project rebuilds, the new fragment will appear as a destination within the graph, as shown in Figure 50-7:

Figure 50-7

The home icon above the destination node indicates this is the *start destination*. This means the destination will be the first displayed when the NavHostFragment activity is created. To change the start destination to another, select that node in the graph and click on the home button in the toolbar.

Review the XML content of the navigation graph by switching the editor to Code mode:

```
<?xml version="1.0" encoding="utf-8"?>
<navigation xmlns:android="http://schemas.android.com/apk/res/android"
    xmlns:app="http://schemas.android.com/apk/res-auto"
    xmlns:tools="http://schemas.android.com/tools"
    android:id="@+id/navigation_graph"
    app:startDestination="@id/firstFragment">

    <fragment
        android:id="@+id/firstFragment"
        android:name="com.ebookfrenzy.navigationdemo.FirstFragment"
        android:label="fragment_first"
        tools:layout="@layout/fragment_first" />
</navigation>
```

Before any navigation can be performed, the graph needs at least one more destination. Repeat the above steps to add a fragment named *SecondFragment* with the layout file named *fragment_second*. The new fragment will appear as another destination within the graph, as shown in Figure 50-8:

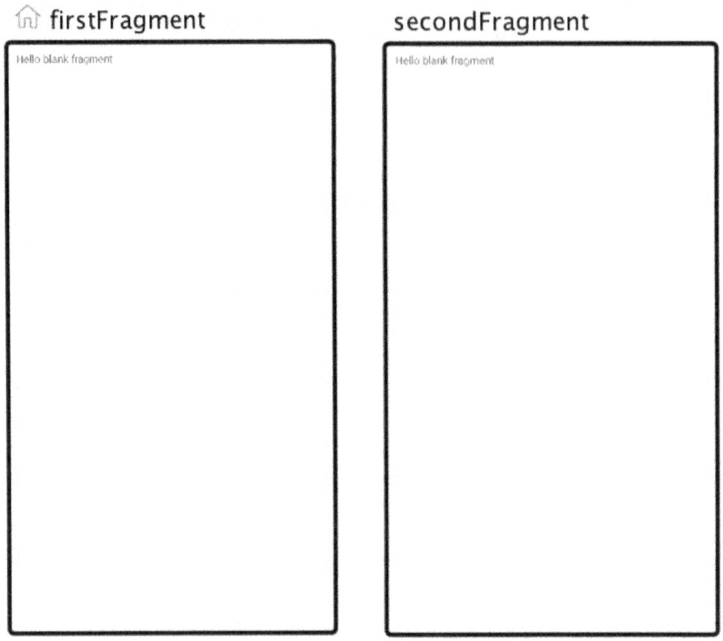

Figure 50-8

50.6 Designing the Destination Fragment Layouts

Before adding actions to navigate between destinations, now is a good time to add some user interface components to the two destination fragments in the graph. Begin by double-clicking on the firstFragment destination so that the *fragment_first.xml* file loads into the layout editor, then select and delete the default TextView instance. Within the Component Tree panel, right-click on the FrameLayout entry and select the *Convert from FrameLayout to ConstraintLayout* menu option, accepting the default settings in the resulting conversion dialog:

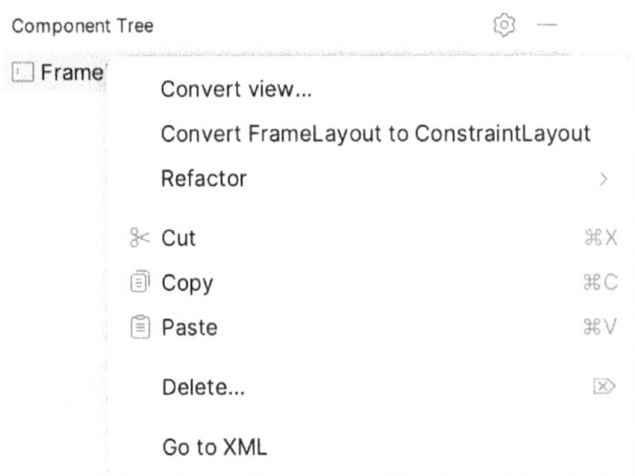

Figure 50-9

Using the Attributes tool window, change the ID of the ConstraintLayout to *constraintLayout*, then drag and drop Button and Plain Text EditText widgets onto the layout so that it resembles that shown in Figure 50-10 below:

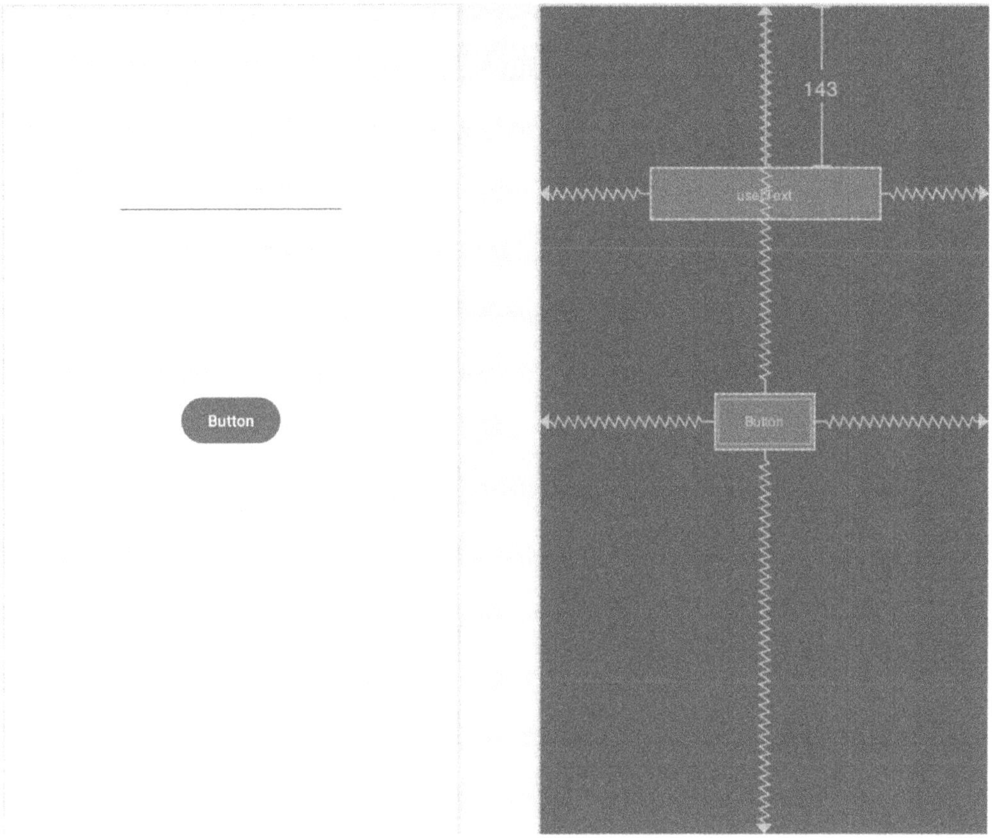

Figure 50-10

Once the views are correctly positioned, click on the *Infer constraints* button in the toolbar to add any missing constraints to the layout. Select the EditText view and use the Attributes tool window to delete the default "Name" text and change the widget's ID to *userText*. Next, change the button text property to read "Navigate" and extract it to a string resource.

Return to the *navigation_graph.xml* file and double-click on the secondFragment destination to load the *fragment_second.xml* file into the layout editor. Select and delete the default TextView instance and repeat the above steps to convert the FrameLayout to a ConstraintLayout, changing the id to *constraintLayout2*. Next, drag and drop a new TextView widget to position it in the center of the layout and click on the *Infer constraints* button to add any missing constraints. With the new TextView selected, use the Attributes panel to change the ID to *argText*.

50.7 Adding an Action to the Navigation Graph

Now that the two destinations have been added to the graph and the corresponding user interface layouts are designed, the project needs a way for the user to navigate from the first fragment to the second. This will be achieved by adding an action to the graph, which can then be referenced from within the app code.

To establish an action connection with the first fragment as the origin and the second fragment as the destination, open the navigation graph and hover the mouse pointer over the vertical center of the right-hand edge of the firstFragment destination so that a circle appears as highlighted in Figure 50-11:

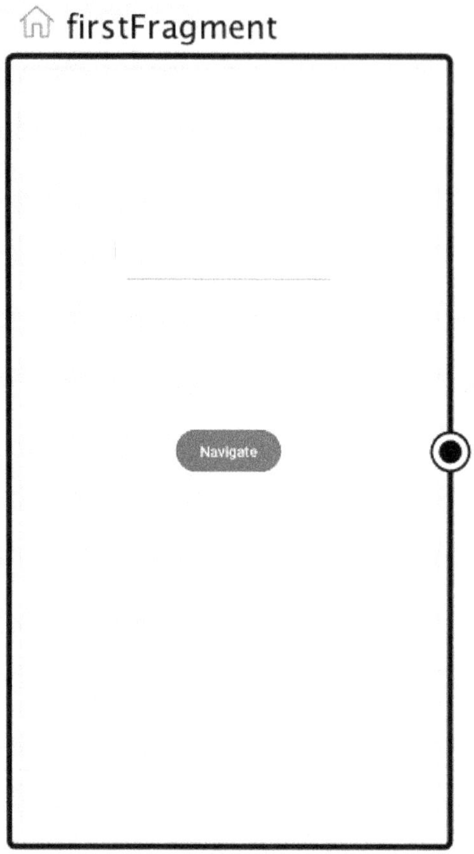

Figure 50-11

Click within the circle and drag the resulting line to the secondFragment destination:

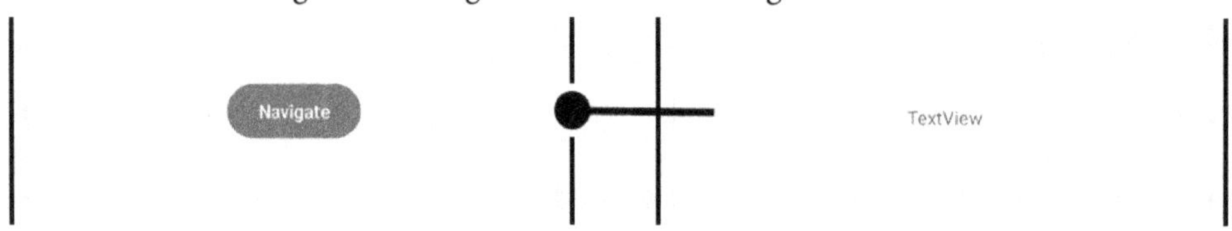

Figure 50-12

Release the line to establish the action connection between the origin and destination, at which point the line will change into an arrow, as shown in Figure 50-13:

Figure 50-13

An action connection may be deleted anytime by selecting it and pressing the keyboard Delete key. With the arrow selected, review the properties available within the Attributes tool window and change the ID to *mainToSecond*. This is the ID by which the action will be referenced within the code. Switch the editor to Code mode and note that the action is now included within the XML:

```
<?xml version="1.0" encoding="utf-8"?>
<navigation xmlns:android="http://schemas.android.com/apk/res/android"
    xmlns:app="http://schemas.android.com/apk/res-auto"
    xmlns:tools="http://schemas.android.com/tools"
    android:id="@+id/navigation_graph"
    app:startDestination="@id/firstFragment">

    <fragment
        android:id="@+id/firstFragment"
        android:name="com.ebookfrenzy.navigationdemo.FirstFragment"
        android:label="fragment_first"
        tools:layout="@layout/fragment_first" >
        <action
            android:id="@+id/mainToSecond"
            app:destination="@id/secondFragment" />
    </fragment>
    <fragment
        android:id="@+id/secondFragment"
        android:name="com.ebookfrenzy.navigationdemo.SecondFragment"
        android:label="fragment_second"
        tools:layout="@layout/fragment_second" />
</navigation>
```

50.8 Implement the OnFragmentInteractionListener

Before adding code to trigger the action, the MainActivity class must be modified to implement the OnFragmentInteractionListener interface. This interface was generated within the Fragment classes when the blank fragments were created within the navigation graph editor. To conform to the interface, the activity needs a method named *onFragmentInteraction()* to implement communication between the fragment and the activity.

Edit the *MainActivity.kt* file and modify it so that it reads as follows:

```
.
.
import android.net.Uri

class MainActivity : AppCompatActivity(),
                     SecondFragment.OnFragmentInteractionListener {
.
.
    override fun onFragmentInteraction(uri: Uri) {
    }
}
```

If Android Studio reports that OnFragmentInteractionListener is undefined (some versions of Android Studio add it automatically, while others do not), edit the *SecondFragment.kt* file and add the following:

```
.
.
```

```
import android.net.Uri
.
.
class SecondFragment : Fragment() {
.
.
   interface OnFragmentInteractionListener {
        // TODO: Update argument type and name
        fun onFragmentInteraction(uri: Uri)
    }
.
.
```

50.9 Adding View Binding Support to the Destination Fragments

Since we will access some views in the fragment layouts, we must modify the current code to enable view binding support. Begin by editing the *FirstFragment.kt* file and making the following changes:

```
.
.
import com.ebookfrenzy.navigationdemo.databinding.FragmentFirstBinding

class FirstFragment : Fragment() {
.
.
    private var _binding: FragmentFirstBinding? = null
    private val binding get() = _binding!!

    override fun onCreateView(
        inflater: LayoutInflater, container: ViewGroup?,
        savedInstanceState: Bundle?
    ): View {

        return inflater.inflate(R.layout.fragment_first, container, false)
        _binding = FragmentFirstBinding.inflate(inflater, container, false)
        return binding.root
    }

    override fun onDestroyView() {
        super.onDestroyView()
        _binding = null
    }
.
.
```

Repeat the above steps for the *SecondFragment.kt* file, referencing FragmentSecondBinding.

50.10 Triggering the Action

Now that the action has been added to the navigation graph, the next step is to add some code within the first fragment to trigger the action when the Button widget is clicked. Locate the *FirstFragment.kt* file, load it into the code editor, and override the *onViewCreated()* method to obtain a reference to the button instance and to configure an onClickListener instance to be called when the user clicks the button:

```
.
.
import androidx.navigation.Navigation
.
.
class FirstFragment : Fragment() {
.
.
    override fun onViewCreated(view: View, savedInstanceState: Bundle?) {
        super.onViewCreated(view, savedInstanceState)

        binding.button.setOnClickListener {
            Navigation.findNavController(it).navigate(
                R.id.mainToSecond)
        }
    }
}
```

The above code obtains a reference to the navigation controller and calls the *navigate()* method on that instance, passing through the resource ID of the navigation action as an argument.

Compile and run the app and verify that clicking the button in the first fragment transitions to the second fragment.

As an alternative to this approach to setting up a listener, the Navigation class also includes a method named *createNavigateOnClickListener()* which provides a more efficient way of setting up a listener and navigating to a destination. The same result can be achieved, therefore, using the following single line of code to initiate the transition:

```
binding.button.setOnClickListener(Navigation.createNavigateOnClickListener(
                                    R.id.mainToSecond, null))
```

50.11 Passing Data Using Safeargs

The next objective is to pass the text entered into the EditText view in the first fragment to the second fragment, where it will be displayed on the TextView widget. As outlined in the previous chapter, the Android Navigation component supports two approaches to passing data. This chapter will make use of type-safe argument passing.

The first step in using safeargs is to add the safeargs plugin to the Gradle build configuration. Using the Project tool window, locate and edit the *Gradle Scripts -> libs.versions.toml* file as follows:

```
.
.
[libraries]
androidx-navigation-safe-args-gradle-plugin = { module = "androidx.
navigation:navigation-safe-args-gradle-plugin", version.ref =
```

```
"navigationFragmentKtx" }
.
.
```

Next, edit project-level *build.gradle.kts* file (*Gradle Scripts -> build.gradle.kts (Project: NavigationDemo)*) to add the plugin dependency as follows:

```
// Top-level build file where you can add configuration options common to all sub-projects/modules.
buildscript {
    dependencies {
        classpath(libs.androidx.navigation.safe.args.gradle.plugin)
    }
}
```

Next, edit the module level *build.gradle.kts* file (*Gradle Scripts -> build.gradle.kts (Module :app)*) to apply the plugin as follows and resync the project:

```
plugins {
    alias(libs.plugins.android.application)
    id ("androidx.navigation.safeargs")
}
```

The next step is to define any arguments that will be received by the destination, which, in this case, is the second fragment. Edit the navigation graph, select the secondFragment destination, and locate the Arguments section within the Attributes tool window. Click on the + button (highlighted in Figure 50-14) to add a new argument to the destination:

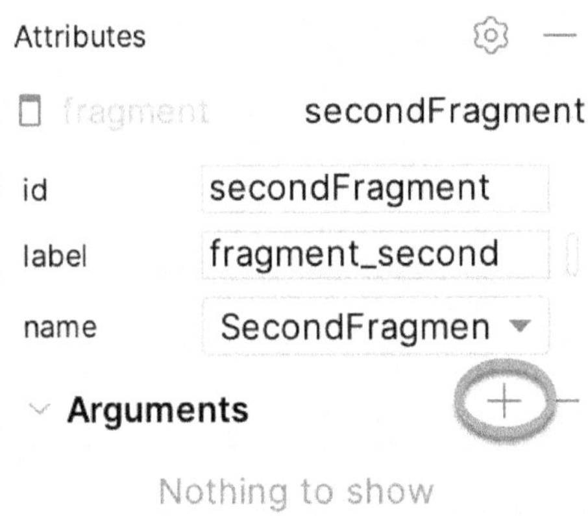

Figure 50-14

After the + button has been clicked, a dialog will appear into which the argument name, type, and default value need to be entered. Name the argument *message*, set the type to *String*, enter *No Message* into the default value field, and click the Add button:

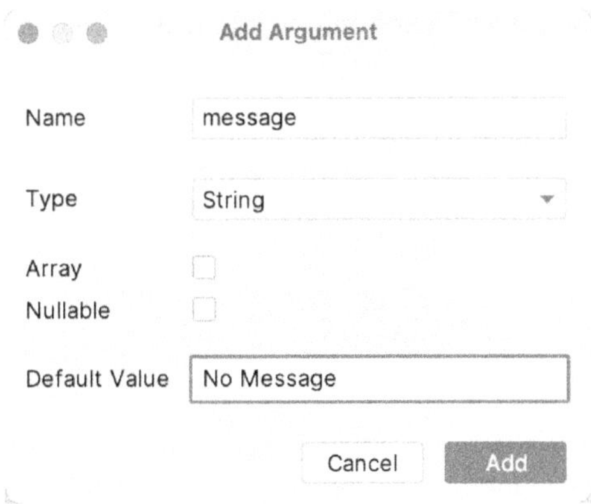

Figure 50-15

The newly configured argument will appear in the secondFragment element of the *navigation_graph.xml* file as follows:

```
<fragment
    android:id="@+id/secondFragment"
    android:name="com.ebookfrenzy.navigationdemo.SecondFragment"
    android:label="fragment_second"
    tools:layout="@layout/fragment_second" >
    <argument
        android:name="message"
        app:argType="string"
        android:defaultValue="No Message" />
</fragment>
```

The next step is to add code to the *FirstFragment.kt* file to extract the text from the EditText view and pass it to the second fragment during the navigation action. This will involve using some special navigation classes generated automatically by the safeargs plugin. Currently, the navigation involves the FirstFragment class, the SecondFragment class, a navigation action named *mainToSecond*, and an argument named *message*.

When the project is built, the safeargs plugin will generate the following additional classes that can be used to pass and receive arguments during navigation.

- **FirstFragmentDirections** - This class represents the origin for the navigation action (named using the class name of the navigation origin with "Directions" appended to the end) and provides access to the action object.
- **ActionMainToSecond** - The class representing the action used to perform the transition (named based on the ID assigned to the action within the navigation graph file prefixed with "Action"). This class contains a setter method for each argument configured on the destination. For example, since the second fragment destination contains an argument named *message*, the class includes a method named *setMessage()*. Once configured, an instance of this class is then passed to the *navigate()* method of the navigation controller to navigate to the destination.
- **SecondFragmentArgs** - The class used in the destination fragment to access the arguments passed from the origin (named using the class name of the navigation destination with "Args" appended to the end). This class includes a getter method for each of the arguments passed to the destination (i.e., *getMessage()*)

Using these classes, the *onClickListener* code within the *onViewCreated()* method of the *FirstFragment.kt* file can be modified as follows to extract the current text from the EditText widget, apply it to the action and initiate the transition to the second fragment:

```
binding.button.setOnClickListener {
    val action: FirstFragmentDirections.MainToSecond  =
                        FirstFragmentDirections.mainToSecond()

    action.message = binding.userText.text.toString()
    Navigation.findNavController(it).navigate(action)
}
```

The above code obtains a reference to the action object, sets the message argument string using the *setMessage()* method, and then calls the *navigate()* method of the navigation controller, passing through the action object. If Android Studio reports FirstFragmentDirections as undefined, rebuild the project using the *Build -> Make Project* menu option to generate the class.

All that remains is to modify the *SecondFragment.kt* class file to receive the argument after the navigation has been performed and display it on the TextView widget. For this example, the code to achieve these tasks will be added using an *onStart()* lifecycle method. Edit the *SecondFragment.kt* file and add this method so that it reads as follows:

```
override fun onStart() {
    super.onStart()
    arguments?.let {
        val args = SecondFragmentArgs.fromBundle(it)
        binding.argText.text = args.message
    }
}
```

The code in the above method begins by obtaining a reference to the TextView widget. Next, the *fromBundle()* method of the SecondFragmentArgs class is called to extract the SecondFragmentArgs object received from the origin. Since the argument in this example was named *message* in the *navigation_graph.xml* file, the corresponding *getMessage()* method is called on the args object to obtain the string value. This string is then displayed on the TextView widget.

Compile and run the app and enter some text before clicking on the Button widget. When the second fragment destination appears, the TextView should display the text entered in the first fragment, indicating that the data was successfully passed between navigation destinations.

50.12 Summary

This chapter has provided a practical example of implementing Android app navigation using the Navigation Architecture Component and the Android Studio navigation graph editor. Topics covered included the creation of a navigation graph containing both existing and new destination fragments, embedding a navigation host fragment within an activity layout, writing code to trigger navigation events, and passing arguments between destinations using the safeargs plugin.

Chapter 51

51. Working with the Floating Action Button and Snackbar

One of the objectives of this chapter is to provide an overview of the concepts of material design. Originally introduced as part of Android 5.0, material design is a set of design guidelines that dictate how the Android user interface, and that of the apps running on Android, appear and behave.

As part of implementing the material design concepts, Google also introduced the Android Design Support Library. This library contains several components that allow many of the key features of material design to be built into Android applications. Two of these components, the floating action button and the Snackbar, will also be covered in this chapter before introducing many of the other components in subsequent chapters.

51.1 The Material Design

The principles of material design define the overall appearance of the Android environment. Material design was created by the Android team at Google and dictates that the elements that make up the user interface of Android and the apps that run on it appear and behave in a certain way in terms of behavior, shadowing, animation, and style. One of the tenets of the material design is that the elements of a user interface appear to have physical depth and a sense that items are constructed in layers of physical material. A button, for example, appears to be raised above the surface of the layout where it resides through shadowing effects. Pressing the button causes the button to flex and lift as though made of a thin material that ripples when released.

Material design also dictates the layout and behavior of many standard user interface elements. A key example is how the app bar located at the top of the screen should appear and how it should behave in relation to scrolling activities taking place within the main content of the activity.

Material design covers a wide range of areas, from recommended color styles to how objects are animated. A full description of the material design concepts and guidelines can be found online at the following link and is recommended reading for all Android developers:

https://material.io/design/introduction

51.2 The Design Library

Many of the building blocks needed to implement Android applications that adopt material design principles are contained within the Android Design Support Library. This library contains a collection of user interface components that can be included in Android applications to implement much of the look, feel, and behavior of material design. Two of the components from this library, the floating action button and Snackbar, will be covered in this chapter, while others will be introduced in later chapters.

51.3 The Floating Action Button (FAB)

The floating action button appears to float above the surface of the user interface of an app. It generally promotes the most common action within a user interface screen. A floating action button could be placed on a screen to allow the user to add an entry to a list of contacts or to send an email from within the app. Figure 51-1, for example, highlights the floating action button that allows the user to add a new contact within the standard Android Contacts app:

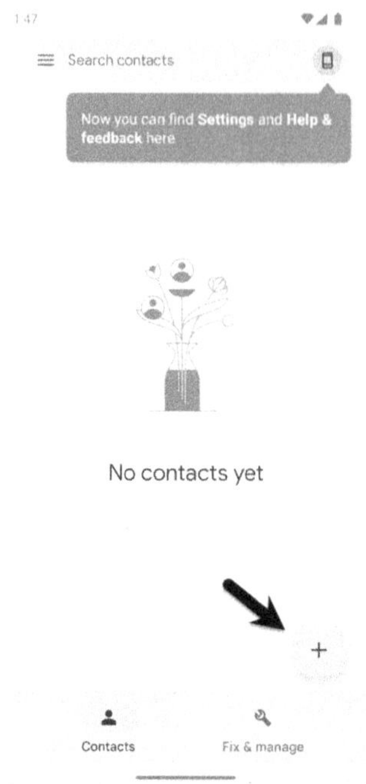

Figure 51-1

Several rules should be followed when using floating action buttons to conform with the material design guidelines. Floating action buttons must be circular and can be either 56 x 56dp (Default) or 40 x 40dp (Mini) in size. The button should be positioned a minimum of 16dp from the edge of the screen on phones and 24dp on desktops and tablet devices. Regardless of the size, the button must contain an interior icon that is 24x24dp in size, and it is recommended that each user interface screen have only one floating action button.

Floating action buttons can be animated or designed to morph into other items when touched. For example, a floating action button could rotate when tapped or morph into another element, such as a toolbar or panel listing related actions.

51.4 The Snackbar

The Snackbar component provides a way to present the user with information as a panel at the bottom of the screen, as shown in Figure 51-2. Snackbar instances contain a brief text message and an optional action button that will perform a task when tapped by the user. Once displayed, a Snackbar will either timeout automatically or can be removed manually by the user via a swiping action. During the appearance of the Snackbar, the app will continue to function and respond to user interactions normally.

Figure 51-2

In the remainder of this chapter, an example application will be created that uses the basic features of the floating action button and Snackbar to add entries to a list of items.

51.5 Creating the Example Project

Select the *New Project* option from the welcome screen and, within the resulting new project dialog, choose the Basic Views Activity template before clicking on the Next button.

Enter *FabExample* into the Name field and specify *com.ebookfrenzy.fabexample* as the package name. Before clicking on the Finish button, change the Minimum API level setting to API 26: Android 8.0 (Oreo) and the Language menu to Kotlin.

51.6 Reviewing the Project

Since the Basic Views Activity template was selected, the activity contains four layout files. The *activity_main.xml* file consists of a CoordinatorLayout manager containing entries for an app bar, a Material toolbar, and a floating action button.

The *content_main.xml* file represents the layout of the content area of the activity and contains a NavHostFragment instance. This file is embedded into the *activity_main.xml* file via the following include directive:

```
<include layout="@layout/content_main" />
```

The floating action button element within the *activity_main.xml* file reads as follows:

```
<com.google.android.material.floatingactionbutton.FloatingActionButton
    android:id="@+id/fab"
    android:layout_width="wrap_content"
    android:layout_height="wrap_content"
    android:layout_gravity="bottom|end"
    android:layout_marginEnd="@dimen/fab_margin"
    android:layout_marginBottom="16dp"
    app:srcCompat="@android:drawable/ic_dialog_email" />
```

This declares that the button is to appear in the bottom right-hand corner of the screen with margins represented by the *fab_margin* identifier in the *values/dimens.xml* file (which, in this case, is set to 16dp). The XML further declares that the interior icon for the button is to take the form of the standard drawable built-in email icon.

The blank template has also configured the floating action button to display a Snackbar instance when tapped by the user. The code to implement this can be found in the *onCreate()* method of the *MainActivity.kt* file and reads as follows:

```
binding.fab.setOnClickListener { view ->
    Snackbar.make(view, "Replace with your own action", Snackbar.LENGTH_LONG)
        .setAction("Action", null).show()
}
```

The code accesses the floating action button via the view binding and adds an onClickListener handler to be called when the button is tapped. This method displays a Snackbar instance configured with a message but no actions.

When the project is compiled and run, the floating action button will appear at the bottom of the screen, as shown in Figure 51-3:

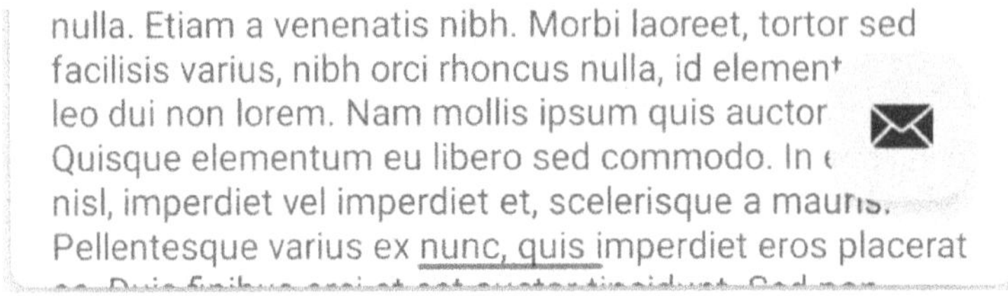

Figure 51-3

Tapping the floating action button will trigger the onClickListener handler method causing the Snackbar to appear at the bottom of the screen:

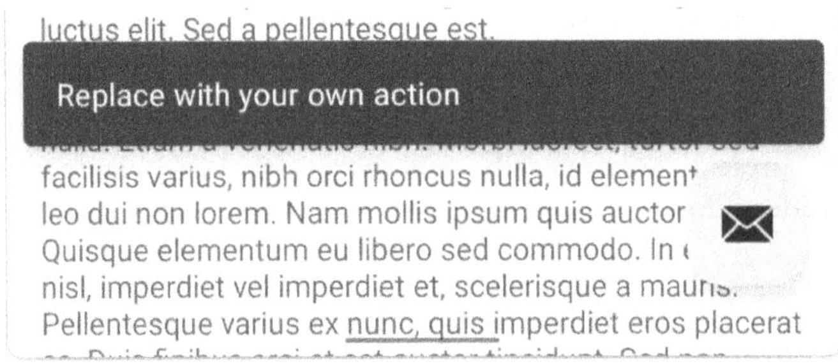

Figure 51-4

51.7 Removing Navigation Features

As *"A Guide to the Android Studio Layout Editor Tool"* outlines, the Basic Views Activity template contains multiple fragments and buttons to navigate from one fragment to the other. These features are unnecessary for this tutorial and will cause problems later if not removed. Before moving ahead with the tutorial, modify the project as follows:

1. Within the Project tool window, navigate to and double-click on the *app -> res -> navigation -> nav_graph.xml* file to load it into the navigation editor.

2. Select the SecondFragment entry in the Component Tree panel within the editor and tap the keyboard delete key to remove it from the graph.

3. Locate and delete the *SecondFragment.kt* (*app -> kotlin+java -> <package name> -> SecondFragment*) and *fragment_second.xml* (*app -> res -> layout -> fragment_second.xml*) files.

4. Locate the *FirstFragment.kt* file, double-click on it to load it into the editor, and remove the code from the *onViewCreated()* method so that it reads as follows:

```
override fun onViewCreated(view: View, savedInstanceState: Bundle?) {
    super.onViewCreated(view, savedInstanceState)

    binding.buttonFirst.setOnClickListener {
        findNavController().navigate(R.id.action_FirstFragment_to_SecondFragment)
    }
}
```

51.8 Changing the Floating Action Button

Since the objective of this example is to configure the floating action button to add entries to a list, the email icon currently displayed on the button needs to be changed to something more indicative of the action being performed. The icon that will be used for the button is named *ic_add_entry.png* and can be found in the *project_icons* folder of the sample code download available from the following URL:

https://www.payloadbooks.com/product/quailkotlin

Locate this image in the file system navigator for your operating system and copy the image file. Right-click on the *app -> res -> drawable* entry in the Project tool window and select Paste from the menu to add the file to the folder:

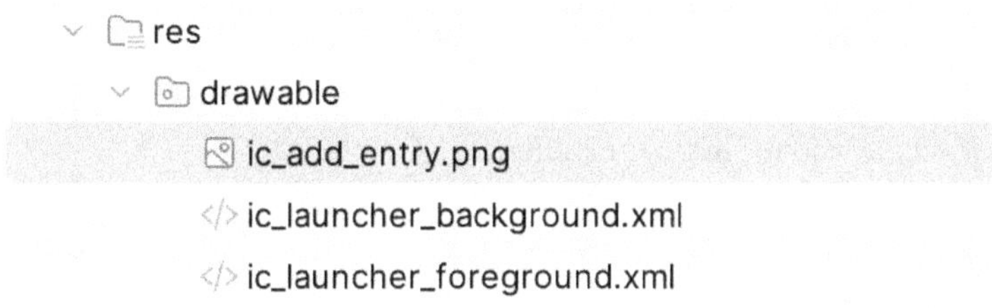

Figure 51-5

Next, edit the *activity_main.xml* file and change the image source for the icon from *@android:drawable/ic_dialog_email* to *@drawable/ic_add_entry* as follows:

```
<com.google.android.material.floatingactionbutton.FloatingActionButton
    android:id="@+id/fab"
    android:layout_width="wrap_content"
    android:layout_height="wrap_content"
    android:layout_gravity="bottom|end"
    android:layout_margin="@dimen/fab_margin"
    android:layout_marginBottom="16dp"
    app:srcCompat="@drawable/ic_add_entry" />
```

Within the layout preview, the interior icon for the button will have changed to a plus sign.

We can also make the floating action button do just about anything when clicked by adding code to the OnClickListener. The following changes to the *MainActivity.kt* file, for example, calls a method named *displayMessage()* to display a toast message each time the button is clicked:

```
.
.
import android.widget.Toast
.
.
binding.fab.setOnClickListener { view ->
    displayMessage("Fab clicked")
    Snackbar.make(view, "Replace with your own action", Snackbar.LENGTH_LONG)
        .setAction("Action", null).show()
}
.
.
fun displayMessage(message: String) {
    Toast.makeText(this@MainActivity,message,Toast.LENGTH_SHORT).show()
}
```

51.9 Adding an Action to the Snackbar

An action may also be added to the Snackbar, which performs a task when tapped by the user. Edit the *MainActivity.kt* file and modify the Snackbar creation code to add an action titled "My Action" configured with an onClickListener named *actionOnClickListener* which, in turn, displays a toast message:

```
binding.fab.setOnClickListener { view ->
    displayMessage("FAB clicked")
    Snackbar.make(view, "Action complete", Snackbar.LENGTH_LONG)
        .setAction("My Action", actionOnClickListener).show()
}
```

Within the *MainActivity.kt* file, add the listener handler:

```
.
.
import android.view.View
.
.
var actionOnClickListener: View.OnClickListener = View.OnClickListener { view ->
    displayMessage("Action clicked")
    Snackbar.make(view, "Action complete", Snackbar.LENGTH_LONG)
            .setAction("My Action", null).show()
}
```

Run the app and tap the floating action button, at which point both the toast message and Snackbar should appear. While the Snackbar is visible, tap the My Action button in the Snackbar and verify that the text on the Snackbar changes to "Action Complete":

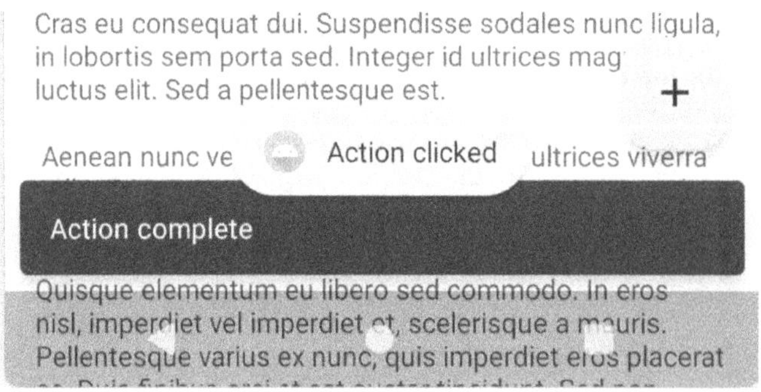

Figure 51-6

51.10 Summary

Before working through an example project that uses these features, this chapter has provided a general overview of material design, the floating action button, and the Snackbar.

The floating action button and the Snackbar are part of Android's material design approach to user interface implementation. The floating action button provides a way to promote the most common action within a particular screen of an Android application. The Snackbar provides a way for an application to present information to the user and allow the user to act upon it.

52. Creating a Tabbed Interface using the TabLayout Component

The previous chapter outlined the concept of material design in Android. It introduced two of the components provided by the design support library in the form of the floating action button and the Snackbar. This chapter will demonstrate how to use another of the design library components, the TabLayout, which can be combined with the ViewPager class to create a tab-based interface within an Android activity.

52.1 An Introduction to the ViewPager2

Although not part of the design support library, ViewPager2 is a useful companion class when used with the TabLayout component to implement a tabbed user interface. The primary role of ViewPager2 is to allow the user to flip through different pages of information where a layout fragment most typically represents each page. The fragments associated with ViewPager2 are managed by an instance of the FragmentStateAdapter class.

At a minimum, the pager adapter assigned to ViewPager2 must implement two methods. The first, named *getItemCount()*, must return the total number of page fragments to be displayed to the user. The second method, *createFragment()*, is passed a page number and must return the corresponding fragment object ready to be presented to the user.

52.2 An Overview of the TabLayout Component

As previously discussed, TabLayout is one of the components introduced in material design and is included in the design support library. The purpose of the TabLayout is to present the user with a row of tabs that can be selected to display different pages to the user. The tabs can be fixed or scrollable, whereby the user can swipe left or right to view more tabs than will currently fit on the display. The information displayed on a tab can be text-based, an image, or a combination of text and images. Figure 52-1, for example, shows the tab bar for an app consisting of four tabs displaying images:

Figure 52-1

Figure 52-2, on the other hand, shows a TabLayout configuration consisting of four tabs displaying text in a scrollable configuration:

Figure 52-2

The remainder of this chapter will work through creating an example project that demonstrates the TabLayout component together with a ViewPager2 and four fragments.

52.3 Creating the TabLayoutDemo Project

Select the *New Project* option from the welcome screen and, within the resulting new project dialog, choose the Basic Views Activity template before clicking on the Next button.

Enter *TabLayoutDemo* into the Name field and specify *com.ebookfrenzy.tablayoutdemo* as the package name. Before clicking on the Finish button, change the Minimum API level setting to API 26: Android 8.0 (Oreo) and the Language menu to Kotlin.

Once the project has been created, load the *content_main.xml* file into the Layout Editor tool, select the *nav_host_fragment_content_main* object, and then delete it. Since we will not be using the navigation features of the Basic Views Activity template, edit the *MainActivity.kt* file and modify the *onCreate()* method to remove the navigation code:

```
override fun onCreate(savedInstanceState: Bundle?) {
    super.onCreate(savedInstanceState)

    binding = ActivityMainBinding.inflate(layoutInflater)
    setContentView(binding.root)

    setSupportActionBar(binding.toolbar)

    val navController = findNavController(R.id.nav_host_fragment_content_main)
    appBarConfiguration = AppBarConfiguration(navController.graph)
    setupActionBarWithNavController(navController, appBarConfiguration)

    binding.fab.setOnClickListener { view ->
        Snackbar.make(view, "Replace with your own action", Snackbar.LENGTH_LONG)
            .setAnchorView(R.id.fab)
            .setAction("Action", null).show()
    }
}
```

Finally, delete the *onSupportNavigateUp()* method:

```
override fun onSupportNavigateUp(): Boolean {
    val navController = findNavController(R.id.nav_host_fragment_content_main)
    return navController.navigateUp(appBarConfiguration)
            || super.onSupportNavigateUp()
}
```

52.4 Creating the First Fragment

Each tab on the TabLayout will display a different fragment when selected. Create the first of these fragments by right-clicking on the *app -> kotlin+java -> com.ebookfrenzy.tablayoutdemo* entry in the Project tool window and selecting the *New -> Fragment -> Fragment (Blank)* option. In the resulting dialog, enter *Tab1Fragment* into the *Fragment Name:* field and *fragment_tab1* into the *Fragment Layout Name:* field. Click on the *Finish* button to create the new fragment:

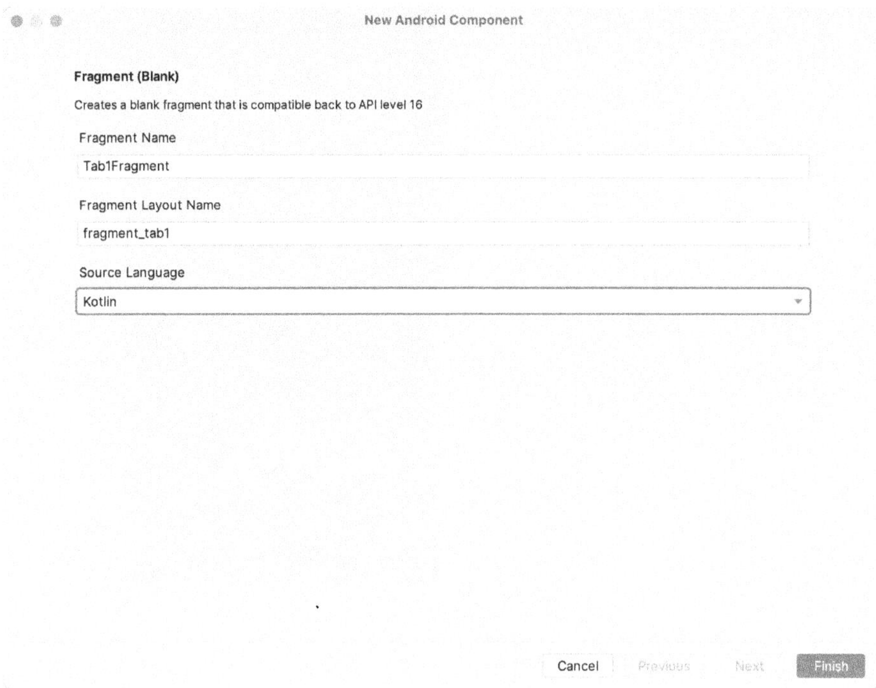

Figure 52-3

Edit the *Tab1Fragment.kt* file, and if Android Studio has not added one automatically, add an OnFragmentInteractionListener interface declaration as follows:

```
.
.
import android.net.Uri
.
.
    interface OnFragmentInteractionListener {
        fun onFragmentInteraction(uri: Uri)
    }
.
.
```

Load the newly created *fragment_tab1.xml* file (located under *app -> res -> layout*) into the Layout Editor tool, right-click on the FrameLayout entry in the Component Tree panel, and select the *Convert FrameLayout to ConstraintLayout* menu option. In the resulting dialog, verify that all conversion options are selected before clicking on OK. Change the ID of the layout to *constraintLayout*.

Once the layout has been converted to a ConstraintLayout, delete the TextView from the layout. From the Palette, locate the TextView widget and drag and drop it so it is positioned in the center of the layout. Edit the object's text property to read "Tab 1 Fragment", extract the string to a resource named *tab_1_fragment*, and click the *Infer Constraints* toolbar button. At this point, the layout should match that of Figure 52-4:

Figure 52-4

52.5 Duplicating the Fragments

So far, the project contains one of the four required fragments. It would be quicker to duplicate the first fragment instead of creating the remaining three fragments using the previous steps. Each fragment consists of a layout XML file and a Kotlin class file, each needing to be duplicated.

Right-click on the *fragment_tab1.xml* file in the Project tool window and select the Copy option from the resulting menu. Right-click on the *layout* entry, this time selecting the Paste option. Name the new layout file *fragment_tab2.xml* in the resulting dialog before clicking the OK button. Edit the new *fragment_tab2.xml* file and change the text on the Text View to "Tab 2 Fragment", following the usual steps to extract the string to a resource named *tab_2_fragment*.

To duplicate the Tab1Fragment class file, right-click on the class listed under *app -> kotlin+java -> com.ebookfrenzy.tablayoutdemo* and select Copy. Right-click on the *com.ebookfrenzy.tablayoutdemo* entry and select Paste. In the Copy Class dialog, enter Tab2Fragment into the *New name:* field and click OK. If a dialog appears reporting issues with ARG_PARAM values, click Continue to complete the copying.

Edit the new *Tab2Fragment.kt* file and modify the *onCreateView()* method to inflate the *fragment_tab2* layout file (only add the ARG_PARAM declarations if Android Studio reported them as inaccessible during the copying process):

```
.
.
private const val ARG_PARAM1 = "param1"
private const val ARG_PARAM2 = "param2"

class Tab2Fragment : Fragment() {
.
.
override fun onCreateView(inflater: LayoutInflater, container: ViewGroup?,
                          savedInstanceState: Bundle?): View? {
```

```
        // Inflate the layout for this fragment
        return inflater.inflate(R.layout.fragment_tab2, container, false)
    }
```

Perform the above duplication steps twice to create the fragment layout and class files for the remaining two fragments. On completion of these steps, the project structure should match that of Figure 52-5:

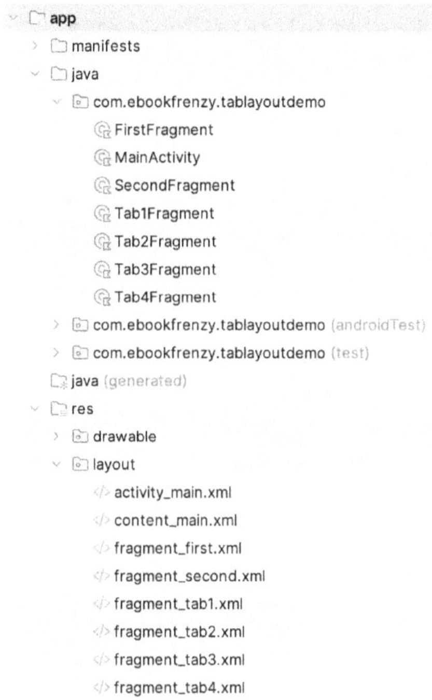

Figure 52-5

52.6 Adding the TabLayout and ViewPager2

With the fragment creation process now complete, the next step is to add the TabLayout and ViewPager2 to the main activity layout file. Edit the *activity_main.xml* file and add these elements as outlined in the following XML listing. Note that the TabLayout component is embedded into the AppBarLayout element while the ViewPager2 is placed after the AppBarLayout:

```
<?xml version="1.0" encoding="utf-8"?>
<androidx.coordinatorlayout.widget.CoordinatorLayout xmlns:android="http://
schemas.android.com/apk/res/android"
    xmlns:app="http://schemas.android.com/apk/res-auto"
    xmlns:tools="http://schemas.android.com/tools"
    android:layout_width="match_parent"
    android:layout_height="match_parent"
    android:fitsSystemWindows="true"
    tools:context=".MainActivity">

    <com.google.android.material.appbar.AppBarLayout
        android:layout_width="match_parent"
        android:layout_height="wrap_content"
        android:fitsSystemWindows="true">
```

```
        <com.google.android.material.appbar.MaterialToolbar
            android:id="@+id/toolbar"
            android:layout_width="match_parent"
            android:layout_height="?attr/actionBarSize" />

        <com.google.android.material.tabs.TabLayout
            android:id="@+id/tabLayout"
            android:layout_width="match_parent"
            android:layout_height="wrap_content"
            app:tabMode="fixed"
            app:tabGravity="fill"/>

    </com.google.android.material.appbar.AppBarLayout>

    <androidx.viewpager2.widget.ViewPager2
        android:id="@+id/view_pager"
        android:layout_width="match_parent"
        android:layout_height="match_parent"
        app:layout_behavior="@string/appbar_scrolling_view_behavior" />

    <include layout="@layout/content_main" />

    <com.google.android.material.floatingactionbutton.FloatingActionButton
        android:id="@+id/fab"
        android:layout_width="wrap_content"
        android:layout_height="wrap_content"
        android:layout_gravity="bottom|end"
        android:layout_marginEnd="@dimen/fab_margin"
        android:layout_marginBottom="16dp"
        app:srcCompat="@android:drawable/ic_dialog_email" />

</androidx.coordinatorlayout.widget.CoordinatorLayout>
```

52.7 Creating the Pager Adapter

This example will use the ViewPager2 approach to handling the fragments assigned to the TabLayout tabs, with ViewPager2 added to the layout resource file, a new class which subclasses FragmentStateAdapter needs to be added to the project to manage the fragments that will be displayed when the user selects the tab items.

Add a new class to the project by right-clicking on the *com.ebookfrenzy.tablayoutdemo* entry in the Project tool window and selecting the *New -> Kotlin Class/File* menu option. In the new class dialog, enter *TabPagerAdapter* into the *Name:* field, select the Class item in the list, and press the keyboard Return key.

Edit the *TabPagerAdapter.kt* file so that it reads as follows:

```
package com.ebookfrenzy.tablayoutdemo

import androidx.fragment.app.*
```

```
import androidx.viewpager2.adapter.FragmentStateAdapter

class TabPagerAdapter(fa: FragmentActivity,
                private var tabCount: Int): FragmentStateAdapter(fa) {

    override fun createFragment(position: Int): Fragment {
        return when (position) {
            0 -> Tab1Fragment()
            1 -> Tab2Fragment()
            2 -> Tab3Fragment()
            3 -> Tab4Fragment()
            else -> Tab1Fragment()
        }
    }

    override fun getItemCount(): Int {
        return tabCount
    }
}
```

The class is declared as extending the FragmentStateAdapter class, and a primary constructor is implemented, allowing the number of pages required to be passed to the class when an instance is created. The *createFragment()* method will be called when a specific page is required. A switch statement is used to identify the page number being requested and to return a corresponding fragment instance. Finally, the *getItemCount()* method returns the count value passed through when the object instance was created.

52.8 Performing the Initialization Tasks

The remaining tasks involve initializing the TabLayout, ViewPager2, and TabPagerAdapter instances and declaring the main activity class as implementing fragment interaction listeners for each of the four tab fragments. Edit the *MainActivity.kt* file so that it reads as follows:

```
package com.ebookfrenzy.tablayoutdemo
.
.
import android.net.Uri
import com.google.android.material.tabs.TabLayoutMediator

class MainActivity : AppCompatActivity(),
          Tab1Fragment.OnFragmentInteractionListener,
          Tab2Fragment.OnFragmentInteractionListener,
          Tab3Fragment.OnFragmentInteractionListener,
          Tab4Fragment.OnFragmentInteractionListener {

    override fun onCreate(savedInstanceState: Bundle?) {
.
.
        configureTabLayout()
    }
```

```
    private fun configureTabLayout() {
        repeat (4) {
            binding.tabLayout.addTab(binding.tabLayout.newTab())
        }

        val adapter = TabPagerAdapter(this, binding.tabLayout.tabCount)
        binding.viewPager.adapter = adapter

        TabLayoutMediator(binding.tabLayout, binding.viewPager) {
                                              tab, position ->
            tab.text = "Tab ${(position + 1)} Item"
        }.attach()
    }

    override fun onFragmentInteraction(uri: Uri) {
    }
.
.
}
```

The code begins by creating four tabs and adding them to the TabLayout instance as follows:

```
.
.
repeat (4) {
    binding.tabLayout.addTab(binding.tabLayout.newTab())
}
.
.
```

Next, an instance of the TabPagerAdapter class is created. Note that the code to create the TabPagerAdapter instance passes through the number of tabs assigned to the TabLayout component. The TabPagerAdapter instance is then assigned as the adapter for the ViewPager2 instance:

```
.
.
val adapter = TabPagerAdapter(this, binding.tabLayout.tabCount)
binding.viewPager.adapter = adapter
.
.
```

Finally, an instance of the TabLayoutMediator class is used to connect the TabLayout with the ViewPager2 object:

```
.
.
TabLayoutMediator(binding.tabLayout, binding.viewPager) { tab, position ->
    tab.text = "Tab ${(position + 1)} Item"
}.attach()
```

.

.

This class ensures that the TabLayout tabs remain synchronized with the currently selected fragment. This process involves ensuring that the correct text is displayed on each tab. In this case, the text is configured to read "Tab <*n*> Item" where <*n*> is replaced by the number of the currently selected tab.

52.9 Testing the Application

Compile and run the app on a device or emulator and make sure that selecting a tab causes the corresponding fragment to appear in the content area of the screen:

Figure 52-6

52.10 Customizing the TabLayout

The TabLayout in this example project is configured using *fixed* mode. This mode works well for a limited number of tabs with short titles. A greater number of tabs or longer titles can quickly become a problem when using fixed mode, as illustrated by Figure 52-7:

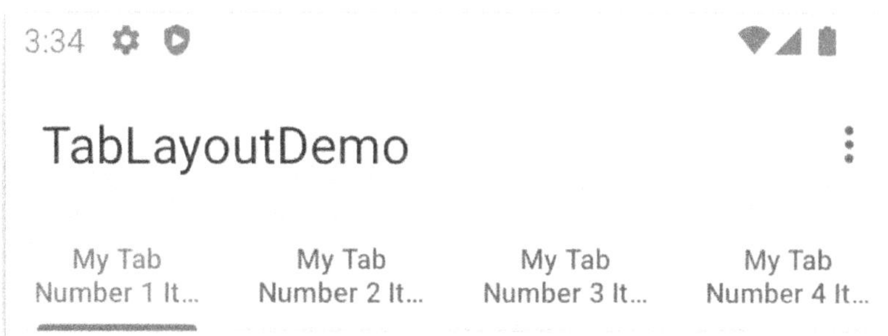

Figure 52-7

To fit the tabs into the available display width, the TabLayout has used multiple lines of text. Even so, the second line is truncated, making it impossible to see the full title. The best solution to this problem is to switch the TabLayout to scrollable mode. In this mode, the titles appear in full-length, single-line format allowing the user to swipe to scroll horizontally through the available items, as demonstrated in Figure 52-8:

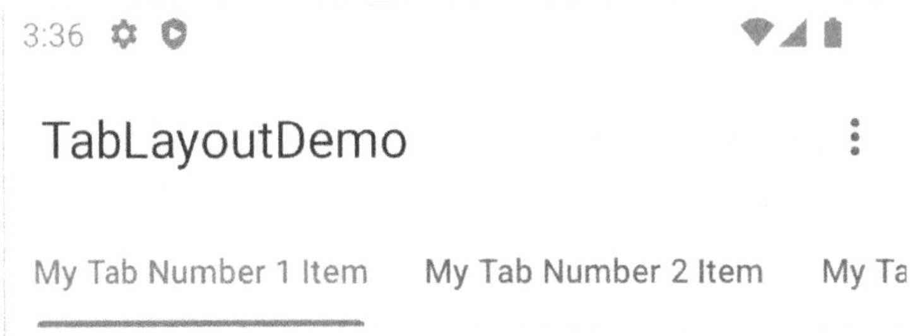

Figure 52-8

To switch a TabLayout to scrollable mode, change the *app:tabMode* property in the *activity_main.xml* layout resource file from "fixed" to "scrollable":

```
<android.support.design.widget.TabLayout
    android:id="@+id/tabLayout"
    android:layout_width="match_parent"
    android:layout_height="wrap_content"
    app:tabMode="scrollable"
    app:tabGravity="fill"/>
</android.support.design.widget.AppBarLayout>
```

When in fixed mode, the TabLayout may be configured to control how the tab items are displayed to take up the available space on the screen. This is controlled via the *app:tabGravity* property, the results of which are more noticeable on wider displays such as tablets in landscape orientation. When set to "fill", for example, the items will be distributed evenly across the width of the TabLayout, as shown in Figure 52-9:

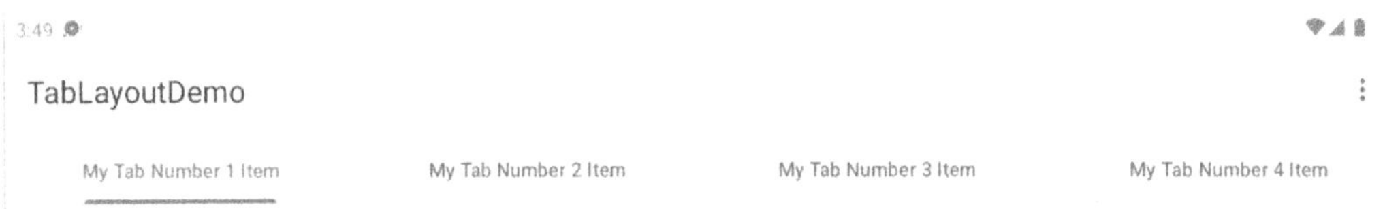

Figure 52-9

Changing the property value to "center" will cause the items to be positioned relative to the center of the tab bar:

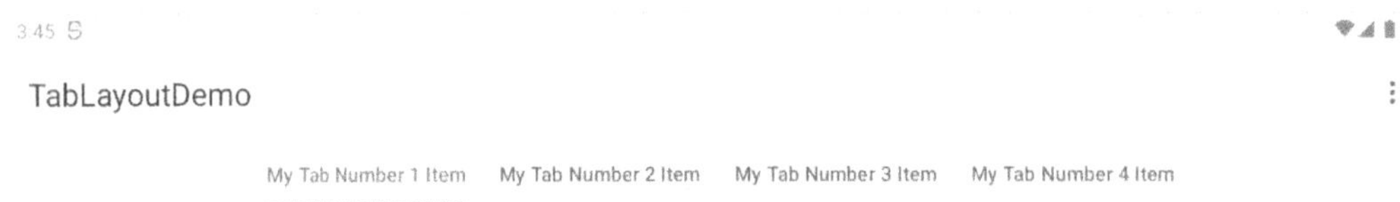

Figure 52-10

52.11 Summary

TabLayout is one of the components introduced in the Android material design implementation. The purpose of the TabLayout component is to present a series of tab items that display different content to the user when selected. The tab items can display text, images, or a combination. When combined with the ViewPager2 class and fragments, tab layouts can be created relatively easily, with each tab item selection displaying a different fragment.

53. Working with the RecyclerView and CardView Widgets

The RecyclerView and CardView widgets work together to provide scrollable lists of information to the user in which the information is presented as individual cards. Details of both classes will be covered in this chapter before working through the design and implementation of an example project.

53.1 An Overview of the RecyclerView

Much like the ListView class outlined in the chapter entitled *"Working with the Floating Action Button and Snackbar"*, the RecyclerView's purpose is to allow information to be presented to the user as a scrollable list. The RecyclerView, however, provides several advantages over the ListView. In particular, the RecyclerView is significantly more efficient in managing the views that make up a list, reusing existing views that makeup list items as they scroll off the screen instead of creating new ones (hence the name "recycler"). This increases the performance and reduces the resources a list uses, a feature of particular benefit when presenting large amounts of data to the user.

Unlike the ListView, the RecyclerView also provides a choice of three built-in layout managers to control how the list items are presented to the user:

- **LinearLayoutManager** – The list items are presented as horizontal or vertical scrolling lists.

Figure 53-1

- **GridLayoutManager** – The list items are presented in grid format. This manager is best used when the list items are of uniform size.

Figure 53-2

- **StaggeredGridLayoutManager** - The list items are presented in a staggered grid format. This manager is best used when the list items are of different sizes.

Figure 53-3

For situations where none of the three built-in managers provide the necessary layout, custom layout managers may be implemented by subclassing the RecyclerView.LayoutManager class.

Each list item displayed in a RecyclerView is created as an instance of the ViewHolder class. The ViewHolder instance contains everything necessary for the RecyclerView to display the list item, including the information to be displayed and the view layout used to display the item.

As with the ListView, the RecyclerView depends on an adapter to act as the intermediary between the RecyclerView instance and the data to be displayed to the user. The adapter is created as a subclass of the RecyclerView.Adapter class and must, at a minimum, implement the following methods, which will be called at various points by the RecyclerView object to which the adapter is assigned:

- **getItemCount()** – This method must return a count of the number of items to be displayed in the list.
- **onCreateViewHolder()** – This method creates and returns a ViewHolder object initialized with the view that is to be used to display the data. This view is typically created by inflating the XML layout file.
- **onBindViewHolder()** – This method is passed the ViewHolder object created by the *onCreateViewHolder()* method together with an integer value indicating the list item that is about to be displayed. Contained within the ViewHolder object is the layout assigned by the *onCreateViewHolder()* method. The *onBindViewHolder()* method is responsible for populating the views in the layout with the text and graphics corresponding to the specified item and returning the object to the RecyclerView, where it will be presented to the user.

Adding a RecyclerView to a layout is a matter of adding the appropriate element to the XML content layout file of the activity in which it is to appear. For example:

```
<?xml version="1.0" encoding="utf-8"?>
<androidx.constraintlayout.widget.ConstraintLayout
    xmlns:android="http://schemas.android.com/apk/res/android"
    xmlns:app="http://schemas.android.com/apk/res-auto"
    xmlns:tools="http://schemas.android.com/tools"
    android:layout_width="match_parent"
    android:layout_height="match_parent"
    app:layout_behavior="@string/appbar_scrolling_view_behavior"
    tools:context=".MainActivity"
    tools:showIn="@layout/activity_card_demo">

    <androidx.recyclerview.widget.RecyclerView
        android:id="@+id/recycler_view"
```

```
        android:layout_width="0dp"
        android:layout_height="0dp"
        app:layout_constraintBottom_toBottomOf="parent"
        app:layout_constraintEnd_toEndOf="parent"
        app:layout_constraintStart_toStartOf="parent"
        app:layout_constraintTop_toTopOf="parent"
        tools:listItem="@layout/card_layout" />

</androidx.constraintlayout.widget.ConstraintLayout>
.
.
```

The RecyclerView has been embedded into the CoordinatorLayout of a main activity layout file along with the AppBar and Toolbar in the above example. This provides some additional features, such as configuring the Toolbar and AppBar to scroll off the screen when the user scrolls up within the RecyclerView (a topic covered in more detail in the chapter entitled *"Working with the AppBar and Collapsing Toolbar Layouts"*).

53.2 An Overview of the CardView

The CardView class is a user interface view that allows information to be presented in groups using a card metaphor. Cards are usually presented in lists using a RecyclerView instance and may be configured to appear with shadow effects and rounded corners. Figure 53-4, for example, shows three CardView instances configured to display a layout consisting of an ImageView and two TextViews:

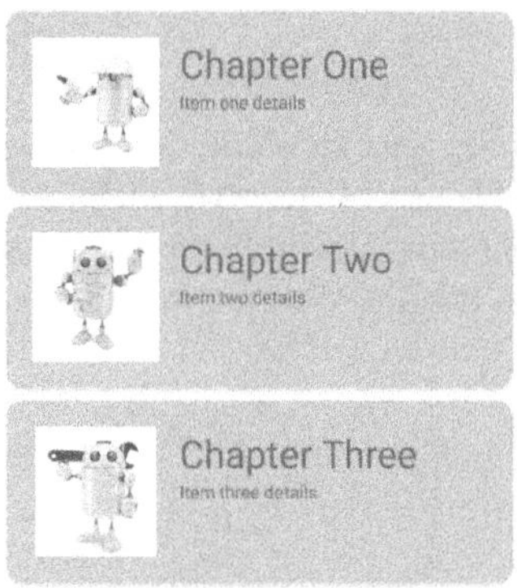

Figure 53-4

The user interface layout to be presented with a CardView instance is defined within an XML layout resource file and loaded into the CardView at runtime. The CardView layout can contain a layout of any complexity using the standard layout managers such as RelativeLayout and LinearLayout. The following XML layout file represents a card view layout consisting of a RelativeLayout and a single ImageView. The card is configured to be elevated to create a shadowing effect and to appear with rounded corners:

```
<?xml version="1.0" encoding="utf-8"?>
    <androidx.cardview.widget.CardView
        xmlns:card_view="http://schemas.android.com/apk/res-auto"
        xmlns:android="http://schemas.android.com/apk/res/android"
        android:id="@+id/card_view"
        android:layout_width="match_parent"
        android:layout_height="wrap_content"
        android:layout_margin="5dp"
```

```
        card_view:cardCornerRadius="12dp"
        card_view:cardElevation="3dp"
        card_view:contentPadding="4dp">

        <RelativeLayout
            android:layout_width="match_parent"
            android:layout_height="wrap_content"
            android:padding="16dp" >

            <ImageView
                android:layout_width="100dp"
                android:layout_height="100dp"
                android:id="@+id/item_image"
                android:layout_alignParentLeft="true"
                android:layout_alignParentTop="true"
                android:layout_marginRight="16dp" />
        </RelativeLayout>
</androidx.cardview.widget.CardView>
```

When combined with the RecyclerView to create a scrollable list of cards, the *onCreateViewHolder()* method of the recycler view inflates the layout resource file for the card, assigns it to the ViewHolder instance and returns it to the RecyclerView instance.

53.3 Summary

This chapter has introduced the Android RecyclerView and CardView components. The RecyclerView provides a resource-efficient way to display scrollable lists of views within an Android app. The CardView is useful when presenting groups of data (such as a list of names and addresses) in the form of cards. As previously outlined and demonstrated in the tutorial contained in the next chapter, RecyclerView and CardView are particularly useful when combined.

Chapter 54

54. An Android RecyclerView and CardView Tutorial

This chapter will create an example project that uses both the CardView and RecyclerView components to create a scrollable list of cards. The completed app will display a list of cards containing images and text. In addition to displaying the list of cards, the project will be implemented such that selecting a card causes messages to be displayed to the user indicating which card was tapped.

54.1 Creating the CardDemo Project

Select the *New Project* option from the welcome screen and, within the resulting new project dialog, choose the Basic Views Activity template before clicking on the Next button.

Enter *CardDemo* into the Name field and specify *com.ebookfrenzy.carddemo* as the package name. Before clicking on the Finish button, change the Minimum API level setting to API 26: Android 8.0 (Oreo) and the Language menu to Kotlin.

54.2 Modifying the Basic Views Activity Project

Since the Basic Views Activity was selected, the layout includes a floating action button which is not required for this project. Load the *activity_main.xml* layout file into the Layout Editor tool, select the floating action button, and tap the keyboard delete key to remove the object from the layout. Edit the *MainActivity.kt* file and remove the floating action button and navigation controller code from the onCreate method as follows:

```
override fun onCreate(savedInstanceState: Bundle?) {
    super.onCreate(savedInstanceState)

    binding = ActivityMainBinding.inflate(layoutInflater)
    setContentView(binding.root)

    setSupportActionBar(binding.toolbar)

    val navController = findNavController(R.id.nav_host_fragment_content_main)
    appBarConfiguration = AppBarConfiguration(navController.graph)
    setupActionBarWithNavController(navController, appBarConfiguration)

    binding.fab.setOnClickListener { view ->
        Snackbar.make(view, "Replace with your own action", Snackbar.LENGTH_LONG)
               .setAnchorView(R.id.fab)
               .setAction("Action", null).show()
    }
}
```

Also, remove the *onSupportNavigateUp()* method, then open the *content_main.xml* file and delete the *nav_host_fragment_content_main* object from the layout so that only the ConstraintLayout parent remains.

54.3 Designing the CardView Layout

The layout of the views contained within the cards will be defined within a separate XML layout file. Within the Project tool window, right-click on the *app -> res -> layout* entry and select the *New -> Layout Resource File* menu option. In the New Resource Dialog, enter *card_layout* into the *File name:* field and *androidx.cardview.widget.CardView* into the root element field before clicking on the *OK* button.

Load the *card_layout.xml* file into the Layout Editor tool, switch to Code mode, and modify the layout so that it reads as follows:

```
<?xml version="1.0" encoding="utf-8"?>
<androidx.cardview.widget.CardView
    xmlns:android="http://schemas.android.com/apk/res/android"
    xmlns:app="http://schemas.android.com/apk/res-auto"
    android:layout_width="match_parent"
    android:layout_height="wrap_content"
    android:id="@+id/card_view"
    android:layout_margin="5dp"
    app:cardBackgroundColor="#80B3EF"
    app:cardCornerRadius="12dp"
    app:cardElevation="3dp"
    app:contentPadding="4dp" >

    <androidx.constraintlayout.widget.ConstraintLayout
        android:id="@+id/relativeLayout"
        android:layout_width="match_parent"
        android:layout_height="wrap_content"
        android:padding="16dp">

        <ImageView
            android:id="@+id/itemImage"
            android:layout_width="100dp"
            android:layout_height="100dp"
            app:layout_constraintLeft_toLeftOf="parent"
            app:layout_constraintStart_toStartOf="parent"
            app:layout_constraintTop_toTopOf="parent" />

        <TextView
            android:id="@+id/itemTitle"
            android:layout_width="236dp"
            android:layout_height="39dp"
            android:layout_marginStart="16dp"
            android:textSize="30sp"
            app:layout_constraintLeft_toRightOf="@+id/itemImage"
            app:layout_constraintStart_toEndOf="@+id/itemImage"
            app:layout_constraintTop_toTopOf="parent" />
```

```
        <TextView
            android:id="@+id/itemDetail"
            android:layout_width="236dp"
            android:layout_height="16dp"
            android:layout_marginStart="16dp"
            android:layout_marginTop="8dp"
            app:layout_constraintLeft_toRightOf="@+id/itemImage"
            app:layout_constraintStart_toEndOf="@+id/itemImage"
            app:layout_constraintTop_toBottomOf="@+id/itemTitle" />
    </androidx.constraintlayout.widget.ConstraintLayout>
</androidx.cardview.widget.CardView>
```

54.4 Adding the RecyclerView

Select the *content_main.xml* layout file and drag a RecyclerView object from the *Containers* section of the palette onto the layout so that it is positioned in the center of the screen, where it should automatically resize to fill the entire screen. Use the *Infer constraints* toolbar button to add any missing layout constraints to the view. Using the Attributes tool window, change the ID of the RecyclerView instance to *recyclerView* and the layout_width and layout_height properties to *match_constraint*.

54.5 Adding the Image Files

In addition to the two TextViews, the card layout contains an ImageView on which the Recycler adapter has been configured to display images. Before the project can be tested, these images must be added. The images that will be used for the project are named *android_image_<n>.jpg* and can be found in the *project_icons* folder of the sample code download available from the following URL:

https://www.payloadbooks.com/product/quailkotlin

Locate these images in the file system navigator for your operating system and select and copy the eight images. Right click on the *app -> res -> drawable* entry in the Project tool window and select Paste to add the files to the folder:

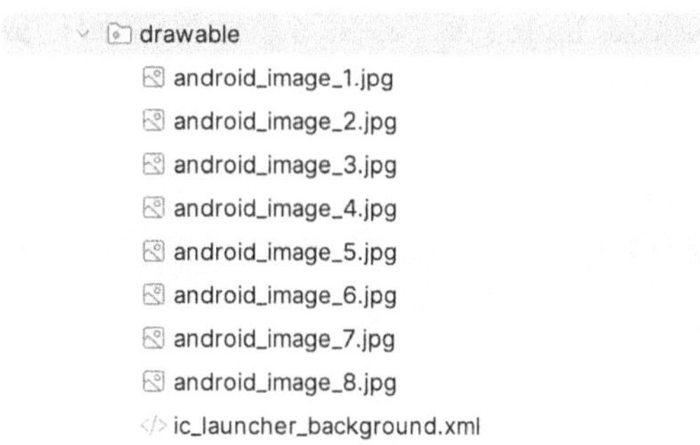

Figure 54-1

54.6 Creating the RecyclerView Adapter

As outlined in the previous chapter, the RecyclerView needs to have an adapter to handle the creation of the list items. Add this new class to the project by right-clicking on the *app -> kotlin+java -> com.ebookfrenzy.carddemo* entry in the Project tool window and selecting the *New -> Kotlin Class/File* menu option. In the new class dialog, enter *RecyclerAdapter* into the *Name* field and select *Class* from the list before tapping the Return keyboard key to create the new Kotlin class file.

Edit the new *RecyclerAdapter.kt* file to add some import directives and to declare that the class now extends *RecyclerView.Adapter*. Rather than create a separate class to provide the data to be displayed, some basic arrays will also be added to the adapter to act as the data for the app:

```
package com.ebookfrenzy.carddemo

import android.view.LayoutInflater
import android.widget.ImageView
import android.widget.TextView
import android.view.View
import android.view.ViewGroup

import androidx.recyclerview.widget.RecyclerView

class RecyclerAdapter : RecyclerView.Adapter<RecyclerAdapter.ViewHolder>() {

    private val titles = arrayOf("Chapter One",
            "Chapter Two", "Chapter Three", "Chapter Four",
            "Chapter Five", "Chapter Six", "Chapter Seven",
            "Chapter Eight")

    private val details = arrayOf("Item one details", "Item two details",
            "Item three details", "Item four details",
            "Item five details", "Item six details",
            "Item seven details", "Item eight details")

    private val images = intArrayOf(R.drawable.android_image_1,
                  R.drawable.android_image_2, R.drawable.android_image_3,
                  R.drawable.android_image_4, R.drawable.android_image_5,
                  R.drawable.android_image_6, R.drawable.android_image_7,
                  R.drawable.android_image_8)
}
```

Within the RecyclerAdapter class, we now need our own implementation of the ViewHolder class configured to reference the view elements in the *card_layout.xml* file. Remaining within the *RecyclerAdapter.kt*, file implement this class as follows:

```
.
.
class RecyclerAdapter : RecyclerView.Adapter<RecyclerAdapter.ViewHolder>() {
.
.
    inner class ViewHolder(itemView: View) : RecyclerView.ViewHolder(itemView) {

        var itemImage: ImageView
        var itemTitle: TextView
        var itemDetail: TextView
```

```
        init {
            itemImage = itemView.findViewById(R.id.itemImage)
            itemTitle = itemView.findViewById(R.id.itemTitle)
            itemDetail = itemView.findViewById(R.id.itemDetail)
        }
    }
.
.
}
.
.
```

The ViewHolder class contains an ImageView and two TextView variables together with a constructor method that initializes those variables with references to the three view items in the *card_layout.xml* file.

The next item to be added to the *RecyclerAdapter.kt* file is the implementation of the *onCreateViewHolder()* method:

```
override fun onCreateViewHolder(viewGroup: ViewGroup, i: Int): ViewHolder {
    val v = LayoutInflater.from(viewGroup.context)
            .inflate(R.layout.card_layout, viewGroup, false)
    return ViewHolder(v)
}
```

This method will be called by the RecyclerView to obtain a ViewHolder object. It inflates the view hierarchy *card_layout.xml* file and creates an instance of our ViewHolder class initialized with the view hierarchy before returning it to the RecyclerView.

The purpose of the *onBindViewHolder()* method is to populate the view hierarchy within the ViewHolder object with the data to be displayed. It is passed the ViewHolder object and an integer value indicating the list item that is to be displayed. This method should now be added, using the item number as an index into the data arrays. This data is then displayed on the layout views using the references created in the constructor method of the ViewHolder class:

```
override fun onBindViewHolder(viewHolder: ViewHolder, i: Int) {
    viewHolder.itemTitle.text = titles[i]
    viewHolder.itemDetail.text = details[i]
    viewHolder.itemImage.setImageResource(images[i])
}
```

The final requirement for the adapter class is an implementation of the *getItem()* method which, in this case, returns the number of items in the *titles* array:

```
override fun getItemCount(): Int {
    return titles.size
}
```

54.7 Initializing the RecyclerView Component

At this point, the project consists of a RecyclerView instance, an XML layout file for the CardView instances and an adapter for the RecyclerView. The last step before testing the progress so far is to initialize the RecyclerView with a layout manager, create an instance of the adapter and assign that instance to the RecyclerView object. For the purposes of this example, the RecyclerView will be configured to use the LinearLayoutManager layout option.

There is a slight complication here because we need to be able to use view binding to access the recyclerView component from within the MainActivity class. The problem is that recyclerView is contained within the *content_main.xml* layout file which is, in turn, included in the *activity_main.xml* file. To be able to reach down into the *content_main.xml* file, we need to assign it an id at the point that it is included. To do this, edit the *activity_main.xml* file and modify the *include* element so that it reads as follows:

```
.
.
   <include
        android:id="@+id/contentMain"
        layout="@layout/content_main" />
.
.
```

With an id assigned to the included file, the recyclerView component can be accessed using the following binding:

```
binding.contentMain.recyclerView
```

Now edit the *MainActivity.kt* file and modify the *onCreate()* method to implement the initialization code:

```
package com.ebookfrenzy.carddemo
.
.
import androidx.recyclerview.widget.LinearLayoutManager
import androidx.recyclerview.widget.RecyclerView

class MainActivity : AppCompatActivity() {
.
.
    private var layoutManager: RecyclerView.LayoutManager? = null
    private var adapter: RecyclerView.Adapter<RecyclerAdapter.ViewHolder>? = null

    override fun onCreate(savedInstanceState: Bundle?) {
.
.
        layoutManager = LinearLayoutManager(this)
        binding.contentMain.recyclerView.layoutManager = layoutManager
        adapter = RecyclerAdapter()
        binding.contentMain.recyclerView.adapter = adapter
    }
.
.
}
```

54.8 Testing the Application

Compile and run the app on a physical device or emulator session and scroll through the different card items in the list:

Figure 54-2

54.9 Responding to Card Selections

The last phase of this project is to make the cards in the list selectable so that clicking on a card triggers an event within the app. For this example, the cards will be configured to present a message on the display when tapped by the user. To respond to clicks, the ViewHolder class needs to be modified to assign an onClickListener on each item view. Edit the *RecyclerAdapter.kt* file and modify the ViewHolder class declaration so that it reads as follows:

```
.
.
    inner class ViewHolder(itemView: View) : RecyclerView.ViewHolder(itemView) {

        var itemImage: ImageView
        var itemTitle: TextView
        var itemDetail: TextView

        init {
            itemImage = itemView.findViewById(R.id.item_image)
            itemTitle = itemView.findViewById(R.id.item_title)
            itemDetail = itemView.findViewById(R.id.item_detail)

            itemView.setOnClickListener { v: View  ->

            }
        }
    }
.
.
}
```

Within the body of the onClick handler, code can now be added to display a message indicating that the card has been clicked. Given that the actions performed as a result of a click will likely depend on which card was tapped, it is also important to identify the selected card. This information can be obtained via a call to the *getAdapterPosition()* method of the *RecyclerView.ViewHolder* class. Remaining within the *RecyclerAdapter.kt* file, add code to the *onClick* handler so it reads as follows:

```
.
.
import com.google.android.material.snackbar.Snackbar
.
.
itemView.setOnClickListener { v: View  ->
    val position: Int = adapterPosition

    Snackbar.make(v, "Click detected on item $position",
            Snackbar.LENGTH_LONG).setAction("Action", null).show()
}
```

The last task is to enable the material design ripple effect that appears when items are tapped within Android applications. This involves the addition of some properties to the declaration of the CardView instance in the *card_layout.xml* file as follows:

```
<?xml version="1.0" encoding="utf-8"?>
<androidx.cardview.widget.CardView
    xmlns:android="http://schemas.android.com/apk/res/android"
    xmlns:card_view="http://schemas.android.com/apk/res-auto"
    android:layout_width="match_parent"
    android:layout_height="match_parent"
    android:id="@+id/card_view"
    android:layout_margin="5dp"
    app:cardBackgroundColor="#80B3EF"
    app:cardCornerRadius="12dp"
    app:cardElevation="3dp"
    app:contentPadding="4dp"
    android:foreground="?selectableItemBackground"
    android:clickable="true" >
```

Run the app once again and verify that tapping a card in the list triggers both the standard ripple effect at the point of contact and the appearance of a Snackbar reporting the number of the selected item.

54.10 Summary

This chapter has worked through the steps involved in combining the CardView and RecyclerView components to display a scrollable list of card-based items. The example also covered the detection of clicks on list items, including the identification of the selected item and the enabling of the ripple effect visual feedback on the tapped CardView instance.

Chapter 55

55. Working with the AppBar and Collapsing Toolbar Layouts

In this chapter, we will explore how the app bar within an activity layout can be customized and made to react to the scrolling events occurring within other screen views. Using the CoordinatorLayout in conjunction with the AppBarLayout and CollapsingToolbarLayout containers, the app bar can be configured to display an image and to animate in and out of view. For example, an upward scrolling motion on a list can be configured so that the app bar recedes from view and reappears when a downward scrolling motion is performed.

Beginning with an overview of the elements that can comprise an app bar, this chapter will work through various examples of app bar configuration.

55.1 The Anatomy of an AppBar

The app bar is the area that appears at the top of the display when an app is running and can be configured to contain various items, including the status bar, toolbar, tab bar, and a flexible space area. Figure 55-1, for example, shows an app bar containing a status bar, toolbar, and tab bar:

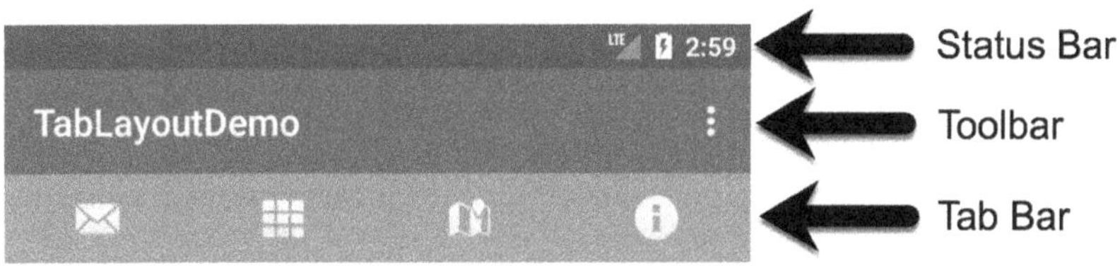

Figure 55-1

A blank background color can fill the flexible space area, or as shown in Figure 55-2, an image displayed on an ImageView object:

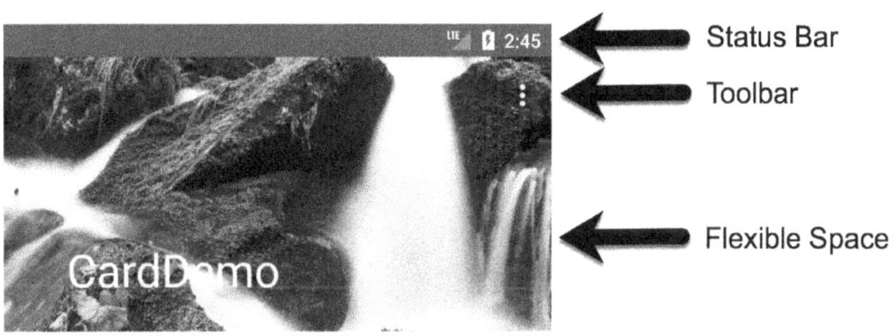

Figure 55-2

As will be demonstrated in the remainder of this chapter, if the main content area of the activity user interface layout contains scrollable content, the elements of the app bar can be configured to expand and contract as the content on the screen is scrolled.

55.2 The Example Project

For this example, changes will be made to the CardDemo project created in the earlier chapter entitled *"An Android RecyclerView and CardView Tutorial"*. Begin by launching Android Studio and loading this project.

Once the project has loaded, run the app and note when scrolling the list upwards that the toolbar remains visible, as shown in Figure 55-3:

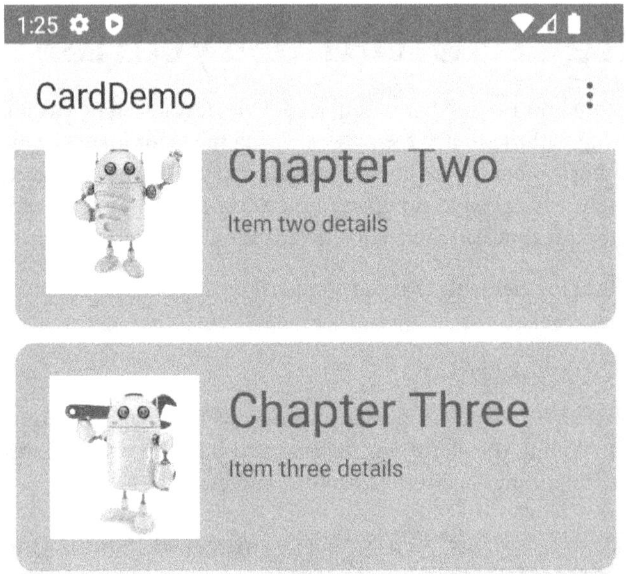

Figure 55-3

The first step is to make configuration changes so the toolbar contracts during an upward scrolling motion and then expands on a downward scroll.

55.3 Coordinating the RecyclerView and Toolbar

Load the *activity_main.xml* file into the Layout Editor tool, switch to Code mode, and review the XML layout design, the hierarchy of which is represented by the diagram in Figure 55-4:

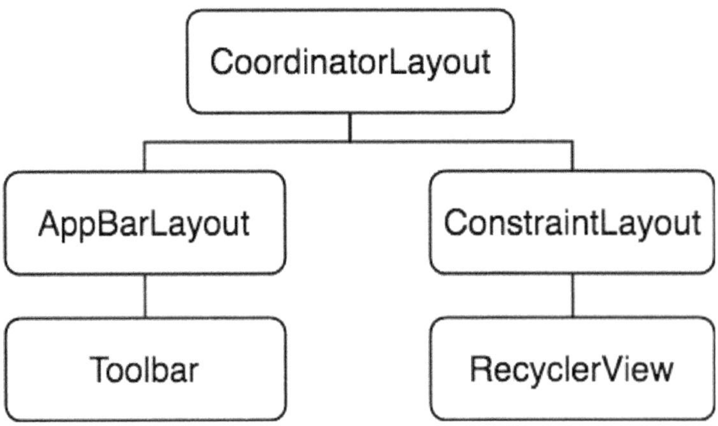

Figure 55-4

At the top level of the hierarchy is the CoordinatorLayout, which, as the name suggests, coordinates the interactions between the various child view elements it contains. As highlighted in *"Working with the Floating*

Action Button and Snackbar" for example, the CoordinatorLayout automatically slides the floating action button upwards to accommodate the appearance of a Snackbar when it appears, then moves the button back down after the bar is dismissed.

The CoordinatorLayout can similarly be used to cause elements of the app bar to slide in and out of view based on the scrolling action of certain views within the view hierarchy. One element within the layout hierarchy shown in Figure 55-4 is the ConstraintLayout. To achieve this coordinated behavior, it is necessary to set properties on the element on which scrolling takes place and the elements with which the scrolling is to be coordinated.

On the scrolling element (in this case, the RecyclerView), the *android:layout_behavior* property must be set to *appbar_scrolling_view_behavior*. Within the *content_main.xml* file, locate the top-level ConstraintLayout element and note that this property has been set by default:

```
<androidx.constraintlayout.widget.ConstraintLayout
    xmlns:android="http://schemas.android.com/apk/res/android"
    xmlns:app="http://schemas.android.com/apk/res-auto"
    xmlns:tools="http://schemas.android.com/tools"
    android:layout_width="match_parent"
    android:layout_height="match_parent"
    app:layout_behavior="@string/appbar_scrolling_view_behavior" >
```

Next, open the *activity_main.xml* file in the layout editor, switch to Code mode, and locate the AppBarLayout element. Note that the only child of AppBarLayout in the view hierarchy is the Toolbar. To make the toolbar react to the scroll events occurring in the RecyclerView, the *app:layout_scrollFlags* property must be set on this element. The value assigned to this property will depend on the nature of the interaction required and must consist of one or more of the following:

- **scroll** – Indicates that the view is to be scrolled off the screen. If this is not set, the view will remain pinned at the top of the screen during scrolling events.

- **enterAlways** – When used with the *scroll* option, an upward scrolling motion will cause the view to retract. Any downward scrolling motion in this mode will cause the view to reappear.

- **enterAlwaysCollapsed** – When set on a view, that view will not expand from the collapsed state until the downward scrolling motion reaches the limit of the list. If the *minHeight* property is set, the view will appear during the initial scrolling motion but only until the minimum height is reached. It will then remain at that height and will not expand fully until the top of the list is reached. Note that this option only works when used with both the *enterAlways* and *scroll* options. For example:

```
app:layout_scrollFlags="scroll|enterAlways|enterAlwaysCollapsed"
android:minHeight="20dp"
```

- **exitUntilCollapsed** – When set, the view will collapse during an upward scrolling motion until the minHeight threshold is met. At that point, it will remain at that height until the scroll direction changes.

For this example, the *scroll* and *enterAlways* options will be set on the Toolbar as follows:

```
<com.google.android.material.appbar.MaterialToolbar
    android:id="@+id/toolbar"
    android:layout_width="match_parent"
    android:layout_height="?attr/actionBarSize"
    app:layout_scrollFlags="scroll|enterAlways" />
```

With the appropriate properties set, rerun the app and make an upward scrolling motion in the RecyclerView list. This should cause the toolbar to collapse out of view (Figure 55-5). A downward scrolling motion should cause the toolbar to reappear.

Figure 55-5

55.4 Introducing the Collapsing Toolbar Layout

The CollapsingToolbarLayout container enhances the standard toolbar by providing a greater range of options and control over the collapsing of the app bar and its children in response to coordinated scrolling actions. The CollapsingToolbarLayout class is intended to be added as a child of the AppBarLayout. It provides features such as automatically adjusting the font size of the toolbar title as the toolbar collapses and expands. A *parallax* mode allows designated content in the app bar to fade from view as it collapses, while a *pin* mode allows elements of the app bar to remain in a fixed position during the contraction.

A *scrim* option is also available to designate the color to which the toolbar should transition during the collapse sequence.

To see these features in action, the app bar contained in the *activity_main.xml* file will be modified to use the CollapsingToolbarLayout class together with the addition of an ImageView to demonstrate the effect of parallax mode better. The new view hierarchy that makes use of the CollapsingToolbarLayout is represented by the diagram in Figure 55-6:

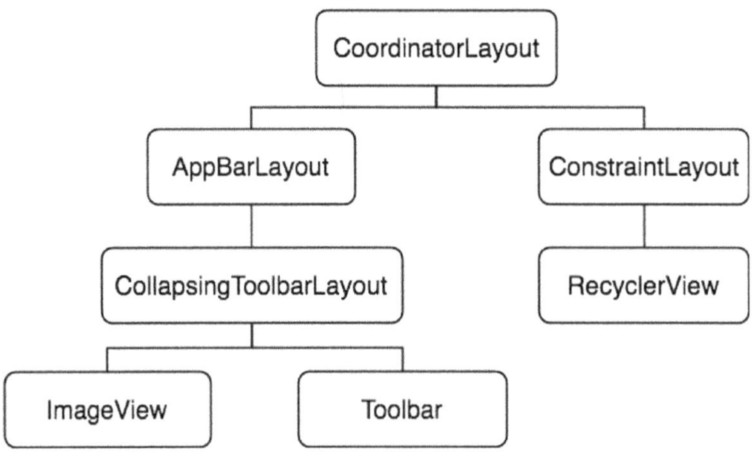

Figure 55-6

Load the *activity_main.xml* file into the Layout Editor tool in Code mode and modify the layout so that it reads as follows:

```
<?xml version="1.0" encoding="utf-8"?>
<androidx.coordinatorlayout.widget.CoordinatorLayout xmlns:android="http://
schemas.android.com/apk/res/android"
    xmlns:app="http://schemas.android.com/apk/res-auto"
    xmlns:tools="http://schemas.android.com/tools"
    android:layout_width="match_parent"
    android:layout_height="match_parent"
    android:fitsSystemWindows="true"
    tools:context=".MainActivity">

    <com.google.android.material.appbar.AppBarLayout
        android:layout_width="match_parent"
        android:layout_height="wrap_content"
        android:fitsSystemWindows="true">

        <com.google.android.material.appbar.CollapsingToolbarLayout
            android:id="@+id/collapsing_toolbar"
            android:layout_width="match_parent"
            android:layout_height="match_parent"
            app:layout_scrollFlags="scroll|enterAlways"
            android:fitsSystemWindows="true"
            app:expandedTitleMarginBottom="30dp"
            app:expandedTitleMarginStart="15dp"
            app:expandedTitleMarginEnd="64dp">

            <ImageView
                android:id="@+id/backdrop"
                android:layout_width="match_parent"
                android:layout_height="200dp"
                android:scaleType="centerCrop"
                android:fitsSystemWindows="true"
                app:layout_collapseMode="parallax"
                android:src="@drawable/appbar_image" />

            <com.google.android.material.appbar.MaterialToolbar
                android:id="@+id/toolbar"
                android:layout_width="match_parent"
                android:layout_height="?attr/actionBarSize"
                app:layout_scrollFlags="scroll|enterAlways"
                app:layout_collapseMode="pin" />
        </com.google.android.material.appbar.CollapsingToolbarLayout>

    </com.google.android.material.appbar.AppBarLayout>

    <include
```

```
        android:id="@+id/contentMain"
        layout="@layout/content_main" />

</androidx.coordinatorlayout.widget.CoordinatorLayout>
```

Using the file system navigator for your operating system, locate the *appbar_image.jpg* image file in the *project_icons* folder of the code sample download for the book and copy it. Right-click on the *app -> res -> drawable* entry in the Project tool window and select *Paste* from the resulting menu.

When run, the app bar should appear as illustrated in Figure 55-7:

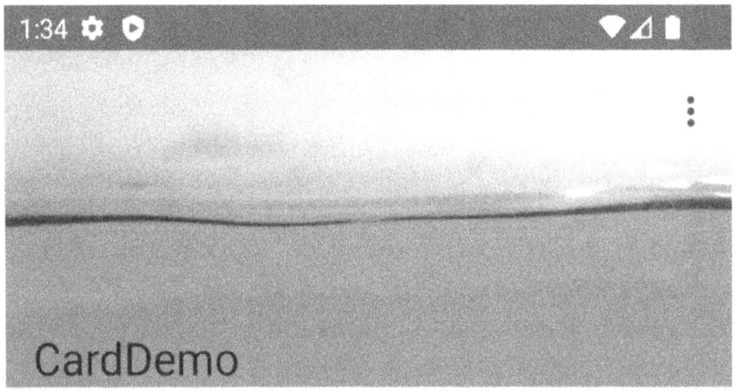

Figure 55-7

Scrolling the list upwards will cause the app bar to collapse gradually. During the contraction, the image will fade to the color defined by the scrim property while the title text font size reduces at a corresponding rate until only the toolbar is visible:

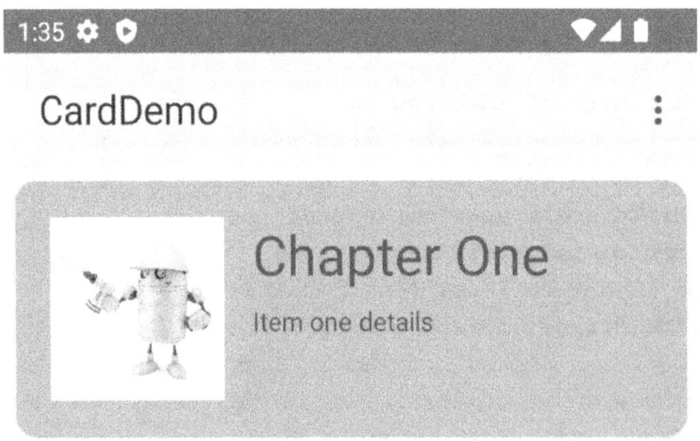

Figure 55-8

The toolbar has remained visible during the initial stages of the scrolling motion (the toolbar will also recede from view if the upward scrolling motion continues) as the flexible area collapses because the toolbar element in the *activity_main.xml* file was configured to use pin mode:

```
app:layout_collapseMode="pin"
```

Had the collapse mode been set to parallax, the toolbar would have retracted along with the image view.

Continuing the upward scrolling motion will cause the toolbar also to collapse, leaving only the status bar visible:

Figure 55-9

Since the scroll flags property for the CollapsingToolbarLayout element includes the enterAlways option, a downward scrolling motion will cause the app bar to expand again.

To fix the toolbar in place so that it no longer recedes from view during the upward scrolling motion, replace *enterAlways* with *exitUntilCollapsed* in the *layout_scrollFlags* property of the CollapsingToolbarLayout element in the *activity_main.xml* file as follows:

```
<com.google.android.material.appbar.CollapsingToolbarLayout
    android:id="@+id/collapsing_toolbar"
    android:layout_width="match_parent"
    android:layout_height="match_parent"
    app:layout_scrollFlags="scroll|exitUntilCollapsed"
    android:fitsSystemWindows="true"
    app:expandedTitleMarginBottom="30dp"
    app:expandedTitleMarginStart="15dp"
    app:expandedTitleMarginEnd="64dp">
```

55.5 Changing the Title and Scrim Color

As a final task, edit the *MainActivity.kt* file and add some code to the *onCreate()* method to change the title text on the collapsing layout manager instance and to set a different scrim color (note that the scrim color may also be set within the layout resource file):

```
package com.ebookfrenzy.carddemo
.
.
import android.graphics.Color
.
.
class MainActivity : AppCompatActivity() {
.
.
    override fun onCreate(savedInstanceState: Bundle?) {
        WindowCompat.setDecorFitsSystemWindows(window, false)
        super.onCreate(savedInstanceState)

        binding = ActivityMainBinding.inflate(layoutInflater)
        setContentView(binding.root)
```

```
        setSupportActionBar(binding.toolbar)

        binding.collapsingToolbar.title = "My Toolbar Title"
        binding.collapsingToolbar.setContentScrimColor(Color.GREEN)

        layoutManager = LinearLayoutManager(this)
        binding.contentMain.recyclerView.layoutManager = layoutManager
        adapter = RecyclerAdapter()
        binding.contentMain.recyclerView.adapter = adapter
    }
.
.
}
```

Run the app one last time and note that the new title appears in the app bar and that scrolling now causes the toolbar to transition to green as it retracts from view.

55.6 Summary

The app bar at the top of most Android apps can consist of several elements, including a toolbar, tab layout, and image view. When embedded in a CoordinatorLayout parent, several different options are available to control how the app bar behaves in response to scrolling events in the main content of the activity. For greater control over this behavior, the CollapsingToolbarLayout manager provides a range of additional levels of control over how the app bar content expands and contracts relative to scrolling activity.

Chapter 56

56. An Overview of Android Intents

By this stage of the book, it should be clear that Android applications comprise one or more activities, among other things. However, an area that has yet to be covered in extensive detail is the mechanism by which one activity can trigger the launch of another activity. As outlined briefly in the chapter entitled *"The Anatomy of an Android App"*, this is achieved primarily using *Intents*.

Before working through some Android Studio-based example implementations of intents in the following chapters, this chapter aims to provide an overview of intents in the form of *explicit intents* and *implicit intents*, together with an introduction to *intent filters*.

56.1 An Overview of Intents

Intents (*android.content.Intent*) are the messaging system by which one activity can launch another activity. An activity can, for example, issue an intent to request the launch of another activity contained within the same application. Intents also go beyond this concept by allowing an activity to request the services of any other appropriately registered activity on the device for which permissions are configured. Consider, for example, an activity contained within an application that requires a web page to be loaded and displayed to the user. Rather than the application having to contain a second activity to perform this task, the code can send an intent to the Android runtime requesting the services of any activity that has registered the ability to display a web page. The runtime system will match the request to available activities on the device and either launch the activity that matches or, in the event of multiple matches, allow the user to decide which activity to use.

Intents also allow data transfer from the sending to the receiving activity. In the previously outlined scenario, for example, the sending activity would need to send the URL of the web page to be displayed to the second activity. Similarly, the receiving activity may be configured to return data to the sending activity when the required tasks are completed.

Though not covered until later chapters, it is also worth highlighting that, in addition to launching activities, intents are also used to launch and communicate with services and broadcast receivers.

Intents are categorized as either *explicit* or *implicit.*

56.2 Explicit Intents

An *explicit intent* requests the launch of a specific activity by referencing the target activity's component name (which is the class name). This approach is most common when launching an activity residing in the same application as the sending activity (since the class name is known to the developer).

An explicit intent is issued by creating an instance of the Intent class, passing through the activity context and the component name of the activity to be launched. A call is then made to the *startActivity()* method, passing the intent object as an argument. For example, the following code fragment issues an intent for the activity with the class name ActivityB to be launched:

```
val i = Intent(this, ActivityB::class.java)
startActivity(i)
```

Data may be transmitted to the receiving activity by adding it to the intent object before it is started via calls to the *putExtra()* method of the intent object. Data must be added in the form of key-value pairs. The following code extends the previous example to add String and integer values with the keys "myString" and "myInt" respectively, to the intent:

```
val i = Intent(this, ActivityB::class.java)
i.putExtra("myString", "This is a message for ActivityB")
i.putExtra("myInt", 100)

startActivity(i)
```

The target activity receives the data as part of a Bundle object which can be obtained via a call to *getIntent().getExtras()*. The *getIntent()* method of the Activity class returns the intent that started the activity, while the *getExtras()* method (of the Intent class) returns a Bundle object containing the data. For example, to extract the data values passed to ActivityB:

```
val extras = intent.extras ?: return

val myString = extras.getString("myString")
int myInt = extras.getInt("MyInt")
```

When using intents to launch other activities within the same application, those activities must be listed in the application manifest file. The following *AndroidManifest.xml* contents are correctly configured for an application containing activities named ActivityA and ActivityB:

```
<?xml version="1.0" encoding="utf-8"?>
<manifest xmlns:android="http://schemas.android.com/apk/res/android"
    package="com.ebookfrenzy.intent1.intent1" >

    <application
        android:icon="@mipmap/ic_launcher"
        android:label="@string/app_name" >
        <activity
            android:label="@string/app_name"
            android:name="com.ebookfrenzy.intent1.intent1.ActivityA" >
            <intent-filter>
              <action android:name="android.intent.action.MAIN" />
              <category android:name="android.intent.category.LAUNCHER" />
            </intent-filter>
        </activity>
        <activity
            android:name="ActivityB"
            android:label="ActivityB" >
        </activity>
    </application>
</manifest>
```

56.3 Returning Data from an Activity

As the example in the previous section stands, while data is transferred to ActivityB, there is no way for data to be returned to the first activity (which we will call ActivityA). This can, however, be achieved by launching ActivityB as a *sub-activity* of ActivityA. An activity is started as a sub-activity by creating an ActivityResultLauncher instance. An ActivityResultLauncher instance is created by a call to the *registerForActivityResult()* method and is passed a callback handler in the form of a lambda. This handler will be called and passed return data when the sub-activity returns. Once an ActivityResultLauncher instance has been created, it can be called with an intent parameter to launch the sub-activity. The code to create an ActivityResultLauncher instance typically reads as follows:

```
val startForResult = registerForActivityResult(
                ActivityResultContracts.StartActivityForResult()) {
                            result: ActivityResult ->
    if (result.resultCode == Activity.RESULT_OK) {
        val data = result.data
        data?.let {
            // Code to handle returned data
        }
    }
}
```

Once the launcher is ready, it can be called and passed the intent to be launched as follows:

```
val i = Intent(this, ActivityB::class.java)
.
.
startForResult(intent)
```

To return data to the parent activity, the sub-activity must implement the *finish()* method, the purpose of which is to create a new intent object containing the data to be returned and then call the *setResult()* method of the enclosing activity, passing through a *result code* and the intent containing the return data. The result code is typically *RESULT_OK*, or *RESULT_CANCELED*, but it may also be a custom value subject to the developer's requirements. If a sub-activity crashes, the parent activity will receive a *RESULT_CANCELED* result code.

The following code, for example, illustrates the code for a typical sub-activity *finish()* method:

```
override fun finish() {
    val data = Intent()

    data.putExtra("returnString1", "Message to parent activity")

    setResult(RESULT_OK, data)
    super.finish()
}
```

56.4 Implicit Intents

Unlike explicit intents, which reference the class name of the activity to be launched, implicit intents identify the activity to be launched by specifying the action to be performed and the type of data to be handled by the receiving activity. For example, an action type of ACTION_VIEW accompanied by the URL of a web page in the form of a URI object will instruct the Android system to search for and, subsequently, launch a web browser-capable activity. The following implicit intent will, when executed on an Android device, result in the designated web page appearing in a web browser activity:

```
val intent = Intent(Intent.ACTION_VIEW,
        Uri.parse("http://www.ebookfrenzy.com"))

startActivity(intent)
```

When an activity issues the above implicit intent, the Android system will search for activities on the device that have registered the ability to handle ACTION_VIEW requests on HTTP scheme data using a process referred to as *intent resolution*. Before the system launches an activity using an implicit intent, the user must either verify or enable that activity. If neither of these conditions has been met, the activity will not be launched by the intent. Before exploring these two options, we first need to talk about intent filters.

56.5 Using Intent Filters

Intent filters are the mechanism by which activities "advertise" supported actions and data handling capabilities to the Android intent resolution process. These declarations also include the settings required to perform the link verification process. The following *AndroidManifest.xml* file illustrates a configuration for an activity named *WebActivity* within an app named *MyWebView* with an appropriately configured intent filter:

```
<?xml version="1.0" encoding="utf-8"?>
.
.
    <application
        android:allowBackup="true"
        android:icon="@mipmap/ic_launcher"
        android:label="@string/app_name"
        android:roundIcon="@mipmap/ic_launcher_round"
        android:supportsRtl="true"
        android:theme="@style/Theme.MyWebView">
        <activity
            android:name="WebActivity"
            android:exported="true">
            <intent-filter android:autoVerify="true">
                <action android:name="android.intent.action.VIEW" />
                <category android:name="android.intent.category.BROWSABLE" />
                <category android:name="android.intent.category.DEFAULT" />
                <data android:scheme="https" />
                <data android:host="www.ebookfrenzy.com"/>
            </intent-filter>
        </activity>
    </application>
</manifest>
```

This manifest file configures the WebActivity activity to be launched in response to an implicit intent from another activity when the intent contains the *https://www.ebookfrenzy.com* URL. The following code, for example, would launch the WebActivity activity (assuming that the MyWebView app has been verified or enabled by the user as a support link):

```
val intent = Intent(Intent.ACTION_VIEW,
    Uri.parse("https://www.ebookfrenzy.com"))
startActivity(intent)
```

56.6 Automatic Link Verification

Using a web link to launch an activity on an Android device is considered a potential security hazard. To minimize this risk, the link used to launch an intent must either be automatically verified or manually added as a supported link on the device by the user. To enable automatic verification, the corresponding intent declaration in the target activity must set autoVerify to true as follows:

```
<intent-filter android:autoVerify="true">
.
.
</intent-filter>
```

Next, the link URL must be associated with the website on which the app link is based. This is achieved by creating a Digital Assets Link file named *assetlinks.json* and installing it within the website's *.well-known* folder.

A digital asset link file comprises a *relation* statement granting permission for a target app to be launched using the website's link URLs and a target statement declaring the companion app package name and SHA-256 certificate fingerprint for that project. A typical asset link file might, for example, read as follows:

```
[{
  "relation": ["delegate_permission/common.handle_all_urls"],
  "target": {
    "namespace": "android_app",
    "package_name": "com.ebookfrenzy.mywebview",
    "sha256_cert_fingerprints":
    ["<your certificate fingerprint here>"]
  }
}]
```

Note that you can either create this file manually or generate it using the online tool available at the following URL:

https://developers.google.com/digital-asset-links/tools/generator

When working with Android, the namespace value is always set to "android_app", while the package name corresponds to the app package to be launched by the intent. Finally, the certificate fingerprint is the hash code used to build the app. When you are testing an app, this will be the debug certificate contained within the *debug.keystore* file. On Windows systems, Android Studio stores this file at the following location:

```
\Users\<your user name>\.android\debug.keystore
```

On macOS and Linux systems, the file can be found at:

```
$HOME/.android/debug.keystore
```

Once you have located the file, the SHA 256 fingerprint can be obtained by running the following command in a terminal or command prompt window:

```
keytool -list -v -keystore <path to debug.keystore file here>
```

When prompted for a password, enter "android" after which output will appear, including the SHA 256 fingerprint:

```
Certificate fingerprints:
        SHA1: 11:E8:66:11:B6:94:3D:AA:7E:50:63:99:77:B8:6A:90:FF:B6:9C:6D
        SHA256: 7F:EE:E3:C8:38:41:C3:EA:11:56:83:94:2A:4C:D2:EA:A0:69:F8:96:D1:17
:77:02:46:EC:AD:6E:3C:64:A9:29
```

When you are ready to build your app's release version, you must ensure you add the release SHA 256 fingerprint to the asset file. Details on generating release keystore files are covered in the chapter entitled *"Creating, Testing, and Uploading an Android App Bundle"*. Once you have a release keystore file, run the above keytool command to access the fingerprint.

Once you have placed the digital asset file in the correct location on the website, install the app on a device or emulator and wait 30 seconds for the link to be verified. To check the verification status, run the following at a command or terminal prompt:

```
adb shell pm get-app-links --user cur com.example.mywebview
```

The resulting output should include confirmation that the link has been verified:

```
com.example.mywebview:
    ID: 0e399bca-bf58-4cfc-8c7b-d1a6c3b065ec
    Signatures: [7F:EE:E3:C8:38:41:C3:EA:11:56:83:94:2A:4C:D2:EA:A0:69:F8:96:D1:1
7:77:02:46:EC:AD:6E:3C:64:A9:29]
    Domain verification state:
      www.ebookfrenzy.com: verified
    User 0:
      Verification link handling allowed: true
      Selection state:
        Disabled:
          www.ebookfrenzy.com
```

You can also check the status from within the Settings app on the device or emulator using the following steps:

1. Launch the Settings app.
2. Select *Apps* from the main list.
3. Locate and select your app from the list of installed apps.
4. On the settings page for your app, choose the *Open by Default* option.

Choose the Open by Default option on your app's settings page.

Once displayed, the page should indicate that a link has been verified, as shown in Figure 56-1:

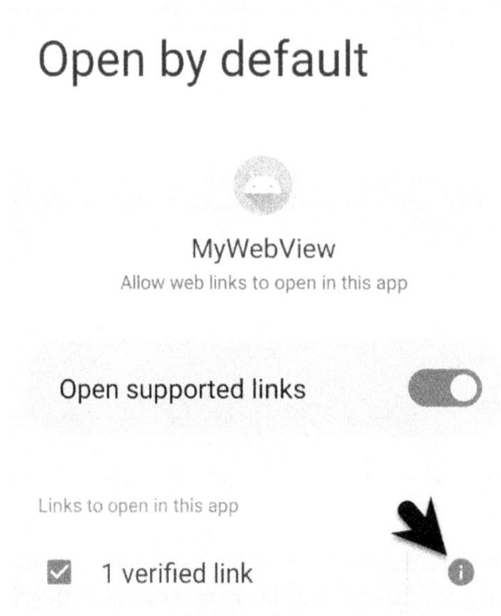

Figure 56-1

To review which links have been verified, tap on the info button indicated by the arrow in the above figure to display the following panel:

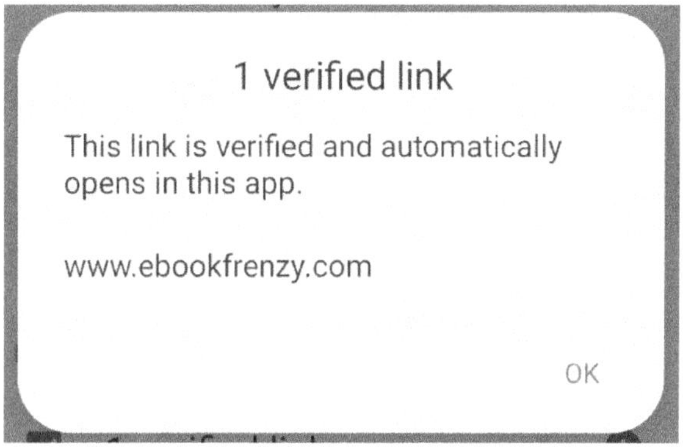

Figure 56-2

The *assetlinks.json* file can contain multiple digital asset links, allowing a single website to be associated with more than one app. If you cannot use auto link verification, add code to your app to prompt the user to enable the link manually.

56.7 Manually Enabling Links

Where it is not possible to auto-verify links using the steps outlined above, the only option is to request that the user manually enable app links. This involves launching the Open by Default screen of the Settings app for the target app where the user can enable the link.

Since the sudden appearance of the Open by Default screen may be confusing to the average user, it is recommended that an explanatory dialog be displayed before launching the Settings app.

To provide the user with the option to enable a link manually, the following code needs to be executed before attempting to launch the intent:

```
.
.
// Code here to display a dialog explaining that the link needs to be enabled
.
.
val intent = Intent(
    Settings.ACTION_APP_OPEN_BY_DEFAULT_SETTINGS,
    Uri.parse("package:com.ebookfrenzy.mywebview"))

startActivity(intent)
.
.
```

The above example code will display the Open by Default settings screen for our target MyWebView app, where the user can click on the Add Link button:

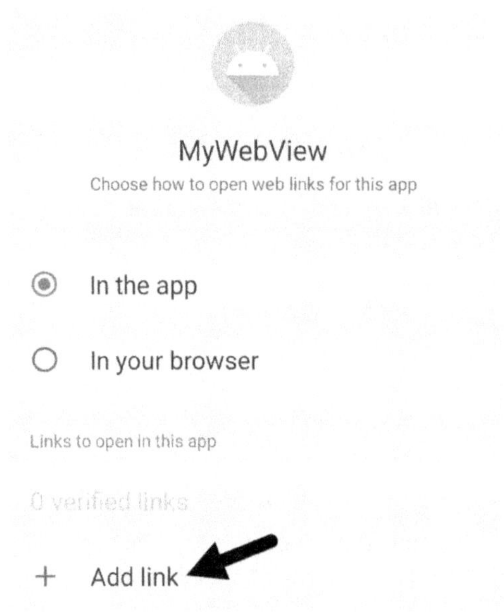

Figure 56-3

Once clicked, a dialog will appear initialized with the link passed in the intent. This can be enabled by setting the checkbox as shown in Figure 56-4:

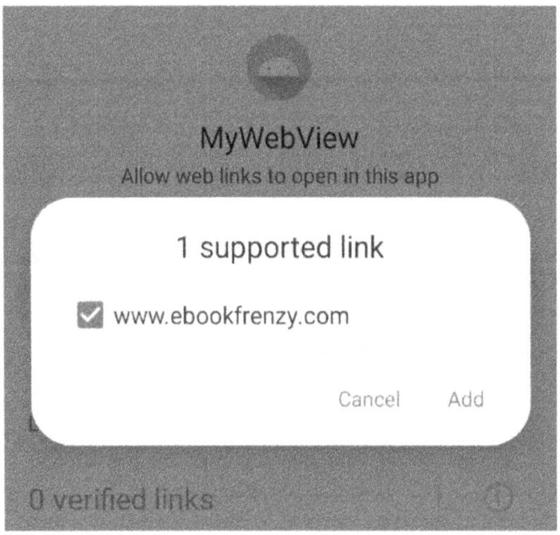

Figure 56-4

56.8 Checking Intent Availability

It is generally unwise to assume that an activity will be available for a particular intent, especially since the absence of a matching action typically results in the application crashing. Fortunately, it is possible to identify the availability of an activity for a specific intent before it is sent to the runtime system. The following method can be used to identify the availability of an activity for a specified intent action type:

```
fun isIntentAvailable(context: Context, action: String): Boolean {
    val packageManager = context.packageManager
    val intent = Intent(action)
    val list = packageManager.queryIntentActivities(intent,
```

```
            PackageManager.MATCH_DEFAULT_ONLY)
    return list.size > 0
}
```

56.9 Summary

Intents are the messaging mechanism by which one Android activity can launch another. An explicit intent references a specific activity to be launched by referencing the receiving activity by class name. Explicit intents are typically, though not exclusively, used when launching activities within the same application. An implicit intent specifies the action to be performed and the type of data to be handled and lets the Android runtime find a matching activity to launch. Implicit intents are generally used when launching activities that reside in different applications.

When working with implicit intents, security restrictions require the user to automatically verify or manually enable the app containing the intent activity target before launching the intent. Automatic verification involves the placement of a Digital Assets Link file on the website corresponding to the link URL.

An activity can send data to the receiving activity by bundling data into the intent object as key-value pairs. Data can only be returned from an activity if it is started as a sub-activity of the sending activity.

Activities advertise capabilities to the Android intent resolution process by specifying intent filters in the application manifest file. Both sending and receiving activities must also request appropriate permissions to perform tasks such as accessing the device contact database or the internet.

Having covered the theory of intents, the next few chapters will work through creating some examples in Android Studio that put both explicit and implicit intents into action.

Chapter 57

57. Android Explicit Intents – A Worked Example

The chapter entitled *"An Overview of Android Intents"* covered the theory of using intents to launch activities. This chapter will put that theory into practice by creating an example application.

The example Android Studio application project created in this chapter will demonstrate the use of an explicit intent to launch an activity, including the transfer of data between sending and receiving activities. The next chapter (*"Android Implicit Intents – A Worked Example"*) will demonstrate using implicit intents.

57.1 Creating the Explicit Intent Example Application

Select the *New Project* option from the welcome screen and, within the resulting new project dialog, choose the Empty Views Activity template before clicking on the Next button.

Enter *ExplicitIntent* into the Name field and specify *com.ebookfrenzy.explicitintent* as the package name. Before clicking on the Finish button, change the Minimum API level setting to API 26: Android 8.0 (Oreo) and the Language menu to Kotlin. Using the Gemini Agent or the steps outlined in section *18.8 Migrating a Project to View Binding*, convert the project to use view binding.

57.2 Designing the User Interface Layout for MainActivity

The user interface for MainActivity will consist of a ConstraintLayout view containing EditText (Plain Text), TextView, and Button views named *editText1*, *textView1*, and *button1*, respectively. Using the Project tool window, locate the *activity_main.xml* resource file for MainActivity (under *app -> res -> layout*) and double-click on it to load it into the Android Studio Layout Editor tool. Select the default "Hello World!" TextView and use the Attributes tool window to assign an ID of *textView1*.

Drag a Button object from the palette and position it to be horizontally centered and located beneath the bottom edge of the TextView. Change the text property to read "Send Text" and configure the *onClick* property to call a method named *sendText*.

Next, add a Plain Text object to be centered horizontally and positioned above the top edge of the TextView. Using the Attributes tool window, remove the "Name" string assigned to the text property and set the ID to *editText1*. With the layout completed, click on the toolbar *Infer constraints* button to add appropriate constraints:

Figure 57-1

Finally, click the red warning button in the top right-hand corner of the Layout Editor window and use the resulting panel to extract the "Send Text" string to a resource named *send_text*. Once the layout is complete, the user interface should resemble that illustrated in Figure 57-2:

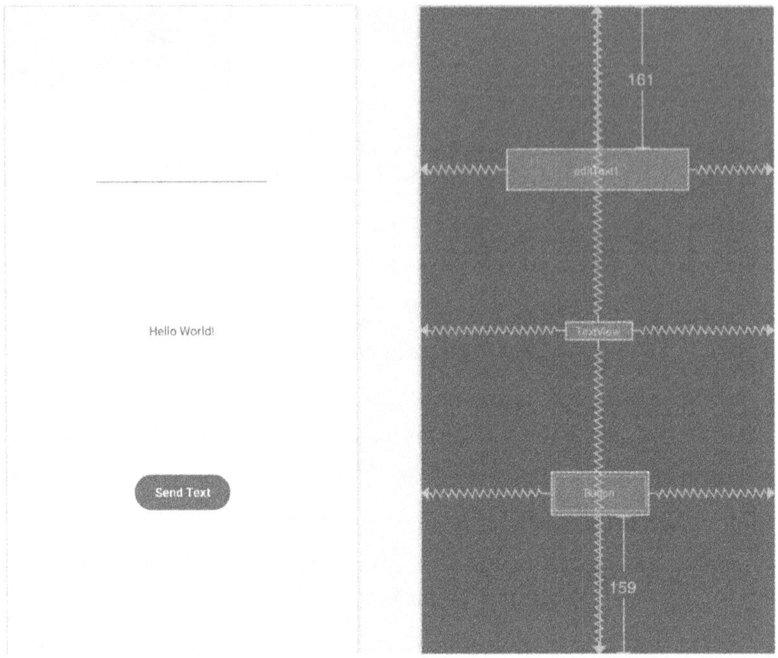

Figure 57-2

57.3 Creating the Second Activity Class

When the "Send Text" button is touched by the user, an intent will be issued requesting that a second activity be launched into which the user can enter a response. The next step, therefore, is to create the second activity. Within the Project tool window, right-click on the *com.ebookfrenzy.explicitintent* package name located in *app -> kotlin+java* and select the *New -> Activity -> Empty Views Activity* menu option to display the *New Android Activity* dialog as shown in Figure 57-3:

Figure 57-3

Enter *SecondActivity* into the Activity Name and Title fields, name the layout file *activity_second*, and change the Language menu to Kotlin. Since this activity will not be started when the application is launched (it will instead be launched via an intent by MainActivity when the button is pressed), ensure the *Launcher Activity* option is disabled before clicking the Finish button.

57.4 Designing the User Interface Layout for SecondActivity

The elements required for the second activity's user interface are a Plain Text EditText, TextView, and Button view. With these requirements in mind, load the *activity_second.xml* layout into the Layout Editor tool, and add the views.

During the design process, note that the *onClick* property on the button view has been configured to call a method named *returnText*, and the TextView and EditText views have been assigned IDs *textView2* and *editText2*, respectively. Once completed, the layout should resemble Figure 57-4. Note that the text on the button ("Return Text") has been extracted to a string resource named *return_text*.

With the layout complete, click on the Infer constraints toolbar button to add the necessary constraints to the layout:

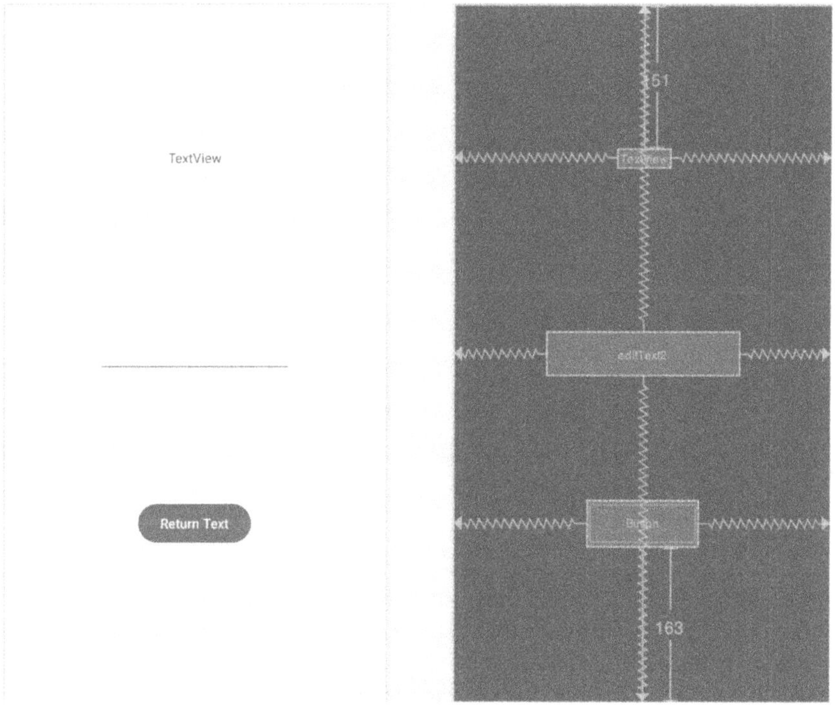

Figure 57-4

57.5 Reviewing the Application Manifest File

For MainActivity to be able to launch SecondActivity using an intent, an entry for SecondActivity needs to be present in the *AndroidManifest.xml* file. Locate this file within the Project tool window (*app -> manifests*), double-click on it to load it into the editor, and verify that Android Studio has automatically added an entry for the activity:

```
<?xml version="1.0" encoding="utf-8"?>
<manifest xmlns:android="http://schemas.android.com/apk/res/android"
    xmlns:tools="http://schemas.android.com/tools">

    <application
        android:allowBackup="true"
        android:dataExtractionRules="@xml/data_extraction_rules"
```

```
        android:fullBackupContent="@xml/backup_rules"
        android:icon="@mipmap/ic_launcher"
        android:label="@string/app_name"
        android:roundIcon="@mipmap/ic_launcher_round"
        android:supportsRtl="true"
        android:theme="@style/Theme.ExplicitIntent"
        tools:targetApi="31">

        <activity
            android:name=".SecondActivity"
            android:exported="false" />
        <activity
            android:name=".MainActivity"
            android:exported="true">
            <intent-filter>
                <action android:name="android.intent.action.MAIN" />

                <category android:name="android.intent.category.LAUNCHER" />
            </intent-filter>
        </activity>
    </application>

</manifest>
```

With the second activity created and listed in the manifest file, it is time to write some code in the MainActivity class to issue the intent.

57.6 Creating the Intent

The objective for MainActivity is to create and start an intent when the user touches the "Send Text" button. As part of the intent creation process, the question string entered by the user into the EditText view will be added to the intent object as a key-value pair. When the user interface layout was created for MainActivity, the button object was configured to call a method named *sendText()* when "clicked" by the user. This method now needs to be added to the MainActivity class *MainActivity.kt* source file as follows:

```
package com.ebookfrenzy.explicitintent
.
.
import android.view.View
import android.content.Intent

class MainActivity : AppCompatActivity() {
.
.
    fun sendText(view: View) {

        val i = Intent(this, SecondActivity::class.java)
```

```
        val myString = binding.editText1.text.toString()
        i.putExtra("qString", myString)
        startActivity(i)
    }
}
```

The code for the *sendText()* method follows the techniques outlined in *"An Overview of Android Intents"*. First, a new Intent instance is created, passing through the current activity and the class name of SecondActivity as arguments. Next, the text entered into the EditText object is added to the intent object as a key-value pair, and the intent started via a call to *startActivity()*, passing through the intent object as an argument.

Compile and run the application and touch the "Send Text" button to launch SecondActivity. Return to the MainActivity screen using either the back button (located in the toolbar along the bottom of the display) or by swiping right from the edge of the screen on newer Android versions.

57.7 Extracting Intent Data

Now that SecondActivity is being launched from MainActivity, the next step is to extract the String data value included in the intent and assign it to the TextView object in the SecondActivity user interface. This involves adding some code to the *onCreate()* method of SecondActivity in the *SecondActivity.kt* source file in addition to adapting the activity to use view binding:

```
package com.ebookfrenzy.explicitintent

import androidx.appcompat.app.AppCompatActivity
import android.os.Bundle
import android.view.View
import android.content.Intent

import com.ebookfrenzy.explicitintent.databinding.ActivitySecondBinding

class SecondActivity : AppCompatActivity() {

    private lateinit var binding: ActivitySecondBinding

    override fun onCreate(savedInstanceState: Bundle?) {
        super.onCreate(savedInstanceState)
        enableEdgeToEdge()
        setContentView(R.layout.second_activity)
        binding = ActivitySecondBinding.inflate(layoutInflater)
        setContentView(binding.root)
        ViewCompat.setOnApplyWindowInsetsListener(binding.main) { v, insets ->
            val systemBars = insets.getInsets(WindowInsetsCompat.Type.
                                                systemBars())
            v.setPadding(systemBars.left, systemBars.top, systemBars.right,
                                          systemBars.bottom)
            insets
        }
        val extras = intent.extras ?: return
```

```
        val qString = extras.getString("qString")
        binding.textView2.text = qString
    }
}
```

Compile and run the application either within an emulator or on a physical Android device. Enter some text into the text box in MainActivity before touching the "Send Text" button. The message should now appear on the TextView component in the SecondActivity user interface.

57.8 Launching SecondActivity as a Sub-Activity

For SecondActivity to be able to return data to MainActivity, SecondActivity must be started as a *sub-activity* of MainActivity. This means we need to call *registerForActivityResult()* and declare a callback handler to be called when SecondActivity returns. This callback will extract the data returned by SecondActivty and display it on textView1.

The call to *registerForActivityResult()* returns an ActivtyResultLauncher instance which can be called from within *sendText()* to launch the intent. Edit the *MainActivity.kt* file so that it reads as follows:

```
.
.
import android.app.Activity
import androidx.activity.result.ActivityResult
import androidx.activity.result.contract.ActivityResultContracts
.
.
class MainActivity : AppCompatActivity() {
.
.
    val startForResult = registerForActivityResult(
                    ActivityResultContracts.StartActivityForResult()) {
            result: ActivityResult ->
        if (result.resultCode == Activity.RESULT_OK) {
            val data = result.data
            data?.let {
                if (it.hasExtra("returnData")) {
                    val returnString = it.extras?.getString("returnData")
                    binding.textView1.text = returnString
                }
            }
        }
    }

    fun sendText(view: View) {
        val i = Intent(this, SecondActivity::class.java)

        val myString = binding.editText1.text.toString()
        i.putExtra("qString", myString)
```

```
        startActivity(i)
        startForResult.launch(i)
    }
}
.
.
```

57.9 Returning Data from a Sub-Activity

SecondActivity is now launched as a sub-activity of MainActivity, which has, in turn, been modified to handle data returned from SecondActivity. All that remains is to modify *SecondActivity.kt* to implement the *finish()* method and to add a method named *returnText()*. The *finish()* method is triggered when an activity exits (for example, when the user selects the back button on the device):

```
fun returnText(view: View) {
    finish()
}

override fun finish() {
    val data = Intent()

    val returnString = binding.editText2.text.toString()
    data.putExtra("returnData", returnString)

    setResult(RESULT_OK, data)
    super.finish()
}
```

The *finish()* method creates a new intent, adds the return data as a key-value pair, and then calls the *setResult()* method, passing through a result code and the intent object. The *returnText()* method calls the *finish()* method.

Open the *activity_second.xml* file, select the button widget, and configure the onClick attribute to call the *returnText()* method.

57.10 Testing the Application

Compile and run the application, enter a question into the text field on MainActivity, and touch the "Send Text" button. When SecondActivity appears, enter the text to the EditText view and use either the back button or the "Return Text" button to return to MainActivity where the response should appear in the text view object.

57.11 Summary

Having covered the basics of intents in the previous chapter, the goal of this chapter was to work through the creation of an application project in Android Studio designed to demonstrate the use of explicit intents together with the concepts of data transfer between a parent activity and sub-activity.

The next chapter will use an example to demonstrate implicit intents in action.

Chapter 58

58. Android Implicit Intents – A Worked Example

This chapter will create an example application in Android Studio designed to demonstrate a practical implementation of implicit intents. The goal will be to create and send an intent requesting that the content of a particular web page be loaded and displayed to the user. Since the example application itself will not contain an activity capable of performing this task, an implicit intent will be issued so that the Android intent resolution algorithm can be engaged to identify and launch a suitable activity from another application. This will likely be an activity from the Chrome web browser bundled with the Android operating system.

Having successfully launched the built-in browser, a new project will be created with an activity capable of displaying web pages. This will be installed onto the device or emulator to demonstrate implicit intents and link verification.

58.1 Creating the Android Studio Implicit Intent Example Project

Select the *New Project* option from the welcome screen and, within the resulting new project dialog, choose the Empty Views Activity template before clicking on the Next button.

Enter *ImplicitIntent* into the Name field and specify *com.ebookfrenzy.implicitintent* as the package name. Since this example will use features only available in recent Android versions, change the Minimum API level setting to API 31: Android 12.0 (S) and the Language menu to Kotlin before clicking the Finish button.

58.2 Designing the User Interface

The user interface for the *MainActivity* class is straightforward, consisting solely of a ConstraintLayout and two Button objects. Within the Project tool window, locate the *app -> res -> layout -> activity_main.xml* file and double-click on it to load it into the Layout Editor tool.

Delete the default TextView and, with Autoconnect mode enabled, position Button widgets within the layout so that it appears as shown below:

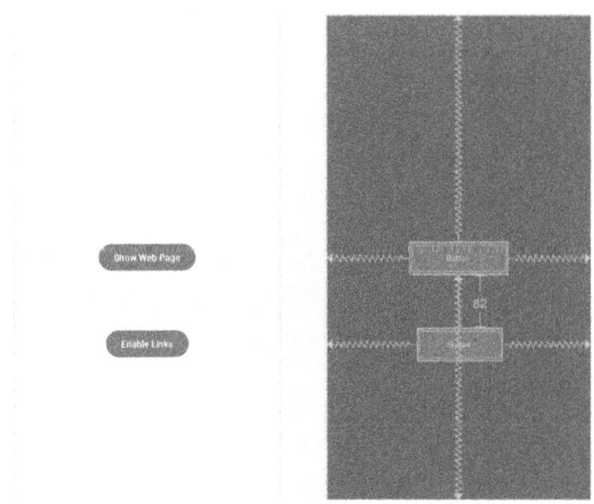

Figure 58-1

Set the text on the buttons to Show Web Page and Enable Links and extract the text to string resources.

Select each Button and use the Attributes tool window to configure the onClick property to call methods named *showWebPage* and *enableLink*, respectively.

58.3 Creating the Implicit Intent

As outlined above, the implicit intent will be created and issued from within a method named *showWebPage()*, which, in turn, needs to be implemented in the *MainActivity* class, the code for which resides in the *MainActivity.kt* source file. Locate this file in the Project tool window and double-click on it to load it into an editing pane. Once loaded, modify the code to add the *showWebPage()* and *enableLink()* methods together with a few requisite imports:

```
package com.ebookfrenzy.implicitintent

import androidx.appcompat.app.AppCompatActivity
import android.os.Bundle
import android.content.Intent
import android.view.View
import android.net.Uri

class MainActivity : AppCompatActivity() {
.
.
    fun showWebPage(view: View) {
        val intent = Intent(Intent.ACTION_VIEW,
            "https://www.payloadbooks.com".toUri())

        startActivity(intent)
    }

    fun enableLink(view: View) {

    }
}
```

The tasks performed by the *showWebPage()* method are very simple. First, a new intent object is created. Instead of specifying the class name of the intent, however, the code indicates the nature of the intent (to display something to the user) using the ACTION_VIEW option. The intent object also includes a URI containing the URL to be displayed. This indicates to the Android intent resolution system that the activity is requesting that a web page be displayed. The intent is then issued via a call to the *startActivity()* method.

Compile and run the application on either an emulator or a physical Android device, and once running, touch the *Show Web Page* button. When touched, a web browser view should appear and load the web page designated by the URL. A successful implicit intent has now been executed.

58.4 Adding a Second Matching Activity

The remainder of this chapter will demonstrate the effect of more than one activity installed on the device matching the requirements for an implicit intent. A second application will be created and installed on the device or emulator to achieve this. Begin by creating a new project within Android Studio with the application name set to *MyWebView*, using the same SDK configuration options used when creating the ImplicitIntent project earlier in this chapter and once again selecting an Empty Views Activity.

If you have a website to host a Digital Asset Links file and want to try out auto verification, use your website URL when specifying the package name. For example, if your website is hosted at *www.mycompany.com*, the package name needs to be set as follows:

```
com.mycompany.mywebview
```

If you do not have a website or do not plan on using auto verification, use the following package name:

```
com.ebookfrenzy.mywebview
```

Click Finish to create the project, then convert the project to use view bindings using the Gemini Agent or the steps in section *18.8 Migrating a Project to View Binding.*

58.5 Adding the Web View to the UI

The user interface for the sole activity contained within the new *MyWebView* project will consist of an instance of the Android WebView widget. Within the Project tool window, locate the *activity_main.xml* file, which contains the user interface description for the activity, and double-click on it to load it into the Layout Editor tool.

With the Layout Editor tool in Design mode, select the default TextView widget and remove it from the layout using the keyboard delete key.

Drag and drop a WebView object from the *Widgets* section of the palette onto the existing ConstraintLayout view, as illustrated in Figure 58-2:

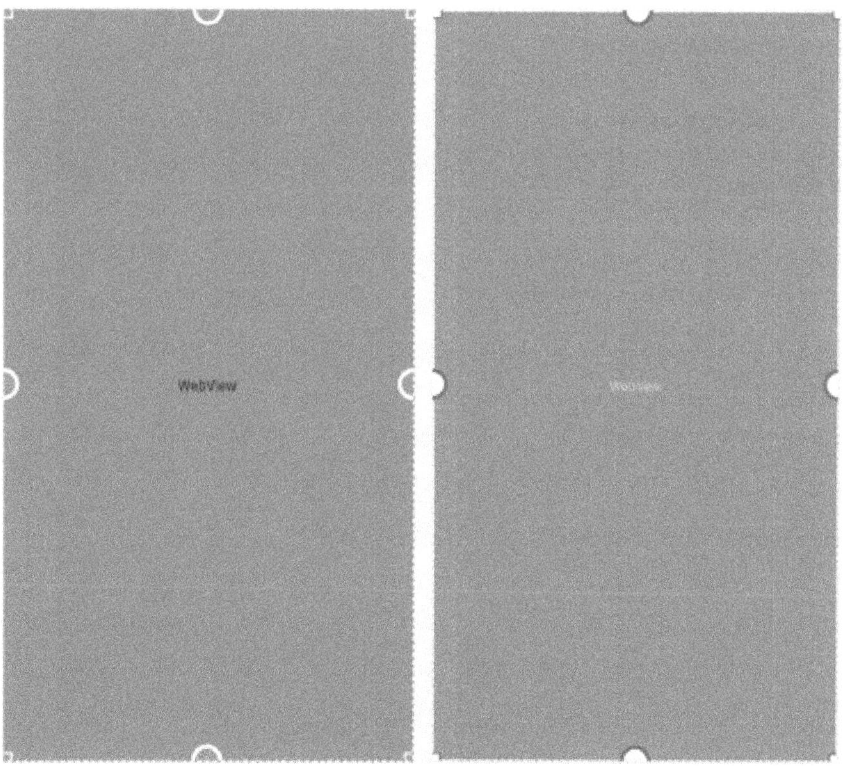

Figure 58-2

Before continuing, change the ID of the WebView instance to *webView1* and use the Infer constraints button to add any missing constraints.

58.6 Obtaining the Intent URL

When the implicit intent object is created to display a web browser window, the web page URL will be bundled into the intent object within a Uri object. The task of the *onCreate()* method within the *MainActivity* class is to extract this Uri from the intent object, convert it into a URL string and assign it to the WebView object. To implement this functionality, modify the *MainActivity.kt* file so that it reads as follows:

```
package com.ebookfrenzy.mywebview
.
.
import java.net.URL

class MainActivity : AppCompatActivity() {

    private lateinit var binding: ActivityMainBinding

    override fun onCreate(savedInstanceState: Bundle?) {
.
.
        handleIntent()
    }

    private fun handleIntent() {

        val intent = this.intent
        val data = intent.data
        var url: URL? = null

        try {
            url = URL(data?.scheme,
                    data?.host,
                    data?.path)
        } catch (e: Exception) {
            e.printStackTrace()
        }

        binding.webView1.loadUrl(url.toString())
    }
.
.
}
```

The new code added to the *onCreate()* method performs the following tasks:

- Obtains a reference to the intent which caused this activity to be launched
- Extracts the Uri data from the intent object

- Converts the Uri data to a URL object
- Loads the URL into the web view, converting the URL to a String in the process

The coding part of the MyWebView project is now complete. All that remains is to modify the manifest file.

58.7 Modifying the MyWebView Project Manifest File

A number of changes must be made to the MyWebView manifest file before it can be tested. In the first instance, the activity will need to seek permission to access the internet (since it will be required to load a web page). This is achieved by adding the appropriate permission line to the manifest file:

```
<uses-permission android:name="android.permission.INTERNET" />
```

Further, a review of the contents of the intent filter section of the *AndroidManifest.xml* file for the MyWebView project will reveal the following settings:

```
<intent-filter>
        <action android:name="android.intent.action.MAIN" />
        <category android:name="android.intent.category.LAUNCHER" />
</intent-filter>
```

In the above XML, the *android.intent.action.MAIN* entry indicates that this activity is the application's entry point when launched without data input - the *android.intent.category.LAUNCHER* directive, on the other hand, indicates that the activity should be listed within the application launcher screen of the device.

Since the activity is not required to be launched as the entry point to an application, cannot be run without data input (in this case, a URL), and is not required to appear in the launcher, neither the MAIN nor LAUNCHER directives are required in the manifest file for this activity.

The intent filter for the *MainActivity* activity does, however, need to be modified to indicate that it is capable of handling ACTION_VIEW intent actions for HTTP data schemes.

Android also requires that activities that handle implicit intents that do not include MAIN and LAUNCHER entries include the so-called *browsable* and *default* categories in the intent filter. The modified intent filter section should therefore read as follows where *<website url>* is replaced either by your website address or *www.payloadbooks.com*, depending on the package name you used when the MyWebView project was created:

```
<intent-filter android:autoVerify="true">
    <action android:name="android.intent.action.VIEW" />
    <category android:name="android.intent.category.BROWSABLE" />
    <category android:name="android.intent.category.DEFAULT" />
    <data android:scheme="https" />
    <data android:host="<website url>"/>
</intent-filter>
```

Bringing these requirements together results in the following complete *AndroidManifest.xml* file:

```
<?xml version="1.0" encoding="utf-8"?>
<manifest xmlns:android="http://schemas.android.com/apk/res/android"
    package="com.ebookfrenzy.mywebview">

    <uses-permission android:name="android.permission.INTERNET" />

    <application
```

```
        android:allowBackup="true"
        android:icon="@mipmap/ic_launcher"
        android:label="@string/app_name"
        android:roundIcon="@mipmap/ic_launcher_round"
        android:supportsRtl="true"
        android:theme="@style/Theme.MyWebView">
        <activity
            android:name=".MainActivity"
            android:exported="true">
            <intent-filter android:autoVerify="true">
                <action android:name="android.intent.action.VIEW" />
                <category android:name="android.intent.category.BROWSABLE" />
                <category android:name="android.intent.category.DEFAULT" />
                <data android:scheme="https" />
                <data android:host="<website url>"/>
            </intent-filter>
        </activity>
    </application>

</manifest>
```

Load the *AndroidManifest.xml* file into the manifest editor by double-clicking on the file name in the Project tool window. Once loaded, modify the XML to match the above changes, remembering to enter the correct website URL.

Having made the appropriate modifications to the manifest file, the new activity is ready to be installed on the device.

58.8 Installing the MyWebView Package on a Device

Before the MyWebView main activity can be used as the recipient of an implicit intent, it must first be installed onto the device. This is achieved by running the application in the normal manner. Because the manifest file contains neither the *android.intent.action.MAIN* nor the *android.intent.category.LAUNCHER* settings, Android Studio must be instructed to install but not launch the app. To configure this behavior, select the *app -> Edit configurations…* menu from the toolbar as illustrated in Figure 58-3:

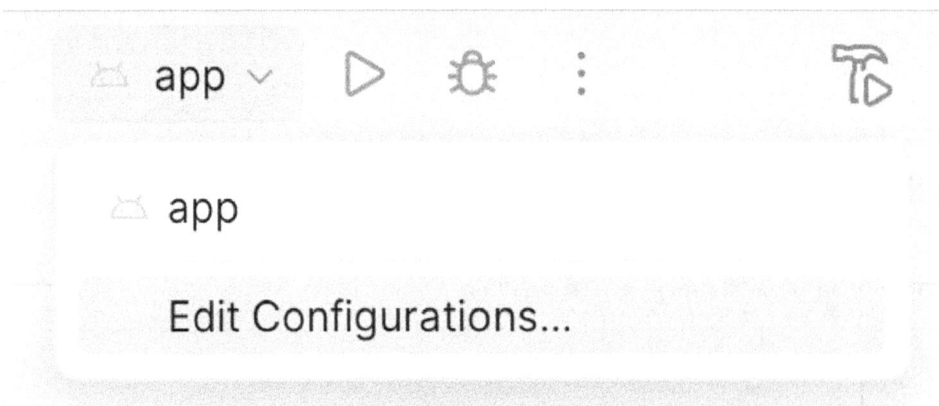

Figure 58-3

Within the Run/Debug Configurations dialog, change the Launch option located in the *Launch Options* section of the panel to *Nothing* and click on Apply followed by OK:

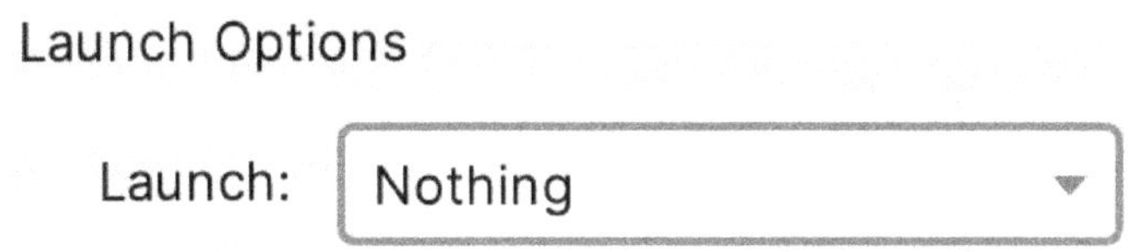

Figure 58-4

With this setting configured, run the app as usual. With this setting configured, run the app as usual. Note that the app is installed on the device but has yet to launch.

58.9 Testing the Application

With the MyWebView app installed, rerun ImplicitIntent and click the Show Web Page button. Note that the web page is still loaded into the Chrome browser instead of the main activity of the MyWebView app. This is because the MyWebView activity has not been verified or enabled to open the link contained in the launch intent. Some code must be added to the *enableLink()* method to enable the link manually.

58.10 Manually Enabling the Link

Within the *enableLink()* method, we need to create and launch an intent to display the Open by Default settings screen for the MyWebView app. Load the *MainActivity.kt* file into the code editor and modify the *enableLink()* method so that it reads as follows, making sure to replace *<reverse domain>* with either com.ebookfrenzy or your own reverse domain depending on the package name you chose when creating the MyWebView project:

```
.
.
import android.provider.Settings
.
.
fun enableLink(view: View) {
    val intent = Intent(
        Settings.ACTION_APP_OPEN_BY_DEFAULT_SETTINGS,
            "package:<reverse domain>.mywebview".toURI())

    startActivity(intent)
}
.
.
```

Rerun the ImpicitIntent app and click on the Enable Link button to display the Open by Default settings screen for the MyWebView app:

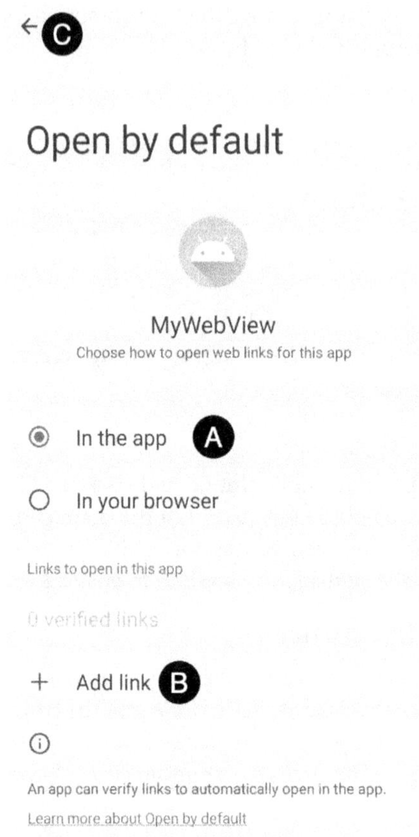

Figure 58-5

Enable the *In the app* option (marked A above), then click the *Add link* (B) button. In the resulting dialog, enable the link before clicking the Add button:

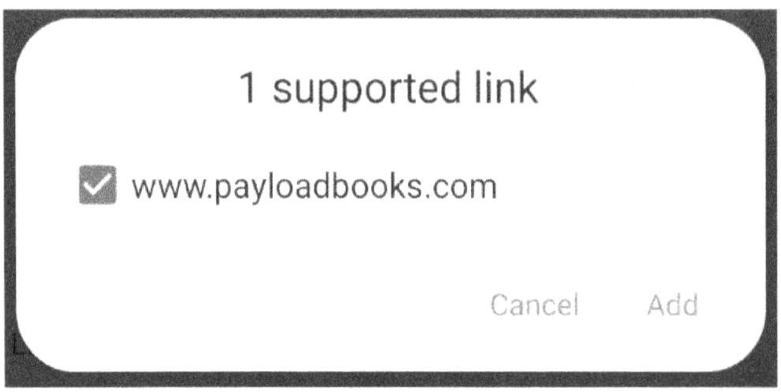

Figure 58-6

Confirm that the link is now listed as being supported before clicking on the back arrow (marked C in Figure 58-5 above) to return to the ImplicitIntent app. Clicking the Open Web Page should now load the page into the MyWebView app instead of the Chrome browser:

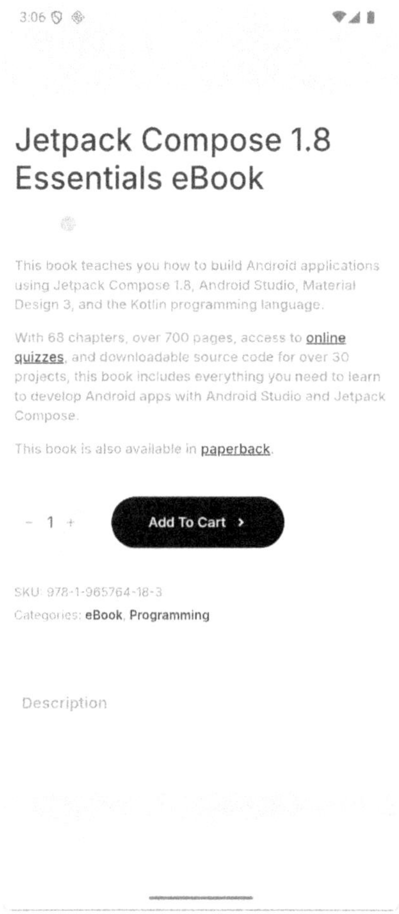

Figure 58-7

58.11 Automatic Link Verification

If you chose to use your own website URL for the MyWebView package name, you can now take the additional step of using automatic link verification. Begin by uninstalling the MyWebView app from the device or emulator on which you have been testing. After placing the Digital Asset Links file on the website, we will reinstall the app to trigger the verification process.

Using the steps outlined in the chapter entitled *"An Overview of Android Intents"*, locate your *debug.keystore* file and obtain your SHA-256 certificate fingerprint using the *keytool* utility as follows:

```
keytool -list -v -keystore <path to debug.keystore file here>
```

Next, open the following page in a web browser:

https://developers.google.com/digital-asset-links/tools/generator

Once the page has loaded, enter your website URL into the *Hosting site domain* field, *com.<domain here>.mywebview* as the *App package name,* and your SHA-256 fingerprint into the *App package fingerprint (SHA256)* field:

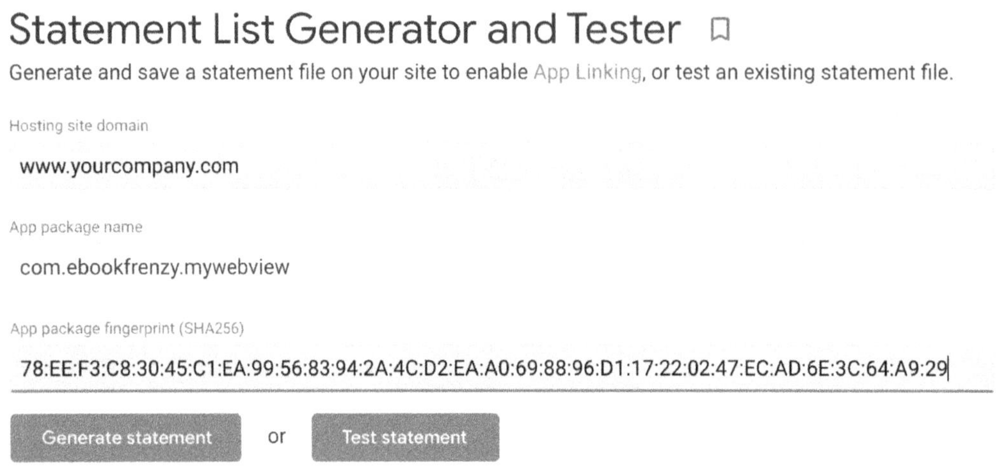

Figure 58-8

Click the *Generate statement* button to display the generated statement and place it in a file named *assetlinks.json* in a folder named *.well-known* on your web server. Return to the generator page and click on the *Test statement* button to verify that the file is valid and in the correct location.

Assuming a successful test, we are ready to try out the app link, reinstall the MyWebView app on your device or emulator and use the Settings app to navigate to the Open by Default page for MyWebView. The page should indicate that a link has been verified:

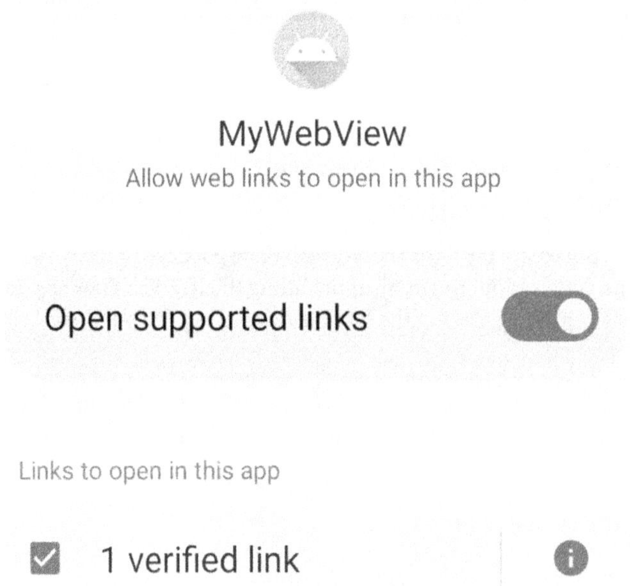

Figure 58-9

Run the ImplicitIntent app again, click the Open Web Page button, and verify that the page content appears in the MyWebView app instead of the Chrome browser.

58.12 Summary

Implicit intents provide a mechanism by which one activity can request the service of another by specifying an action type and, optionally, the data on which that action is to be performed. To be eligible as a target candidate for an implicit intent, however, an activity must be configured to extract the appropriate data from the inbound intent object and be included in a correctly configured manifest file, including appropriate permissions and intent filters. The app containing the target activity must also be verified using a Digital Asset Links file or manually enabled by the user.

Within this chapter, an example was created to demonstrate both the issuing of an implicit intent, the creation of an example activity capable of handling such an intent, and the link verification process.

Chapter 59

59. Android Broadcast Intents and Broadcast Receivers

In addition to providing a mechanism for launching application activities, intents are also used to broadcast system-wide messages to other components on the system. This involves the implementation of Broadcast Intents and Broadcast Receivers, both of which are the topic of this chapter.

59.1 An Overview of Broadcast Intents

Broadcast intents are Intent objects that are broadcast via a call to the *sendBroadcast()*, *sendStickyBroadcast()*, or *sendOrderedBroadcast()* methods of the Activity class (the latter being used when results are required from the broadcast). In addition to providing a messaging and event system between application components, broadcast intents are also used by the Android system to notify interested applications about key system events (such as the external power supply or headphones being connected or disconnected).

When a broadcast intent is created, it must include an action string, optional data, and a category string. As with standard intents, data is added to a broadcast intent using key-value pairs in conjunction with the *putExtra()* method of the intent object. The optional category string may be assigned to a broadcast intent via a call to the *addCategory()* method.

The action string, which identifies the broadcast event, must be unique and typically uses the application's package name syntax. For example, the following code fragment creates and sends a broadcast intent, including a unique action string and data:

```
val intent = Intent()
intent.action = "com.example.Broadcast"
intent.putExtra("MyData", 1000)
sendBroadcast(intent)
```

The above code would successfully launch the corresponding broadcast receiver on an Android device earlier than 3.0. On more recent versions of Android, however, the broadcast receiver would not receive the intent. This is because Android 3.0 introduced a launch control security measure that prevents components of *stopped* applications from being launched via an intent. An application is considered to be in a stopped state if the application has either just been installed and not previously launched or been manually stopped by the user using the application manager on the device. To get around this, however, a flag can be added to the intent before it is sent to indicate that the intent is to be allowed to start a component of a stopped application. This flag is FLAG_INCLUDE_STOPPED_PACKAGES and would be used as outlined in the following adaptation of the previous code fragment:

```
val intent = Intent()
intent.action = "com.example.Broadcast"
intent.putExtra("MyData", 1000)
intent.flags = Intent.FLAG_INCLUDE_STOPPED_PACKAGES
sendBroadcast(intent)
```

59.2 An Overview of Broadcast Receivers

An application listens for specific broadcast intents by registering a *broadcast receiver*. Broadcast receivers are implemented by extending the Android BroadcastReceiver class and overriding the *onReceive()* method. The broadcast receiver may then be registered within code (for example, within an activity) or a manifest file. Part of the registration implementation involves the creation of intent filters to indicate the specific broadcast intents the receiver is required to listen for. This is achieved by referencing the *action string* of the broadcast intent. When a matching broadcast is detected, the *onReceive()* method of the broadcast receiver is called, at which point the method has 5 seconds to perform any necessary tasks before returning. It is important to note that a broadcast receiver does not need to run continuously. If a matching intent is detected, the Android runtime system automatically starts the broadcast receiver before calling the *onReceive()* method.

The following code outlines a template Broadcast Receiver subclass:

```
package com.ebookfrenzy.sendbroadcast

import android.content.BroadcastReceiver
import android.content.Context
import android.content.Intent

class MyReceiver : BroadcastReceiver() {

    override fun onReceive(context: Context, intent: Intent) {
        // TODO: This method is called when the BroadcastReceiver is receiving
        // an Intent broadcast.
        throw UnsupportedOperationException("Not yet implemented")
    }
}
```

When registering a broadcast receiver within a manifest file, a *<receiver>* entry must be added for the receiver.

The following example manifest file registers the above example broadcast receiver:

```
<?xml version="1.0" encoding="utf-8"?>
<manifest xmlns:android="http://schemas.android.com/apk/res/android"
    package="com.example.broadcastdetector.broadcastdetector"
    android:versionCode="1"
    android:versionName="1.0" >

    <uses-sdk android:minSdkVersion="33" />

    <application
        android:icon="@mipmap/ic_launcher"
        android:label="@string/app_name" >
        <receiver android:name="MyReceiver" >
        </receiver>
    </application>
</manifest>
```

When running on versions of Android older than Android 8.0, the intent filters associated with a receiver can be placed within the receiver element of the manifest file as follows:

```
<receiver android:name="MyReceiver" >
    <intent-filter>
        <action android:name="com.example.Broadcast" >
        </action>
    </intent-filter>
</receiver>
```

On Android 8.0 or later, the receiver must be registered in code using the *registerReceiver()* method of the Activity class together with an appropriately configured IntentFilter object:

```
val filter = IntentFilter()
filter.addAction("com.example.Broadcast")
val receiver: MyReceiver = MyReceiver()
registerReceiver(receiver, filter, RECEIVER_EXPORTED)
```

When a broadcast receiver registered in code is no longer required, it may be unregistered via a call to the *unregisterReceiver()* method of the activity class, passing through a reference to the receiver object as an argument. For example, the following code will unregister the above broadcast receiver:

```
unregisterReceiver(receiver)
```

It is important to remember that some system broadcast intents can only be detected by a broadcast receiver if it is registered in code rather than in the manifest file. Check the Android Intent class documentation for a detailed overview of the system broadcast intents and corresponding requirements online at:

https://developer.android.com/reference/android/content/Intent

59.3 Obtaining Results from a Broadcast

When a broadcast intent is sent using the *sendBroadcast()* method, there is no way for the initiating activity to receive results from any broadcast receivers that pick up the broadcast. If return results are required, it is necessary to use the *sendOrderedBroadcast()* method instead. When a broadcast intent is sent using this method, it is delivered sequentially to each broadcast receiver with a registered interest.

The *sendOrderedBroadcast()* method is called several arguments, including a reference to another broadcast receiver (known as the *result receiver*) which is to be notified when all other broadcast receivers have handled the intent, together with a set of data references into which those receivers can place result data. When all broadcast receivers have been given the opportunity to handle the broadcast, the *onReceive()* method of the *result receiver* is called and passed the result data.

59.4 Sticky Broadcast Intents

By default, broadcast intents disappear once they have been sent and handled by interested broadcast receivers. A broadcast intent can, however, be defined as being "sticky". A sticky intent and the data contained therein remain in the system after it has completed. The data stored within a sticky broadcast intent can be obtained via the return value of a call to the *registerReceiver()* method using the usual arguments (references to the broadcast receiver and intent filter object). Many of the Android system broadcasts are sticky, a prime example being those broadcasts relating to battery level status.

A sticky broadcast may be removed at any time via a call to the *removeStickyBroadcast()* method, passing through as an argument a reference to the broadcast intent to be removed.

59.5 The Broadcast Intent Example

The remainder of this chapter will work through creating an Android Studio-based example of broadcast intents in action. In the first instance, a simple application will be created to issue a custom broadcast intent. A corresponding broadcast receiver will then be created to display a message on the display of the Android device when the broadcast is detected. Finally, the broadcast receiver will be modified to detect notification by the system that external power has been disconnected from the device.

59.6 Creating the Example Application

Select the *New Project* option from the welcome screen and, within the resulting new project dialog, choose the Empty Views Activity template before clicking on the Next button.

Enter *SendBroadcast* into the Name field and specify *com.ebookfrenzy.sendbroadcast* as the package name. Before clicking on the Finish button, change the Minimum API level setting to API 33: Android 13.0 (Tiramisu) and the Language menu to Kotlin.

Once the new project has been created, locate and load the *activity_main.xml* layout file located in the Project tool window under *app -> res -> layout* and, with the Layout Editor tool in Design mode, replace the TextView object with a Button view and set the text property so that it reads "Send Broadcast". Once the text value has been set, follow the usual steps to extract the string to a resource named *send_broadcast*.

With the button still selected in the layout, locate the *onClick* property in the Attributes panel and configure it to call a method named *broadcastIntent*.

59.7 Creating and Sending the Broadcast Intent

Having created the framework for the *SendBroadcast* application, it is now time to implement the code to send the broadcast intent. This involves implementing the *broadcastIntent()* method specified previously as the *onClick* target of the Button view in the user interface. Locate and double-click on the *MainActivity.kt* file and modify it to add the code to create and send the broadcast intent. Once modified, the source code for this class should read as follows:

```
package com.ebookfrenzy.sendbroadcast
.
.
import android.content.Intent
import android.view.View

class MainActivity : AppCompatActivity() {
.
.
    fun broadcastIntent(view: View) {
        val intent = Intent()
        intent.action = "com.ebookfrenzy.sendbroadcast"
        intent.flags = Intent.FLAG_INCLUDE_STOPPED_PACKAGES
        sendBroadcast(intent)
    }
}
```

Note that in this instance, the action string for the intent is com.ebookfrenzy.sendbroadcast. When the broadcast receiver class is created in later sections of this chapter, the intent filter declaration must match this action string.

This concludes the creation of the application to send the broadcast intent. All that remains is to build a matching broadcast receiver.

59.8 Creating the Broadcast Receiver

To create the broadcast receiver, a new class needs to be created, which subclasses the BroadcastReceiver superclass. Within the Project tool window, navigate to *app -> kotlin+java* and right-click on the package name. Select the *New -> Other -> Broadcast Receiver* menu option from the resulting menu, name the class *MyReceiver*, and ensure the Exported and Enabled options are selected. These settings allow the Android system to launch the receiver when needed and ensure that the class can receive messages sent by other applications. With the class configured, click on *Finish*.

Once created, Android Studio will automatically load the new *MyReceiver.kt* class file into the editor, where it should read as follows:

```
package com.ebookfrenzy.sendbroadcast

import android.content.BroadcastReceiver
import android.content.Context
import android.content.Intent

class MyReceiver : BroadcastReceiver() {

    override fun onReceive(context: Context, intent: Intent) {
        // This method is called when the BroadcastReceiver is receiving an
Intent broadcast.
        TODO("MyReceiver.onReceive() is not implemented")
    }
}
```

As seen in the code, Android Studio generated a template for the new class and a stub for the *onReceive()* method. Some changes now need to be made to the class to implement the required behavior. Remaining in the *MyReceiver.kt* file, therefore, modify the code so that it reads as follows:

```
package com.ebookfrenzy.sendbroadcast

import android.content.BroadcastReceiver
import android.content.Context
import android.content.Intent
import android.widget.Toast

class MyReceiver : BroadcastReceiver() {

    override fun onReceive(context: Context, intent: Intent) {
        // TODO: This method is called when the BroadcastReceiver is receiving
        // an Intent broadcast.
        throw UnsupportedOperationException("Not yet implemented")

        Toast.makeText(context, "Broadcast Intent Detected.",
                Toast.LENGTH_LONG).show()
    }
}
```

The code for the broadcast receiver is now complete.

59.9 Registering the Broadcast Receiver

The project needs to publicize the presence of the broadcast receiver and must include an intent filter to specify the broadcast intents in which the receiver is interested. When the BroadcastReceiver class was created in the previous section, Android Studio automatically added a <receiver> element to the manifest file. All that remains, therefore, is to add code within the *MainActivity.kt* file to create an intent filter and to register the receiver:

```
package com.ebookfrenzy.sendbroadcast

import androidx.appcompat.app.AppCompatActivity
import android.os.Bundle
import android.content.Intent
import android.view.View
import android.content.IntentFilter
import android.content.BroadcastReceiver

class MainActivity : AppCompatActivity() {

    private var receiver: BroadcastReceiver? = null

    override fun onCreate(savedInstanceState: Bundle?) {
.
.
        configureReceiver()
    }

    private fun configureReceiver() {
        val filter = IntentFilter()
        filter.addAction("com.ebookfrenzy.sendbroadcast")
        receiver = MyReceiver()
        registerReceiver(receiver, filter, RECEIVER_EXPORTED)
    }
.
.
}
```

It is also important to unregister the broadcast receiver when it is no longer needed:

```
override fun onDestroy() {
    super.onDestroy()
    unregisterReceiver(receiver)
}
```

59.10 Testing the Broadcast Example

To test the broadcast sender and receiver, run the SendBroadcast app on a device or AVD and wait for it to appear on the display. Once running, touch the button, at which point the toast message reading "Broadcast Intent Detected." should pop up for a few seconds before fading away.

59.11 Listening for System Broadcasts

The final stage of this example is to modify the intent filter for the broadcast receiver to listen for the system intent that is broadcast when external power is disconnected from the device. That action is *android.intent.action.ACTION_POWER_DISCONNECTED*. Modify the *configureReceiver()* method in the *MainActivity.kt* file to add this additional filter:

```
private fun configureReceiver() {
    val filter = IntentFilter()
    filter.addAction("com.ebookfrenzy.sendbroadcast")
    filter.addAction("android.intent.action.ACTION_POWER_DISCONNECTED")
    receiver = MyReceiver()
    registerReceiver(receiver, filter)
}
```

Since the *onReceive()* method in the MyReceiver.kt file will now be listening for two types of broadcast intent, it is worthwhile to modify the code so that the action string of the current intent is also displayed in the toast message. This string can be obtained via a call to the *getAction()* method of the intent object passed as an argument to the *onReceive()* method:

```
override fun onReceive(context: Context, intent: Intent) {

    val message = "Broadcast intent detected " + intent.action

    Toast.makeText(context, message,
            Toast.LENGTH_LONG).show()
}
```

Test the receiver by re-installing the modified *SendBroadcast* package. Touching the button in the *SendBroadcast* application should now result in a new message containing the custom action string:

```
Broadcast intent detected com.ebookfrenzy.sendbroadcast
```

Next, remove the USB connector currently supplying power to the Android device, at which point the receiver should report the following in the toast message (the message may be truncated on devices in portrait orientation). If the app is running on an emulator, display the extended controls, select the *Battery* option and change the *Charger connection* setting to *None*.

```
Broadcast intent detected android.intent.action.ACTION_POWER_DISCONNECTED
```

To avoid this message appearing whenever the device is disconnected from a power supply, launch the Settings app and select the *Apps* option. Select the SendBroadcast app from the resulting list and tap the *Uninstall* button.

59.12 Summary

Broadcast intents are a mechanism by which an intent can be issued for consumption by multiple components on an Android system. Broadcasts are detected by registering a Broadcast Receiver, which, in turn, is configured to listen for intents that match particular action strings. In general, broadcast receivers remain dormant until woken up by the system when a matching intent is detected. The Android system also uses broadcast intents to issue notifications of events such as a low battery warning or the connection or disconnection of external power to the device.

In addition to providing an overview of Broadcast intents and receivers, this chapter has also worked through an example of sending broadcast intents and implementing a broadcast receiver to listen for both custom and system broadcast intents.

Chapter 60

60. An Introduction to Kotlin Coroutines

When an Android application is first started, the runtime system creates a single thread in which all components will run by default. This thread is generally referred to as the *main thread*. The primary role of the main thread is to handle the user interface in terms of event handling and interaction with views in the user interface. Any additional components started within the application will, by default, also run on the main thread.

Any code within an application that performs a time-consuming task using the main thread will cause the entire application to appear to lock up until the task is completed. This typically results in the operating system displaying an "Application is not responding" warning to the user. This is far from the desired behavior for any application. Fortunately, Kotlin provides a lightweight alternative in the form of Coroutines. This chapter will introduce Coroutines, including terminology such as dispatchers, coroutine scope, suspend functions, coroutine builders, and structured concurrency. The chapter will also explore channel-based communication between coroutines.

60.1 What are Coroutines?

Coroutines are blocks of code that execute asynchronously without blocking the thread from which they are launched. Coroutines can be implemented without worrying about building complex AsyncTask implementations or directly managing multiple threads. Because of the way they are implemented, coroutines are much more efficient and less resource intensive than using traditional multi-threading options. Coroutines also make for code that is much easier to write, understand and maintain since it allows code to be written sequentially without having to write callbacks to handle thread-related events and results.

Although a relatively recent addition to Kotlin, there is nothing new or innovative about coroutines. Coroutines, in one form or another, have existed in programming languages since the 1960s and are based on a model known as Communicating Sequential Processes (CSP). Though it does so efficiently, Kotlin still uses multi-threading behind the scenes.

60.2 Threads vs. Coroutines

A problem with threads is that they are a finite resource and expensive in terms of CPU capabilities and system overhead. In the background, much work is involved in creating, scheduling, and destroying a thread. Although modern CPUs can run large numbers of threads, the actual number of threads that can be run in parallel at any one time is limited by the number of CPU cores (though newer CPUs have 8 cores, most Android devices contain CPUs with 4 cores). When more threads are required than there are CPU cores, the system has to perform thread scheduling to decide how the execution of these threads is to be shared between the available cores.

To avoid these overheads, instead of starting a new thread for each coroutine and destroying it when the coroutine exits, Kotlin maintains a pool of active threads and manages how coroutines are assigned to those threads. When an active coroutine is suspended, the Kotlin runtime saves it, and another coroutine resumes to take its place. When the coroutine is resumed, it is restored to an existing unoccupied thread within the pool to continue executing until it either completes or is suspended. Using this approach, a limited number of threads are used efficiently to execute asynchronous tasks with the potential to perform large numbers of concurrent tasks without the inherent performance degeneration that would occur using standard multi-threading.

60.3 Coroutine Scope

All coroutines must run within a specific scope, allowing them to be managed as groups instead of as individual ones. This is particularly important when canceling and cleaning up coroutines, for example, when a Fragment or Activity is destroyed, and ensuring that coroutines do not "leak" (in other words, continue running in the background when the app no longer needs them). By assigning coroutines to a scope, they can, for example, all be canceled in bulk when they are no longer needed.

Kotlin and Android provide built-in scopes and the option to create custom scopes using the CoroutineScope class. The built-in scopes can be summarized as follows:

- **GlobalScope** – GlobalScope is used to launch top-level coroutines tied to the entire application lifecycle. Since this has the potential for coroutines in this scope to continue running when not needed (for example, when an Activity exits), use of this scope is not recommended for Android applications. Coroutines running in GlobalScope are considered to be using *unstructured concurrency*.

- **ViewModelScope** – Provided specifically for ViewModel instances when using the Jetpack architecture ViewModel component. Coroutines launched in this scope from within a ViewModel instance are automatically canceled by the Kotlin runtime system when the corresponding ViewModel instance is destroyed.

- **LifecycleScope** - Every lifecycle owner has associated with it a LifecycleScope. This scope is canceled when the corresponding lifecycle owner is destroyed, making it particularly useful for launching coroutines from within activities and fragments.

For all other requirements, a custom scope will likely be used. The following code, for example, creates a custom scope named *myCoroutineScope*:

```
private val myCoroutineScope = CoroutineScope(Dispatchers.Main)
```

The coroutineScope declares the dispatcher that will be used to run coroutines (though this can be overridden) and must be referenced each time a coroutine is started if it is to be included within the scope. All of the running coroutines in a scope can be canceled via a call to the *cancel()* method of the scope instance:

```
myCoroutineScope.cancel()
```

60.4 Suspend Functions

A suspend function is a special type of Kotlin function that contains the code of a coroutine. It is declared using the Kotlin *suspend* keyword, which indicates to Kotlin that the function can be paused and resumed later, allowing long-running computations to execute without blocking the main thread.

The following is an example suspend function:

```
suspend fun mySlowTask() {
    // Perform long-running tasks here
}
```

60.5 Coroutine Dispatchers

Kotlin maintains threads for different types of asynchronous activity, and when launching a coroutine, it will be necessary to select the appropriate dispatcher from the following options:

- **Dispatchers.Main** – Runs the coroutine on the main thread and is suitable for coroutines that need to make changes to the UI and as a general-purpose option for performing lightweight tasks.

- **Dispatchers.IO** – Recommended for coroutines that perform network, disk, or database operations.

- **Dispatchers.Default** – Intended for CPU-intensive tasks such as sorting data or performing complex calculations.

The dispatcher is responsible for assigning coroutines to appropriate threads and suspending and resuming the coroutine during its lifecycle. In addition to the predefined dispatchers, it is also possible to create dispatchers for your own custom thread pools.

60.6 Coroutine Builders

The coroutine builders bring together all of the components covered so far and launch the coroutines so that they start executing. For this purpose, Kotlin provides the following six builders:

- **launch** – Starts a coroutine without blocking the current thread and does not return a result to the caller. Use this builder when calling a suspend function from within a traditional function and when the results of the coroutine do not need to be handled (sometimes referred to as "fire and forget" coroutines).

- **async** – Starts a coroutine and allows the caller to wait for a result using the await() function without blocking the current thread. Use async when you have multiple coroutines that need to run in parallel. The async builder can only be used from within another suspend function.

- **withContext** – Allows a coroutine to be launched in a different context from that used by the parent coroutine. Using this builder, a coroutine running using the Main context could launch a child coroutine in the Default context. The withContext builder also provides a useful alternative to async when returning results from a coroutine.

- **coroutineScope** – The coroutineScope builder is ideal for situations where a suspend function launches multiple coroutines that will run in parallel and where some action must occur only when all the coroutines reach completion. If those coroutines are launched using the coroutineScope builder, the calling function will not return until all child coroutines have completed. When using coroutineScope, a failure in any coroutine will cancel all other coroutines.

- **supervisorScope** – Similar to the coroutineScope outlined above, except that a failure in one child does not result in the cancellation of the other coroutines.

- **runBlocking** - Starts a coroutine and blocks the current thread until the coroutine reaches completion. This is typically the exact opposite of what is wanted from coroutines but is useful for testing code and when integrating legacy code and libraries. Otherwise to be avoided.

60.7 Jobs

Each call to a coroutine builder, such as launch or async, returns a Job instance which can, in turn, be used to track and manage the lifecycle of the corresponding coroutine. Subsequent builder calls from within the coroutine create new Job instances, which will become children of the immediate parent Job, forming a parent-child relationship tree where canceling a parent Job will recursively cancel all its children. Canceling a child does not, however, cancel the parent, though an uncaught exception within a child created using the launch builder may result in the cancellation of the parent (this is not the case for children created using the async builder, which encapsulates the exception in the result returned to the parent).

The status of a coroutine can be identified by accessing the isActive, isCompleted, and isCancelled properties of the associated Job object. In addition to these properties, several methods are also available on a Job instance. For example, a Job and all of its children may be canceled by calling the cancel() method of the Job object, while a call to the *cancelChildren()* method will cancel all child coroutines.

The *join()* method can be called to suspend the coroutine associated with the job until all of its child jobs have completed. To perform this task and cancel the Job once all child jobs have completed, call the *cancelAndJoin()*

method.

This hierarchical Job structure, together with coroutine scopes, form the foundation of structured concurrency, which aims to ensure that coroutines do not run longer than required without manually keeping references to each coroutine.

60.8 Coroutines – Suspending and Resuming

It helps to see some coroutine examples in action to understand coroutine suspension better. To start with, let's assume a simple Android app containing a button that, when clicked, calls a function named *startTask()*. This function calls a suspend function named *performSlowTask()* using the Main coroutine dispatcher. The code for this might read as follows:

```
private val myCoroutineScope = CoroutineScope(Dispatchers.Main)

fun startTask(view: View) {
    myCoroutineScope.launch(Dispatchers.Main) {
        performSlowTask()
    }
}
```

In the above code, a custom scope is declared and referenced in the call to the launch builder, which, in turn, calls the *performSlowTask()* suspend function. Since *startTask()* is not a suspend function, the coroutine must be started using the launch builder instead of the async builder.

Next, we can declare the *performSlowTask()* suspend function as follows:

```
suspend fun performSlowTask() {
    Log.i(TAG, "performSlowTask before")
    delay(5_000) // simulates long-running task
    Log.i(TAG, "performSlowTask after")
}
```

As implemented, all the function does is output diagnostic messages before and after performing a 5-second delay, simulating a long-running task. While the 5-second delay is in effect, the user interface will continue to be responsive because the main thread is not being blocked. To understand why it helps to explore what is happening behind the scenes.

First, the *startTask()* function is executed and launches the *performSlowTask()* suspend function as a coroutine. This function then calls the Kotlin *delay()* function passing through a time value. The built-in Kotlin *delay()* function is implemented as a suspend function, so it is also launched as a coroutine by the Kotlin runtime environment. The code execution has now reached what is referred to as a suspend point which will cause the *performSlowTask()* coroutine to be suspended while the delay coroutine is running. This frees up the thread on which *performSlowTask()* was running and returns control to the main thread so that the UI is unaffected.

Once the *delay()* function reaches completion, the suspended coroutine will be resumed and restored to a thread from the pool where it can display the Log message and return to the *startTask()* function.

When working with coroutines in Android Studio suspend points within the code editor are marked as shown in the figure below:

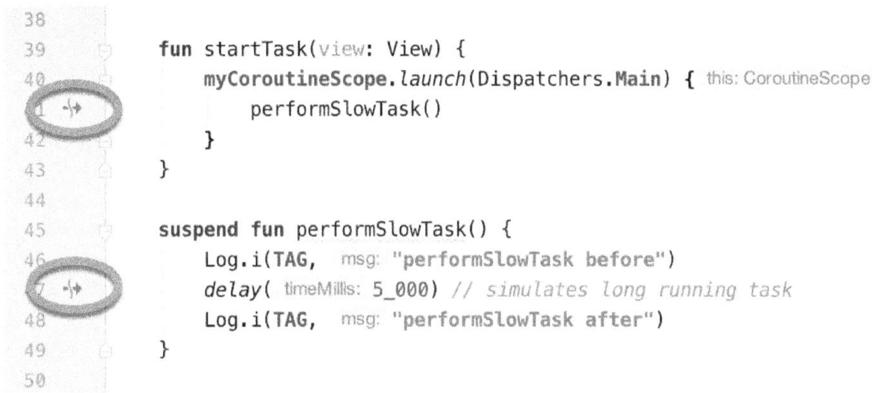

Figure 60-1

60.9 Returning Results from a Coroutine

The above example ran a suspend function as a coroutine but did not demonstrate how to return results. However, suppose the *performSlowTask()* function is required to return a string value to be displayed to the user via a TextView object.

To do this, we must rewrite the suspend function to return a Deferred object. A Deferred object is a commitment to provide a value at some point in the future. By calling the *await()* function on the Deferred object, the Kotlin runtime will deliver the value when the coroutine returns it. The code in our *startTask()* function might, therefore, be rewritten as follows:

```
fun startTask(view: View) {

    coroutineScope.launch(Dispatchers.Main) {
        statusText.text = performSlowTask().await()
    }
}
```

The problem now is that we are having to use the launch builder to start the coroutine since *startTask()* is not a suspend function. As outlined earlier in this chapter, it is only possible to return results when using the async builder. To get around this, we have to adapt the suspend function to use the async builder to start another coroutine that returns a Deferred result:

```
suspend fun performSlowTask(): Deferred<String> =
    coroutineScope.async(Dispatchers.Default) {
        Log.i(TAG, "performSlowTask before")
        delay(5_000)
        Log.i(TAG, "performSlowTask after")
    return@async "Finished"
}
```

When the app runs, the "Finished" result string will be displayed on the TextView object when the *performSlowTask()* coroutine completes. Once again, the wait for the result will occur in the background without blocking the main thread.

60.10 Using withContext

As we have seen, coroutines are launched within a specified scope and using a specific dispatcher. By default, any child coroutines will inherit the same dispatcher as that used by the parent. Consider the following code designed to call multiple functions from within a suspend function:

```
fun startTask(view: View) {

    coroutineScope.launch(Dispatchers.Main) {
        performTasks()
    }
}

suspend fun performTasks() {
    performTask1()
    performTask2()
    performTask3()
}

suspend fun performTask1() {
    Log.i(TAG, "Task 1 ${Thread.currentThread().name}")
}

suspend fun performTask2() {
    Log.i(TAG, "Task 2 ${Thread.currentThread().name}")
}

suspend fun performTask3 () {
    Log.i(TAG, "Task 3 ${Thread.currentThread().name}")
}
```

Since the *performTasks()* function was launched using the Main dispatcher, all three functions will default to the main thread. To prove this, the functions have been written to output the name of the thread in which they are running. On execution, the Logcat panel will contain the following output:

```
Task 1 main
Task 2 main
Task 3 main
```

However, imagine that the *performTask2()* function performs network-intensive operations more suited to the IO dispatcher. This can easily be achieved using the withContext launcher, which allows the context of a coroutine to be changed while still staying in the same coroutine scope. The following change switches the *performTask2()* coroutine to an IO thread:

```
suspend fun performTasks() {
    performTask1()
    withContext(Dispatchers.IO) { performTask2() }
    performTask3()
}
```

When executed, the output will read as follows, indicating that the Task 2 coroutine is no longer on the main thread:

```
Task 1 main
Task 2 DefaultDispatcher-worker-1
```

```
Task 3 main
```

The withContext builder also provides an interesting alternative to using the async builder and the Deferred object *await()* call when returning a result. Using withContext, the code from the previous section can be rewritten as follows:

```
fun startTask(view: View) {

    coroutineScope.launch(Dispatchers.Main) {
          statusText.text = performSlowTask()
    }
}

suspend fun performSlowTask(): String =
    withContext(Dispatchers.Main) {
        Log.i(TAG, "performSlowTask before")
        delay(5_000)
        Log.i(TAG, "performSlowTask after")

        return@withContext "Finished"
    }
}
```

60.11 Coroutine Channel Communication

Channels provide a simple way to implement communication between coroutines, including streams of data. In the simplest form, this involves the creation of a Channel instance and calling the *send()* method to send the data. Once sent, transmitted data can be received in another coroutine via a call to the *receive()* method of the same Channel instance.

The following code, for example, passes six integers from one coroutine to another:

```
.
.
import kotlinx.coroutines.channels.*
.
.
val channel = Channel<Int>()

suspend fun channelDemo() {
    coroutineScope.launch(Dispatchers.Main) { performTask1() }
    coroutineScope.launch(Dispatchers.Main) { performTask2() }
}

suspend fun performTask1() {
    (1..6).forEach {
        channel.send(it)
    }
}
```

```
suspend fun performTask2() {
    repeat(6) {
        Log.d(TAG, "Received: ${channel.receive()}")
    }
}
```

When executed, the following logcat output will be generated:

```
Received: 1
Received: 2
Received: 3
Received: 4
Received: 5
Received: 6
```

60.12 Summary

Kotlin coroutines provide a simpler and more efficient approach to performing asynchronous tasks than traditional multi-threading. Coroutines allow asynchronous tasks to be implemented in a structured way without implementing the callbacks associated with typical thread-based tasks. This chapter has introduced the basic concepts of coroutines, including jobs, scope, builders, suspend functions, structured concurrency, and channel-based communication.

Chapter 61

61. An Android Kotlin Coroutines Tutorial

The previous chapter introduced the key concepts of performing asynchronous tasks within Android apps using Kotlin coroutines. This chapter will build on this knowledge to create an example app that launches thousands of coroutines at the touch of a button.

61.1 Creating the Coroutine Example Application

Select the *New Project* option from the welcome screen and, within the resulting new project dialog, choose the Empty Views Activity template before clicking on the Next button.

Enter *CoroutineDemo* into the Name field and specify *com.ebookfrenzy.coroutinedemo* as the package name. Before clicking on the Finish button, change the Minimum API level setting to API 26: Android 8.0 (Oreo) and the Language menu to Kotlin. Migrate the project to view binding using the steps outlined in section *18.8 Migrating a Project to View Binding.*

61.2 Designing the User Interface

The user interface will consist of a button to launch coroutines and a Seekbar to specify how many coroutines will be launched asynchronously each time the button is clicked. As the coroutines execute, a TextView will update when individual coroutines start and end.

Begin by loading the *activity_main.xml* layout file and add the Button, TextView, and SeekBar objects so that the layout resembles that shown in Figure 61-1:

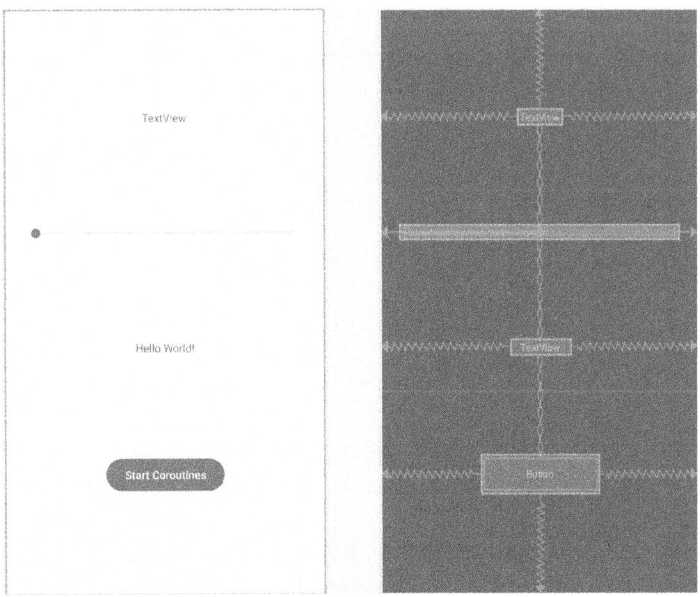

Figure 61-1

To implement the layout constraints shown above, begin by clearing all constraints on the layout using the toolbar button. Shift-click on the four objects so all are selected, right-click over the top-most TextView, and select the *Center -> Horizontally* menu option. Right-click again, this time selecting the *Chains -> Create Vertical Chain* option.

Select the SeekBar and change the layout_width property to 0dp (match_constraint) before adding a 24dp margin on the left and right-hand sides, as shown in Figure 61-2:

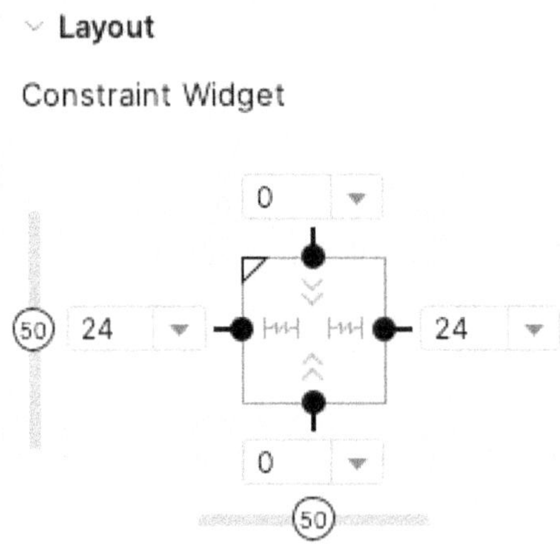

Figure 61-2

Modify the onClick attribute for the Button to call a method named *launchCoroutines* and change the ids of the top-most TextView, the SeekBar, and the lower TextView to *countText*, *seekBar*, and *statusText* respectively. Finally, change the text on the Button to read "Launch Coroutines" and extract the text to a string resource.

61.3 Implementing the SeekBar

The SeekBar controls the number of asynchronous coroutines, ranging from 1 to 2000, launched each time the button is clicked. In the *activity_main.xml* file, select the SeekBar and use the Attributes tool window to change the max property to 2000. Next, edit the *MainActivity.kt* file, add a variable in which to store the current slider setting, and modify the *onCreate()* method to add a SeekBar listener:

```
.
.
import android.widget.SeekBar

class MainActivity : AppCompatActivity() {

    private lateinit var binding: ActivityMainBinding
    private var count: Int = 1

    override fun onCreate(savedInstanceState: Bundle?) {
.
.
        binding.seekBar.setOnSeekBarChangeListener(object :
            SeekBar.OnSeekBarChangeListener {
            override fun onProgressChanged(seek: SeekBar,
```

```
                                                progress: Int, fromUser: Boolean) {
                count = progress
                val message = "${count} coroutines"
                binding.countText.text = message
            }

            override fun onStartTrackingTouch(seek: SeekBar) {
            }

            override fun onStopTrackingTouch(seek: SeekBar) {
            }
        })
    }
.
.
```

When the seekbar slides, the current value will be stored in the count variable and displayed on the countText view.

61.4 Adding the Suspend Function

When the user taps the button, the app will launch the number of coroutines selected in the SeekBar. The *launchCoroutines()* onClick method will achieve this using the coroutine *launch* builder to execute a suspend function. Since the suspend function will return a status string to be displayed on the statusText TextView object, it must be implemented using the async builder. All of these actions will need to be performed within a coroutine scope which must be declared. Within the *MainActivity.kt* file, make the following changes:

```
.
.
import kotlinx.coroutines.*

class MainActivity : AppCompatActivity() {

    private val coroutineScope = CoroutineScope(Dispatchers.Main)
.
.
    private suspend fun performTaskAsync(tasknumber: Int): Deferred<String> =
        coroutineScope.async(Dispatchers.Main) {
            delay(5_000)
            return@async "Finished Coroutine $tasknumber"
        }
.
.
}
```

Given that the function only performs a small task and involves changes to the user interface, the coroutine is executed using the Main dispatcher. It is passed the sequence number of the coroutine to be launched, delays for 5 seconds, and then returns a string indicating that the numbered coroutine has finished.

61.5 Implementing the launchCoroutines Method

The final task before testing the app is to add the *launchCoroutines()* method, which is called when the Button object is clicked. This method should be added to the *MainActivity.kt* file as follows:

```
.
.
import android.view.View
.
.
    fun launchCoroutines(view: View) {

        (1..count).forEach {
            val message = "Started Coroutine ${it}"
            binding.statusText.text = message
            coroutineScope.launch(Dispatchers.Main) {
                binding.statusText.text = performTaskAsync(it).await()
            }
        }
    }
.
.
```

The method implements a loop to launch the requested number of coroutines. It updates the status TextView each time a result is returned from a completed coroutine via an *await()* method call.

61.6 Testing the App

Build and run the app on a device or emulator and move the SeekBar to a low number (for example, 10) before tapping the launch button. The status text will update when a coroutine is launched until the maximum is reached. After each coroutine completes the 5-second delay, the status text will update until all ten have completed (in practice, these status updates will happen so quickly that it will be difficult to see the status changes).

Repeat the process with the SeekBar set to 2000, sliding the Seekbar back and forth as the coroutines run to verify that the main thread is still running and has not been blocked.

Finally, with the Logcat panel displayed, set the SeekBar to 2000 and repeatedly click on the launch button. After about 15 clicks, the Logcat panel will begin displaying messages similar to the following:

```
I/Choreographer: Skipped 52 frames!  The application may be doing too much work
on its main thread.
```

Although the app continues to function, the volume of coroutines running within the app is beginning to overload the main thread. The fact that this only occurs when tens of thousands of coroutines are executing concurrently is a testament to the efficiency of Kotlin coroutines. However, when this message appears in your own apps, it may be a sign that too many coroutines are running or that the asynchronous workload is too heavy for the main thread. That being the case, a different dispatcher may need to be used, perhaps using the *withContext* builder.

61.7 Summary

Building on the information covered in *"An Introduction to Kotlin Coroutines"*, this chapter has created an example app that demonstrates the use of Kotlin Coroutines within an Android app. The example demonstrated the use of the Main dispatcher to launch thousands of asynchronous Coroutines, including returning results.

Chapter 62

62. An Overview of Android Services

The Android Service class is designed to allow applications to initiate and perform background tasks. Unlike broadcast receivers, which are intended to perform a task quickly and then exit, services are designed to perform tasks that take a long time to complete (such as downloading a file over an internet connection or streaming music to the user) but do not require a user interface.

This chapter will provide an overview of the services available, including *bound* and *intent services*. Once these basics have been covered, subsequent chapters will work through some examples of services in action.

62.1 Intent Service

As previously outlined, services run by default within the same main thread as the component from which they are launched. As such, any CPU-intensive tasks that need to be performed by the service should occur within a new thread, thereby avoiding impacting the performance of the calling application.

The *JobIntentService* class is a convenience class (subclassed from the Service class) that sets up a worker thread for handling background tasks and handles each request asynchronously. Once the service has handled all queued requests, it exits. All that is required when using the JobIntentService class is to implement the *onHandleWork()* method, containing the code to be executed for each request.

For services that do not require synchronous processing of requests, JobIntentService is the recommended option. However, services requiring synchronous handling of requests will need to subclass from the Service class and manually implement and manage threading to handle any CPU-intensive tasks efficiently.

62.2 Bound Service

A bound service allows a launching component to interact with and receive results from the service. This interaction can also occur across process boundaries through the implementation of interprocess communication (IPC). An activity might, for example, start a service to handle audio playback. The activity will, in all probability, include a user interface providing controls to the user to pause playback or skip to the next track. Similarly, the service will likely need to communicate information to the calling activity to indicate that the current audio track has ended and provide details of the next track that is about to start playing.

A component (referred to in this context as a *client*) starts and *binds* to a bound service via a call to the *bindService()* method. Also, multiple components may bind to a service simultaneously. When a client no longer requires the service binding, a call should be made to the *unbindService()* method. When the last bound client unbinds from a service, the Android runtime system will terminate the service. It is important to remember that a bound service may also be started via a call to *startService()*. Once started, components may then bind to it via *bindService()* calls. When a bound service is launched via a call to *startService()*, it will continue to run even after the last client unbinds from it.

A bound service must include an implementation of the *onBind()* method, which is called both when the service is initially created and when other clients subsequently bind to the running service. The purpose of this method is to return to binding clients an object of type *IBinder* containing the information needed by the client to communicate with the service.

When implementing the communication between a client and a bound service, the recommended technique depends on whether the client and service reside in the same or different processes and whether or not the service is private to the client. Local communication can be achieved by extending the Binder class and returning an instance from the *onBind()* method. Interprocess communication, on the other hand, requires Messenger and Handler implementation. Details of both of these approaches will be covered in later chapters.

62.3 The Anatomy of a Service

As has already been mentioned, a service must be created as a subclass of the Android Service class (more specifically, *android.app.Service*) or a sub-class thereof (such as *android.app.IntentService*). As part of the subclassing procedure, one or more of the following superclass callback methods must be overridden, depending on the exact nature of the service being created:

- **onStartCommand()** – This method is called when another component starts the service via a call to the *startService()* method. This method does not need to be implemented for bound services.
- **onBind()** – Called when a component binds to the service via a call to the *bindService()* method. When implementing a bound service, this method must return an *IBinder* object facilitating communication with the client.
- **onCreate()** – Intended as a location to perform initialization tasks, this method is called immediately before the call to either *onStartCommand()* or the *first* call to the *onBind()* method.
- **onDestroy()** – Called when the service is being destroyed.
- **onHandleWork()** – Applies only to JobIntentService subclasses. This method is called to handle the processing for the service. It is executed in a separate thread from the main application.

Note that the IntentService class includes its own implementations of the *onStartCommand()* and *onBind()* callback methods, so these do not need to be implemented in subclasses.

62.4 Controlling Destroyed Service Restart Options

The *onStartCommand()* callback method is required to return an integer value to define what should happen with regard to the service if the Android runtime system destroys it. Possible return values for these methods are as follows:

- **START_NOT_STICKY** – Indicates to the system that the service should not be restarted if it is destroyed unless there are pending intents awaiting delivery.
- **START_STICKY** – Indicates that the service should be restarted as soon as possible after it has been destroyed if the destruction occurred after the *onStartCommand()* method returned. If no pending intents are waiting to be delivered, the *onStartCommand()* callback method is called with a NULL intent value. The intent being processed when the service was destroyed is discarded.
- **START_REDELIVER_INTENT** – Indicates that if the service was destroyed after returning from the *onStartCommand()* callback method, the service should be restarted with the current intent redelivered to the *onStartCommand()* method followed by any pending intents.

62.5 Declaring a Service in the Manifest File

For a service to be usable, it must first be declared within a manifest file. This involves embedding an appropriately configured *<service>* element into an existing *<application>* entry. At a minimum, the <service> element must contain a property declaring the class name of the service, as illustrated in the following XML fragment:

```
.
.
    <application
```

```
        android:icon="@mipmap/ic_launcher"
        android:label="@string/app_name" >
        <activity
            android:label="@string/app_name"
            android:name=".MainActivity" >
            <intent-filter>
              <action android:name="android.intent.action.MAIN" />
              <category android:name="android.intent.category.LAUNCHER" />
            </intent-filter>
        </activity>
        <service android:name=".MyService>
           </service>
    </application>
</manifest>
```

By default, services are declared public in that they can be accessed by components outside the application package in which they reside. To make a service private, the *android:exported* property must be declared as *false* within the <service> element of the manifest file. For example:

```
<service android:name="MyService"
              android:exported="false">
</service>
```

When working with JobIntentService, the manifest Service declaration must also request the BIND_JOB_SERVICE permission as follows:

```
<service
    android:name=".MyJobIntentService"
    android:permission="android.permission.BIND_JOB_SERVICE" />
```

As previously discussed, services run within the same process as the calling component by default. To force a service to run within its own process, add an *android:process* property to the <service> element, declaring a name for the process prefixed with a colon (:):

```
<service android:name=".MyService"
    android:exported="false"
    android:process=":myprocess">
</service>
```

The colon prefix indicates that the new process is private to the local application. If the process name begins with a lowercase letter instead of a colon, however, the process will be global and available for use by other components.

Finally, using the same intent filter mechanisms outlined for activities, a service may also advertise capabilities to other applications running on the device. For more details on intent filters, refer to the chapter *"An Overview of Android Intents"*.

62.6 Starting a Service Running on System Startup

Given the background nature of services, it is not uncommon for a service to need to be started when an Android-based system first boots up. This can be achieved by creating a broadcast receiver with an intent filter configured to listen for the system *android.intent.action.BOOT_COMPLETED* intent. When such an intent is detected, the broadcast receiver would invoke the necessary service and then return. Note that, to function, such a broadcast receiver must request the *android.permission.RECEIVE_BOOT_COMPLETED* permission.

62.7 Summary

Android services are a powerful mechanism that allows applications to perform tasks in the background. A service, once launched, will continue to run regardless of whether the calling application is the foreground task or not and even if the component that initiated the service is destroyed.

Services are subclassed from the Android Service class. Bound services provide a communication interface to other client components and generally run until the last client unbinds from the service.

By default, services run locally within the same process and main thread as the calling application. A new thread should, therefore, be created within the service to handle CPU-intensive tasks. Remote services may be started within a separate process by making a minor configuration change to the corresponding <service> entry in the application manifest file.

The IntentService class (a subclass of the Android Service class) provides a convenient mechanism for handling asynchronous service requests within a separate worker thread.

63. Android Local Bound Services – A Worked Example

As outlined in the previous chapter, Bound services provide a mechanism for implementing communication between an Android service and one or more client components. This chapter builds on the overview of bound services provided in *"An Overview of Android Services"* before embarking on an example implementation of a *local* bound service.

63.1 Understanding Bound Services

Bound services are provided to allow applications to perform tasks in the background. Multiple client components may *bind* to a bound service and, once bound, interact with that service using various mechanisms.

Bound services are created as sub-classes of the Android Service class and must, at a minimum, implement the *onBind()* method. Client components bind to a service via a call to the *bindService()* method. The first bind request to a bound service will result in a call to that service's *onBind()* method (subsequent bind requests do not trigger an *onBind()* call). Clients wishing to bind to a service must also implement a ServiceConnection subclass containing *onServiceConnected()* and *onServiceDisconnected()* methods, which will be called once the client-server connection has been established or disconnected, respectively. In the case of the *onServiceConnected()* method, this will be passed an IBinder object containing the information needed by the client to interact with the service.

63.2 Bound Service Interaction Options

Two recommended mechanisms for implementing interaction between client components and a bound service exist. Suppose the bound service is local and private to the same application as the client component (in other words, it runs within the same process and is not available to components in other applications). In that case, the recommended method is to create a subclass of the Binder class and extend it to provide an interface to the service. An instance of this Binder object is then returned by the *onBind()* method and subsequently used by the client component to access methods and data held within the service directly.

When the bound service is not local to the application (in other words, it is running in a different process from the client component), interaction is best achieved using a Messenger/Handler implementation.

In the remainder of this chapter, an example will be created to demonstrate the steps involved in creating, starting, and interacting with a local, private bound service.

63.3 A Local Bound Service Example

The example application created in the remainder of this chapter will consist of a single activity and a bound service. The purpose of the bound service is to obtain the current time from the system and return that information to the activity, where it will be displayed to the user. The bound service will be local and private to the same application as the activity.

Select the *New Project* option from the welcome screen and, within the resulting new project dialog, choose the Empty Views Activity template before clicking on the Next button.

Enter *LocalBound* into the Name field and specify *com.ebookfrenzy.localbound* as the package name. Before clicking on the Finish button, change the Minimum API level setting to API 26: Android 8.0 (Oreo) and the Language menu to Kotlin. Use the Gemini Agent or the steps in section *18.8 Migrating a Project to View Binding* to migrate the project to view binding.

Once the project has been created, the next step is to add a new class to act as the bound service.

63.4 Adding a Bound Service to the Project

To add a new class to the project, right-click on the package name (located under *app -> kotlin+java -> com.ebookfrenzy.localbound*) within the Project tool window and select the *New -> Service -> Service* menu option. Specify *BoundService* as the class name and make sure that both the *Exported* and *Enabled* options are selected before clicking on *Finish* to create the class. Android Studio will load the *BoundService.kt* file into the editor, where it will read as follows:

```
package com.ebookfrenzy.localbound

import android.app.Service
import android.content.Intent
import android.os.IBinder

class BoundService : Service() {

    override fun onBind(intent: Intent): IBinder {
        TODO("Return the communication channel to the service.")
    }
}
```

63.5 Implementing the Binder

As previously outlined, local bound services can communicate with bound clients by passing an appropriately configured Binder object to the client. This is achieved by creating a Binder subclass within the bound service class and extending it by adding one or more new methods the client can call. This usually involves implementing a method that returns a reference to the bound service instance. With a reference to this instance, the client can then access data and call methods within the bound service directly.

For this example, some changes are needed to the template *BoundService* class created in the preceding section. In the first instance, a Binder subclass needs to be declared. This class will contain a single method named *getService()* which will return a reference to the current service object instance (represented by the *this* keyword). With these requirements in mind, edit the *BoundService.kt* file and modify it as follows:

```
package com.ebookfrenzy.localbound

import android.app.Service
import android.content.Intent
import android.os.IBinder
import android.os.Binder

class BoundService : Service() {

    private val myBinder = MyLocalBinder()

    override fun onBind(intent: Intent): IBinder {
```

```
        TODO("Return the communication channel to the service.")
    }

    inner class MyLocalBinder : Binder() {
        fun getService() : BoundService {
            return this@BoundService
        }
    }
}
```

Having made the changes to the class, it is worth taking a moment to recap the steps performed here. First, a new subclass of Binder (named *MyLocalBinder*) is declared. This class contains a single method to return a reference to the current instance of the *BoundService* class. A new instance of the *MyLocalBinder* class is created and assigned to the *myBinder* IBinder reference (since Binder is a subclass of IBinder, there is no type mismatch in this assignment).

Next, the *onBind()* method needs to be modified to return a reference to the *myBinder* object, and a new public method implemented to return the current time when called by any clients that bind to the service:

```
package com.ebookfrenzy.localbound

import android.app.Service
import android.content.Intent
import android.os.IBinder
import android.os.Binder
import java.text.SimpleDateFormat
import java.util.*

class BoundService : Service() {

    private val myBinder = MyLocalBinder()

    override fun onBind(intent: Intent): IBinder {
        return myBinder
    }

    fun getCurrentTime(): String {
        val dateformat = SimpleDateFormat("HH:mm:ss MM/dd/yyyy",
                Locale.US)
        return dateformat.format(Date())
    }

    inner class MyLocalBinder : Binder() {
        fun getService() : BoundService {
            return this@BoundService
        }

    }
```

```
}
```

At this point, the bound service is complete and is ready to be added to the project manifest file. Locate and double-click on the *AndroidManifest.xml* file for the *LocalBound* project in the Project tool window and, once loaded into the Manifest Editor, verify that Android Studio has already added a <service> entry for the service as follows:

```
<?xml version="1.0" encoding="utf-8"?>
<manifest xmlns:android="http://schemas.android.com/apk/res/android"
    package="com.ebookfrenzy.localbound.localbound" >

    <application
        android:allowBackup="true"
        android:icon="@mipmap/ic_launcher"
        android:label="@string/app_name"
        android:theme="@style/AppTheme" >
        <service
            android:name=".BoundService"
            android:enabled="true"
            android:exported="true" >
        </service>
        <activity
            android:name=".MainActivity" >
            <intent-filter>
                <action android:name="android.intent.action.MAIN" />

                <category android:name="android.intent.category.LAUNCHER" />
            </intent-filter>
        </activity>
     </application>

</manifest>
```

The next phase is writing the code within the activity to bind to the service and call the *getCurrentTime()* method.

63.6 Binding the Client to the Service

For this tutorial, the client is the *MainActivity* instance of the running application. As previously noted, to successfully bind to a service and receive the IBinder object returned by the service's *onBind()* method, it is necessary to create a ServiceConnection subclass and implement *onServiceConnected()* and *onServiceDisconnected()* callback methods. Edit the *MainActivity.kt* file and modify it as follows:

```
package com.ebookfrenzy.localbound

import androidx.appcompat.app.AppCompatActivity
import android.os.Bundle
import android.content.ComponentName
import android.content.Context
import android.content.ServiceConnection
import android.os.IBinder
```

```
import android.content.Intent

class MainActivity : AppCompatActivity() {

    private lateinit var binding: ActivityMainBinding
    var myService: BoundService? = null
    var isBound = false
.
.
    private val myConnection = object : ServiceConnection {
        override fun onServiceConnected(className: ComponentName,
                                        service: IBinder) {
            val binder = service as BoundService.MyLocalBinder
            myService = binder.getService()
            isBound = true
        }

        override fun onServiceDisconnected(name: ComponentName) {
            isBound = false
        }
    }
}
```

The *onServiceConnected()* method will be called when the client binds successfully to the service. The method is passed as an argument the IBinder object returned by the *onBind()* method of the service. This argument is cast to an object of type MyLocalBinder. Then the *getService()* method of the binder object is called to obtain a reference to the service instance, which, in turn, is assigned to *myService*. A Boolean flag indicates that the connection has been successfully established.

The *onServiceDisconnected()* method is called when the connection ends and sets the Boolean flag to false.

Having established the connection, the next step is to modify the activity to bind to the service. This involves the creation of an intent and a call to the *bindService()* method, which can be performed in the *onCreate()* method of the activity:

```
override fun onCreate(savedInstanceState: Bundle?) {
.
.
    val intent = Intent(this, BoundService::class.java)
    bindService(intent, myConnection, Context.BIND_AUTO_CREATE)
}
```

63.7 Completing the Example

All that remains is to add a mechanism for calling the *getCurrentTime()* method and displaying the result to the user. As is now customary, Android Studio will have created a template *activity_main.xml* file for the activity containing only a TextView. Load this file into the Layout Editor tool and, using Design mode, select the TextView component and change the ID to *myTextView*. Add a Button view beneath the TextView and change the text on the button to read "Show Time", extracting the text to a string resource named *show_time*. On completion of these changes, the layout should resemble that illustrated in Figure 63-1. If any constraints are missing, click on the Infer Constraints button in the Layout Editor toolbar.

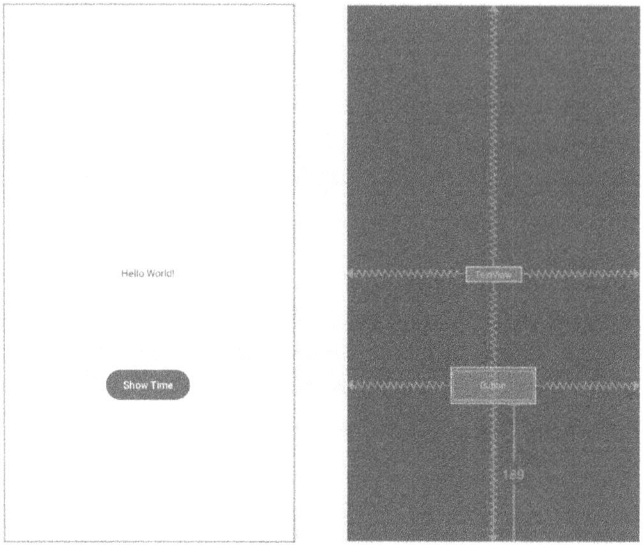

Figure 63-1

Complete the user interface design by selecting the Button and configuring the *onClick* property to call a method named *showTime*.

Finally, edit the *MainActivity.kt* file code to implement the *showTime()* method. This method calls the *getCurrentTime()* method of the service (which, thanks to the *onServiceConnected()* method, is now available from within the activity via the *myService* reference) and assigns the resulting string to the TextView:

```
package com.ebookfrenzy.localbound
.
.
class MainActivity : AppCompatActivity() {

    var myService: BoundService? = null
    var isBound = false

    fun showTime(view: View) {
        val currentTime = myService?.getCurrentTime()
        binding.myTextView.text = currentTime
    }
.
.
}
```

63.8 Testing the Application

With the code changes complete, perform a test run of the application. Once visible, touch the button and note that the text view changes to display the current date and time. The example has successfully started and bound to a service and then called a method of that service to cause a task to be performed, and the results returned to the activity.

63.9 Summary

When a bound service is local and private to an application, components within that application can interact with the service without resorting to inter-process communication (IPC). In general terms, the service's *onBind()* method returns an IBinder object containing a reference to the running service instance. The client component implements a ServiceConnection subclass containing callback methods that are called when the service is connected and disconnected. The former method is passed the IBinder object returned by the *onBind()* method, allowing public methods within the service to be called.

Having covered the implementation of local bound services, the next chapter will focus on using IPC to interact with remote bound services.

Chapter 64

64. Android Remote Bound Services – A Worked Example

In this final chapter dedicated to Android services, an example application will be developed to demonstrate the use of a messenger and handler configuration to facilitate interaction between a client and remote bound service of a messenger and handler configuration to facilitate interaction between a client and a remote bound service.

64.1 Client to Remote Service Communication

As outlined in the previous chapter, the interaction between a client and a local service can be implemented by returning to the client an IBinder object containing a reference to the service object. In the case of remote services, however, this approach does not work because the remote service is running in a different process and, as such, cannot be reached directly from the client.

In the case of remote services, a Messenger and Handler configuration must be created, which allows messages to be passed across process boundaries between client and service.

Specifically, the service creates a Handler instance that will be called when a message is received from the client. In terms of initialization, it is the job of the Handler to create a Messenger object which, in turn, creates an IBinder object to be returned to the client in the *onBind()* method. The client uses This IBinder object to create an instance of the Messenger object and, subsequently, to send messages to the service handler. Each time a message is sent by the client, the *handleMessage()* method of the handler is called, passing through the message object.

The example created in this chapter will consist of an activity and a bound service running in separate processes. The Messenger/Handler mechanism will send a string to the service, which will display in the Logcat output.

64.2 Creating the Example Application

Select the *New Project* option from the welcome screen and, within the resulting new project dialog, choose the Empty Views Activity template before clicking on the Next button.

Enter *RemoteBound* into the Name field and specify *com.ebookfrenzy.remotebound* as the package name. Before clicking on the Finish button, change the Minimum API level setting to API 26: Android 8.0 (Oreo) and the Language menu to Kotlin.

64.3 Designing the User Interface

Locate the *activity_main.xml* file in the Project tool window and double-click on it to load it into the Layout Editor tool. With the Layout Editor tool in Design mode, right-click on the default TextView instance, choose the *Convert view...* menu option, select the Button view from the resulting dialog and click Apply. Change the button's text property to read "Send Message" and extract the string to a new resource named *send_message*.

Finally, configure the *onClick* property to call a method named *sendMessage*.

64.4 Implementing the Remote Bound Service

To implement the remote bound service for this example, add a new class to the project by right-clicking on the package name (located under *app -> kotlin+java*) within the Project tool window and selecting the *New ->*

Service -> Service menu option. Specify *RemoteService* as the class name and make sure that both the *Exported* and *Enabled* options are selected before clicking on *Finish* to create the class.

The next step is to implement the handler class for the new service. This is achieved by extending the Handler class and implementing the *handleMessage()* method. This method will be called when a message is received from the client. It will be passed a Message object as an argument containing any data that the client needs to pass to the service. In this instance, this will be a Bundle object containing a string to be displayed to the user. The modified class in the *RemoteService.kt* file should read as follows once this has been implemented:

```
package com.ebookfrenzy.remotebound

import android.app.Service
import android.content.Intent
import android.os.IBinder
import android.os.Handler
import android.os.Looper
import android.os.Message
import android.os.Messenger
import android.util.Log

class RemoteService : Service() {

    class IncomingHandler : Handler(Looper.getMainLooper()) {

        val TAG = "RemoteService"

        override fun handleMessage(msg: Message) {
            val data = msg.data
            val dataString = data.getString("MyString")
            Log.i(TAG, "Message = $dataString")
        }
    }

    override fun onBind(intent: Intent): IBinder? {
        TODO("Return the communication channel to the service.")
    }
}
```

With the handler implemented, the only remaining task in terms of the service code is to modify the *onBind()* method such that it returns an IBinder object containing a Messenger object which, in turn, contains a reference to the handler:

```
.
.
private val myMessenger = Messenger(IncomingHandler())

override fun onBind(intent: Intent): IBinder {
    return myMessenger.binder
}
```

The first line of the above code fragment creates a new instance of our handler class and passes it through to the constructor of a new Messenger object. Within the *onBind()* method, the *getBinder()* method of the messenger object is called to return the messenger's IBinder object.

64.5 Configuring a Remote Service in the Manifest File

To accurately portray the communication between a client and remote service, it will be necessary to configure the service to run separately from the rest of the application. This is achieved by adding an *android:process* property within the <service> tag for the service in the manifest file. To launch a remote service, it is also necessary to provide an intent filter for the service. To implement this change, modify the *AndroidManifest.xml* file to add the required entry:

```
<?xml version="1.0" encoding="utf-8"?>
<manifest xmlns:android="http://schemas.android.com/apk/res/android"
    package="com.ebookfrenzy.remotebound" >

    <application
        android:allowBackup="true"
        android:icon="@mipmap/ic_launcher"
        android:label="@string/app_name"
        android:supportsRtl="true"
        android:theme="@style/AppTheme" >
        <service
            android:name=".RemoteService"
            android:enabled="true"
            android:exported="true"
            android:process=":my_process" >
        </service>

        <activity
            android:name=".MainActivity" >
            <intent-filter>
                <action android:name="android.intent.action.MAIN" />

                <category android:name="android.intent.category.LAUNCHER" />
            </intent-filter>
        </activity>
     </application>

</manifest>
```

64.6 Launching and Binding to the Remote Service

As with a local bound service, the client component needs to implement an instance of the ServiceConnection class with *onServiceConnected()* and *onServiceDisconnected()* methods. Also, in common with local services, the *onServiceConnected()* method will be passed the IBinder object returned by the *onBind()* method of the remote service, which will be used to send messages to the server handler. In the case of this example, the client is *MainActivity*, the code for which is located in *MainActivity.kt*. Load this file and modify it to add the ServiceConnection class and a variable to store a reference to the received Messenger object together with a Boolean flag to indicate whether or not the connection is established:

```
package com.ebookfrenzy.remotebound

import androidx.appcompat.app.AppCompatActivity
import android.os.Bundle
import android.content.ComponentName
import android.content.ServiceConnection
import android.os.*
import android.view.View

class MainActivity : AppCompatActivity() {

    var myService: Messenger? = null
    var isBound: Boolean = false
.
.
    private val myConnection = object : ServiceConnection {
        override fun onServiceConnected(
                className: ComponentName,
                service: IBinder) {
            myService = Messenger(service)
            isBound = true
        }

        override fun onServiceDisconnected(
                className: ComponentName) {
            myService = null
            isBound = false
        }
    }
}
```

Next, some code must be added to bind to the remote service. This involves creating an intent that matches the intent filter for the service as declared in the manifest file and then making a call to the *bindService()* method, providing the intent and a reference to the ServiceConnection instance as arguments. For this example, this code will be implemented in the activity's *onCreate()* method:

```
.
.
import android.content.Context
import android.content.Intent
.
.
override fun onCreate(savedInstanceState: Bundle?) {
.
.
    val intent = Intent(applicationContext, RemoteService::class.java)
    bindService(intent, myConnection, Context.BIND_AUTO_CREATE)
```

```
}
```

64.7 Sending a Message to the Remote Service

Before testing the application, all that remains is to implement the *sendMessage()* method in the MainActivity class, which is configured to be called when the user touches the button in the user interface. This method needs to check that the service is connected, create a bundle object containing the string to be displayed by the server, add it to a Message object, and send it to the server:

```
fun sendMessage(view: View) {

    if (!isBound) return

    val msg = Message.obtain()

    val bundle = Bundle()
    bundle.putString("MyString", "Message Received")

    msg.data = bundle

    try {
        myService?.send(msg)
    } catch (e: RemoteException) {
        e.printStackTrace()
    }
}
```

With the code changes complete, compile and run the application. Once loaded, open the Logcat tool window and enter the following into the filter field:

```
package:mine tag:RemoteService
```

With the Logcat tool window still visible, tap the button in the user interface, at which point the log message should appear as follows:

```
Message = Message Received
```

64.8 Summary

To implement interaction between a client and remote bound service, an app must implement a handler/message communication framework. The basic concepts behind this technique have been covered in this chapter, together with the implementation of an example application designed to demonstrate communication between a client and a bound service, each running in a separate process.

Chapter 65

65. An Introduction to Kotlin Flow

The earlier chapter, *"An Introduction to Kotlin Coroutines"* taught us about Kotlin Coroutines and explained how they can perform multiple tasks concurrently without blocking the main thread. As we have seen, coroutine suspend functions are ideal for performing tasks that return a single result value. In this chapter, we will introduce Kotlin Flows and explore how these can be used to return sequential streams of results from coroutine-based tasks.

By the end of the chapter, you should understand the Flow, StateFlow, and SharedFlow Kotlin types and appreciate the difference between hot and cold flow streams. In the next chapter (*"An Android SharedFlow Tutorial"*), we will look more closely at using SharedFlow within the context of Android app development.

65.1 Understanding Flows

Flows are a part of the Kotlin programming language and are designed to allow multiple values to be returned sequentially from coroutine-based asynchronous tasks. A stream of data arriving over time via a network connection is ideal for using a Kotlin flow.

Flows are comprised of *producers*, *intermediaries*, and *consumers*. Producers are responsible for providing the data that makes up the flow. For example, the code that retrieves the stream of data from our hypothetical network connection would be considered a producer. As each data value becomes available, the producer emits that value to the flow. The consumer sits at the opposite end of the flow stream and *collects* the values as the producer emits them.

Intermediaries may be placed between the producer and consumer to perform additional operations on the data, such as filtering the stream, performing additional processing, or transforming the data in other ways before it reaches the consumer. Figure 65-1 illustrates the typical structure of a Kotlin flow:

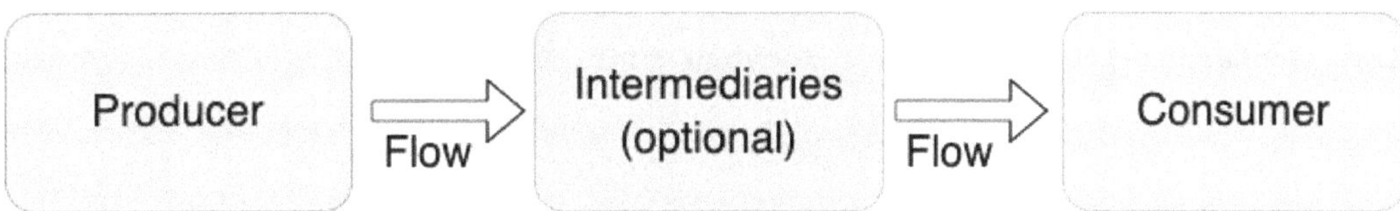

Figure 65-1

The flow shown in the above diagram consists of a single producer and a consumer. In practice, multiple consumers can collect emissions from a single producer, and a single consumer can collect data from multiple producers.

The remainder of this chapter will demonstrate many of the key features of Kotlin flows.

65.2 Creating the Sample Project

Select the *New Project* option from the Android Studio welcome screen and, within the resulting new project dialog, choose the Empty Views Activity template before clicking on the Next button.

Enter *FlowDemo* into the Name field and specify *com.ebookfrenzy.flowdemo* as the package name. Before clicking on the Finish button, change the Minimum API level setting to API 26: Android 8.0 (Oreo) and the Language menu to Kotlin.

Once the new project has been created, locate and load the *activity_main.xml* layout file located in the Project tool window under *app -> res -> layout* and, with the Layout Editor tool in Design mode, replace the TextView object with a Button view and set the text property so that it reads "Start". Once the text value has been set, follow the usual steps to extract the string to a resource.

With the button still selected in the layout, locate the *onClick* property in the Attributes panel and configure it to call a method named *handleFlow*.

65.3 Adding the Kotlin Lifecycle Library

Kotlin flow requires that the Kotlin extensions lifecycle library is included as a dependency, so edit the *Gradle Scripts -> libs.versions.toml* version catalog file and add an entry for the lifecycle runtime library as follows:

```
[versions]
.
.
lifecycleRuntimeKtx = "2.8.7"

[libraries]
.
.
androidx-lifecycle-runtime-ktx = { group = "androidx.lifecycle", name =
"lifecycle-runtime-ktx", version.ref = "lifecycleRuntimeKtx" }
.
.
```

Next, edit the *build.gradle.kts (Module :app)* file and add the lifecycle library to the dependencies section as follows before clicking on the *Sync Now* link at the top of the editor panel:

```
dependencies {
.
.
    implementation(libs.androidx.lifecycle.runtime.ktx)
.
.
```

When prompted, click the Sync Now button at the top of the editor panel to commit to the change.

65.4 Declaring a Flow

The Kotlin Flow type represents the most basic form of flow. Each flow can only emit data of a single type which must be specified when the flow is declared. The following declaration, for example, declares a Flow instance designed to stream String-based data:

```
Flow<String>
```

When declaring a flow, we need to assign to it the code that will generate the data stream. This code is referred to as the *producer block*. This can be achieved using the *flow builder*, which takes a coroutine suspend block containing the producer block code as a parameter. Add the following code to the *MainActivity.kt* file to declare a flow named *myFlow* designed to emit a stream of integer values:

```
.
.
```

```
import kotlinx.coroutines.*
import kotlinx.coroutines.flow.*
.
.
fun myFlow(): Flow<Int> = flow {
    // Producer block
}
```

As an alternative to the flow builder, the *flowOf()* builder can be used to convert a fixed set of values into a flow:

```
val myFlow2 = flowOf(2, 4, 6, 8)
```

Also, many Kotlin collection types now include an *asFlow()* extension function that can be called to convert the contained data to a flow. The following code, for example, converts an array of string values to a flow:

```
val myArrayFlow = arrayOf<String>("Red", "Green", "Blue").asFlow()
```

65.5 Emitting Flow Data

Once a flow has been built, the next step is to make sure the data is emitted to reach any consumers observing the flow. Of the three flow builders we looked at in the previous section, only the *flowOf()* and *asFlow()* builders create flows that automatically emit the data as soon as a consumer starts collecting. In the case of the flow builder, however, we need to write code to emit each value as it becomes available manually. We achieve this by making calls to the *emit()* function and passing through as an argument the current value to be streamed. The following changes to our *myFlow* declaration implement a loop that emits the value of an incrementing counter. To demonstrate the asynchronous nature of flow streams, a two-second delay is performed on each loop iteration:

```
fun myFlow(): Flow<Int> = flow {
    var counter = 1

    while (counter < 6) {
        emit(counter)
        counter++
        delay(2000)
    }
}
```

65.6 Collecting Flow Data

A consumer can collect the streaming data within a flow by calling the *collect()* method on the flow instance. This will continue to collect data from the stream either until the stream ends or the lifecycle scope in which the collection is being performed is destroyed. For example, we can collect the data from the *myFlow* stream and output each value by adding the *handleFlow()* onClick function:

```
.
.
import android.view.View
import androidx.lifecycle.lifecycleScope
.
.
fun handleFlow(view: View) {
    lifecycleScope.launch {
        myFlow().collect() { value ->
```

```
                println("Collected value = $value")
            }
        }
}
```

Note that *collect()* is a suspend function, so it must be called from within a coroutine scope.

Compile and run the app on a device or emulator and display the Logcat tool window. When the Start button is clicked in the running app, the following output should appear with a two-second delay between each output:

```
Collected value = 1
Collected value = 2
Collected value = 3
Collected value = 4
Collected value = 5
```

To add code to be executed when the stream ends, the collection can be performed in a *try/finally* construct, for example:

```
fun handleFlow(view: View) {
    lifecycleScope.launch {
        try {
            myFlow().collect() { value ->
                println("Collected value = $value")
            }
        } finally {
            println("Flow stream ended.")
        }
    }
}
```

The *collect()* operator will collect every value the producer emits, even if new values are emitted while the consumer is still processing the last value. For example, our producer is configured to emit a new value every two seconds. Suppose, however, that we simulate our consumer taking 2.5 seconds to process each collected value as follows:

```
fun handleFlow(view: View) {
    lifecycleScope.launch {
        myFlow().collect() { value ->
            println("Collected value = $value")
            delay(2500)
        }
    }
}
```

When executed, we will still see all the values listed in the output because *collect()* does not discard any uncollected values, regardless of whether more recent ones have been emitted since the last collection. This type of behavior is essential to avoid data loss within the flow. In some situations, however, the consumer may be uninterested in any intermediate values emitted between the most recently processed value and the latest emitted value. In this case, the *collectLatest()* operator can be called on the flow instance. This operator works by canceling the current collection if a new value arrives before processing completes on the previous value and restarts the process on the latest value.

The *conflate()* operator is similar to the *collectLatest()* operator except that instead of canceling the current collection operation when a new value arrives, *conflate()* allows the current operation to complete but discards intermediate values that arrive during this process. When the current operation completes, the most recent value is then collected.

Another collection operator is the *single()* operator. This operator collects a single value from the flow and throws an exception if it finds another value in the stream. This operator is generally only useful where the appearance of a second stream value indicates that something else has gone wrong somewhere in the app or data source.

65.7 Adding a Flow Buffer

When a consumer takes time to process the values emitted by a producer, there is the potential for execution time inefficiencies. Suppose, for example, that in addition to the two-second delay between each emission from our *myFlow* producer, the collection process in our consumer takes an additional second to complete. We can simulate this behavior as follows:

```
.
.
import kotlin.system.measureTimeMillis
.
.
fun handleFlow(view: View) {
    lifecycleScope.launch {
        val elapsedTime = measureTimeMillis {
            myFlow()
                .collect() { value ->
                    println("Collected value = $value")
                    delay(1000)
                }
        }
        println("Duration = $elapsedTime")
    }
}
```

To allow us to measure the total time to process the flow fully, the consumer code has been placed in the closure of a call to the Kotlin *measureTimeMillis()* function. After execution completes, a duration similar to the following will be reported:

```
Duration = 15024
```

This accounts for approximately ten seconds to process the five values within *myFlow* and another five seconds to collect those values. There is an inefficiency here because the producer waits for the consumer to process each value before starting on the next value. This would be much more efficient if the producer did not have to wait for the consumer. We could use the *collectLatest()* or *conflate()* operators, but only if the loss of intermediate values is not a concern. To speed up the processing while collecting emitted values, we can use the *buffer()* operator. This operator buffers values as they are emitted and passes them to the consumer when it is ready to receive them. This allows the producer to continue emitting values while the consumer processes preceding values while ensuring that every emitted value is collected. The *buffer()* operator may be applied to a flow as follows:

```
val elapsedTime = measureTimeMillis {
    myFlow()
```

```
            .buffer()
            .collect() { value ->
            println("Collected value = $value")
            delay(1000)
    }
}
println("Duration = $elapsedTime")
```

Execution of the above code indicates that we have now reclaimed the five seconds previously lost in the collection code:

```
Duration = 10323
```

65.8 Transforming Data with Intermediaries

All of the examples we have looked at in this chapter have passed the data values to the consumer without any modifications. Changes to the data can be made between the producer and consumer by applying one or more *intermediate flow operators*. In this section, we will look at some of these operators.

The *map()* operator can convert the value to some other value. We can use *map()*, for example, to convert our integer value to a string:

```
fun handleFlow(view: View) {
    lifecycleScope.launch {
        myFlow()
            .map {
                "Collected value = $it"
            }
            .collect() {
                println(it)
            }
        }
    }
}
```

When the code is executed, it will give us the following output:

```
Collected value = 1
Collected value = 2
Collected value = 3
Collected value = 4
Collected value = 5
```

The *map()* operator will perform the conversion on every collected value. The *filter()* operator can control which values get collected. The filter code block must contain an expression that returns a Boolean value. Only if the expression evaluates to true does the value pass through to the collection. The following code filters odd numbers out of the data flow (note that we've left the *map()* operator in place to demonstrate the chaining of operators):

```
fun handleFlow(view: View) {
    lifecycleScope.launch {
        myFlow()
            .filter {
```

```
                    it % 2 == 0
                }
                .map {
                    "Collected value $it"
                }
                .collect() {
                    println(it)
                }
            }
        }
    }
```

The above changes will generate the following output:

```
Collected value = 2
Collected value = 4
```

The *transform()* operator serves a similar purpose to *map()* but provides more flexibility. The *transform()* operator also needs to emit the modified result manually. A particular advantage of *transform()* is that it can emit multiple values, as demonstrated below:

```
.
.
myFlow()
    .transform {
        emit("Value = $it")
        var doubled = it * 2
        emit("Value doubled = $doubled")
    }
    .collect {
        println(it)
    }
}
.
.
// Output
Value = 1
Value doubled = 2
Value = 2
Value doubled = 4
Value = 3
Value doubled = 6
Value = 4
Value doubled = 8
Value = 5
Value doubled = 10
```

65.9 Terminal Flow Operators

All the collection operators covered previously are referred to as *terminal flow operators*. The *reduce()* operator is one of several other terminal flow operators that can be used in place of a collection operator to make changes to the flow data. The *reduce()* operator takes two parameters in the form of an *accumulator* and a *value*. The first flow value is placed in the accumulator, and a specified operation is performed between the accumulator and the current value (with the result stored in the accumulator):

```
.
.
myFlow()
    .reduce { accumulator, value ->
        println("accumulator = $accumulator, value = $value")
        accumulator + value
    }
}
.
.
// Output
accumulator = 1, value = 2
accumulator = 3, value = 3
accumulator = 6, value = 4
accumulator = 10, value = 5
```

The *fold()* operator works similarly to the *reduce()* operator, with the exception that it is passed an initial accumulator value:

```
.
.
myFlow()
    .fold(10) { accumulator, value ->
        println("accumulator = $accumulator, value = $value")
        accumulator * value
    }
}
.
.
// Output
accumulator = 10, value = 1
accumulator = 10, value = 2
accumulator = 20, value = 3
accumulator = 60, value = 4
accumulator = 240, value = 5
```

65.10 Flow Flattening

As we have seen in earlier examples, we can use operators to perform tasks on values collected from a flow. However, an interesting situation occurs when that task creates one or more flows resulting in a "flow of flows". In such situations, these streams can be *flattened* into a single stream.

Consider the following example code, which declares two flows:

```
fun myFlow(): Flow<Int> = flow {
    for (i in 1..5) {
        emit(i)
    }
}

fun doubleIt(value: Int) = flow {
    emit(value)
    delay(1000)
    emit(value + value)
}
```

If we were to call *doubleIt()* for each value in the *myFlow* stream, we would end up with a separate flow for each value. This problem can be solved by concatenating the *doubleIt()* streams into a single flow using the *flatMapConcat()* operator as follows:

```
.
.
myFlow()
    .flatMapConcat { doubleIt(it) }
    .collect { println(it) }
.
.
```

When this modified code executes, we will see the following output from the *collect()* operator:

```
1
2
2
4
3
6
4
8
5
10
```

As we can see from the output, the *doubleIt()* flow has emitted the value provided by *myFlow*, followed by the doubled value. When using the *flatMapConcat()* operator, the *doubleIt()* calls are being performed synchronously, causing execution to wait until *doubleIt()* has emitted both values before processing the next flow value. The emitted values can instead be collected asynchronously using the *flatMapMerge()* operator as follows:

```
myFlow()
    .flatMapMerge { doubleIt(it) }
    .collect { println(it) }
}
```

When executed, the following output will appear:

```
1
2
3
```

```
4
5
2
4
6
8
10
```

65.11 Combining Multiple Flows

Multiple flows can be combined into a single flow using the *zip()* and *combine()* operators. The following code demonstrates the *zip()* operator being used to convert two flows into a single flow:

```
fun handleFlow(view: View) {
    lifecycleScope.launch {
        val flow1 = (1..5).asFlow()
            .onEach { delay(1000) }
        val flow2 = flowOf("one", "two", "three", "four")
            .onEach { delay(1500) }
        flow1.zip(flow2) { value, string -> "$value, $string" }
            .collect { println(it) }
    }
}
// Output
1, one
2, two
3, three
4, four
```

We have applied the *onEach()* operator to both flows in the above code. This is a useful operator for performing a task on receipt of each stream value.

The *zip()* operator will wait until both flows have emitted a new value before performing the collection. The *combine()* operator works slightly differently in that it proceeds as soon as either flow emits a new value, using the last value emitted by the other flow in the absence of a new value:

```
.
.
val flow1 = (1..5).asFlow()
    .onEach { delay(1000) }
val flow2 = flowOf("one", "two", "three", "four")
    .onEach { delay(1500) }
flow1.combine(flow2) { value, string -> "$value, $string" }
    .collect { println(it) }
.
.
// Output
1, one
2, one
3, one
```

```
3, two
4, two
4, three
5, three
5, four
```

As we can see from the output, multiple instances have occurred where the last value was reused on one flow because a new value was emitted on the other.

65.12 Hot and Cold Flows

So far, in this chapter, we have looked exclusively at the Kotlin Flow type. Kotlin also provides additional types in the form of StateFlow and SharedFlow. Before exploring these, however, it is important to understand the concept of *hot* and *cold* flows.

A stream declared using the Flow type is called a *cold flow* because the code within the producer does not begin executing until a consumer begins collecting values. StateFlow and SharedFlow, on the other hand, are referred to as *hot flows* because they begin emitting values immediately, regardless of whether consumers are collecting the values.

Once a consumer begins collecting from a hot flow, it will receive the latest value emitted by the producer, followed by any subsequent values. Any previous values emitted before the collection starts will be lost unless steps are taken to implement caching.

Another important difference between Flow, StateFlow, and SharedFlow is that a Flow-based stream cannot have multiple collectors. Each Flow collector launches a new flow with its own independent data stream. With StateFlow and SharedFlow, on the other hand, multiple collectors share access to the same flow.

65.13 StateFlow

StateFlow, as the name suggests, is primarily used to observe a state change within an app, such as the current setting of a counter, toggle button, or slider. Each StateFlow instance stores a single value likely to change over time and notifies all consumers when those changes occur. This enables you to write code that reacts to changes in the state instead of code that checks whether or not a state value has changed continually. StateFlow behaves the same way as LiveData except that LiveData has lifecycle awareness and does not require an initial value (LiveData was covered previously beginning with the chapter titled *"Modern Android App Architecture with Jetpack"*).

To create a StateFlow stream, create an instance of MutableStateFlow, passing through a mandatory initial value. This is the variable that will be used to change the current state value from within the app code:

```
private val _stateFlow = MutableStateFlow(0)
```

Next, call *asStateFlow()* on the MutableStateFlow instance to convert it into a StateFlow from which changes in state can be collected:

```
val stateFlow = _stateFlow.asStateFlow()
```

Once created, any changes to the state are made via the *value* property of the mutable state instance. The following code, for example, increments the state value:

```
_stateFlow.value += 1
```

Once the flow is active, the state can be consumed in the usual ways, though it is generally recommended to collect from StateFlow using the *collectLatest()* operator, for example:

```
stateFlow.collectLatest {
    println("Counter = $it")
```

```
}
```

To try out this example, make the following modifications to the *MainActivity.kt* file:

```
.
.
class MainActivity : AppCompatActivity() {

    private val _stateFlow = MutableStateFlow(0)
    val stateFlow = _stateFlow.asStateFlow()

    override fun onCreate(savedInstanceState: Bundle?) {
.
.
        lifecycleScope.launch {
            stateFlow.collectLatest {
                println("Counter = $it")
            }
        }
    }

    fun handleFlow(view: View) {
        _stateFlow.value += 1
    }
}
```

Run the app and verify that the Start button outputs the incremented counter value each time it is clicked.

65.14 SharedFlow

SharedFlow provides a more general-purpose streaming option than that offered by StateFlow. Some of the key differences between StateFlow and SharedFlow are as follows:

- Consumers are generally referred to as *subscribers.*
- An initial value is not provided when creating a SharedFlow instance.
- SharedFlow allows values emitted before collection started to be "replayed" to the collector.
- SharedFlow *emits* values instead of using a *value* property.

SharedFlow instances are created using MutableSharedFlow as the backing property on which we call the *asSharedFlow()* to obtain a SharedFlow reference:

```
.
.
import kotlinx.coroutines.channels.BufferOverflow
.
.
class MainActivity : AppCompatActivity() {

private val _sharedFlow = MutableSharedFlow<Int>(
```

```
        replay = 10, onBufferOverflow = BufferOverflow.DROP_OLDEST)
val sharedFlow = _sharedFlow.asSharedFlow()
.
.
```

As configured above, new flow subscribers will receive the last ten values before receiving any new values. The above flow is configured to discard the oldest value when more than ten values are buffered. The full set of options for handling buffer overflows is as follows:

- **DROP_LATEST** - The latest value is dropped when the buffer is full, leaving the buffer unchanged as new values are processed.
- **DROP_OLDEST** - Treats the buffer as a "last-in, first-out" stack where the oldest value is dropped to make room for a new value when the buffer is full.
- **SUSPEND** - The flow is suspended when the buffer is full.

Values are emitted on a SharedFlow stream by calling the *emit()* method of the MutableSharedFlow instance:

```
fun handleFlow(view: View) {

    var counter = 1

    lifecycleScope.launch {
        while (counter < 6) {
            _sharedFlow.emit(counter)
            counter++
            delay(2000)
        }
    }
}
```

Once the flow is active, subscribers can collect values using the usual techniques on the SharedFlow instance. For example, we can add the following collection code to the *onCreate()* method of our example project to output the flow values:

```
override fun onCreate(savedInstanceState: Bundle?) {
.
.
    lifecycleScope.launch {
        sharedFlow.collect {
            println("$it")
        }
    }
}
```

Also, the current number of subscribers to a SharedFlow stream can be obtained via the *subscriptionCount* property of the mutable instance:

```
val subCount = _sharedFlow.subscriptionCount
```

65.15 Summary

Kotlin flows allow sequential data or state changes to be returned over time from asynchronous tasks. A flow consists of a producer that emits a sequence of values and consumers that collect and process those values. The flow stream can be manipulated between the producer and consumer by applying one or more intermediary operators, including transformations and filtering. Flows are created based on the Flow, StateFlow, and SharedFlow types. A Flow-based stream can only have a single collector, while StateFlow and SharedFlow can have multiple collectors.

Flows are categorized as being hot or cold. A cold flow does not begin emitting values until a consumer begins collection. On the other hand, hot flows begin emitting values as soon as they are created, regardless of whether or not the values are being collected. In the case of SharedFlow, a predefined number of values may be buffered and replayed to new subscribers when they begin collecting values.

Chapter 66

66. An Android SharedFlow Tutorial

The previous chapter introduced Kotlin flows and explored how these can be used to return multiple sequential values from within coroutine-based asynchronous code. This tutorial will look at a more detailed flow implementation, this time using SharedFlow within a ViewModel. The tutorial will also demonstrate how to ensure that flow collection responds correctly to an app switching between background and foreground modes.

66.1 About the Project

The app created in this chapter will consist of a RecyclerView located in the user interface layout of the main fragment. A shared flow located within a ViewModel will be activated as soon as the view model is created and will emit an integer value every two seconds. Code within the main fragment will collect the values from the flow and list them in the RecyclerView. The project will then be modified to suspend the collection process while the app is placed in the background.

66.2 Creating the SharedFlowDemo Project

Begin by launching Android Studio, selecting the *New Project* option from the welcome screen, and, within the new project dialog, choose the Empty Views Activity template before clicking the Next button.

Enter *SharedFlowDemo* into the Name field and specify *com.ebookfrenzy.sharedflowdemo* as the package name. Before clicking on the Finish button, change the Minimum API level setting to API 26: Android 8.0 (Oreo) and the Language menu to Kotlin. Migrate the project to view binding using the steps outlined in section *18.8 Migrating a Project to View Binding.*

66.3 Adding the Lifecycle Libraries

Edit the *Gradle Scripts -> libs.versions.toml* version catalog file and add entries for the lifecycle runtime and viewmodel libraries as follows:

```
[versions]
.
.
lifecycleRuntimeKtx = "2.11.0"
lifecycleViewmodelKtx = "2.11.0"

[libraries]
.
.
androidx-lifecycle-runtime-ktx = { group = "androidx.lifecycle", name =
"lifecycle-runtime-ktx", version.ref = "lifecycleRuntimeKtx" }
androidx-lifecycle-viewmodel-ktx = { group = "androidx.lifecycle", name =
"lifecycle-viewmodel-ktx", version.ref = "lifecycleViewmodelKtx" }
```

Next, edit the *build.gradle.kts (Module :app)* file and add the lifecycle libraries to the dependencies section as follows before clicking on the *Sync Now* link at the top of the editor panel:

```
dependencies {
.
```

```
.
    implementation(libs.androidx.lifecycle.runtime.ktx)
    implementation(libs.androidx.lifecycle.viewmodel.ktx)
.
.
}
```

66.4 Designing the User Interface Layout

Locate the *res -> layout -> activity_main.xml* file, load it into the layout editor, and delete the default TextView component. From the Containers section of the widget palette, drag and drop a RecyclerView onto the center of the layout canvas. Add constraints so the view fills the entire canvas, and each side is attached to the corresponding side of the parent container. With the RecyclerView selected, refer to the Attributes tool window, change the id to *recyclerView* if it does not already have this id, and set layout_height and layout_width to *match_constraint*.

66.5 Adding the List Row Layout

We now need to add a layout resource file containing a TextView to be used for each row in the list. Add this file now by right-clicking on the *app -> res -> layout* entry in the Project tool window and selecting the *New -> Layout resource file* menu option. Name the file *list_row* and change the root element to LinearLayout before clicking OK to create the file and load it into the layout editor. With the layout editor in Design mode, drag a TextView object from the palette onto the layout, where it will appear by default at the top of the layout:

Figure 66-1

With the TextView selected in the layout, use the Attributes tool window to set the view id to *itemText,* the layout_height to 50dp, and the textSize attribute to 20sp. With the text view still selected, unfold the gravity settings and set *center* to true and all other values to false:

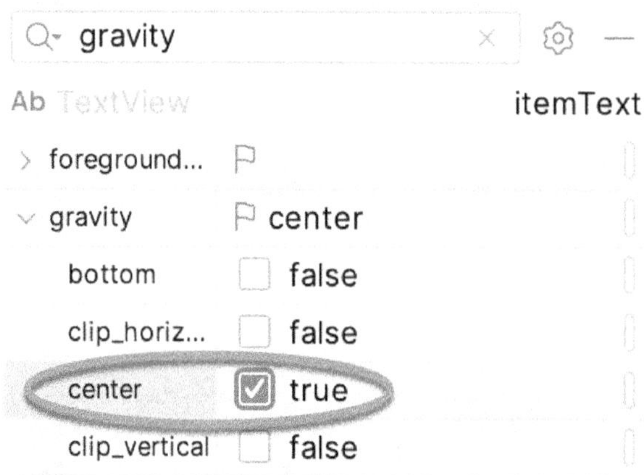

Figure 66-2

Select the LinearLayout entry in the Component Tree window and set the layout_height attribute to *wrap_ content.*

66.6 Adding the RecyclerView Adapter

Add the RecyclerView adapter class to the project by right-clicking on the *app -> kotlin+java -> com.ebookfrenzy.sharedflowdemo* entry in the Project tool window and selecting the *New -> Kotlin Class/File...* menu. In the dialog, name the class *ListAdapter* and choose *Class* from the list before pressing the keyboard Return key. With the resulting *ListAdapter.kt* class file loaded into the editor, implement the class as follows:

```
package com.ebookfrenzy.sharedflowdemo

import android.view.LayoutInflater
import android.view.View
import android.view.ViewGroup
import android.widget.TextView
import androidx.annotation.NonNull
import androidx.recyclerview.widget.RecyclerView
import com.ebookfrenzy.sharedflowdemo.R

class ListAdapter(private var itemsList: List<String>) :
    RecyclerView.Adapter<ListAdapter.MyViewHolder>() {

    class MyViewHolder(view: View) : RecyclerView.ViewHolder(view) {
        var itemText: TextView = view.findViewById(R.id.itemText)
    }

    override fun onCreateViewHolder(parent: ViewGroup,
                                    viewType: Int): MyViewHolder {
        val itemView = LayoutInflater.from(parent.context)
            .inflate(R.layout.list_row, parent, false)
        return MyViewHolder(itemView)
    }

    override fun onBindViewHolder(holder: MyViewHolder, position: Int) {
        val item = itemsList[position]
        holder.itemText.text = item
    }

    override fun getItemCount(): Int {
        return itemsList.size
    }
}
```

66.7 Adding the ViewModel

The next step is to add the view model and write some code to create and start the SharedFlow instance. Begin by locating the *com.ebookfrenzy.sharedflowdemo* entry in the Project tool window, right-clicking on it, and selecting the *New -> Kotlin Class/File* menu option. Name the new class MainViewModel and press the keyboard enter key. Edit the new class file so that it reads as follows:

```
package com.ebookfrenzy.sharedflowdemo
```

```
import androidx.lifecycle.ViewModel
import androidx.lifecycle.viewModelScope
import kotlinx.coroutines.delay
import kotlinx.coroutines.flow.MutableSharedFlow
import kotlinx.coroutines.flow.asSharedFlow
import kotlinx.coroutines.launch

class MainViewModel : ViewModel() {

    init {
        sharedFlowInit()
    }

    private fun sharedFlowInit() {
    }
}
```

When the ViewModel instance is created, the initializer will call the *sharedFlowInit()* function. The purpose of this function is to launch a new coroutine containing a loop in which new values are emitted using a shared flow. Before adding this code, we first need to declare the flow as follows:

```
.
.
class MainViewModel : ViewModel() {

    private val _sharedFlow = MutableSharedFlow<Int>()
    val sharedFlow = _sharedFlow.asSharedFlow()
.
.
```

With the flow declared, code can now be added to the *sharedFlowInit()* function to launch the flow using the view model's own scope. This will ensure that the flow ends when the view model is destroyed:

```
fun sharedFlowInit() {
    viewModelScope.launch {
        for (i in 1..1000) {
            delay(2000)
            _sharedFlow.emit(i)
        }
    }
}
```

66.8 Configuring the ViewModelProvider

Later in this chapter, we will require access to the view model from within the *MainActivity.kt* file. As outlined in *"An Android ViewModel Tutorial"*, this is achieved using a ViewModelProvider instance. Edit the *MainActivity.kt* file and modify it as follows to access the view model:

```
.
.
```

```
import androidx.lifecycle.ViewModelProvider
.
.
class MainActivity : AppCompatActivity() {

    private lateinit var binding: ActivityMainBinding
    private lateinit var viewModel: MainViewModel

   override fun onCreate(savedInstanceState: Bundle?) {
.
.
        viewModel = ViewModelProvider(this)[MainViewModel::class.java]
}
```

66.9 Collecting the Flow Values

Before testing the app for the first time, we need to add some code to perform the flow collection and display those values in the RecyclerView list. The intention is for collection to start automatically when the app launches, so this code will be placed in the *onCreate()* method of the *MainActivity.kt* file.

Start by adding some variables to store a reference to our list adapter and the array of items to be displayed in the RecyclerView. Now is also a good time to add the imports we will need to complete the app:

```
.
.
import androidx.lifecycle.Lifecycle
import kotlinx.coroutines.flow.*
import kotlinx.coroutines.launch
import androidx.lifecycle.repeatOnLifecycle
import androidx.lifecycle.lifecycleScope
import androidx.recyclerview.widget.LinearLayoutManager
.
.
class MainActivity : AppCompatActivity() {

    private lateinit var binding: ActivityMainBinding
    private lateinit var viewModel: MainViewModel

    private val itemList = ArrayList<String>()
    private lateinit var listAdapter: ListAdapter
.
.
```

Next, add a new method named *collectFlow()* and call if from the *onCreate()* method:

```
override fun onCreate(savedInstanceState: Bundle?) {
.
.
    collectFlow()
}
```

```
fun collectFlow() {

}
```

Add code to the *collectFlow()* method to create a list adapter instance and assign it to the RecyclerView. We also need to configure the RecyclerView to use a LinearLayout manager:

```
fun collectFlow() {
    listAdapter = ListAdapter(itemList)
    val layoutManager = LinearLayoutManager(this)
    binding.recyclerView.layoutManager = layoutManager
    binding.recyclerView.adapter = listAdapter
}
```

With these changes, we are ready to collect the values emitted by the shared flow and add them to the RecyclerView. Add code to the *collectFlow()* method so that it now reads as follows:

```
fun collectFlow() {
    listAdapter = ListAdapter(itemList)
    val layoutManager = LinearLayoutManager(this)
    binding.recyclerView.layoutManager = layoutManager
    binding.recyclerView.adapter = listAdapter

    lifecycleScope.launch {
        viewModel.sharedFlow.collect { value ->
            itemList.add(value.toString())
            listAdapter.notifyItemInserted(itemList.lastIndex)
            binding.recyclerView.smoothScrollToPosition(listAdapter.itemCount)
        }
    }
}
```

This code accesses the shared flow instance within the view model and begins collecting values from the stream. Each collected value is added to the *itemList* array used when the ListAdapter was initialized. We then notify the adapter that a new item has been added to the end of the list. This will cause the RecyclerView to update so that the new value appears in the list. We have also added code to instruct the RecyclerView to scroll smoothly to the last position in the list so that the most recent values are automatically visible.

66.10 Testing the SharedFlowDemo App

Compile and run the app on a device or emulator and verify that values appear within the RecyclerView list as the shared flow emits them. Rotate the device into landscape orientation to trigger a configuration change and confirm that the sequence of values continues without restarting from zero:

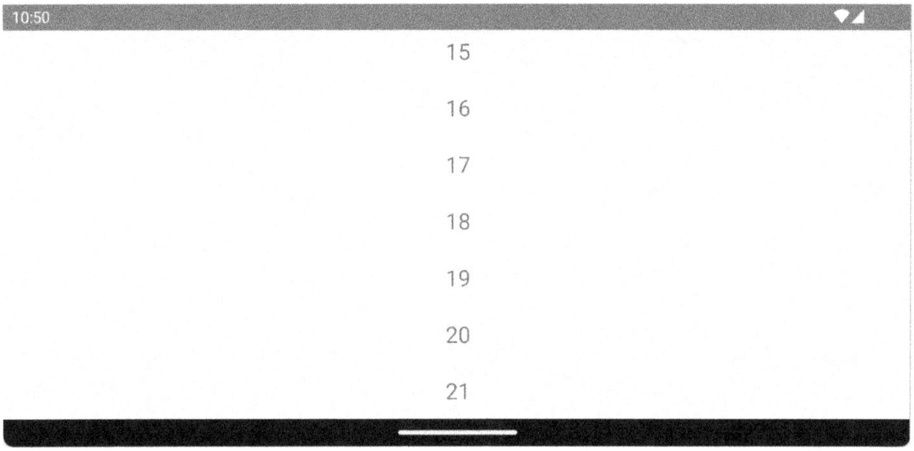

Figure 66-3

With the app now working, it is time to look at what happens when it is placed in the background.

66.11 Handling Flows in the Background

Our app has a shared flow that feeds values to the user interface in the form of a RecyclerView. By performing the collection in a coroutine scope, the user interface remains responsive while the flow is being collected (you can verify this by scrolling up and down within the list of values while the list is updating). This raises the question of what happens when the app is placed in the background. We can add some diagnostic output to the emitter and collector code to find out. First, edit the *MainViewModel.kt* file and add a *Log()* call within the body of the emission *for* loop:

```
.
.
import android.util.Log
.
.
class MainViewModel : ViewModel() {

    private val TAG = "SharedFlowDemo"
.
.
    private fun sharedFlowInit() {
        viewModelScope.launch {
            for (i in 1..1000) {
                delay(2000)
                Log.i(TAG, "Emitting $i")
                _sharedFlow.emit(i)
            }
        }
    }
.
.
```

Make a similar change to the collection code block in the *MainActivity.kt* file as follows:

```
.
.
import android.util.Log
.
.
class MainActivity : AppCompatActivity() {

    private val TAG = "SharedFlowDemo"
.
.
    fun collectFlow() {
.
.
        lifecycleScope.launch {
            viewModel.sharedFlow.collect { value ->
                Log.i(TAG, "Collecting $value")
                itemList.add(value.toString())
                listAdapter.notifyItemInserted(itemList.lastIndex)
                binding.recyclerView.smoothScrollToPosition(
                                        listAdapter.itemCount)
            }
        }
    }
}
```

Once these changes have been made, display the Logcat tool window and enter the following keys into the filter field:

```
package:mine tag:SharedFlowDemo
```

Run the app, and as the list of values updates, output similar to the following should appear in the Logcat panel:

```
Emitting 1
Collecting 1
Emitting 2
Collecting 2
Emitting 3
Collecting 3
.
.
```

Now place the app in the background and note that both the emission and collection operations continue to run, even though the app is no longer visible to the user. The continued emission is to be expected and is the correct behavior for a shared flow residing within a view model. However, it is wasteful of resources to collect data and update a user interface that is not currently visible to the user. We can resolve this problem by executing the collection using the *repeatOnLifecycle* function.

The repeatOnLifecycle function is a suspend function that runs a specified block of code each time the current lifecycle reaches or exceeds one of the following states (a topic covered previously in the *"Working with Android Lifecycle-Aware Components"* chapter):

- Lifecycle.State.INITIALIZED
- Lifecycle.State.CREATED
- Lifecycle.State.STARTED
- Lifecycle.State.RESUMED
- Lifecycle.State.DESTROYED

Conversely, the coroutine is canceled when the lifecycle drops below the target state.

In this case, we want the collection to start each time *Lifecycle.State.START* is reached and to stop when the lifecycle is suspended. To implement this, modify the collection code as follows:

```
lifecycleScope.launch {
    repeatOnLifecycle(Lifecycle.State.STARTED) {
        viewModel.sharedFlow.collect { value ->
            Log.i(TAG, "Collecting $value")
            itemList.add(value.toString())
            listAdapter.notifyDataSetChanged()
            binding.recyclerView.smoothScrollToPosition(listAdapter.itemCount)
        }
    }
}
```

Rerun the app, place it in the background, and note that only the emission diagnostic messages appear in the Logcat output, confirming that the main fragment is no longer collecting values and adding them to the RecyclerView list. When the app is brought to the foreground, the collection will resume at the latest emitted value since replay was not configured on the shared flow.

66.12 Summary

In this chapter, we created a SharedFlow instance within a view model. We then collected the streamed values within the main fragment and used that data to update the user interface. We also outlined the importance of avoiding unnecessary flow-driven user interface updates when an app is placed in the background. This problem can easily be resolved using the repeatOnLifecycle function. This function can be used to cancel and restart asynchronous tasks such as flow collection when the containing lifecycle reaches a target lifecycle state.

67. An Overview of Android SQLite Databases

Mobile applications that do not need to store at least some amount of persistent data are few and far between. The use of databases is an essential aspect of most applications, ranging from applications that are almost entirely data-driven, to those that simply need to store small amounts of data such as the prevailing score of a game.

The importance of persistent data storage becomes even more evident when taking into consideration the somewhat transient lifecycle of the typical Android application. With the ever-present risk that the Android runtime system will terminate an application component to free up resources, a comprehensive data storage strategy to avoid data loss is a key factor in the design and implementation of any application development strategy.

This chapter will provide an overview of the SQLite database management system bundled with the Android operating system, together with an outline of the Android SDK classes that are provided to facilitate persistent SQLite-based database storage from within an Android application. Before delving into the specifics of SQLite in the context of Android development, however, a brief overview of databases and SQL will be covered.

67.1 Understanding database tables

Database *tables* provide the most basic level of data structure in a database. Each database can contain multiple tables and each table is designed to hold information of a specific type. For example, a database may contain a *customer* table that contains the name, address, and telephone number for each of the customers of a particular business. The same database may also include a *products* table used to store the product descriptions with associated product codes for the items sold by the business.

Each table in a database is assigned a name that must be unique within that particular database. A table name, once assigned to a table in one database, may not be used for another table except within the context of another database.

67.2 Introducing database schema

Database Schemas define the characteristics of the data stored in a database table. For example, the table schema for a customer database table might define that the customer name is a string of no more than 20 characters in length and that the customer phone number is a numerical data field of a certain format.

Schemas are also used to define the structure of entire databases and the relationship between the various tables contained in each database.

67.3 Columns and data types

It is helpful at this stage to begin to view a database table as being similar to a spreadsheet where data is stored in rows and columns.

Each column represents a data field in the corresponding table. For example, the name, address, and telephone data fields of a table are all *columns*.

Each column, in turn, is defined to contain a certain type of data. A column designed to store numbers would, therefore, be defined as containing numerical data.

67.4 Database rows

Each new record that is saved to a table is stored in a row. Each row, in turn, consists of the columns of data associated with the saved record.

Once again, consider the spreadsheet analogy described earlier in this chapter. Each entry in a customer table is equivalent to a row in a spreadsheet and each column contains the data for each customer (name, address, telephone, etc). When a new customer is added to the table, a new row is created and the data for that customer is stored in the corresponding columns of the new row.

Rows are also sometimes referred to as *records* or *entries* and these terms can generally be used interchangeably.

67.5 Introducing primary keys

Each database table should contain one or more columns that can be used to identify each row in the table uniquely. This is known in database terminology as the *Primary Key*. For example, a table may use a bank account number column as the primary key. Alternatively, a customer table may use the customer's social security number as the primary key.

Primary keys allow the database management system to identify a specific row in a table uniquely. Without a primary key, it would not be possible to retrieve or delete a specific row in a table because there can be no certainty that the correct row has been selected. For example, suppose a table existed where the customer's last name had been defined as the primary key. Imagine then the problem that might arise if more than one customer named "Smith" were recorded in the database. Without some guaranteed way to identify a specific row uniquely, it would be impossible to ensure the correct data was being accessed at any given time.

Primary keys can comprise a single column or multiple columns in a table. To qualify as a single column primary key, no two rows can contain matching primary key values. When using multiple columns to construct a primary key, individual column values do not need to be unique, but all the columns' values combined must be unique.

67.6 What is SQLite?

SQLite is an embedded, relational database management system (RDBMS). Most relational databases (Oracle, SQL Server, and MySQL being prime examples) are standalone server processes that run independently, and in cooperation with, applications that require database access. SQLite is referred to as *embedded* because it is provided in the form of a library that is linked into applications. As such, there is no standalone database server running in the background. All database operations are handled internally within the application through calls to functions contained in the SQLite library.

The developers of SQLite have placed the technology into the public domain with the result that it is now a widely deployed database solution.

SQLite is written in the C programming language and as such, the Android SDK provides a Java-based "wrapper" around the underlying database interface. This essentially consists of a set of classes that may be utilized within the Java or Kotlin code of an application to create and manage SQLite-based databases.

For additional information about SQLite refer to *https://www.sqlite.org*.

67.7 Structured Query Language (SQL)

Data is accessed in SQLite databases using a high-level language known as Structured Query Language. This is usually abbreviated to SQL and pronounced *sequel*. SQL is a standard language used by most relational database management systems. SQLite conforms mostly to the SQL-92 standard.

SQL is essentially a very simple and easy-to-use language designed specifically to enable the reading and writing of database data. Because SQL contains a small set of keywords, it can be learned quickly. In addition, SQL syntax is more or less identical between most DBMS implementations, so having learned SQL for one system, your skills will likely transfer to other database management systems.

While some basic SQL statements will be used within this chapter, a detailed overview of SQL is beyond the scope of this book. There are, however, many other resources that provide a far better overview of SQL than we could ever hope to provide in a single chapter here.

67.8 Trying SQLite on an Android Virtual Device (AVD)

For readers unfamiliar with databases in general and SQLite in particular, diving right into creating an Android application that uses SQLite may seem a little intimidating. Fortunately, Android is shipped with SQLite pre-installed, including an interactive environment for issuing SQL commands from within an *adb shell* session connected to a running Android AVD emulator instance. This is both a useful way to learn about SQLite and SQL and also an invaluable tool for identifying problems with databases created by applications running in an emulator.

To launch an interactive SQLite session, begin by running an AVD session. This can be achieved from within Android Studio by launching the Device Manager (*Tools -> Device Manager*), selecting a previously configured AVD, and clicking on the start button.

Once the AVD is up and running, open a Terminal or Command-Prompt window and connect to the emulator using the *adb* command-line tool as follows (note that the –e flag directs the tool to look for an emulator with which to connect, rather than a physical device):

```
adb -e shell
```

Once connected, the shell environment will provide a command prompt at which commands may be entered. Begin by obtaining superuser privileges using the *su* command:

```
Generic_x86:/ su
root@android:/ #
```

If a message appears indicating that superuser privileges are not allowed, the AVD instance likely includes Google Play support. To resolve this create a new AVD and, on the "Choose a device definition" screen, select a device that does not have a marker in the "Play Store" column.

Data stored in SQLite databases are stored in database files on the file system of the Android device on which the application is running. By default, the file system path for these database files is as follows:

```
/data/data/<package name>/databases/<database filename>.db
```

For example, if an application with the package name *com.example.MyDBApp* creates a database named *mydatabase.db*, the path to the file on the device would read as follows:

```
/data/data/com.example.MyDBApp/databases/mydatabase.db
```

For this exercise, therefore, change directory to /data/data within the adb shell and create a sub-directory hierarchy suitable for some SQLite experimentation:

```
cd /data/data
mkdir com.example.dbexample
cd com.example.dbexample
mkdir databases
cd databases
```

With a suitable location created for the database file, launch the interactive SQLite tool as follows:

```
root@android:/data/data/databases # sqlite3 ./mydatabase.db
sqlite3 ./mydatabase.db
SQLite version 3.8.10.2 2015-05-20 18:17:19
Enter ".help" for usage hints.
sqlite>
```

At the *sqlite>* prompt, commands may be entered to perform tasks such as creating tables and inserting and retrieving data. For example, to create a new table in our database with fields to hold ID, name, address, and phone number fields the following statement is required:

```
create table contacts (_id integer primary key autoincrement, name text, address text, phone text);
```

Note that each row in a table should have a *primary key* that is unique to that row. In the above example, we have designated the ID field as the primary key, declared it as being of type *integer,* and asked SQLite to increment the number automatically each time a row is added. This is a common way to make sure that each row has a unique primary key. On most other platforms, the choice of name for the primary key is arbitrary. In the case of Android, however, the key must be named *_id* for the database to be fully accessible using all of the Android database-related classes. The remaining fields are each declared as being of type *text.*

To list the tables in the currently selected database, use the *.tables* statement:

```
sqlite> .tables
contacts
```

To insert records into the table:

```
sqlite> insert into contacts (name, address, phone) values ("Bill Smith", "123 Main Street, California", "123-555-2323");
sqlite> insert into contacts (name, address, phone) values ("Mike Parks", "10 Upping Street, Idaho", "444-444-1212");
```

To retrieve all rows from a table:

```
sqlite> select * from contacts;
1|Bill Smith|123 Main Street, California|123-555-2323
2|Mike Parks|10 Upping Street, Idaho|444-444-1212
```

To extract a row that meets specific criteria:

```
sqlite> select * from contacts where name="Mike Parks";
2|Mike Parks|10 Upping Street, Idaho|444-444-1212
```

To exit from the sqlite3 interactive environment:

```
sqlite> .exit
```

When running an Android application in the emulator environment, any database files will be created on the file system of the emulator using the previously discussed path convention. This has the advantage that you can connect with adb, navigate to the location of the database file, load it into the sqlite3 interactive tool and perform tasks on the data to identify possible problems occurring in the application code.

It is also important to note that, while it is possible to connect with an adb shell to a physical Android device, the shell is not granted sufficient privileges by default to create and manage SQLite databases. Debugging of database problems is, therefore, best performed using an AVD session. Alternatively, databases can be inspected on both emulators and devices using the Android Studio Database Inspector, a topic that will be covered later.

67.9 The Android Room persistence library

SQLite is, as previously mentioned, written in the C programming language while Android applications are primarily developed using Java or Kotlin. To bridge this "language gap" in the past, the Android SDK included a set of classes that provide a layer on top of the SQLite database management system. Although still available in the SDK, the use of these classes involves writing a considerable amount of code and does not take advantage of the new architecture guidelines and features such as view models and LiveData. To address these shortcomings, the Android Jetpack Architecture Components include the Room persistent library. This library provides a high-level interface on top of the SQLite database system that makes it easy to store data locally on Android devices with minimal coding while also conforming to the recommendations for modern application architecture.

The next few chapters will provide an overview and tutorial of SQLite database management using the Room persistence library.

67.10 Summary

SQLite is a lightweight, embedded relational database management system that is included as part of the Android framework and provides a mechanism for implementing organized persistent data storage for Android applications. When combined with the Room persistence library, Android provides a modern way to implement data storage from within an Android app.

The goal of this chapter was to provide an overview of databases in general and SQLite in particular within the context of Android application development. The next chapters will provide an overview of the Room persistence library, after which we will work through the creation of an example application.

68. An Android SQLite Database Tutorial

The chapter entitled *"An Overview of Android SQLite Databases"* covered the basic principles of integrating relational database storage into Android applications using the SQLite database management system. In this chapter, we will create a project using SQLite databases to store and retrieve data.

68.1 About the Database Example

The example project is a simple data entry and retrieval application that allows users to add, query, and delete database entries. The idea behind this application is a simple contact database containing customer names and phone numbers.

The name of the database file will be *customerDB.db*, which, in turn, will contain a single table named *customers*. Each record in the database table will contain a unique customer ID, a customer name, and the customer's phone number, corresponding to column names "customername" and "customerphone", respectively. The customer ID column will act as the primary key and automatically be assigned and incremented by the database management system.

68.2 Creating the SQLDemo Project

Start Android Studio, select the *New Project* option from the welcome screen, and, within the resulting new project dialog, choose the Empty Views Activity template before clicking the Next button.

Enter *SQLDemo* into the Name field and specify *com.ebookfrenzy.sqldemo* as the package name. Before clicking on the Finish button, change the Minimum API level setting to API 26: Android 8.0 (Oreo) and the Language menu to Kotlin. Use the Gemini Agent or the steps in section *18.8 Migrating a Project to View Binding,* to enable view binding for the project.

68.3 Designing the User interface

Open the *activity_main.xml* file and delete the default TextView component. Add two Plain Text fields, three Buttons, and a TextView to the layout and position them as shown in Figure 68-1:

Figure 68-1

Change the hint property of the Plain Text views to "name" and "phone" respectively, and remove the default "Name" text property. Modify the buttons so that they read "Add", "Find," and "Delete", and the TextView text to "Database Ready," extract all the string values to resources, and apply layout constraints either manually or using the *Infer constraints* button.

Change the IDs of the Plain Text views and TextView to *customerName, customerPhone*, and *statusText*, respectively. Finally, configure the buttons to call methods named *addCustomer*, *findCustomer,* and *deleteCustomer.*

68.4 Creating the Data Model

Once completed, the application will consist of an activity and a database handler class. The database handler will be a subclass of SQLiteOpenHelper and will provide an abstract layer between the underlying SQLite database and the activity class, with the activity calling on the database handler to interact with the database (adding, removing, and querying database entries). To implement this interaction in a structured way, a third class will need to be implemented to hold the database entry data as it is passed between the activity and the handler. This is actually a very simple class capable of holding customer ID, name, and phone values, together with getter and setter methods for accessing these values. Instances of this class can then be created within the activity and database handler and passed back and forth as needed. Essentially, this class represents the database model.

Navigate within the Project tool window to *app -> kotlin+java* and right-click on the package name. From the popup menu, choose the *New -> Kotlin File/Class* option and, in the Create New Class dialog, name the class Customer and change the Kind menu to Class before tapping Enter on your keyboard.

Once created, the *Customer.kt* source file will automatically load into the Android Studio editor. Once loaded, modify the code to add the appropriate constructors:

```
package com.ebookfrenzy.sqldemo

class Customer {

    var id: Int = 0
    var customerName: String?  = null
    var customerPhone: String? = null

    constructor(id: Int, name: String, phone: String ) {
        this.id = id
        this.customerName = name
        this.customerPhone = phone
    }
    constructor(name: String, phone: String) {
        this.customerName = name
        this.customerPhone = phone
    }
}
```

The completed class contains data members for the internal storage of data columns from database entries.

68.5 Implementing the Data Handler

The data handler will be implemented by subclassing from the Android SQLiteOpenHelper class and, as outlined in *"An Overview of Android SQLite Databases"*, adding the constructor, *onCreate()* and *onUpgrade()*

methods. Since the handler will be required to add, query, and delete data on behalf of the activity component, corresponding methods will also need to be added to the class.

Begin by adding a second new class to the project to act as the handler, named MyDBHandler. Once the new class has been created, modify it so that it reads as follows:

```
package com.ebookfrenzy.sqldemo

import android.database.sqlite.SQLiteDatabase
import android.database.sqlite.SQLiteOpenHelper
import android.content.Context
import android.content.ContentValues

class MyDBHandler(context: Context, name: String?,
                  factory: SQLiteDatabase.CursorFactory?, version: Int) :
    SQLiteOpenHelper(context, DATABASE_NAME, factory, DATABASE_VERSION) {

    override fun onCreate(db: SQLiteDatabase) {
    }

    override fun onUpgrade(db: SQLiteDatabase, oldVersion: Int,
                           newVersion: Int) {
    }
}
```

Having now pre-populated the source file with template *onCreate()* and *onUpgrade()* methods, the next task is to modify the code to declare constants for the database name, table name, table columns, and database version as follows:

```
.
.
class MyDBHandler(context: Context?, name: String?,
                  factory: SQLiteDatabase.CursorFactory?, version: Int) :
    SQLiteOpenHelper(context, DATABASE_NAME, factory, DATABASE_VERSION) {

    override fun onCreate(db: SQLiteDatabase) {
    }

    override fun onUpgrade(db: SQLiteDatabase, oldVersion: Int,
                           newVersion: Int) {
    }

    companion object {
        private val DATABASE_VERSION = 1
        private val DATABASE_NAME = "customerDB.db"
        val TABLE_CUSTOMERS = "customers"
        val COLUMN_ID = "_id"
        val COLUMN_CUSTOMERNAME = "customername"
```

```
        val COLUMN_CUSTOMERPHONE = "customerphone"
    }
}
```

Next, the *onCreate()* method needs to be implemented so that the customers table is created when the database is first initialized. This involves constructing a SQL CREATE statement containing instructions to create a new table with the appropriate columns and then passing that through to the *execSQL()* method of the SQLiteDatabase object passed as an argument to *onCreate()*:

```
override fun onCreate(db: SQLiteDatabase) {
    val CREATE_CUSTOMERS_TABLE = ("CREATE TABLE " +
            TABLE_CUSTOMERS + "("
            + COLUMN_ID + " INTEGER PRIMARY KEY," +
            COLUMN_CUSTOMERNAME
            + " TEXT," + COLUMN_CUSTOMERPHONE + " TEXT" + ")")

    db.execSQL(CREATE_CUSTOMERS_TABLE)
}
```

The *onUpgrade()* method is called when the handler is invoked with a greater database version number than the one previously used. The exact steps to be performed in this instance will be application-specific, so for this example, we will remove the old database and create a new one:

```
override fun onUpgrade(db: SQLiteDatabase, oldVersion: Int,
                       newVersion: Int) {
    db.execSQL("DROP TABLE IF EXISTS " + TABLE_CUSTOMERS)
    onCreate(db)
}
```

All that remains to be implemented in the *MyDBHandler.kt* handler class are the methods to add, query, and remove database table entries.

68.6 The Add Handler Method

The method to insert database records will be named *addCustomer()* and will take an instance of our Customer data model class as an argument. A ContentValues object will be created in the method's body and primed with key-value pairs for the data columns extracted from the Customer object. Next, a reference to the database will be obtained via a call to *getWritableDatabase()* followed by a call to the *insert()* method of the returned database object. Finally, once the insertion has been performed, the database needs to be closed:

```
fun addCustomer(customer: Customer) {
    val values = ContentValues()

    values.put(COLUMN_CUSTOMERNAME, customer.customerName)
    values.put(COLUMN_CUSTOMERPHONE, customer.customerPhone)
    val db = this.writableDatabase
    db.insert(TABLE_CUSTOMERS, null, values)
    db.close()
}
```

68.7 The Query Handler Method

The method to query the database will be named *findCustomer()* and will take a String object containing the customer's name to be located as an argument. Using this string, a SQL SELECT statement will be constructed to find all matching records in the table. For this example, only the first match will then be returned, contained within a new instance of our Customer data model class:

```
fun findCustomer(customername: String): Customer? {
    val query =
        "SELECT * FROM $TABLE_CUSTOMERS WHERE $COLUMN_CUSTOMERNAME =
\"$customername\""

    val db = this.writableDatabase
    val cursor = db.rawQuery(query, null)
    var customer: Customer? = null

    if (cursor.moveToFirst()) {
        cursor.moveToFirst()
        val id = Integer.parseInt(cursor.getString(0))
        val name = cursor.getString(1)
        val phone = cursor.getString(2)
        customer = Customer(id, name, phone)
        cursor.close()
    }
    db.close()
    return customer
}
```

68.8 The Delete Handler Method

The deletion method will be named *deleteCustomer()* and will accept the entry to be deleted in the form of a Customer object as an argument. The method will use a SQL SELECT statement to search for the entry based on the customer name and, if located, delete it from the table. The success or otherwise of the deletion will be reflected in a Boolean return value:

```
fun deleteCustomer(customername: String): Boolean {
    var result = false
    val query =
        "SELECT * FROM $TABLE_CUSTOMERS WHERE $COLUMN_CUSTOMERNAME =
\"$customername\""

    val db = this.writableDatabase
    val cursor = db.rawQuery(query, null)

    if (cursor.moveToFirst()) {
        val id = Integer.parseInt(cursor.getString(0))
        db.delete(
            TABLE_CUSTOMERS, COLUMN_ID + " = ?",
            arrayOf(id.toString()))
        cursor.close()
```

```
            result = true
        }
        db.close()
        return result
}
```

68.9 Implementing the Activity Event Methods

The final task before testing the application is to write the onClick event handlers for the three buttons in the user interface. Load the *MainActivity.kt* source file into the editor and add the onClick target methods as follows:

```
package com.ebookfrenzy.sqldemo
.
.
import android.view.View
.
.
class MainActivity : AppCompatActivity() {

    private lateinit var binding: ActivityMainBinding
    private lateinit var dbHandler: MyDBHandler
.
.
   override fun onCreate(savedInstanceState: Bundle?) {
        super.onCreate(savedInstanceState)
.
.
        dbHandler = MyDBHandler(this, null, null, 1)
    }

    fun addCustomer(view: View) {
        val name = binding.customerName.text.toString()
        val phone = binding.customerPhone.text.toString()
        val customer = Customer(name, phone)

        dbHandler.addCustomer(customer)
        binding.customerName.setText("")
        binding.customerPhone.setText("")
    }

    fun findCustomer(view: View) {
        val customer =
              dbHandler.findCustomer(binding.customerName.text.toString())

        if (customer != null) {
            binding.customerPhone.setText(
                customer.customerPhone)
            binding.statusText.text = "Match Found"
```

```
        } else {
            binding.statusText.text = "No Match Found"
        }
    }

    fun deleteCustomer(view: View) {
        val result = dbHandler.deleteCustomer(
            binding.customerName.text.toString())
        if (result) {
            binding.statusText.text = "Record Deleted"
            binding.customerName.setText("")
            binding.customerPhone.setText("")
        } else
            binding.statusText.text = "No Match Found"
    }
}
```

68.10 Testing the Application

With the coding changes completed, compile and run the application either in an AVD session or on a physical Android device. Once the application runs, enter a customer name and phone number into the user interface form and touch the Add button. Once the record has been added, the text boxes will clear. Repeat these steps to add a second customer to the database. Next, enter the name of one of the newly added customers into the customer name field and touch the Find button. The form should update with the customer ID and phone number for the selected customer. Touch the Delete button to delete the selected record. A subsequent search by customer name should indicate that the record no longer exists.

68.11 Summary

This chapter worked step by step through a practical application of SQLite-based database storage in Android applications. To develop your new database skill set further, consider extending the example to include the ability to update existing records in the database table.

69. Understanding Android Content Providers

The previous chapter worked on creating an example application designed to store data using a SQLite database. When implemented this way, the data is private to the application and, as such, inaccessible to other applications running on the same device. While this may be the desired behavior for many application types, situations will inevitably arise whereby the data stored on behalf of an application could benefit other applications. A prime example is the data stored by the built-in Contacts application on an Android device. While the Contacts application is primarily responsible for managing the user's address book details, this data is also made accessible to any other applications needing access. This data sharing between Android applications is achieved through implementing *content providers*.

69.1 What is a Content Provider?

A content provider provides access to structured data between different Android applications. This data is exposed to applications either as tables of data (in much the same way as a SQLite database) or as a handle to a file. This essentially involves the implementation of a client/server arrangement whereby the application seeking access to the data is the client and the content provider is the server, performing actions and returning results on behalf of the client.

A successful content provider implementation involves several elements, each of which will be covered in detail in the remainder of this chapter.

69.2 The Content Provider

A content provider is created as a subclass of the *android.content.ContentProvider* class. Typically, the application responsible for managing the data to be shared will implement a content provider to facilitate sharing of that data with other applications.

Creating a content provider involves implementing methods to manage the data on behalf of other client applications. These methods are as follows:

69.2.1 onCreate()

This method is called when the content provider is first created and should be used to perform any initialization tasks required by the content provider.

69.2.2 query()

This method will be called when a client requests that data be retrieved from the content provider. This method identifies the data to be retrieved (single or multiple rows), performs the data extraction, and returns the results wrapped in a Cursor object.

69.2.3 insert()

This method is called when a new row needs to be inserted into the provider database. This method must identify the destination for the data, perform the insertion and return the full URI of the newly added row.

69.2.4 update()

The method called when existing rows need to be updated on behalf of the client. The method uses the arguments passed through to update the appropriate table rows and return the number of rows updated as a result of the operation.

69.2.5 delete()

Called when rows are to be deleted from a table. This method deletes the designated rows and returns a count of the number of rows deleted.

69.2.6 getType()

Returns the MIME type of the data stored by the content provider.

It is important when implementing these methods in a content provider to keep in mind that, with the exception of the *onCreate()* method, they can be called from many processes simultaneously and must, therefore, be thread safe.

Once a content provider has been implemented, the issue that then arises is how the provider is identified within the Android system. This is where the *content URI* comes into play.

69.3 The Content URI

An Android device will potentially contain several content providers. The system must, therefore, provide some way of identifying one provider from another. Similarly, a single content provider may provide access to multiple forms of content (typically in the form of database tables). Client applications, therefore, need a way to specify the underlying data for which access is required. This is achieved using content URIs.

The content URI is used to identify specific data within a specific content provider. The Authority section of the URI identifies the content provider and usually takes the form of the package name of the content provider. For example:

```
com.example.mydbapp.myprovider
```

A specific database table within the provider data structure may be referenced by appending the table name to the authority. For example, the following URI references a table named *products* within the content provider:

```
com.example.mydbapp.myprovider/products
```

Similarly, a specific row within the specified table may be referenced by appending the row ID to the URI. The following URI, for example, references the row in the products table in which the value stored in the ID column equals 3:

```
com.example.mydbapp.myprovider/products/3
```

When implementing the insert, query, update and delete methods in the content provider, it will be the responsibility of these methods to identify whether the incoming URI is targeting a specific row in a table, or references multiple rows, and act accordingly. This can potentially be a complex task given that a URI can extend to multiple levels. This process can, however, be eased significantly using the *UriMatcher* class, as will be outlined in the next chapter.

69.4 The Content Resolver

Access to a content provider is achieved via a ContentResolver object. An application can obtain a reference to its content resolver by calling the *getContentResolver()* method of the application context.

The content resolver object contains a set of methods that mirror those of the content provider (insert, query, delete etc.). The application simply makes calls to the methods, specifying the URI of the content on which the operation is to be performed. The content resolver and content provider objects then communicate to perform the requested task on behalf of the application.

69.5 The <provider> Manifest Element

For a content provider to be visible within an Android system, it must be declared within the Android manifest file for the application in which it resides. This is achieved using the <provider> element, which must contain the following items:

- **android:authority** – The full authority URI of the content provider. For example com.example.mydbapp.mydbapp.myprovider.
- **android:name** – The name of the class that implements the content provider. In most cases, this will use the same value as the authority.

Similarly, the <provider> element may be used to define the permissions that must be held by client applications in order to qualify for access to the underlying data. If no permissions are declared, the default behavior is for permission to be allowed for all applications.

Permissions can be set to cover the entire content provider, or limited to specific tables and records.

69.6 Summary

The data belonging to an application is typically private to the application and inaccessible to other applications. Setting up a content provider is necessary when the data needs to be shared. This chapter has covered the basic elements that combine to enable data sharing between applications and outlined the concepts of the content provider, content URI, and content resolver.

In the next chapter, the SQLDemo project created previously will be extended to make the underlying customer data available via a content provider.

70. An Android Content Provider Tutorial

As outlined in the previous chapter, content providers provide a mechanism through which the data stored by one Android application can be made accessible to other applications. Having provided a theoretical overview of content providers, this chapter will continue the coverage of content providers by extending the SQLDemo project created in the chapter entitled *"An Android SQLite Database Tutorial"* to implement content provider-based access to the database.

70.1 Copying the SQLDemo Project

To keep the original SQLDemo project intact, we will make a backup copy of the project before modifying it to implement content provider support for the application. If the SQLDemo project is currently open within Android Studio, close it using the *File -> Close Project* menu option.

Using the file system explorer for your operating system type, navigate to the directory containing your Android Studio projects and copy the SQLDemo project folder to a new folder named SQLDemo_provider.

Within the Android Studio welcome screen, open the SQLDemo_provider project so that it loads into the main window.

70.2 Adding the Content Provider Package

The next step is to add a new package to the SQLDemo project to contain the content provider class. Add this new package by navigating within the Project tool window to *app -> kotlin+java*, right-clicking on it, and selecting the *New -> Package* menu option. When the Choose Destination Directory dialog appears, select the *..\app\src\main\java* option from the Directory Structure panel and click OK.

In the New Package dialog, enter the following package name into the name field before pressing the enter key:

```
com.ebookfrenzy.sqldemo.provider
```

The new package should now be listed within the Project tool window, as illustrated in Figure 70-1:

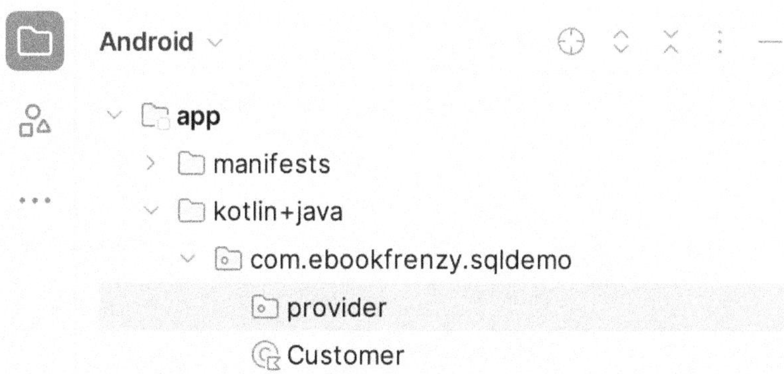

Figure 70-1

70.3 Creating the Content Provider Class

As discussed in *"Understanding Android Content Providers"*, content providers are created by subclassing the android.content.ContentProvider class. Consequently, the next step is to add a class to the new provider package to serve as the content provider for this application. Locate the new package in the Project tool window, right-click on it and select the *New -> Other -> Content Provider* menu option. In the Configure Component dialog, enter MyContentProvider into the Class Name field and the following into the URI Authorities field:

```
com.ebookfrenzy.sqldemo.provider.MyContentProvider
```

Ensure that the new content provider class is exported and enabled before clicking on Finish to create the new class.

Once the new class has been created, the *MyContentProvider.kt* file should be listed beneath the provider package in the Project tool window and automatically loaded into the editor, where it will appear as outlined in the following listing:

```
package com.ebookfrenzy.sqldemo.provider

import android.content.ContentProvider
import android.content.ContentValues
import android.database.Cursor
import android.net.Uri

class MyContentProvider : ContentProvider() {

    override fun delete(uri: Uri, selection: String?,
                selectionArgs: Array<String>?): Int {
        TODO("Implement this to handle requests to delete one or more rows")
    }

    override fun getType(uri: Uri): String? {
        TODO(
            "Implement this to handle requests for the MIME type of the data" +
                    "at the given URI"
        )
    }

    override fun insert(uri: Uri, values: ContentValues?): Uri? {
        TODO("Implement this to handle requests to insert a new row.")
    }

    override fun onCreate(): Boolean {
        TODO("Implement this to initialize your content provider on startup.")
    }

    override fun query(
        uri: Uri, projection: Array<String>?, selection: String?,
        selectionArgs: Array<String>?, sortOrder: String?
```

```
    ): Cursor? {
        TODO("Implement this to handle query requests from clients.")
    }

    override fun update(
        uri: Uri, values: ContentValues?, selection: String?,
        selectionArgs: Array<String>?
    ): Int {
        TODO("Implement this to handle requests to update one or more rows.")
    }
}
```

As is evident from a quick review of the code in this file, Android Studio has already populated the class with stubs for each of the methods that a subclass of ContentProvider is required to implement. It will soon be necessary to begin implementing these methods, but first some constants relating to the provider's content authority and URI need to be declared.

70.4 Constructing the Authority and Content URI

As outlined in the previous chapter, all content providers must have associated with them an authority and a content uri. In practice, the authority is typically the full package name of the content provider class itself, in this case com.ebookfrenzy.sqldemo.provider.MyContentProvider as declared when the new Content Provider class was created in the previous section.

The content URI will vary depending on application requirements, but for this example it will comprise the authority with the name of the database table appended at the end. Within the *MyContentProvider.kt* file, make the following modifications:

```
package com.ebookfrenzy.sqldemo.provider
.
.
class MyContentProvider : ContentProvider() {
.
.
   companion object {
        val AUTHORITY = "com.ebookfrenzy.sqldemo.provider.MyContentProvider"
        private val CUSTOMERS_TABLE = "customers"
        val CONTENT_URI : Uri = Uri.parse("content://" + AUTHORITY + "/" +
                CUSTOMERS_TABLE)
    }
}
```

The above statements begin by creating a new String object named AUTHORITY and assigning the authority string to it. Similarly, a second String object named CUSTOMERS_TABLE is created and initialized with the name of our database table (customers).

Finally, these two string elements are combined, prefixed with *content://* and converted to a Uri object using the *parse()* method of the Uri class. The result is assigned to a variable named CONTENT_URI.

70.5 Implementing URI Matching in the Content Provider

When the methods of the content provider are called, they will be passed as an argument a URI indicating the data on which the operation is to be performed. This URI may take the form of a reference to a specific row in a specific table. It is also possible that the URI will be more general, for example specifying only the database table. It is the responsibility of each method to identify the Uri type and to act accordingly. This task can be eased considerably by making use of a UriMatcher instance. Once a UriMatcher instance has been created, it can be configured to return a specific integer value corresponding to the type of URI it detects when asked to do so. For this tutorial, we will be configuring our UriMatcher instance to return a value of 1 when the URI references the entire customers table, and a value of 2 when the URI references the ID of a specific row in the customers table. Before working on creating the URIMatcher instance, we will first create two integer variables to represent the two URI types:

```
package com.ebookfrenzy.sqldemo.provider

import android.content.ContentProvider
import android.content.ContentValues
import android.database.Cursor
import android.net.Uri
import android.content.UriMatcher
import android.database.sqlite.SQLiteDatabase
import android.database.sqlite.SQLiteQueryBuilder
import android.text.TextUtils

import com.ebookfrenzy.sqldemo.MyDBHandler

class MyContentProvider : ContentProvider() {

    private val CUSTOMERS = 1
    private val CUSTOMER_ID = 2
.
.
```

With the Uri type variables declared, it is now time to add code to create a UriMatcher instance and configure it to return the appropriate variables:

```
class MyContentProvider : ContentProvider() {

    private var myDB: MyDBHandler? = null
    private val CUSTOMERS = 1
    private val CUSTOMER_ID = 2

    private val sURIMatcher = UriMatcher(UriMatcher.NO_MATCH)

    init {
        sURIMatcher.addURI(AUTHORITY, CUSTOMERS_TABLE, CUSTOMERS)
        sURIMatcher.addURI(AUTHORITY, CUSTOMERS_TABLE + "/#",
            CUSTOMER_ID)
    }
```

.

.

The UriMatcher instance (named sURIMatcher) is now primed to return the value of CUSTOMER when just the customers table is referenced in a URI, and CUSTOMER_ID when the URI includes the ID of a specific row in the table.

70.6 Implementing the Content Provider onCreate() Method

When the content provider class is created and initialized, a call will be made to the *onCreate()* method of the class. Within this method, any initialization tasks for the class must be performed. For this example, all that needs to be performed is for an instance of the MyDBHandler class implemented in *"An Android SQLite Database Tutorial"* to be created. Once this instance has been created, it will need to be accessible from the other methods in the class, so a declaration for the database handler also needs to be declared, resulting in the following code changes to the *MyContentProvider.kt* file:

```
class MyContentProvider : ContentProvider() {
.
.
    override fun onCreate(): Boolean {
        myDB = context?.let { MyDBHandler(it, null, null, 1) }
        return false
    }
.
.
```

70.7 Implementing the Content Provider insert() Method

When a client application or activity requests that data be inserted into the underlying database, the *insert()* method of the content provider class will be called. At this point, however, all that exists in the *MyContentProvider.kt* file of the project is a stub method, which reads as follows:

```
override fun insert(uri: Uri, values: ContentValues?): Uri? {
    TODO("Implement this to handle requests to insert a new row.")
}
```

Passed as arguments to the method are a URI specifying the destination of the insertion and a ContentValues object containing the data to be inserted.

This method now needs to be modified to perform the following tasks:

- Use the sUriMatcher object to identify the URI type.
- Throw an exception if the URI is not valid.
- Obtain a reference to a writable instance of the underlying SQLite database.
- Perform a SQL insert operation to insert the data into the database table.
- Notify the corresponding content resolver that the database has been modified.
- Return the URI of the newly added table row.

Bringing these requirements together results in a modified *insert()* method, which reads as follows:

```
override fun insert(uri: Uri, values: ContentValues?): Uri? {
    val uriType = sURIMatcher.match(uri)
```

```
    val sqlDB = myDB!!.writableDatabase
    val id: Long

    when (uriType) {
        CUSTOMERS -> id = sqlDB.insert(MyDBHandler.TABLE_CUSTOMERS, null, values)
        else -> throw IllegalArgumentException("Unknown URI: " + uri)
    }

    context?.contentResolver?.notifyChange(uri, null)
    return Uri.parse(CUSTOMERS_TABLE + "/" + id)
}
```

70.8 Implementing the Content Provider query() Method

When a content provider is called upon to return data, the *query()* method of the provider class will be called. When called, this method is passed some or all of the following arguments:

- **URI** – The URI specifying the data source on which the query is to be performed. This can take the form of a general query with multiple results, or a specific query targeting the ID of a single table row.
- **Projection** – A row within a database table can comprise multiple columns of data. In the case of this application, for example, these correspond to the ID, customer name and phone number. The projection argument is simply a String array containing the name for each column that is to be returned in the result data set.
- **Selection** – The "where" element of the selection to be performed as part of the query. This argument controls which rows are selected from the specified database. For example, if the query was required to select only customers named "John Andrews" then the selection string passed to the *query()* method would read customername = "John Andrews".
- **Selection Args** – Any additional arguments that need to be passed to the SQL query operation to perform the selection.
- **Sort Order** – The sort order for the selected rows.

When called, the *query()* method is required to perform the following operations:

- Use the sUriMatcher to identify the Uri type.
- Throw an exception if the URI is not valid.
- Construct a SQL query based on the criteria passed to the method. For convenience, the SQLiteQueryBuilder class can be used to construct the query.
- Execute the query operation on the database.
- Notify the content resolver of the operation.
- Return a Cursor object containing the results of the query.

With these requirements in mind, the code for the *query()* method in the *MyContentProvider.kt* file should now read as outlined in the following listing:

```
override fun query(
    uri: Uri, projection: Array<String>?, selection: String?,
```

```
    selectionArgs: Array<String>?, sortOrder: String?
): Cursor? {

    val queryBuilder = SQLiteQueryBuilder()
    queryBuilder.tables = MyDBHandler.TABLE_CUSTOMERS
    val uriType = sURIMatcher.match(uri)

    when (uriType) {
        CUSTOMER_ID -> queryBuilder.appendWhere(MyDBHandler.COLUMN_ID + "="
                + uri.lastPathSegment)
        CUSTOMERS -> {
        }
        else -> throw IllegalArgumentException("Unknown URI")
    }

    val cursor = queryBuilder.query(myDB?.readableDatabase,
        projection, selection, selectionArgs, null, null,
        sortOrder)
    cursor.setNotificationUri(context?.contentResolver, uri)
    return cursor
}
```

70.9 Implementing the Content Provider update() Method

The *update()* method of the content provider is called when changes are being requested to existing database table rows. The method is passed a URI with the new values in the form of a ContentValues object and the usual selection argument strings.

When called, the *update()* method would typically perform the following steps:

- Use the sUriMatcher to identify the URI type.
- Throw an exception if the URI is not valid.
- Obtain a reference to a writable instance of the underlying SQLite database.
- Perform the appropriate update operation on the database, depending on the selection criteria and the URI type.
- Notify the content resolver of the database change.
- Return a count of the number of rows that were changed due to the update operation.

A general-purpose *update()* method, and the one we will use for this project, would read as follows:

```
override fun update(
    uri: Uri, values: ContentValues?, selection: String?,
    selectionArgs: Array<String>?
): Int {
    val uriType = sURIMatcher.match(uri)
    val sqlDB: SQLiteDatabase = myDB!!.writableDatabase
    val rowsUpdated: Int
```

```
    when (uriType) {
        CUSTOMERS -> rowsUpdated = sqlDB.update(MyDBHandler.TABLE_CUSTOMERS,
            values,
            selection,
            selectionArgs)
        CUSTOMER_ID -> {
            val id = uri.lastPathSegment
            rowsUpdated = if (TextUtils.isEmpty(selection)) {
                sqlDB.update(MyDBHandler.TABLE_CUSTOMERS,
                    values,
                    MyDBHandler.COLUMN_ID + "=" + id, null)
            } else {
                sqlDB.update(MyDBHandler.TABLE_CUSTOMERS,
                    values,
                    MyDBHandler.COLUMN_ID + "=" + id
                            + " and "
                            + selection,
                    selectionArgs)
            }
        }
        else -> throw IllegalArgumentException("Unknown URI: " + uri)
    }
    context?.contentResolver?.notifyChange(uri, null)
    return rowsUpdated
}
```

70.10 Implementing the Content Provider delete() Method

In common with a number of other content provider methods, the *delete()* method is passed a URI, a selection string and an optional set of selection arguments. A typical *delete()* method will also perform the following, and by now largely familiar, tasks when called:

- Use the sUriMatcher to identify the URI type.
- Throw an exception if the URI is not valid.
- Obtain a reference to a writable instance of the underlying SQLite database.
- Perform the appropriate delete operation on the database depending on the selection criteria and the Uri type.
- Notify the content resolver of the database change.
- Return a count of the number of rows that were changed due to the update operation.

A typical *delete()* method is in many ways similar to the *update()* method and may be implemented as follows:

```
override fun delete(uri: Uri, selection: String?, selectionArgs: Array<String>?):
Int {
    val uriType = sURIMatcher.match(uri)
    val sqlDB = myDB!!.writableDatabase
```

```
    val rowsDeleted: Int

    when (uriType) {
        CUSTOMERS -> rowsDeleted = sqlDB.delete(MyDBHandler.TABLE_CUSTOMERS,
        selection,
        selectionArgs)
        CUSTOMER_ID -> {
        val id = uri.lastPathSegment
        rowsDeleted = if (TextUtils.isEmpty(selection)) {
            sqlDB.delete(MyDBHandler.TABLE_CUSTOMERS,
            MyDBHandler.COLUMN_ID + "=" + id,
            null)
        } else {
            sqlDB.delete(MyDBHandler.TABLE_CUSTOMERS,
            MyDBHandler.COLUMN_ID + "=" + id
                + " and " + selection,
            selectionArgs)
        }
        }
        else -> throw IllegalArgumentException("Unknown URI: " + uri)
    }
    context?.contentResolver?.notifyChange(uri, null)
    return rowsDeleted
}
```

With these methods implemented, the content provider class, in terms of the requirements for this example, is complete. The next step is to ensure that the content provider is declared in the project manifest file to be visible to any content resolvers seeking access.

70.11 Declaring the Content Provider in the Manifest File

Unless a content provider is declared in the manifest file of the application to which it belongs, it will not be possible for a content resolver to locate and access it. As outlined, content providers are declared using the <provider> tag and the manifest entry must correctly reference the content provider authority and content URI.

For this project, therefore, locate the *manifests -> AndroidManifest.xml* file within the Project tool window and double-click on it to load it into the editing panel. Within the editing panel, make sure that the content provider declaration has already been added by Android Studio when the MyContentProvider class was added to the project:

```
<?xml version="1.0" encoding="utf-8"?>
<manifest xmlns:android="http://schemas.android.com/apk/res/android"
    xmlns:tools="http://schemas.android.com/tools">

    <application
        android:allowBackup="true"
        android:dataExtractionRules="@xml/data_extraction_rules"
        android:fullBackupContent="@xml/backup_rules"
        android:icon="@mipmap/ic_launcher"
```

```
        android:label="@string/app_name"
        android:roundIcon="@mipmap/ic_launcher_round"
        android:supportsRtl="true"
        android:theme="@style/Theme.SQLDemo"
        tools:targetApi="31">
        <provider
            android:name=".provider.MyContentProvider"
            android:authorities="com.ebookfrenzy.sqldemo.provider.
MyContentProvider"
            android:enabled="true"
            android:exported="true"></provider>

        <activity
            android:name=".MainActivity"
            android:exported="true">
            <intent-filter>
                <action android:name="android.intent.action.MAIN" />

                <category android:name="android.intent.category.LAUNCHER" />
            </intent-filter>
        </activity>
    </application>

</manifest>
```

All that remains before testing the application is to modify the database handler class to use the content provider instead of directly accessing the database.

70.12 Modifying the Database Handler

When this application was originally created, it was designed to use a database handler to access the underlying database directly. Now that a content provider has been implemented, the database handler needs to be modified to perform all database operations using the content provider via a content resolver.

The first step is to modify the *MyDBHandler.kt* class so that it obtains a reference to a ContentResolver instance. This can be achieved in the constructor method of the class:

```
.
.
import android.content.ContentResolver

import com.ebookfrenzy.sqldemo.provider.MyContentProvider
.
.
class MyDBHandler(context: Context, name: String?,
                factory: SQLiteDatabase.CursorFactory?, version: Int) :
    SQLiteOpenHelper(context, DATABASE_NAME,
        factory, DATABASE_VERSION) {
```

```
    private val myCR: ContentResolver

    init {
        myCR = context.contentResolver
    }
.
.
```

Next, the *addCustomer()*, *findCustomer()*, and *removeCustomer()* methods need to be rewritten to use the content resolver and content provider for data management purposes:

```
fun addCustomer(customer: Customer) {
    val values = ContentValues()
    values.put(COLUMN_CUSTOMERNAME, customer.customerName)
    values.put(COLUMN_CUSTOMERPHONE, customer.customerPhone)

    myCR.insert(MyContentProvider.CONTENT_URI, values)
}

fun findCustomer(customername: String): Customer? {
    val projection = arrayOf(COLUMN_ID, COLUMN_CUSTOMERNAME,
            COLUMN_CUSTOMERPHONE)
    val selection = "customername = \"" + customername + "\""

    val cursor = myCR.query(MyContentProvider.CONTENT_URI,
        projection, selection, null, null)
    var customer: Customer? = null
    if (cursor != null) {
        if (cursor.moveToFirst()) {
            cursor.moveToFirst()
            val id = Integer.parseInt(cursor.getString(0))
            val customerName = cursor.getString(1)
            val customerPhone = cursor.getString(2)
            customer = Customer(id, customername, customerPhone)
            cursor.close()
        }
    }
    return customer
}

fun deleteCustomer(customername: String): Boolean {
    var result = false
    val selection = "customername = \"" + customername + "\""
    val rowsDeleted = myCR.delete(MyContentProvider.CONTENT_URI,
        selection, null)

    if (rowsDeleted > 0)
```

```
            result = true
        return result
}
```

With the database handler class updated to use a content resolver and content provider, the application is now ready to be tested. Compile and run the application and perform operations to add, find, and remove customer entries. In terms of operation and functionality, the application should behave exactly as it did when directly accessing the database, except it now uses the content provider.

As we will see in the next chapter, with the content provider now implemented and declared in the manifest file, any other applications can potentially access that data (since no permissions were declared, the default full access is in effect). The only information the other applications need to know to gain access is the content URI and the names of the columns in the customers table.

70.13 Summary

The goal of this chapter was to provide a more detailed overview of the exact steps involved in implementing an Android content provider with a particular emphasis on the structure and implementation of the query, insert, delete, and update methods of the content provider class. Practical use of the content resolver class to access data in the content provider was also covered, and the Database project was modified to use both a content provider and a content resolver.

Chapter 71

71. An Android Content Provider Client Tutorial

In this final chapter devoted to Content Providers, we will build an app that accesses the data contained in our SQLDemo content provider and displays the list of customer contacts.

71.1 Creating the SQLDemoClient Project

Start Android Studio, select the *New Project* option from the welcome screen, and choose the Empty Views Activity template within the resulting new project dialog before clicking on the Next button.

Enter *SQLDemoClient* into the Name field and specify *com.ebookfrenzy.sqldemoclient* as the package name. Before clicking on the Finish button, change the Minimum API level setting to API 26: Android 8.0 (Oreo) and the Language menu to Kotlin. Use the Gemini Agent or the steps in section *18.8 Migrating a Project to View Binding* to enable view binding for the project.

71.2 Designing the User interface

Open the *activity_main.xml* file and remove the default TextView. Add a button and a TextView to the layout, change the button text to read "Reload", and position the views so that the layout resembles Figure 71-1:

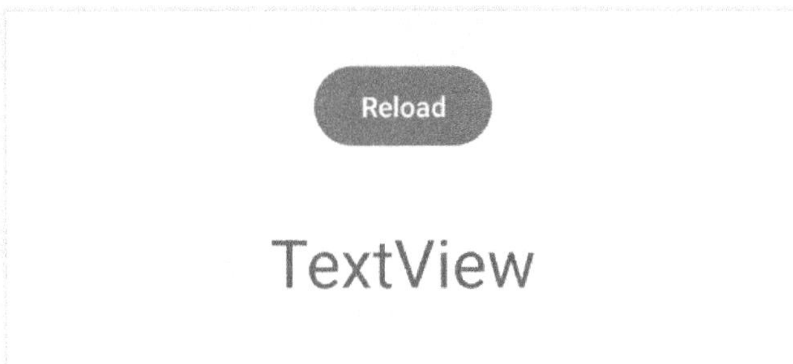

Figure 71-1

Use the *Infer constraints* button to configure the layout constraints, change the textAppearance property of the TextView to *Display1* and set the onClick attribute on the button to a method named *reload()*.

71.3 Accessing the Content Provider

The code to access the content provider will be contained in the *reload()* method. The first step is to obtain a Cursor object by calling the *query()* method of the Content Resolver instance. When calling *query()*, we need to provide the content URI for the customers table managed by SQLDemo's content provider, which will read as follows:

```
content://com.ebookfrenzy.sqldemo.provider.MyContentProvider/customers
```

Once we have a reference to the Cursor object, we can step through the database records and display the data using our TextView component. Edit the *MainActivity.kt* file and add the *reload()* method as follows:

```
.
.
```

```
import android.net.Uri
import android.view.View

class MainActivity : AppCompatActivity() {
.
.
    fun reload(view: View?) {
        val cursor = contentResolver.query(
      "content://com.ebookfrenzy.sqldemo.provider.MyContentProvider/customers"
                                .toUri(),
            null, null, null, null)

        if (cursor != null) {
            if (cursor.moveToFirst()) {
                val stringBldr = StringBuilder()

                while (!cursor.isAfterLast) {
                    val nameindex = cursor.getColumnIndex("customername")
                    val phoneindex = cursor.getColumnIndex("customerphone")

                    if ((nameindex != -1) && (phoneindex != -1)) {
                        val string = cursor.getString(nameindex) + " " +
                            cursor.getString(phoneindex)

                        stringBldr.append("""

                            ${string}

                        """.trimIndent())
                        binding.textView.text = stringBldr
                    }
                    cursor.moveToNext()
                }
            }
            cursor.close()
        }
    }
}
```

71.4 Adding the Query Permission

Before we can test the app, the final task is to request permission to query the content provider. To request permission, edit the *manifests -> AndroidManifest.xml* file and modify it as follows:

```
<?xml version="1.0" encoding="utf-8"?>
<manifest xmlns:android="http://schemas.android.com/apk/res/android"
    xmlns:tools="http://schemas.android.com/tools">
```

```
    <queries>
        <provider android:authorities="com.ebookfrenzy.sqldemo.provider.
MyContentProvider" />
    </queries>
.
.
```

71.5 Testing the Project

Build and run the app on the device or emulator you used to test the SQLDemo app and tap the Reload button. The app should query the records in the customers database and display them on the TextView:

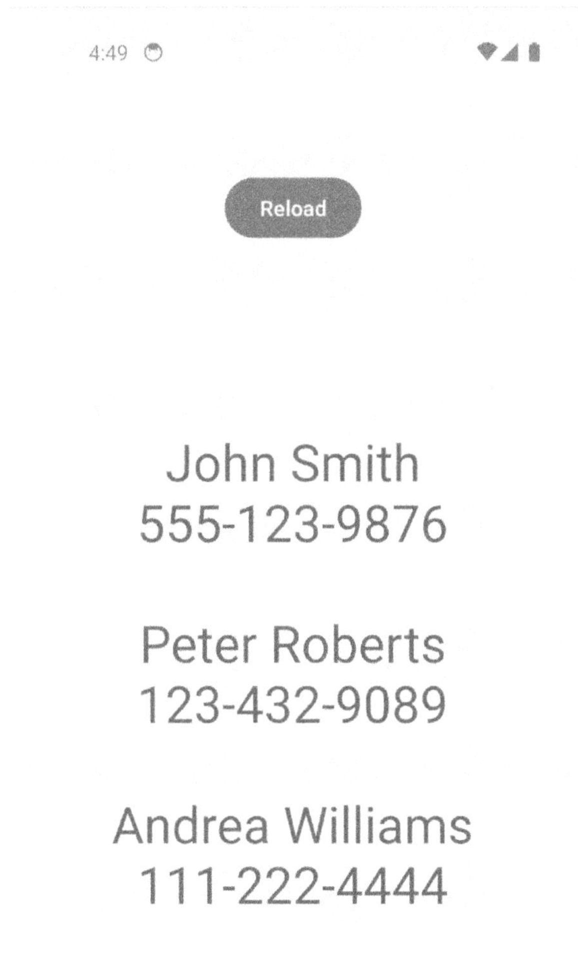

Figure 71-2

71.6 Summary

In this chapter, we created a simple app to demonstrate accessing the data stored in a content provider from a client app. This involved passing the provider's content URI to the *query()* method of the content resolver instance and requesting query permission from the content provider in the project manifest file. The *query()* call returned a Cursor object we used to step through the database records.

Chapter 72

72. The Android Room Persistence Library

Included with the Android Architecture Components, the Room persistence library is designed to make it easier to add database storage support to Android apps in a way consistent with the Android architecture guidelines. With the basics of SQLite databases covered in the previous chapters, this chapter will explore Room-based database management, the key elements that work together to implement Room support within an Android app, and how these are implemented in terms of architecture and coding. Having covered these topics, the next two chapters will put this theory into practice with an example Room database project.

72.1 Revisiting Modern App Architecture

The chapter entitled *"Modern Android App Architecture with Jetpack"* introduced the concept of modern app architecture and stressed the importance of separating different areas of responsibility within an app. The diagram illustrated in Figure 72-1 outlines the recommended architecture for a typical Android app:

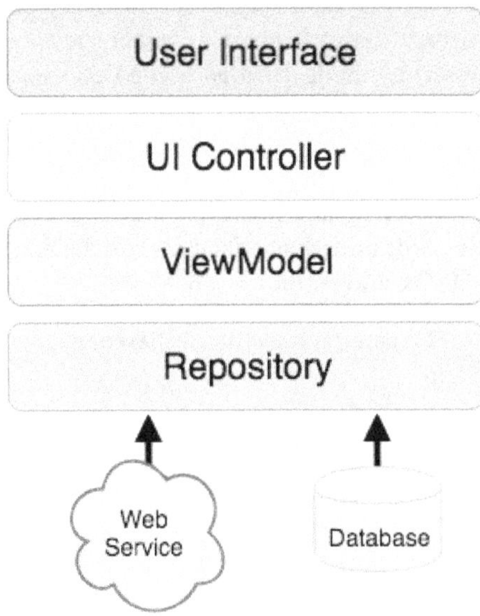

Figure 72-1

With the top three levels of this architecture covered in some detail in earlier chapters of this book, it is time to explore the repository and database architecture levels in the context of the Room persistence library.

72.2 Key Elements of Room Database Persistence

Before going into greater detail later in the chapter, it is first worth summarizing the key elements involved in working with SQLite databases using the Room persistence library:

72.2.1 Repository

As previously discussed, the repository module contains all of the code necessary for directly handling all data sources used by the app. This avoids the need for the UI controller and ViewModel to contain code directly accessing sources such as databases or web services.

72.2.2 Room Database

The room database object provides the interface to the underlying SQLite database. It also provides the repository with access to the Data Access Object (DAO). An app should only have one room database instance, which may be used to access multiple database tables.

72.2.3 Data Access Object (DAO)

The DAO contains the SQL statements required by the repository to insert, retrieve and delete data within the SQLite database. These SQL statements are mapped to methods which are then called from within the repository to execute the corresponding query.

72.2.4 Entities

An entity is a class that defines the schema for a table within the database, defines the table name, column names, and data types, and identifies which column is to be the primary key. In addition to declaring the table schema, entity classes contain getter and setter methods that provide access to these data fields. The data returned to the repository by the DAO in response to the SQL query method calls will take the form of instances of these entity classes. The getter methods will then be called to extract the data from the entity object. Similarly, when the repository needs to write new records to the database, it will create an entity instance, configure values on the object via setter calls, then call insert methods declared in the DAO, passing through entity instances to be saved.

72.2.5 SQLite Database

The SQLite database is responsible for storing and providing access to the data. The app code, including the repository, should never directly access this underlying database. All database operations are performed using a combination of the room database, DAOs, and entities.

The architecture diagram in Figure 72-2 illustrates how these different elements interact to provide Room-based database storage within an Android app:

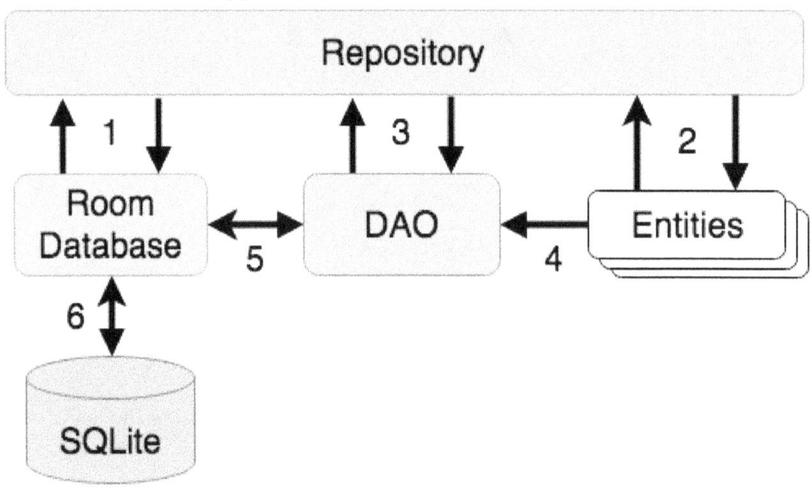

Figure 72-2

The numbered connections in the above architecture diagram can be summarized as follows:

1. The repository interacts with the Room Database to get a database instance which, in turn, is used to obtain references to DAO instances.
2. The repository creates entity instances and configures them with data before passing them to the DAO for use in search and insertion operations.
3. The repository calls methods on the DAO passing through entities to be inserted into the database and receives entity instances back in response to search queries.
4. When a DAO has results to return to the repository, it packages them into entity objects.
5. The DAO interacts with the Room Database to initiate database operations and handle results.
6. The Room Database handles all low-level interactions with the underlying SQLite database, submitting queries and receiving results.

With a basic outline of the key elements of database access using the Room persistent library covered, it is time to explore entities, DAOs, room databases, and repositories in more detail.

72.3 Understanding Entities

Each database table will have associated with it an entity class. This class defines the schema for the table and takes the form of a standard Kotlin class interspersed with some special Room annotations. An example Kotlin class declaring the data to be stored within a database table might read as follows:

```
class Customer {

    var id: Int = 0
    var name: String? = null
    var address: String? = null

    constructor() {}

    constructor(id: Int, name: String, address: String) {
        this.id = id
        this.name = name
        this.address = address
    }
    constructor(name: String, address: String) {
        this.name = name
        this.address = address
    }
}
```

As currently implemented, the above code declares a basic Kotlin class containing several variables representing database table fields and a collection of getter and setter methods. This class, however, is not yet an entity. To make this class into an entity and to make it accessible within SQL statements, some Room annotations need to be added as follows:

```
@Entity(tableName = "customers")
class Customer {
```

```
    @PrimaryKey(autoGenerate = true)
    @NonNull
    @ColumnInfo(name = "customerId")
    var id: Int = 0

    @ColumnInfo(name = "customerName")
    var name: String? = null
    var address: String? = null

    constructor() {}

    constructor(id: Int, name: String, address: String) {
        this.id = id
        this.name = name
        this.address = address
    }

    constructor(name: String, address: String) {
        this.name = name
        this.address = address
    }
}
```

The above annotations begin by declaring that the class represents an entity and assigns a table name of "customers". This is the name by which the table will be referenced in the DAO SQL statements:

```
@Entity(tableName = "customers")
```

Every database table needs a column to act as the primary key. In this case, the customer id is declared as the primary key. Annotations have also been added to assign a column name to be referenced in SQL queries and to indicate that the field cannot be used to store null values. Finally, the id value is configured to be auto-generated. This means the system automatically generates the id assigned to new records to avoid duplicate keys:

```
@PrimaryKey(autoGenerate = true)
@NonNull
@ColumnInfo(name = "customerId")
var id: Int = 0
```

A column name is also assigned to the customer name field. Note, however, that no column name was assigned to the address field. This means that the address data will still be stored within the database but is not required to be referenced in SQL statements. If a field within an entity is not required to be stored within a database, use the @Ignore annotation:

```
@Ignore
var MyString: String? = null
```

Annotations may also be included within an entity class to establish relationships with other entities using a relational database concept referred to as *foreign keys*. Foreign keys allow a table to reference the primary key in another table. For example, a relationship could be established between an entity named Purchase and our existing Customer entity as follows:

```
@Entity(foreignKeys = arrayOf(ForeignKey(entity = Customer::class,
    parentColumns = arrayOf("customerId"),
    childColumns = arrayOf("buyerId"),
    onDelete = ForeignKey.CASCADE,
    onUpdate = ForeignKey.RESTRICT)))

class Purchase {

    @PrimaryKey(autoGenerate = true)
    @NonNull
    @ColumnInfo(name = "purchaseId")
    var purchaseId: Int = 0

    @ColumnInfo(name = "buyerId")
    var buyerId: Int = 0
.
.
}
```

Note that the foreign key declaration also specifies the action to be taken when a parent record is deleted or updated. Available options are CASCADE, NO_ACTION, RESTRICT, SET_DEFAULT, and SET_NULL.

72.4 Data Access Objects

A Data Access Object allows access to the data stored within a SQLite database. A DAO is declared as a standard Kotlin interface with additional annotations that map specific SQL statements to methods that the repository may then call.

The first step is to create the interface and declare it as a DAO using the @Dao annotation:

```
@Dao
interface CustomerDao {
}
```

Next, entries are added consisting of SQL statements and corresponding method names. The following declaration, for example, allows all of the rows in the customers table to be retrieved via a call to a method named *getAllCustomers()*:

```
@Dao
interface CustomerDao {
   @Query("SELECT * FROM customers")
   fun getAllCustomers(): LiveData<List<Customer>>
}
```

The *getAllCustomers()* method returns a List object containing a Customer entity object for each record retrieved from the database table. The DAO is also using LiveData so that the repository can observe changes to the database.

Arguments may also be passed into the methods and referenced within the corresponding SQL statements. Consider the following DAO declaration, which searches for database records matching a customer's name (note that the column name referenced in the WHERE condition is the name assigned to the column in the entity class):

```
@Query("SELECT * FROM customers WHERE name = :customerName")
fun findCustomer(customerName: String): List<Customer>
```

In this example, the method is passed a string value which is, in turn, included within an SQL statement by prefixing the variable name with a colon (:).

A basic insertion operation can be declared as follows using the @Insert *convenience annotation*:

```
@Insert
fun addCustomer(Customer customer)
```

This is referred to as a convenience annotation because the Room persistence library can infer that the Customer entity passed to the *addCustomer()* method is to be inserted into the database without the need for the SQL insert statement to be provided. Multiple database records may also be inserted in a single transaction as follows:

```
@Insert
fun insertCustomers(Customer... customers)
```

The following DAO declaration deletes all records matching the provided customer name:

```
@Query("DELETE FROM customers WHERE name = :name")
fun deleteCustomer(String name)
```

As an alternative to using the @Query annotation to perform deletions, the @Delete convenience annotation may also be used. In the following example, all of the Customer records that match the set of entities passed to the *deleteCustomers()* method will be deleted from the database:

```
@Delete
fun deleteCustomers(Customer... customers)
```

The @Update convenience annotation provides similar behavior when updating records:

```
@Update
fun updateCustomers(Customer... customers)
```

The DAO methods for these types of database operations may also be declared to return an int value indicating the number of rows affected by the transaction, for example:

```
@Delete
fun deleteCustomers(Customer... customers): int
```

72.5 The Room Database

The Room database class is created by extending the RoomDatabase class and acts as a layer on top of the actual SQLite database embedded into the Android operating system. The class is responsible for creating and returning a new room database instance and providing access to the database's associated DAO instances.

The Room persistence library provides a database builder for creating database instances. Each Android app should only have one room database instance, so it is best to implement defensive code within the class to prevent more than one instance from being created.

An example Room Database implementation for use with the example customer table is outlined in the following code listing:

```
import android.content.Context
import android.arch.persistence.room.Database
import android.arch.persistence.room.Room
import android.arch.persistence.room.RoomDatabase
```

```
@Database(entities = [(Customer::class)], version = 1)
abstract class CustomerRoomDatabase: RoomDatabase() {
    abstract fun customerDao(): CustomerDao

    companion object {

        private var INSTANCE: CustomerRoomDatabase? = null

        internal fun getDatabase(context: Context): CustomerRoomDatabase? {
            if (INSTANCE == null) {
                synchronized(CustomerRoomDatabase::class.java) {
                    if (INSTANCE == null) {
                        INSTANCE =
                              Room.databaseBuilder(
                               context.applicationContext,
                                 CustomerRoomDatabase::class.java,
                                    "customer_database").build()
                    }
                }
            }
            return INSTANCE
        }
    }
}
```

Important areas to note in the above example are the annotation above the class declaration declaring the entities with which the database is to work, the code to check that an instance of the class has not already been created and the assignment of the name "customer_database" to the instance.

72.6 The Repository

The repository is responsible for getting a Room Database instance, using that instance to access associated DAOs, and then making calls to DAO methods to perform database operations. A typical constructor for a repository designed to work with a Room Database might read as follows:

```
class CustomerRepository(application: Application) {

    private var customerDao: CustomerDao?

    init {
        val db: CustomerRoomDatabase? =
                    CustomerRoomDatabase.getDatabase(application)
        customerDao = db?.customerDao()
    }
.
.
```

Once the repository can access the DAO, it can call the data access methods. The following code, for example, calls the *getAllCustomers()* DAO method:

```
val allCustomers: LiveData<List<Customer>>?
allCustomers = customerDao.getAllCustomers()
```

When calling DAO methods, it is important to note that unless the method returns a LiveData instance (which automatically runs queries on a separate thread), the operation cannot be performed on the app's main thread. Attempting to do so will cause the app to crash with the following diagnostic output:

```
Cannot access database on the main thread since it may potentially lock the UI
for a long period of time
```

Since some database transactions may take a longer time to complete, running the operations on a separate thread avoids the app appearing to lock up. As will be demonstrated in the chapter entitled *"An Android Room Database and Repository Tutorial"*, this problem can be easily resolved by making use of coroutines (for more information or a reminder of how to use coroutines, refer back to the chapter entitled *"An Introduction to Kotlin Coroutines"*).

72.7 In-Memory Databases

The examples outlined in this chapter use a SQLite database that exists as a database file on the persistent storage of an Android device. This ensures that the data persists even after the app process is terminated.

The Room database persistence library also supports *in-memory* databases. These databases reside entirely in memory and are lost when the app terminates. The only change necessary to work with an in-memory database is to call the *Room.inMemoryDatabaseBuilder()* method of the Room Database class instead of *Room.databaseBuilder()*. The following code shows the difference between the method calls (note that the in-memory database does not require a database name):

```
// Create a file storage-based database
INSTANCE = Room.databaseBuilder<CustomerRoomDatabase>(context.applicationContext,
        CustomerRoomDatabase::class.java, "customer_database")
        .build()
// Create an in-memory database
INSTANCE = Room.inMemoryDatabaseBuilder<CustomerRoomDatabase>(
                        context.getApplicationContext(),
                            CustomerRoomDatabase.class)
                            .build()
```

72.8 Database Inspector

Android Studio includes a Database Inspector tool window which allows the Room databases associated with running apps to be viewed, searched, and modified, as shown in Figure 72-3:

Figure 72-3

The Database Inspector will be covered in the chapter *"An Android Room Database and Repository Tutorial"*.

72.9 Summary

The Android Room persistence library is bundled with the Android Architecture Components and acts as an abstract layer above the lower-level SQLite database. The library is designed to make it easier to work with databases while conforming to the Android architecture guidelines. This chapter has introduced the elements that interact to build Room-based database storage into Android app projects, including entities, repositories, data access objects, annotations, and Room Database instances.

With the basics of SQLite and the Room architecture component covered, the next step is to create an example app that puts this theory into practice. Since the user interface for the example application will require a forms-based layout, the next chapter, entitled *"An Android TableLayout and TableRow Tutorial"*, will detour slightly from the core topic by introducing the basics of the TableLayout and TableRow views.

Chapter 73

73. An Android TableLayout and TableRow Tutorial

When the work began on the next chapter of this book (*"An Android Room Database and Repository Tutorial"*), it was originally intended to include the steps to design the user interface layout for the Room database example application. It quickly became evident, however, that the best way to implement the user interface was to use the Android TableLayout and TableRow views and that this topic area deserved a self-contained chapter. As a result, this chapter will focus solely on the user interface design of the database application to be completed in the next chapter, and in doing so, take some time to introduce the basic concepts of table layouts in Android Studio.

73.1 The TableLayout and TableRow Layout Views

The TableLayout container view allows user interface elements to be organized on the screen in a table format consisting of rows and columns. Each row within a TableLayout is occupied by a TableRow instance which, in turn, is divided into cells, with each cell containing a single child view (which may be a container with multiple view children).

The number of columns in a table is dictated by the row with the most columns, and, by default, the width of each column is defined by the widest cell in that column. Columns may be configured to be shrinkable or stretchable (or both) such that they change in size relative to the parent TableLayout. In addition, a single cell may be configured to span multiple columns.

Consider the user interface layout shown in Figure 73-1:

Figure 73-1

From the visual appearance of the layout, it is difficult to identify the TableLayout structure used to design the interface. The hierarchical tree illustrated in Figure 73-2, however, makes the structure a little easier to understand:

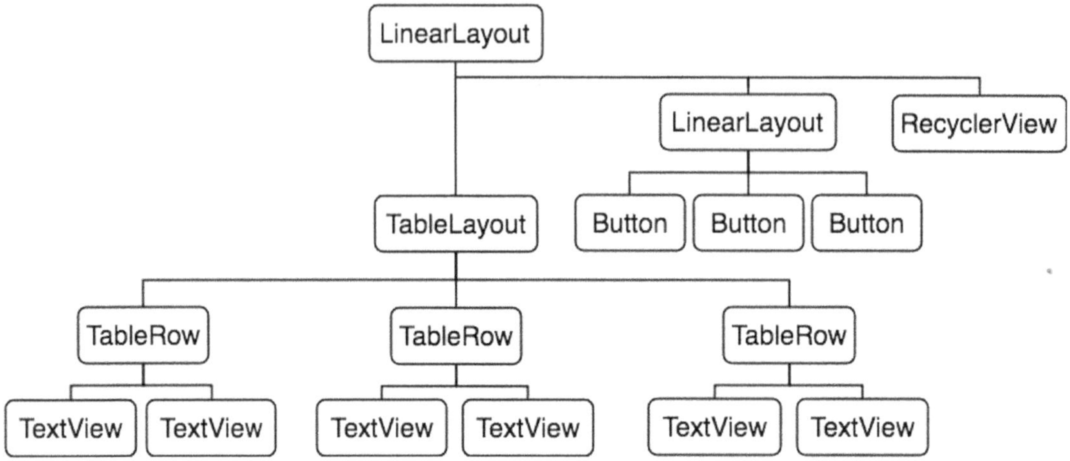

Figure 73-2

The layout comprises a parent LinearLayout view with TableLayout, LinearLayout, and RecyclerView children. The TableLayout contains three TableRow children representing three rows in the table. The TableRows contain two child views, each representing the contents of a table column cell. The LinearLayout child view contains three Button children.

The layout shown in Figure 73-2 is the exact layout required for the database example that will be completed in the next chapter. Therefore, the remainder of this chapter will be used to work step by step through the design of this user interface using the Android Studio Layout Editor tool.

73.2 Creating the Room Database Project

Select the *New Project* menu option from the welcome screen and, within the resulting new project dialog, choose the Empty Views Activity template before clicking on the Next button.

Enter *RoomDemo* into the Name field and specify *com.ebookfrenzy.roomdemo* as the package name. Before clicking on the Finish button, change the Minimum API level setting to API 26: Android 8.0 (Oreo) and the Language menu to Kotlin.

Migrate the project to view binding using the Gemini Agent or the steps outlined in section *18.8 Migrating a Project to View Binding.*

73.3 Converting to a LinearLayout

Locate the *activity_main.xml* file in the Project tool window (*app -> res -> layout*) and double-click on it to load it into the Layout Editor tool. By default, Android Studio has used a ConstraintLayout as the root layout element in the user interface. This needs to be converted to a vertically oriented LinearLayout.

With the Layout Editor tool in Design mode, locate the ConstraintLayout component in the Component Tree panel, right-click on it to display the menu shown in Figure 73-3, and select the *Convert view...* option:

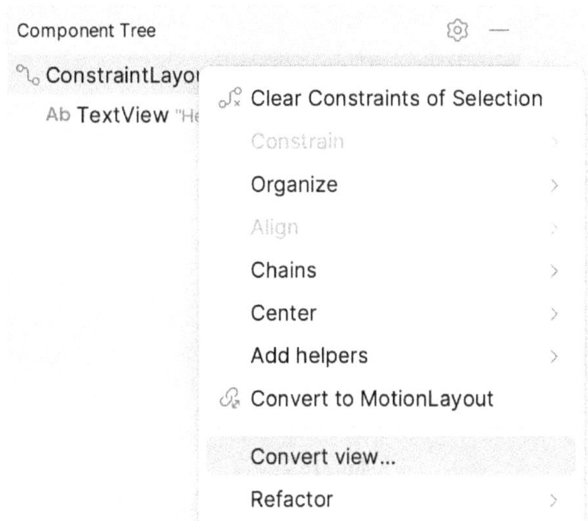

Figure 73-3

In the resulting dialog (Figure 73-4), select the option to convert to a LinearLayout before clicking on the Apply button:

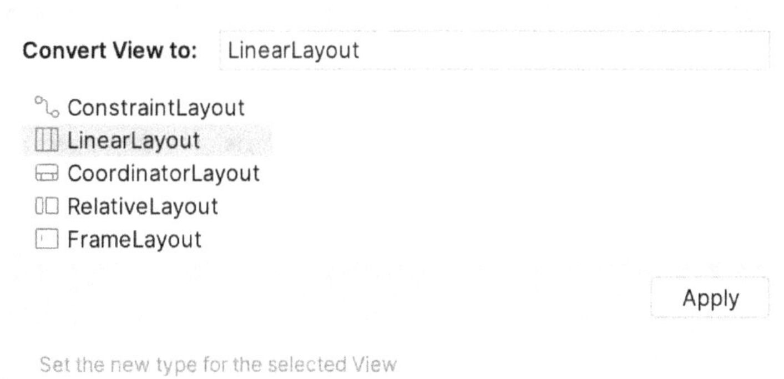

Figure 73-4

By default, the layout editor will have converted the ConstraintLayout to a horizontal LinearLayout, so select the layout component in the Component Tree window, refer to the Attributes tool window, and change the orientation property to *vertical*:

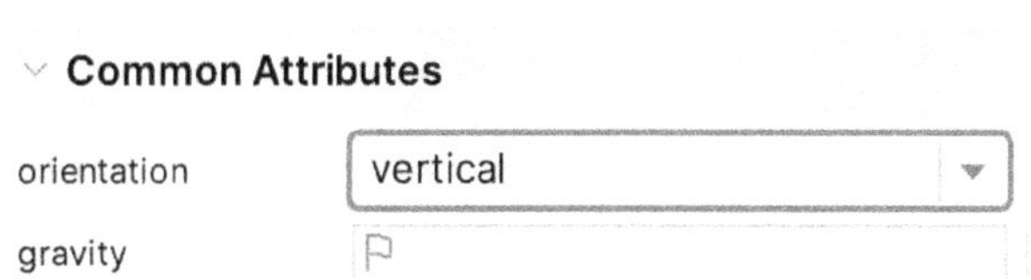

Figure 73-5

With the conversion complete, select and delete the default TextView widget from the layout.

73.4 Adding the TableLayout to the User Interface

Remaining in the *activity_main.xml* file and referring to the Layouts category of the Palette, drag a TableLayout view to position it at the top of the LinearLayout canvas area.

Once these initial steps are complete, the Component Tree for the layout should resemble that shown in Figure 73-6.

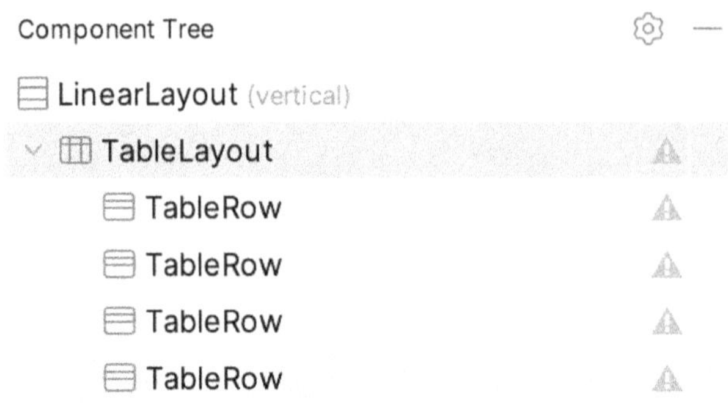

Figure 73-6

Android Studio has automatically added four TableRow instances to the TableLayout. Since only three rows are required for this example, select and delete the fourth TableRow instance. Additional rows may be added to the TableLayout at any time by dragging the TableRow object from the palette and dropping it onto the TableLayout entry in the Component Tree tool window.

With the TableLayout selected, use the Attributes tool window to change the layout_height property to *wrap_content* and layout_width to *match_parent*.

73.5 Configuring the TableRows

From within the *Text* section of the palette, drag two TextView objects onto the uppermost TableRow entry in the Component Tree (Figure 73-7):

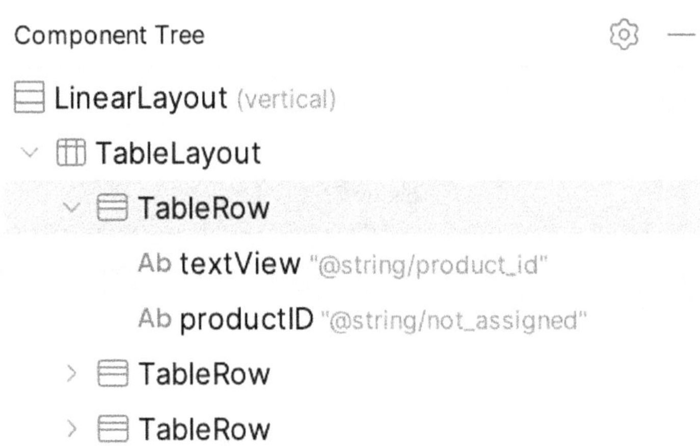

Figure 73-7

Select the left-most TextView within the screen layout and change the text property to "Product ID" in the Attributes tool window. Repeat this step for the rightmost TextView, changing the text to "Not assigned" and specifying an ID value of *productID*.

Drag and drop another TextView widget onto the second TableRow entry in the Component Tree and change the text on the view to read "Product Name". Locate the Plain Text object in the palette and drag and drop it to position it beneath the Product Name TextView within the Component Tree as outlined in Figure 73-8. Next, delete the "Name" string from the text property and set the ID to *productName*.

Figure 73-8

Drag and drop another TextView and a Number (Decimal) Text Field onto the third TableRow to position the TextView above the EditText in the hierarchy. Change the text on the TextView to "Product Quantity" and the ID of the EditText object to *productQuantity*.

Shift-click to select all of the widgets in the layout as shown in Figure 73-9 below, and use the Attributes tool window to set the textSize property on all of the objects to 18sp:

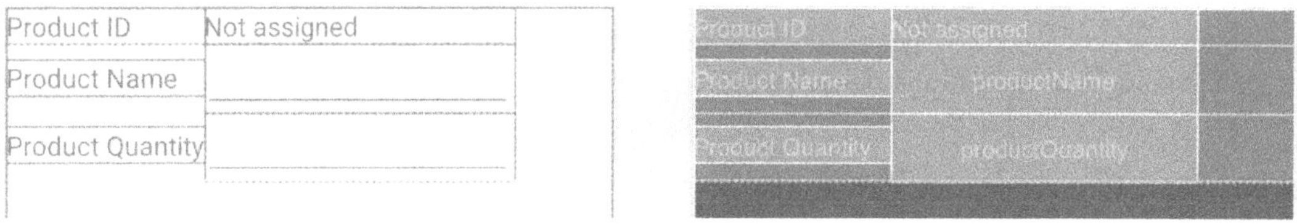

Figure 73-9

73.6 Adding the Button Bar to the Layout

The next step is to add a LinearLayout (Horizontal) view to the parent LinearLayout view, positioned immediately below the TableLayout view. Begin by clicking on the small disclosure arrow to the left of the TableLayout entry in the Component Tree so that the TableRows are folded away from view. Drag a *LinearLayout (horizontal)* instance from the *Layouts* section of the Layout Editor palette, drop it immediately beneath the TableLayout entry in the Component Tree panel, and change the layout_height property to *wrap_content*:

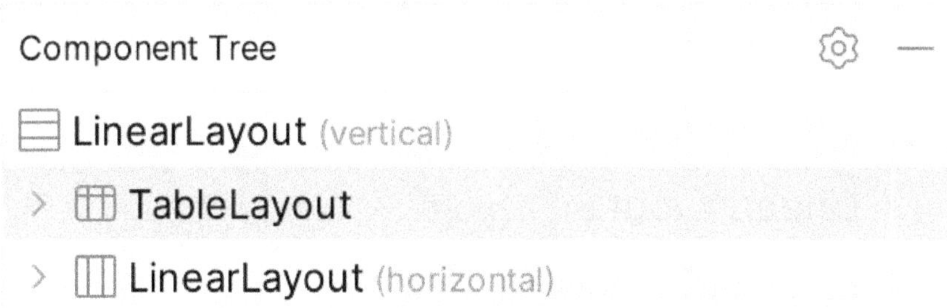

Figure 73-10

Drag three Button objects onto the new LinearLayout and assign string resources for each button that read "Add", "Find" and "Delete" respectively. Buttons in this type of button bar arrangement should generally be displayed with a borderless style. Use the Attributes tool window for each button to change the *style* setting to *Widget.AppCompat.Button.Borderless* and the *textColor* attribute to *?attr/colorPrimary*. Change the IDs for the buttons to *addButton*, *findButton*, and *deleteButton*, respectively.

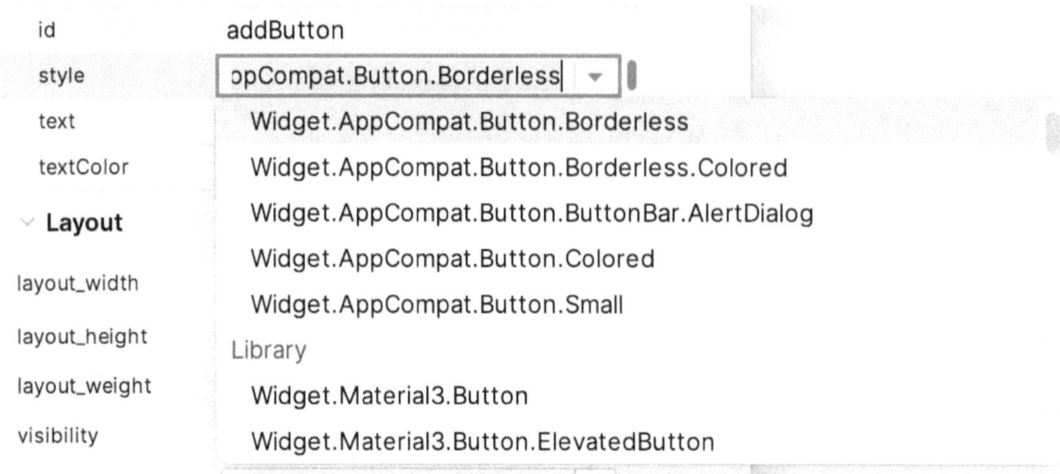

Figure 73-11

With the new horizontal LinearLayout view selected in the Component Tree, change the gravity property to *center_horizontal* so that the buttons are centered horizontally within the display. Before proceeding, extract all of the text properties added in the above steps to string resources.

73.7 Adding the RecyclerView

In the Component Tree, click on the disclosure arrow to the left of the newly added horizontal LinearLayout entry to fold all the children from view.

From the Containers section of the Palette, drag a RecyclerView instance onto the Component Tree to position it beneath the button bar LinearLayout as shown in Figure 73-12. Ensure the RecyclerView is added as a direct child of the parent vertical LinearLayout view and not as a child of the horizontal button bar LinearLayout.

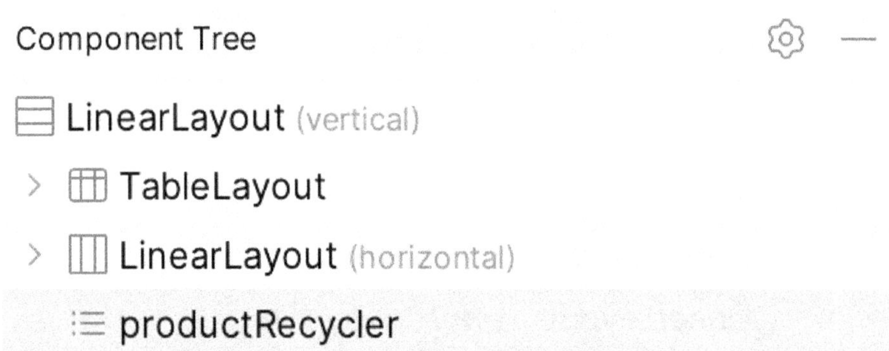

Figure 73-12

With the RecyclerView selected in the layout, change the ID of the view to *product_recycler* and set the layout_height property to *match_parent*. Before proceeding, check that the hierarchy of the layout in the Component Tree panel matches that shown in the following figure:

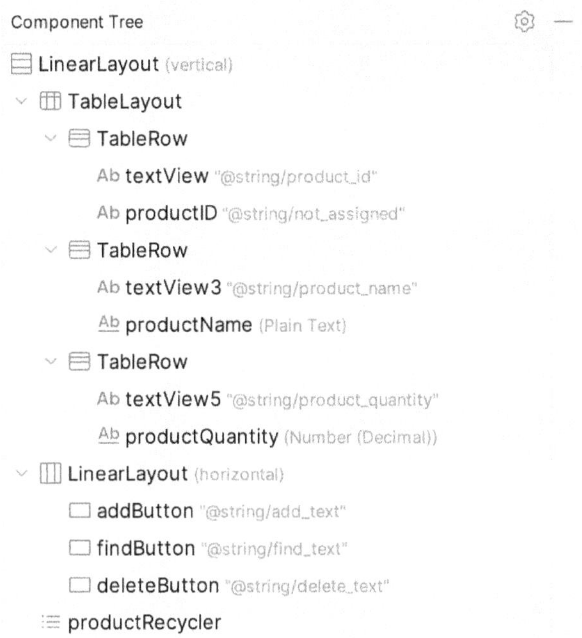

Figure 73-13

73.8 Adjusting the Layout Margins

All that remains is to adjust some of the layout settings. Begin by clicking on the first TableRow entry in the Component Tree panel so that it is selected. Hold down the Cmd/Ctrl-key on the keyboard and click on the second and third TableRows, the horizontal LinearLayout, and the RecyclerView so that all five items are selected. In the Attributes panel, locate the *layout_margin* attributes category and, once located, change the value to 10dp as shown in Figure 73-14:

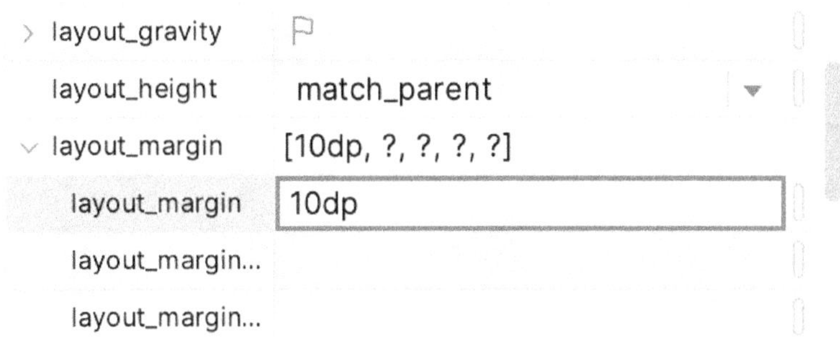

Figure 73-14

With margins set, the user interface should appear as illustrated in Figure 73-1.

73.9 Summary

The Android TableLayout container view provides a way to arrange view components in a row and column configuration. While the TableLayout view provides the overall container, each row and the cells contained therein are implemented via instances of the TableRow view. In this chapter, a user interface has been designed in Android Studio using the TableLayout and TableRow containers. The next chapter will add the functionality behind this user interface to implement the SQLite database capabilities using a repository and the Room persistence library.

74. An Android Room Database and Repository Tutorial

This chapter will combine the knowledge gained in *"The Android Room Persistence Library"* with the initial project created in the previous chapter to provide a detailed tutorial demonstrating how to implement SQLite-based database storage using the Room persistence library. In keeping with the Android architectural guidelines, the project will use a view model and repository. The tutorial will use all the elements covered in *"The Android Room Persistence Library"* including entities, a Data Access Object, a Room Database, and asynchronous database queries.

74.1 About the RoomDemo Project

The user interface layout created in the previous chapter was the first step in creating a rudimentary inventory app to store product names and quantities. When completed, the app will provide the ability to add, delete and search for database entries while displaying a scrollable list of all products currently stored in the database. This product list will update automatically as database entries are added or deleted.

74.2 Modifying the Build Configuration

Launch Android Studio and open the RoomDemo project started in the previous chapter. Before adding any new classes to the project, the first step is to add some additional libraries and plugins to the build configuration, including the Room persistence library.

Using the Project tool window, locate and edit the *Gradle Scripts -> libs.versions.toml* file as follows:

```
[versions]
.
.
roomRuntime = "2.8.4"
fragmentKtx = "1.8.9"
ksp = "2.3.5"

[libraries]
.
.
androidx-room-compiler = { module = "androidx.room:room-compiler", version.ref =
"roomRuntime" }
androidx-room-runtime = { group = "androidx.room", name = "room-runtime",
version.ref = "roomRuntime" }
androidx-fragment-ktx = { group = "androidx.fragment", name = "fragment-ktx",
version.ref = "fragmentKtx" }

[plugins]
.
.
```

```
devtoolsKsp = { id = "com.google.devtools.ksp", version.ref = "ksp"}
```

Click the Sync Now link to commit the changes. Finally, make the following changes to the module level *build.gradle.kts* file (*app -> Gradle Scripts -> build.gradle.kts (Module :app)*):

```
plugins {
    alias(libs.plugins.androidApplication)
    alias(libs.plugins.devtoolsKsp)
}

android {
.
.
dependencies {
.
.
    implementation(libs.androidx.room.runtime)
    implementation(libs.androidx.fragment.ktx)
    ksp(libs.androidx.room.compiler)
.
.
}
```

74.3 Building the Entity

This project will begin by creating the entity defining the database table schema. The entity will consist of an integer for the product id, a string column to hold the product name, and another integer value to store the quantity.

The product id column will serve as the primary key and will be auto-generated. Table 74-1 summarizes the structure of the entity:

Column	Data Type
productid	Integer / Primary Key / Auto Increment
productname	String
productquantity	Integer

Table 74-1

Add a class file for the entity by right-clicking on the *app -> kotlin+java -> com.ebookfrenzy.roomdemo* entry in the Project tool window and selecting the *New -> Kotlin Class/File* menu option. In the new class dialog, name the class *Product*, select the Class entry in the list, and press the keyboard return key to generate the file.

When the *Product.kt* file opens in the editor, modify it so that it reads as follows:

```
package com.ebookfrenzy.roomdemo

class Product {
```

```
    var id: Int = 0
    var productName: String? = null
    var quantity: Int = 0

    constructor() {}

    constructor(id: Int, productname: String, quantity: Int) {
        this.productName = productname
        this.quantity = quantity
    }
    constructor(productname: String, quantity: Int) {
        this.productName = productname
        this.quantity = quantity
    }
}
```

The class now has variables for the database table columns and matching getter and setter methods. Of course, this class does not become an entity until it has been annotated. With the class file still open in the editor, add annotations and corresponding import statements:

```
package com.ebookfrenzy.roomdemo

import androidx.room.ColumnInfo
import androidx.room.Entity
import androidx.room.PrimaryKey

@Entity(tableName = "products")
class Product {

    @PrimaryKey(autoGenerate = true)
    @ColumnInfo(name = "productId")
    var id: Int = 0

    @ColumnInfo(name = "productName")
    var productName: String? = null
    var quantity: Int = 0

    constructor() {}

    constructor(id: Int, productname: String, quantity: Int) {
        this.id = id
        this.productName = productname
        this.quantity = quantity
    }
    constructor(productname: String, quantity: Int) {
        this.productName = productname
        this.quantity = quantity
```

```
    }
}
```

These annotations declare this as the entity for a table named *products* and assign column names for the *id* and *name* variables. The id column is also configured to be the primary key and auto-generated. Since it will not be necessary to reference the quantity column in SQL queries, a column name has not been assigned to the *quantity* variable.

74.4 Creating the Data Access Object

With the product entity defined, the next step is to create the DAO interface. Referring again to the Project tool window, right-click on the *app -> kotlin+java -> com.ebookfrenzy.roomdemo* entry and select the *New -> Kotlin Class/File* menu option. In the new class dialog, enter *ProductDao* into the Name field and select *Interface* from the list as highlighted in Figure 74-1:

Figure 74-1

Press the Return key to generate the new interface and, with the *ProductDao.kt* file loaded into the code editor, make the following changes:

```
package com.ebookfrenzy.roomdemo

import androidx.lifecycle.LiveData
import androidx.room.Dao
import androidx.room.Insert
import androidx.room.Query

@Dao
interface ProductDao {

    @Insert
    fun insertProduct(product: Product)

    @Query("SELECT * FROM products WHERE productName = :name")
    fun findProduct(name: String): List<Product>

    @Query("DELETE FROM products WHERE productName = :name")
```

```
    fun deleteProduct(name: String)

    @Query("SELECT * FROM products")
    fun getAllProducts(): LiveData<List<Product>>
}
```

The DAO implements methods to insert, find and delete records from the products database. The insertion method is passed a Product entity object containing the data to be stored, while the methods to find and delete records are passed a string containing the name of the product on which to perform the operation. The *getAllProducts()* method returns a LiveData object containing all of the records within the database. This method will be used to keep the RecyclerView product list in the user interface layout synchronized with the database.

74.5 Adding the Room Database

The last task before adding the repository to the project is implementing the Room Database instance. Add a new class to the project named *ProductRoomDatabase*, this time with the *Class* option selected.

Once the file has been generated, modify it as follows using the steps outlined in the *"The Android Room Persistence Library"* chapter:

```
package com.ebookfrenzy.roomdemo

import android.content.Context
import androidx.room.Database
import androidx.room.Room
import androidx.room.RoomDatabase

@Database(entities = [(Product::class)], version = 1)
abstract class ProductRoomDatabase: RoomDatabase() {

    abstract fun productDao(): ProductDao

    companion object {

        private var INSTANCE: ProductRoomDatabase? = null

        internal fun getDatabase(context: Context): ProductRoomDatabase? {
            if (INSTANCE == null) {
                synchronized(ProductRoomDatabase::class.java) {
                    if (INSTANCE == null) {
                        INSTANCE =
                           Room.databaseBuilder(
                            context.applicationContext,
                                ProductRoomDatabase::class.java,
                                    "product_database").build()
                    }
                }
            }
            return INSTANCE
```

```
        }
    }
}
```

74.6 Adding the Repository

Add a new class named *ProductRepository* to the project, with the *Class* option selected.

The repository class will be responsible for interacting with the Room database on behalf of the ViewModel. It must provide methods that use the DAO to insert, delete, and query product records. Except for the *getAllProducts()* DAO method (which returns a LiveData object), these database operations must be performed on separate threads from the main thread.

Remaining within the *ProductRepository.kt* file, make the following changes :

```
package com.ebookfrenzy.roomdemo

import android.app.Application
import androidx.lifecycle.LiveData
import androidx.lifecycle.MutableLiveData
import kotlinx.coroutines.*

class ProductRepository(application: Application) {

    val searchResults = MutableLiveData<List<Product>>()
}
```

The above declares a MutableLiveData variable named *searchResults* into which the results of a search operation are stored whenever an asynchronous search task completes (later in the tutorial, an observer within the ViewModel will monitor this live data object).

The repository class must now provide some methods the ViewModel can call to initiate these operations. However, the repository needs to obtain the DAO reference via a ProductRoomDatabase instance to do this. Add a constructor method to the ProductRepository class to perform these tasks:

```
.
.
class ProductRepository(application: Application) {

    val searchResults = MutableLiveData<List<Product>>()
    private var productDao: ProductDao?

    init {
        val db: ProductRoomDatabase? =
                    ProductRoomDatabase.getDatabase(application)
        productDao = db?.productDao()
    }
.
.
```

With a reference to DAO stored, the methods are ready to be added to the ProductRepository class file as follows:

```
.
```

```
.
val searchResults = MutableLiveData<List<Product>>()
private var productDao: ProductDao?
private val coroutineScope = CoroutineScope(Dispatchers.Main)
.
.
fun insertProduct(newproduct: Product) {
    coroutineScope.launch(Dispatchers.IO) {
        asyncInsert(newproduct)
    }
}

private fun asyncInsert(product: Product) {
    productDao?.insertProduct(product)
}

fun deleteProduct(name: String) {
    coroutineScope.launch(Dispatchers.IO) {
        asyncDelete(name)
    }
}

private fun asyncDelete(name: String) {
    productDao?.deleteProduct(name)
}

fun findProduct(name: String) {

    coroutineScope.launch(Dispatchers.Main) {
        searchResults.value = asyncFind(name).await()
    }
}

private fun asyncFind(name: String): Deferred<List<Product>?> =

    coroutineScope.async(Dispatchers.IO) {
        return@async productDao?.findProduct(name)
    }
.
.
```

For the add and delete database operations, the above code adds two methods: a standard method and a coroutine suspend method. In each case, the standard method calls the suspend method to execute the coroutine outside of the main thread (using the IO dispatcher) so as not to block the app while the task is being performed. In the case of the find operation, the *asyncFind()* suspend method uses a deferred value to return the search results to the *findProduct()* method. Because the *findProduct()* method needs access to the searchResults variable, the call to the *asyncFind()* method is dispatched to the main thread, which, in turn, performs the database operation using the IO dispatcher.

One final task remains to complete the repository class. The RecyclerView in the user interface layout must keep up to date with the current list of products stored in the database. The ProductDao class already includes a method named *getAllProducts()* which uses a SQL query to select all of the database records and return them wrapped in a LiveData object. The repository needs to call this method once on initialization and store the result within a LiveData object that can be observed by the ViewModel and, in turn, by the UI controller. Once this has been set up, the UI controller observer will be notified each time a change occurs to the database table, and the RecyclerView can be updated with the latest product list. Remaining within the *ProductRepository.kt* file, add a LiveData variable and call to the DAO *getAllProducts()* method within the constructor:

```
.
.
class ProductRepository(application: Application) {
.
.
    val allProducts: LiveData<List<Product>>?

    init {
        val db: ProductRoomDatabase? =
                ProductRoomDatabase.getDatabase(application)
        productDao = db?.productDao()
        allProducts = productDao?.getAllProducts()
    }
.
.
```

74.7 Adding the ViewModel

The ViewModel is responsible for creating an instance of the repository and providing methods, and LiveData objects that the UI controller can utilize to keep the user interface synchronized with the underlying database. As implemented in *ProductRepository.kt*, the repository constructor requires access to the application context to get a Room Database instance. To make the application context accessible within the ViewModel so it can be passed to the repository, the ViewModel needs to subclass AndroidViewModel instead of ViewModel.

Begin by locating the *com.ebookfrenzy.viewmodeldemo* entry in the Project tool window, right-clicking it, and selecting the *New -> Kotlin Class/File* menu option. Next, name the new class MainViewModel and press the keyboard Enter key. Finally, edit the new class file to change the class to extend AndroidViewModel and implement the default constructor:

```
package com.ebookfrenzy.roomdemo

import android.app.Application
import androidx.lifecycle.AndroidViewModel
import androidx.lifecycle.LiveData
import androidx.lifecycle.MutableLiveData

class MainViewModel(application: Application) : AndroidViewModel(application) {

    private val repository: ProductRepository = ProductRepository(application)
```

```
    private val allProducts: LiveData<List<Product>>?
    private val searchResults: MutableLiveData<List<Product>>

    init {
        allProducts = repository.allProducts
        searchResults = repository.searchResults
    }
}
```

The constructor creates a repository instance and then uses it to get references to the results and live data objects so that the UI controller can observe them. All that now remains within the ViewModel is to implement the methods that will be called from within the UI controller in response to button clicks and when setting up observers on the LiveData objects:

```
fun insertProduct(product: Product) {
    repository.insertProduct(product)
}

fun findProduct(name: String) {
    repository.findProduct(name)
}

fun deleteProduct(name: String) {
    repository.deleteProduct(name)
}

fun getSearchResults(): MutableLiveData<List<Product>> {
    return searchResults
}

fun getAllProducts(): LiveData<List<Product>>? {
    return allProducts
}
```

74.8 Creating the Product Item Layout

The name of each product in the database will appear within the RecyclerView list in the main user interface. This will require a layout resource file containing a TextView for each row in the list. Add this file now by right-clicking on the *app -> res -> layout* entry in the Project tool window and selecting the *New -> Layout Resource File* menu option. Name the file *product_list_item* and change the root element to a vertical LinearLayout before clicking on OK to create the file and load it into the layout editor. With the layout editor in Design mode, drag a TextView object from the palette onto the layout, where it will appear by default at the top of the layout:

Figure 74-2

With the TextView selected in the layout, use the Attributes tool window to set the ID of the view to *product_* *row* and the layout_height to 30dp. Select the LinearLayout entry in the Component Tree window and set the layout_height attribute to *wrap_content*.

74.9 Adding the RecyclerView Adapter

As outlined in detail in the chapter entitled *"Working with the RecyclerView and CardView Widgets"*, a RecyclerView instance requires an adapter class to provide the data to be displayed. Add this class by right-clicking on the *app -> kotlin+java -> com.ebookfrenzy.roomdemo* entry in the Project tool window and selecting the *New -> Kotlin Class* menu. In the dialog, name the class *ProductListAdapter* and choose *Class* from the list before pressing the keyboard Return key. With the resulting *ProductListAdapter.kt* class loaded into the editor, implement the class as follows:

```
package com.ebookfrenzy.roomdemo

import android.view.LayoutInflater
import android.view.View
import android.view.ViewGroup
import android.widget.TextView
import androidx.recyclerview.widget.RecyclerView
import com.ebookfrenzy.roomdemo.Product
import com.ebookfrenzy.roomdemo.R

class ProductListAdapter(private val productItemLayout: Int) :
            RecyclerView.Adapter<ProductListAdapter.ViewHolder>() {

    private var productList: List<Product>? = null

    override fun onBindViewHolder(holder: ViewHolder, listPosition: Int) {
        val item = holder.item
        productList.let {
            item.text = it!![listPosition].productName
        }
    }

    override fun onCreateViewHolder(parent: ViewGroup, viewType: Int):
                                                          ViewHolder {
        val view = LayoutInflater.from(parent.context).inflate(
                                    productItemLayout, parent, false)
        return ViewHolder(view)
    }

    fun setProductList(products: List<Product>) {
        productList = products
        notifyDataSetChanged()
    }

    override fun getItemCount(): Int {
        return if (productList == null) 0 else productList!!.size
```

```
    }

    class ViewHolder(itemView: View) : RecyclerView.ViewHolder(itemView) {
        var item: TextView = itemView.findViewById(R.id.product_row)
    }
}
```

74.10 Preparing the Main Activity

The last remaining component to modify is the MainActivity class which needs to configure listeners on the Button views and observers on the live data objects in the ViewModel class. Before adding this code, some preparation work must be performed to add some imports and variables. Edit the *MainActivity.kt* file and modify it as follows:

```
package com.ebookfrenzy.roomdemo
.
.
import androidx.activity.viewModels
import androidx.recyclerview.widget.LinearLayoutManager
import com.ebookfrenzy.roomdemo.Product

import java.util.*

class MainActivity : AppCompatActivity() {

   private lateinit var binding: ActivityMainBinding
   private var adapter: ProductListAdapter? = null
   private val viewModel: MainViewModel by viewModels()

    override fun onCreate(savedInstanceState: Bundle?) {
.
.
         listenerSetup()
         observerSetup()
         recyclerSetup()
    }
.
.
```

At various stages in the code, the app will need to clear the product information displayed in the user interface. To avoid code repetition, add the following *clearFields()* convenience function:

```
private fun clearFields() {
    binding.productID.text = ""
    binding.productName.setText("")
    binding.productQuantity.setText("")
}
```

Before the app can be built and tested, the three setup methods called from the *onCreate()* method above need to be added to the class.

74.11 Adding the Button Listeners

The user interface layout for the main fragment contains three buttons, each needing to perform a specific task when clicked by the user. Edit the *MainActivity.kt* file and add the *listenerSetup()* method:

```
private fun listenerSetup() {

    binding.addButton.setOnClickListener {
        val name = binding.productName.text.toString()
        val quantity = binding.productQuantity.text.toString()

        if (name != "" && quantity != "") {
            val product = Product(name, Integer.parseInt(quantity))
            viewModel.insertProduct(product)
            clearFields()
        } else {
            binding.productID.text = "Incomplete information"
        }
    }

    binding.findButton.setOnClickListener { viewModel.findProduct(
                                binding.productName.text.toString()) }

    binding.deleteButton.setOnClickListener {
        viewModel.deleteProduct(binding.productName.text.toString())
        clearFields()
    }
}
```

The addButton listener performs some basic validation to ensure that the user has entered a product name and quantity and uses this data to create a new Product entity object (note that the quantity string is converted to an integer to match the entity data type). The ViewModel *insertProduct()* method is then called and passed the Product object before the fields are cleared.

The findButton and deleteButton listeners pass the product name to either the ViewModel *findProduct()* or *deleteProduct()* method.

74.12 Adding LiveData Observers

The user interface now needs to add observers to remain synchronized with the *searchResults* and *allProducts* live data objects within the ViewModel. Remaining in the *MainActivity.kt* file, implement the observer setup method as follows:

```
private fun observerSetup() {

    viewModel.getAllProducts()?.observe(this) { products ->
        products?.let {
            adapter?.setProductList(it)
        }
    }
```

```
    viewModel.getSearchResults().observe(this) { products ->

        products?.let {
            if (it.isNotEmpty()) {
                binding.productID.text = String.format(Locale.US, "%d", it[0].id)
                binding.productName.setText(it[0].productName)
                binding.productQuantity.setText(
                    String.format(
                        Locale.US, "%d",
                        it[0].quantity
                    )
                )
            } else {
                binding.productID.text = "No Match"
            }
        }
    }
}
```

The "all products" observer passes the current list of products to the *setProductList()* method of the RecyclerAdapter where the displayed list will be updated.

The "search results" observer checks that at least one matching result has been located in the database, extracts the first matching Product entity object from the list, gets the data from the object, converts it where necessary, and assigns it to the TextView and EditText views in the layout. If the product search fails, the user is notified via a message displayed on the product ID TextView.

74.13 Initializing the RecyclerView

Add the final setup method to initialize and configure the RecyclerView and adapter as follows:

```
private fun recyclerSetup() {
    adapter = ProductListAdapter(R.layout.product_list_item)
    binding.productRecycler.layoutManager = LinearLayoutManager(this)
    binding.productRecycler.adapter = adapter
}
```

74.14 Testing the RoomDemo App

Compile and run the app on a device or emulator, add some products, and ensure they appear automatically in the RecyclerView. Perform a search for an existing product and verify that the product ID and quantity fields update accordingly. Finally, enter the name of an existing product, delete it from the database, and confirm that it is removed from the RecyclerView product list.

74.15 Using the Database Inspector

As previously outlined in *"The Android Room Persistence Library"*, the Database Inspector tool may be used to inspect the content of Room databases associated with a running app and to perform minor data changes. After adding some database records using the RoomDemo app, display the Database Inspector tool using the *View -> Tool Windows -> App Inspection* menu option:

From within the inspector window, select the running app from the menu marked A in Figure 74-3 below:

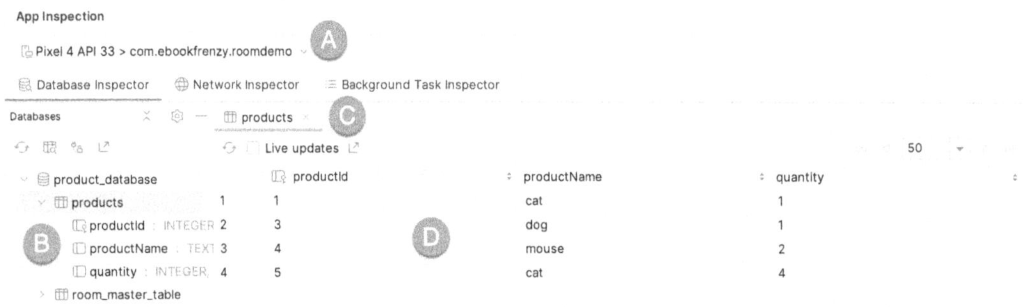

Figure 74-3

From the Databases panel (B), double-click on the *products* table to view the table rows currently stored in the database. Enable the *Live updates* option (C) and then use the running app to add more records to the database. Note that the Database Inspector updates the table data (D) in real-time to reflect the changes.

Turn off Live updates so that the table is no longer read-only, double-click on the quantity cell for a table row, and change the value before pressing the keyboard Enter key. Return to the running app and search for the product to confirm that the change made to the quantity in the inspector was saved to the database table.

Finally, click on the table query button (indicated by the arrow in Figure 74-4 below) to display a new query tab (A), make sure that *product_database* is selected (B), and enter a SQL statement into the query text field (C) and click the Run button(D):

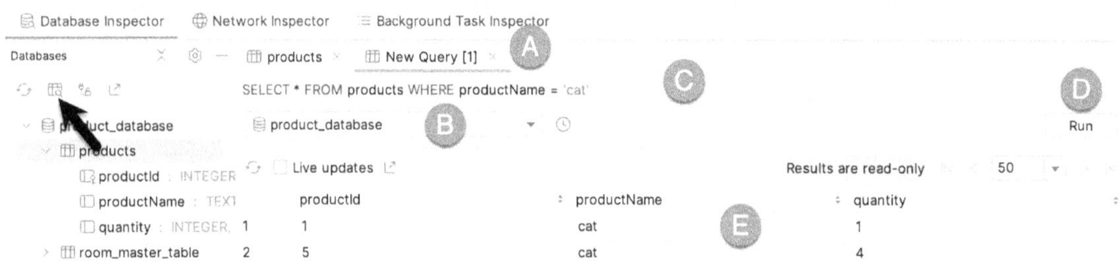

Figure 74-4

The list of rows should update to reflect the SQL query (E) results.

74.16 Summary

This chapter has demonstrated the use of the Room persistence library to store data in a SQLite database. The finished project used a repository to separate the ViewModel from all database operations. It demonstrated the creation of entities, a DAO, and a room database instance, including the use of asynchronous tasks when performing some database operations.

Chapter 75

75. Making Runtime Permission Requests in Android

In a number of the example projects created in preceding chapters, changes have been made to the *AndroidManifest.xml* file to request permission for the app to perform a specific task. In a couple of instances, for example, internet access permission has been requested to allow the app to download and display web pages. In each case up until this point, adding the request to the manifest was all that was required for the app to obtain permission from the user to perform the designated task.

However, there are several permissions for which additional steps are required for the app to function when running on Android 6.0 or later. The first of these so-called "dangerous" permissions will be encountered in the next chapter. Before reaching that point, however, this chapter will outline the steps involved in requesting such permissions when running on the latest generations of Android.

75.1 Understanding Normal and Dangerous Permissions

Android enforces security by requiring the user to grant permission for an app to perform certain tasks. Before the introduction of Android 6, permission was always sought when the app was installed on the device. Figure 75-1, for example, shows a typical screen seeking a variety of permissions while installing an app via Google Play.

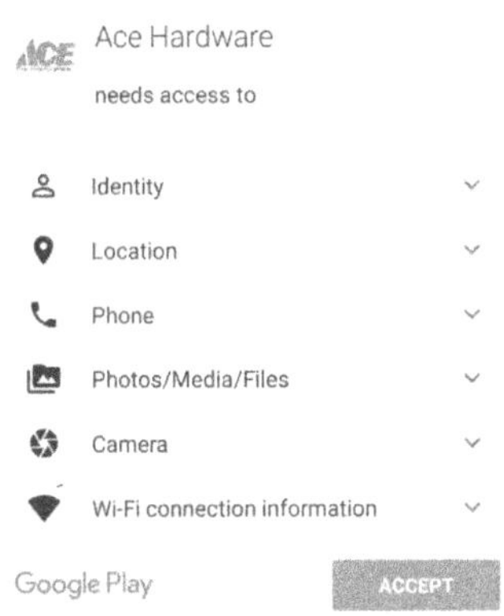

Figure 75-1

For many types of permissions, this scenario still applies to apps on Android 6.0 or later. These permissions are referred to as *normal permissions* and are still required to be accepted by the user at the point of installation. A second type of permission, called *dangerous permissions*, must also be declared within the manifest file in the same way as a normal permission but must also be requested from the user when the application is first launched. When such a request is made, it appears in the form of a dialog box, as illustrated in Figure 75-2:

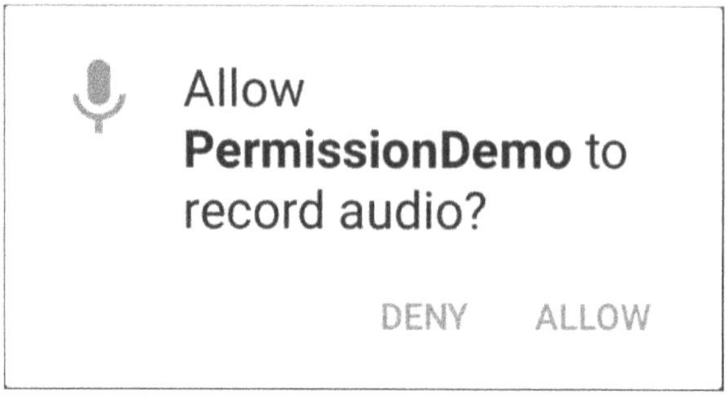

Figure 75-2

The full list of permissions that fall into the dangerous category is contained in Table 75-1:

Permission Group	**Permission**
Calendar	READ_CALENDAR WRITE_CALENDAR
Camera	CAMERA
Contacts	READ_CONTACTS WRITE_CONTACTS GET_ACCOUNTS
Location	ACCESS_FINE_LOCATION ACCESS_COARSE_LOCATION
Microphone	RECORD_AUDIO
Notifications	POST_NOTIFICATIONS
Phone	READ_PHONE_STATE CALL_PHONE READ_CALL_LOG WRITE_CALL_LOG ADD_VOICEMAIL USE_SIP PROCESS_OUTGOING_CALLS
Sensors	BODY_SENSORS
SMS	SEND_SMS RECEIVE_SMS READ_SMS RECEIVE_WAP_PUSH RECEIVE_MMS

Storage	MANAGE_EXTERNAL_STORAGE READ_EXTERNAL_STORAGE WRITE_EXTERNAL_STORAGE

Table 75-1

The MANAGE_EXTERNAL_STORAGE permission gives the app access to all files on the device's external storage, including those belonging to other apps. Consequently, permission will only be enabled for your app once Google has verified during the review process that this level of access is needed. To test your app in advance of submitting it to the Google Play store, the following *adb* command can be executed to enable access for the app on the testing device temporarily:

```
adb shell appops set --uid <package name> MANAGE_EXTERNAL_STORAGE allow
```

This mode can be turned off as follows:

```
adb shell appops set --uid <package name> MANAGE_EXTERNAL_STORAGE default
```

75.2 Creating the Permissions Example Project

Select the *New Project* option from the welcome screen and, within the resulting new project dialog, choose the Empty Views Activity template before clicking on the Next button.

Enter *PermissionDemo* into the Name field and specify *com.ebookfrenzy.permissiondemo* as the package name. Before clicking on the Finish button, change the Minimum API level setting to API 26: Android 8.0 (Oreo) and the Language menu to Kotlin.

75.3 Checking for a Permission

The Android Support Library contains several methods that can be used to seek and manage dangerous permissions within the code of an Android app. These API calls can be made safely regardless of the version of Android on which the app is running but will only perform meaningful tasks when executed on Android 6.0 or later.

Before an app attempts to use a feature that requires approval of a dangerous permission, and regardless of whether or not permission was previously granted, the code must check that the permission has been granted. This can be achieved via a call to the *checkSelfPermission()* method of the ContextCompat class, passing through as arguments a reference to the current activity and the requested permission. The method will check whether the permission has been previously granted and return an integer value matching *PackageManager.PERMISSION_GRANTED* or *PackageManager.PERMISSION_DENIED*.

Within the *MainActivity.kt* file of the example project, modify the code to check whether permission has been granted for the app to record audio:

```
.
.
import android.content.pm.PackageManager
import android.util.Log
import android.Manifest
import androidx.core.content.ContextCompat

class MainActivity : AppCompatActivity() {

    private val TAG = "PermissionDemo"
```

```
    override fun onCreate(savedInstanceState: Bundle?) {
        super.onCreate(savedInstanceState)
.
.
        setupPermissions()
    }
.
.
    private fun setupPermissions() {
        val permission = ContextCompat.checkSelfPermission(this,
                Manifest.permission.RECORD_AUDIO)

        if (permission != PackageManager.PERMISSION_GRANTED) {
            Log.i(TAG, "Permission to record denied")
        }
    }
}
```

Edit the *AndroidManifest.xml* file (located in the Project tool window under *app -> manifests*) and add a line to request recording permission as follows:

```
<?xml version="1.0" encoding="utf-8"?>
<manifest xmlns:android="http://schemas.android.com/apk/res/android"
    package="com.ebookfrenzy.permissiondemoactivity" >

    <uses-permission android:name="android.permission.RECORD_AUDIO" />

    <application
        android:allowBackup="true"
.
.
    </application>
</manifest>
```

Run the app on a device or emulator and open the Logcat tool window. Note that even though the permission has been added to the manifest file, the permission denied message appears. This is because Android requires that in addition to adding the request to the manifest file, the app must also request dangerous permissions at runtime.

75.4 Requesting Permission at Runtime

A permission request is made via a call to the *requestPermissions()* method of the ActivityCompat class. When this method is called, the permission request is handled asynchronously, and a method named *onRequestPermissionsResult()* is called when the task is completed.

The *requestPermissions()* method takes as arguments a reference to the current activity, the identifier of the requested permission, and a request code. The request code can be any integer value and will be used to identify which request has triggered the call to the *onRequestPermissionsResult()* method. Modify the *MainActivity.kt* file to declare a request code and request recording permission if the permission check fails:

```
.
.
import androidx.core.app.ActivityCompat

class MainActivity : AppCompatActivity() {

    private val TAG = "PermissionDemo"
    private val RECORD_REQUEST_CODE = 101
.
.
    private fun setupPermissions() {
        val permission = ContextCompat.checkSelfPermission(this,
                Manifest.permission.RECORD_AUDIO)

        if (permission != PackageManager.PERMISSION_GRANTED) {
            Log.i(TAG, "Permission to record denied")
            makeRequest()
        }
    }

    private fun makeRequest() {
        ActivityCompat.requestPermissions(this,
                arrayOf(Manifest.permission.RECORD_AUDIO),
                RECORD_REQUEST_CODE)
    }
}
```

Next, implement the *onRequestPermissionsResult()* method so that it reads as follows:

```
override fun onRequestPermissionsResult(requestCode: Int,
              permissions: Array<String>, grantResults: IntArray) {
    super.onRequestPermissionsResult(requestCode, permissions, grantResults)

    when (requestCode) {
        RECORD_REQUEST_CODE -> {

            if (grantResults.isEmpty() || grantResults[0] !=
                                 PackageManager.PERMISSION_GRANTED) {

                Log.i(TAG, "Permission has been denied by user")
            } else {
                Log.i(TAG, "Permission has been granted by user")
            }
        }
    }
}
```

Compile and run the app on an emulator or device and note that a dialog seeking permission to record audio appears as shown in Figure 75-3:

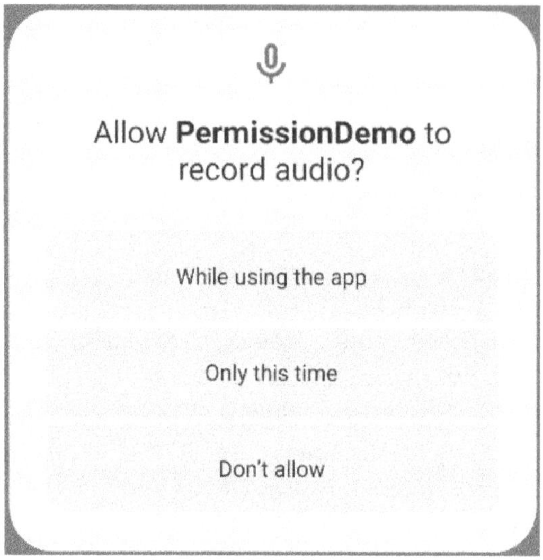

Figure 75-3

Tap the *While using the app* button and check that the "Permission has been granted by user" message appears in the Logcat panel.

Once the user has granted the requested permission, the *checkSelfPermission()* method call will return a PERMISSION_GRANTED result on future app invocations until the user uninstalls and re-installs the app or changes the permissions for the app in Settings.

75.5 Providing a Rationale for the Permission Request

As evident from Figure 75-3, the user can deny the requested permission. In this case, the app will continue to request permission each time the user launches it unless the user selects the "Never ask again" option before clicking the Deny button. Repeated denials by the user may indicate that the user doesn't understand why the app requires permission. The user might, therefore, be more likely to grant permission if the reason for the requirements is explained when the request is made. Unfortunately, it is not possible to change the content of the request dialog to include such an explanation.

An explanation is best included in a separate dialog which can be displayed before the request dialog is presented to the user. This raises the question of when to display this explanation dialog. The Android documentation recommends that an explanation dialog only be shown if the user has previously denied the permission and provides a method to identify when this is the case.

A call to the *shouldShowRequestPermissionRationale()* method of the ActivityCompat class will return a true result if the user has previously denied a request for the specified permission and a false result if the request has not previously been made. In the case of a true result, the app should display a dialog containing a rationale for needing permission, and once the dialog has been read and dismissed by the user, the permission request should be repeated.

To add this functionality to the example app, modify the *onCreate()* method so that it reads as follows:

```
.
.
import android.app.AlertDialog
```

```
.
.
private fun setupPermissions() {
    val permission = ContextCompat.checkSelfPermission(this,
            Manifest.permission.RECORD_AUDIO)

    if (permission != PackageManager.PERMISSION_GRANTED) {
        Log.i(TAG, "Permission to record denied")
        if (ActivityCompat.shouldShowRequestPermissionRationale(this,
                Manifest.permission.RECORD_AUDIO)) {
            val builder = AlertDialog.Builder(this)
            builder.setMessage("Permission to access the microphone is required
for this app to record audio.")
                    .setTitle("Permission required")

            builder.setPositiveButton("OK") { dialog, id ->
                makeRequest()
            }

            val dialog = builder.create()
            dialog.show()
        } else {
            makeRequest()
        }
    }
}
```

The method still checks whether or not the permission has been granted but now also identifies whether a rationale needs to be displayed. If the user has previously denied the request, a dialog is displayed containing an explanation and an OK button on which a listener is configured to call the *makeRequest()* method when the button is tapped. If the permission request has not previously been made, the code moves directly to seeking permission.

75.6 Testing the Permissions App

On the device or emulator session on which testing is being performed, launch the Settings app, select the *Apps* option, and scroll to and select the PermissionDemo app. On the app settings screen, tap the uninstall button to remove the app.

Rerun the app, and click on the *Don't allow* button when the permission request dialog appears. Stop and restart the app and verify that the rationale dialog appears. Tap the OK button, and tap the *While using the app* button when the permission request dialog appears.

Return to the Settings app, select the Apps option, and choose the PermissionDemo app again from the list. Once the settings for the app are listed, verify that the Permissions section lists the Microphone permission.

Return to the Settings app, select the Apps option, and choose the PermissionDemo app again from the list. Once the settings for the app are listed, verify that the Permissions section lists the *Microphone* permission:

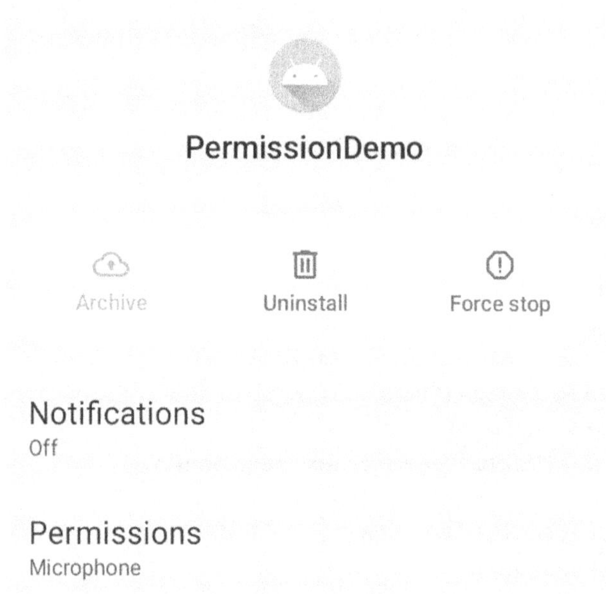

Figure 75-4

75.7 Summary

Before the introduction of Android 6.0, the only step necessary for an app to request permission to access certain functionality was to add an appropriate line to the application's manifest file. The user would then be prompted to approve the permission when installing the app. This is still the case for most permissions, except for a set of permissions considered dangerous. Permissions that are considered dangerous usually have the potential to allow an app to violate the user's privacy, such as allowing access to the microphone, contacts list, or external storage.

As outlined in this chapter, apps based on Android 6 or later must now request dangerous permission approval from the user when the app launches and include the permission request in the manifest file.

Chapter 76

76. An Android Notifications Tutorial

Notifications provide a way for an app to convey a message to the user when the app is either not running or is currently in the background. For example, a messaging app might notify the user that a new message has arrived from a contact. Notifications can be categorized as being either local or remote. A local notification is triggered by the app itself on the device on which it is running. On the other hand, remote notifications are initiated by a remote server and delivered to the device for presentation to the user.

Notifications appear in the notification drawer that is pulled down from the screen's status bar, and each notification can include actions such as a button to open the app that sent the notification. Android also supports Direct Reply notifications, a feature that allows the user to type in and submit a response to a notification from within the notification panel.

This chapter outlines the implementation of local notifications within an Android app. The next chapter (*"An Android Direct Reply Notification Tutorial"*) will cover the implementation of direct reply notifications.

76.1 An Overview of Notifications

When a notification is initiated on an Android device, it appears as an icon in the status bar. Figure 76-1, for example, shows a status bar with several notification icons:

Figure 76-1

To view the notifications, the user makes a downward swiping motion starting at the status bar to pull down the notification drawer, as shown in Figure 76-2:

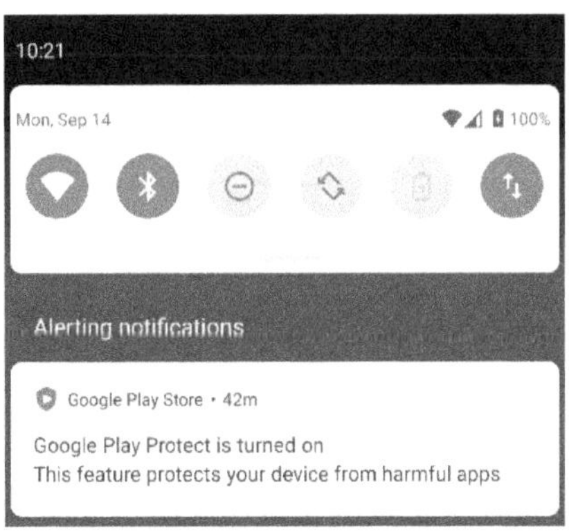

Figure 76-2

In devices running Android 8 or newer, performing a long press on an app launcher icon will display any pending notifications associated with that app, as shown in Figure 76-3:

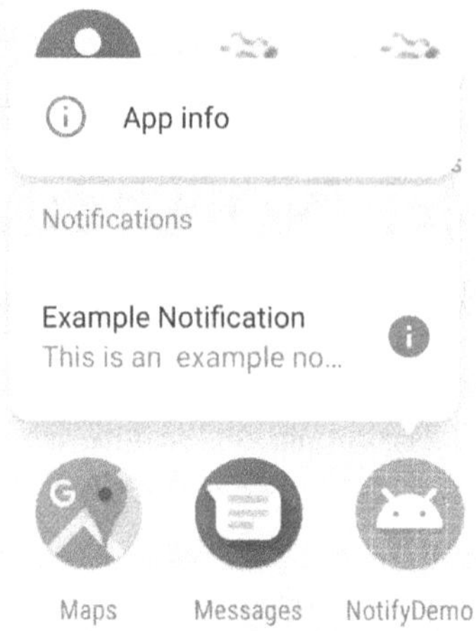

Figure 76-3

Android 8 and later also supports notification dots that appear on app launcher icons when a notification is waiting to be seen by the user.

A typical notification will display a message and, when tapped, launch the app responsible for issuing the notification. Notifications may also contain action buttons that perform a task specific to the corresponding app when tapped. Figure 76-4, for example, shows a notification containing two action buttons allowing the user to delete or save an incoming message:

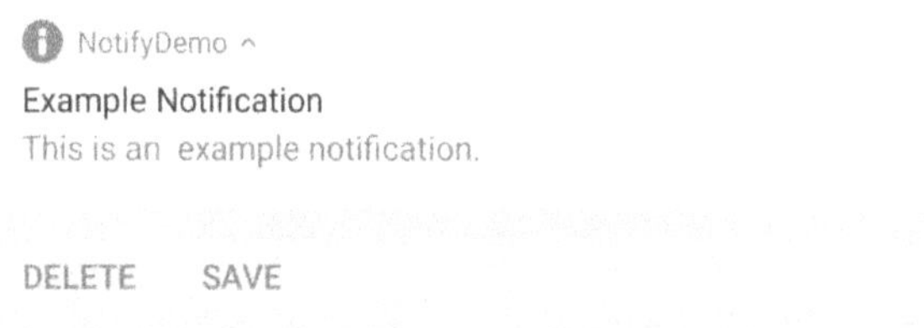

Figure 76-4

It is also possible for the user to enter an in-line text reply into the notification and send it to the app, as is the case in Figure 76-5 below. This allows the user to respond to a notification without launching the corresponding app into the foreground:

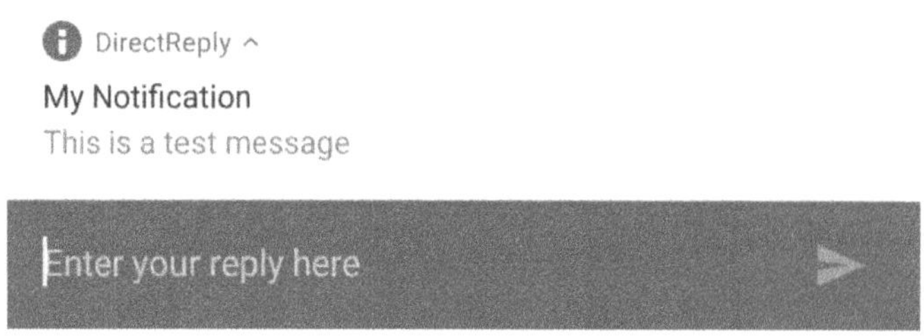

Figure 76-5

The remainder of this chapter will work through creating and issuing a simple notification containing actions. The topic of direct reply support will be covered in the next chapter entitled *"An Android Direct Reply Notification Tutorial"*.

76.2 Creating the NotifyDemo Project

Select the *New Project* option from the welcome screen and, within the resulting new project dialog, choose the Empty Views Activity template before clicking on the Next button.

Enter *NotifyDemo* into the Name field and specify *com.ebookfrenzy.notifydemo* as the package name. Before clicking on the Finish button, change the Minimum API level setting to API 33: Android 13 (Tiramisu) and the Language menu to Kotlin.

76.3 Designing the User Interface

The main activity will contain a single button, the purpose of which is to create and issue an intent. Locate and load the *activity_main.xml* file into the Layout Editor tool and delete the default TextView widget.

With Autoconnect enabled, drag and drop a Button object from the panel onto the center of the layout canvas, as illustrated in Figure 76-6.

With the Button widget selected in the layout, use the Attributes panel to configure the onClick property to call a method named *sendNotification*.

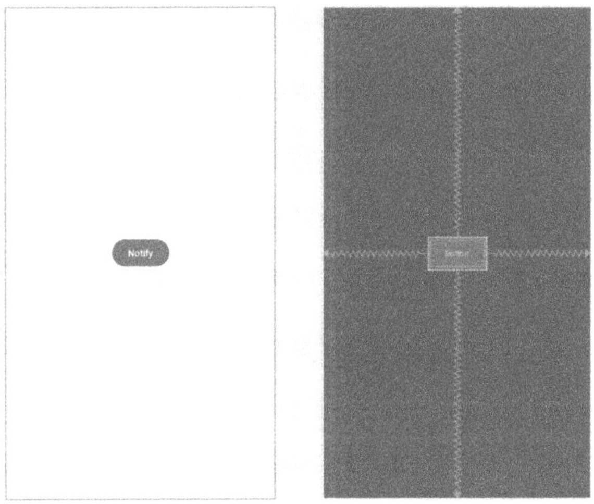

Figure 76-6

Select the Button widget, change the text property in the Attributes tool window to "Notify" and extract the property value to a string resource.

76.4 Creating the Second Activity

In this example, the app will contain a second activity which will be launched by the user from within the notification. Add this new activity to the project by right-clicking on the *com.ebookfrenzy.notifydemo* package name located in *app -> kotlin+java* and selecting the *New -> Activity -> Empty Views Activity* menu option to display the *New Android Activity* dialog.

Enter *ResultActivity* into the Activity Name field and name the layout file *activity_result*. Since this activity will not be started when the application is launched (it will instead be launched via an intent from within the notification), it is important to make sure that the *Launcher Activity* option is disabled before clicking on the Finish button.

Open the layout for the second activity (*app -> res -> layout -> activity_result.xml*) and drag and drop a TextView widget so that it is positioned in the center of the layout. Edit the text of the TextView so that it reads "Result

Activity" and extract the property value to a string resource.

76.5 Creating a Notification Channel

Before an app can send a notification, it must create a notification channel. A notification channel consists of an ID that uniquely identifies the channel within the app, a channel name, and a channel description (only the latter two will be seen by the user). Channels are created by configuring a NotificationChannel instance and then passing that object through to the *createNotificationChannel()* method of the NotificationManager class. For this example, the app will contain a single notification channel named "NotifyDemo News". Edit the *MainActivity.kt* file and implement code to create the channel when the app starts:

```
.
.
import android.app.NotificationChannel
import android.app.NotificationManager
import android.content.Context
import android.graphics.Color

class MainActivity : AppCompatActivity() {

    private var notificationManager: NotificationManager? = null

    override fun onCreate(savedInstanceState: Bundle?) {
.
.
        notificationManager =
                  getSystemService(
                   Context.NOTIFICATION_SERVICE) as NotificationManager

        createNotificationChannel(
                "com.ebookfrenzy.notifydemo.news",
                "NotifyDemo News",
                "Example News Channel")
    }

    private fun createNotificationChannel(id: String, name: String,
                                             description: String) {

        val importance = NotificationManager.IMPORTANCE_LOW
        val channel = NotificationChannel(id, name, importance)

        channel.description = description
        channel.enableLights(true)
        channel.lightColor = Color.RED
        channel.enableVibration(true)
        channel.vibrationPattern =
            longArrayOf(100, 200, 300, 400, 500, 400, 300, 200, 400)
        notificationManager?.createNotificationChannel(channel)
```

```
    }
}
```

The code declares and initializes a NotificationManager instance and then creates the new channel with a low importance level (other options are high, max, min, and none) configured with the name and description properties. A range of optional settings are also added to the channel to customize how the user is alerted to the arrival of a notification. These settings apply to all notifications sent to this channel. Finally, the channel is created by passing the notification channel object through to the *createNotificationChannel()* method of the notification manager instance.

76.6 Requesting Notification Permission

Before testing the application, the appropriate permissions must be requested within the manifest file for the application. Specifically, the application will require permission to post notifications to the user. Within the Project tool window, locate and double-click on the *AndroidManifest.xml* file to load it into the editor and modify the XML to add the permission:

```
<?xml version="1.0" encoding="utf-8"?>
<manifest xmlns:android="http://schemas.android.com/apk/res/android"
    package="com.ebookfrenzy.audioapp" >

    <uses-permission android:name="android.permission.POST_NOTIFICATIONS" />
.
.
```

The above step will be adequate to ensure that the user enables notification permission when the app is installed on devices running versions of Android predating Android 6.0. Notification access is categorized in Android as a dangerous permission because it gives the app the potential to compromise the user's privacy. For the example app to function on Android 6 or later devices, code must be added to request permission at app runtime.

Edit the *MainActivity.kt* file and begin by adding some additional import directives and a constant to act as request identification codes for the permission being requested:

```
.
.
import android.Manifest
import android.content.pm.PackageManager
import android.widget.Toast
import androidx.core.app.ActivityCompat
import androidx.core.content.ContextCompat

class MainActivity : AppCompatActivity() {
.
.
    private val NOTIFICATION_REQUEST_CODE = 101
.
.
```

Next, a method needs to be added to the class, the purpose of which is to take as arguments the permission to be requested and the corresponding request identification code. Remaining with the *MainActivity.kt* class file, implement this method as follows:

```
private fun requestPermission(permissionType: String, requestCode: Int) {
```

```
    val permission = ContextCompat.checkSelfPermission(this,
            permissionType)

    if (permission != PackageManager.PERMISSION_GRANTED) {
        ActivityCompat.requestPermissions(this,
                arrayOf(permissionType), requestCode
        )
    }
}
```

Using the steps outlined in the *"Making Runtime Permission Requests in Android"* chapter of this book, the above method verifies that the specified permission has not already been granted before making the request, passing through the identification code as an argument.

When the request has been handled, the *onRequestPermissionsResult()* method will be called on the activity, passing through the identification code and the request results. The next step, therefore, is to implement this method within the *MainActivity.kt* file as follows:

```
override fun onRequestPermissionsResult(requestCode: Int,
                permissions: Array<String>, grantResults: IntArray) {
    super.onRequestPermissionsResult(requestCode, permissions, grantResults)

    when (requestCode) {
        NOTIFICATION_REQUEST_CODE -> {
            if (grantResults.isEmpty() || grantResults[0]
                != PackageManager.PERMISSION_GRANTED
            ) {

                Toast.makeText(
                    this,
                    "Notification permission required",
                    Toast.LENGTH_LONG
                ).show()
            }
        }
    }
}
```

The above code checks the request identifier code to identify which permission request has returned before checking whether or not the corresponding permission was granted. If permission is denied, a message is displayed to the user indicating that the app will not function and the record button is disabled.

Before testing the app, all that remains is to call the newly added requestPermission() method when the app launches. Remaining in the *MainActivity.kt* file, modify the *onCreate()* method as follows:

```
override fun onCreate(savedInstanceState: Bundle?) {
    super.onCreate(savedInstanceState)
.
.
    requestPermission(Manifest.permission.POST_NOTIFICATIONS,
```

```
        NOTIFICATION_REQUEST_CODE)

    notificationManager =
        getSystemService(
            Context.NOTIFICATION_SERVICE) as NotificationManager
.
.
```

With the code changes complete, compile and run the app on a device or emulator running Android 13 or later. When the dialog shown in Figure 76-7 appears, click on the Allow button to enable notifications:

Figure 76-7

After launching the app, place it in the background and open the Settings app. Within the Settings app, select the *Apps* option, select the NotifyDemo project, and, on the subsequent screen, tap the *Notifications* entry. The notification screen should list the NotifyDemo News category as being active for the user:

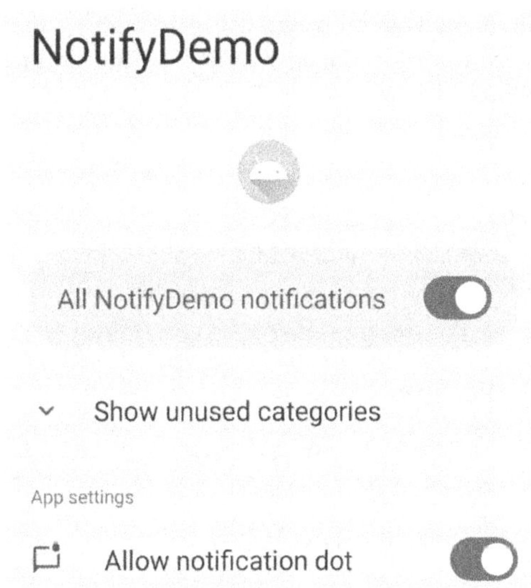

Figure 76-8

Before proceeding, ensure that notification dots are enabled for the app.

Although not a requirement for this example, it is worth noting that a channel can be deleted from within the app via a call to the *deleteNotificationChannel()* method of the notification manager, passing through the ID of the channel to be deleted:

```
val channelID = "com.ebookfrenzy.notifydemo.news"
notificationManager?.deleteNotificationChannel(channelID)
```

76.7 Creating and Issuing a Notification

Notifications are created using the Notification.Builder class and must contain an icon, title, and content. Open the *MainActivity.kt* file and implement the *sendNotification()* method as follows to build a basic notification:

```
.
.
import android.app.Notification
import android.view.View
.
.
fun sendNotification(view: View) {

    val channelID = "com.ebookfrenzy.notifydemo.news"

    val notification = Notification.Builder(this@MainActivity,
            channelID)
            .setContentTitle("Example Notification")
            .setContentText("This is an example notification.")
            .setSmallIcon(android.R.drawable.ic_dialog_info)
            .setChannelId(channelID)
            .build()
}
```

Once a notification has been built, it needs to be issued using the *notify()* method of the NotificationManager instance. The code to access the NotificationManager and issue the notification needs to be added to the *sendNotification()* method as follows:

```
fun sendNotification(view: View) {

    val notificationID = 101
    val channelID = "com.ebookfrenzy.notifydemo.news"

    val notification = Notification.Builder(this@MainActivity,
            channelID)
            .setContentTitle("Example Notification")
            .setContentText("This is an example notification.")
            .setSmallIcon(android.R.drawable.ic_dialog_info)
            .setChannelId(channelID)
            .build()

    notificationManager?.notify(notificationID, notification)
}
```

Note that when the notification is issued, it is assigned a notification ID. This can be any integer and may be used later when updating the notification.

Compile and run the app and tap the button on the main activity. When the notification icon appears in the status bar, touch and drag down from the status bar to view the full notification:

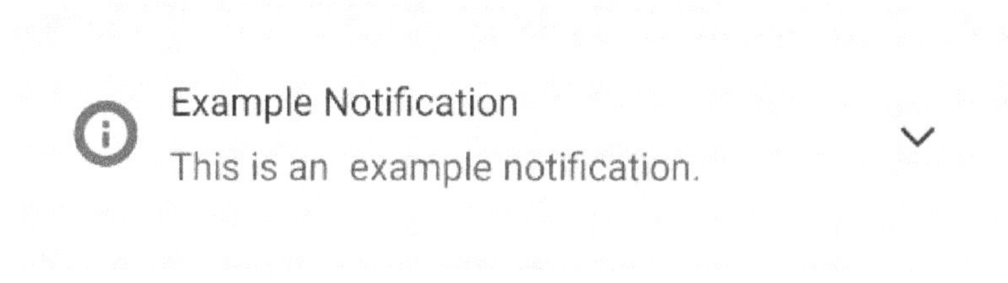

Figure 76-9

Click and hold on the notification to view additional information:

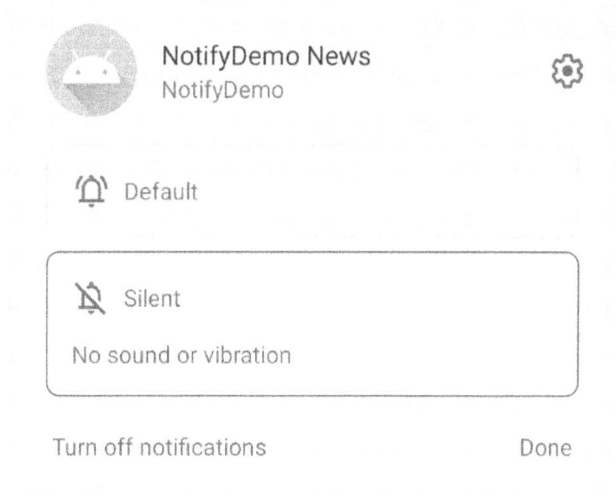

Figure 76-10

Next, place the app in the background, navigate to the home screen displaying the launcher icons for all of the apps, and note that a notification dot has appeared on the NotifyDemo launcher icon as indicated by the arrow in Figure 76-11:

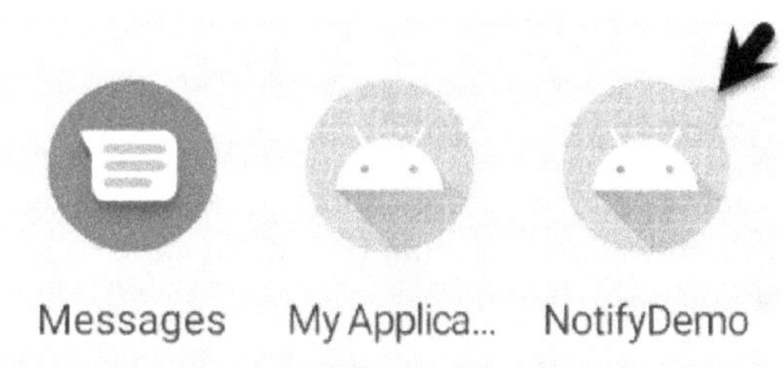

Figure 76-11

If the dot is not present, check the notification options for NotifyDemo in the Settings app to confirm that notification dots are enabled, as outlined earlier in the chapter. If the dot still does not appear, touch and hold over a blank area of the device home screen, select the *Home Settings* option from the resulting menu, and enable the *Notification dots* option.

Performing a long press over the launcher icon will display a popup containing the notification:

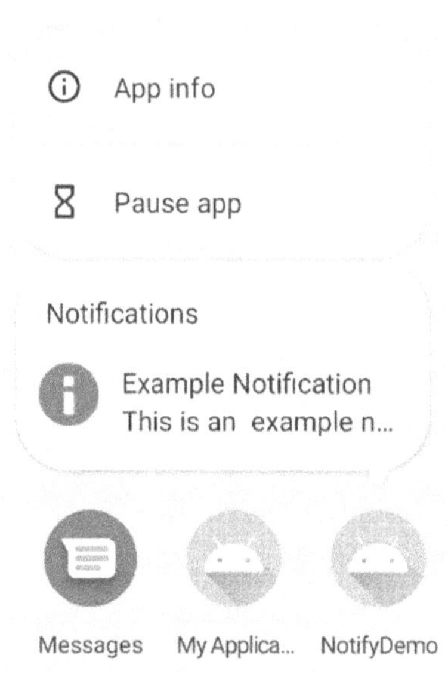

Figure 76-12

If more than one notification is pending for an app, the long press menu popup will contain a count of notifications (highlighted in the above figure). This number may be configured from within the app by making a call to the *setNumber()* method when building the notification:

```
val notification = Notification.Builder(this@MainActivity,
        channelID)
        .setContentTitle("Example Notification")
        .setContentText("This is an  example notification.")
        .setSmallIcon(android.R.drawable.ic_dialog_info)
        .setChannelId(channelID)
        .setNumber(10)
        .build()
```

As currently implemented, tapping on the notification has no effect regardless of where it is accessed. The next step is configuring the notification to launch an activity when tapped.

76.8 Launching an Activity from a Notification

A notification should allow the user to perform some action, such as launching the corresponding app or taking another action in response to the notification. A common requirement is to launch an activity belonging to the app when the user taps the notification.

This approach requires an activity to be launched and an Intent configured to launch that activity. Assuming an app that contains an activity named ResultActivity, the intent would be created as follows:

```
val resultIntent = Intent(this, ResultActivity::class.java)
```

This intent needs to then be wrapped in a PendingIntent instance. PendingIntent objects are designed to allow an intent to be passed to other applications, essentially granting those applications permission to perform the intent at some point in the future. In this case, the PendingIntent object is being used to provide the Notification system with a way to launch the ResultActivity activity when the user taps the notification panel:

```
val pendingIntent = PendingIntent.getActivity(
                this,
```

```
                0,
                resultIntent,
                PendingIntent.FLAG_IMMUTABLE)
```

All that remains is to assign the PendingIntent object during the notification build process using the *setContentIntent()* method.

Bringing these changes together results in a modified *sendNotification()* method, which reads as follows:

```
.
.
import android.app.PendingIntent
import android.content.Intent
import android.graphics.drawable.Icon

class MainActivity : AppCompatActivity() {

    fun sendNotification(view: View) {

        val notificationID = 101
        val channelID = "com.ebookfrenzy.notifydemo.news"
        val resultIntent = Intent(this, ResultActivity::class.java)

        val pendingIntent = PendingIntent.getActivity(
                this,
                0,
                resultIntent,
                PendingIntent.FLAG_IMMUTABLE
        )

        val notification = Notification.Builder(this@MainActivity,
                channelID)
                .setContentTitle("Example Notification")
                .setContentText("This is an  example notification.")
                .setSmallIcon(android.R.drawable.ic_dialog_info)
                .setChannelId(channelID)
                .setContentIntent(pendingIntent)
                .build()

        notificationManager?.notify(notificationID, notification)
    }
.
.
```

Compile and rerun the app, tap the button, and display the notification drawer. This time, however, tapping the notification will cause the ResultActivity to launch.

76.9 Adding Actions to a Notification

Another way to add interactivity to a notification is to create actions. These appear as buttons beneath the notification message and are programmed to trigger specific intents when tapped by the user. The following code, if added to the *sendNotification()* method, will add an action button labeled "Open" which launches the referenced pending intent when selected:

```
val icon: Icon = Icon.createWithResource(this, android.R.drawable.ic_dialog_info)

val action: Notification.Action =
        Notification.Action.Builder(icon, "Open", pendingIntent).build()

val notification = Notification.Builder(this@MainActivity,
        channelID)
        .setContentTitle("Example Notification")
        .setContentText("This is an  example notification.")
        .setSmallIcon(android.R.drawable.ic_dialog_info)
        .setChannelId(channelID)
        .setContentIntent(pendingIntent)
        .setActions(action)
        .build()

notificationManager?.notify(notificationID, notification)
```

Add the above code to the method and run the app. Issue the notification and note the appearance of the Open action within the notification (depending on the Android version, it may be necessary to pull down on the notification panel to reveal the Open action):

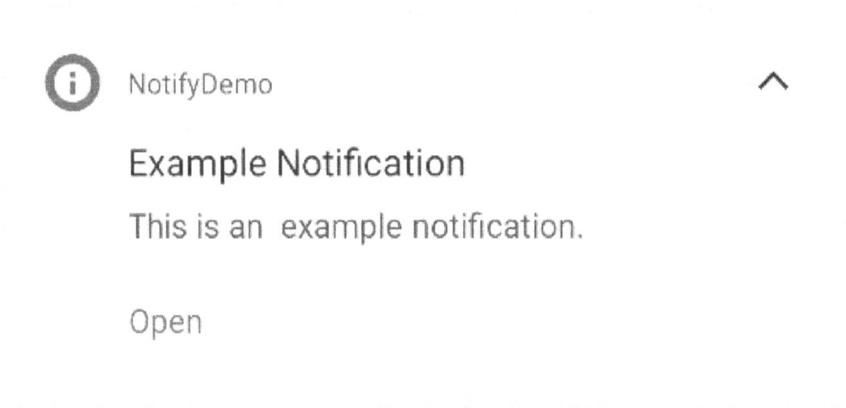

Figure 76-13

Tapping the action will trigger the pending intent and launch the ResultActivity.

76.10 Bundled Notifications

If an app tends to issue notifications regularly, there is a danger that those notifications will rapidly clutter both the status bar and the notification drawer providing a less-than-optimal experience for the user. This can be particularly true of news or messaging apps that send a notification every time a breaking news story or a new message arrives from a contact. Consider, for example, the notifications in Figure 76-14:

Figure 76-14

Now imagine if ten or even twenty new messages had arrived. To avoid this problem, Android allows notifications to be bundled into groups.

To bundle notifications, each notification must be designated as belonging to the same group via the *setGroup()* method, and an additional notification must be issued and configured as the *summary notification*. The following code, for example, creates and issues the three notifications shown in Figure 76-14 above but bundles them into the same group. The code also issues a notification to act as the summary:

```
val GROUP_KEY_NOTIFY = "group_key_notify"

var builderSummary: Notification.Builder = Notification.Builder(this, channelID)
        .setSmallIcon(android.R.drawable.ic_dialog_info)
        .setContentTitle("A Bundle Example")
        .setContentText("You have 3 new messages")
        .setGroup(GROUP_KEY_NOTIFY)
        .setGroupSummary(true)

var builder1: Notification.Builder = Notification.Builder(this, channelID)
        .setSmallIcon(android.R.drawable.ic_dialog_info)
        .setContentTitle("New Message")
        .setContentText("You have a new message from Kassidy")
        .setGroup(GROUP_KEY_NOTIFY)

var builder2: Notification.Builder = Notification.Builder(this, channelID)
        .setSmallIcon(android.R.drawable.ic_dialog_info)
        .setContentTitle("New Message")
        .setContentText("You have a new message from Caitlyn")
        .setGroup(GROUP_KEY_NOTIFY)

var builder3: Notification.Builder = Notification.Builder(this, channelID)
        .setSmallIcon(android.R.drawable.ic_dialog_info)
        .setContentTitle("New Message")
        .setContentText("You have a new message from Jason")
        .setGroup(GROUP_KEY_NOTIFY)
```

```
var notificationId0 = 100
var notificationId1 = 101
var notificationId2 = 102
var notificationId3 = 103

notificationManager?.notify(notificationId1, builder1.build())
notificationManager?.notify(notificationId2, builder2.build())
notificationManager?.notify(notificationId3, builder3.build())
notificationManager?.notify(notificationId0, builderSummary.build())
```

When the code is executed, a single notification icon will appear in the status bar even though the app has issued four notifications. Within the notification drawer, a single summary notification is displayed listing the information in each of the bundled notifications:

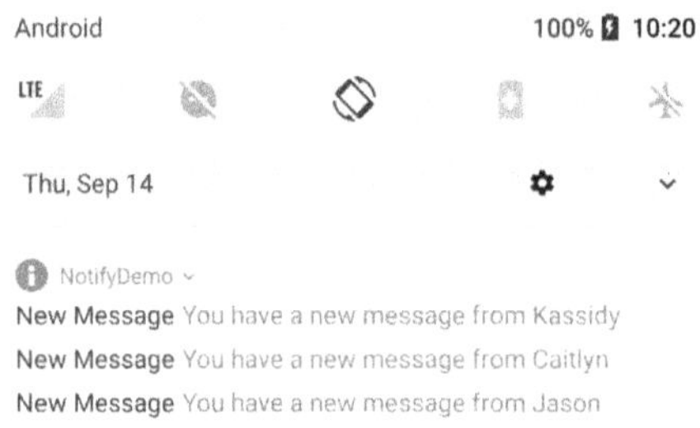

Figure 76-15

Pulling further downward on the notification entry expands the panel to show the details of each of the bundled notifications:

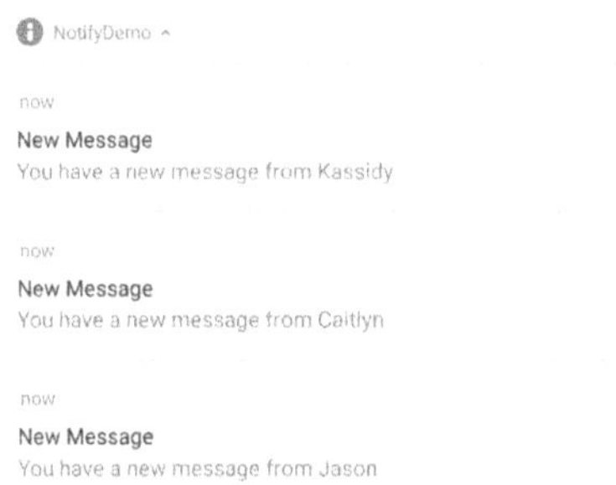

Figure 76-16

76.11 Summary

Notifications provide a way for an app to deliver a message to the user when the app is not running or is currently in the background. Notifications appear in the status bar and notification drawer. Local notifications are triggered on the device by the running app, while remote notifications are initiated by a remote server and delivered to the device. Local notifications are created using the NotificationCompat.Builder class and issued using the NotificationManager service.

As demonstrated in this chapter, notifications can be configured to provide users with options (such as launching an activity or saving a message) by using actions, intents, and the PendingIntent class. Notification bundling provides a mechanism for grouping notifications to provide an improved experience for apps that issue more notifications.

Chapter 77

77. An Android Direct Reply Notification Tutorial

Direct reply is an Android feature that allows the user to enter text into a notification and send it to the app associated with that notification. This allows the user to reply to a message in the notification without launching an activity within the app. This chapter will build on the knowledge gained in the previous chapter to create an example app that uses this notification feature.

77.1 Creating the DirectReply Project

Select the *New Project* option from the welcome screen and, within the resulting new project dialog, choose the Empty Views Activity template before clicking on the Next button.

Enter *DirectReply* into the Name field and specify *com.ebookfrenzy.directreply* as the package name. Before clicking on the Finish button, change the Minimum API level setting to API 33: Android 13 and the Language menu to Kotlin. Modify the project to support view binding using the Gemini Agent or the steps outlined in section *18.8 Migrating a Project to View Binding.*

77.2 Designing the User Interface

Load the *activity_main.xml* layout file into the layout tool. With Autoconnect enabled, add a Button object beneath the existing "Hello World!" label, as shown in Figure 77-1. With the Button widget selected in the layout, use the Attributes tool window to set the onClick property to call a method named *sendNotification*. Use the Infer Constraints button to add any missing constraints to the layout if necessary. Before continuing, select the "Hello World!" TextView, change the id attribute to *textView*, and modify the text on the button to read "Notify":

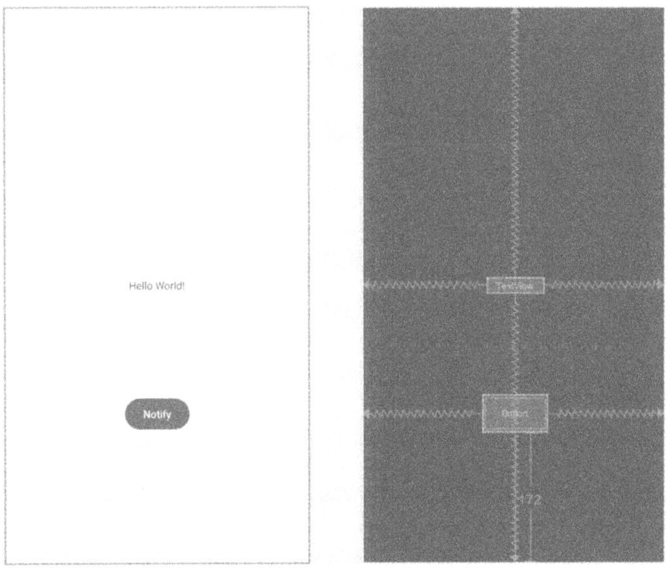

Figure 77-1

77.3 Requesting Notification Permission

Within the Project tool window, locate and double-click on the *AndroidManifest.xml* file to load it into the editor and modify the XML to add the permission element:

```
<?xml version="1.0" encoding="utf-8"?>
<manifest xmlns:android="http://schemas.android.com/apk/res/android"
    package="com.ebookfrenzy.audioapp" >

    <uses-permission android:name="android.permission.POST_NOTIFICATIONS" />
.
.
```

Edit the *MainActivity.kt* file and begin by adding some additional import directives and a constant to act as request identification codes for the permission being requested:

```
.
.
import android.Manifest
import android.content.pm.PackageManager
import android.widget.Toast
import androidx.core.app.ActivityCompat
import androidx.core.content.ContextCompat
.
.
class MainActivity : AppCompatActivity() {
.
.
    private val NOTIFICATION_REQUEST_CODE = 101
.
.
```

Next, a method needs to be added to the class, the purpose of which is to take as arguments the permission to be requested and the corresponding request identification code. Remaining with the *MainActivity.kt* class file, implement this method as follows:

```
private fun requestPermission(permissionType: String, requestCode: Int) {
    val permission = ContextCompat.checkSelfPermission(this,
            permissionType)

    if (permission != PackageManager.PERMISSION_GRANTED) {
        ActivityCompat.requestPermissions(this,
                arrayOf(permissionType), requestCode
        )
    }
}
```

When the request has been handled, the *onRequestPermissionsResult()* method will be called on the activity, passing through the identification code and the request results. The next step, therefore, is to implement this method within the *MainActivity.kt* file as follows:

```
override fun onRequestPermissionsResult(requestCode: Int,
```

```
                permissions: Array<String>, grantResults: IntArray) {
    super.onRequestPermissionsResult(requestCode, permissions, grantResults)

    when (requestCode) {
        NOTIFICATION_REQUEST_CODE -> {
            if (grantResults.isEmpty() || grantResults[0]
                != PackageManager.PERMISSION_GRANTED
            ) {

                Toast.makeText(
                    this,
                    "Notification permission required",
                    Toast.LENGTH_LONG
                ).show()
            }
        }
    }
}
```

Before testing the app, all that remains is to call the newly added *requestPermission()* method when the app launches. Remaining in the *MainActivity.kt* file, modify the *onCreate()* method as follows:

```
override fun onCreate(savedInstanceState: Bundle?) {
    super.onCreate(savedInstanceState)
.
.
    requestPermission(Manifest.permission.POST_NOTIFICATIONS,
        NOTIFICATION_REQUEST_CODE)
}
```

77.4 Creating the Notification Channel

As with the example in the previous chapter, a channel must be created before a notification can be sent. Edit the *MainActivity.kt* file and add code to create a new channel as follows:

```
.
.
import android.app.NotificationChannel
import android.app.NotificationManager
import android.content.Context
import android.graphics.Color

class MainActivity : AppCompatActivity() {

    private lateinit var binding: ActivityMainBinding
    private val NOTIFICATION_REQUEST_CODE = 101
    private var notificationManager: NotificationManager? = null
    private val channelID = "com.ebookfrenzy.directreply.news"
```

```
    override fun onCreate(savedInstanceState: Bundle?) {
        super.onCreate(savedInstanceState)
        binding = ActivityMainBinding.inflate(layoutInflater)
        setContentView(binding.root)
        requestPermission(Manifest.permission.POST_NOTIFICATIONS,
            NOTIFICATION_REQUEST_CODE)

        notificationManager =
                  getSystemService(
                   Context.NOTIFICATION_SERVICE) as NotificationManager

        createNotificationChannel(channelID,
                "DirectReply News", "Example News Channel")
    }

    private fun createNotificationChannel(id: String,
                                           name: String, description: String) {

        val importance = NotificationManager.IMPORTANCE_HIGH
        val channel = NotificationChannel(id, name, importance)

        channel.description = description
        channel.enableLights(true)
        channel.lightColor = Color.RED
        channel.enableVibration(true)
        channel.vibrationPattern =
                  longArrayOf(100, 200, 300, 400, 500, 400, 300, 200, 400)

        notificationManager?.createNotificationChannel(channel)
    }
.
.
}
```

77.5 Building the RemoteInput Object

The key element that makes direct reply in-line text possible within a notification is the RemoteInput class. The previous chapters introduced the PendingIntent class and explained how it allows one application to create an intent and then grant other applications or services the ability to launch that intent from outside the original app. In that chapter, entitled *"An Android Notifications Tutorial"*, a pending intent was created that allowed an activity in the original app to be launched from within a notification. The RemoteInput class allows a request for user input to be included in the PendingIntent object along with the intent. When the intent within the PendingIntent object is triggered, for example, launching an activity, that activity is also passed any input provided by the user.

The first step in implementing a direct reply within a notification is to create the RemoteInput object. This is achieved using the *RemoteInput.Builder()* method. To build a RemoteInput object, a key string is required that will be used to extract the input from the resulting intent. The object also needs a label string that will appear within the text input field of the notification. Edit the *MainActivity.kt* file and add the *sendNotification()* method.

Note also the addition of some import directives and variables that will be used later as the chapter progresses:

```
package com.ebookfrenzy.directreply
.
.
import android.content.Intent
import android.app.RemoteInput
import android.view.View
import android.app.PendingIntent

class MainActivity : AppCompatActivity() {

    private val notificationId = 101
    private val KEY_TEXT_REPLY = "key_text_reply"
.
.
    fun sendNotification(view: View) {

        val replyLabel = "Enter your reply here"
        val remoteInput = RemoteInput.Builder(KEY_TEXT_REPLY)
                .setLabel(replyLabel)
                .build()
    }
.
.
}
```

Now that the RemoteInput object has been created and initialized with a key and a label string, it will need to be placed inside a notification action object. Before that step can be performed, however, the PendingIntent instance needs to be created.

77.6 Creating the PendingIntent

The steps to creating the PendingIntent are the same as those outlined in the *"An Android Notifications Tutorial"* chapter, except that the intent will be configured to launch MainActivity. Remaining within the *MainActivity.kt* file, add the code to create the PendingIntent as follows:

```
fun sendNotification(view: View) {
.
.
    val resultIntent = Intent(this, MainActivity::class.java)

    val resultPendingIntent = PendingIntent.getActivity(
            this,
            0,
            resultIntent,
            PendingIntent.FLAG_MUTABLE
    )
}
```

77.7 Creating the Reply Action

The in-line reply will be accessible within the notification via an action button. This action needs to be created and configured with an icon, a label to appear on the button, the PendingIntent object, and the RemoteInput object. Modify the *sendNotification()* method to add the code to create this action:

```
.
.
import android.graphics.drawable.Icon
import android.app.Notification
.
.
fun sendNotification(view: View) {
.
.
    val icon = Icon.createWithResource(this@MainActivity,
            android.R.drawable.ic_dialog_info)

    val replyAction = Notification.Action.Builder(
            icon,
            "Reply", resultPendingIntent)
            .addRemoteInput(remoteInput)
            .build()
}
.
.
```

At this stage in the tutorial, we have the RemoteInput, PendingIntent, and Notification Action objects built and ready to be used. The next stage is to build the notification and issue it:

```
.
.
import com.google.android.material.R.color
.
.
fun sendNotification(view: View) {
.
.
    val newMessageNotification = Notification.Builder(this, channelID)
            .setColor(ContextCompat.getColor(this,
                            color.design_default_color_primary))
            .setSmallIcon(
                    android.R.drawable.ic_dialog_info)
            .setContentTitle("My Notification")
            .setContentText("This is a test message")
            .addAction(replyAction).build()

    val notificationManager = getSystemService(
```

```
        Context.NOTIFICATION_SERVICE) as NotificationManager

    notificationManager.notify(notificationId,
            newMessageNotification)
}
```

With the changes made, compile and run the app, allow notifications, and test that tapping the button issues the notification successfully. When viewing the notification drawer, the notification should appear as shown in Figure 77-2:

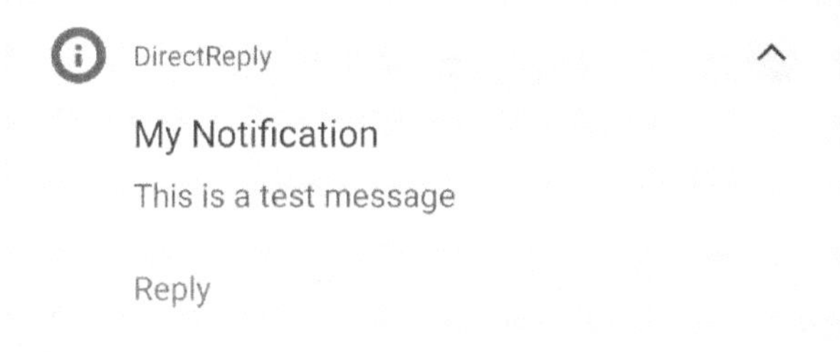

Figure 77-2

Tap the Reply action button so that the text input field appears, displaying the reply label embedded into the RemoteInput object when it was created.

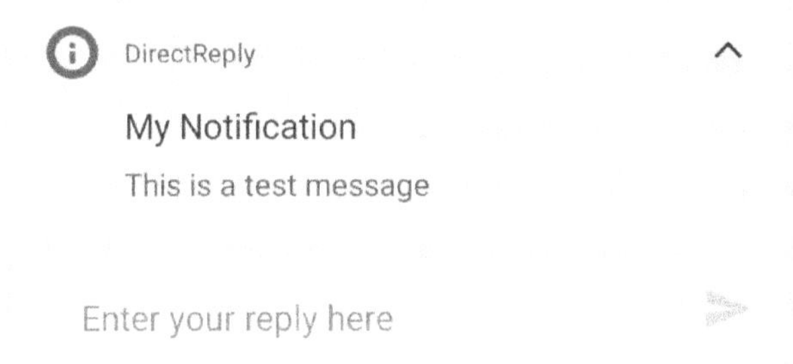

Figure 77-3

Enter some text and tap the send arrow button at the end of the input field.

77.8 Receiving Direct Reply Input

Now that the notification is successfully seeking input from the user, the app needs to do something with that input. This tutorial's objective is to have the text entered by the user into the notification appear on the TextView widget in the activity user interface.

When the user enters text and taps the send button, the MainActivity is launched via the intent in the PendingIntent object. Embedded in this intent is the text entered by the user via the notification. Within the *onCreate()* method of the activity, a call to the *getIntent()* method will return a copy of the intent that launched the activity. Passing this through to the *RemoteInput.getResultsFromIntent()* method will, in turn, return a Bundle object containing the reply text, which can be extracted and assigned to the TextView widget. This results in a modified *onCreate()* method within the *MainActivity.kt* file, which reads as follows:

```
.
.
```

```
override fun onCreate(savedInstanceState: Bundle?) {
.
.
    handleIntent()
}

private fun handleIntent() {

    val intent = this.intent

    val remoteInput = RemoteInput.getResultsFromIntent(intent)

    if (remoteInput != null) {

        val inputString = remoteInput.getCharSequence(
                KEY_TEXT_REPLY).toString()

        binding.textView.text = inputString
    }
}
.
```

. After making these code changes build and run the app once again. Click the button to issue the notification and enter and send some text from within the notification panel. Note that the TextView widget in the MainActivity is updated to display the in-line text that was entered.

77.9 Updating the Notification

After sending the reply within the notification, you may have noticed that the progress indicator continues to spin within the notification panel, as highlighted in Figure 77-4:

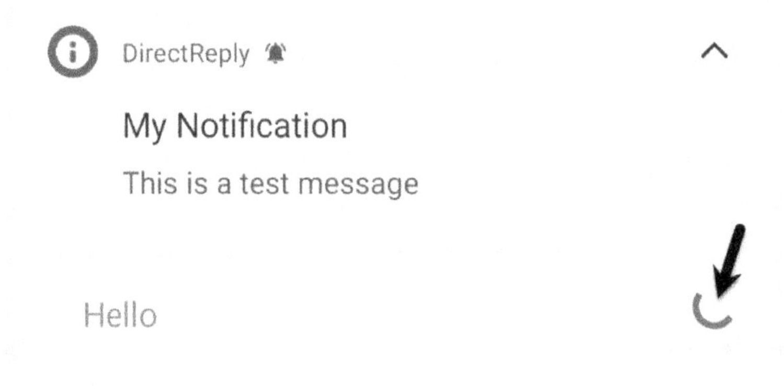

Figure 77-4

The notification shows this indicator because it is waiting for a response from the activity confirming receipt of the sent text. The recommended approach to performing this task is to update the notification with a new message indicating that the reply has been received and handled. Since the original notification was assigned an ID when it was issued, it can be used again to perform an update. Add the following code to the *handleIntent()* method to perform this task:

```
private fun handleIntent() {
.
.
    if (remoteInput != null) {

        val inputString = remoteInput.getCharSequence(
                KEY_TEXT_REPLY).toString()

        binding.textView.text = inputString

        val repliedNotification = Notification.Builder(this, channelID)
                .setSmallIcon(
                        android.R.drawable.ic_dialog_info)
                .setContentText("Reply received")
                .build()

        notificationManager?.notify(notificationId,
                repliedNotification)
    }
}
```

Test the app one last time and verify that the progress indicator goes away after the in-line reply text has been sent and that a new panel appears, indicating that the reply has been received:

Figure 77-5

77.10 Summary

The direct reply notification feature allows text to be entered by the user within a notification and passed via an intent to an activity of the corresponding application. Direct reply is made possible by the RemoteInput class, an instance of which can be embedded within an action and bundled with the notification. When working with direct reply notifications, it is important to let the NotificationManager service know that the reply has been received and processed. The best way to achieve this is to update the notification message using the notification ID provided when the notification was first issued.

78. An Android Biometric Authentication Tutorial

Touch sensors are now built into many Android devices to identify the user and provide access to the device and application functionality, such as in-app payment options using fingerprint recognition. Fingerprint recognition is just one of several authentication methods, including passwords, PINs, and, more recently, facial recognition.

Although only a few Android devices currently on the market provide facial recognition, this will likely become more common in the future. In recognition of this, Google has begun to transition away from a fingerprint-centric approach to adding authentication to apps to a less specific approach called *biometric authentication*.

This chapter provides an overview of biometric authentication and a detailed, step-by-step tutorial demonstrating a practical approach to implementing biometric authentication within an Android app project.

78.1 An Overview of Biometric Authentication

The key biometric authentication component is the BiometricPrompt class. This class performs much of the work that previously had to be performed by writing code in earlier Android versions, including displaying a standard dialog to guide the user through the authentication process, performing the authentication, and reporting the results to the app. The class also handles excessive failed authentication attempts and enforces a timeout before the user can try again.

The BiometricPrompt class includes a companion Builder class that can be used to configure and create BiometricPrompt instances, including defining the text that is to appear within the biometric authentication dialog and the customization of the cancel button (also referred to as the *negative button*) that appears in the dialog.

The BiometricPrompt instance is also assigned a set of authentication callbacks that will be called to provide the app with the results of an authentication operation. A CancellationSignal instance is also used to allow the app to cancel the authentication while it is in process.

With these basics covered, the remainder of this chapter will implement fingerprint-based biometric authentication within an example project.

78.2 Creating the Biometric Authentication Project

Select the *New Project* option from the welcome screen and, within the resulting new project dialog, choose the Empty Views Activity template before clicking on the Next button.

Enter *BiometricDemo* into the Name field and specify *com.ebookfrenzy.biometricdemo* as the package name. Before clicking on the Finish button, change the Minimum API level setting to API 29: Android (Q) and the Language menu to Kotlin.

78.3 Configuring Device Fingerprint Authentication

Fingerprint authentication is only available on devices containing a touch sensor and on which the appropriate configuration steps have been taken to secure the device and enroll at least one fingerprint. For steps on configuring an emulator session to test fingerprint authentication, refer to the chapter *"Using and Configuring the Android Studio AVD Emulator"*.

Configure fingerprint authentication on a physical device by opening the Settings app and selecting the *Security* option. Within the Security settings screen, select the *Fingerprint* option. Tap the Next button on the resulting information screen to proceed to the Fingerprint setup screen. Before fingerprint security can be enabled, a backup screen unlocking method (such as a PIN) must be configured. If the lock screen is not secured, follow the steps to configure PIN, pattern, or password security.

With the lock screen secured, proceed to the fingerprint detection screen and touch the sensor when prompted lock screen secured, proceed to the fingerprint detection screen and touch the sensor when prompted (Figure 78-1), repeating the process to add additional fingerprints if required.

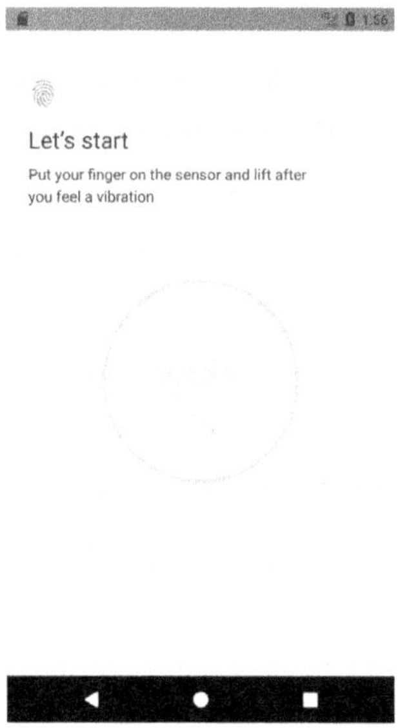

Figure 78-1

78.4 Adding the Biometric Permission to the Manifest File

Biometric authentication requires that the app request the *USE_BIOMETRIC* permission within the project manifest file. Within the Android Studio Project tool window, locate and edit the *app* -> *manifests* -> *AndroidManifest.xml* file to add the permission request as follows:

```
<?xml version="1.0" encoding="utf-8"?>
<manifest xmlns:android="http://schemas.android.com/apk/res/android"
    package="com.ebookfrenzy.biometricdemo">

    <uses-permission
        android:name="android.permission.USE_BIOMETRIC" />
.
.
```

78.5 Designing the User Interface

To keep the example as simple as possible, the only visual element within the user interface will be a Button view. Locate and select the *activity_main.xml* layout resource file to load it into the Layout Editor tool.

Delete the sample TextView object, drag and drop a Button object from the *Common* category of the palette and position it in the center of the layout canvas. Using the Attributes tool window, change the text property on the button to "Authenticate" and extract the string to a resource. Finally, configure the onClick property to call a method named *authenticateUser*.

On completion of the above steps, the layout should match that shown in Figure 78-2:

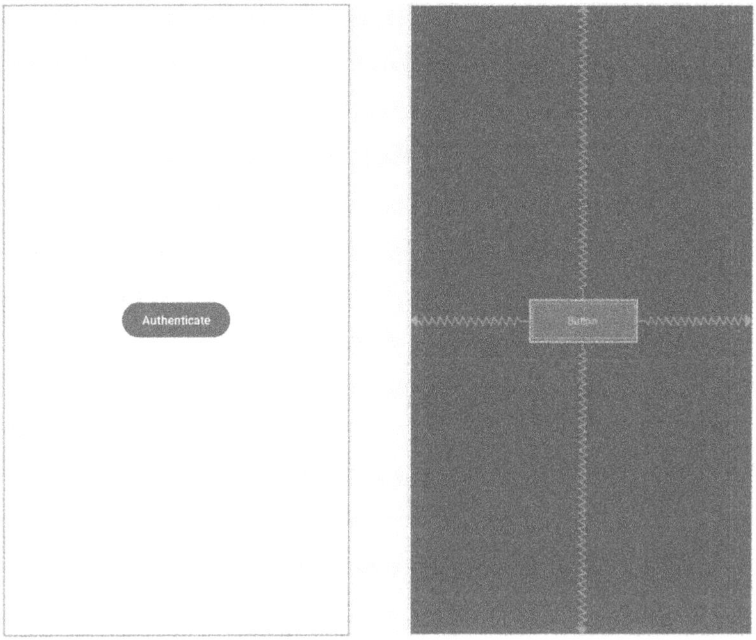

Figure 78-2

78.6 Adding a Toast Convenience Method

At various points throughout the code in this example, the app will be designed to display information to the user via Toast messages. Rather than repeat the same Toast code multiple times, a convenience method named *notifyUser()* will be added to the main activity. This method will accept a single String value and display it to the user as a Toast message. Edit the *MainActivity.kt* file now and add this method as follows:

```
.
.
import android.widget.Toast
.
.
private fun notifyUser(message: String) {
    Toast.makeText(this,
            message,
            Toast.LENGTH_LONG).show()
}
```

78.7 Checking the Security Settings

Earlier in this chapter, steps were taken to configure the lock screen and register fingerprints on the device or emulator on which the app will be tested. It is important, however, to include defensive code in the app to ensure these requirements have been met before attempting to seek fingerprint authentication. These steps will be performed within the onCreate method residing in the *MainActivity.kt* file, using the Keyguard and PackageManager manager services. Note that code has also been added to verify that the USE_BIOMETRIC permission has been configured for the app:

```
.
.
import androidx.core.app.ActivityCompat
import android.Manifest
import android.app.KeyguardManager
import android.content.Context
import android.content.pm.PackageManager
.
.
class MainActivity : AppCompatActivity() {

    override fun onCreate(savedInstanceState: Bundle?) {
        super.onCreate(savedInstanceState)
.
.
        checkBiometricSupport()
    }

    private fun checkBiometricSupport(): Boolean {

        val keyguardManager = getSystemService(Context.KEYGUARD_SERVICE)
                                          as KeyguardManager

        if (!keyguardManager.isKeyguardSecure) {

            notifyUser("Lock screen security not enabled in Settings")
            return false
        }

        if (ActivityCompat.checkSelfPermission(this,
                        Manifest.permission.USE_BIOMETRIC) !=
                                PackageManager.PERMISSION_GRANTED) {

            notifyUser("Fingerprint authentication permission not enabled")
            return false
        }

        return if (packageManager.hasSystemFeature(
```

```
                    PackageManager.FEATURE_FINGERPRINT)) {
                true
            } else true
        }
.
.
}
```

The above code changes begin by using the Keyguard manager to verify that a backup screen unlocking method has been configured (in other words, a PIN or other authentication method can be used as an alternative to fingerprint authentication to unlock the screen). If the lock screen is not secured, the code reports the problem to the user and returns from the method.

The method then checks that the user has biometric authentication permission enabled for the app before using the package manager to verify that fingerprint authentication is available on the device.

78.8 Configuring the Authentication Callbacks

When the biometric prompt dialog is configured, it will need to be assigned a set of authentication callback methods that can be called to notify the app of the success or failure of the authentication process. These methods need to be wrapped in a BiometricPrompt.AuthenticationCallback class instance. Remaining in the *MainActivity.kt* file, add a method to create and return an instance of this class with the appropriate methods implemented:

```
.
.
import android.hardware.biometrics.BiometricPrompt
.
.
private val authenticationCallback: BiometricPrompt.AuthenticationCallback
    get() = object : BiometricPrompt.AuthenticationCallback() {
        override fun onAuthenticationError(errorCode: Int,
                                           errString: CharSequence) {
            super.onAuthenticationError(errorCode, errString)
            notifyUser("Authentication error: $errString")
        }

        override fun onAuthenticationHelp(helpCode: Int,
                                 helpString: CharSequence) {
            super.onAuthenticationHelp(helpCode, helpString)
        }

        override fun onAuthenticationFailed() {
            super.onAuthenticationFailed()
            notifyUser("Authentication Failed")
        }

        override fun onAuthenticationSucceeded(result:
                      BiometricPrompt.AuthenticationResult) {
```

```
            super.onAuthenticationSucceeded(result)
            notifyUser("Authentication Succeeded")

        }
    }
.
.
```

78.9 Adding the CancellationSignal

Once initiated, the biometric authentication process is performed independently of the app. To provide the app with a way to cancel the operation, an instance of the CancellationSignal class is created and passed to the biometric authentication process. This CancellationSignal instance can then be used to cancel the process if necessary. The cancellation signal instance may be configured with a listener, which will be called when the cancellation is completed. Add a new method to the activity class to configure and return a CancellationSignal object as follows:

```
.
.
import android.os.CancellationSignal
.
.
private var cancellationSignal: CancellationSignal? = null
.
.
private fun getCancellationSignal(): CancellationSignal {

    cancellationSignal = CancellationSignal()
    cancellationSignal?.setOnCancelListener {
        notifyUser("Canceled via signal")
    }
    return cancellationSignal as CancellationSignal
}
.
.
```

78.10 Starting the Biometric Prompt

All that remains is to add code to the *authenticateUser()* method to create and configure a BiometricPrompt instance and initiate the authentication. Add the *authenticateUser()* method as follows:

```
.
.
import android.view.View
.
.
fun authenticateUser(view: View) {
    val biometricPrompt = BiometricPrompt.Builder(this)
            .setTitle("Biometric Demo")
            .setSubtitle("Authentication is required to continue")
```

```
            .setDescription("This app uses biometric authentication to protect
your data.")
            .setNegativeButton("Cancel", this.mainExecutor)
                { _, _ ->
                    notifyUser("Authentication canceled") }.build()

    biometricPrompt.authenticate(getCancellationSignal(), mainExecutor,
                        authenticationCallback)
}
```

The BiometricPrompt.Builder class creates a new BiometricPrompt instance configured with title, subtitle, and description text to appear in the prompt dialog. The negative button is configured to display text which reads "Cancel" and a listener is configured to display a message when this button is clicked. Finally, the *authenticate()* method of the BiometricPrompt instance is called and passed the AuthenticationCallback and CancellationSignal instances. The Biometric prompt also needs to know which thread to perform the authentication on. This is defined by passing through an Executor object configured for the required thread. In this case, the *getMainExecutor()* method is used to pass a main Executor object to the BiometricPrompt instance so that the authentication process occurs on the app's main thread.

78.11 Testing the Project

With the project now complete, run the app on a physical Android device or emulator session and click on the Authenticate button to display the BiometricPrompt dialog as shown in Figure 78-3:

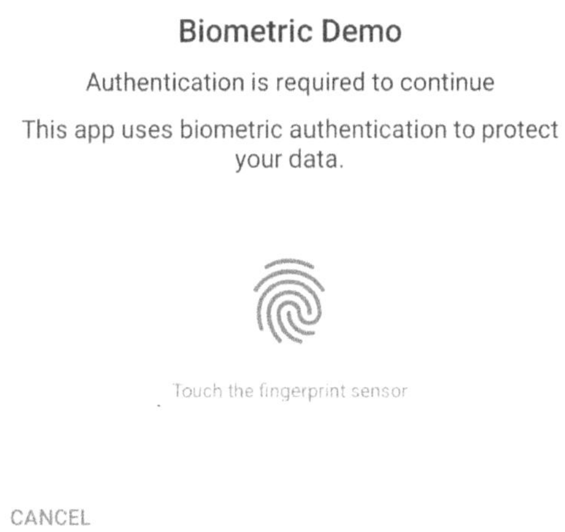

Figure 78-3

Once running, either touch the fingerprint sensor or use the extended controls panel within the emulator to simulate a fingerprint touch as outlined in the chapter entitled *"Using and Configuring the Android Studio AVD Emulator"*. Assuming a registered fingerprint is detected, the prompt dialog will return to the main activity, where the toast message from the successful authentication callback method will appear.

Click the Authenticate button again, using an unregistered fingerprint to attempt the authentication. This time the biometric prompt dialog will indicate that the fingerprint was not recognized:

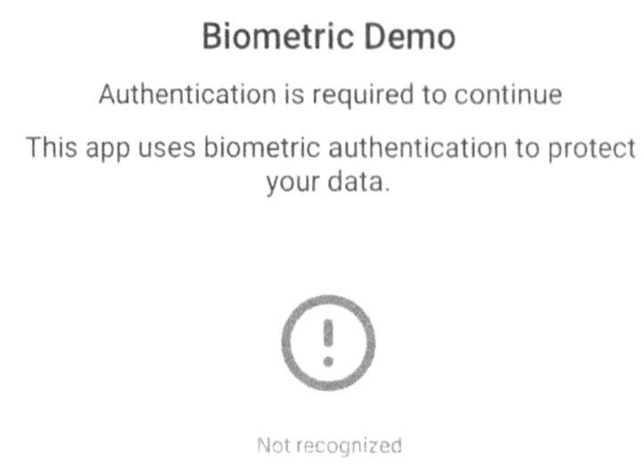

Figure 78-4

Verify that the error handling callback works by clicking on the activity outside the biometric prompt dialog. The prompt dialog will disappear, and the toast message will appear with the following message:

```
Authentication error: Fingerprint operation canceled by user.
```

Check that canceling the prompt dialog using the Cancel button triggers the "Authentication Canceled" toast message. Finally, attempt to authenticate multiple times using an unregistered fingerprint and note that after several attempts, the prompt dialog indicates that too many failures have occurred and that future attempts cannot be made until later.

78.12 Summary

This chapter has outlined how to integrate biometric authentication into an Android app project. This involves using the BiometricPrompt class, which automatically handles most of the authentication process once configured with appropriate message text and callbacks.

Chapter 79

79. Creating, Testing, and Uploading an Android App Bundle

Once an Android project is complete and tested on a wide range of Android devices, the next step is to prepare the application for submission to Google Play. Before submission can take place, however, the application must be packaged for release and signed with a private key. This chapter will work through obtaining a private key, preparing the Android App Bundle for the project, and uploading it to Google Play.

79.1 The Release Preparation Process

Up until now, we have been building application projects in a mode suitable for testing and debugging. On the other hand, building an application package for release to customers via Google Play requires additional steps. The first requirement is to compile the application in release mode instead of *debug mode*. Secondly, the application must be signed with a private key that uniquely identifies you as the developer of the application. Finally, the application must be packaged into an *Android App Bundle*.

While these tasks can be performed outside of the Android Studio environment, they can be performed more easily using the Android Studio build mechanism, as outlined in the remainder of this chapter. First, however, it is essential to understand more about Android App Bundles.

79.2 Android App Bundles

When a user installs an app from Google Play, the app is downloaded in the form of an APK file. This file contains everything needed to install and run the app on the user's device. Before the introduction of Android Studio 3.2, the developer would generate one or more APK files using Android Studio and upload them to Google Play. Supporting multiple device types, screen sizes, and locales would require creating and uploading multiple APK files customized for each target device and locale or generating a large *universal APK* containing all of the different configuration resources and platform binaries within a single package.

Creating multiple APK files involved a significant amount of work that had to be repeated each time the app needed to be updated, imposing a considerable time overhead on the app release process.

The universal APK option, although less burdensome to the developer, caused an entirely unexpected problem. By analyzing app installation metrics, Google discovered that the larger an installation APK file becomes (resulting in longer download times and increased storage use), the fewer conversions the app receives. The conversion rate is calculated as the percentage of users who complete the app installation after viewing it on Google Play. Google estimates that the conversion rate for an app drops by 1% for each 6MB increase in APK file size.

Android App Bundles solve these problems by allowing the developer to create a single package from within Android Studio and have custom APK files automatically generated by Google Play for each individual supported configuration (a concept called *Dynamic Delivery*).

An Android App Bundle is a ZIP file containing all the files necessary to build APK files for the devices and locales for which support has been provided within the app project. The project might, for example, include resources and images for different screen sizes. When a user installs the app, Google Play receives information about the device, including the display, processor architecture, and locale. Using this information, the appropriate pre-generated APK files are transferred onto the user's device.

An additional benefit of Dynamic Delivery is the ability to split an app into multiple modules, referred to as *dynamic feature modules*, where each module contains the code and resources for a particular area of functionality within the app. Each dynamic feature module is contained within a separate APK file from the base module and is downloaded to the device only when the user requires that feature. Dynamic Delivery and app bundles also enable the creation of *instant dynamic feature modules*, which can be run instantly on a device without the need to install an entire app.

Although it is still possible to generate APK files from Android Studio, app bundles are now the recommended method for uploading apps to Google Play.

79.3 Register for a Google Play Developer Console Account

The first step in the application submission process is to create a Google Play Developer Console account. To do so, navigate to *https://play.google.com/apps/publish/signup/* and follow the instructions to complete the registration process. Note that there is a one-time $25 fee to register. Once an application goes on sale, Google will keep 30% of all revenues associated with the application. After creating the account, the developer console can be accessed at *https://play.google.com/console.*

The next step is to gather together information about the application. To bring your application to market, the following information will be required:

- **Title** – The title of the application.
- **Short Description** - Up to 80 words describing the application.
- **Full Description** – Up to 4000 words describing the application.
- **Screenshots** – Up to 8 screenshots of your application running (a minimum of two is required). Google recommends submitting screenshots of the application running on a 7" or 10" tablet.
- **Language** – The language of the application (the default is US English).
- **Promotional Text** – The text that will be used when your application appears in special promotional features within the Google Play environment.
- **Application Type** – Whether your application is considered a *game* or an *application.*
- **Category** – The category that best describes your application (for example, finance, health and fitness, education, sports, etc.).
- **Locations** – The geographical locations into which you wish your application to be made available for purchase.
- **Contact Details** – Methods by which users may contact you for support relating to the application. Options include web, email, and phone.
- **Pricing & Distribution** – Information about the price of the application and the geographical locations where it is to be marketed and sold.

Having collected the above information, click the *Create app* link within the Google Play Console to begin the creation process:

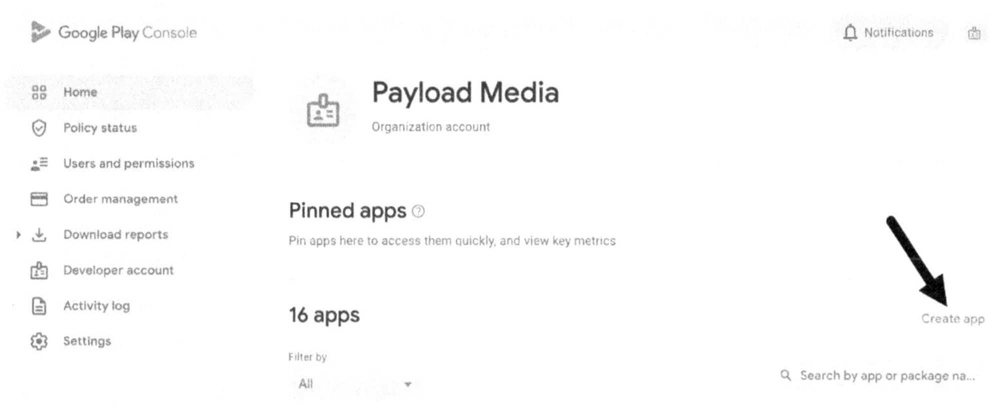

Figure 79-1

79.4 Configuring the App in the Console

When the *Create app* button is first clicked, the app details and declarations screen will appear as shown in Figure 79-2 below:

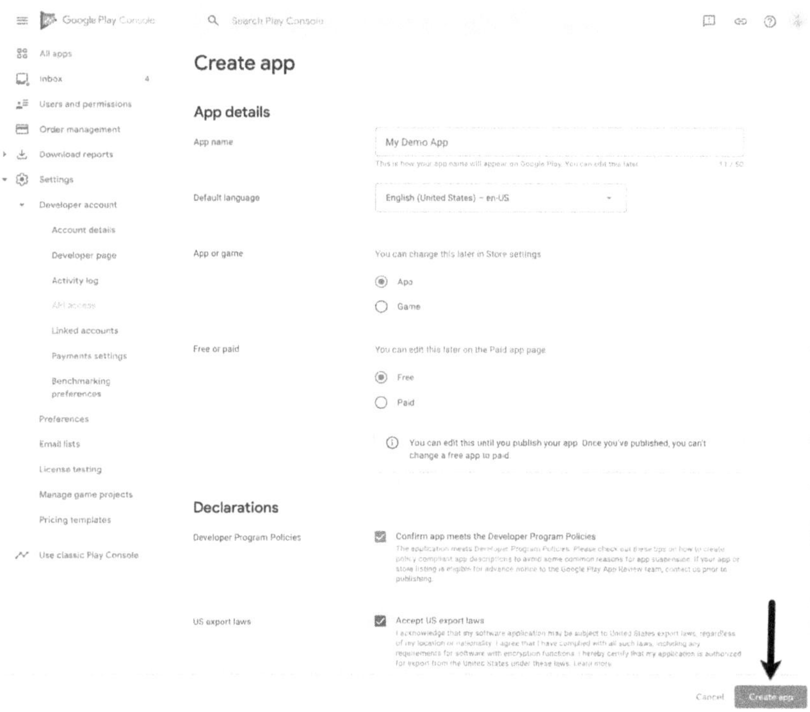

Figure 79-2

Once the app entry has been fully configured, click on the *Create app* button (highlighted in the above figure) to add the app and display the dashboard screen. Within the dashboard, locate the *Set up your app* section and unfold the list of tasks to configure the app store listing:

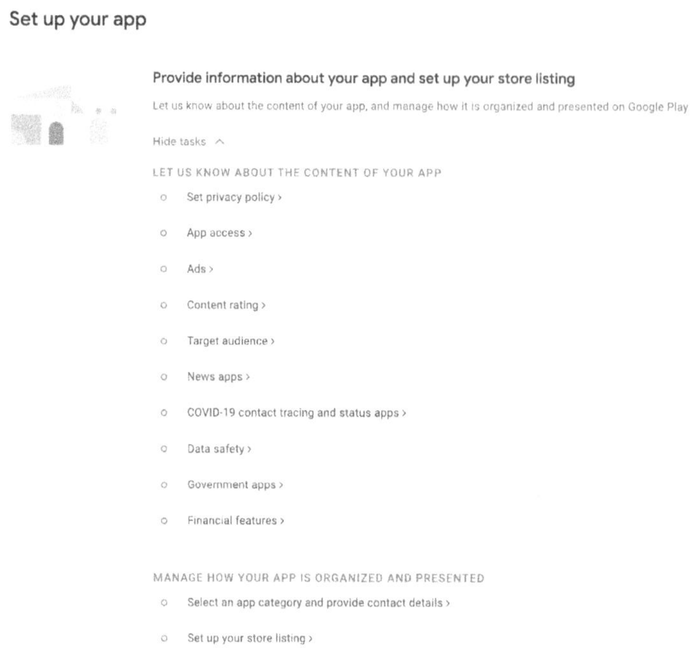

Figure 79-3

Work through the list of links and provide the requested information for your app, making sure to save the changes at each step.

79.5 Creating a Keystore File

To create a keystore file, select the Android Studio *Build -> Generate Signed Bundle / APK…* menu option to display the Generate Signed Bundle or APK Wizard dialog as shown in Figure 79-4:

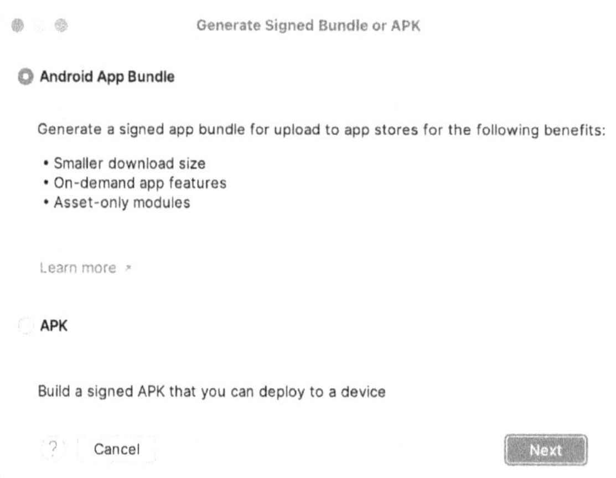

Figure 79-4

Verify that the *Android App Bundle* option is selected before clicking the *Next* button.

If you have an existing release keystore file, click on the *Choose existing…* button on the next screen and navigate to and select the file. If you have not created a keystore file, click the *Create new…* button to display the *New Key Store* dialog (Figure 79-5). Click on the button to the right of the Key store path field and navigate to a suitable location on your file system, enter a name for the keystore file (for example, *release.keystore.jks*) and click the OK button.

The New Key Store dialog is divided into two sections. The top section relates to the keystore file. In this section, enter a strong password to protect the keystore file into both the *Password* and *Confirm* fields. The lower section of the dialog relates to the upload key that will be stored in the key store file.

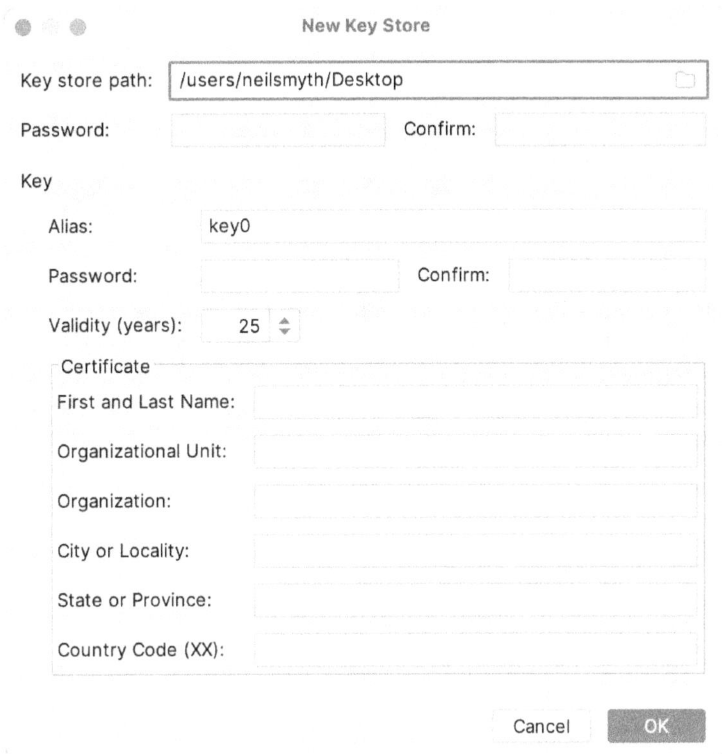

Figure 79-5

Within the *Key* section of the New Key Store dialog, enter the following details:

- An alias by which the key will be referenced. This can be any sequence of characters, though the system uses only the first eight.
- A suitably strong password to protect the key.
- The number of years for which the key is to be valid (Google recommends a duration in excess of 25 years).

In addition, information must be provided for at least one of the remaining fields (for example, your first and last name or organization name).

Once the information has been entered, click the OK button to create the bundle.

79.6 Creating the Android App Bundle

The next step is instructing Android Studio to build the application app bundle file in release mode and sign it with the newly created private key. At this point, the *Generate Signed Bundle or APK* dialog should still be displayed with the keystore path, passwords, and key alias fields populated with information:

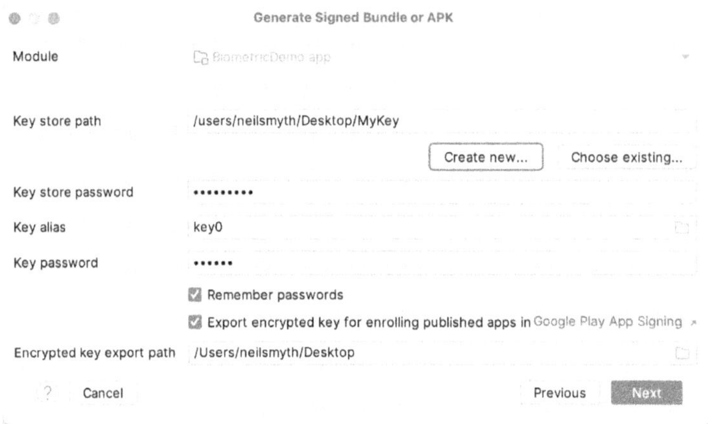

Figure 79-6

Ensure that the Export Encrypted Key option is enabled and, assuming the other settings are correct, click on the Next button to proceed to the app bundle generation screen (Figure 79-7). Within this screen, review the *Destination Folder:* setting to verify that the location into which the app bundle file will be generated is acceptable. If another location is preferred, click on the button to the right of the text field and navigate to the desired file system location.

Figure 79-7

Click the *Create* button and wait for the Gradle system to build the app bundle. Once the build is complete, a dialog will appear providing the option to open the folder containing the app bundle file in an explorer window or to load the file into the APK Analyzer:

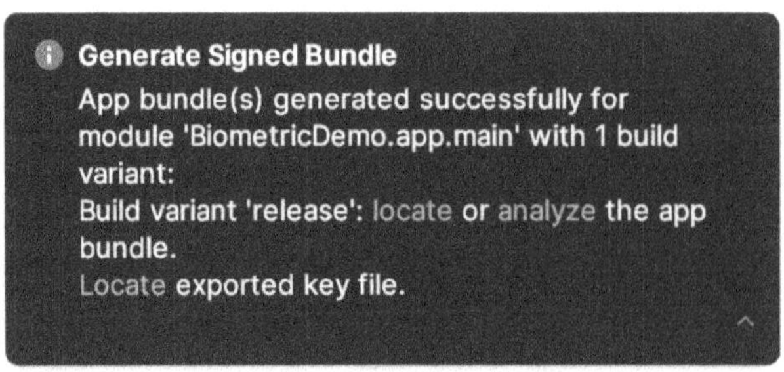

Figure 79-8

At this point, the application is ready to be submitted to Google Play. Click on the locate link to open a filesystem browser window. The file should be named *app-release.aab* and located in the project folder's *app/release* subdirectory unless another location is specified.

The private key generated as part of this process should be used when signing and releasing future applications and, as such, should be kept in a safe place and securely backed up.

79.7 Generating Test APK Files

An optional step at this stage is to generate APK files from the app bundle and install and run them on devices or emulator sessions. Google provides a command-line tool called *bundletool* designed specifically for this purpose which can be downloaded from the following URL:

https://github.com/google/bundletool/releases

At the time of writing, bundletool is provided as a .jar file which can be executed from the command line as follows (noting that the version number may have changed since this book was published):

```
java -jar bundletool-all-0.9.0.jar
```

Running the above command will list all of the options available within the tool. To generate the APK files from the app bundle, the *build-apks* option is used. The files will also need to be signed to generate APK files that can be installed onto a device or emulator. To achieve this, include the *--ks* option specifying the path of the keystore file created earlier in the chapter and the *--ks-key-alias* option specifying the alias provided when the key was generated.

Finally, the *--output* flag must be used to specify the path of the file (called the APK Set) into which the APK files will be generated. This file must not already exist and is required to have a *.apks* filename extension. Bringing these requirements together results in the following command line (allowing for differences in your operating system path structure):

```
java -jar bundletool-all-0.9.0.jar build-apks --bundle=/tmp/MyApps/app/release/
bundle.aab --output=/tmp/MyApks.apks --ks=/MyKeys/release.keystore.jks --ks-key-
alias=MyReleaseKey
```

When this command is executed, a prompt will appear requesting the keystore password before the APK files are generated into the specified APK Set file. The APK Set file is a ZIP file containing all the APK files generated from the app bundle.

To install the appropriate APK files onto a connected device or emulator, use a command similar to the following:

```
java -jar bundletool-all-0.9.0.jar install-apks --apks=/tmp/MyApks.apks
```

This command will instruct the tool to identify the appropriate APK files for the connected device and install them so that the app can be launched and tested.

It is also possible to extract the APK files from the APK Set for the connected device without installing them. The first step in this process is to obtain the specification of the connected device as follows:

```
java -jar bundletool-all-0.9.0.jar get-device-spec --output=/tmp/device.json
```

The above command will generate a JSON file similar to the following:

```
{
  "supportedAbis": ["x86"],
  "supportedLocales": ["en-US"],
  "screenDensity": 420,
  "sdkVersion": 27
```

```
}
```

Next, this specification file is used to extract the matching APK files from the APK Set:

```
java -jar bundletool-all-0.9.0.jar extract-apks --apks=/tmp/MyApks.apks --output-dir=/tmp/nexus5_apks --device-spec=/tmp/device.json
```

When executed, the directory specified via the *--output-dir* flag will contain the correct APK files for the specified device configuration.

The next step in bringing an Android application to market involves submitting it to the Google Play Developer Console to make it available for testing.

79.8 Uploading the App Bundle to the Google Play Developer Console

Return to the Google Play Console and select the *Internal testing* option (marked A in Figure 79-9) located in the *Testing* section of the navigation panel before clicking on the *Create new release* button (B):

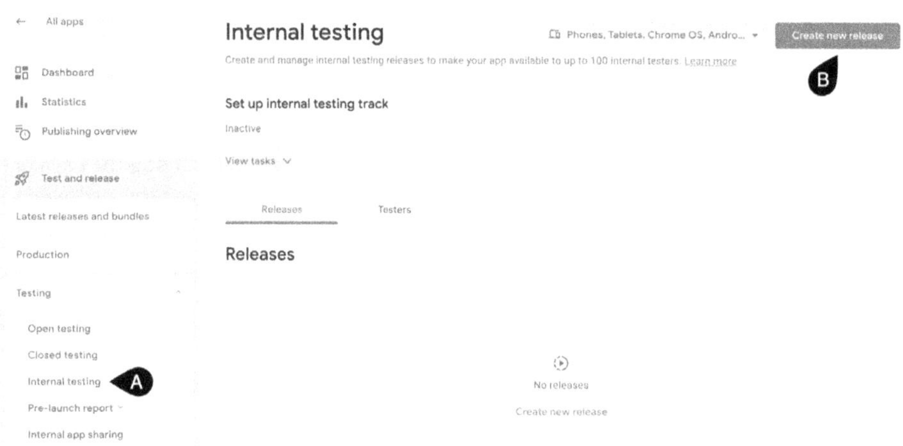

Figure 79-9

On the resulting screen, drag and drop the bundle file generated by Android Studio onto the upload drop point (A):

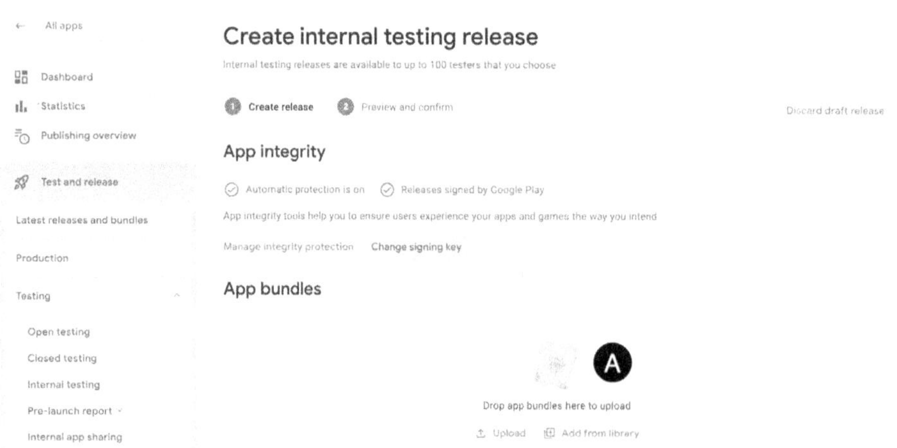

Figure 79-10

When the upload is complete, scroll down the screen and enter the release name and optional release notes. The release name can be any information you need to help you recognize the release, and it is not visible to users.

After the app bundle file is uploaded, Google Play will generate all the necessary APK files ready for testing. Once the APK files have been generated, scroll down to the bottom of the screen and click on the *Next* button to review the app bundle.

79.9 Exploring the App Bundle

On the review screen, click on the arrow to the right of the uploaded bundle as indicated in Figure 79-11:

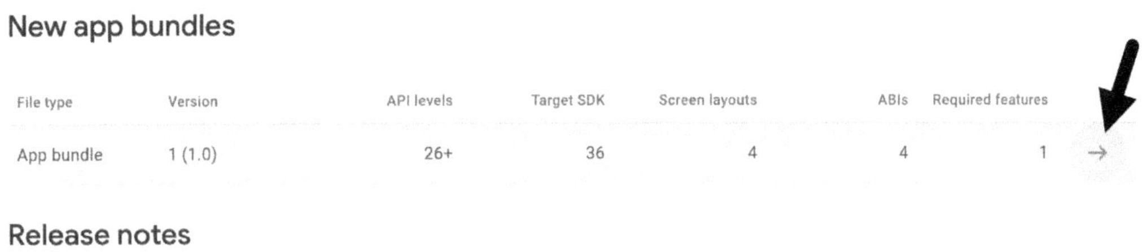

Figure 79-11

This panel provides summary information relating to the API levels, screen layouts, and platforms supported by the app bundle:

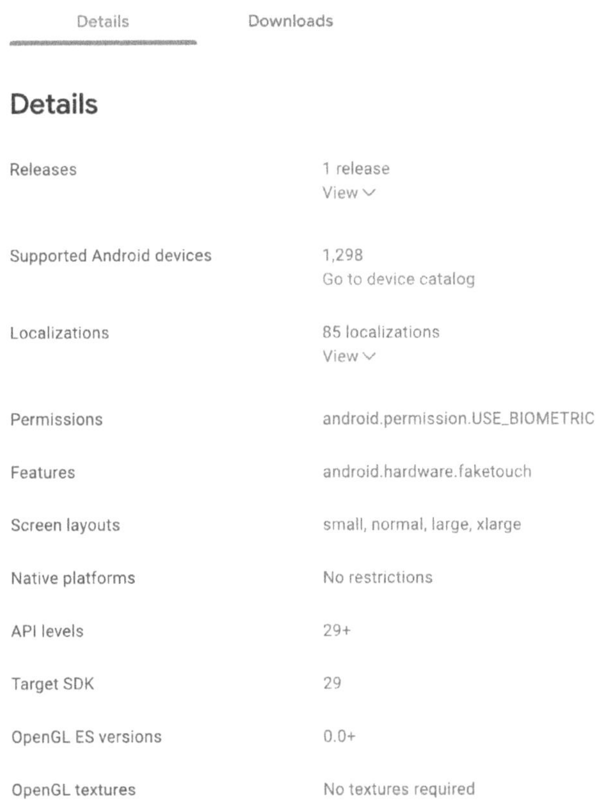

Figure 79-12

Clicking on the *Go to device catalog* link will display the devices that are supported by the bundle file:

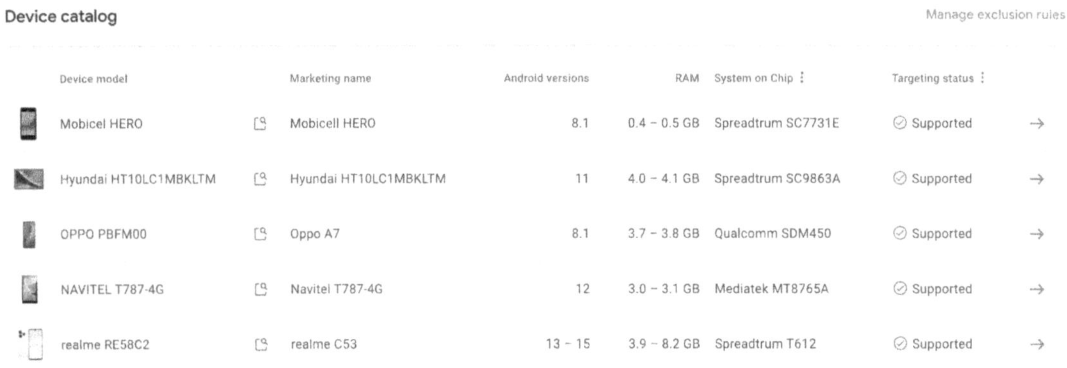

Figure 79-13

Close the review panel, then click the *Save and Publish* button located at the bottom of the screen, and confirm the selection in the verification dialog:

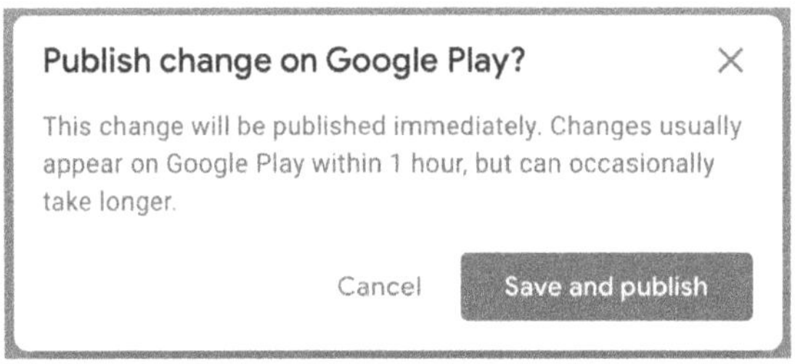

Figure 79-14

Currently, the app is ready for testing but can only be rolled out once some testers have been set up within the console.

79.10 Managing Testers

If the app is still in the Internal, Alpha, or Beta testing phase, a list of authorized testers may be specified by selecting the app from within the Google Play console, clicking on *Internal testing* in the navigation panel, and selecting the *Testers* tab as shown in Figure 79-15:

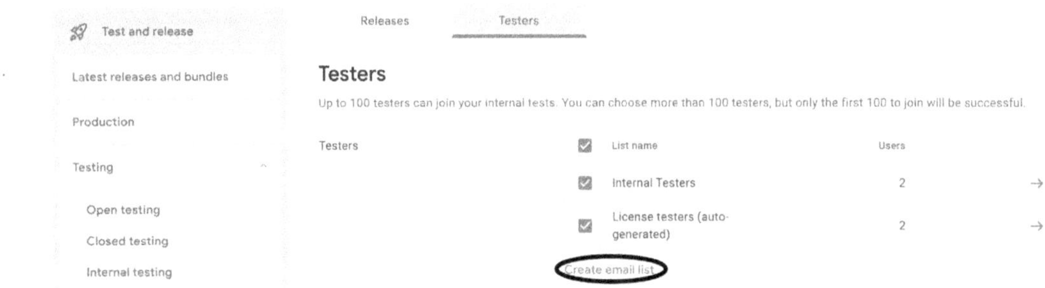

Figure 79-15

To add testers, click the *Create email list* button, name the list, and specify the test users' email addresses manually or by uploading a CSV file.

The "Join on the web" URL can now be copied from the screen and provided to test users, allowing them to accept the testing invitation and download the app:

Figure 79-16

79.11 Uploading New App Bundle Revisions

The first app bundle file uploaded for your application will invariably have a version code of 1. If an attempt is made to upload another bundle file with the same version code number, the console will reject the file with the following error:

```
You need to use a different version code for your APK because you already have
one with version code 1.
```

To resolve this problem, the version code embedded into the bundle file needs to be increased. This is performed in the *module* level *build.gradle.kts* file of the project, shown highlighted in Figure 79-17:

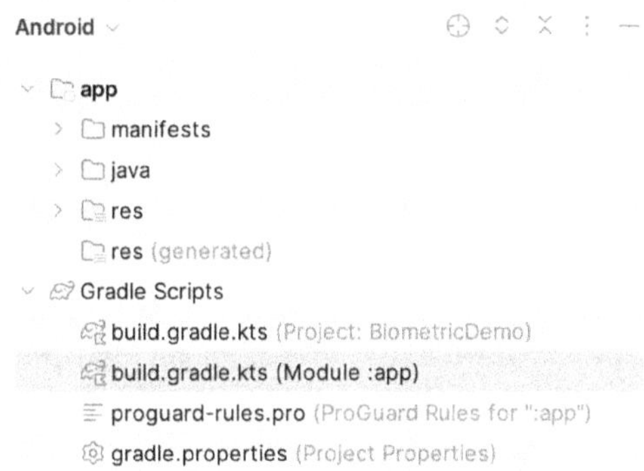

Figure 79-17

This file will typically read as follows:

```
plugins {
    alias(libs.plugins.android.application)
.
.
}

android {
    namespace = "com.example.myapp"
.
.
    defaultConfig {
        applicationId = "com.example.myapp"
        minSdk = 26
        targetSdk = 36
        versionCode = 1
        versionName = "1.0"
.
```

To change the version code, change the number declared next to *versionCode*. To also change the version number displayed to users of your application, change the *versionName* string. For example:

```
versionCode 2
versionName "2.0"
```

After making these changes, rebuild the app bundle file and perform the upload again.

79.12 Analyzing the App Bundle File

Android Studio provides the ability to analyze the content of an app bundle file. To analyze a bundle file, select the Android Studio *Build -> Analyze APK...* menu option and navigate to and choose the bundle file to be reviewed. Once loaded into the tool, information will be displayed about the raw and download size of the package together with a listing of the file structure of the package as illustrated in Figure 79-18:

Figure 79-18

Selecting the *classes.dex* file will display the class structure of the file in the lower panel. Within this panel, details of the individual classes may be explored down to the level of the methods within a class:

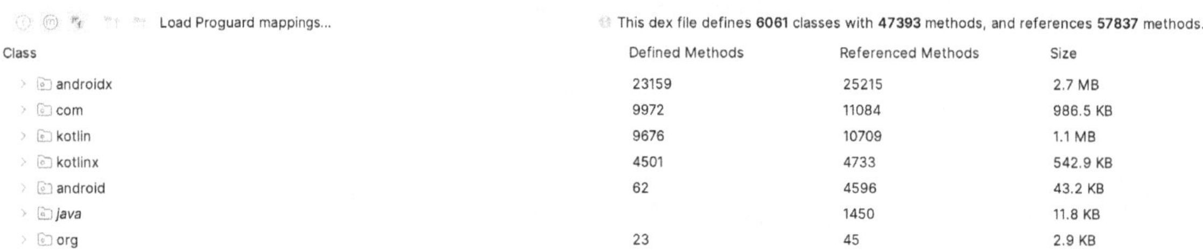

Figure 79-19

Similarly, selecting a resource or image file within the file list will display the file content within the lower panel. The size differences between two bundle files may be reviewed by clicking on the *Compare with previous APK...* button and selecting a second bundle file.

79.13 Summary

Once an app project is complete or ready for user testing, it can be uploaded to the Google Play console and published for production, internal, alpha, or beta testing. Before the app can be uploaded, an app entry must be created within the console, including information about the app and screenshots for use within the Play Store. A release Android App Bundle file is generated and signed with an upload key within Android Studio. After the bundle file has been uploaded, Google Play removes the upload key and replaces it with the securely stored app signing key, and the app is ready to be published.

The content of a bundle file can be reviewed at any time by loading it into the Android Studio APK Analyzer tool.

Chapter 80

80. An Overview of Android In-App Billing

n the early days of mobile applications for operating systems such as Android and iOS, the most common method for earning revenue was to charge an upfront fee to download and install the application. Another revenue opportunity was soon introduced by embedding advertising within applications. The most common and lucrative option is to charge the user for purchasing items from within the application after installing it. This typically takes the form of access to a higher level in a game, acquiring virtual goods or currency, or subscribing to premium content in the digital edition of a magazine or newspaper.

Google supports integrating in-app purchasing through the Google Play In-App Billing API and the Play Console. This chapter will provide an overview of in-app billing and outline how to integrate in-app billing into your Android projects. Once these topics have been explored, the next chapter will walk you through creating an example app that includes in-app purchasing features.

80.1 Preparing a Project for In-App Purchasing

Building in-app purchasing into an app will require a Google Play Developer Console account, details of which were covered previously in the *"Creating, Testing, and Uploading an Android App Bundle"* chapter. You must also register a Google merchant account. These settings can be found by navigating to *Setup -> Payments profile* in the Play Console. Note that merchant registration is not available in all countries. For details, refer to the following page:

https://support.google.com/googleplay/android-developer/answer/9306917

The app must then be uploaded to the console and enabled for in-app purchasing. However, the console will not activate in-app purchasing support for an app unless the Google Play Billing Library has been added to the module-level *build.gradle.kts* file:

```
dependencies {
.
.
    implementation(libs.billingclient.ktx)
.
.
}
```

Once the build file has been modified and the app bundle uploaded to the console, the next step is to add in-app products or subscriptions for the user to purchase.

80.2 Creating In-App Products and Subscriptions

Products and subscriptions are created and managed using the options listed beneath the Monetize section of the Play Console navigation panel, as highlighted in Figure 80-1 below:

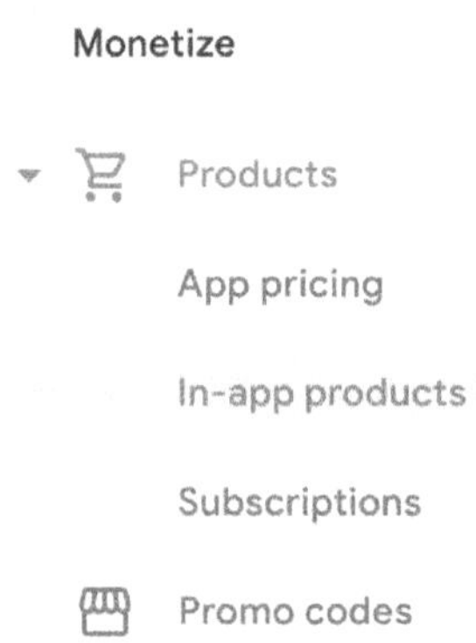

Figure 80-1

Each product or subscription needs an ID, title, description, and pricing information. Purchases fall into the categories of *consumable* (the item must be purchased each time it is required by the user, such as virtual currency in a game), *non-consumable* (only needs to be purchased once by the user, such as content access), and *subscription*-based. Consumable and non-consumable products are collectively referred to as *managed products.*

Subscriptions are useful for selling an item that needs to be renewed regularly, such as access to news content or the premium features of an app. When creating a subscription, a *base plan* specifies the price, renewal period (monthly, annually, etc.), and whether the subscription auto-renews. Users can also be given discount offers and the option of pre-purchasing a subscription.

80.3 Billing Client Initialization

Communication between your app and the Google Play Billing Library is handled by a BillingClient instance. In addition, BillingClient includes a set of methods that can be called to perform both synchronous and asynchronous billing-related activities. When the billing client is initialized, it will need to be provided with a reference to a PurchasesUpdatedListener callback handler. The client will call this handler to notify your app of the results of any purchasing activity. To avoid duplicate notifications, it is recommended to have only one BillingClient instance per app.

A BillingClient instance can be created using the *newBuilder()* method, passing through the current activity or fragment context. The purchase update handler is then assigned to the client via the *setListener()* method:

```
private val purchasesUpdatedListener =
    PurchasesUpdatedListener { billingResult, purchases ->
        if (billingResult.responseCode ==
            BillingClient.BillingResponseCode.OK
            && purchases != null
        ) {
            for (purchase in purchases) {
                // Process the purchases
            }
        } else if (billingResult.responseCode ==
            BillingClient.BillingResponseCode.USER_CANCELED
        ) {
            // Purchase canceled by the user
        } else {
```

```
            // Handle errors here
        }
    }

billingClient = BillingClient.newBuilder(this)
    .setListener(purchasesUpdatedListener)
    .enablePendingPurchases(
        PendingPurchasesParams.newBuilder()
            .enableOneTimeProducts().build()
    )
    .build()
```

80.4 Connecting to the Google Play Billing Library

After successfully creating the Billing Client, the next step is initializing a connection to the Google Play Billing Library. A call must be made to the *startConnection()* method of the billing client instance to establish this connection. Since the connection is performed asynchronously, a BillingClientStateListener must be implemented to receive a callback indicating whether the connection was successful. Code should also be added to override the *onBillingServiceDisconnected()* method. This is called if the connection to the Billing Library is lost and can be used to report the problem to the user and retry the connection.

Once the setup and connection tasks are complete, the BillingClient instance will make a call to the *onBillingSetupFinished()* method, which can be used to check that the client is ready:

```
billingClient.startConnection(object : BillingClientStateListener {
    override fun onBillingSetupFinished(
        billingResult: BillingResult
    ) {
        if (billingResult.responseCode ==
            BillingClient.BillingResponseCode.OK
        ) {
            // Connection successful
        } else {
            // Connection failed
        }
    }

    override fun onBillingServiceDisconnected() {
        // Connection to billing service lost
    }
})
```

80.5 Querying Available Products

Once the billing environment is initialized and ready to go, the next step is to request the details of the products or subscriptions available for purchase. This is achieved by making a call to the *queryProductDetailsAsync()* method of the BillingClient and passing through an appropriately configured QueryProductDetailsParams instance containing the product ID and type (ProductType.SUBS for a subscription or ProductType.INAPP for a managed product):

```
val queryProductDetailsParams = QueryProductDetailsParams.newBuilder()
```

```
    .setProductList(
        ImmutableList.of(
            Product.newBuilder()
                .setProductId(productId)
                .setProductType(
                    BillingClient.ProductType.INAPP
                )
                .build()
        )
    )
    .build()

billingClient.queryProductDetailsAsync(
    queryProductDetailsParams
) { billingResult: BillingResult?, productDetailsResult:
                                 QueryProductDetailsResult? ->
    val queriedProductDetailsList = productDetailsResult?.productDetailsList
    if (!queriedProductDetailsList.isNullOrEmpty()) {
        // Process list of matching products
    } else {
        // No product matches found
    }
}
```

The *queryProductDetailsAsync()* method is passed a ProductDetailsResponseListener handler (in this case, as a trailing lambda). When the asynchronous query completes, the handler is called and passed a QueryProductDetailsResult object. The *productDetailsList* property of this object contains a list of ProductDetail objects, each containing information about a matching product. For example, we can call methods on these Product Detail instances to get information such as the product name, title, description, price, and offer details.

80.6 Starting the Purchase Process

Once a product or subscription has been queried and selected for purchase by the user, the purchase process is ready to be launched. We do this by calling the *launchBillingFlow()* method of the BillingClient, passing through as arguments the current activity and a BillingFlowParams instance configured with the ProductDetail object for the purchased item.

```
val billingFlowParams = BillingFlowParams.newBuilder()
    .setProductDetailsParamsList(
        ImmutableList.of(
            BillingFlowParams.ProductDetailsParams.newBuilder()
                .setProductDetails(productDetails)
                .build()
        )
    )
    .build()

billingClient.launchBillingFlow(this, billingFlowParams)
```

The success or otherwise of the purchase operation will be reported via a call to the PurchasesUpdatedListener callback handler outlined earlier in the chapter.

80.7 Completing the Purchase

When purchases are successful, the PurchasesUpdatedListener handler will be passed a list containing a Purchase object for each item. You can verify that the item has been purchased by calling the *getPurchaseState()* method of the Purchase instance as follows:

```
if (purchase.getPurchaseState() == Purchase.PurchaseState.PURCHASED) {
    // Purchase completed.
} else if (purchase.getPurchaseState() == Purchase.PurchaseState.PENDING) {
    // Payment is still pending
}
```

Note that your app will only support pending purchases if a call is made to the *enablePendingPurchases()* method during initialization. A pending purchase will remain so until the user completes the payment process.

When the purchase of a non-consumable item is complete, it must be acknowledged to prevent a refund from being issued to the user. This requires the *purchase token* for the item, which is obtained via a call to the *getPurchaseToken()* method of the Purchase object. This token is used to create an AcknowledgePurchaseParams instance and an AcknowledgePurchaseResponseListener handler. Managed product purchases and subscriptions are acknowledged by calling the BillingClient's *acknowledgePurchase()* method as follows:

```
billingClient.acknowledgePurchase(acknowledgePurchaseParams,
                             acknowledgePurchaseResponseListener);
val acknowledgePurchaseParams = AcknowledgePurchaseParams.newBuilder()
    .setPurchaseToken(purchase.purchaseToken)
    .build()

val acknowledgePurchaseResponseListener = AcknowledgePurchaseResponseListener {
    // Check acknowledgement result
}

billingClient.acknowledgePurchase(
    acknowledgePurchaseParams,
    acknowledgePurchaseResponseListener
)
```

For consumable purchases, you will need to notify Google Play when the item has been consumed so that it is available to be repurchased by the user. This requires a configured ConsumeParams instance containing a purchase token and a call to the billing client's *consumePurchase()* method:

```
val consumeParams = ConsumeParams.newBuilder()
    .setPurchaseToken(purchase.purchaseToken)
    .build()

coroutineScope.launch {
    val result = billingClient.consumePurchase(consumeParams)
    if (result.billingResult.responseCode ==
                     BillingClient.BillingResponseCode.OK) {
        // Purchase successfully consumed
```

```
    }
}
```

80.8 Querying Previous Purchases

When working with in-app billing, checking whether a user has already purchased a product or subscription is a common requirement. A list of all the user's previous purchases of a specific type can be generated by calling the *queryPurchasesAsync()* method of the BillingClient instance and implementing a PurchaseResponseListener. The following code, for example, obtains a list of all previously purchased items that have not yet been consumed:

```
val queryPurchasesParams = QueryPurchasesParams.newBuilder()
    .setProductType(BillingClient.ProductType.INAPP)
    .build()

billingClient.queryPurchasesAsync(
    queryPurchasesParams,
    purchasesListener
)
.
.
private val purchasesListener =
    PurchasesResponseListener { billingResult, purchases ->

        if (!purchases.isEmpty()) {
            // Access existing active purchases
        } else {
            // No products found
        }
    }
```

To obtain a list of active subscriptions, change the ProductType value from INAPP to SUBS. Alternatively, to obtain a list of the most recent purchases for each product, make a call to the BillingClient *queryPurchaseHistoryAsync()* method:

```
val queryPurchaseHistoryParams = QueryPurchaseHistoryParams.newBuilder()
    .setProductType(BillingClient.ProductType.INAPP)
    .build()

billingClient.queryPurchaseHistoryAsync(queryPurchaseHistoryParams) {
billingResult, historyList ->
    // Process purchase history list
}
```

80.9 Summary

In-app purchases provide a way to generate revenue from within Android apps by selling virtual products and subscriptions to users. This chapter explored managed products and subscriptions and explained the difference between consumable and non-consumable products. In-app purchasing support is added to an app using the Google Play In-app Billing Library. It involves creating and initializing a billing client on which methods are called to perform tasks such as making purchases, listing available products, and consuming existing purchases. The next chapter contains a tutorial demonstrating the addition of in-app purchases to an Android Studio project.

Chapter 81

81. An Android In-App Purchasing Tutorial

In the previous chapter, we explored how to integrate in-app purchasing into an Android project and also looked at some code samples that can be used when working on your own projects. This chapter will put this theory into practice by creating an example project demonstrating how to add a consumable in-app product to an Android app. The tutorial will also show how in-app products are added and managed within the Google Play Console and explain how to enable test payments to make purchases during testing without having to spend real money.

81.1 About the In-App Purchasing Example Project

The simple concept behind this project is an app in which an in-app product must be purchased before a button can be clicked. This in-app product is consumed each time the button is clicked, requiring the user to repurchase the product each time they want to be able to click the button. On initialization, the app will connect to the app store, obtain product details, and display the product name. Once the app has established that the product is available, a purchase button will be enabled, which will step through the purchase process when clicked. Upon completion of the purchase, a second button will be enabled so the user can click on it and consume the purchase.

81.2 Creating the InAppPurchase Project

The first step in this exercise is to create a new project. Launch Android Studio and select the *New Project* option from the welcome screen. Choose the Empty Views Activity template in the new project dialog before clicking the Next button.

Enter InAppPurchase into the Name field and specify a package name that uniquely identifies your app within the Google Play ecosystem (for example, *com.<your company>.InAppPurchase).* Before clicking on the Finish button, change the Minimum API level setting to API 26: Android 8.0 (Oreo) and the Language menu to Kotlin. Once the project has been created, use the Gemini Agent or the steps outlined in section *18.8 Migrating a Project to View Binding* to convert the project to use view binding.

81.3 Adding Libraries to the Project

Before writing code, some libraries must be added to the project build configuration, including the standard Android billing client library. Later in the project, we will also need to use the ImmutableList class, part of Google's Guava Core Java libraries. Edit the version catalog (*Gradle Scripts -> libs.versions.toml*) and make the following additions:

```
[versions]
billingKtx = "9.1.0"
gauvaJre = "33.6.0-jre"
gauvaAndroid = "33.6.0-android"

[libraries]
.
.
```

```
billingclient-ktx = { group = "com.android.billingclient", name = "billing-ktx",
version.ref = "billingKtx" }
guava-jre = { group = "com.google.guava", name="guava", version.ref = "gauvaJre"}
guava-android = { group = "com.google.guava", name="guava", version.ref =
"gauvaAndroid"}
```

After making the changes, click on the *Sync Now* link at the top of the editor panel before modifying the *Gradle Scripts -> build.gradle.kts (Module: app)* file as follows:

```
dependencies {
    implementation(libs.billingclient.ktx)
    implementation(libs.guava.jre)
    implementation(libs.guava.android)
.
.
```

Click on the *Sync Now* link at the top of the editor panel again to commit these changes.

81.4 Designing the User Interface

The user interface will consist of the existing TextView and two Buttons. With the *activity_main.xml* file loaded into the editor, drag and drop two Button views onto the layout so that one is above and the other below the TextView. Select the TextView and change the id attribute to *statusText*.

Click on the *Clear all Constraints* button in the toolbar and shift-click to select all three views. Right-click on the top-most Button view and select the *Center -> Horizontally in Parent* menu option. Repeat this step once more, selecting *Chains -> Create Vertical Chain*. Change the text attribute of the top button so that it reads "Consume Purchase" and the id to *consumeButton*. Also, configure the onClick property to call a method named *consumePurchase*.

Select the bottom-most button and repeat the above steps, setting the text to "Buy Product", the id to *buyButton*, and the onClick callback to *makePurchase*. Once completed, the layout should match that shown in Figure 81-1:

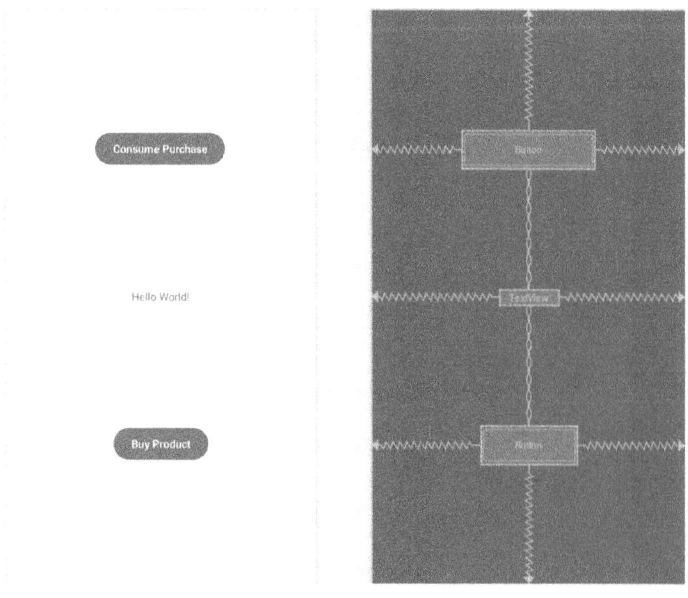

Figure 81-1

81.5 Adding the App to the Google Play Store

Using the steps outlined in the chapter entitled *"Creating, Testing, and Uploading an Android App Bundle"*, sign into the Play Console, create a new app, and set up a new internal testing track, including the email addresses of designated testers. Return to Android Studio and generate a signed release app bundle for the project. Once the bundle file has been generated, upload it to the internal testing track and roll it out for testing.

Now that the app is in the Google Play Store, we are ready to create an in-app product for the project.

81.6 Creating an In-App product

With the app selected in the Play Console, scroll down the left-hand panel list until the Monetize with Play section comes into view. Within this section, select the One-time products option listed under Products as shown in Figure 81-2:

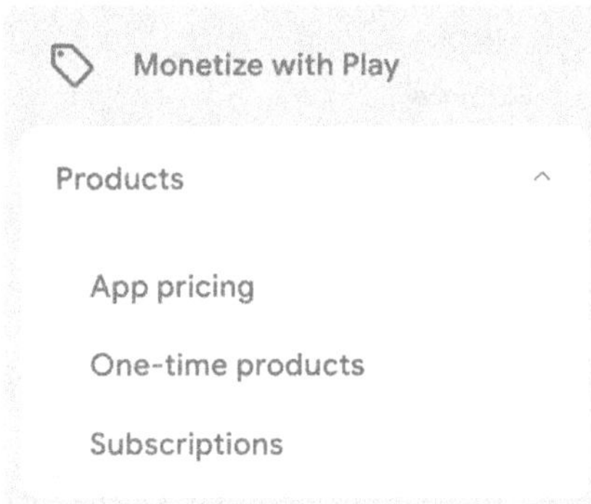

Figure 81-2

On the One-time products page, click on the *Create one-time product* button:

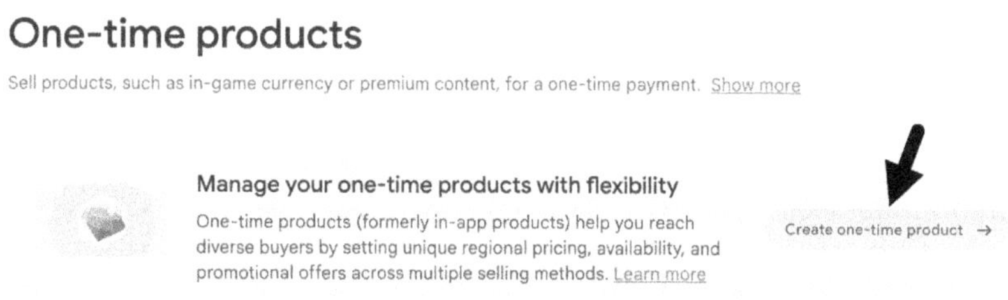

Figure 81-3

On the new product screen, enter the following information before saving the new product:

- **Product ID:** one_button_click
- **Name:** A Button Click
- **Description:** This is a test in-app product that allows a button to be clicked once.

Click the Next button and enter the following information:

- **Purchase option ID:** This can be any string that starts with a number or lowercase letter and is limited to numbers, lowercase letters, and hyphens.
- **Purchase type:** Buy

In the availability and pricing section, hover the mouse pointer over your country and click the edit icon indicated in Figure 81-4:

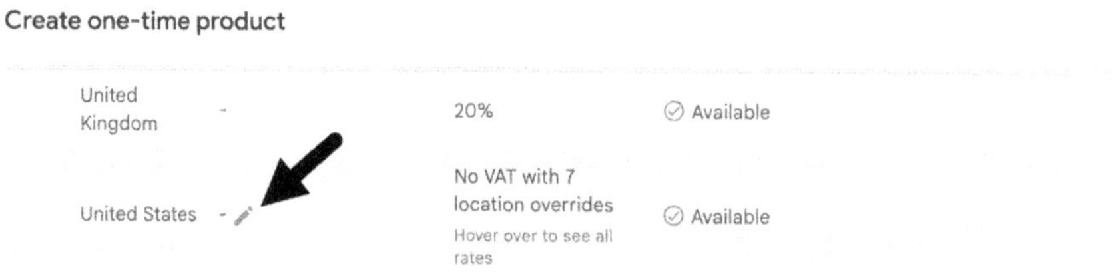

Figure 81-4

In the resulting dialog, enter a low price in your currency before clicking the Save button:

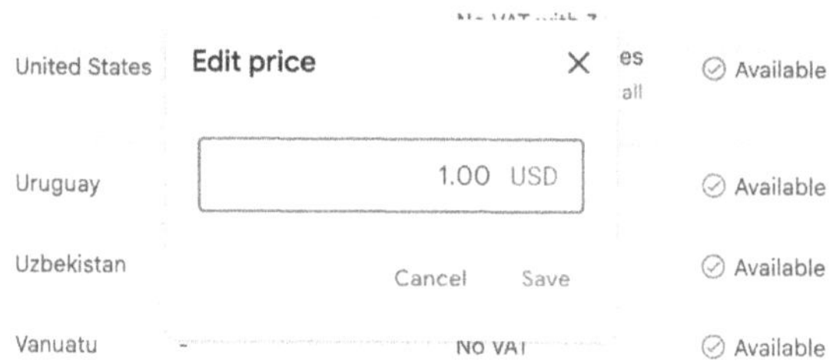

Figure 81-5

Scroll to the bottom of the page and click the Activate button to create the product.

81.7 Enabling license testers

When testing in-app billing it is useful to be able to make test purchases without spending any money. This can be achieved by enabling license testing for the internal track testers. License testers can use a test payment card when making purchases so that they are not charged.

Within the Play Console, return to the main home screen and select the *Setup -> License testing* option.

Within the license testing screen, add the testers that were added for the internal testing track, change the *License response* setting to RESPOND_NORMALLY, and save the changes:

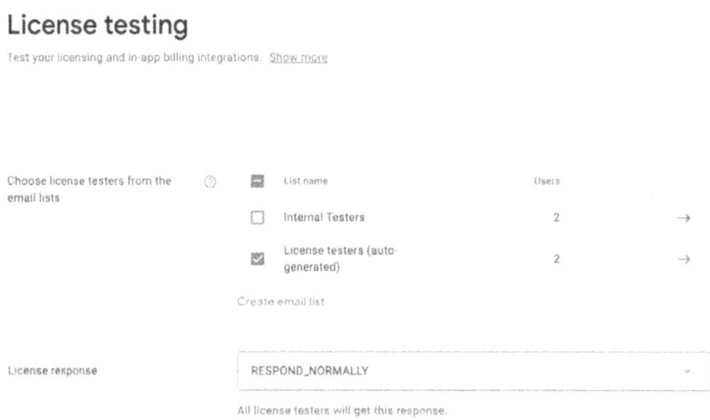

Figure 81-6

Now that both the app and the in-app product have been set up in the Play Console, we can start adding code to the project.

81.8 Initializing the Billing Client

Edit the *MainActivity.kt* file and make the following changes to begin implementing the in-app purchase functionality:

```
.
.
import android.util.Log
import com.android.billingclient.api.*
.
.
class MainActivity : AppCompatActivity() {

    private lateinit var binding: ActivityMainBinding
    private lateinit var billingClient: BillingClient
    private lateinit var productDetails: ProductDetails
    private lateinit var purchase: Purchase
    private val demo_product = "one_button_click"

    val TAG = "InAppPurchaseTag"

    override fun onCreate(savedInstanceState: Bundle?) {
.
.
        billingSetup()
    }

    private fun billingSetup() {
        billingClient = BillingClient.newBuilder(this)
            .setListener(purchasesUpdatedListener)
            .enablePendingPurchases(
                PendingPurchasesParams.newBuilder()
                    .enableOneTimeProducts().build()
            )
            .build()

        billingClient.startConnection(object : BillingClientStateListener {
            override fun onBillingSetupFinished(
                billingResult: BillingResult
            ) {
                if (billingResult.responseCode ==
                    BillingClient.BillingResponseCode.OK
                ) {
                    Log.i(TAG, "OnBillingSetupFinish connected")
                    queryProduct(demo_product)
                } else {
                    Log.i(TAG, "OnBillingSetupFinish failed")
```

```
                }
            }

            override fun onBillingServiceDisconnected() {
                Log.i(TAG, "OnBillingSetupFinish connection lost")
            }
        })
    }
.
.
```

When the app starts, the *onCreate()* method will now call *billingSetup()*, which will, in turn, create a new billing client instance and attempt to connect to the Google Play Billing Library. The *onBillingSetupFinished()* listener will be called when the connection attempt completes and output Logcat messages indicating the success or otherwise of the connection attempt. Finally, we have also implemented the *onBillingServiceDisconnected()* callback which will be called if the Google Play Billing Library connection is lost.

If the connection is successful, *queryProduct()* is called. This method and the purchasesUpdatedListener assigned to the billing client must be added.

81.9 Querying the Product

To make sure the product is available for purchase, we need to create a QueryProductDetailsParams instance configured with the product ID that was specified in the Play Console and pass it to the *queryProductDetailsAsync()* method of the billing client. This will require that we also add the *onProductDetailsResponse()* callback method, where we will check that the product exists, extract the product name, and display it on the status TextView. Now that we have obtained the product details, we can also safely enable the buy button. Within the *MainActivity.kt* file, add the *queryProduct()* method so that it reads as follows:

```
.
.
import com.android.billingclient.api.QueryProductDetailsParams.Product
import com.google.common.collect.ImmutableList
.
.
private fun queryProduct(productId: String) {
    val queryProductDetailsParams = QueryProductDetailsParams.newBuilder()
        .setProductList(
            ImmutableList.of(
                Product.newBuilder()
                    .setProductId(productId)
                    .setProductType(
                        BillingClient.ProductType.INAPP
                    )
                    .build()
            )
        )
        .build()
```

```
    billingClient.queryProductDetailsAsync(
        queryProductDetailsParams
    ) { billingResult: BillingResult?, productDetailsResult:
                                     QueryProductDetailsResult? ->
        val queriedProductDetailsList = productDetailsResult?.productDetailsList
        if (!queriedProductDetailsList.isNullOrEmpty()) {
            productDetails = queriedProductDetailsList[0]
            runOnUiThread {
                binding.buyButton.isEnabled = true
                binding.statusText.text = productDetails.name
            }
        } else {
            Log.i(TAG, "onProductDetailsResponse: No products.")
        }
    }
}
```

Much of the code used here should be familiar from the previous chapter. The listener code checks that at least one product matches the query criteria. The ProductDetails object is then extracted from the first matching product, stored in the *productDetails* variable, and the product name property is displayed on the TextView.

One point of note is that when we display the product name on the status TextView, we do so by calling *runOnUiThread()*. This is necessary because the listener is not running on the main thread, so it cannot safely make direct changes to the user interface. The *runOnUiThread()* method provides a quick and convenient way to execute code on the main thread.

81.10 Launching the Purchase Flow

When the user clicks the buy button, *makePurchase()* will be called to start the purchase process. We can now add this method as follows:

```
.
.
import com.android.billingclient.api.BillingFlowParams.ProductDetailsParams
import android.view.View
.
.
fun makePurchase(view: View?) {
    val billingFlowParams = BillingFlowParams.newBuilder()
        .setProductDetailsParamsList(
            ImmutableList.of(
                ProductDetailsParams.newBuilder()
                    .setProductDetails(productDetails)
                    .build()
            )
        )
        .build()

    billingClient.launchBillingFlow(this, billingFlowParams)
```

```
}
```

81.11 Handling Purchase Updates

The results of the purchase process will be reported to the app via the PurchaseUpdatedListener assigned to the billing client during the initialization phase. Add this handler now as follows:

```
private val purchasesUpdatedListener =
    PurchasesUpdatedListener { billingResult, purchases ->
        if (billingResult.responseCode ==
            BillingClient.BillingResponseCode.OK
            && purchases != null
        ) {
            for (purchase in purchases) {
                completePurchase(purchase)
            }
        } else if (billingResult.responseCode ==
            BillingClient.BillingResponseCode.USER_CANCELED
        ) {
            Log.i(TAG, "onPurchasesUpdated: Purchase Canceled")
        } else {
            Log.i(TAG, "onPurchasesUpdated: Error")
        }
    }
```

The handler will output log messages if the user cancels the purchase or another error occurs. However, a successful purchase results in a call to the *completePurchase()* method, which is passed the current Purchase object. Add this method as outlined below:

```
private fun completePurchase(item: Purchase) {
    purchase = item
    if (purchase.purchaseState == Purchase.PurchaseState.PURCHASED) {
        runOnUiThread {
            binding.consumeButton.isEnabled = true
            binding.statusText.text = "Purchase Complete"
            binding.buyButton.isEnabled = false
        }
    }
}
```

This method stores the purchase before verifying that the product has indeed been purchased and that payment is not still pending. The "consume" button is enabled, and the user is notified of the successful purchase. The buy button is also disabled to prevent the user from repurchasing before consuming the purchase.

81.12 Consuming the Product

With the user now able to click on the "consume" button, the next step is to ensure the product is consumed so that only one click can be performed before another button click is purchased. This requires that we now write the *consumePurchase()* method:

```
.
.
```

```
import kotlinx.coroutines.*
.
.
class MainActivity : AppCompatActivity() {

    private val coroutineScope = CoroutineScope(Dispatchers.IO)
.
.
    fun consumePurchase(view: View?) {

        val consumeParams = ConsumeParams.newBuilder()
            .setPurchaseToken(purchase.purchaseToken)
            .build()

         coroutineScope.launch {
            val result = billingClient.consumePurchase(consumeParams)
            if (result.billingResult.responseCode ==
                     BillingClient.BillingResponseCode.OK) {
                runOnUiThread() {
                    binding.consumeButton.isEnabled = false
                    binding.statusText.text = "Purchase consumed"
                    binding.buyButton.isEnabled = true
                }
            }
        }
    }
.
.
```

This method creates a ConsumeParams instance and configures it with the purchase token for the current purchase (obtained from the Purchase object previously saved in the *completePurchase()* method). This is passed to the *consumePurchase()* method, which is launched within a coroutine using the IO dispatcher. If the product is successfully consumed, code is executed in the main thread to disable the consume button, enable the buy button, and update the status text.

81.13 Restoring a Previous Purchase

With the code added so far, we can purchase and consume a product within a single session. If we were to make a purchase and exit the app before consuming it, the purchase would be lost when the app restarts. We can solve this problem by configuring a QueryPurchasesParams instance to search for the unconsumed In-App product and passing it to the *queryPurchasesAsync()* method of the billing client together with a reference to a listener that will be called with the results. Add a new function and the listener to the *MainActivity.kt* file as follows:

```
private fun reloadPurchase() {

    val queryPurchasesParams = QueryPurchasesParams.newBuilder()
        .setProductType(BillingClient.ProductType.INAPP)
        .build()
```

```
    billingClient.queryPurchasesAsync(
        queryPurchasesParams,
            purchasesListener
    )
}

private val purchasesListener =
    PurchasesResponseListener { billingResult, purchases ->
        if (purchases.isNotEmpty()) {
            purchase = purchases.first()
            binding.consumeButton.isEnabled = true
            binding.buyButton.isEnabled = false
        } else {
            binding.consumeButton.isEnabled = false
        }
    }
```

If the list of purchases passed to the listener is not empty, the first purchase in the list is assigned to the *purchase* variable, and the consume button is enabled (in a more complete implementation, code should be added to check this is the correct product by comparing the product id and to handle the return of multiple purchases). If no purchases are found, the consume button is disabled until another purchase is made. All that remains is to call our new *reloadPurchase()* method during the billing setup process as follows:

```
private fun billingSetup() {
.
.
            if (billingResult.responseCode ==
                BillingClient.BillingResponseCode.OK
            ) {
                Log.i(TAG, "OnBillingSetupFinish connected")
                queryProduct(demo_product)
                reloadPurchase()
            } else {
                Log.i(TAG, "OnBillingSetupFinish failed")
            }
.
.
}
```

81.14 Testing the app

Before we can test the app we need to upload this latest version to the Play Console. As we already have version 1 uploaded, we first need to increase the version number in the *build.gradle.kts (Module: app)* file:

```
.
.
defaultConfig {
    applicationId "com.ebookfrenzy.inapppurchase"
    minSdk 26
```

```
    targetSdk 36
    versionCode 2
    versionName "2.0"
.
.
```

Sync the build configuration, then follow the steps in the *"Creating, Testing, and Uploading an Android App Bundle"* chapter to generate a new app bundle, upload it to the internal test track, and roll it out to the testers. Next, using the internal testing link, install the app on a device or emulator where one of the test accounts is signed in. To locate the testing link, select the app in the Google Play Console and choose the Internal testing option from the navigation panel followed by the Testers tab, as shown in Figure 81-7:

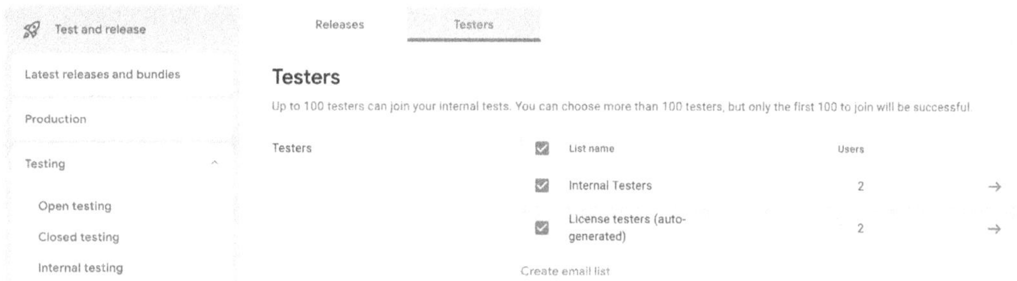

Figure 81-7

Scroll to the "How testers join your test" section of the screen and click on *Copy link*:

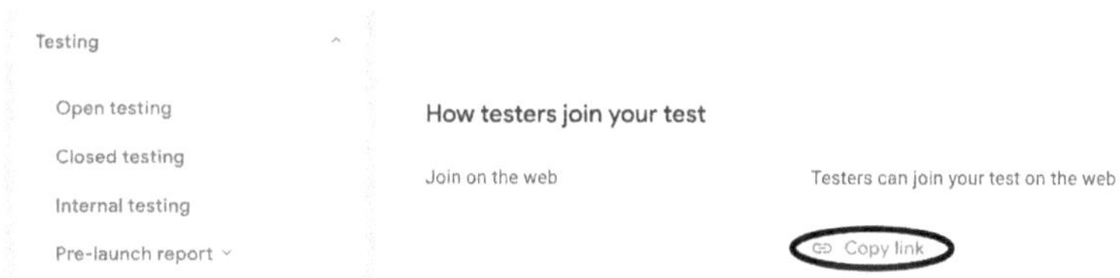

Figure 81-8

Open the Chrome browser on the testing device or emulator, enter the testing link, and follow the instructions to install the app from the Play Store. After the app starts, the user interface should appear as shown in Figure 81-9 below with the billing client connected, the product name displayed, and the Purchase button enabled:

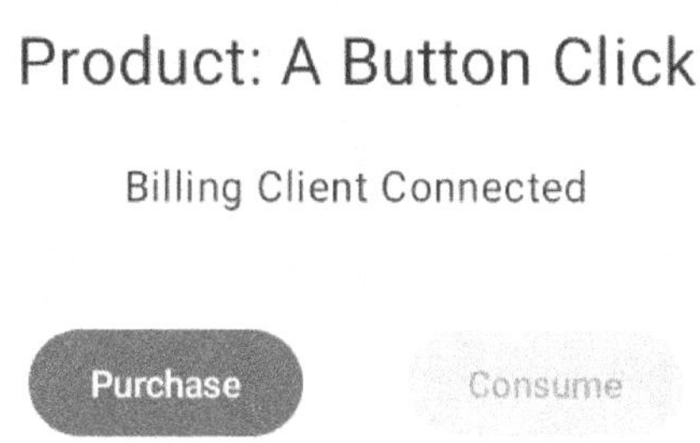

Figure 81-9

Clicking the Purchase button will begin the purchase flow as shown in Figure 81-10:

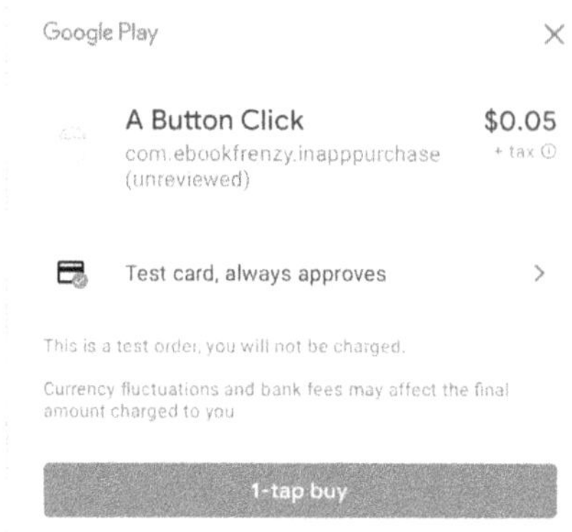

Figure 81-10

Tap the buy button to complete the purchase using the test card and wait for the Consume button to be enabled.

Tap the Consume button and wait for the "Purchase Consumed" status message to appear. With the product consumed, it should now be possible to purchase it again. Make another purchase, then terminate and restart the app. The app should locate the previous unconsumed purchase and enable the consume button.

81.15 Troubleshooting

If you encounter problems with the purchase, make sure the device is attached to Android Studio via a USB cable or WiFi, and select it from within the Logcat panel. Enter InAppPurchaseTag into the Logcat search bar and check the diagnostic output, adding additional Log calls in the code if necessary. For additional information about failures, a useful trick is to access the debug message from BillingResult instances, for example:

```
.
.
} else if (billingResult.responseCode ==
    BillingClient.BillingResponseCode.USER_CANCELED
) {
    Log.i(TAG, "onPurchasesUpdated: Purchase Canceled")
} else {
    Log.i(TAG, billingResult.getDebugMessage())
}
```

Note that as long as you leave the app version number unchanged in the module-level *build.gradle.kts* file, you should now be able to run modified versions of the app directly on the device or emulator without having to re-bundle and upload it to the console.

If the test payment card is not listed, ensure the device user account has been added to the license testers list. If the app is running on a physical device, try it on an emulator. If all else fails, you can enter a valid payment method to make test purchases and then refund yourself using the Order Management screen accessible from the Play Console home page.

81.16 Summary

In this chapter, we created a project demonstrating adding an in-app product to an Android app. This included the creation of the product within the Google Play Console and writing code to initialize and connect to the billing client, querying available products, and purchasing and consuming the product. We also explained how to add license testers using the Play Console to make purchases during testing without spending money.

82. Integrating Gemini AI into Android Apps

As artificial intelligence becomes an increasingly integral part of our personal and professional lives, the inevitable question arises of whether to integrate it into the apps we develop. The answer, of course, depends on the type of app, but as the capabilities of AI continue to evolve and improve, it is likely that most apps will eventually utilize AI to some degree. As a company at the forefront of AI research and development, it should come as no surprise that Google has introduced an impressive set of tools, APIs, and frameworks for directly integrating AI capabilities into Android apps. This chapter provides an overview of how to utilize these services to integrate AI into your own applications.

82.1 Gemini models

From the perspective of an Android developer, the two main components for integrating AI capabilities into an app are the AI model and an application programming interface (API) that interacts with it. Gemini provides multiple models, each tailored to specific requirements. Though the capabilities of each model can change between versions, they are currently categorized as follows:

- **Gemini Pro** - The most powerful AI model for generating fast and accurate text responses to image, audio, video, and text inputs. Gemini Pro is best suited for solving complex problems or those involving large data volumes.
- **Gemini Flash** - A cost-efficient model for generating text results in response to image, audio, video, and text inputs.
- **Gemini Flash Live** - This model implements live interaction with Gemini and provides text and audio responses to text, video, and audio inputs.
- **Nano Banana** - Models designed to generate and edit images based on text descriptions.
- **Veo** - Generates video content in response to text and image inputs.

For detailed information on the latest models and their capabilities, refer to the following web page:

https://ai.google.dev/gemini-api/docs/models

82.2 Firebase AI Logic and Gemini API providers

To access Gemini AI features from within an Android app, we integrate the Firebase AI Logic client SDK libraries and use them to interact with your choice of Gemini *API provider* (also called the *generative backend*). Gemini currently supports the following API providers:

- **Gemini Developer API** - The Gemini Developer API provides free access to many Gemini AI features (subject to quota limitations). Access to paid features, such as image generation, is charged on a pay-as-you-go basis and requires a Google Cloud Billing account.
- **Gemini Enterprise Agent Platform** - Used to build and deploy enterprise-level autonomous AI agents.

Integrating an Android Studio project with Firebase and enabling the provider APIs is a multi-step process covered in detail beginning with the *"Preparing the Gemini Firebase AI Logic Project"* chapter. Once an app is integrated, it can access all of Gemini AI's features, including text prompts, video analysis, and image generation.

82.3 Initializing AI models

Regardless of the API, the first step in integrating Gemini AI into an Android app is initializing the generative model. This is a two-step process beginning with the creation of a FirebaseAI instance configured for provider API selection. The following code, for example, creates a FirebaseAI instance based on the Gemini Developer API:

```
val firebaseAI = Firebase.ai(backend = GenerativeBackend.googleAI())
```

The *generativeModel()* method of the FirebaseAI instance is then called to create the GenerativeModel instance, passing as an argument the name of the required model:

```
val generativeModel = firebaseAI
        .generativeModel("gemini-flash-latest")
```

In practice, the above steps are generally performed in a single statement, for example:

```
val generativeModel = Firebase.ai(backend = GenerativeBackend.googleAI())
        .generativeModel(modelName = "gemini-flash-latest")
```

Once a generative model has been initialized, it is ready to receive input and generate content. Before exploring content output generation, we first need to understand how the input content is packaged.

82.4 Multi-modal content

When working with Gemini AI, there are two categories of content: *input content* and *output content*. Input content refers to the data sent to the generative model, including elements such as text, images, documents, video, and data. The model uses this data to generate the output content (text, images, videos, etc.).

The input content can be as simple as a single text string containing a question or instruction. For more complex requests, Gemini also supports *multi-modal* input content. This means a single request to generate content can include multiple input values of varying types. For example, the input content of a generative request could include an image and a text prompt referencing the image. A user might upload an image of a vintage car and ask Gemini to identify its make and model, or upload a video and ask for a transcript.

Multi-modal input content is packaged into a Content object before it is passed to the model. Content objects can be created using the *Content.Builder()* method, but a more efficient option is to use the Kotlin Domain Specific Language (DSL) builder *content {}* block provided by the Gemini API. For example, a Content object containing image, video, and text inputs might be declared as follows:

```
val input = content {
    image(bitmap)
    inlineData(bytes, "video/mp4")
    text(prompt)
}
```

82.5 Generating content

Once the model has been initialized and the input content is ready, the next step is to send the request to the model for processing. This involves calling a generation method, such as *generateContent()*, on the model and waiting for a response. The response is returned as a GenerateContentResponse object from which the output content can be retrieved.

It can take a while for the model to return the output content, and requests may throw errors. Therefore, content generation calls should be performed in a coroutine and include error handling. The following code, for example, calls the *generateContent()* model method and handles the response:

```
scope.launch(Dispatchers.IO) {

    val prompt = content {
        // define input content
    }

    try {
        val response = model.generateContent(prompt)
        response.text?.let { outputContent ->
            // handle output content
        }
    } catch (e: Exception) {
        // handle errors
    }
}
```

The *generateContent()* method generates content as a single response and is one of several content generation methods. For example, the *generateContentStream()* method returns the response as a stream that is updated as more content is generated. This is useful for displaying early sections of the response while the model continues to process the remaining content, for example, while analyzing a long video. The model produces the stream as a Kotlin flow, the content of which can be collected in the method lambda, for example:

```
val prompt = content {
    // define input content
}

model.generateContentStream(prompt)
        .collect { responseBlock ->
    // handle output content stream
}
```

82.6 Starting a chat session

The options we have covered so far do not retain context between individual content generation requests. Consider, for example, the following Gemini AI interaction:

Question: *"Who were the first mountaineers to reach the summit of Mount Everest?"*

Response: *"The first mountaineers to reach the summit of Mount Everest were Sir Edmund Hilary and Tenzing Norgay. They reached the summit on May 29, 1953."*

Question: *"How old were they?"*

Response: *"Please provide context! I need to know who "they" refers to in order to tell you their age."*

From the transcript, we can see that Gemini has not retained the context from the first question when asked to elaborate on the previous answer. To maintain context between inputs, we must initiate a chat session with the model. Chat sessions are created by calling the *startChat()* method of the generative model, which returns a Chat object. Input content is sent to the model by calling the Chat object's *sendMessage()* method, and the output content is returned as a GenerateContentResponse object, as shown in the code below:

```
val chat = model.startChat()

val prompt = content {
    // define input content
}

val response = chat.sendMessage(prompt)

response.text?.let { outputContent ->
    // handle output content
}
```

With chat enabled, the previous questions would generate output similar to the following:

Question: *"Who were the first mountaineers to reach the summit of Mount Everest?"*

Response: *"The first mountaineers to reach the summit of Mount Everest were Sir Edmund Hilary and Tenzing Norgay. They reached the summit on May 29, 1953."*

Question: *"How old were they?"*

Response: *"Edmund Hilary was 33 years old when he reached the summit of Everest. Tenzing Norgay was approximately 39 years when he reached the summit of Everest. His exact birth date is unknown, so his age is an approximation."*

82.7 Image Generation

Image generation is provided by the Gemini AI image models (currently called Nano Banana), which generate and edit images based on text descriptions. An example statement to initialize a Gemini image model is as follows:

```
val imageModel = Firebase.ai(backend = GenerativeBackend.googleAI())
                     .generativeModel(modelName = "gemini-3.1-flash-image")
```

The above statement creates an image model with the default configuration settings. However, the Gemini image models include several configuration options that can be defined during initialization using the following syntax:

```
private val imageModel =
    Firebase.ai(
        backend = GenerativeBackend.googleAI()
    ).generativeModel(
        modelName = "gemini-3.1-flash-image",
        safetySettings = listOf(
            SafetySetting(HarmCategory.HARASSMENT, HarmBlockThreshold.ONLY_HIGH)
        ),
        generationConfig = generationConfig {
            responseModalities = listOf(ResponseModality.IMAGE)

            imageConfig = imageConfig {
                aspectRatio = AspectRatio.LANDSCAPE_4x3
                imageSize = ImageSize.SIZE_1K
            }
```

```
        }
    )
```

The model is created by calling the API provider's *generativeModel()* method, which requires the model name, as well as optional GenerationConfig and SafetySettings list objects.

Once the model is created and initialized, content is generated by passing the prompt text to the model's *generateContent()* method:

```
viewModelScope.launch(Dispatchers.IO) {

    try {
        val response = imageModel.generateContent(prompt)

        // extract images from response
    } catch (e: Exception) {
        // Handle error (typically, generation was blocked by a filter)
    }
}
```

The response returned by the Gemini model can contain one or more candidate responses. Each candidate contains a Content object, which in turn contains a list of Part objects representing the different types of content generated by the model, such as text or images. The following statement navigates this hierarchy to retrieve the first image generated by the model:

```
val image = response.candidates
    .firstOrNull()
    ?.content
    ?.parts
    ?.filterIsInstance<ImagePart>()
    ?.firstOrNull()
    ?.image
```

The expression begins by calling *firstOrNull()* on the candidates list to retrieve the first candidate response. If no candidates were returned, *firstOrNull()* returns *null* instead of throwing an exception. The safe call operator (?.) is then used throughout the remainder of the expression so that, if any step returns *null*, evaluation stops and the entire expression evaluates to *null*.

Next, the code accesses the candidate's content property and then its parts collection. Since a response may contain different types of content, *filterIsInstance<ImagePart>()* creates a new list containing only those parts that represent images. The subsequent call to *firstOrNull()* retrieves the first image part, if one exists, and the final *.image* property extracts the Bitmap object. If the response contains no image, the image variable is simply assigned *null*.

82.8 Summary

Google offers tools and APIs for integrating AI into Android apps, including Gemini models for text, image, and video generation. To access Gemini AI, apps must be integrated with Firebase and use the Firebase Logic AI client SDKs to access the Gemini API providers.

The input content sent to the model can be either a single text prompt or multi-modal values of mixed types packaged into a Content object. The *generateContent()* method generates content as a single response, while *generateContentStream()* returns it as a stream for incremental processing. By default, Gemini does not retain context between requests. To maintain context, a chat session must be initiated with the model using the *startChat()* and *sendMessage()* methods. Image generation is provided by the Gemini image models and generated using the *generateContent()* method.

Chapter 83

83. Preparing the Gemini Firebase AI Logic Project

The previous chapter provided a high-level overview of Gemini AI in the context of Android app development. In this chapter and those that follow, we will use an example project to learn about the Gemini Developer API and explore Gemini AI features, including image generation and video analysis.

Upon completion, the example app will comprise three screens, each showcasing a distinct Gemini AI feature. This chapter covers the initial project setup, including accessing Google Cloud and AI Studio accounts, and enabling the Gemini Developer API in the Firebase console.

83.1 Opening the GeminiDemo starter project

To save time, we will use a starter project containing the screen layouts and navigation logic and extend it to include the Gemini AI features. If you have not already done so, download the project source code using the following link:

https://www.payloadbooks.com/product/quailkotlin

Within the sample code folder, make a copy of the "GeminiDemo_start" folder and name it "GeminiDemo", then start Android Studio and open the GeminiDemo project folder.

The project includes a navigation bar, three screen fragments, and a view model. The majority of the Gemini AI integration will take place within the GeminiViewModel class, which utilizes LiveData to update the user interface with responses from the generative model.

Run the GeminiDemo app and navigate through the screens, including options to select images and videos from your Photo library. If you are using an emulator, instructions for adding images and videos to the library will be provided later.

83.2 Creating a Google Cloud account

The Gemini AI projects you create will be stored and managed in your Google Cloud account. If you do not already have an account, you can set one up for free using the following link:

https://cloud.google.com/

During registration, you may need to enter a payment method, such as a credit card. This is used solely to verify your identity, and you will not be charged unless you start using the billable services covered in later chapters.

83.3 Generating the Gemini API key

Apps that use the Gemini APIs must be authenticated using an API key generated using Google AI Studio. Open a browser window and use the following URL to access the AI Studio dashboard:

https://aistudio.google.com

Sign in using your Google Cloud account credentials and accept the terms of service if prompted. When the dialog shown in Figure 83-1 appears, select the Get API key option:

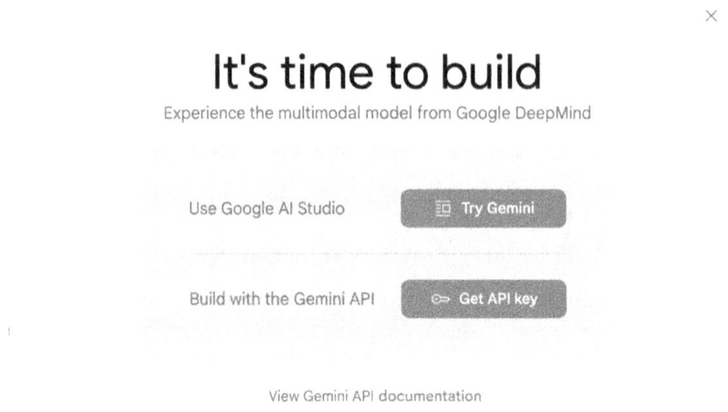

Figure 83-1

If you already have a Google Cloud project set up for working with Gemini, locate and select it using the search field (A) in the dialog below and click button B . Alternatively, if you click the "Create API key in new project" button (C), AI Studio will create a Google Cloud project for you named "Gemini API":

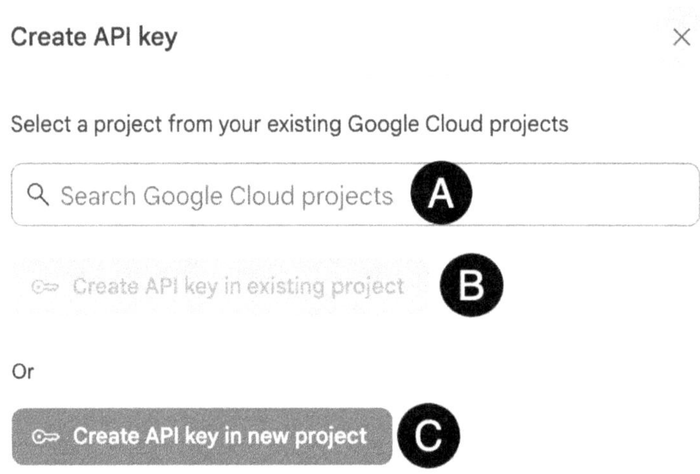

Figure 83-2

Once the key has been generated, it will appear in the dialog shown in Figure 83-3. We do not need to copy the key, so close the dialog:

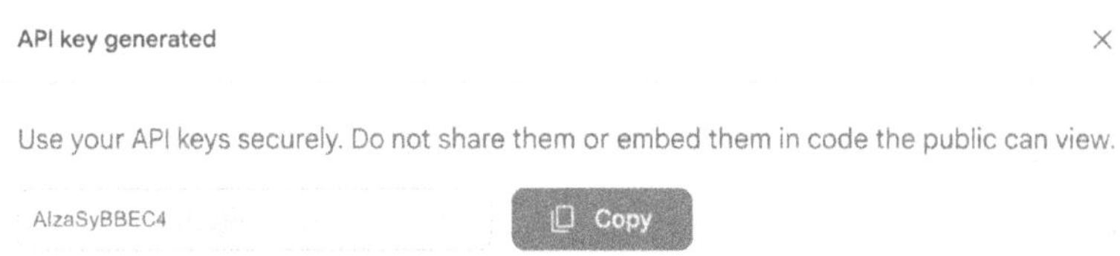

Figure 83-3

A list of your API keys is available on AI Studio's API Keys screen (*https://aistudio.google.com/api-keys*):

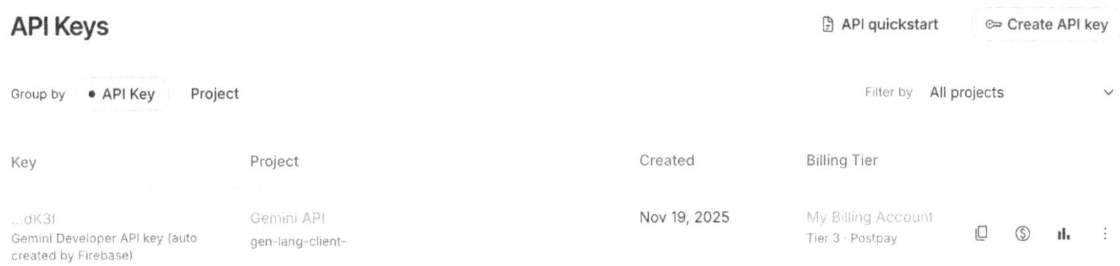

Figure 83-4

83.4 Adding the Google Cloud project to Firebase

When we generated the API key previously, AI Studio created a Google Cloud project named "Gemini API." This project must be connected to Firebase before the Gemini APIs can be enabled. Open a browser window and navigate to the Firebase console at the following URL:

https://console.firebase.google.com/

Within the console, select the option to create a new Firebase project:

Figure 83-5

On the project creation screen, locate and click the "Add Firebase to Google Cloud project" link, as highlighted in Figure 83-6:

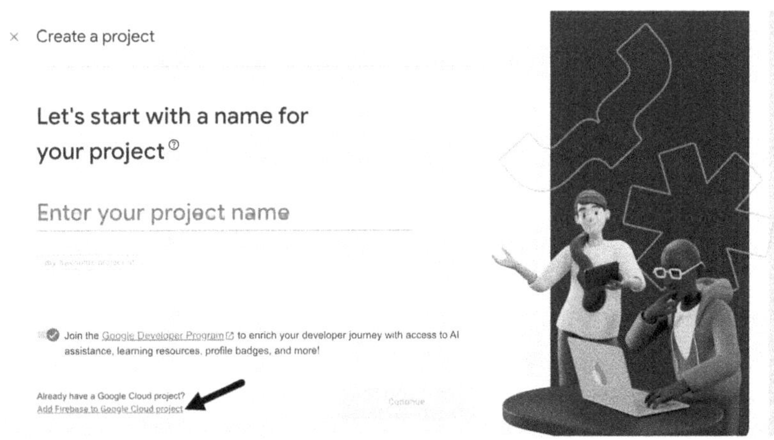

Figure 83-6

On the next screen, select your "Gemini API" project from the drop-down menu before clicking the Continue button:

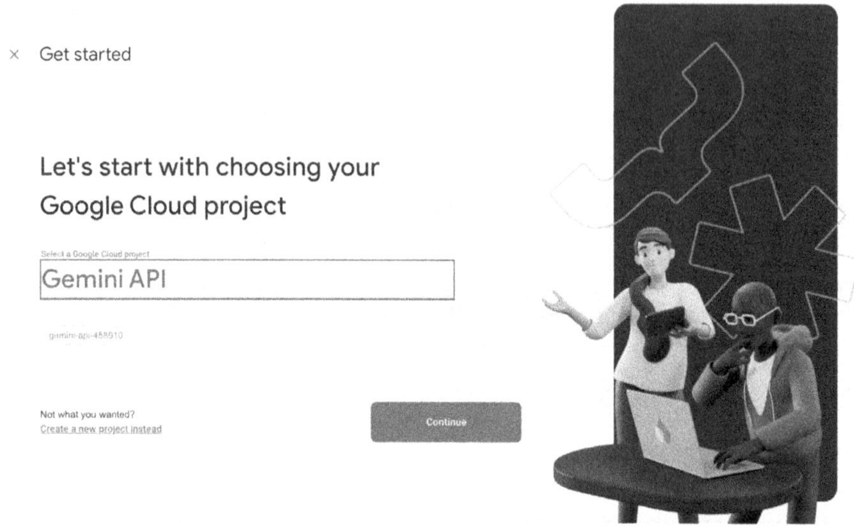

Figure 83-7

Proceed through the screens, disabling Google Analytics when prompted (they won't be used in this example), and clicking the Add Firebase button on the final screen. Once the integration process is complete, the screen shown in Figure 83-8 will appear:

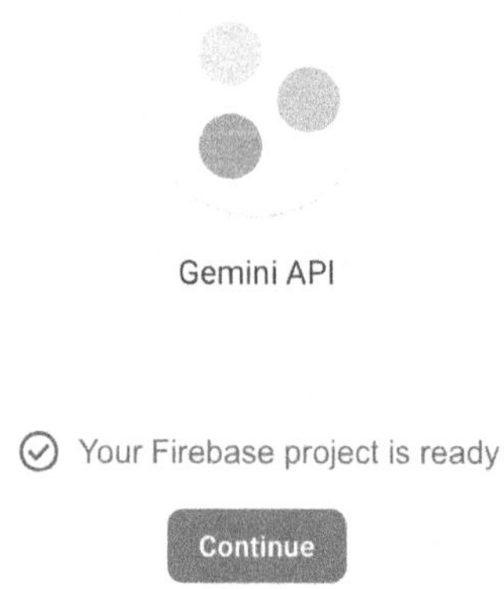

Figure 83-8

Click Continue to return to the Firebase console.

83.5 Registering the app with Firebase

Now that the Google Cloud project is integrated with Firebase, the next step is registering the GeminiDemo app. In the Firebase console, use the menu marked A in Figure 83-9 to select the Gemini API project, then click the Add App button (B) to begin registering the app:

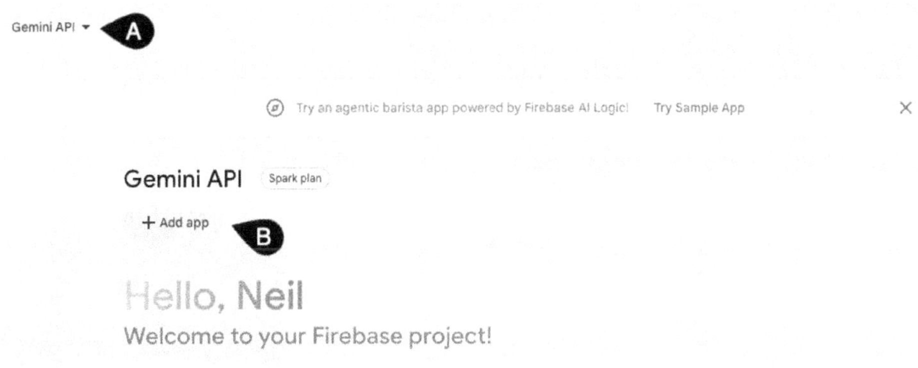

Figure 83-9

When prompted, select the Android option from the platform selection list:

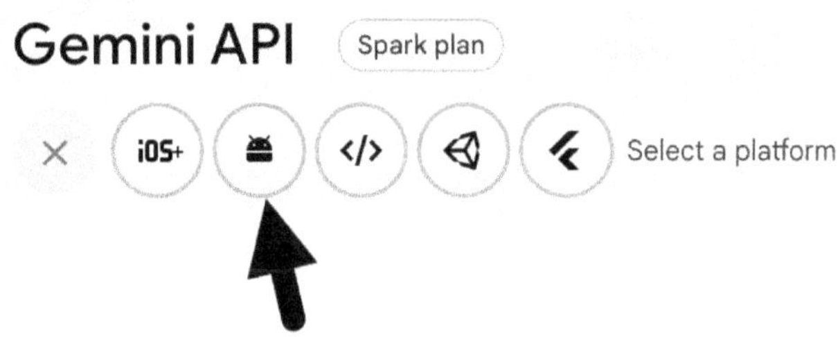

Figure 83-10

The app registration screen will take you through several steps, beginning with entering the app's package name (*com.example.geminidemo*) and an optional nickname (for example, "Gemini Demo").

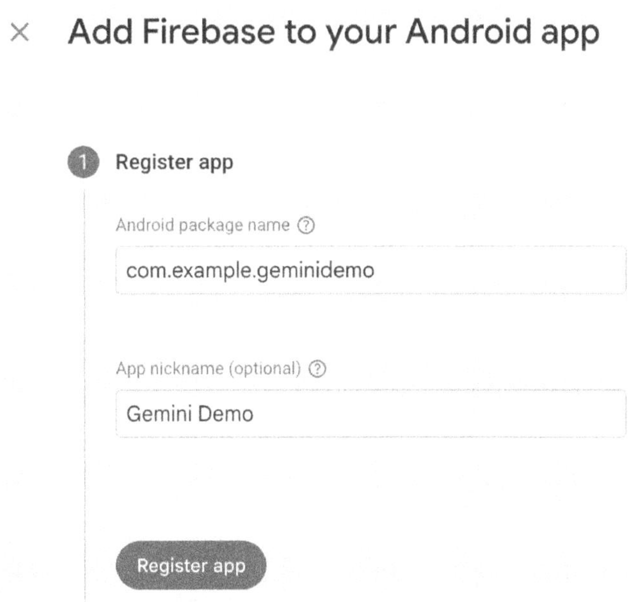

Figure 83-11

After entering the information, click the "Register app" button. The next step is to download the Google Services file and include it in the Android Studio project. This JSON file contains the project ID and API keys for each registered app. Click to download the file and save it for later:

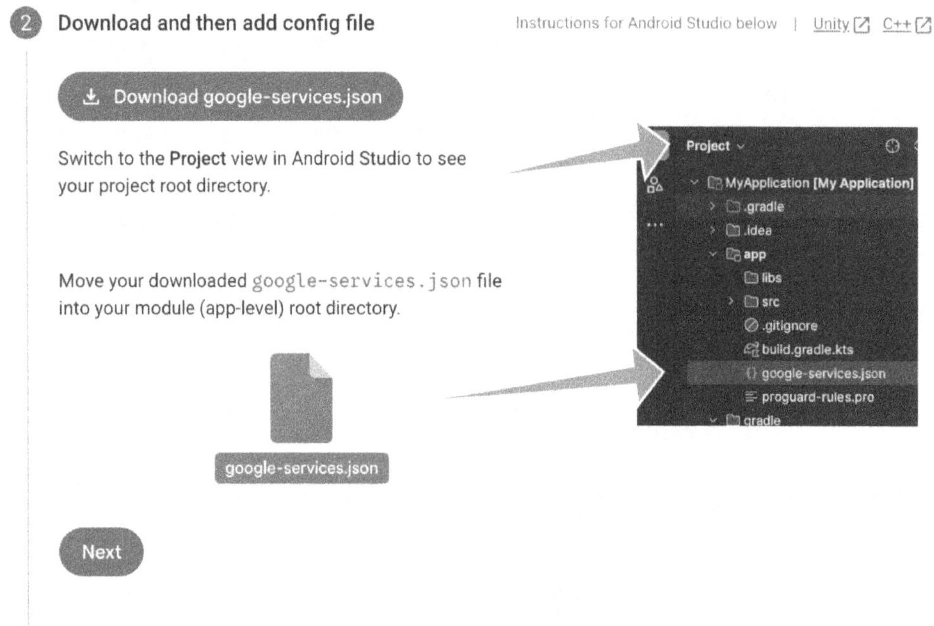

Figure 83-12

The third step outlines the changes required to the Android Studio build configuration. We will cover this later, so click Next, followed by the "Continue to console" button:

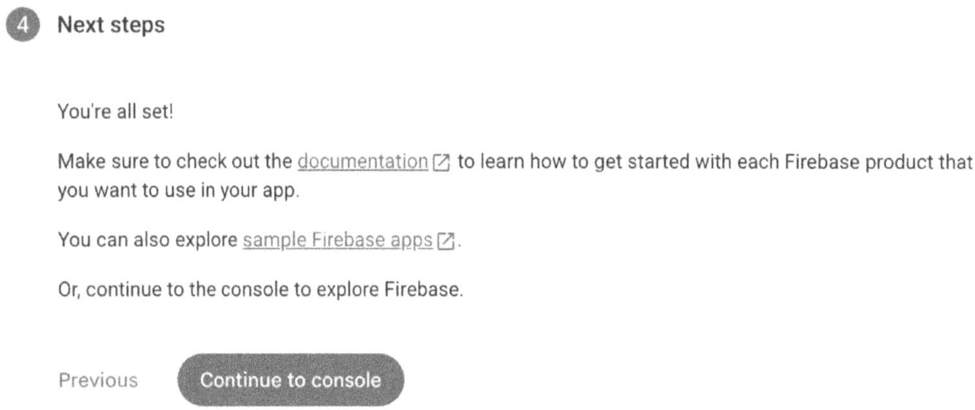

Figure 83-13

83.6 Enabling the Gemini API provider

Before using Gemini to generate content, we must enable the Gemini Developer API for the project within the Firebase console. Open the Firebase console, select the Gemini API project from the menu marked A in Figure 83-14, select the AI Logic entry in the navigation panel (B), followed by the Get Started button (C):

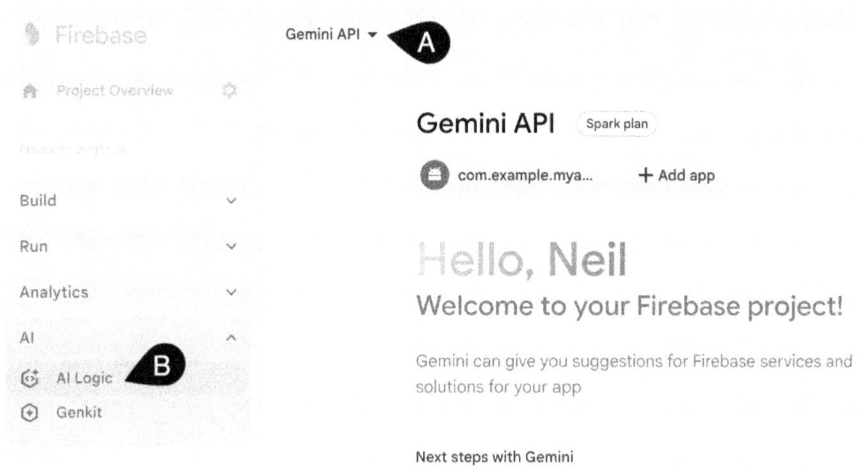

Figure 83-14

On the provider selection screen, click the "Get started with this API" button located in the Gemini Developer API box:

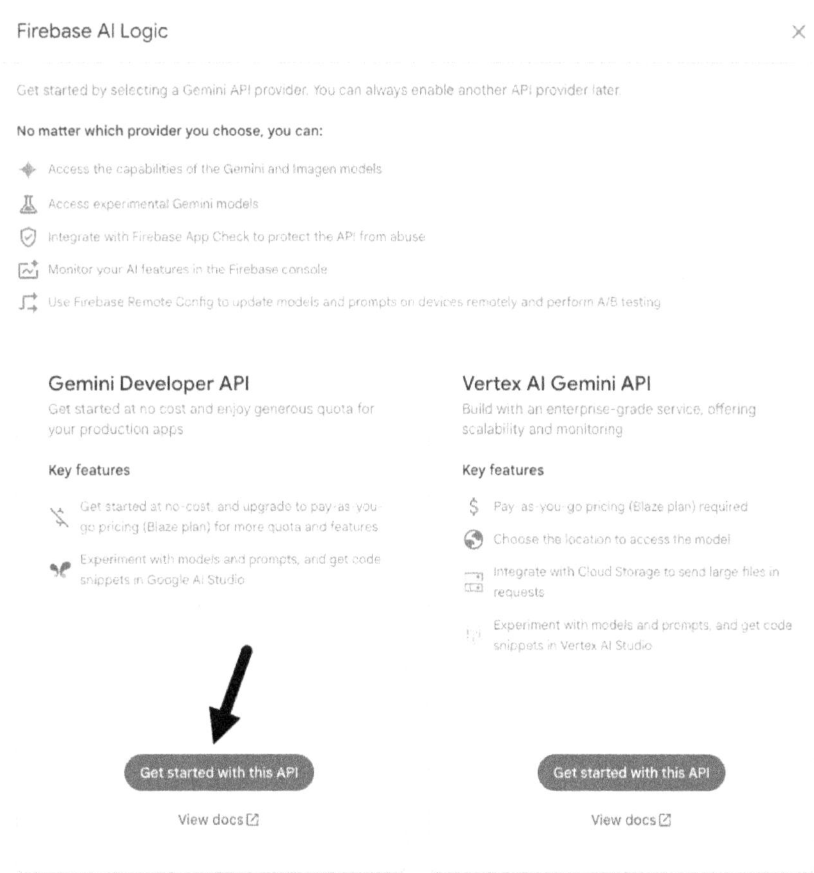

Figure 83-15

Once the API is enabled, click Continue to display the list of enabled apps. To review or change the provider selection, click on the Settings tab highlighted in Figure 83-16, keeping in mind that the Gemini Developer and Vertex AI APIs can be enabled simultaneously:

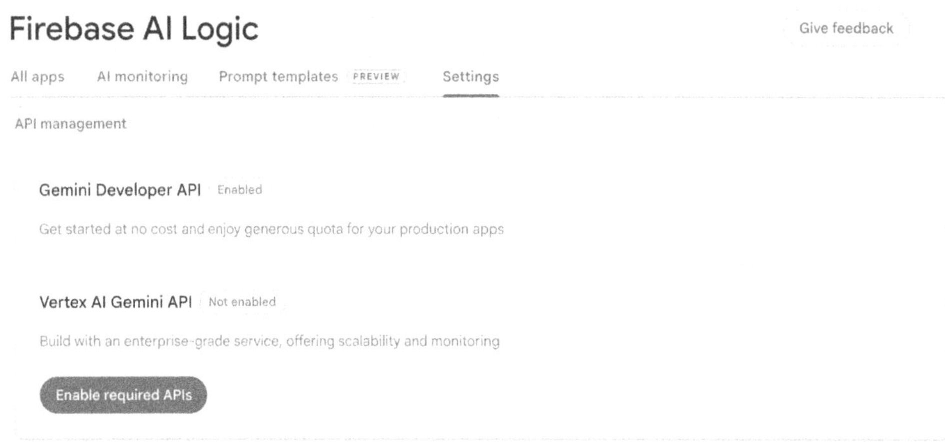

Figure 83-16

83.7 Adding the JSON services file

We are now ready to add the previously downloaded *google-services.json* file to the project build configuration. With the GeminiDemo project loaded in Android Studio, switch the Project tool window to Project mode using the menu shown in Figure 83-17 below:

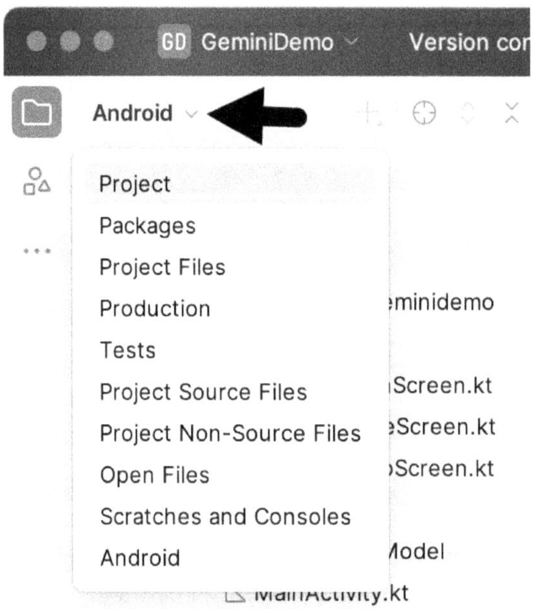

Figure 83-17

Open the file system browser for your operating system, navigate to the location where you saved the *google-services.json* file, and drag it onto the *app* folder in the Project tool window:

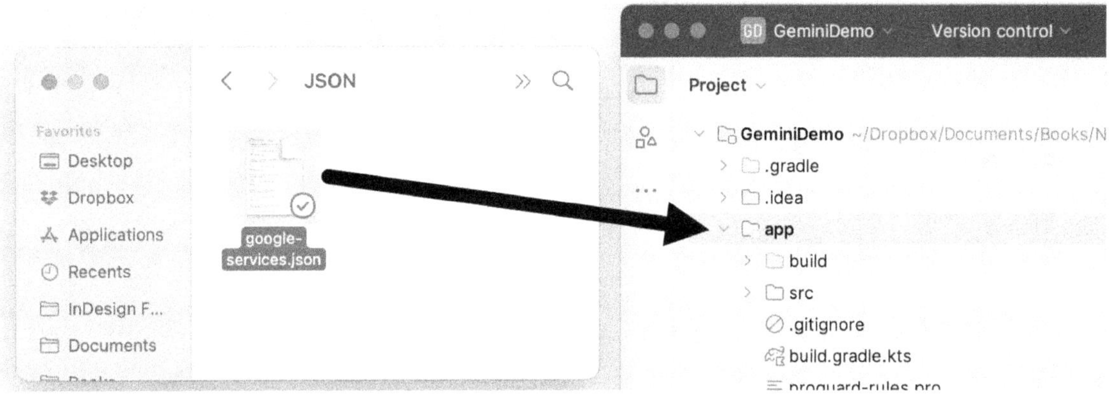

Figure 83-18

When the *app* folder highlights, release the mouse button to drop the file into position:

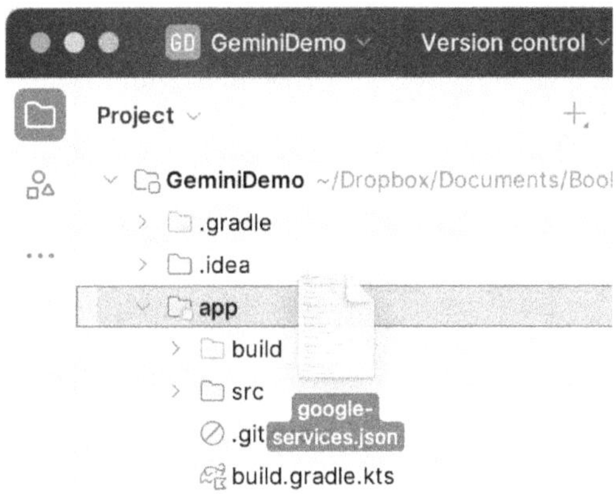

Figure 83-19

Once it has been added, the location of the file in the *app* folder must match that shown below:

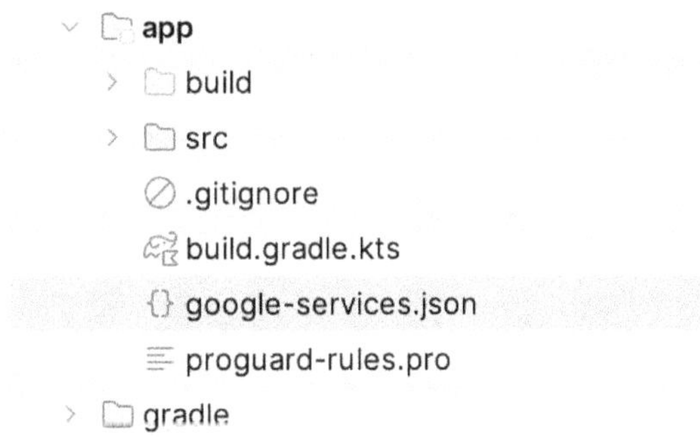

Figure 83-20

Click and drag the file within the tool window to reposition it if necessary, then revert the Project tool window to Android mode using the menu in Figure 83-17 above.

83.8 Adding libraries

Libraries and plugin dependencies must be added to the project before we can start writing code. These include the Firebase, AI Logic, image handling, and navigation libraries. First, modify the *Gradle Scripts -> libs.versions.*

toml file as follows:

```
[versions]
.
.
firebaseBom = "34.17.0"

[libraries]
.
.
firebase-bom = { module = "com.google.firebase:firebase-bom", version.ref =
"firebaseBom" }
google-firebase-ai = { module = "com.google.firebase:firebase-ai" }
.
.
```

Synchronize the project, then add plugins and corresponding library dependencies to the module-level Gradle build file (*Gradle Scripts -> build.gradle.kts (Module: app)*). Also, make sure the *compileSdk* and *targetSdk* values are set to API 37 or later:

```
plugins {
.
.
    id("com.google.gms.google-services")
}

android {
.
.
    compileSdk {
        version = release(37)
    }

    defaultConfig {
        applicationId = "com.ebookfrenzy.geminidemo"
        minSdk = 26
        targetSdk = 37
.
.
dependencies {
    implementation(platform(libs.firebase.bom))
    implementation(libs.google.firebase.ai)
.
.
```

Edit the project-level *build.gradle.kts* file and modify it as follows before synchronizing the project:

```
plugins {
.
```

```
.
    id("com.google.gms.google-services") version "4.5.0" apply false
}
```

83.9 Initializing the generative model

Edit the *GeminiViewModel.kt* file and make the following modifications to declare the generative model and use it to initialize a generative futures instance. For this example, we will use the Gemini 2.5 Flash model:

```
.
.
import com.google.firebase.Firebase
import com.google.firebase.ai.ai
import com.google.firebase.ai.type.GenerativeBackend

class GeminiViewModel: ViewModel() {
.
.
    val generatedImage: StateFlow<Bitmap?> = _generatedImage.asStateFlow()

    private val generativeModel =
        Firebase.ai(backend = GenerativeBackend.googleAI())
            .generativeModel(modelName = "gemini-flash-latest")
.
.
```

With the above steps completed, the project is ready for us to begin implementing the Gemini AI features.

83.10 Summary

In this chapter, we prepared an Android app project to integrate with the Gemini Developer API. These steps included creating a Google Cloud account and using Google AI Studio to generate an API key, which is required to authenticate the app. We then used the Firebase console to register the app and enable the Gemini Developer API provider. Finally, the chapter detailed the initialization of a generative model.

Chapter 84

84. A Gemini AI Tutorial

Now that the preparation stage is complete, work can begin on the first screen of the GeminiDemo project. The Text + Image screen will integrate AI capabilities using the Gemini Developer API to allow the user to interact with Gemini by entering text prompts and uploading images for analysis.

84.1 Opening the GeminiDemo project

If you are reading the AI chapters sequentially, launch Android Studio and open the GeminiDemo project from the previous chapter. Alternatively, open the *GeminiDemo_step1* project from the source code samples download. If you have not already done so, you can download the sample code using the following link:

https://www.payloadbooks.com/product/quailkotlin

Before proceeding, follow the steps in the *"Preparing the Gemini Firebase AI Logic Project"* chapter to add your *google-services.json* file to the project.

84.2 Getting started

The first step is to test that images are available in the photo library for testing the Gemini API code we will add later. Launch Android Studio and run the app on a device or emulator. With the "Text + Image" screen displayed, click the Select a Photo button to test that the visual media picker activity appears:

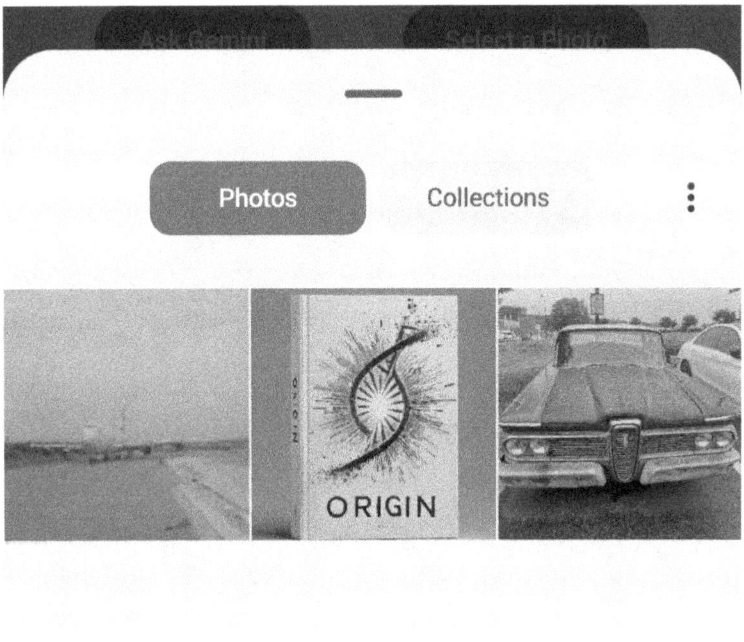

Figure 84-1

If you are using an emulator, the photo library may be empty. To add photos, drag and drop them from the host computer onto the emulator home screen. Next, open the Files app in the emulator, navigate to the Downloads folder, and perform a long press on the image to select it (marked A in Figure 84-2). Select the menu button (B) followed by the *Open with* option (C):

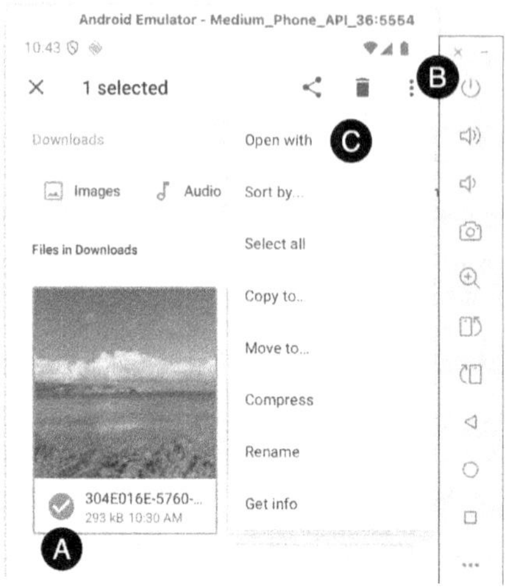

Figure 84-2

When prompted, select the Photos app. Stop and restart the GeminiDemo app, and open the media picker to access the added image.

When an image is selected, the app displays it on the ImageView located above the prompt text field, and the corresponding Uri is stored in the *selectedImageUri* variable declared within the *TextImageFragment.kt* class file:

```
class TextImageFragment : Fragment() {
.
.
    private var selectedImageUri: Uri? = null
.
.
    override fun onCreate(savedInstanceState: Bundle?) {
        super.onCreate(savedInstanceState)

        imagePickerLauncher = registerForActivityResult<String?, Uri?>(
            GetContent()
        ) { uri: Uri? ->
            binding.imageView.setImageURI(uri)
            selectedImageUri = uri
        }
    }
.
.
```

84.3 Calling the Gemini API

The Ask Gemini button is pre-configured to call a method called *askGemini()*, the code for which reads as follows:

```
fun askGemini(message: String) {
    binding.resultText.setText(R.string.generating_response)
```

```
    val bitmap: Bitmap? = uriToBitmap(requireContext(), selectedImageUri)
    viewModel?.sendTextAndImage(bitmap, message)
}
```

The method displays a message that the request is processing before converting the selected image to a bitmap. Both the prompt text and bitmap are then passed to the stub *sendTextAndImage()* method declared in the *GeminiViewModel.kt* file:

```
fun sendTextAndImage(bitmap: Bitmap?, prompt: String) {


}
```

Edit the *GeminiViewModel.kt* file and make the following modifications:

```
.
.
import androidx.lifecycle.viewModelScope
import kotlinx.coroutines.Dispatchers
import kotlinx.coroutines.launch
import com.google.firebase.ai.type.content
.
.
class GeminiViewModel: ViewModel() {
.
.
   fun sendTextAndImage(bitmap: Bitmap?, prompt: String) {

        viewModelScope.launch(Dispatchers.IO) {
            val content = content {
                bitmap?.let {
                    image(bitmap)
                }
                text(prompt)
            }

            try {
                val response = generativeModel.generateContent(content)

                response.text?.let { outputContent ->
                    _stateFlow.value = outputContent
                }
            } catch (e: Exception) {
                _stateFlow.value = e.localizedMessage ?: ""
            }
        }
    }
```

The function launches a coroutine to perform the Gemini request asynchronously, then creates a Content object containing the text prompt and the image if one was selected:

```
viewModelScope.launch(Dispatchers.IO) {
    val content = content {
        bitmap?.let {
            image(bitmap)
        }
        text(prompt)
    }
```

Next, the content is passed to the generative model's *generateContent()* method for processing:

```
try {
    val response = generativeModel.generateContent(content)
```

The response is then assigned to the state flow instance for presentation to the user:

```
response.text?.let { outputContent ->
    _stateFlow.value = outputContent
}
```

If an error occurs, the try-catch statement extracts the error message and sends it to the state flow:

```
} catch (e: Exception) {
    _stateFlow.value = e.localizedMessage ?: ""
}
```

84.4 Testing the app

The first stage of the GeminiDemo project is now ready for testing. Run the app, ask Gemini a question, and await a response. Next, select a photo and ask Gemini questions related to the image:

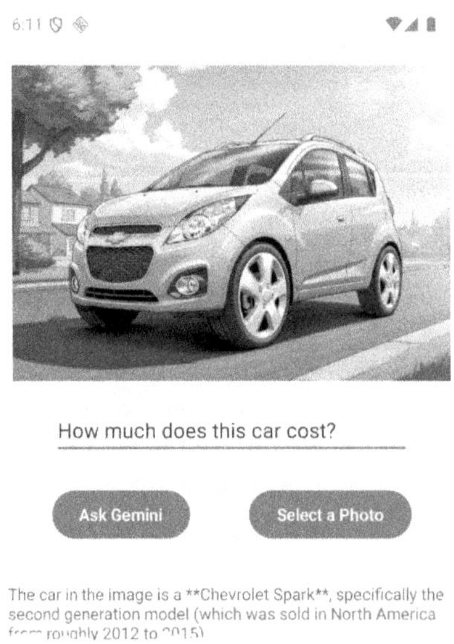

Figure 84-3

84.5 Migrating to chat

If we were to ask a follow-up question on the same topic without providing context, the model would be unable to answer it because it doesn't remember the previous interaction. As the final step in this chapter, we will convert the example to a chat session. Edit the *GeminiViewModel.kt* file and make the following changes:

```
private val generativeModel =
        Firebase.ai(backend = GenerativeBackend.googleAI())
            .generativeModel(modelName = "gemini-2.5-flash")

val chatSession = generativeModel.startChat()

fun askGemini(
    bitmap: Bitmap?,
    prompt: String
) {
        viewModelScope.launch(Dispatchers.IO) {
.
.
            try {
                val response = generativeModel.generateContent(content)
                val response = chatSession.sendMessage(content)

                response.text?.let { outputContent ->
                _stateFlow.value = outputContent
            }
        } catch (e: Exception) {
            _stateFlow.value = e.localizedMessage ?: ""
        }
```

Rerun the app and repeat the previous steps to select an image and ask a question. Ask a follow-up question without providing context and verify that the model can provide an answer:

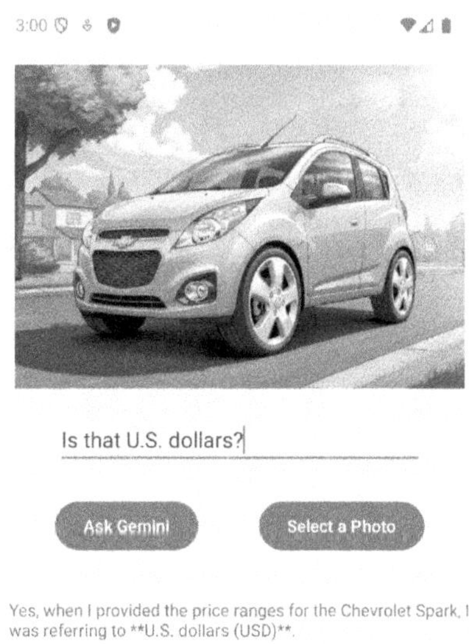

Figure 84-4

84.6 Summary

This chapter completed the first screen of our GeminiDemo project, allowing a text prompt and an image to be passed to the Gemini model using the Client SDK. The content generation code was then changed to retain context between requests using a chat session.

85. Using Gemini AI for Video Analysis

Now that the GeminiDemo app can answer questions and analyze images, this chapter will complete work on the Text + Video screen, enabling us to enter text prompts and upload video content for Gemini to analyze.

85.1 Opening the GeminiDemo project

If you are reading the AI chapters sequentially, launch Android Studio and open the GeminiDemo project from the previous chapter. Alternatively, open the *GeminiDemo_step2* project from the source code samples download. If you have not already done so, you can download the sample code using the following link:

https://www.payloadbooks.com/product/quailkotlin

Before proceeding, follow the steps in the *"Preparing the Gemini Firebase AI Logic Project"* chapter to add your *google-services.json* file to the project.

85.2 Updating the view model

The GeminiViewModel class contains a stub method named *sendTextAndVideo(),* which is called when the Ask Gemini button is clicked in the Text + Video app screen. The method is passed the application context, the Uri of the selected video, and the prompt text, and reads as follows:

```
fun sendTextAndVideo(context: Context?, videoUri: Uri?, prompt: String) {

}
```

The purpose of the method is to ask the Gemini model to analyze the video within the context of the prompt text and present the response to the user. Edit the *GeminiViewModel.kt* file as follows to complete the *sendTextAndVideo()* method:

```
public void sendTextAndVideo(Context context, Uri videoUri, String prompt) {
.
.
fun sendTextAndVideo(context: Context?, videoUri: Uri?, prompt: String) {

    val contentResolver = context?.contentResolver

    viewModelScope.launch(Dispatchers.IO) {
        try {
            videoUri?.let {
                contentResolver?.openInputStream(videoUri).use { stream ->
                    stream?.let {
                        val bytes = stream.readBytes()

                        val prompt = content {
```

```
                        inlineData(bytes, "video/mp4")
                        text(prompt)
                    }

                    var fullResponse = ""

                    generativeModel.generateContentStream(prompt)
                        .collect { responseBlock ->
                            fullResponse += responseBlock.text
                        }
                    _stateFlow.value = fullResponse
                }
            }
        }
    } catch (e: Exception) {
        _stateFlow.value = e.localizedMessage ?: "An error occurred."
    }
  }
}
```

Before proceeding to the next step, we need to take some time to explain the *sendTextAndVideo()* method. When the method is called, it is passed the application context, the URI of the selected video, and the text prompt string.

The application context provides us with access to the ContentResolver instance, which, in turn, grants the app access to content stored on the device. Using the content resolver, we open an input stream from the video URI and convert the video to an array of bytes:

```
videoUri?.let {
    contentResolver?.openInputStream(videoUri).use { stream ->
        stream?.let {
            val bytes = stream.readBytes()
```

Next, the prompt and video byte array are used to build a content object, which is then passed to the *generateContentStream()* method of the generative model:

```
val prompt = content {
    inlineData(bytes, "video/mp4")
    text(prompt)
}
```

The model will analyze the byte stream and generate a sequence of responses until the analysis is complete, at which point the full response is applied to the state flow:

```
generativeModel.generateContentStream(prompt)
        .collect { responseBlock ->
    fullResponse += responseBlock.text
}
_stateFlow.value = fullResponse
```

As with the *sendTextAndImage()* function, these tasks are performed asynchronously within a coroutine using a try-catch construct.

85.3 Testing the app

Run the app, select the Text + Video screen, and choose a video from your Photo library. Videos can be added to the emulator by dragging and dropping them from the host computer onto the emulator's home screen. Large high-definition video files can cause the app on the emulator to crash due to memory limitations. Try using short videos or a lower resolution to reduce file size.

Open the Files app in the emulator, navigate to the Downloads folder, and play the video for a few seconds. Restart the app and select the video from the library.

Use the prompt field to ask Gemini questions about the video. For example, you can ask Gemini to describe the video, identify elements such as clothing, or provide a dialog transcript. Be patient, as it can sometimes take a few minutes for Gemini to provide a complete response:

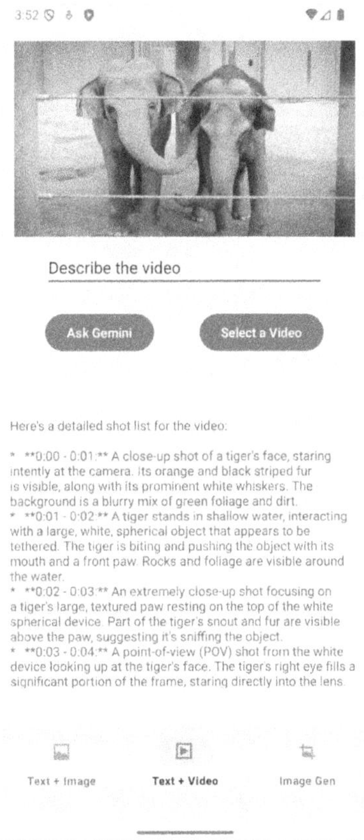

Figure 85-1

85.4 Summary

In this chapter, we utilized the Gemini Developer API to incorporate video analysis features into the GeminiDemo project. We used the PickVisualMedia activity to provide the app access to videos stored on the device. The selected video was then converted to a byte stream and bundled with the text prompt into a Content object. The input content was then passed to the model using the *generateContent()* method.

Chapter 86

86. Gemini AI Image Generation

This chapter will complete the GeminiDemo project by extending the view model to add text-to-image generation support using the Gemini Image models. The steps in this chapter will demonstrate how to create and configure an image model instance and use it to generate images based on text descriptions.

86.1 Opening the GeminiDemo project

If you are reading the AI chapters sequentially, launch Android Studio and open the GeminiDemo project from the previous chapter. Alternatively, open the *GeminiDemo_step3* project from the source code samples download. If you have not already done so, you can download the sample code using the following link:

https://www.payloadbooks.com/product/quailkotlin

Before proceeding, follow the steps in the *"Preparing the Gemini Firebase AI Logic Project"* chapter to add your *google-services.json* file to the project.

86.2 Initializing the image model

Before generating images, we need to create an image model instance by calling the *generativeModel()* method, passing the model name and configuration options, including aspect ratio, image size and content type. Safety settings may also be included to control how strictly Gemini should enforce objectionable content filters. Edit the *GeminiViewModel.kt* file and add the following code to create the image model:

```
.
.
import com.google.firebase.ai.type.SafetySetting
import com.google.firebase.ai.type.HarmCategory
import com.google.firebase.ai.type.HarmBlockThreshold
import com.google.firebase.ai.type.generationConfig
import com.google.firebase.ai.type.ImagenSafetySettings
import com.google.firebase.ai.type.ResponseModality
import com.google.firebase.ai.type.imageConfig
import com.google.firebase.ai.type.AspectRatio
import com.google.firebase.ai.type.ImageSize
import com.google.firebase.ai.type.ImagePart

class GeminiViewModel: ViewModel() {

    private val _stateFlow = MutableStateFlow("")
    val stateFlow: StateFlow<String> = _stateFlow.asStateFlow()

    private val _generatedImage = MutableStateFlow<Bitmap?>(null)
    val generatedImage: StateFlow<Bitmap?> = _generatedImage.asStateFlow()

    private val imageModel =
```

```
        Firebase.ai(
            backend = GenerativeBackend.googleAI()
        ).generativeModel(
            modelName = "gemini-3.1-flash-image",
            safetySettings = listOf(
                SafetySetting(
                    HarmCategory.HARASSMENT,
                    HarmBlockThreshold.ONLY_HIGH
                )
            ),
            generationConfig = generationConfig {
                responseModalities = listOf(ResponseModality.IMAGE)

                imageConfig = imageConfig {
                    aspectRatio = AspectRatio.LANDSCAPE_4x3
                    imageSize = ImageSize.SIZE_1K
                }
            }
        )
.
.
```

86.3 Sending the image generation request

With the Imagen model initialized, the next requirement is a method to send the image generation prompt to the model. This method will be called from the image generation screen (*ImageGenFragment.kt*) and passed the description of the required image. The generated image will be assigned to a StateFlow variable for display on the image generation screen. With these requirements in mind, make the following additions to the GeminiViewModel class:

```
fun generateImageFromText(prompt: String) {

    viewModelScope.launch(Dispatchers.IO) {
        try {
            _stateFlow.value = "Generating image..."
            _generatedImage.value = null

            val response = imageModel.generateContent(prompt)

            val image = response.candidates
                .firstOrNull()
                ?.content
                ?.parts
                ?.filterIsInstance<ImagePart>()
                ?.firstOrNull()
                ?.image

            if (image != null) {
```

```
                _generatedImage.value = image
                _stateFlow.value = "Image complete"
            } else {
                _stateFlow.value = "The model did not return an image."
            }

        } catch (e: Exception) {
            _stateFlow.value =
                e.localizedMessage ?: "Image generation failed."
        }
    }
}
```

The above function calls the *generateContent()* model method from within a coroutine and passes it the image description text:

```
viewModelScope.launch(Dispatchers.IO) {

    try {
        _stateFlow.value = "Generating image..."
        _generatedImage.value = null

        val response = imageModel.generateContent(prompt)
```

Next, the *candidates* property of the response object is used to access the first image generated by the model:

```
val image = response.candidates
    .firstOrNull()
    ?.content
    ?.parts
    ?.filterIsInstance<ImagePart>()
    ?.firstOrNull()
    ?.image
```

If the request succeeds, the generated image is emitted via the generatedImage state flow:

```
if (image != null) {
    _generatedImage.value = image
    _stateFlow.value = "Image complete"
} else {
    _stateFlow.value = "The model did not return an image."
}
```

Alternatively, if the generation request fails, the catch statement displays the error message via the stateFlow instance:

```
} catch (e: Exception) {
    _stateFlow.value =
        e.localizedMessage ?: "Image generation failed."
}
```

86.4 Upgrading to the Firebase Blaze plan

Before generating images, you may need to upgrade from the free Firebase Spark plan to the Blaze pay-as-you-go plan linked to a Google Cloud Billing account. If an upgrade is necessary, the GeminiDemo app will display the following message similar to the following when image generation is requested:

```
You exceeded your quota, please check your plan and billing details.
```

Your current plan level is displayed in the bottom left-hand corner of the Firebase console, as shown in Figure 86-1:

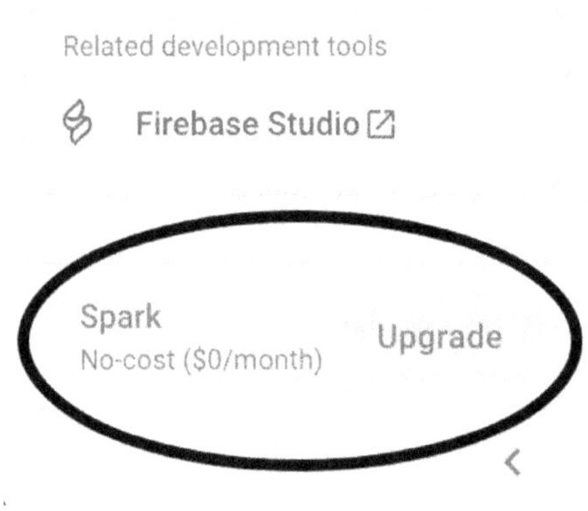

Figure 86-1

Click the Upgrade button and select the Blaze plan option in the resulting dialog:

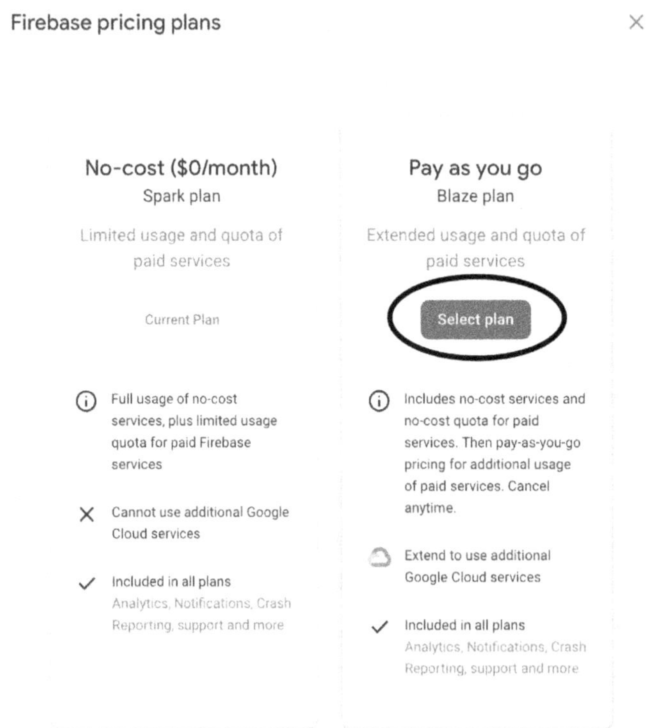

Figure 86-2

On the screen shown in Figure 86-3, follow the steps to set up a billing account and complete the upgrade:

Figure 86-3

Firebase AI Logic prices are very low (cents rather than dollars or the equivalent in your local currency), and the costs incurred should be minimal.

86.5 Testing image generation

Run the app, select Image Gen in the bottom navigation bar, and enter a description before clicking the Generate Image button. If the request violates the model's safety settings or Google's mandatory content filters, the error will be reported on the Text component. If the image is generated successfully, it will appear on the screen as shown in Figure 86-4:

Figure 86-4

86.6 Summary

The Gemini image model generates images from text descriptions. Several options are available for configuring the model, including the aspect ratio and image size. The models also include safety options to prevent the generation of harmful content. Once the model has been initialized and configured, the *generateContent()* method is called and passed the image description. The generated image is returned as a GenerateContentResponse object from which the image bitmap can be accessed.

Chapter 87

87. Working with Material Design 3 Theming

The appearance of an Android app is intended to conform to a set of guidelines defined by Material Design. Google developed Material Design to provide a level of design consistency between different apps while also allowing app developers to include their own branding in terms of color, typography, and shape choices (a concept referred to as Material theming). In addition to design guidelines, Material Design also includes a set of UI components for use when designing user interface layouts, many of which we have used throughout this book.

This chapter will provide an overview of how theming works within an Android Studio project and explore how the default design configurations provided for newly created projects can be modified to meet your branding requirements.

87.1 Material Design 2 vs. Material Design 3

Before beginning, it is important to note that Google is transitioning from Material Design 2 to Material Design 3 and that Android Studio Quail projects default to Material Design 3. Material Design 3 provides the basis for Material You, a feature introduced in Android 12 that allows an app to automatically adjust theme elements to complement preferences configured by the user on the device. For example, dynamic color support provided by Material Design 3 allows the colors used in apps to adapt automatically to match the user's wallpaper selection.

87.2 Understanding Material Design Theming

We know that Android app user interfaces are created by assembling components such as layouts, text fields, and buttons. These components appear using default colors unless we specifically override a color attribute in the XML layout resource file or by writing code. The project's theme defines these default colors. The theme consists of a set of color slots (declared in *themes.xml* files) which are assigned color values (declared in the *colors.xml* file). Each UI component is programmed internally to use theme color slots as the default color for specific attributes (such as the foreground and background colors of the Text widget). It follows, therefore, that we can change the application-wide theme of an app by changing the colors assigned to specific theme slots. When the app runs, the new default colors will be used for all widgets when the user interface is rendered.

87.3 Material Design 3 Theming

Before exploring Material Design 3, we must consider how it is used in an Android Studio project. The theme used by an application project is declared as a property of the *application* element within the *AndroidManifest.xml* file, for example:

```
<?xml version="1.0" encoding="utf-8"?>
<manifest xmlns:android="http://schemas.android.com/apk/res/android"
    xmlns:tools="http://schemas.android.com/tools">

    <application
.
.
```

```
        android:supportsRtl="true"
        android:theme="@style/Theme.MyDemoApp"
        tools:targetApi="31">
        <activity
.
.
```

As previously discussed, all of the files associated with the project theme are contained within the *colors.xml* and *themes.xml* files located in the *res* -> *values* folder, as shown in Figure 87-1:

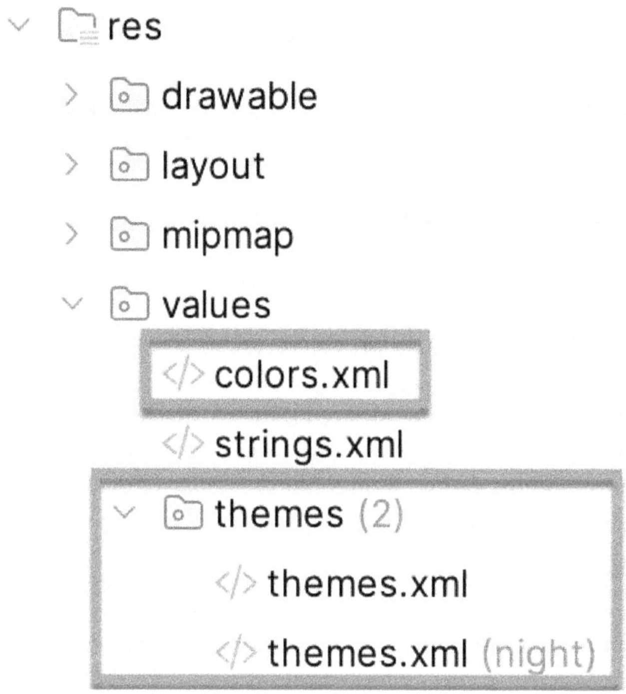

Figure 87-1

The theme itself is declared in the two *themes.xml* files located in the *themes* folder. These resource files declare different color palettes containing Material Theme color slots for use when the device is in light or dark (night) mode. Note that the style name property in each file must match that referenced in the *AndroidManifest.xml* file, for example:

```
<resources xmlns:tools="http://schemas.android.com/tools">
    <!-- Base application theme. -->
    <style name="Base.Theme.MyDemoApp" parent="Theme.Material3.DayNight.
NoActionBar">
        <!-- Customize your light theme here. -->
        <!-- <item name="colorPrimary">@color/my_light_primary</item> -->
    </style>

    <style name="Theme.MyDemoApp" parent="Base.Theme.MyDemoApp" />
</resources>
```

These color slots (also referred to as *color attributes*) are used by the Material components to set colors when they are rendered on the screen. For example, the *colorPrimary* color slot is used as the background color for the Material Button component.

Color slots in MD3 are grouped as Primary, Secondary, Tertiary, Error, Background, and Surface. These slots are further divided into pairs consisting of a *base color* and an *"on" base color*. This generally translates to the background and foreground colors of a Material component.

The particular group used for coloring will differ between widgets. A Material Button widget, for example, will use the *colorPrimary* base color for the background color and *colorOnPrimary* for its content (i.e., the text or icon it displays). The FloatingActionButton component, on the other hand, uses *colorPrimaryContainer* as the background color and *colorOnPrimaryContainer* for the foreground. The correct group for a specific widget type can usually be identified quickly by changing color settings in the theme files and reviewing the rendering in the layout editor.

Suppose that we need to change *colorPrimary* to red. We achieve this by adding a new entry to the *colors.xml* file for the red color and then assigning it to the *colorPrimary* slot in the *themes.xml* file. The *colorPrimary* slot in an MD3 theme night, therefore, read as follows:

```
<resources xmlns:tools="http://schemas.android.com/tools">
    <!-- Base application theme. -->
    <style name="Base.Theme.MyDemoApp" parent="Theme.Material3.DayNight.
NoActionBar">
        <item name="colorPrimary">@color/my_bright_primary</item>
    </style>

    <style name="Theme.MyDemoApp" parent="Base.Theme.MyDemoApp" />
</resources>
```

This color is then declared in the *colors.xml* file:

```
<?xml version="1.0" encoding="utf-8"?>
<resources>
.
.
    <color name="my_bright_primary">#FC0505</color>
.
.
</resources>
```

87.4 Building a custom theme

As we have seen, the coding work in implementing a theme is relatively simple. The difficult part, however, is often choosing complementary colors to make up the theme. Fortunately, Google has developed a tool that makes it easy to design custom color and font themes for your apps. This tool is called the Material Theme Builder and is available at:

https://m3.material.io/theme-builder

Figure 87-2 shows a recent version of the Theme Builder. However, Google redesigns the builder every few weeks, so it is possible that the user interface you see will not match the current design:

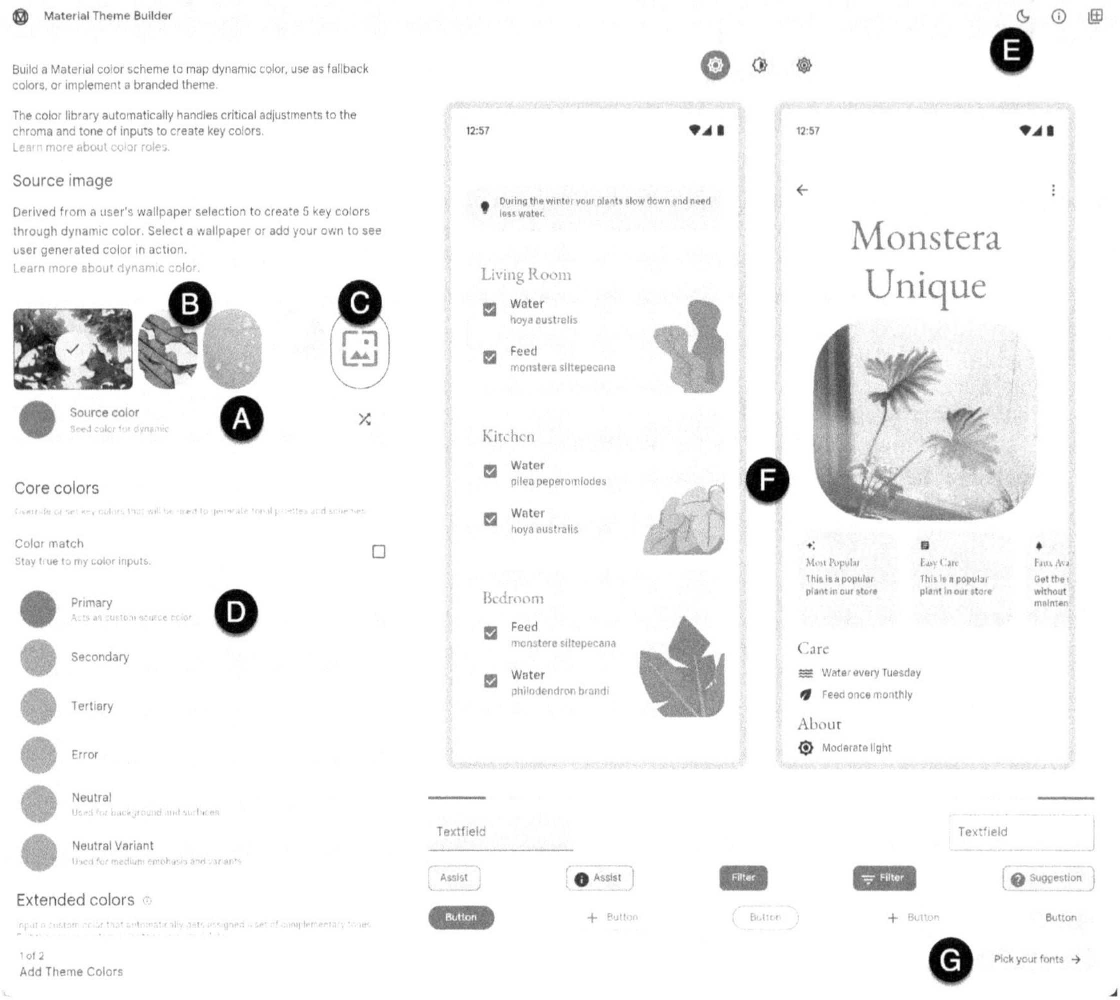

Figure 87-2

A custom Material color theme can be generated by providing a source color of your own choosing (marked A) in the figure above, selecting a standard wallpaper (B), uploading a source image (C), or making individual core color selections (D). The button marked E previews the color scheme in light and dark modes.

The area marked F displays example app interfaces, light and dark color scheme charts, and widgets that update to preview your color selections. Since the panel is longer than the typical browser window, you must scroll down to see all the information.

Once the theme colors have been defined, clicking on the Pick your fonts button (G) button will display the screen shown in Figure 87-3, where you can select the fonts to be used by your app:

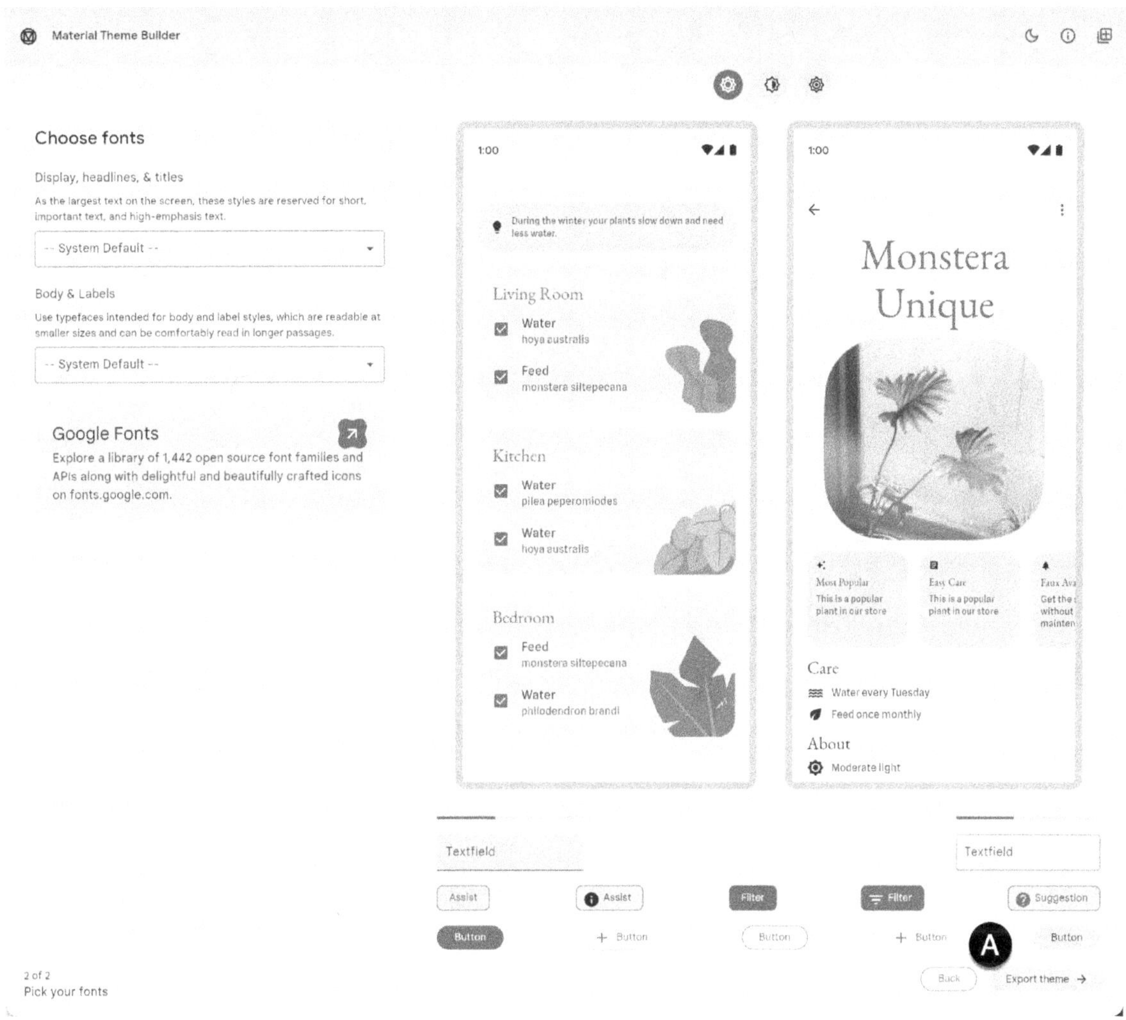

Figure 87-3

To incorporate the theme into your design, click the *Export theme* button (marked A above) and select the *Android Views (XML)* option. Once downloaded, the *themes.xml* and *colors.xml* files can replace the existing files in your project. Note that the theme name in the exported *themes.xml* files must be changed to match your project.

87.5 Summary

Material Design provides guidelines and components defining how Android apps appear. Individual branding can be applied to an app by designing themes that specify the colors, fonts, and shapes used when displaying the app. Google recently introduced Material Design 3, which replaces Material Design 2 and supports the new features of Material You, including dynamic colors. Google also provides the Material Theme Builder for designing your own themes, which eases the task of choosing complementary theme colors. Once this tool has been used to design a theme, the corresponding files can be exported and used within an Android Studio project.

88. A Material Design 3 Theming and Dynamic Color Tutorial

This chapter will show you how to create a new Material Design 3 theme using the Material Theme Builder tool and integrate it into an Android Studio project. The tutorial will also demonstrate how to add support for and test dynamic theme colors to an app.

88.1 Creating the ThemeDemo Project

Select the *New Project* option from the welcome screen and, within the resulting new project dialog, choose the Empty Views Activity template before clicking on the Next button.

Enter *ThemeDemo* into the Name field and specify *com.ebookfrenzy.themedemo* as the package name. Before clicking on the Finish button, change the Minimum API level setting to API 26: Android 8.0 (Oreo) and the Language menu to Kotlin.

88.2 Designing the User Interface

The main activity will consist of a simple layout containing some user interface components that will enable us to see the effects of the theming work performed later in the chapter. For information on MD3 components, refer to the following web page:

https://material.io/blog/migrating-material-3

The layout will be designed within the *activity_main.xml* file, which currently contains a single Text view. Open this file in the layout editor, delete the Text view, turn off Autoconnect mode (marked A in Figure 88-1), and click on the button to clear all constraints from the layout (B).

Figure 88-1

From the Buttons section of the Palette, drag Chip, CheckBox, Switch, and Button views onto the layout canvas. Next, drag a FloatingActionButton onto the layout canvas to position it beneath the Button component. When prompted to choose an icon to appear on the FloatingActionButton, select the *ic_lock_power_off* icon from within the resource tool window, as illustrated in Figure 88-2:

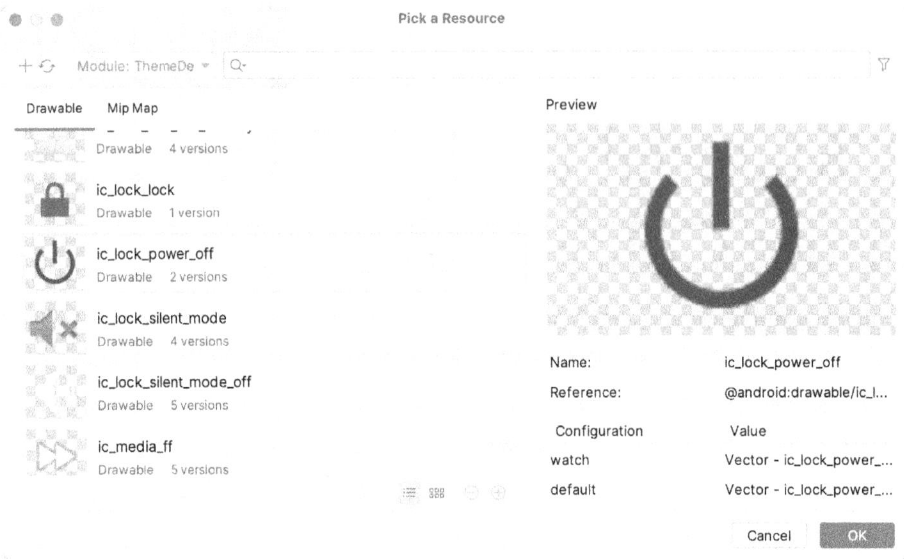

Figure 88-2

Change the text attribute for the Chip widget to "This is my chip" and set the chipIcon attribute to @ *android:drawable/ic_btn_speak_now* so that the layout resembles that shown to the left in Figure 88-3:

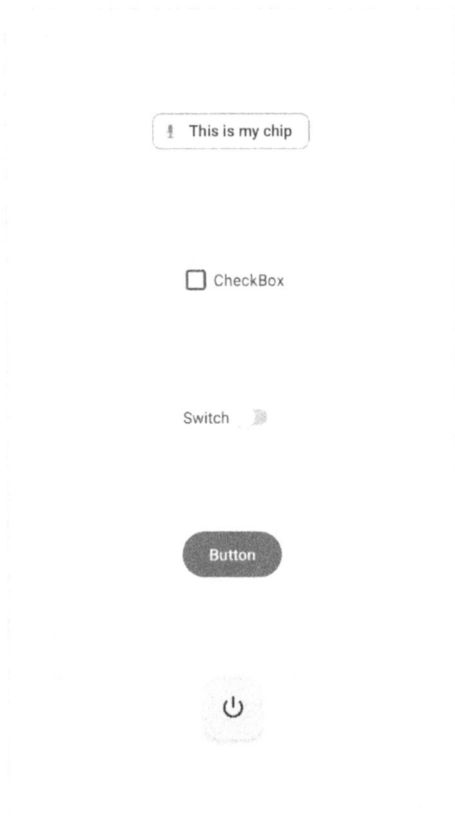

Figure 88-3

To set up the constraints, select all the components, right-click on the Chip view, and select *Chains -> Create Vertical Chain* from the resulting menu. Repeat this step, this time selecting the *Center -> Horizontally in Parent* menu option.

Compile and run the app on a device or emulator and verify that the user interface matches that shown in Figure 88-3 above. The next step is to create a custom theme and apply it to the project.

88.3 Building a new theme

The theme for the project will be designed and generated using the Material Theme Builder. Open a browser window and navigate to the following URL to access the builder tool:

https://m3.material.io/theme-builder

Once you have loaded the builder, select a wallpaper, then click the Primary color circle in the Core colors section to display the color selector. From the color selector, choose any color you feel like using as the basis for your theme before clicking on the Apply button:

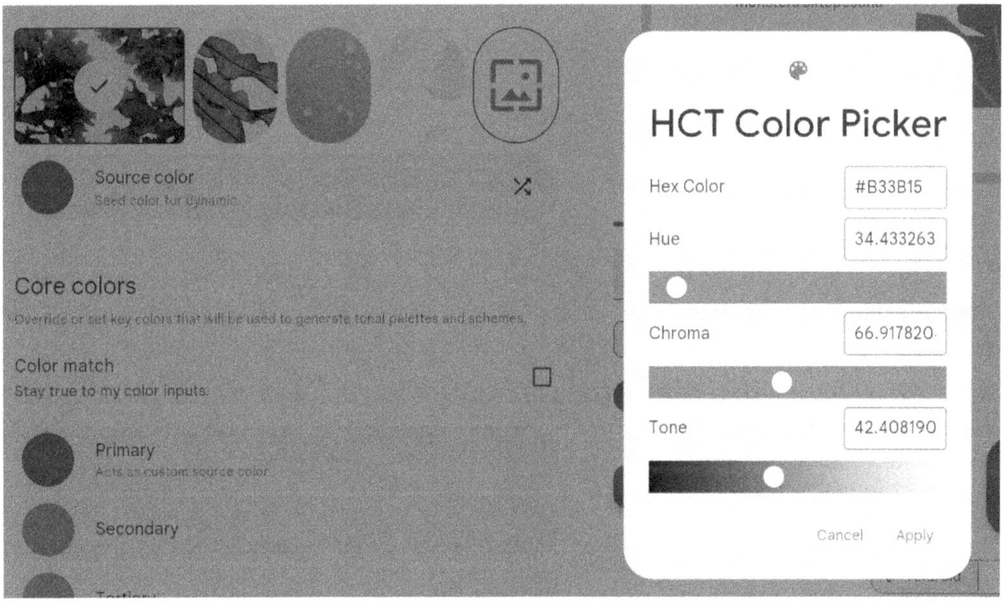

Figure 88-4

Review the color scheme and make any necessary color adjustments using the Core colors panel until you are happy with the color slots. Once the theme is ready, click on the *Pick your fonts* button and make font selections.

Click on the *Export theme* button. In the resulting panel, click Export and select the select the *Jetpack Compose (Theme.kt)* option. When prompted, save the file to a suitable location on your computer filesystem. The theme will be saved as a compressed file named *material-theme.zip*.

Using the appropriate tool for your operating system, unpack the theme file, which should contain the following folders and files in a folder named *material-theme*:

- **values/colors.xml** - The color definitions for light mode.
- **values/themes.xml** - The theme for the light mode.
- **values/colors.xml** - The color definitions for dark mode.

- **values-night/themes.xml** - The theme for dark mode.

Now that the theme files have been generated, they need to be integrated into the Android Studio project.

88.4 Adding the Theme to the Project

Before adding the new theme to the project, we first need to remove the old theme files. This is easier if the Project tool window is in Project Files mode. To switch mode, use the menu at the top of the tool Project tool window as shown below and select the Project Files option:

Figure 88-5

With Project Files mode selected, navigate to the *app -> src -> main -> res -> values* folder and select and delete the *colors.xml* and *themes.xml* files. Also, delete the *themes.xml* file located in the *values-night* folder.

Open the filesystem navigation tool for your operating system, locate the *colors.xml* and *themes.xml* files in the *values* folder of the new material theme, and copy and paste them into the *values* folder within the Project tool window. Repeat this step to copy the *themes.xml* and *colors.xml* files in the *values-night* folder, this time pasting them into the *values-night* folder.

Switch the Project tool window back to Android mode, at which point the value resource files section should match Figure 88-6:

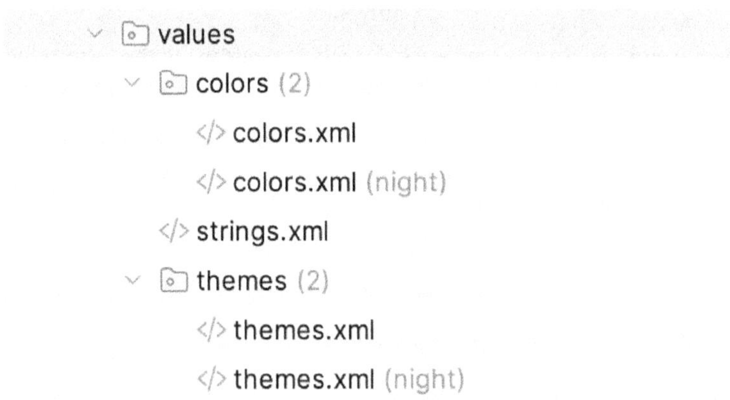

Figure 88-6

Next, modify the light *themes.xml* file to match the current project as follows:

```
<resources>
    <style name="Base.Theme.ThemeDemo" parent="Theme.Material3.Light.
NoActionBar">
        <item name="colorPrimary">@color/md_theme_light_primary</item>
        <item name="colorOnPrimary">@color/md_theme_light_onPrimary</item>
.
.
    </style>

    <style name="Theme.ThemeDemo" parent="Base.Theme.ThemeDemo" />

</resources>
```

Repeat these steps to make the same modifications to the *themes.xml (night)* file.

Return to the *activity_main.xml* file to confirm that the user interface is rendered using the custom theme colors, using the button highlighted below to switch between light and dark modes:

Figure 88-7

88.5 Enabling Dynamic Color Support

The app will need to be run on a device or emulator running Android 12 or later with the correct Wallpaper settings to test dynamic colors. On the device or emulator, launch the Settings app and select *Wallpaper & style* from the list of options. On the wallpaper settings screen, click the option to browse wallpapers (marked A in Figure 88-8) and select a wallpaper image containing colors that differ significantly from the colors in your theme. Once selected, assign the wallpaper to the Home screen.

Return to the Wallpaper & styles screen and make sure that a *Wallpaper color* option is selected (B). As each option is clicked, the wallpaper example will change to reflect the selection:

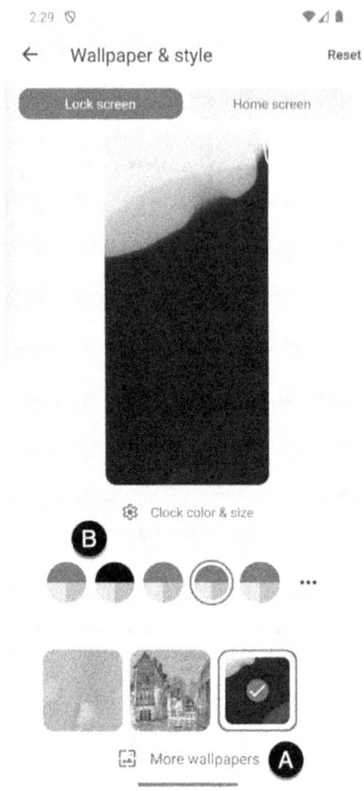

Figure 88-8

To enable dynamic colors, we need to call the *applyToActivitiesIfAvailable()* method of the DynamicColors class. To enable dynamic color support for the entire app, this needs to be called from within the *onCreate()* method of a custom Application instance. Begin by adding a new Kotlin class file to the project under *app -> kotlin+java -> com.ebookfrenzy.themedemo* named *ThemeDemoApplication.kt* and modifying it so that it reads as follows:

```
package com.ebookfrenzy.themedemo

import android.app.Application
import com.google.android.material.color.DynamicColors

class ThemeDemoApplication: Application() {
    override fun onCreate() {
        super.onCreate()
        DynamicColors.applyToActivitiesIfAvailable(this)
    }
}
```

With the custom Application class created, we must configure the project to use this class instead of the default Application instance. To do this, edit the *AndroidManifest.xml* file and add an *android:name* element referencing the new class:

```
<?xml version="1.0" encoding="utf-8"?>
<manifest xmlns:android="http://schemas.android.com/apk/res/android"
    package="com.ebookfrenzy.themedemo">

    <application
```

```
        android:name=".ThemeDemoApplication"
        android:allowBackup="true"
.
.
```

Build and run the app and note that the layout uses a theme matching the wallpaper color. Place the ThemeDemo app into the background, return to the *Wallpaper & styles* settings screen, and choose a different wallpaper. Bring the ThemeDemo app to the foreground again. At this point, it will have dynamically adapted to match the new wallpaper.

88.6 Summary

In this chapter, we have used the Material Theme Builder to design a new theme and explained the steps to integrate the generated theme files into an Android Studio project. Finally, the chapter demonstrated how to implement and use the Material You dynamic colors feature.

Chapter 89

89. An Overview of Gradle in Android Studio

In the *"A Guide to Gradle Version Catalogs"* chapter, we introduced the library version catalog and explained how the Gradle build system relies on it to ensure that projects are built using the correct libraries and versions. Aside from some modifications to the version catalog and library decencies in the intervening chapters, it has been taken for granted that Android Studio will take the necessary steps to compile and run the application projects that have been created. Android Studio has been achieving this in the background using a system known as *Gradle*.

It is time to look at how Gradle is used to compile and package an application project's various elements and begin exploring how to configure this system when more advanced requirements are needed for building projects in Android Studio.

89.1 An Overview of Gradle

Gradle is an automated build toolkit that allows how projects are built to be configured and managed through a set of build configuration files. This includes defining how a project will be built, what dependencies need to be fulfilled to build successfully, and what the build process's end result (or results) should be.

The strength of Gradle lies in the flexibility that it provides to the developer. The Gradle system is a self-contained, command-line-based environment that can be integrated into other environments using plugins. In the case of Android Studio, Gradle integration is provided through the appropriately named Android Studio Plugin.

Although the Android Studio Plug-in allows Gradle tasks to be initiated and managed from within Android Studio, the Gradle command-line wrapper can still be used to build Android Studio-based projects, including on systems on which Android Studio is not installed.

The configuration rules to build a project are declared in Gradle build files and scripts based on the Groovy programming language.

89.2 Gradle and Android Studio

Gradle brings many powerful features to building Android application projects. Some of the key features are as follows:

89.2.1 Sensible Defaults

Gradle implements a concept referred to as *convention over configuration*. This means that Gradle has a predefined set of sensible default configuration settings that will be used unless settings in the build files override them. This means that builds can be performed with the minimum configuration required by the developer. Changes to the build files are only needed when the default configuration does not meet your build needs.

89.2.2 Dependencies

Another key area of Gradle functionality is that of dependencies. Consider, for example, a module within an Android Studio project which triggers an intent to load another module in the project. The first module has, in effect, a dependency on the second module since the application will fail to build if the second module cannot be located and launched at runtime. This dependency can be declared in the Gradle build file for the first module so that the second module is included in the application build, or an error flagged if the second module cannot be found or built. Other examples of dependencies are libraries and JAR files on which the project depends to compile and run.

Gradle dependencies can be categorized as *local* or *remote*. A local dependency references an item that is present on the local file system of the computer system on which the build is being performed. A remote dependency refers to an item that is present on a remote server (typically referred to as a *repository*).

Remote dependencies are handled for Android Studio projects using another project management tool named *Maven*. If a remote dependency is declared in a Gradle build file using Maven syntax, then the dependency will be downloaded automatically from the designated repository and included in the build process. The following dependency declaration, for example, causes the AppCompat library to be added to the project from the Google repository:

```
implementation(libs.androidx.appcompat)
```

89.2.3 Build Variants

In addition to dependencies, Gradle also provides *build variant* support for Android Studio projects. This allows multiple variations of an application to be built from a single project. Android runs on many different devices encompassing a range of processor types and screen sizes. To target as wide a range of device types and sizes as possible, it will often be necessary to build several variants of an application (for example, one with a user interface for phones and another for tablet-sized screens). Through the use of Gradle, this is now possible in Android Studio.

89.2.4 Manifest Entries

Each Android Studio project has associated with it an *AndroidManifest.xml* file containing configuration details about the application. Several manifest entries can be specified in Gradle build files which are then auto-generated into the manifest file when the project is built. This capability complements the build variants feature, allowing elements such as the application version number, application ID, and SDK version information to be configured differently for each build variant.

89.2.5 APK Signing

The chapter *"Creating, Testing, and Uploading an Android App Bundle"* covered creating a signed release APK file using the Android Studio environment. It is also possible to include the signing information entered through the Android Studio user interface within a Gradle build file to generate signed APK files from the command line.

89.2.6 ProGuard Support

ProGuard is a tool included with Android Studio that optimizes, shrinks, and obfuscates Java byte code to make it more efficient and harder to reverse engineer (the method by which others can identify the logic of an application through analysis of the compiled Java byte code). The Gradle build files allow you to control whether or not ProGuard is run on your application when it is built.

89.3 The Property and Settings Gradle Build File

The gradle build configuration consists of configuration, property, and settings files. The *gradle.properties* file, for example, contains mostly esoteric settings relating to the command-line flags used by the Java Virtual Machine (JVM), whether or not the project uses the AndroidX libraries and Kotlin coding style support. As a typical user, it is unlikely that you will need to change any of these settings in this file.

The *settings.gradle.kts* file, on the other hand, defines which online repositories are to be searched when the build system needs to download and install any additional libraries and plugins required to build the project and the project name. A typical *settings.gradle.kts* file will read as follows:

```
pluginManagement {
```

```
    repositories {
        google {
            content {
                includeGroupByRegex("com\\.android.*")
                includeGroupByRegex("com\\.google.*")
                includeGroupByRegex("androidx.*")
            }
        }
        mavenCentral()
        gradlePluginPortal()
    }
}
plugins {
    id("org.gradle.toolchains.foojay-resolver-convention") version "1.0.0"
}
dependencyResolutionManagement {
    repositoriesMode.set(RepositoriesMode.FAIL_ON_PROJECT_REPOS)
    repositories {
        google()
        mavenCentral()
    }
}

rootProject.name = "AndroidSample"
include(":app")
```

As with the *gradle.properties* file, it is unlikely that changes will need to be made to this file.

89.4 The Top-level Gradle Build File

A completed Android Studio project contains everything needed to build an Android application and consists of modules, libraries, manifest files, and Gradle build files.

Each project contains one top-level Gradle build file. This file is listed as *build.gradle.kts (Project: <project name>)* and can be found in the project tool window as highlighted in Figure 89-1:

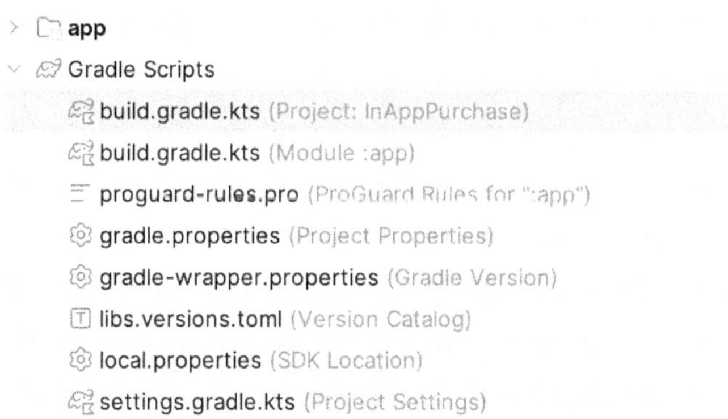

Figure 89-1

By default, the contents of the top-level Gradle build file reads as follows:

```
plugins {
    alias(libs.plugins.android.application) apply false
}
```

In most situations, making any changes to this build file is unnecessary.

89.5 Module Level Gradle Build Files

An Android Studio application project is made up of one or more modules. Take, for example, a hypothetical application project named GradleSample which contains modules named Module1 and Module2, respectively. In this scenario, each module will require its own Gradle build file. In terms of the project structure, these would be located as follows:

- Module1/build.gradle.kts
- Module2/build.gradle.kts

By default, the Module1 *build.gradle.kts* file would resemble that of the following listing:

```
plugins {
    alias(libs.plugins.android.application)
}

android {
    namespace = "com.example.gradlesample"
    compileSdk {
        version = release(37)
    }

    defaultConfig {
        applicationId = "com.example.gradlesample"
        minSdk = 26
        targetSdk = 37
        versionCode = 1
        versionName = "1.0"

        testInstrumentationRunner = "androidx.test.runner.AndroidJUnitRunner"
    }

    buildTypes {
        release {
            optimization {
                enable = false
            }
        }
    }
    compileOptions {
        sourceCompatibility = JavaVersion.VERSION_11
        targetCompatibility = JavaVersion.VERSION_11
```

```
    }
}

dependencies {
    implementation(libs.androidx.activity.ktx)
    implementation(libs.androidx.appcompat)
    implementation(libs.androidx.constraintlayout)
    implementation(libs.androidx.core.ktx)
    implementation(libs.material)
    testImplementation(libs.junit)
    androidTestImplementation(libs.androidx.espresso.core)
    androidTestImplementation(libs.androidx.junit)
}
```

As is evident from the file content, the build file begins by declaring the use of the Gradle Android application plug-in:

```
plugins {
    alias(libs.plugins.android.application)
}
```

The *android* section of the file declares the project namespace and then states the version of the SDK to be used when building Module1.

```
android {
    namespace = "com.example.gradlesample"
    compileSdk {
        version = release(37) {
            minorApiLevel = 1
        }
```

The items declared in the defaultConfig section define elements to be generated into the module's *AndroidManifest.xml* file during the build. These settings, which may be modified in the build file, are taken from the settings entered within Android Studio when the module was first created:

```
defaultConfig {
    applicationId = "com.example.gradlesample"
    minSdk = 26
    targetSdk = 37
    versionCode = 1
    versionName = "1.0"

    testInstrumentationRunner = "androidx.test.runner.AndroidJUnitRunner"
}
```

The buildTypes section contains instructions on whether and how to run ProGuard on the APK file when a release version of the application is built:

```
buildTypes {
    release {
        isMinifyEnabled = false
        proguardFiles(
```

```
                getDefaultProguardFile("proguard-android-optimize.txt"),
                "proguard-rules.pro"
            )
        }
}
```

As currently configured, ProGuard will not be run when Module1 is built. To enable ProGuard, the *minifyEnabled* entry must be changed from *false* to *true*. The *proguard-rules.pro* file can be found in the module directory of the project. Changes made to this file override the default settings in the *proguard-android.txt* file, which is located in the Android SDK installation directory under *sdk/tools/proguard*.

Since no debug buildType is declared in this file, the defaults will be used (built without ProGuard, signed with a debug key, and debug symbols enabled).

An additional section, entitled *productFlavors*, may also be included in the module build file to enable multiple build variants to be created.

Next, directives are included to specify the version of the Java compiler to be used when building the project:

```
compileOptions {
    sourceCompatibility JavaVersion.VERSION_11
    targetCompatibility JavaVersion.VERSION_11
}
```

Finally, the dependencies section lists any local and remote dependencies on which the module depends. The dependency lines in the above example file designate the Android libraries that need to be included from the Android Repository:

```
dependencies {
    implementation(libs.androidx.core.ktx)
    implementation(libs.androidx.appcompat)
    implementation(libs.material)
.
.
}
```

Note that the dependency declarations include version numbers to indicate which library version should be included.

89.6 Configuring Signing Settings in the Build File

The *"Creating, Testing, and Uploading an Android App Bundle"* chapter of this book covered the steps involved in setting up keys and generating a signed release APK file using the Android Studio user interface. These settings may also be declared within a *signingConfigs* section of the *build.gradle.kts* file. For example:

```
.
.
    defaultConfig {
.
.
    }
    signingConfigs {
        release {
```

```
            storeFile file("keystore.release")
            storePassword "your keystore password here"
            keyAlias "your key alias here"
            keyPassword "your key password here"
        }
    }
    buildTypes {
.
.
}
```

The above example embeds the key password information directly into the build file. An alternative to this approach is to extract these values from system environment variables:

```
signingConfigs {
    release {
        storeFile file("keystore.release")
        storePassword System.getenv("KEYSTOREPASSWD")
        keyAlias "your key alias here"
        keyPassword System.getenv("KEYPASSWD")
    }
}
```

Yet another approach is to configure the build file so that Gradle prompts for the passwords to be entered during the build process:

```
signingConfigs {
    release {
        storeFile file("keystore.release")
        storePassword System.console().readLine
                ("\nEnter Keystore password: ")
        keyAlias "your key alias here"
        keyPassword System.console().readLIne("\nEnter Key password: ")
    }
}
```

89.7 Running Gradle Tasks from the Command Line

Each Android Studio project contains a Gradle wrapper tool to invoke Gradle tasks from the command line. This tool is located in the root directory of each project folder. While this wrapper is executable on Windows systems, it may need to have execute permission enabled on Linux and macOS before it can be used. To enable execute permission, open a terminal window, change directory to the project folder for which the wrapper is needed, and execute the following command:

```
chmod +x gradlew
```

Once the file has execute permissions, the location of the file will either need to be added to your $PATH environment variable or the name prefixed by ./ to run. For example:

```
./gradlew tasks
```

Gradle views project building in terms of several different tasks. A full listing of tasks that are available for the current project can be obtained by running the following command from within the project directory (remembering to prefix the command with a ./ if running on macOS or Linux):

```
gradlew tasks
```

To build a debug release of the project suitable for device or emulator testing, use the assembleDebug option:

```
gradlew assembleDebug
```

Alternatively, to build a release version of the application:

```
gradlew assembleRelease
```

89.8 Summary

For the most part, Android Studio performs application builds in the background without any intervention from the developer. This build process is handled using the Gradle system, an automated build toolkit designed to allow how projects are built to be configured and managed through a set of build configuration files. While the default behavior of Gradle is adequate for many basic project build requirements, the need to configure the build process is inevitable with more complex projects. This chapter has provided an overview of the Gradle build system and configuration files within the context of an Android Studio project.

Index

Symbols

A

B

C

D

H

I

J

K

M

N

O

P

U

V

W

X

Z

www.ingramcontent.com/pod-product-compliance
Lightning Source LLC
LaVergne TN
LVHW060008210926
848481LV00013B/3673
9781965764473